A Practical Guide to Service Management

Insights from industry experts for uncovering, implementing, and improving service management practices

Keith D. Sutherland

Lawrence J. "Butch" Sheets

BIRMINGHAM—MUMBAI

A Practical Guide to Service Management

Group Product Manager: Preet Ahuja

Publishing Product Manager: Suwarna Rajput

Senior Editor: Runcil Rebello

Technical Editor: Arjun Varma

Copy Editor: Safis Editing

Project Coordinator: Ashwin Kharwa

Proofreader: Safis Editing

Indexer: Pratik Shirodkar

Production Designer: Aparna Bhagat

Marketing Coordinator: Rohan Dobhal

First published: October 2023

Production reference: 1150923

Published by Packt Publishing Ltd.
Grosvenor House
11 St Paul's Square
Birmingham
B3 1RB

ISBN 978-1-80461-250-7

www.packtpub.com

To all of our family, friends, and colleagues, this book is dedicated to you – all of the people who have contributed to our success over the last 40+ years. Special recognition goes to our wives, Holly Sutherland and Debbie Sheets, who have been there with their love and support through our journey. Thank you to Lisa Schwartz, our long-time friend and partner, for contributing the foreword to this book. Finally, thanks to the Packt team for asking us to share our knowledge and experience with the world, while also providing the guidance and support to make this happen.

– Keith D. Sutherland and Lawrence J. "Butch" Sheets

Foreword

As organizations strive to meet the ever-changing demands of their customers, the art of service management has emerged as a critical discipline that bridges the gap between vision and execution. *A Practical Guide to Service Management* is an essential compass for navigating this dynamic terrain.

This guide is not just another theoretical exploration of service management; it is a pragmatic roadmap crafted for those who seek practical solutions and tangible results. In these pages, you will find a treasure trove of insights, strategies, and proven methodologies that will empower you to revolutionize how services are conceived, designed, delivered, and continuously improved.

Drawing upon a wealth of real-world experiences and battle-tested wisdom, this book encapsulates the collective expertise of professionals who have successfully navigated the intricate landscape of service management. It seamlessly blends time-tested principles with cutting-edge practices, ensuring that whether you're a seasoned practitioner or just embarking on this journey, you will find actionable guidance that can be applied immediately.

From the strategic considerations that underpin effective service design to the nuts and bolts of service transition and daily operations, *A Practical Guide to Service Management* leaves no stone unturned. This guide is more than a compendium of methodologies; it's a call to action. It invites you to embrace a culture of continuous improvement, cultivate collaboration across teams, and view service management as a dynamic and adaptive discipline that responds to the evolving needs of both customers and organizations.

As you embark on this journey through the pages ahead, I encourage you to approach each chapter not just as a theoretical exercise, but as a toolkit for transformation. The challenges and opportunities presented by service management are as diverse as the organizations that strive to excel in it. With this guide in hand, you have a trusted companion to help you overcome obstacles, unlock new possibilities, and forge a path toward service excellence.

May *A Practical Guide to Service Management* empower you to create services that inspire, innovate, and make a lasting impact. Your commitment to mastering this discipline will not only drive operational efficiency but also foster customer loyalty and propel your organization toward a future where service is not just a function but a strategic cornerstone.

Lisa Schwartz

Founder and CEO, ITSM Academy

Contributors

About the authors

Keith D. Sutherland serves as a principal consultant in service management and is a co-founder/ managing partner of Service Management Dynamix, LLC, a South Carolina-based company. As a fully licensed and accredited instructor and service management consultant, he has facilitated numerous sessions for organizations interested in the value of a formal **Service Management** (**SM**) capability. Keith's varied background allows him to share real and practical experiences with customers, while his dynamic presentation style aids them in absorbing the concept of service management.

It has been a long-running IT career for me, with my first paid position in IT in 1973. I have been blessed and enabled by the many companies and people I have been privileged to work for and with over these decades. In many ways, this book that Butch and I have written is one way for us to give back, considering all that we have received.

Lawrence J. "Butch" Sheets serves as a principal consultant in service management and is a co-founder of Service Management Dynamix, LLC, a South Carolina-based company. As a licensed and accredited instructor and Service Management consultant, he has facilitated numerous sessions for organizations interested in the value of a formal SM capability. Butch's 45+ years of IT experience and 20+ years in formal SM allow him to share real and practical lessons with customers. His no-nonsense approach enables customers and practitioners to understand and apply SM concepts.

Since 1972, IT has been a part of my working career. I want to thank all those that guided my career over the last 50 years and this book is a tribute to those people. This book is a chance for Keith and me to give something back to the industry that has given us so much.

About the reviewer

Ian Keith MacDonald is a chartered IT professional recognized for his thought leadership in IT service management. An ITIL-accredited author and multiple IT award winner, he is a regular contributor and speaker at industry bodies and forums on IT best practice.

With over 40 years of experience in IT gained across the UK financial services industry, he has gained leadership expertise from running large IT service departments across the UK and Europe and has a proven track record of creating high-performance teams and delivering IT and organizational performance improvement through the adoption of IT and quality management best practice frameworks.

After gaining significant experience in the IT workplace, he is now established as an independent IT consultant and trainer.

In my career, I've been surrounded by great people who've inspired, encouraged, and given me the permission to think differently and make a difference.

Table of Contents

4

Systems Thinking in Terms of Service Management   29

Part 2: Essential Process Capabilities for Effective Service Management

5

Service Management Key Concepts   43

6

Incident Management   55

7

Problem Management 77

8

Change Management 99

9

Release and Deployment Management   125

10

Request Management   143

11

Service Catalog Management 161

12

Service Asset Management 175

13

Configuration Management   191

14

Business Relationship Management   207

15

Service Level Management   221

Part 3: How to Apply a Pragmatic, Customized Service Management Capability

16

Pragmatic Application of Service Management   239

17

Implementing a Successful Service Management Capability with Key Artifacts 251

18

Reviewing Critical Success Factors for Service Management Capability 269

19

Realizing CSFs for Service Management Implementation 277

20

Sustaining a Service Management Practice 285

Appendix A

SLA Template   297

Appendix B

SLR Template   303

Index   311

Preface

After more than 80 years' combined experience and involvement in IT, including over 50 years directly engaged in educating and helping customers implement service management disciplines, we felt we could share our knowledge and experience in a broader context. Thus, this book was developed to communicate key elements of a formal service management capability.

Within the content of this book, the reader will be introduced to the various methods, frameworks, and standards characterized by best practices for service management. From 1972 to the present, IT and service management have continued to evolve but the basic tenets of delivering and supporting services have remained constant. Customers define what is valuable and determine what provider does the best job of meeting the customers' needs and delivering value for the money being spent. Whether delivering a business service such as a restaurant dinner, auto repair, or IT service, it is essential to understand what the customer wants from the service and how the provider can meet those needs to produce a satisfactory experience.

It is our objective to help the reader understand the basis for the effective development of a service management capability. Although the guidance focuses on IT, the information shared can be applied to a variety of businesses and services. You will find information about the key processes to consider, process activities, important terms and definitions, key governance to apply, roles and responsibilities, technology considerations, and process interactions. We, having been directly involved in implementing and executing service management, also provide practical information on how to successfully establish and maintain a service management capability.

It is our desire to provide the necessary information and guidance to allow an organization or individual to develop an efficient and effective service management program that delivers value to their stakeholders and benefit to the business. We hope that you enjoy the knowledge and experience we have shared but more importantly, that you will find value in the lessons you have learned and feel enabled to apply them to your situation to make your life better and more productive. Thank you for taking the time to read our book. It represents an opportunity for us to leave some level of legacy and to give back to the community we have operated in for so many years! Besides, we have been involved in this discipline for so long that there is no way we could not have contributed to a book on this subject.

Who this book is for

This book covers information that will benefit C-level executives wanting to understand the value of service management in their organizations. It provides managers and practitioners within a service provider organization with guidance and information about delivering and supporting services, be it in IT or any other service organization.

What this book covers

Chapter 1, Understanding Service Management, provides an understanding of what ingredients are required to construct and maintain a service management capability.

Chapter 2, Getting to Grips with Service Management Frameworks, introduces the various methods, frameworks, movements, and standards for service management.

Chapter 3, Working with the "Design Thinking" Aspect of Service Management, is a concept that integrates the key factors in service management: people, process, and technology.

Chapter 4, Systems Thinking in Terms of Service Management, elaborates on the approach that aligns strategies with results and the frameworks, methods, movements, and standards that enable those results.

Chapter 5, Service Management Key Concepts, offers foundational concepts that are critical for understanding service management.

Chapter 6, Incident Management, is an introduction to the incident management process, including governance, execution, and enablement.

Chapter 7, Problem Management, is an introduction to the problem management process, including governance, execution, and enablement.

Chapter 8, Change Management, is an introduction to the change management process, including governance, execution, and enablement.

Chapter 9, Release and Deployment Management, is an introduction to the release and deployment management processes, including governance, execution, and enablement.

Chapter 10, Request Management, is an introduction to the service request management process, including governance, execution, and enablement.

Chapter 11, Service Catalog Management, is an introduction to the service catalog management process, including governance, execution, and enablement.

Chapter 12, Service Asset Management, is an introduction to the asset management process, including governance, execution, and enablement.

Chapter 13, Configuration Management, is an introduction to the configuration management process, including governance, execution, and enablement.

Chapter 14, Business Relationship Management, is an introduction to the business relationship management process, including governance, execution, and enablement.

Chapter 15, Service Level Management, is an introduction to the service level management process, including governance, execution, and enablement.

Chapter 16, Pragmatic Application of Service Management, explores the usage and benefit of using a continual improvement approach.

Chapter 17, Implementing a Successful Service Management Capability with Key Artifacts, reviews the key artifacts required for a successful implementation of a service management capability.

Chapter 18, Reviewing Critical Success Factors for Service Management Capability, reviews the critical success factors for initiating and sustaining a service management capability.

Chapter 19, Realizing CSFs for Service Management Implementation, discusses the critical success factors that will increase an organization's chances of success at successfully implementing a service management capability.

Chapter 20, Sustaining a Service Management Practice, describes the practices of continual improvement, management commitment, and monitoring, measuring, and reporting on managing the service management capability.

Appendix A, SLA Template, describes the content that could appear in a service-level agreement.

Appendix B, SLR Template, describes the information a service-level manager needs to develop a service-level agreement between the customer and the service provider.

Conventions used

There are a number of text conventions used throughout this book.

Bold: Indicates a new term, an important word, or words that you see onscreen. For instance, words in menus or dialog boxes appear in **bold**. Here is an example: "With respect to stakeholders, the terms **user** and **customer** have been alluded to, both separately and interchangeably."

> Tips or important notes
> Appear like this.

Get in touch

Feedback from our readers is always welcome.

General feedback: If you have questions about any aspect of this book, email us at customercare@ packtpub.com and mention the book title in the subject of your message.

Errata: Although we have taken every care to ensure the accuracy of our content, mistakes do happen. If you have found a mistake in this book, we would be grateful if you would report this to us. Please visit www.packtpub.com/support/errata and fill in the form.

Piracy: If you come across any illegal copies of our works in any form on the internet, we would be grateful if you would provide us with the location address or website name. Please contact us at copyright@packtpub.com with a link to the material.

If you are interested in becoming an author: If there is a topic that you have expertise in and you are interested in either writing or contributing to a book, please visit authors.packtpub.com.

Share Your Thoughts

Once you've read *A Practical Guide to Service Management*, we'd love to hear your thoughts! Scan the QR code below to go straight to the Amazon review page for this book and share your feedback.

https://packt.link/r/1804612502

Your review is important to us and the tech community and will help us make sure we're delivering excellent quality content.

Download a free PDF copy of this book

Thanks for purchasing this book!

Do you like to read on the go but are unable to carry your print books everywhere? Is your eBook purchase not compatible with the device of your choice?

Don't worry, now with every Packt book you get a DRM-free PDF version of that book at no cost.

Read anywhere, any place, on any device. Search, copy, and paste code from your favorite technical books directly into your application.

The perks don't stop there, you can get exclusive access to discounts, newsletters, and great free content in your inbox daily

Follow these simple steps to get the benefits:

1. Scan the QR code or visit the link below

https://packt.link/free-ebook/9781804612507

2. Submit your proof of purchase

3. That's it! We'll send your free PDF and other benefits to your email directly

Part 1:
The Importance of
Service Management

Part 1 elaborates on the understanding that service management serves as a structure from which other complementary frameworks, methods, movements, and standards can be harmonized, providing value for customers in the form of desired outcomes.

This part has the following chapters:

- *Chapter 1, Understanding Service Management*
- *Chapter 2, Getting to Grips with Service Management Frameworks*
- *Chapter 3, Working with the "Design Thinking" Aspect of Service Management*
- *Chapter 4, Systems Thinking in Terms of Service Management*

1
Understanding Service Management

Many of the concepts that are adopted in service management have their origins in other industries (for example, the building industry, emergency response, and others). Service management is not, in and of itself, a concept born in **information technology** (IT). All of us, in our daily lives, are surrounded by service management applications all the time. Understanding this perspective helps set the stage for what it means to be a service provider.

Through a *play-on-words* approach, you will understand what aspects make up the ingredients to construct and maintain a service management capability. We will explain why non-IT resources (for example, the director of marketing, administrative assistants, auditors, and others) can understand and be successful with service management education and certification, at least at a foundation level. Many, after attending education, have said "*This just seems like common sense!*"

In this chapter, we're going to cover the following main topics:

- The origins of many service management aspects
- Common service management examples and *wordplay* for service management
- Service management can improve life personally and professionally
- Common sense aspects of service management

Delving into the origins of many service management aspects

Compared to other industries (such as manufacturing, building, healthcare, and so on), where the date of origin isn't known, most believe that IT emerged in or around 1965. Common concepts such as capacity management and incident management did not originate in IT. For instance, capacity management has its origin in the building industry, while incident management is largely accepted to have originated in the field of emergency response (that is, firefighters, emergency medical technicians, and so on). As you may be aware, the role of incident commander has proven useful in many IT organizations. The manufacturing industry has had a significant influence on IT, especially when you recognize the many quality improvement methodologies (for example, Six Sigma, Lean, and Kaizen), where those concepts that have proven useful on the manufacturing floor, such as value stream mapping and Gemba walks, have been brought into the IT field.

Many baby boomers, those born between 1946 to 1964, who sought careers in what we call IT today, started in the mainframe arena. The mainframe brought standards and structure to how IT was implemented and maintained. **Information Systems Management Architecture (ISMA)**, which originated in the early '80s and was attributed to IBM (a highly recognizable name in the mainframe arena), largely spoke to those standards and structure. In fact, at the 2004 annual service management conference, sponsored by the US chapter of the **IT Service Management Forum (itSMF)**, held in Long Beach, CA, there was an informal gathering that included many of the original **IT Infrastructure Library (ITIL)** authors. They spoke to the influence of ISMA on the development of the ITIL framework. Though the recognized term today is just service management, its origins date back to the mid-1980s. All these decades later, the concept of service management has evolved, and many organizations still depend on it to gain a broad perspective on how best to be a provider of IT services. Also, as the decades have passed, more generations have entered the workforce (for example, Gen-X, Millennials, Gen-Z, and soon, Gen-Alpha). The evolution of service management has had to reflect the makeup of the workforce as these generations want (need) to be able to see themselves in the framework.

It is important to recognize the concept of ITIL as a **framework** for managing services versus a **standard**, **methodology**, or **movement**. The very mention of a framework implies that there is more than one way to apply it and experience success, which also means there is more than one way to apply it and experience failure. This statement alone should give us all pause, presuming success is desired. The origins of formal service management for IT date back decades. The first formal standard for IT service management, BSi15000, was developed by the British Standards Institution in approximately 2000. The ISO/IEC 20000 standard for service management emerged in 2005. Many are familiar with a framework for IT service management, called ITIL, which emerged years before the release of BSI15000. The real point is that service management, and its many respected authors along the way, continued to evolve as the newly developed solutions and trends in IT emerged. It is fair to say that sometimes, these standards, frameworks, methods, and movements trail behind emerging technologies and trends.

Collating common service management examples and understanding wordplay

All service providers implement and manage services. Perhaps the most generally accepted service provider example is any restaurant. As educators and consultants in the service management discipline, it is common, with a bit of *wordplay*, to challenge customers to reverse the words service management to *managing services*, and then ask what is involved in doing that. It doesn't take long to realize the emergence of the following words: customers, demand, specialized resources, suppliers, point of sale, menus, financial capital, success factors, methods, and organizational culture.

In truth, an IT service provider deals with the same scenarios, but the names may be slightly different (for example, service catalog instead of a menu, IT services instead of meals, and process instead of work methods) or the same (for example, customers, suppliers, demand, and so on). Besides restaurants and IT service providers, other examples of service providers include quick oil change providers, car washes, car dealership service departments, and more. Note that for any of these examples, whether the company itself is a service provider, the company has a service provider within it, or both, the challenge is the same – to be as efficient and effective as possible.

Given the many different types of service providers that are encountered across multiple industries and countries, what has been the perception of the quality of service received? It doesn't take long to recognize the quality of a given service management experience. When asking any group what constitutes a quality experience from a service provider, expect the response to be varied. Take a restaurant, for example. Some may say it was the quality of the food, or that it was affordable, or timely, or it helped to foster a great conversation within the group. All of these different responses represent what the participant (that is, the stakeholder) valued in their respective experience with the service provider. It is important, as a service provider, to recognize that different stakeholders may have different perspectives on what they value in their interaction with the service. What these stakeholders valued with the service largely comes down to what they were intending to accomplish (that is, outcomes), which, in the case of the restaurant service provider, may have been as simple as a great meal experience.

Service providers must remember two very key aspects of providing services:

- Stakeholder preferences can change over time
- Different stakeholders have differing perspectives, even against the same service offerings (for example, two customers order the same meal, but for different reasons, such as cost, dietary restrictions, and so on)

In keeping with the restaurant service provider example, there could be multiple franchises with the same name, yet the same stakeholder going to two different franchises could have a different experience with the service, even though the same meal was ordered at both locations. For the same service, the experience can be different! There are varying reasons for this, including differing skills and competencies across the staff, differing suppliers for the meal ingredients, differing cultures based on the location, and more. Even in a so-called *cookie-cutter* arrangement with the service provider, there can be a distinct experience for the customer (one type of stakeholder). With differing experiences over time with service providers, it doesn't take long to recognize what constitutes a great service management experience from one that is not so great, even from the same service provider.

When considering preferences, service providers should recognize that those customer preferences may change over time – that is, just because the service meets the needs of stakeholders today does not mean the same level of satisfaction will be in place tomorrow. As important as it is to continue to provide an expected level of service, it is also critical to consider how that same service experience might be improved. With this in mind, it is always important to maintain a stance that services can always be improved.

In that same restaurant service provider example, note the frequency at which a different representative of the provider (someone other than the server) checks in near the end of the meal experience to understand what the customer experience has been so far. These providers recognize the need to do a final check with that customer before they leave the meal experience. Why does this happen? It is an opportunity for the provider to identify what the customer enjoyed, what could be improved, or even present a last chance to fix something (if this is necessary). Most understand that there can be an unsatisfactory experience with the service, yet the customer is still willing to engage with the service provider going forward. This is especially true if that customer has had multiple prior satisfactory experiences with the service provider. Traits such as empathy and emotional intelligence help here, as well as knowledge of that customer and their preferences. So, skills such as relationship management help here. Though a negative experience with a first-time customer can have an impact on whether they return to that same restaurant service provider in the future, the best service providers still attempt to make things right, presenting a chance that the customer will return for a repeat visit. In these situations, that restaurant service provider might offer a discount on the service, a gift card for a return visit, or take a personal approach with a senior member of the service provider (for example, the owner, on-site manager, and so on).

Improving your personal and professional life with service management

For years, it has been maintained that an IT service provider with as few as 20 people can benefit from adopting a formal service management capability. With the availability of automation, **machine learning (ML)**, **artificial intelligence (AI)**, and deep learning, this statement suggests that how services are delivered and the interaction between the service provider and service consumer has become more significant to stakeholder satisfaction.

It was mentioned earlier that there are many generations in the workforce (whether Baby Boomers, Gen-X, Millennials, or Gen-Z), making culture a key consideration for any initiative. Creating and maintaining a formal service management practice, when done well, brings long-term predictability and innovation to any organization, making it a key program. The combination of culture and the service management program creates the best opportunity for long-term viability while using our human resources optimally. For instance, no matter the generation, there needs to be integration across, and common alignment with, the organization's mission, goals, objectives, and values. Gone should be the days of being awakened in the middle of the night by a database error, while still having to be onsite at the start of business. Gone are the days of the requirements changing because a new functionality went live, resulting in new necessities. Gone are the days of putting changes in over the weekend and having service outages on Monday morning. If these examples are, indeed, gone, then the human resources individuals that design, develop, transition, support, and improve services are more likely to thrive in their skills at work and their lives at home. Every generation has a *home* in this scenario as each can adopt and adapt to their differing needs. These needs include more time with family, improved work/life balance, diverse circumstances, skill specialization, and innovation.

Identifying common sense aspects of service management

In the delivery of service management education, which primarily focused on IT resources, it has long been obvious that the concepts discussed do not approach rocket science complexity. Many may come to the education event thinking that it will be an IT class. That's a natural inference from the name ITSM.

In actuality, this education, at a foundational level, focuses on what it takes to be a valued service provider. Although the education event is largely attended by IT resources, it is not unusual to see participation by resources from human resources, sales, marketing, finance, administration, and even customer-vendor relationships. Many of these non-IT-specific resources refer to the phrase "*This seems like common sense.*" Presumably, effectively using analogies (for example, the restaurant as a service provider) helps in driving understanding of the concepts. While helping the resources visualize a scenario outside of their own lives with the help of analogies, it also makes sense to transition to a situation where the resource connects these analogies naturally to their work, such as an actual business process (for example, close a sales order, procure to pay, onboard a new employee, and so on).

A significant aspect of education on formal service management – that is, why participants attend – is the exposure to best practices. In years past, this education included a focus on the difference between *best practice* and *good practice*, with the real goal being the latter. A best practice represents leveraging what other service providers have done to drive efficiency and effectiveness in provisioning IT services. Good practice, on the other hand, represents tailoring those concepts to your organization's culture and needs. This is where common sense must prevail. An example is a healthcare organization with multiple hospitals that has adopted service management concepts in the areas of service desk and incident management. The service desk is staffed with healthcare-related resources, who bring knowledge of healthcare-related disciplines (such as nursing, radiology, and others). The common-sense aspect of this is the service desk agent's ability to speak the same language as the users most likely to contact them (for example, a hospital nursing station). At the same time, a manufacturing organization is not likely to staff its service desk with healthcare-related competencies. Common sense must prevail!

Once service management education has been attained, participants can judge their organization's current service management capabilities against the learned criteria. Whether a formal practice or not, all service providers practice service management. It is a matter of what level of maturity they are at, contrasted and compared with where the business of the larger company is going. Is the IT organization (service provider) optimally positioned to support that vision? Is the IT organization exercising an improvement culture, demonstrating an ability to increase service delivery capabilities? Can IT map the services it delivers to business outcomes and values? These questions represent common sense aspects of being a valued service provider.

The real work begins once formal service management education has been completed. The current question then becomes "*What should the participant do differently now?*" Though not rocket science concepts, the sheer number of concepts is comprehensive and begs a practical (short-term set of actions – *low-hanging fruit*) and pragmatic (long-term character attribute – think *program*) approach.

Summary

Service management, no matter the level of formality, is in play at all times and is all around us in many different scenarios. It is incumbent upon service providers to maintain this capability, especially for those that have formalized their practice. That said, a service provider's market consists of stakeholders that are key to the success of a formal service management capability. Formal service management is not specific to IT. In fact, and as mentioned, many of its included concepts originate from other industries. Culture also plays a key role in the success of managing services. Once human resources get entrenched in formal service management situations across an ecosystem of service providers, it becomes contagious, in that the quality of the service being delivered is judged. Applying common sense concepts from formal service management can have a significant impact on work/life balance.

In the coming chapters, we will build on these concepts of service management, including related frameworks/standards/methods, systems thinking, and design thinking. Now that your curiosity has been piqued by the general idea of service management, let's explore what is meant by formalizing these concepts from an IT service management perspective, often referred to as ITSM.

2

Getting to Grips with Service Management Frameworks

Today, multiple service management frameworks and related standards, specific to IT or highly related, have emerged, and have achieved significant adoption. What are the other service management frameworks, and why should you be aware of them? What were the reasons behind their emergence?

In this chapter, we're going to cover the following main topics:

- Distinguishing between frameworks, methods, standards, and movements
- Tracing the evolution of service management
- What are the service management frameworks for IT?
- What are the service management frameworks for enterprises?

Distinguishing between frameworks, methods, standards, and movements

In discussing the difference between frameworks, methods, standards, and movements, it is important to define each of them and also support those definitions with familiar examples. One of the related factors is the concept of **systems thinking**, where an IT service provider leverages a number of these based on their strategy and level of current maturity. The fact is that no one framework, standard, methodology, or even movement on its own would be enough to implement and maintain a thriving service management capability. The analogy would be that a favorite meal, or any meal, requires several ingredients to be part of the recipe. In keeping with the concept of systems thinking, a generally accepted definition of **architecture** is the interrelationship between systems (for example, business architecture, supported by IT service architecture, supported by application architecture, and so on) with **systems** simply defined as a set of integrated components (for example, an application made up of modules, a server made up of component pieces, a service management technology platform made up of modules with applications within, and so on). Any framework, method, or standard can be looked at as a system, where multiple are in use to help meet and sustain a capability – such as a service management capability. Systems thinking will be discussed in greater detail in *Chapter 3*.

Frameworks are generally defined as conceptual support structures or systems that hold parts together. A key word in this simple definition is *conceptual*, which brings the word *interpretation* into the mix. How one entity interprets and uses a framework is based on its level of understanding, need, and maturity. The challenge with frameworks, and their use, is that there are multiple ways of applying them and realizing success. At the same time, ineffectively applying frameworks can result in failure. The sagest advice encourages organizations to bring in a framework for use (**adopt**) and also customize its use in a way that respects the existing strategy and maturity (**adapt**). Within IT, several frameworks can be used for service management, including ITIL®, COBIT®, IT4IT™, Scrum, SFIA, SAFe®, and VeriSM™ – this is not an exhaustive list. Many have found that the concepts from these frameworks can be adopted by not only IT service providers but also other departments within a company, such as sales, legal, finance, and human resources. At least for the large majority of CIOs, there has been a realization that the adoption of best practices is critical to the success of IT in its ability to service its market. Frameworks play a critical role. Given the lack of straightforward guidance in the application of frameworks, organizations seeking education or consulting in this area should consider due diligence in selecting a provider to assist them.

Methods (that is, methodologies) are different from frameworks. While frameworks, as mentioned previously, can be applied in multiple ways, this is not the case with methods. **Methods** are described as a technique, systematic procedure, or process for getting something done. From that description alone, it is clear that it is not *conceptual* or subject to varying interpretations (such as the description of frameworks). Familiar methods are Six Sigma, Lean Six Sigma, **Capability Maturity Model Integration (CMMI®)**, **Software Development Life Cycle (SDLC)**, **Projects in a Controlled Environment (PRINCE2®)**, **Knowledge-Centered Service (KCS®)**, and many others. All of these methods can be applied to IT, though IT may not have been the origin (for example, Six Sigma has its origins in manufacturing). Specific to service management, methods such as Lean, PRINCE2®, and USM have proven to be of significant adoption.

Standards respect both frameworks and methods since, in many cases, it is critical to comprehensively adopt and apply frameworks or methods to achieve a standard. For instance, you may have to adopt a particular framework to achieve the standard. For this book, **standards** are defined as a model or technical-specific criteria, designed to be used consistently as a rule, guideline, or definition. They help make things simpler, while also increasing the reliability and effectiveness of many of the products and services we use (for example, a service provider's service offerings). Standards also tend to have associated naming conventions. For instance, international standards are prefixed with *ISO/IEC*, American standards are prefixed with *ANSI*, and British standards are prefixed with *BSI*. The standard for service management is ISO/IEC 20000, which did not start that way. It was born from the British Standards Institute standard BS 15000. Other commonly known standards are the international standard ISO/IEC 9000 family (quality standard), international standard ISO/IEC 15504 (for process assessments), and ISO/IEC 27001 (information security management). Also, though it is not an established formal organization (like ANSI, BSI, or ISO/IEC) per se, FitSM refers to itself as a standard that wishes to achieve service management effectiveness without the complexity of other standards (especially across integrated organizations).

This publication would be remiss if it did not mention bodies of knowledge or **movements**. For instance, DevOps is not described as a framework, method, or standard. It is described as a movement, where its key components are culture, collaboration (sharing), use of automation, lean thinking, and measurement. These all represent DevOps principles. Developing IT applications under these principles allows for faster implementation to production with appropriate levels of quality. This makes DevOps part of Agile thinking (as is the Scrum framework). A **body of knowledge (BoK)** is a type of knowledge typically sponsored by an organization with a specific area of specialization with its own purpose, concepts, terms, and activities. For instance, certified project managers (**Project Management Professionals** or **PMPs**) are familiar with the **Project Management Body of Knowledge (PMBOK®)**, which doesn't apply to just IT (neither does the PRINCE2® method).

Also emerging in a significant way is the **Business Relationship Management Body of Knowledge (BRMBoK™)**. **Service Integration and Management (SIAM)** is also considered a BoK and focuses on suppliers and integration, given the prevalence of external provider involvement in the delivery of IT services. One of the longest-standing bodies of knowledge specific to service management is the **Universal Service Management Body of Knowledge (USMBOK)**, which was initially published in 2008.

As this publication focuses on the concept of formal service management capabilities, it is important to know that there are complementary aspects of various other frameworks, methods, standards, movements, and BoKs – hence the concept of not only systems thinking but also *design thinking*.

Though a formal service management capability touts the approach of integrating multiple disciplines, it also recalibrates toward value co-creation, as will be discussed in *Chapter 3*. Service management professionals must understand that a blended approach is critical to the success of implementing a formal service management capability. No one system will be adequate for initial and sustained success, raising the importance of strategy and design (architecture) involvement throughout the journey. In *Chapters 3* and *4*, the subjects of systems thinking and design thinking, respectively, will illustrate the concept of combining standards, methods, movements, and frameworks, and how they integrate. It's this integration that produces a formal service management capability for a service provider and, therefore, the organization. To this point, it is about understanding that success in service management cannot be optimally achieved without considering different facets of multiple solutions and must be pragmatic to a specific organization's needs.

Tracing the evolution of service management

Since the late 1990s and early 2000s, the international not-for-profit organization promoting service management, known as **IT Service Management Forum (itSMF)**, has held annual conferences on the subject of service management. Many countries have their own chapter (for example, itSMF USA), where interested parties gather as a collective to present and discuss the subject of service management. Even within a specific country's chapter, there is the concept of **Local Interest Groups (LIGs)**, where smaller instances or segments gather in the interest of furthering their knowledge of service management. This was a brilliant arrangement, in that it significantly furthered the spread and adoption of formal service management capabilities within these countries. In the United States, of note was the significant adoption of ITIL® by large Midwest-based corporations, resulting in permeation east, west, and south. The establishment of LIGs across the country had a direct correlation, enabling a local, community-based approach to service management adoption.

In 2004, at the national itSMF USA conference, in Long Beach, CA, many of the original authors and pundits of service management gathered in an informal meeting to discuss *all things service management*.

The origins of IT service management (dating back to the mid-80s) came up in that discussion. It was noted that IBM had a significant influence on what led to formal IT service management. In 1980, **Information Systems Management Architecture (ISMA)** was published, detailing IBM's approach to defining and managing IT services. IBM had also published a series of books, referred to as **yellow books**. A careful look at some of the diagrams within these publications provides evidence of what became formal processes in service management. Familiarity with the origins and objectives helps provide an understanding of the intent of service management.

Service management, which spans decades, has continued to evolve to remain relevant. Given the concepts of service management overall, in that they are subject to interpretation and have undergone significant criticism (for example, for being rigorous, inflexible, and bureaucratic), skilled service management educators and consultants can readily identify prior evidence of concepts that are popular today. Since the very beginning, the prevailing theme has always been to *do what makes sense!*

Service management was also respected as a process capability, where each process consisted of three aspects – governance (control), execution (roles, activities, and metrics), and enablement (resources and integration with other complements). From the very beginning, the following process capabilities were readily actioned upon (these are considered the most significant):

- Incident management
- Problem management
- Change management
- Access management
- Software control and distribution
- Configuration management
- Service-level management
- Availability management
- IT service continuity management
- Capacity management

All of these processes are still in place.

In truth, many contributions across the industry had occurred, and the complexity of service management increased dramatically. By this point, the popularity and adoption of formal service management had grown far beyond its initial use. In correlation with the international growth of country chapters regarding itSMF (and corresponding LIGs), having a formal service management capability was now accepted as the best practice approach for IT service providers to become more efficient and effective.

With the emergence and adoption of Agile thinking (in around 2012 in the United States market), within a few years, there was a shift away from formal service management in many organizations.

The functionality (utility) of IT services is largely based on (comes from) applications. Therefore, development looms large. Perhaps for most organizations, getting to market quicker with business solutions proves differentiation, hence the need to be more agile. Formal service management had begun to be perceived as too structured, too bureaucratic, latent with rigor, and getting in the way of getting to the market quicker. Also, along the way, the concept of **bi-modal IT** emerged, where there were, in essence, two approaches to bringing solutions to market – via an SDLC (for example, Waterfall) or Agile. It seemed the traditional SDLC approach to development was consistent with service management, while SAFe, DevOps, Scrum, and **Site Reliability Engineering** (**SRE**) made more sense for organizations that wanted to demonstrate velocity. What became perplexing was if an organization was committed to both approaches, which were still in place in many organizations. In these cases, companies moved away from formal service management capabilities.

In this movement, among multiple sets of guidance, what was missed, and later realized, was that there was still a need for governance, some level of structure, and many of the concepts where formal service management excelled. The most knowledgeable, and importantly, the most pragmatic, never wavered on the value that service management could bring an organization. At the same time, it was imperative to change the perception of being bureaucratic and too rigid. Formal service management, the real subject of this book, takes the history of service management, and in some ways serves an orchestration role, blends the other needed approaches, and enables a customized and pragmatic service management capability. This does not discount that service management, in and of itself, also brings significant historic contributions, along with newer concepts, to the service management landscape.

The term ITSM has been used from the very beginning and, in essence, has translated directly to value for all stakeholders in the ecosystem. These varying stakeholder groups can be inside or outside of IT (for example, a product team composed of business partners and IT resources) and are all involved in managing services.

What are the service management frameworks for IT?

Formal service management, for an organization, is defined as the specialized internal consultancy for providing value to stakeholders and customers in the form of services (for example, a service management practice). **ITSM** is defined as the strategic, tactical, and operational approach to managing IT within the organization and delivering IT services to customers.

It is important to note the strategic, tactical, and operational aspects of service management. When organizations start with a formal service management capability (and no matter what framework(s) they adopt), they tend to focus on the operational aspects (for example, incident, problem, change, request, and more). These areas tend to produce efficiency with a relatively quick turnaround (time to market). Though these are important, being operational, they don't get visibility at the higher leadership levels. Later in this book, we will focus on the need to get closer to the business partners at higher levels of service management in the organization. Organizations should strive to define and follow a roadmap, composed of strategic, tactical, and operational aspects throughout. It does take longer to show results with the strategic and tactical aspects, but they are critical components as they create the visibility of the IT service provider as a service provider, a trusted advisor, and (potentially) a strategic partner.

Just as service management technology platform capabilities continue to evolve, so do the frameworks, methods, standards, and bodies of knowledge. From an ITSM-specific perspective, the following frameworks, internationally, have garnered significant service management use:

- **ITIL®**: From Axelos
- **COBIT®**: From **Information Systems Audit & Control Association (ISACA)**
- **VeriSM™**: From **International Foundation of Digital Competencies (IFDC)**
- **FitSM®**: From **IT Education Management Organization (ITEMO)**
- **USM**: The **Unified Service Management** model from the SURVUZ Foundation
- **BRM**: From the Business Relationship Management Institute
- **IT4IT™**: From the Open Group®

As mentioned previously, there is a standard associated with service management, known as ISO/IEC 20000, which is commonly referred to as ISO 20K. FitSM®, mentioned in the preceding list, is more referred to as a standard versus a framework and is advertised as complementary access. All of the preceding frameworks have associated certifications and credentials. Any of these approaches could further a service provider's goal of implementing and maintaining a formal service management capability. This book focuses on formal service management, but we will call out some of these others as complements.

What are the service management frameworks for enterprises?

Enterprise service management (**ESM**) is defined as the practice of applying IT best practices across the business to improve effectiveness, efficiency, and overall service delivery. The result is improved customer experience and business outcomes. Though the concept of ESM has emerged over recent years, it is not new. There is evidence dating back to the early 2000s. Business partners saw the gains their IT departments made in managing services, by adopting formal ITSM, and worked with IT to bring some of those very concepts (for example, change management) into their business units. This is an example of where those IT service providers had proven their worth before they were looked upon as business partners (versus just IT).

Another proof point that's seen with ESM is non-IT resources attending service management platform (technology) conferences. It is because these platforms now tout functionality (utility), which helps with other shared service aspects of the business (for example, human resources, customer service, legal, procurement, governance/risk and compliance, and more).

From an ESM-specific perspective, the following frameworks allow us to go beyond IT (but are IT-inclusive):

- **ITIL®**: From Axelos
- **COBIT®**: From ISACA
- **VeriSM™**: From IFDC
- **USM**: From the SURVUZ Foundation
- **BRM**: From the Business Relationship Management Institute

Even though these frameworks can mature existing capabilities in business partner areas, it is likely that IT service provider resources would be involved in helping business partners move forward with the concepts. The fact that ESM has emerged is proof that service management is not only applicable to IT service providers. Given the many examples of service providers that exist (for example, a restaurant), it follows that many can benefit from service management thinking. Within an overall business, the IT service provider can provide a leadership role in helping their business partners benefit from sound service management concepts.

Summary

Just in absorbing this chapter, it is apparent that there are many moving parts in the service management ecosystem. Yet, the appropriate level of understanding, coupled with a pragmatic approach, will likely result in success with formal service management. Whether it's a framework, a standard, a method, a movement, or a BoK, all of these approaches and disciplines represent part of managing a service and therefore are key contributors associated with service management.

As presented earlier, understanding the history of service management (how we got here) can be a significant factor in learning the best approach toward applying it in an organization. In the most successful applications of service management, there is a strong commitment to understanding the business of the company, and what aspects of formal service management guidance apply to the current and proposed future state. No two organizations are the same, even in the same line of business. Culture, strategy, skills, and competencies are key factors of consideration moving forward. *Chapter 20* will explain why formal service management initiatives/programs succeed, but also why they fail.

Both systems thinking and design thinking will be discussed in the next two chapters and are critical to the success of formal service management. Related to our discussion regarding the various frameworks, methods, standards, and more, there is a need to integrate within and across them. We will discuss the required integration across these elements in the next two chapters.

3

Working with the "Design Thinking" Aspect of Service Management

Design thinking is a concept that predates service management but has become an important facet of it. In terms of service management, it largely deals with the *people* aspect of *people, process, and technology*. This includes the attitude, behavior, and culture on the success of a service management capability within an organization. Terms such as *co-creation*, *user experience*, and *customer experience* are relevant here. Additional important terms are *trust*, *safe environment*, *collaboration*, and *no fear of conflict* – all are critical to pay attention to.

In this chapter, we will cover the following main topics:

- Defining design thinking in terms of service management
- Why is user experience important?
- Why is customer experience important?
- What is customer journey mapping?

Defining design thinking in terms of service management

In previous chapters, we have discussed formal service management as being a *specialized organizational capability* (an internal consultancy, of sorts, on how best to provide products and services). Service management frameworks, though having some scientific aspects, are far more of an art form than a science, given that it is the people, the culture, and the governance that are all critical to the success of the service provider. Recall that any service management framework on its own is not enough, and not intended to be the only ingredient, to foster an optimized service management capability. It is the integration across multiple approaches that makes the difference – hence, the concept of design thinking.

For clarity, understanding the difference between design thinking and systems thinking (the subject of the next chapter) makes sense. **Systems thinking**, as a *holistic approach*, is used to analyze the relationship across multiple systems and their respective components (there is systemic interaction.). Decisions are made on how best to meet customer requirements through the use of systems and components. This will be discussed in more detail in the next chapter, which focuses on systems thinking.

Though there is a connection between systems thinking and design thinking, the latter is more focused on the stakeholders involved *and* a balance of their collective concerns. Many aspects of service management frameworks (e.g., governance, principles, people, processes, and technology) all have an expressed connection to stakeholders. This is evidenced by words, phrases, and concepts, such as *collaboration, engagement, relationship, customer journey mapping,* and *feedback*. Although design thinking is a method that continually encourages real users to define what constitutes value to them, the economic aspects must also be considered. Service providers do not tend to have unlimited budgets and resources, so working closely with key stakeholders to determine the most pragmatic solution (which delivers the most appropriate benefits) is key. Giving stakeholders the ability to contribute collectively affords the benefits of better digital products and better customer experiences, resulting in better capability for customers and users to get their jobs done. Lastly, for the service provider, there is also an opportunity to gather feedback on what works and what doesn't.

With respect to stakeholders, the terms **user**, **consumer**, and **customer** have been alluded to, separately and interchangeably. These will be discussed more specifically in most of all of the upcoming chapters in this book. The point to be made here is that it is pretty common for organizations, by practice and/or policy, to stipulate the appropriate use of these terms. For instance, an organization may determine that the use of *consumer* is confined to stakeholders that purchase products and/or services from the company, whereas *customer* and *user* are considered to be used preferably as internal terms. This is important as part of design thinking, given its objective to understand the requirements and concerns of the collective stakeholder ecosystem. As the service provider, it is viability, feasibility, and desirability that matter most.

The design thinking approach is highly dependent on collaboration, where the service provider and its market collaborate closely and work together to architect a solution that meets the expectations of all involved (e.g., economy of scale, governance, operational excellence, and security and IT compliance). DevOps, discussed as a movement in earlier chapters, embraces this concept by specifying the stakeholders that tend to be on the **dev** (e.g., business partners) side and those that tend to be on the **ops** side (e.g., suppliers). These collaboration aspects will have only marginal success without a *safe* environment, where the attributes of trust, commitment, and no fear of conflict are all key ingredients. Consider these attributes, along with the different value perspectives (i.e., strategic, financial, economic, operational, and technical) that different stakeholders bring. This highlights not only the opportunity for success but also the challenges that must be overcome. The culture of the organization is always a factor.

All stakeholders, whether on the service provider side or the consumer side, must keep at the top of their minds the organization's mission, goals, values, and objectives. The following diagram, shown previously in *Chapter 2*, which is open to interpretation, shows how an organization is structured and designed, the criticality of strategies, where service management tends to fit in, and how those strategies (plans) are interconnected:

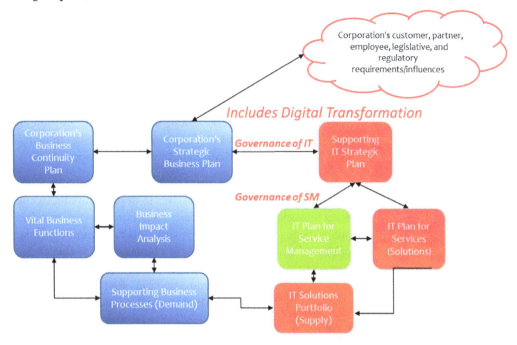

Figure 3.1 – The strategy/plan cascade

We can determine, at least, some of the stakeholders that need to be represented as part of design thinking. Consider the word *architecture* whenever the word *design* appears. As part of design thinking, it is the experience with the service offerings, from concept to retirement, that is architected. That includes an understanding of the requirements (what stakeholders are needed?), the design of the service/product solutions (what stakeholders are needed?), the development of the solution (what stakeholders are needed?), the deployment of the solution (what stakeholders are needed?), the support of the solution (what stakeholders are needed?), and lastly, the improvement of the solution (what stakeholders are needed?). The interpretation here should be that design thinking is never really completed. Interaction with stakeholders should always be there throughout the life cycle of a service offering.

As important as understanding the mission, goals, values, and objectives is, the service provider must also be equally concerned about how its market gets exposure to its products and services. Think of a service offering outside of work, such as your favorite restaurant, store, or entertainment experience:

- How did you find out about the provider (**touchpoint**)? How do you feel about that?

- How do you interact with the provider (**an interaction**), including how you feel about it or how it could be improved?

In terms of how you know about your favorite restaurant, it could be that you visited its website, walked/drove by it, or perhaps the restaurant directly contacted you in some way (e.g., a flyer to your mailbox, a phone call, or a television commercial). Think of these as *touchpoints*.

Now, if you actively use the service provider's product/service, what are the various ways that you interact with it? For the store, it may be that you order online (and it may be your only option), you physically visit it, or maybe they do the shopping for you. To put this into the context of service management and being a service provider, there are a myriad of options for creating awareness of your services/products (touchpoints) and also a myriad of ways for your market to engage with you (and you with them), called *interactions*. It is meritable to understand, based on its culture, how an organization is structured and the technology in place (versus what's available). In design thinking, two of the keywords are *touchpoints* and *interactions* (as discussed throughout this chapter).

For service providers practicing formal service management, there are a number of aforementioned frameworks, methods, and bodies of knowledge that lend themselves to design thinking (while others lend themselves more to systems thinking). Also, as previously mentioned, service providers should look to leverage multiple options, taking an integrated approach. This requires not only the skills and competencies of these capabilities but also the knowledge of a business and its culture. So, as alluded to earlier, is service management an *art form* or a *science*? There are scientific aspects, but more predominantly, it is an art form, where creativity and innovation can often flourish. Design thinking compels the service provider to learn more about the business of their stakeholders. Done well, there is a measurable positive impact on customer satisfaction levels, retaining those customers while attracting new ones, and improving opportunities to meet business objectives.

Consider the following diagram, which, although not exhaustive and randomly selected, illustrates multiple frameworks and methods as tools that can be used for design thinking:

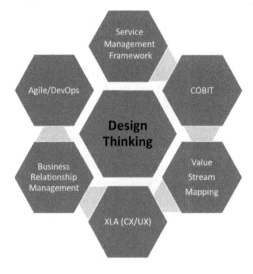

Figure 3.2 – (Random) tools for design thinking

Each of the tools shown represents areas (within the tool) where there is a focus on understanding, architecting, testing, managing, measuring, or improving the experience of a service provider's product/service:

- **Business relationship management (BRM)** can be used to understand how the service provider market perceives value and the current state versus the desired state of value realization

- **Agile/DevOps** can be used to ensure a co-creative, collaborative nature from requirements through to delivery

- **Value stream mapping** can help with cohesion across multiple stakeholder groups in understanding the current state and defining a future state, along with a plan to evolve

- **Experience-level agreement (XLA)** (i.e., **customer experience (CX)** and **user experience (UX)**) can be used to understand experience trends, at a user and customer level

- **COBIT** can be used proactively to provide assurance of policies to facilitate a design thinking environment, and it can be used reactively to measure how well a method is maturing

- **Respected service management frameworks** can be used as the primary integrator of all of these ingredients, especially and explicitly integrating across multiple frameworks and methods

The preceding diagram and bullet list are not exhaustive, in that other combinations could have been chosen, and even within a given selection, each brings more capability than was exemplified (e.g., BRM does more than what was described). Independent of what approaches (e.g., the framework, body of knowledge, or method) are used to enable design thinking, the service provider must ensure the skills and competencies are mastered prior to use. This might include leveraging an experienced (and potentially external) resource for help. For instance, having an experienced value stream mapping facilitator is critical! A key component of tool adoption is its demonstrated success, given the importance of building a coalition across key stakeholders.

With the design thinking method, a sound approach to co-creating value between the service provider and their market (e.g., customer, consumer, user, or sponsor) is the prime objective. This includes working closer with these stakeholders in the following ways:

- Learning who the key stakeholders are. Know your audience! If the challenge was to distill all of the thousands of pages about service management down to one word, that one word would be **empathy**. As the service provider, do you understand what it is like to consume a product/service that you provide?

- Understanding the demand, which could come in the form of an enhancement to an existing service/product, or could be, although not as likely as an enhancement, a totally new and different product/service. Use collaboration to look at the demand from different aspects, resulting in, at least, a high-level understanding of the requirements. Construct a plan to achieve the desired outcome.

- By this point (in design thinking), the service provider and its market are well into the co-creation of value. Continuing to collaborate, these stakeholders naturally progress to solutioning, where ideas emerge on how the demand can be realized. It is the safe environment that these stakeholders operate within that allows the potential for creative solutions and, perhaps, innovative ideas to emerge.

- Continuing to work together, perhaps with a subset of the broader group, and bringing a proposed concept to an alpha/beta state. Open it up to the broader group and understand how well the requirements are being met, and to what degree things need to change, from a market perspective (versus the service provider perspective). How well are the usability needs met?

- Remembering that business is about differentiation, innovation, and *speed to value*, using and applying the lessons learned from the alpha/beta review. It is important to progress the new solution to a releasable state. Use the concepts of agile/DevOps/**site reliability engineering (SRE)** to test and integrate the new solution, involving the wider audience. Creative approaches are best, as a new solution will not yet be in production. The viability of the new solution should be realized during this time, with all stakeholders understanding the risks.

The following diagram, common to a waterfall approach, speaks to the preceding bullet points:

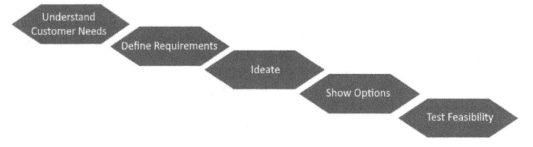

Figure 3.3 – Key activities for design thinking

Do not underestimate the required level of skills and competencies required to be successful with design thinking. This is not just technical knowledge, but also business acumen, cultural knowledge, and the right environment setting (no fear of conflict, trust, or commitment/accountability) across the stakeholder ecosystem. Think of the composition of a product team today. These teams tend to be made up of both business partners and service provider representation. They can be led by a business partner or the service provider – aren't all of the stakeholders there to serve the mission, goals, values, and objectives of the business?

Design thinking did not originate in service management but can certainly be used as part of a formal service management capability. If the mantra for service management is to provide value in the form of realized outcomes for stakeholders, then design thinking is a key component. It must be considered a critical component of success, potentially making the service provider a trusted advisor and strategic partner to the business. That only happens if the consumer/customer/sponsor/user perceives that the service provider demonstrates its ability to understand its market and how its product/services support that market. Consistent analysis of stakeholder interaction is key for design thinking, including the use of experimentation and learning, opening the door for further discovery, improvement opportunity, and, perhaps, innovation.

Why is user experience important?

There can be a clear distinction between a *user, partner, consumer,* or *customer* (or similar), all of which are considered types of consumers and, therefore, stakeholders. Those subjects will be covered in greater detail later in this book (*Chapter 5*). The focus here is the *experience* aspect, in this chapter (*user*) and the next (*customer*).

In a generic sense, think of users as generalists, more closely associated with the day-to-day aspects of operating a company. Practitioners would also be a valid description, considering the competencies they are required to execute in specialized areas. These users are the most likely to interact with the products/services and the service providers. This is where experience matters. The interactions here, good or bad, are measurable and can be tied directly to the experience with the service provider and business indicators.

Here are three user scenarios that can have a significant impact on experience:

- **Scenario 1**: Logic might suggest that a critical product/service outage would directly negatively affect the user's relationship with the service provider; this is not necessarily true. All consumers, at some point in their life, experience a lower quality of product/service but still have a positive relationship with their provider.

- **Scenario 2**: The provider may presume user satisfaction levels are where they need to be, but the actual UX does not agree. Although it is important to understand how well a service performs, it is equally important to understand what the user experiences with the service.

- **Scenario 3**: Customer requirements did not meet user requirements. As part of product/service design, early in the requirement gathering process, although there was customer representation, it didn't prove effective in assuring that user requirements throughout development, testing, and deployment have been met.

As part of the design thinking discussion, each of the preceding scenarios, good or bad, would be considered as part of the cycle. In the establishment of a formal service management capability, it is likely that similar scenarios have occurred. Collaborating on value, done effectively, ensures that user requirements are represented as part of prototyping, prior to testing. Common areas of impact on UX are as follows:

- The service provider, inclusive of its external agents, has the ability to interact with users. This includes the available channels the user can engage through.

- Do users participate in the development of service provider standard operating procedures?

- UX has a significant impact on company bottom-line performance, including employee retention and customer satisfaction levels.

Given the level of user interaction with service provider products/services, effective approaches in gaining feedback from users can prove valuable in understanding UX. There are scientific-based solutions, including supporting technology platforms, that provide you with the ability to measure UX – a convergence of the concepts and technology. With this knowledge – from continued trend analysis, modification of current measures, and/or programs/projects – there should always be an understanding of UX and the ability to efficiently know whether shifts occur. There is an emerging trend of organizations developing XLAs designed to capture much of this subject area. XLAs are not to be confused with **service-level agreements (SLA)**, nor are they a replacement. The general thinking, as previously stated, is to measure both UX and service provision, and subsequently learn from both.

Although there is upcoming coverage on the subject of CX, it is important to understand that UX is closely related to and directly impacted by CX. Presuming that users are part of a customer organization, CX is often tasked with representing the needs of users (as users may not have *a seat at the table*). This situation calls into question CX's ability to represent user needs, where the service provider is now dependent on information from customers. The service provider must do its best to ensure that user needs are represented, as part of design thinking, throughout the life cycle of products/services.

To close, processing incidents and service requests is a key aspect of service management. How do the users at your company feel about their experience with the service provider in the processing of both? Is it predictable? Were they involved in the design? What have you learned from the feedback that can be used to improve UX? It is likely there is an opportunity for improvement, but even if it is not glaring or minimal, understanding what it takes to maintain a desirable experience is also key. Certainly, we want to replicate the positive things done that lead to great UX, tailored for each situation.

Why is customer experience important?

With the presumption that a company internally would have both customers and users, it follows that users would be part of the customer organization. For instance, the service provider, as part of service management, provides products/services for a customer organization. Also, the IT service provider provides services for the human resources customer, in which there are human resources practitioners (users). It then follows that, as part of design thinking, the service provider co-creates value with the human resources customer, meaning that the customer *has a seat at the table* (the phrase **seat at the table** means, in this case, that the customer is an active participant in the governance and decision-making around products/services).

Let's define CX as the touchpoints and interactions with the service provider across the life cycle of a service, including the strategy, design, transition, delivery, support, and improvement of the products/services. This starts to answer the question of why CX is important, given the level of optimization across the product/service life cycle that customers should be directly involved in. Again, the keywords and terms are *collaboration, engagement, working together on what constitutes value, relationship management,* and *customer journey mapping.* In fact, a key aspect of business relationship management (which relates to business partners, also known as customers) is that the IT service provider, if it fashions itself as (or desires to be) a trusted advisor or strategic business partner, should take the lead on assuring value co-creation. It is human nature that when the appropriate level of inclusion occurs, those included feel that they had a voice in the outcome, even if it wasn't exactly what they wanted to occur. Consensus does not mean everyone got what they wanted, but it does mean people had an opportunity to contribute. Think of the positive impact that has on experience.

Customers, who often by default represent users, by definition are experts in their specific area. Remember that practitioners have areas of specialization (e.g., how does this business process work in our area?). It is proven that when service providers spend an appropriate amount of time with business partners (customers), they learn more about a customer's business, including what they are trying to achieve, innovative ways to provide the product/service, and even what customers should be reporting as incidents but are just tolerating (because they thought that was just how it is supposed to work!). Importantly, direct service provider involvement sends a message that the service provider is invested in the success of the customers they are aligned with. The term **alignment** has evolved to **convergence**, as in many cases, the IT service provider is part of the same company as the customer, where both have a duty to be part of the mission, goals, values, and objectives of the company, which cascades to any external entities, helping the company meet its objectives.

The intent is to ensure that the involvement of stakeholders, outside of the service provider, plays a critical role in the products/services created to enhance the ability of the customer to execute the business process(es) that they are accountable for (and are experts at!). It's important that everyone is part of an inclusive environment, including trust, openness, use of business (or layman's) terms, commitment, and accountability – often referred to as a *safe environment.* As mentioned earlier (and in one example), note the emergence of product teams, which can be led by a business customer or a representative of the IT service provider. A phrase that comes to mind is *maintaining an attitude of healthy discontent,* where a group of stakeholders reaches a collective result, even though there may have been intense debate (healthy discourse) prior to doing so. This group of stakeholders works closely together for the benefit of everyone.

The CX is critical. Customers, in essence, are a key factor in the long-term viability of the service provider, making it important in establishing, nurturing, and improving their experience over time. Similar to the questions posed with UX, to what degree do customers engage and participate across the life cycle of a service provider's products/services? To what degree would internal customers indicate that the service provider enhances their relationship with external customers (consumers)? After all, it is the deliverables output (services/products) from the service provider that generates the results that internal customers seek, allowing them to generate deliverables their respective markets seek.

So, it is important to all service providers, IT or otherwise, to not lose sight of who their customers are or the line of sight to their customers. The service provider doesn't win unless the customer wins. This just means that unless the service provider is grounded in the success of the customers they serve, then everyone will lose in the long run – service providers must give their customers the ability to service (customer) markets. There is evidence of customers appreciating the track records and performance of their service providers – to the point where they engage the service provider to educate them on relevant concepts. These situations can lead to the service provider being respected as a trusted advisor or even a strategic partner. Service providers practicing formal service management can gain and sustain high marks by focusing on CX.

What is customer journey mapping?

Having now discussed CX and UX, it is understood that they have a strong connection to design thinking, which primarily focuses on stakeholders and how a service provider engages them throughout the life cycle of a service/product. **Customer journey mapping** is a key aspect of design thinking and is defined as the process of creating a visual story of your customer's interactions with a service provider's products/services (and, therefore, the brand or how a service provider sees itself). Customer journey mapping is an exercise that helps a service provider step into their customer's shoes – to see their business from the customer's perspective. Customer journey mapping is not specific to service management but has become a critical part of it, providing products and services, as *managing services* (the reversal of the words *service management*) is a key component of what customers expect.

It was previously stated that if the challenge was to distill the thousands of pages of service management content down to one word, that one word could very well be *empathy*. Empathy gives us the ability to see things from another perspective. A customer journey map allows for empathy, given the visibility of a customer's experience with a product/service over the course of that product/service life cycle. Consider how a customer or user is even made aware of the service/product, which can be referred to as a *touchpoint*. How is this awareness happening? There is also the concept of customers and users having a formal association with the use of a product/service.

Project managers, for instance, have long used the term **benefits realization** (where the earnings gained from the implementation of the product/service until now are tracked over time). The business relationship management discipline, commonly leveraged in service provisioning, largely focuses on the concept of **value capture** (where the provider retains some profit to reinvest in itself), understanding that the value must be articulated across the stakeholders. The value gained must be articulated in terms that the stakeholders understand. How would the value gained from the product/service be expressed to the **chief financial officer** (**CFO**), versus the **chief information officer** (**CIO**), versus the **chief operating officer** (**COO**)? Different stakeholders have different perspectives of value. This concept of value will be discussed more specifically in *Chapters 5* and *6*.

Again, customer journey mapping is a key aspect of design thinking, allowing for a specific focus on the product/service consumer community. It is a decades-old practice that allows service providers with a service mindset to understand and adjust to the experience of customers and users. The ability to see across the entire spectrum of touchpoints and interactions is the only view that truly presents the opportunity to understand experience in total, and it may also uncover circumstances not readily seen (e.g., there could be **dis-benefits**, a consequence of something else occurring that was not intentional). These activities along the experience landscape (represented as chevrons), each with its own purpose, are integrated as well, and therefore, they are highly dependent on each other.

Summary

Remember that the design thinking method, for a service provider, is about the ability to see the products/services they create through the lens of their consumer audience. There is also a strong relationship between design thinking and systems thinking (the systems thinking method is discussed in the next chapter). Within each of the two, there are various disciplines (e.g., frameworks, methods, and bodies of knowledge) that provide assurance of integration within and across both methods. The prudent skills and competencies must be in place for this to occur and tend to happen through internal and external relationships.

In this chapter, we discussed the concepts of design thinking, UX, CX, and customer (including users) journey mapping. All speak to the concept of empathy and solidify service management more as an art form than a science, although there are scientific aspects. Think of the long-standing reputation of the IT industry, where IT service provider resources have been depicted as speaking a different language than the rest of the business, even though it is a business unit within the business (such as human resources, finance, purchasing, and so on). It is up to the IT service provider to consider formally adopting these concepts, largely positioning IT as a business partner and converging (versus aligning). Most IT service providers desire this convergence to become trusted advisors or strategic business partners in their market (e.g., stakeholders, consumers, customers, or users). However, these IT service providers must first prove they understand their market.

In the next chapter, we will look at systems thinking in terms of service management.

Systems Thinking in Terms of Service Management

The most successful service providers with a formal service management capability in place have long realized that no one framework, method, movement, or standard will be enough to establish and maintain success. At the same time, as there are competitive solutions and continually emerging ways of working, service providers must be diligent in selecting which of these approaches make the most sense for them (e.g., including where they currently are and where they are going). Systems thinking requires that service providers are clear with the business strategy of the enterprise and which approaches make the most sense for both their service management plans and their plan for services.

In this chapter, we're going to cover the following main topics:

- Systems thinking in terms of service management

- The convergence of strategies (e.g., business, IT, service management, and services)

- Evolution in the use of multiple approaches to sustain a successful service management capability

Defining systems thinking in terms of service management

Having discussed design thinking and its relationship with service management in the previous chapter, systems thinking has a similar context in that it can be used to translate stakeholder requirements into IT solutions. Both design thinking and systems thinking are critical to the success of formal service management. Like design thinking, **systems thinking** does not have its origin in service management. It dates back to 1956 from the MIT Sloan School of Management. Think of systems thinking as the activity (or activities) associated with looking at the use of multiple approaches, each with its own components, from which to architect a solution – such as a product or a service. Just like an individual framework can have multiple components, multiple frameworks, standards, and methods can each be seen as a component of a larger system (e.g., a service management system). The very word *analysis* lends itself to thinking – what available systems can be leveraged to create an IT product or service? Generically defined, a laptop computer is a system in and of itself because it is made up of components (e.g., processors, motherboards, memory chips, ports, etc.). These parts make up an assembly to address an outcome. IT is a system of systems, with architecture as the means to bring them together for a higher purpose. As discussed in earlier chapters, no one framework, method, standard, body of knowledge, or movement is enough for sustained success with formal service management. The approaches used ought to be the ones most suitable in generating value for stakeholders (consumers) directly related to desired outcomes.

Systems thinking is about seeing the results of our actions in a larger context. The skills and competencies required are significant, given the sheer number of solution options available and the evolutionary nature of information technology (where progress seems more exponential than incremental). Additionally, there is an art to translating customer requirements or user stories into technical solutions, meaning that the IT service provider must have the knowledge to identify and match the most appropriate solutions to the situation. Matching business knowledge with solution capability, and thus, now operating from its own body of knowledge, presents the best chance to meet a business vision, mission, and objectives. Design/architecture naturally comes to mind, but not strictly just an architecture capability. A myriad of knowledgeable stakeholders is needed as it is not usually likely that one person or even a small contingent of people bring all of the collective skills necessary for success. To acquire that knowledge, the competencies are built through formal education, business knowledge, applying the concepts, and even assistance from external providers.

Most will associate **IT service management** (**ITSM**) with the ITIL framework, speaking directly to the origin in the mid-80s. Keywords from the ITIL definition of service management include a **specialized organizational capability**, meaning that for an IT service provider for an organization, it represents the internal consultancy on how services will be managed (conceived, designed, implemented, maintained, and improved). The inference is that certain approaches will be used for certain situations. Systems thinking represents those approaches. Using a honeycomb depiction, the following diagram shows a sampling of approaches that could be used as part of systems thinking to meet a particular customer outcome:

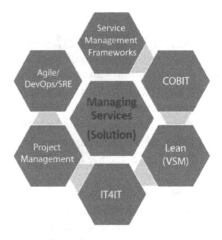

Figure 4.1 – Sample systems thinking ingredients

With so many available approaches, an organization's formal service management capability has to *standardize*, largely through governance decisions, which approaches it adopts. **Organizational change management (OCM)** is also an important aspect, given that these approaches may evolve. Think of different approaches as the ingredients required to meet consumer value and outcomes, where each ingredient has a role to play as part of a capability. Given the nature of these ingredients to evolve or emerge, careful consideration must be made to what sustains them over time. Too often, service providers discard an ingredient in favor of another versus leveraging what can be optimized and reused along with an emerging solution. For instance, an organization discards their previously adopted service management framework in favor of *Agile*. A careful investigation of that very framework may actually allude to or include Agile concepts. As discussed later in this book (*Chapter 5* through *Chapter 10*), service management has more directly connected itself to other ingredients such as Agile, DevOps, **site reliability engineering (SRE)**, and more.

The following diagram, by this book's authors, was developed to show a logical connection between any chosen service management framework and the life that an IT product or service goes through, along with other ingredients (frameworks, standards, bodies of knowledge, simulations, and more). The diagram represents the use of multiple approaches – the very concept of systems thinking. It is nicknamed the **continuous complex closed-loop system**, given the needed cohesion and interaction throughout:

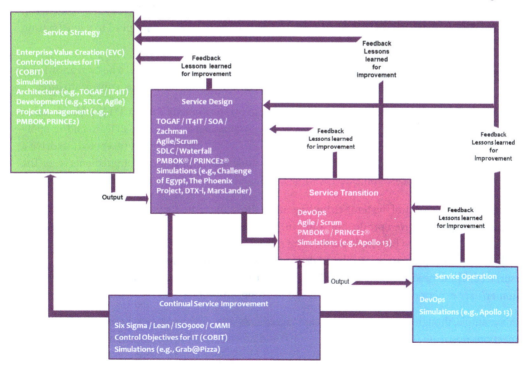

Figure 4.2 – The continuous complex closed-loop system

It is not the intention to imply that all of these approaches would be needed to produce or improve a product or service. In the establishment of a formal service management practice, it is part of governance to involve the proper stakeholders with the appropriate competencies to generate value through outcomes for consumers.

In reviewing the preceding diagram, think of what stakeholders need to be involved along the way. Interrogation of the DevOps movement, for instance, reveals arguably every stakeholder one might imagine (e.g., customers, suppliers, architects, business representatives, developers, project managers, QA, and more). For clarification, let's look at the service design area and the multiple ingredients and understand the relevance of each:

- **TOGAF/IT4IT/SOA/Zachman**: These are all architecture frameworks. All would not be used for a given situation. As part of governance, a formal service management practice would determine which is appropriate for the organization.

- **Agile/Scrum/SDLC/Waterfall**: These are solutions related to development. Agile/Scrum are significantly different approaches than SDLC/Waterfall. Both solution sets would be in place within the same organization, where policy would dictate what is used in which situation. At the same time, an organization could be strictly an Agile/Scrum *shop*. If both solution sets are in place, then the organization is said to be practicing **bi-modal IT** (coined by Gartner in 2014). Generally, organizations are trending to Agile/Scrum, allowing speed to value (getting to market quicker).

- **PMBOK/PRINCE2**: These represent project management, with PMBOK as a body of knowledge and PRINCE2 as a method for managing projects. Both could be used in a given situation.

- **Business simulations such as The Challenge of Egypt/The Phoenix Project/DTX-i/MarsLander**: These are all simulations. Simulations allow the participating stakeholders to learn and/or apply concepts as part of being a learning organization, or they can be crafted (executed) to drive a needed message. They can also be used to drive understanding of specific ingredients (e.g., The Phoenix Project focuses on DevOps while DTX can be used to focus on digital transformation).

Presumably, and as part of systems thinking, all of these ingredients would be used to develop, maintain, or improve a given product or solution. Imagine the skills and competencies across a given set of resources needed to be a high-performing service provider. Now, complement that with other ingredients from the previously introduced design thinking, where the needs and desires of consumers are surfaced. These needs may include business relationship management, customer journey mapping, customer/user experience, experimentation and learning, and more.

In this example, though only the service design ingredients were discussed, bear in mind that there are connections upstream (to the strategy ingredients) and downstream (to the transition, operations, and continual improvement ingredients). This speaks to a holistic approach to formal service management. There is validation that no one ingredient is enough for any service provider to achieve high performance.

It is essential that both systems thinking and design thinking are key aspects of formal service management, with both contributing ingredients toward value and desired outcomes for consumers. With so many considerations on how to culminate in a product or service, whatever is chosen must align with a need for supporting skills and competencies. Service providers must understand their velocity and cadence to adopt these ingredients. Hence, the need to establish a formal service management capability, including an associated pragmatic roadmap that matures both systems thinking and design thinking aspects.

The convergence of strategies (e.g., business, IT, service management, and services)

All organizations, no matter the type, understand their specific market. That is, they understand who their consumers are (and what they value), as well as the legal and regulatory aspects applicable to that market. For instance, a pharmaceutical company strives to not only know who the consumers are of its products and services (e.g., doctors, pharmacies, hospitals, patients, etc.) but also what the legal and regulatory requirements are (e.g., Food & Drug Administration, 211 CFR Part xxx, etc.) to operate in that market. These two factors are likely the most critical in establishing a strategy for the organization. Within the overall organization, there is at least one IT service provider, either internal or external. The following diagram was referenced in an earlier chapter and shows multiple strategies. In this instance, taking a closer look at these strategies (plans) will lend itself to systems thinking in the context of a formal service management capability:

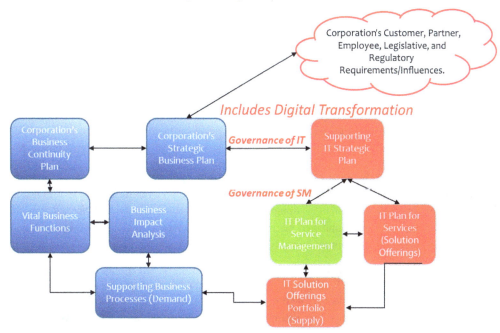

Figure 4.3 – The strategy cascade

In reviewing the preceding diagram, consider the following:

- Areas in blue represent ownership/accountability by the business (e.g., board and CXO levels). This is part of **outside-in thinking**.

- Areas in red and green are owned and accountable to the IT service provider. Green represents service management but must be tightly aligned to IT services, with both consistent with the IT strategic plan.

- Governance of IT happens across the blue and red areas.

- Governance of service management happens between the red and green areas.

- Service management (in green) is not only highly influenced by the strategies and plans above it, but also by **business continuity**, also known as **business continuity management** (BCM).

It is the vital business functions and the supporting business processes (both represented in blue) that represent the closest connection to the IT products and services (represented in red) from the IT service provider. It is governance that ensures that all parties converge to achieve the mission, goals, and objectives of the overall organization. Formal service management plays a key role in helping the organization meet its overall strategy while also respecting what is critical (in its order of importance). Without this structure, the following detriments are likely to occur:

- Internal customer-facing services may often be left undefined. Without quantifying IT efforts against business outcomes, it may be difficult to express the value that an IT service provider contributes or to identify the associated budget needed to support those outcomes.

- Shadow IT (IT systems built without explicit organizational approval) may continue to be pervasive, no matter the industry. Internal IT is perceived as operational but not strategic (e.g., not respected as a business partner).

- Technical debt may abound. There is a trend in lessening investment in the operational aspects (leading to deficiencies in code, skills/competencies, documentation, and computing environments), resulting in the overall inefficiency and ineffectiveness of the IT footprint. This lack of investment has resulted in being unable to keep up with demand from consumers.

The impact of these three trends can be mitigated through stronger governance of service management (not to be confused with the governance of IT), value capture (where IT retains money to reinvest in itself), and a rolling service management roadmap. If a strategy does indeed *begin with the end in mind*, then a defined, documented, and published plan needs to be understood and executed with defined roles and activities, pragmatic timelines, and supported actions, all of which constitute governance.

From the diagram, it is clear that the IT service provider is accountable for three specific plans:

- **IT strategic plan**: This speaks to how the IT service provider supports, and the role IT plays in supporting, the overall business strategy. The IT service provider is a business unit and, preferably, participates in the development of the overall business strategy.

- **IT plan for services**: The product and service solutions required to run the day-to-day operations of the business. From a supply chain concept, this puts IT at the beginning of the value stream for the organization, as almost all business processes are enabled by IT solutions.

- **IT plan for service management**: This is in reference to where the formal service management capability serves as a means to help maintain and optimize the products and services that are part of the plan for services. This was referred to earlier as the **specialized organizational capability**. Whether the IT service provider has formalized service management or not, service management does exist within IT, as it is ultimately how these products and services are presented to its market. It is just a matter of how well it is being done.

The convergence of these three plans represented (showing as red and green) in *Figure 4.3* is intentional and important, as they cascade at or underneath the overall business plans (represented in blue). Although most organizations have a published business strategy, it is not a given that they all have a documented **business continuity plan** (**BCP**). This goes much deeper than a disaster recovery plan, though they are related. A BCP is generically defined as the process a company undergoes to create a prevention and recovery system from potential threats (e.g., a natural disaster or cyberattack). Whether formalized or not, all organizations are subject to the need for continuity planning. In reviewing *Figure 4.3*, note the subsets of **Vital Business Functions** (**VBFs**) and **Business Impact Analysis** (**BIA**). Associate BIA with prioritization based on impact on the business (in a business continuance situation, what areas of the business would be addressed first).

Formal service management needs to have VBFs directly associated with business processes at the top of their mind. A *VBF* is defined as a function of a business process that is critical to the success of the business. All organizations have a VBF, and if it is not formalized as part of a formal BCP, then the formal service management capability has to find an alternate way to understand what the critical services are. Having to guess which IT services (in connection to business processes) are important puts the service management practice at risk, as the resources allocated need to be focused on the right activities at the right time. The way that consumers realize value from an IT product or service lies in how that solution helps them achieve a result. These results tend to be based on the successful execution of a business process. In formal service management, *providing value through helping its market realize outcomes is key*!

So where does systems thinking come in? Let's bear in mind that, for the most part, it is the architecture team that needs to have a holistic view of how products and services are introduced, maintained, and improved. This team typically also has to operate within the elements of time, quality, and cost. So, it is key for this competency to have insight into the overall organizational strategy and to ideally participate in the development of the multiple strategies introduced in *Figure 4.3*. Though it is common for the architecture team to aspire to a particular architecture framework (e.g., TOGAF, IT4IT, etc.) or hybrid, that same team must have access to other areas of specialization that are critical to the success of the IT service provider. These may include governance (e.g., **Control Objectives for Information and Related Technologies** (**COBIT**)), service management (e.g., ITIL), development (e.g., SAFe Agile, DevOps, etc.), project management (e.g., PMBOK, PRINCE2, etc.), and quality improvement (e.g., Lean, Six Sigma, etc.). The areas of specialization mentioned here are not exhaustive. As discussed in earlier chapters, there are many frameworks, standards, methods, bodies of knowledge, and movements that organizations can take advantage of. Note that all of the areas mentioned have direct involvement in the creation, design, maintenance, and improvement of products and services. All are facets of systems thinking. Along with the architecture team, let's consider that the accountability point for the formal service management practice, in essence, is an architect as well, and it is focused on the **specialized organizational capability**. Collaboration across these areas of specialization is key; each of them represents a *component* of a much larger *system*.

Systems thinking, done well, provides a fundamental understanding of what it takes to be able to provide products and services at a strategic level. That understanding has to go beyond the CIO and direct reports. A great question to ask a business partner is whether they consider the IT service provider to be strategic or operational. Actually, this is a trick question because the answer to both ought to be "yes." If the service provider is perceived to be only operational in nature, then IT is not being perceived as a business partner. The real value for your business customers comes with the *strategic* aspects of being a service provider. The shift of the pendulum from operational to strategic allows the IT service provider to provide a needed focus on service solutions that are agile, ever-changing, and deliver more value to the enterprise. It also makes it much easier to apply the concept of value capture, where IT is able to consistently invest in itself and avoid the creation of technical debt.

Customers are more willing to fund when they are receiving both strategic and operational value. The value provided by a service provider should be measurable technically, operationally, economically, financially, and strategically. Enter systems thinking! As discussed, just like there is a combination of approaches to create an IT product or service (the systems thinking concept), there is also a combination of plans/strategies that a formal service management capability must consider and converge with.

Evolution in the use of multiple approaches to sustain a successful service management capability

In upcoming chapters, service management processes will be discussed in detail. They are what bring consistency and predictability across the ingredients of a product or service while ensuring that value is realized and improvement opportunities are surfaced.

Multiple service management frameworks have emerged in recent years (e.g., ITIL, VeriSM, FitSM, USM, and more), representing a continued evolution in best practices for service management. IT service providers must put a stake in the ground in terms of what framework makes the most sense for their respective organizations.

In previous decades, one could debate whether IT advanced incrementally, but today it advances faster than ever. IT must take advantage of new opportunities for value creation. Organizations must balance the need for stability and predictability with operational agility and increased velocity. In terms of **speed to value** (a play on **speed to market**), managing IT products and services is a key strategic capability – a reminder that formal service management is a **specialized organizational capability**.

Systems thinking ensures a flexible, coordinated, and integrated system for the effective governance and management of IT-enabled products and services.

In the following diagram, multiple frameworks, methods, and movements are used to progress requirements (e.g., a significant enhancement to an existing customer-facing service) through to production:

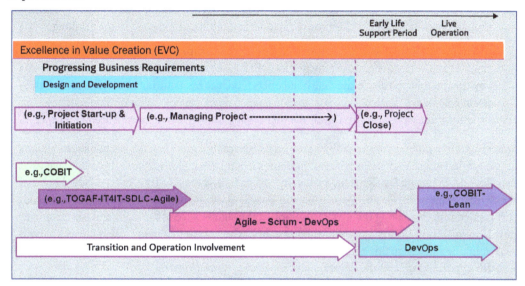

Figure 4.4 – A sample application of systems thinking

Let us look at the components in detail:

- Project management methods and/or frameworks are used to track and manage the project throughout (e.g., initiate, start, manage, and close) its journey. A significant enhancement to an existing IT product or service likely requires a project, perhaps as part of a program, with an associated initiative.

- The COBIT framework is used to provide governance of IT and provides guidance specific to the gathering and management of requirements. As previously mentioned, governance is a key aspect of formal service management. Governance applies not only at a strategic level, but also at tactical and operational ones.

- The TOGAF architecture framework is used to define the specifications on how best to meet the requirements in terms of time, quality, and cost throughout the development, transition, and operational and improvement aspects of the IT service. Architecture frameworks are instrumental in translating consumer needs and wants to various IT-specific disciplines.

- The service management framework is used to progress, through the use of processes, the initiation of the enhancement (request) through to production, serving as a conduit throughout the life cycle of the IT product or service.

- Agile/DevOps/Scrum is used for the development and testing of the new enhancement. The biggest advantage of this area is speed to value, with an acceptable level of quality. Culture, automation, Lean, measurement, and sharing are all factors (what DevOps values) in bringing the enhancement to fruition—all related to both systems thinking and design thinking.

- The **Excellence in Value Creation** (**EVC**) framework is used to capture that value (per different stakeholder perspectives) and is recognized and addressed throughout the cycle (from requirements through to production). EVC is more related to design thinking than systems thinking.

- The COBIT framework/Lean methods are used to assess improvement opportunities going forward (post-introduction to production). COBIT is not restricted to governance, in that it also provides the ability to assess capability and offers guidance on maturing to a higher level. Value-stream mapping, a Lean concept discussed in later chapters, can identify improvements based on current-state observations (from early life support and forward). It relies on trusted information.

Bear in mind that a different organization based on its governance of formal service management may have used different capabilities to address the same circumstance. For instance, it could have used Waterfall for development, Six Sigma for quality improvement, and the ISO/IEC 20000 standard (instead of the COBIT framework) for governance but still used a service management framework (pick one!) for the needed processes along the way. Do not forget the significance of the skills and competencies required, no matter the desired capabilities/approaches. Also, notice that many capabilities have both systems thinking and design thinking aspects to them. For instance, DevOps considers both the human aspects (design thinking) and the development aspects (systems thinking).

In keeping with *Figure 4.4*, and for the same set of circumstances, that very organization could have increased its current formal service management capability with the adoption of **SRE**. In working with Lean methods, SRE can identify opportunities to introduce automation, potentially increasing reliability and speed to value, of which indicators measured by EVC would improve. This is an example of the IT service provider, through formal service management, taking advantage of new opportunities for value creation. This also, again, speaks to both systems thinking (SRE) and design thinking (EVC).

The information in this short section is intentionally far from comprehensive. The high-level descriptions of the shared options to be used as part of systems thinking in the preceding swim lane diagram illustrate the need for multiple solutions to achieve success. Combine that with the evolutionary nature of each, if not the introduction of new options that can provide additional value. Any solution that can provide value should be considered. So, diligence in keeping with market trends makes sense and is part of systems thinking.

Summary

Customers don't really care (and shouldn't care) about the widgets behind the curtain (the supporting services) from the service provider. They care about what they need to interact with (customer-facing products and services) in order to create the business outcomes they seek. As part of systems thinking, the IT service provider integrates point solutions (much like the different stations in the kitchen of a restaurant coming together to produce a meal), so this is how products and services happen! Customer-facing products and services need to continue to evolve (or transform) in order for value to continue to be in place and for outcomes to be realized.

Whether the overall organization is in run mode, grow mode, or transformation mode, the IT service provider should always be in transformation mode. This is a key responsibility for formal service management. This presumes that the IT service provider wants to be perceived as a business partner and not just an operational provider. As such, service management is alive and well – it just requires strong governance, an established, respected, and productive center of gravity (who owns the reins of IT), and most importantly, a strong (outside-in) understanding of business partners and the market that they serve.

IT is at the beginning of the value stream, delivering products and services that support business outcomes, generate positive and measurable value for their customers, and encourage customers to invest in additional services. The result is IT service providers that are able to generate value capture, anticipate customer needs, continually improve to maintain value over time, and ensure a long-term positive relationship with their business partners.

This chapter formally ends the first section of this book, represented by *Chapter 1* through *Chapter 4*. To this point, there has been information shared on the history of service management frameworks and systems/design thinking. Also, throughout this section, information from a variety of guidance has been introduced (e.g., design thinking and systems thinking). The next section, *Chapter 5* through *Chapter 15*, describes the common processes that an organization should consider when starting or improving a service management capability. Grasping the intent of service management, minimally at a foundational level of understanding, positions the reader to understand what it takes to be a great service provider, IT or otherwise.

Part 2:
Essential Process Capabilities for Effective Service Management

In this part, you will be taken on a journey of the key process capabilities needed as part of a formal service management capability. You will become well-grounded in the key elements of service management capability.

This part has the following chapters:

5
Service Management Key Concepts

In this chapter, we will discuss the foundational concepts of service management. These concepts are critical for understanding and are prevalent throughout the capabilities (for example, incident management, problem management, change management, and so on) that will be presented in the coming chapters (*Chapters 6* through *15*).

In this chapter, we're going to cover the following main topics:

- Key definitions
- An IT management system (ISO/IEC 20000:2018)
- Business and IT convergence
- General (IT) universal service management capabilities
- Accelerators for service management

Key definitions

There are many key definitions and best practices that you will need to be familiar with. We will look at each of these beyond the simple definition, defining why these terms are important to the best-practice guidance available and how they would be applied in the implementation of best practices.

One of the more important definitions in service management is the definition of value. **Value** is defined as *the perceived benefits, usefulness, and importance of something*. One of the key characteristics of value is the element of perception. As beauty is in the eye of the beholder, so too is the value as perceived by the recipient of the product or service. The recipient of the product or service will want to determine, *does this result satisfy my need, does it produce the result expected*, and *is the cost reasonable for the result achieved*? A no to any of these questions and there will be concern that the value is not there. The need is characterized by the stated requirements defined by the customer. Perception is what the customer believes they will get by stating their requirements. When expectations and requirements are met, the perception is that a service or product has value. If there is no value in using or consuming the service, then a customer/user will not use the service again and most likely will tell others about their experience. If a service or product does not deliver value, it will be perceived as a cost to be reduced or eliminated. In this instance, a customer may seek to replace a service not providing value with a competitor's product, or a service creating a potential loss of revenue to the service provider. It is critical to understand what a consumer considers important in using the service and ensure that the expected outcome is delivered.

Another term to define from the previous statement is *outcome*. The **outcome** in this context is the resulting benefit that the customer/user wants to achieve by using the product or service. Outcome is not the same as output. **Output** is the statement you receive at the end of each month from your bank showing the transactions executed during that period. The outcome is you reviewing the statement to validate the transactions you executed during the month and to ensure that nothing was done without your knowledge. The outcome is the benefit you derive from having the statement in your possession so that you can review the activity. Understanding outcomes allows you, as a service provider, to validate the service you deliver produces the benefits your customer/user wants to achieve. The outcome is or should be the starting point for defining a service.

So, what is a service? A **service** is defined as the outcome a customer wants to achieve. Services are typically intangible in that the customer/user does not have a physical product to have and hold. So, products represent something you can lay your hands on while a service is delivered without having a physical component or combining one or more products into a deliverable. For example, if you go to a restaurant for a meal, products are used to deliver the service in the form of a meal. As the diner, you do not prepare the food and you do not buy the food – instead, you submit a request to the individual taking your order; they transmit that request to the kitchen staff and then they prepare the meal. Then, the server delivers it to your table, and you consume it. In the end, you are satisfied with the service provided, including the server, hostess, staff, price, and the meal, or not, and if not, you may choose not to eat there again. Your dissatisfaction may be a result of any of the components of the experience. Another example of a service is your service desk. When a request comes to the service desk from a user, the agent determines what kind of request it is, what response to provide, and then provides the appropriate response to satisfy the requestor's need. One of the challenges for IT organizations is understanding what their services are and how to manage them effectively and efficiently.

A **service offering** is what the service provider will deliver to the customer/consumer. A service offering is generally the products and services that are combined to deliver value to the consumer. For example, auto dealers may provide a vehicle with the options the buyer desires and add financing, maintenance plans, and other services to the deal when the buyer has made their purchase decision. This allows the service provider – in this case, the dealer – to customize the service offering to their buyer while still controlling how the service offering is produced. Another example to illustrate a service offering would be a meal at a restaurant; the menu may offer steak and when the diner orders the steak, the wait staff may offer sauteed mushrooms and onions as an add-on to the service defined in the menu. These add-ons provide a means for the restaurant to customize the service offering to the diner's preferences. **Service offerings** are what the service provider delivers to their customer based on the content of the service catalog and service portfolio. These terms will be described in more detail in *Chapters 11* and *15*.

Service provisioning is the action performed by the service provider to deliver an agreed level of service to their customers and users. These actions may involve several products or services necessary to fulfill the commitments made by the service provider to the customer. Service provisioning involves delivering the outputs necessary to meet the needs of the business and satisfy the outcomes the customer wants to achieve. Service provisioning is why the service provider exists and will produce value for the customer and the service provider.

Service consumption is the result of a service provider delivering a product or service to their customers/consumers and the customer/consumer using the product or service to produce the outcome they want to achieve. Service consumption is the act of actually using the service.

Service management is defined as the system used to manage the services defined, developed, built, deployed, delivered, and supported by a service provider to fulfill the needs of its stakeholders and customers. **IT service management** (**ITSM**) is the management system that focuses on managing IT services offered by an IT service provider and delivered to an internal or external customer. **Enterprise service management** is the management system that is applied by the business organization to manage the creation and delivery of products and services to its external customers. All of these definitions reflect the scope of the management system necessary to ensure that what the organization intends to deliver to its customers is aligned with the strategy and culture of the entity, fulfilling the needs of its customers and creating value for all stakeholders. More about the management system will be covered in the *An IT management system (ISO/IEC 20000:2018)* section.

A **capability** is defined as the ability to perform some activity or function effectively and deliver the intended results. Capability must include not only processes but also people and technologies. Culture and the way an organization applies people, processes, and technology will influence how effective an organization will be in delivering and managing its services. A capability could be your ability to effectively manage changes that minimize disruptions to agreed service levels. Capabilities reflect the organization's ability to perform its business functions adequately enough to deliver its products and services to enable value for its customers. Capabilities will expand and mature over time as an organization executes its functions and produces its products and services. Capabilities rely on the effective execution of processes as well as the interactions between processes. Continual improvement is a key factor in maturing an organization's capabilities.

A **process** is defined as one or more activities taking a clearly defined input from a supplier and delivering a clearly defined output to a customer or stakeholder. The process itself provides a high-level definition of the activities being considered to be executed depending on the nature of the input provided by the supplier and what outputs need to be produced for the customer. The supplier in this context is any entity that is providing the input. A supplier could be an individual, group, or another process. The customer or stakeholder receiving the output from the process could be an individual customer, another business unit, or another process. In **SIPOC**, you have the key elements of a process defined. The *S* is the supplier providing the input trigger that initiates the process. In incident management, the **input** is typically a request initiated by a user because something has broken. The *I* is the input that the supplier is providing to the process. The *P* is for the process activities that will be performed on the input provided by the supplier. This is where activities act on the input to transform it into a usable and measurable output that will meet the needs of the customer or stakeholder. The *O* is the output that is produced by the activities performed by the process. The *C* is the customer or stakeholder that will receive the output and take whatever action is appropriate to produce the outcome the stakeholder intended. Although this is pretty straightforward, there is much to discuss in the process area. *Figure 5.1* shows the SIPOC diagram and what is contained in the process area:

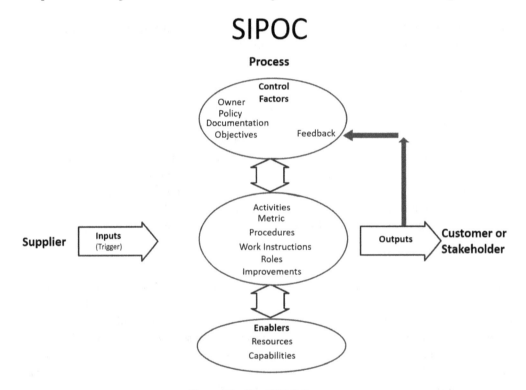

Figure 5.1 – The SIPOC diagram

In the process, there are three key elements: a control element, a process element, and the enabler's element. The **control element** is where governance is applied. So, every process must have an owner – that is, the individual that is accountable for the process. The owner will be responsible for establishing policies that govern the process. The owner will ensure that appropriate documentation is created for the process. The owner will work with other stakeholders to establish the objectives for the process based on the level of maturity of the process and the culture and strategy of the organization. The owner will establish a feedback mechanism so that as the process is being executed, any improvement opportunities or changes to the process based on the feedback can be documented and evaluated for implementation.

In the **process element**, the activities are described at a high level. Here, all the potential activities are described for any situation this process may be applied to. Each activity is defined and criteria are established for when that activity is needed. Metrics for how the performance of the process activities will be determined are defined. These metrics will be established based on the objectives defined in the control element and the level of maturity for the process. In the early deployment of a process, the focus of the metrics will be on the progress of deploying the process and compliance with the policies. As the process matures, metrics will also focus on the effectiveness of the process in producing the outputs expected and the efficiency of the process – that is, how easy it is to produce the expected outputs. As common instances of the process execution are identified, procedures document what activities will be performed for the specific instance you are executing in more detail. For example, a major incident might have a specific procedure defined to handle this instance of an incident. There may also be a specific procedure defined for a security incident. Procedures reflect which of the process activities will be applied for that type of input. Working instructions apply the technology being used to describe in detail how to manage a specific iteration of a procedure. For example, if you are using ServiceNow as your technology for managing a type of service request, work instructions describe how to record an incident in the technology. In the process element, roles and responsibilities are clearly defined and documented. These roles will be assigned to individuals and groups within the organization so that all stakeholders understand their responsibilities when interacting with the process at any level, whether it is a process owner (the individual that owns the process), process manager (the individual(s) that manage the process day to day), process practitioner (the individuals executing one or more activities of a process), or any stakeholder being impacted by the process. Improvement opportunities identified through the feedback loop in the control element are assessed, developed, deployed, and implemented as part of the process element. This ensures that the process will continue to mature and improve its performance throughout its life cycle.

In the **enabler's element**, the key resources involved in making the process effective and efficient are identified and addressed. Some key resources and capabilities include the technology being applied to the process and how effectively the technology enables the process inputs and outputs to be managed efficiently – that is, the individuals that have been assigned roles for the process, how well they understand what to do and when, how easy is it for them to perform the activities assigned, and how effective they are in fulfilling their responsibilities. The effectiveness of your education about the process enables key resources to understand their roles and responsibilities. Many times, a **Responsible, Accountable, Consulted, Informed** (**RACI**) matrix will be used to communicate the key accountabilities and responsibilities of the roles. Enablers enhance and improve the overall efficiency and effectiveness of the process.

The outputs produced by the process activities are the expected results of the execution of the process. The outputs could be in the form of a report or a request to another process or a completed order for a product. These outputs are used by the customer or stakeholder to produce the outcome they want to achieve by triggering the process. A customer may have initiated a request from an external customer for more products. The output would be the completed order request, while the outcome would be the demand for more products to be delivered to the external customer, resulting in revenue for the company. Another example could be a request submitted by a user for a new laptop. This request is common and there is a standard service request procedure and work instructions to fulfill it. The output from the request is a valid order for the new laptop and the outcome is that the user receives the laptop, delivered to their desk, ready to be used to perform their job.

In this section, many definitions were offered for key terms within service management, including value, service, service management, capability, process, procedures, and work instructions. In the next section, we will discuss the management system that's used to manage services.

An IT management system (ISO/IEC 20000:2018)

Service management is the management system that enables any service provider to manage and deliver services that have value efficiently and effectively. A **management system** is defined as the activities, governance, and resources necessary to manage the organization's ability to deliver products or services that meet the needs of its stakeholders and deliver value. It is important to recognize the concept of ITSM as a *framework* for managing services (service management) versus a *standard* or a *methodology* or a *movement*. However, as the ITSM guidance has matured, there are several standards, methodologies, and movements that have contributed to the guidance available. The very mention of the framework implies that there is more than one way to apply it and experience success, which also means there is more than one way to apply it and experience failure. This statement alone should give us all pause, presuming success is desired. The origins of formal service management for IT date back decades. This started in the early to mid-80s as some 40 publications (version 1), each focused on a particular part (process) of service management. Version 1 was revised in Version 2, which was replaced by Version 3 and eventually became ITIL 4. The International Organization for Standards introduced a standard based on these best practices called **ISO/IEC 20000**. **ISO/IEC 20000:2018** is the updated standard as of 2018 and reflects the evolution of best practices. A standard defines the best approach to comply with specific guidance on what and how to do something. Standards enforce guidance through controls that must be met to conform with the guidance. The standards typically provide a means to certify compliance with the standard. The real point is that the framework, and its many respected authors along the way, continued to evolve as the newly developed solutions and trends in IT emerged. It is fair to say that some best practices are tracked behind emerging trends, whether this is technology, other frameworks, standards, or methods. Some of these sources include, but are not limited to, ITIL, IT4IT, FitSM, COBIT19, Agile, Lean, DevOps, and VeriSM – and the list goes on and on. In the current environment, it makes sense to leverage guidance from any and/or all of these sources to develop your IT service management strategy and capability because they all offer guidance that should be adapted to your specific needs. A framework will differ from a standard in that a standard can be adopted while frameworks provide guidance that is recommended; however, an organization must adapt the guidance to their specific needs and requirements. Standards dictate what should be done, while frameworks suggest what should be considered and are intentionally flexible in the application.

Now that you have a better understanding of the management system used to manage services efficiently and effectively, let's talk about why businesses need to apply these management systems appropriately.

Business and IT convergence

For years, it has been maintained that an IT service provider with as few as 20 people can benefit from developing a formal service management capability. With the availability of automation, **machine learning (ML)**, **artificial intelligence (AI)**, and deep learning, this statement suggests that how services are delivered and the interaction between the service provider and service consumer has become more significant to stakeholder satisfaction. The need for technology to support the business has become ubiquitous in that businesses cannot do without the information that IT is the steward of, and if IT cannot provide that information in a usable form, at the right time and place, then the business could suffer loss of revenue and reputation.

There are many generations in the workforce today (whether Baby Boomers, Millennials, or Gen-Z) making culture a key consideration for any initiative. Creating and maintaining a formal service management practice, done well, brings long-term predictability and innovation to any organization, making it a key program. The combination of the culture and the service management program creates the best opportunity for long-term viability while using our human resources optimally. For instance, no matter the generation, there needs to be integration across, and common alignment with, the organization's mission, goals, objectives, and values. Gone should be the days of being awakened in the middle of the night for a database error, while still having to be onsite at the start of business. Gone are the days of the requirements changing because the requirements changed by the time the new functionality went live. Gone are the days of putting changes in over the weekend and having service outages on Monday morning. If these examples are, indeed, gone, then the human resources that design, develop, transition, support, and improve services are more likely to thrive in their skills at work and their lives at home. Every generation has a *home* in that scenario, as each can adopt and adapt to their differing needs. These needs include more time with family, improved work/life balance, diverse circumstances, skill specialization, and innovation.

For business and IT to effectively converge, IT must be an integral part of the organization. IT should be treated the same as every other provider group within the organization, such as the HR department, finance, purchasing, or the executive. If IT is treated as a necessary evil to be tolerated, then the business will not value the interaction and will not provide the necessary information needed for IT to be successful in meeting business needs. If IT is not at the table when the business is planning its strategy and developing its business plans, then IT cannot be effective in offering services that meet the business needs. Only through an effective mutual relationship between IT and the business can convergence be achieved. Then and only then will IT be able to enable business success and deliver services that provide value to all the stakeholders within the organization and out.

Now that we understand that convergence between the business and IT is essential, the next section will cover the common elements of management systems.

General (IT) universal service management capabilities

There are many different management systems out there for service management but they all have many capabilities that are common between them. These common capabilities can be separated into three specific areas: strategic, tactical, and operational. Within each of these areas, we will find common elements that tend to be consistent across all of the methodologies, frameworks, and standards.

Earlier, you were introduced to ITIL, FitSM, VeriSM, COBIT19, IT4IT, and others. Each of these systems has varying nuances but are similar in many aspects. For instance, all of these will have elements of business focus, including business strategies, plans, goals, and objectives. They will recognize that demand comes from the business and customers and that businesses focus on value capture as the key outcome all customers want to achieve. There is evidence in each of these frameworks and standards that suggest demand can take many forms; you could have demand for a new service to support a change in strategic direction, a new product has been introduced that results in tactical changes to an existing service, or an outage has occurred for a mission-critical service and an operational major incident needs to be initiated. The business will want support from the service provider in capturing and analyzing the performance of the company and will want a balanced set of measures to determine how effectively the enterprise management system is working.

The common elements of the service management system focus on strategic, tactical, and operational systems. From a strategic perspective, the focus is on aligning the IT mission, vision, goals, and objectives with the business vision, mission, goals, and objectives. This ensures that IT is focused on what is most important to the business and what IT can potentially do to enable overall business success. IT also ensures that the policies and governance applied to the management system are appropriate and consistent with the overall business governance. The service management system must provide a means to align IT's portfolio of services with what the business needs. All of these management systems contain guidance on how to effectively manage resources to ensure the resources are available and appropriate to meet the needs of the business. These management systems advocate for aligning the organizational structure and culture with the business. This ensures that IT does not violate the norms and mores of the organization in their dealings internally or externally with stakeholders.

From a tactical perspective, these management systems tend to address key areas of concern for IT's ability to deliver services to the business, such as the following:

- Security
- Risk
- Managing assets
- Managing the components necessary to deliver services
- Documenting the services that will be offered
- Maintaining relationships with all stakeholders
- Establishing a means to plan, design, build, test, deploy, and operate new products and services

For each of the preceding items, one or more processes will be defined that enable the management system to deliver the key outcomes necessary to fulfill the objectives of the organization.

From an operational perspective, the management systems will address these key areas of concern for IT's ability to deliver services to the business:

- Respond effectively to any type of request, be it an incident, service, change, or problem

- Provide a means to capture request demand and fulfill and resolve it as appropriate

- Validate that any change introduced into the production environment has been adequately tested and communicated to all stakeholders before being made available for consumption by those stakeholders

The management system will have processes defined to ensure that the operational activities being performed by the IT organization can meet the objectives and ensure satisfactory fulfillment of any demand on IT resources.

Finally, all of these management systems will have a means for monitoring and measuring the performance of the IT organization in meeting its strategies, plans, and objectives. The approach that's applied by the management system will identify appropriate targets, measure what occurred against those targets, report the results to appropriate stakeholders, and identify and document potential improvement opportunities. Each system applies continual improvement techniques to identify the improvement opportunity, document the benefits to make the improvement, and then, if justified, schedule the improvement to be built, tested, deployed, and implemented.

As you continue to review the content of this book, more information will be provided about the processes and activities necessary to be effective in managing your IT services. In the next section of this chapter, we will review some of the accelerators for service management. These accelerators are frameworks or techniques that you can apply to improve the speed of your service management initiative.

Accelerators for service management

There are some key factors to consider when initiating a service management capability and making it happen quickly; generating results that matter is very important. Some techniques can help accelerate the achievement of benefits, including, but certainly not limited to, Lean, Agile, and DevOps. In this section, you will get some exposure on what these techniques do to help move your service management efforts forward.

In our experience, one of the most important factors to consider when initiating or improving your service management capability is understanding your current state and what can be leveraged to make improvements. What is it that you are doing today that works well? How can you make incremental improvements to the things you are already doing to generate benefits? If you can identify some quick wins, this will help you achieve improvements that show value and benefit for the service management effort and generate momentum for making additional improvements. In many organizations, improving the incident response and resolution metrics can be a highly visible improvement that will positively impact the user community and improve user/customer satisfaction. If changes are not well controlled, improving the control of changes can reduce the incidents that result and raise the availability of your services for the customers and users. Using the current state as the starting point to determine what to improve can be a significant opportunity to accelerate the benefits of service management.

If your organization is familiar with Lean and Agile approaches, then these can be leveraged to deliver service management processes in a more timely and appropriate manner. For instance, **Lean** techniques can help you identify where you are currently creating waste in your service management processes and identify how to eliminate or reduce the impact of that waste. By identifying and measuring the waste being created, you can demonstrate the improvements that could be made and the benefit that results from those improvements. Numbers matter to management, so being able to show them the results of the improvements can go a long way in generating momentum and encouraging more opportunities for improvement. Likewise, if you are an **Agile** shop, you will be familiar with creating a **minimum viable product** (**MVP**), and this can be used to identify what minimum improvements could be made that would provide value and improve performance in executing service management processes. It would also ensure that the MVP created would be usable and could be delivered in a timely fashion.

DevOps has been described as a paradigm shift in how IT organizations should operate. Bringing together the development side of the house and the operations side of the house can act as an accelerant by limiting false starts and ensuring that what is developed for the service management processes can be used by operations to fulfill the needs of all stakeholders. DevOps intends to ensure that what is developed can be applied and improve the overall operation of the IT organization. This enables greater synergy between these two elements of the IT organization and results in improvements in delivering value to the stakeholders.

Finally, a major accelerator for any major initiative involves educating the organization about why it is important to perform service management efficiently and effectively. When everyone is on the same page, it is much easier to move forward with pace than if only a few managers know where the organization is going. Educating the organization can take a formal approach, such as ITSM education or informal workshops, to raise awareness about ITSM. An organizational change management plan (that is, a communication plan) can be part of the overall strategy for educating all the various stakeholders that will be impacted by the service management effort. For customers, receiving faster, better service, and more value for the service being delivered are key benefits. For IT professionals, the key benefits are improved skills, easier, better response to demand, growth opportunities, and more satisfied customers and users. All stakeholders will benefit from greater efficiency in delivering and supporting services. In our experience, it is not sufficient to say we are doing service management but also to educate the organization about what that means and how they will be impacted by the initiative. Providing information and knowledge to those impacted by the service management effort will help the stakeholders understand what is in it for them and raise the potential that they will join the effort rather than resist it. Without this effort, the risk of your efforts being limited and delayed increases significantly.

Summary

In this chapter, you saw some key definitions for service management, including value, a service, process, and others. There were descriptions of what a management system was and that service management is about *managing services*, no matter the level of formality, it is in play at all times, and it is all around us in many different scenarios. We also reviewed the various management systems where best practices and guidance can be leveraged to gain knowledge and understanding about how to apply them to your specific needs. There was also a discussion about the common elements of the various service management systems that can be leveraged and adapted to your specific needs and culture. Another area of discussion was how business and IT continue to converge, one relying on the other for overall success. This chapter wrapped up with a review of some key accelerators that can be applied to improve the speed with which you implement service management capabilities.

In the coming chapters, there will be more specific information about the processes that can enable you to improve your overall service management capability. The information contained in these chapters will provide you with practical information and examples of how these processes work. The next chapter will begin by speaking about one of the key operational processes: **incident management**.

6
Incident Management

In this chapter, you will be introduced to the incident management capability, both by itself and as part of formal service management. This includes the capability's governance (purpose, objectives, and policies), execution (roles, responsibilities, activities, and metrics), and enablement (acceleration, integration, and supporting technology).

In this chapter, we're going to cover the following main topics:

- Purpose and objectives
- Policies
- Process terms and definitions
- Process input and output
- Process activities
- Roles and responsibilities
- Key process indicators
- Process integrations
- Technology requirements

Purpose and objectives

Incident management is the process that is responsible for managing all incidents from initiation through closure.

The purpose of incident management is to manage the negative impact of a disruption in the normal operation of a service or service component by restoring the normal operational state of a service or component as soon as possible within the agreed target resolution time. **Normal operation** is typically defined by service levels documented in **service-level agreements** (**SLAs**) or as assumed by the customer and service provider.

An **incident** is defined as an unplanned disruption or potential disruption to the agreed level of service. Something that was working yesterday has broken today. That something could be the service being delivered to the user or consumer, or it could be a component that has reached a threshold. If action is not taken, it will result in a disruption of service to the user. There are instances where a disk array provides redundancy so one disk failure does not cause a service disruption. But the failure of a disk is not normal operation, so it must be handled as an incident to get it back to operating normally. Because incidents result in unplanned work for the service provider and a negative impact on the customer, it is very important to resolve incidents as quickly as possible within the agreed timeframes documented in customer agreements. It is essential to the service provider that this unplanned work is reduced whenever possible.

The objectives for incident management include the following:

- Maintaining the agreed service levels by restoring normal operation as quickly as possible
- Having a consistent and repeatable approach to executing incident management
- Facilitating a rapid resolution of incidents by leveraging previous or similar incidents, known errors, and knowledge bases
- Improving efficiency and effectiveness by leveraging appropriate sources of information about the service and configuration items
- Applying standards to managing incidents, documentation, response, and resolution techniques
- Improving visibility and communication about incidents and their management progress
- Prioritization and response based on business impact and urgency
- Improving user and customer satisfaction with the availability of services

Incident management requires any and all service providers involved to address the incident, whether the service provider is internal or external to the business

Policies

Policies represent the governance being applied to the incident management process. A **policy** describes the rules and boundaries being applied to the process to ensure appropriate controls are in place. This ensures consistency and repeatability but also identifies the level of flexibility a practitioner has when executing the process, procedure, or work instruction. In some instances, a policy could be applied to more than one process, and in the case of policies within incident management, this is true. Some incident management policies include categorization, prioritization, impact, urgency, incident record content, and reporting. Each of these policies will be discussed in more detail with examples ahead.

Categorization

Categorization is one of those policies that will be used by other processes (i.e., change management, request management, or problem management). Categorization is very important to understand what service is failing, what configuration items make up the service, and potentially, how to respond and resolve incidents. Categorization should allow the user to quickly and easily identify what they were doing when the failure occurred and allow the IT response team (typically the service desk) to quickly triage the incident and resolve or escalate it as appropriate. The categorization scheme will typically be multilevel and will allow you to produce reporting that aligns the service with the business.

A typical categorization scheme might start with the service at the highest level. This would be the service recognized by the customer and user. The next level could be the components of the service such as a server cluster, storage devices, the network, application, and so on. The lowest level could be the configuration item. This is illustrated in the following figure:

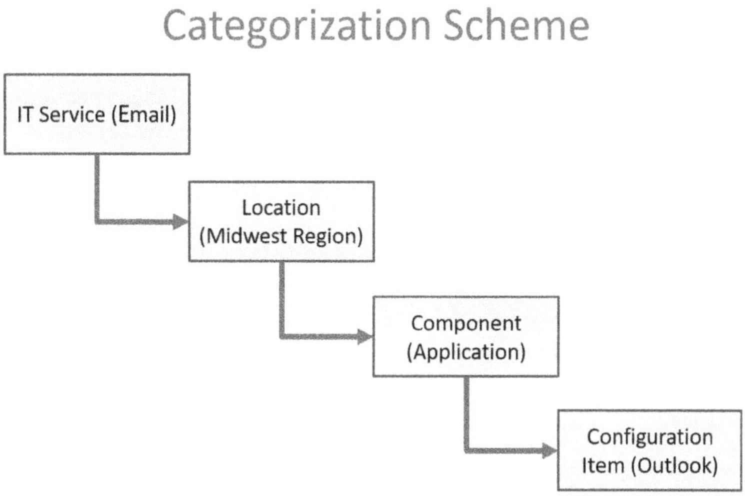

Categorization Scheme

IT Service (Email)

Location
(Midwest Region)

Component
(Application)

Configuration
Item (Outlook)

Figure 6.1 – A simple categorization scheme

The preceding figure shows a simple categorization scheme that includes a location for a widespread organization where the location is significant to managing incidents and providing reporting. A similar example in *Figure 6.2* shows a scheme that helps to align IT services with business processes:

Categorization Scheme

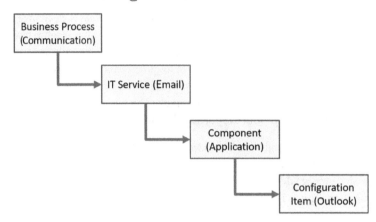

Figure 6.2 – A business-aligned service categorization scheme

When reporting the impact of incidents on the quality of the service, this scheme can allow you to more easily measure the impact on the business process affected. It provides the business with a better understanding of how it was impacted by the disruption in service. The benefit of this kind of reporting is transparency and clarity for the business.

A categorization scheme can be very sophisticated, but it is always a good idea to keep it simple and straightforward. The more levels, the greater reporting detail can be produced, but it can get very difficult for the staff using the categorization to know how to categorize an incident quickly and accurately. Your technology capability is also a consideration when attempting to categorize incidents. Keeping it simple will help to implement a categorization system that will be easy to apply, easy to use, and easier to apply to your technology.

Prioritization

Prioritization is another key policy that will be used by other processes (i.e., change management, problem management, and request management). Once you know what the incident is, you must determine the significance of the incident. How fast should you act? What kind of resources do you need to determine what is wrong and how to fix the incident? Prioritization allows the service desk or resolver group to know how important this particular incident is to the business. Not all incidents need to be resolved immediately, and incidents that have the highest impact on the business need to be resolved first. Since there are limited resources in most organizations for focusing on incident management, it makes sense to ensure that you are focusing on those with the most negative impact on the business. Prioritization is typically related to two specific factors: impact and urgency. There are instances where available resources are also a consideration, but we will start with impact and urgency.

Impact is defined as the consequences resulting from the disruption or potential service disruption. It is focused on how significant this outage is to the business and user in performing their designated function. *Figure 6.3* shows a sample impact matrix and the criteria used:

Impact = Degree of Failure

Impact Example

Factors	High	Medium	Low
Number of People	Big Group	Small Group	1 Person
Scope	Global	Regional	Local
# of Cis	>10	<10	1
Type of Role	Revenue Role	VIP	Normal

Figure 6.3 – Impact criteria matrix

Urgency describes for how long the service can be disrupted before action needs to be taken or how fast the disruption needs to be restored to normal operation. *Figure 6.4* shows a sample urgency matrix and the criteria applied:

Urgency = Time sensitivity in relation to risk and exposure

Note: These would be based on existing scales.
See the following model for an alternative method of establishing High, Medium, and Low

Factors	High	Medium	Low
Revenue Generating	Core	Support	Not Related
Security Classification	Core	Support	Not Related
Brand Exposure	Core	Support	Not Related
Safety Exposure	Core	Support	Not Related

Figure 6.4 – A sample urgency matrix

You could consider developing weighted criteria for urgency and determine, based on the business's needs, what the criteria are and how the weighting would be applied. *Figure 6.5* shows an example using the criteria in *Figure 6.4*:

Incident/Problem/Change/Release Management

Urgency: This model uses a points system to establish a multidimensional view of urgency based on risk

Factors	Points						Total	Weights	WGT*TOT PTS	Comments
	0	1	2	3	4	5				
Revenue Generating	X	1	2	3	4	5	5	100%	5	Scale to measure relationship to revenue generating business process
Security Classification	X	1	X	3	x	5	3	25%	0.75	The range would be indicated of the established security and data sensitivity classification
Brand Exposure	X	x	X	3	4	5	3	100%	3	Media Exposure
Safety Exposure	X	1	2	x	4	5	4	100%	4	Safety classification based on Risk Management model
Total possible points							Total Weighted Points		12.75	

Example Model:	0-5	Low
	6-9	Medium
	>9	High

Figure 6.5 – A complex urgency model

The combination of impact and urgency is the primary element involved in determining the prioritization of an incident, change, problem, or service request. *Figure 6.6* shows a simple matrix for impact and urgency:

Incident/Problem/Change/Release Management

Impact = Degree of failure
Impact Example

Factors	High	Medium	Low
Number of People	Big Group	Small Group	1 Person
Scope	Global	Regional	Local
# of Cis	>10	<10	1
Type of Role	Revenue Role	VIP	Normal

Urgency = Time sensitivity in relationship to risk and exposure

Note: These would be based on existing scales: see model below for Alternative model of establishing High, Medium, and Low

Factors	High	Medium	Low
Revenue Generating	Core	Support	Not Related
Security Classification	Core	Support	Not Related
Brand Exposure	Core	Support	Not Related
Safety Exposure	Core	Support	Not Related

Combination of Impact and Urgency Calculates Priority which points to which Time based SLA applies

	High	Medium	Low
High	1	2	3
Medium	2	2	4
Low	3	4	5

Figure 6.6 – A prioritization matrix based on impact and urgency

The priority relates to how the response and resolution of the incident request will be handled and is based on the commitments either explicitly or implicitly described by the service provider organization and the customers. The explicit commitments are typically documented in SLAs. Once the service desk or resolver group has determined what the priority is, it will identify the SLA commitments and respond and resolve accordingly. *Figure 6.7* shows one example of priority and SLA targets:

Incident/Problem/Change/Release Management

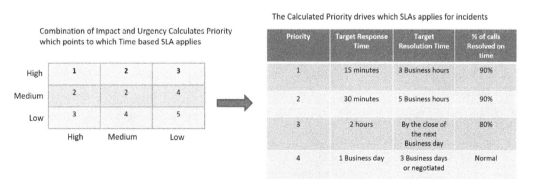

Combination of Impact and Urgency Calculates Priority which points to which Time based SLA applies

	High	Medium	Low
High	1	2	3
Medium	2	2	4
Low	3	4	5

The Calculated Priority drives which SLAs applies for incidents

Priority	Target Response Time	Target Resolution Time	% of calls Resolved on time
1	15 minutes	3 Business hours	90%
2	30 minutes	5 Business hours	90%
3	2 hours	By the close of the next Business day	80%
4	1 Business day	3 Business days or negotiated	Normal

Figure 6.7 – An SLA response and resolution targets based on priority

The prioritization of incidents is essential to ensure that the responders understand what kind of effort and time should be dedicated to the incident request. It also ensures that the providers are focusing on those incidents that have the most impact on the business first. An effective prioritization policy avoids the first-in-first-out approach to managing incidents and improves overall customer satisfaction by addressing the incidents that are most impactful to the business.

Incident logging is another very important policy. A policy statement such as *all incidents must be recorded* is essential to setting expectations with the service provider support teams and the customer/user community. It is necessary to capture information about the incident, have evidence that the incident occurred, and know what the support team's response to the incident was. From a customer/user perspective, it ensures that these stakeholders understand that unless the incident is reported and documented, there is no evidence that it ever happened. Any issues raised about incident response and resolution will be difficult to substantiate if no record of it happening exists. Included in this policy should be the minimum requirements for what gets documented in the incident record. There are a variety of elements that should be considered for the incident record, and the technology used to record incident requests will dictate some of those elements, but at a minimum, the incident record needs to describe the service and component impacted, when the incident occurred, who reported the incident, its priority, what investigation and diagnosis occurred, when it was responded to, who responded, what the resolution was, and when it occurred. Including this information in the incident record provides valuable knowledge that can be used for similar incidents, problem management, and change management activities. Any communication with the requestor should be documented in the incident record. The following table shows some of the data items contained in an incident record:

Incident Record Items	
Item	**Description**
Incident identifier	Typically automated as part of the technology
Date and time logged	Typically, an automated date and time stamp is applied by the technology
Name of agent recording the incident request	May be automated
Name of requestor	
Location (if in multiple locations)	May be automated
Contact information for the requestor	May be automated based on the name of the requestor
Description of the issue	Document as much information about the issue as the requestor can describe
Category of product or service	Document the category of the product or service based on information provided by the requestor

Incident Record Items	
Item	**Description**
Sub-category	Typically, the component that may be failing
Service/product	The name of the service or product that may be failing
Priority of the incident	Prioritization is typically determined automatically based on impact and urgency.
Impact	The impact that the incident has on the business or user's ability to do their job
Urgency	How fast does the incident need to be resolved?
Assign to	What support team will this incident be assigned to for investigation, diagnosis, resolution, recovery, and a return to normal operation?
Diagnostic actions	The assigned support team will document in the incident record all actions taken to diagnose the issue and resolve it.
Resolution description	The resolving support team will document in the incident record what was done to resolve and restore the product or service to normal operation.
Resolution date and time stamp	Document when the resolution was completed.
Classification code	A code used to establish the classification of the incident when it was opened
Closure code	A code used to identify the classification of the incident when it was resolved and closed
Closure date and time stamp	The date and time at which the customer/user was notified of the resolution and recovery and service was confirmed back to normal operation

Table 6.1 – Sample incident record content

In many instances, your technology will dictate what is required and optional in the incident record, but a policy should be documented to reflect the expectations for filling out and completing the incident record.

Here's why an **incident closure policy** should be documented:

- To define what information will be required in the incident record
- To define the effectiveness of the categorization and classification information
- To validate that the information provided clearly documents the activities performed during investigation, diagnosis, recovery, and resolution

When necessary, the service desk could reject and reassign the incident request to the resolving group when the necessary and required information has not been provided to the degree and quality expected.

These are some of the key policies that should be developed, documented, and communicated to all appropriate stakeholders to ensure that the stakeholders understand their responsibilities and realize the expectations when responding to an incident request.

Process terms and definitions

There are a number of key terms related to incident management, including incident, major incident, escalation, response time, resolution time, classification code, closure code, and so on. In this section, you will learn the definitions of these terms:

- An **incident** is defined as an abnormal condition for a service or a component of a service. It could be a situation where the service is not working or the service performance has degraded to the point where the service is unusable. It could be a component is down to the point that the service is no longer performing. There are situations where a component is down but has a redundant capability, so the service is still working but the component is not in a normal operational state. This too will be an incident. Another situation could be missing an agreed target for data/information updates, which can delay other activities and can potentially negatively impact a business. Within your organization, you should clearly define what an incident is and provide examples such as those previously mentioned so there is clarity within the organization about what is and what is not an incident.

- A **major incident** is defined as an incident that has a significant measurable impact on a business. Within your organization, you must define what criteria will be used to determine whether the incident is a normal incident or qualifies as a major incident. Major incidents require greater attention from support teams and need to be dealt with according to a more aggressive timeline. Criteria that might be considered to determine a major incident include a loss of revenue for the business, an incapability to ship or deliver a product to a customer, a negative impact on a business or organization's reputation, and others. These criteria should be specified in a policy and clearly communicated to the organization. Prioritization information should be aligned with the major incident policy. Typically, a major incident will have a specific procedure defined for it that accelerates the investigation and diagnosis while engaging with additional resources to discover the resolution as quickly as possible. In many instances, a major incident will require the engagement of a SWAT team or a swarming event to deal with this incident. The communication chain will also be much greater and potentially include many management levels.

- **Escalation** is defined as getting additional resources involved in the activities of incident management. There are two types of escalation in incident management: functional and hierarchical. **Functional escalation** involves engaging additional resources to assist in the investigation, diagnosis, and resolution of the incident. An example of this type of escalation would be the service desk escalating to a Level 2 support team. **Hierarchical escalation** is up the chain of command. An example of this would be, for a major incident, communicating to the CIO to initiate a swarming event or to communicate about the major incident and the current status of the recovery. It could be a request to management to focus additional resources on the incident or an instance where the incident is not getting the attention necessary to respond according to the SLA commitments. In general, the first group to be informed about the incident (usually the service desk) will own the responsibility for escalating an incident.

- **Response time** is defined as the amount of time it takes to respond to a customer/user when an incident is recorded. This documents how long it takes for the receiver of an incident to acknowledge that the incident has been recorded and is being actively worked on. Response time is one of the measures used to determine how effective the support organization is in capturing information about the incident and beginning work on the incident.

- **Resolution time** is the time from the opening of the incident until the incident issue is resolved and the service is restored to normal operation. This is when the service provider has performed all the activities necessary to restore normal operation. At this point, the service provider will communicate with the customer/user to confirm normal operation has been achieved as part of the closure.

- A **classification code** is a code used to classify the type of incident the service provider believes it is. Classification codes are based on a defined list and reflect what is happening based on the symptoms described by the requestor and understood by the service provider. Some example classification codes might include hardware, application, network, user error, and others. These classification codes are used to assist in the triage of the incident so it can be directed to the appropriate support team for action. Along with a closure code, a classification code can be used to improve the triage scripting used by the first point of contact when an incident is initiated.

- A **closure code** is a code that identifies what the actual issue was with the incident. The closure code uses the same defined list as a classification code. The classification code can be compared with the closure code to determine whether the incident was correctly classified when it was opened. This provides a mechanism for identifying when an incident is misclassified and allows the service provider to make improvements in the triage scripts. The result of making this improvement is a more reliable classification of incidents, a reduction in time to assign to the appropriate support team, and a reduction in time to resolve and restore service or components to a normal operational state.

In this section, we covered some of the key terms related to incident management.

Process input and output

Incidents can occur at any time and can be detected in a variety of ways. The following list identifies much of the input and output for incident management. You may have additional input or output not reflected in the following list:

- A user request to a service desk
- A user request submitted through a portal or self-help option
- A user request submitted by email
- A supplier-identified outage
- An event-generated incident created automatically by monitoring software
- The support team identified an outage resulting from their monitoring of components

Incident output includes the following:

- Service restoration to a normal operational state
- Communications to incident stakeholders
- Incident records
- Problem records:
    - Workarounds
    - Known errors
    - Incident symptoms
    - Incident investigation and diagnosis information
- Change requests
- Service requests
- Incident performance measures

Process activities

Incident management is one of the service management processes that have consistent activities for each incident request. Here are the activities defined for incident management:

- Detecting the incident
- Recording the incident

- Classifying and prioritizing the incident

- Initial investigation and diagnosis

- Escalation

- Investigation and diagnosis

- Resolution and restoration

- Recovery and closure

Figure 6.8 shows the flow for incident management, and the subsequent paragraphs describe what is involved in each of these activities and, in some cases, when an activity may be bypassed. You will also learn what the difference between a normal incident and a major incident is:

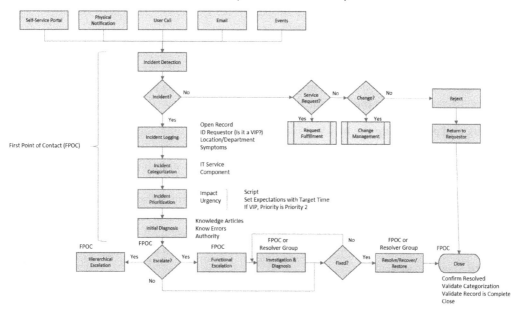

Figure 6.8 – Generic incident request workflow

Detecting an incident can occur in a variety of ways. The input described a number of ways in which the service provider may detect that an incident has occurred. When an incident is detected, the first thing that should be done is to validate that it is actually an incident and not a service request or a request for change. If it is not an incident, then it should be redirected to the appropriate process for action. If it is an incident, then it should be directed to the next activity.

Record the incident in the appropriate mechanism created for that purpose. There should be clear guidance on the information that should be recorded about the incident at this point. The following information should be considered when recording the incident:

- Who reported the incident
- The location of the requestor, if appropriate
- The requestor's impact on the incident
- The urgency of the resolution based on the requestor's expectations
- Symptoms
- The service the incident is related to

This information will be key for the first point of contact to determine how to classify the incident and to establish the priority of the incident, which is the next point.

Classifying and prioritizing the incident is based on a number of factors. When classifying the incident, identify the service or component being impacted, the symptoms described by the requestor, and the triage scripts. This will begin to point to the potential failure and what may be done to resolve the issue. Prioritization is a combination of impact and urgency. The incident may have a high impact but low urgency and should be prioritized appropriately. At this point, if the incident is identified as high-impact and high-urgency, it may be prioritized as a major incident and directed to the major incident procedure for action. *Figure 6.9* shows the major incident request flow, which is basically the same as the normal incident flow but involves more resources and has a higher degree of scrutiny by support groups and management:

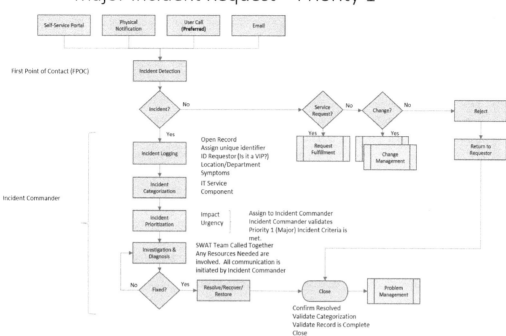

Figure 6.9 – Generic major incident request workflow

Once an incident is classified and prioritized, it is ready for **initial investigation and diagnosis**. Initial investigation and diagnosis are performed by the first point of contact – usually, the service desk. The service desk will review the symptoms and look at previous similar incidents, known errors, and workarounds to determine whether this incident has occurred before and can be resolved and restored at this point. If it can be, then the service desk will proceed to the resolution and restoration activity. If the service desk cannot resolve the incident, or if the incident is being handled in the major incident procedure, the service desk will escalate the incident to a higher level of support.

Escalation is the activity of bringing higher levels of support and experience to the incident response or engaging with the management chain for assistance. The two paths for escalation include functional and hierarchical. Functional escalation involves involving higher levels of experience and capability to investigate and resolve the incident. For example, the Service Desk has determined that it cannot resolve an incident, so it escalates the incident to the second level of support. When escalation occurs, best practice suggests that the first point of contact should retain ownership of the incident request so the requestor always has the first point of contact to get information about the status of their request. Once escalation to the second level has occurred, in best practice, the first point of contact will continue to monitor the progress of the incident until it is resolved and restored.

Hierarchical escalation occurs when the management chain is engaged to get additional resources involved or there is a need to remove a roadblock to restoring service or to communicate the status of a major incident. For example, the service desk has identified a major incident and a SWAT team or swarm has been engaged. The incident manager will communicate to the CIO that a major incident has been identified and is being worked on by the swarm. The incident manager will communicate with the CIO and other stakeholders every 15 minutes until the major incident is resolved and restored to normal service.

Investigation and diagnosis are the actions performed by the support team responsible for the component or service that is failing. During investigation and diagnosis, the support team will review a variety of sources to determine what is failing and what to do about it. Some of the sources used to perform investigation and diagnosis are diagnostic scripts, known errors, knowledge bases, previous similar incidents, changes implemented, workarounds, current open problems, and so on. Whatever sources are used get documented in the incident record so that this knowledge is captured with the incident documentation and can be reused for similar situations in the future. It is also valuable if at some point, this incident or multiple incidents for the same service can be raised to a problem and the root cause(s) can be identified and resolved permanently to improve quality and reduce incidents.

Resolution and restoration of service or a component of service is the activity post-investigation and diagnosis that takes place to return the service or component back to normal operation. As was discussed earlier in the *Prioritization* subsection of the *Policies* section, normal operations are defined in SLAs or some other customer agreement. Resolution is the action performed to resolve whatever has failed with the service or component. In resolving the failure, a change may be required or some type of fix applied. It could be as simple as a reboot of a device. Once the solution has been applied, the service or component needs to be restored to a known state before the failure occurred. For example, if a transaction failed, it may require a backup applied to the data to get back to the known state before the transaction failure occurred. In many cases, when an application failure occurs, there may be datasets that need to be restored to a point prior to the failure before restarting the application. Once the service or component is restored to normal operation, the final step occurs.

Recovery and closure is the final activity in the incident management process. Restoration of the service has occurred and the service provider has determined, as far as they know, that the service or component of the service is up and running. The first point of contact is responsible for following up with the incident requestor to validate that the service has recovered to a normal state and is ready for use. Once the first point of contact has validated this, you will confirm with the requestor that the incident record can be closed. The first point of contact will update the closure code to indicate where the actual failure occurred. The first point of contact will verify that the incident record has been updated appropriately, generate a user satisfaction survey, and close the incident.

If the incident was a major incident or an incident that occurs frequently, the first point of contact may raise a problem record for analysis by problem management. In some instances, if the incident requestor is not available, based on policy, the incident could be closed after a specific period of time. For example, if the requestor does not respond to a contact within 48 business hours, then the incident will be closed. The policy could also offer instances where an incident could be closed using technology automation. Once the incident is closed, no more action should be taken on that instance, and if the issue occurs again, a new incident has occurred.

In this section, we reviewed the activities related to the incident management process. There was a review of generic incident and major incident workflows.

Roles and responsibilities

There are three key roles for incident management: **process owner**, **process manager**, and **process practitioner**. As was discussed in *Chapter 5*, there are common responsibilities for every process owner and process manager. There are some key responsibilities that the incident management roles need to consider. The incident management process owner needs to work very closely with the change, problem, and request process owners to document the policies related to prioritization and categorization. Putting together a consistent policy for these two elements of service management will be critical to maintaining the relationships between these processes. In addition, the incident management process owner needs to establish the right metrics based on the maturity of the process and the capabilities of the technology to provide the data for the metrics. It will be very important for the process owner to have measures that drive the right behavior and produce metrics that effectively measure the performance of the process.

The incident management **process manager** is responsible for ensuring that the resources assigned to the incident management process are properly prepared to execute the process efficiently and effectively and that the practitioners have the necessary tools and resources to be efficient. The incident process manager is responsible for ensuring metrics are captured and reported to the appropriate stakeholders. The process manager is responsible for monitoring the execution of the process and identifying opportunities to improve. They will be the primary focus for communications to stakeholders concerning major incidents. The process manager will manage the major incident or be responsible for appointing a manager for major incidents.

The incident management **process practitioners** include the first point of contact (usually the service desk), specialist support teams (Levels 2 and 3 and suppliers), and management. The service desk is the first point of contact for users according to best practice guidance. A service desk practitioner is responsible for recording, categorizing, prioritizing, and performing initial investigation and diagnosis, and escalating any incident initiated by a user. As the first point of contact, a service desk practitioner is responsible for monitoring and tracking the progress of managing the incident regardless of whether it is escalated or resolved at the service desk. A service desk practitioner is responsible for ensuring that the incident is closed after making an effort to contact the user and validate the service recovered. The service desk is responsible for communication between the service provider organization and the user.

Specialist support teams are responsible for applying their skills and experience to resolve an incident and restore it to normal operation. They are responsible for documenting the activities involved in investigation and diagnosis and resolution and restoration. They are responsible for communicating the progress of the incident to the service desk as it goes through its life cycle. The management team is responsible for ensuring that the support teams have the necessary resources needed to execute the process and to set expectations about the impact on the organization.

Key process indicators

The incident management process has a number of key process indicators. These key process indicators should cover the progress of implementing the process across the service provider organization, compliance with the process policies, the effectiveness of producing the process deliverables, and the efficiency of the execution. A balanced set of metrics will ensure that the process is being measured appropriately and the key areas are covered. Some examples of key process indicators are contained in the following list:

- The total number of incidents as a control measure
- The number of incidents without documentation for investigation, diagnosis, resolution, or restoration
- The number of major incidents and percentage of major incidents compared to all incidents recorded
- The number and percentage of incidents closed within an agreed target time
- The number and percentage of incidents misassigned
- The number and percentage of incidents resolved at the first point of contact
- The number and percentage of incidents incorrectly categorized
- The number of incidents not recorded

It will be important for the organization to focus on a few key metrics based on where you are in the maturity of your process. It is recommended that one or two metrics per focus area is sufficient to provide guidance on performance and where improvement can be considered. It is also important to monitor the behavior being exhibited as a result of the metrics so that you can identify unintended behavior and make adjustments as appropriate. At some point in your process life cycle, it will be appropriate to set targets for key process indicators. Be careful, however, to ensure that the targets are achievable and realistic so that they do not slow down progress. Likewise, monitor the behavior to make sure the targets are driving the right behavior. It is always good to keep in mind that what gets measured gets managed and what you measure is what will be produced.

Process integration

For each process in the best practice frameworks, you will have both primary and secondary relationships and interactions with other processes. Since every process has a relationship with every other process, this section will only cover the primary relationships to key processes. Each process will be described with the key interactions that incident management has with it:

- **Problem management** provides information to incident management in the form of problem symptoms, workarounds, known errors, and potential solutions to the incident. Incident management provides information to problem management for recurring incidents, major incidents, a top-ten list of incidents, and the information related to activities involved in investigating, diagnosing, resolving, and restoring incidents.

- **Change management** provides information to incident management on changes that have been recently implemented that may be the cause of the incident, since when something breaks, the first question is *what changed?* Incident management will initiate an emergency change to restore service, especially for major incidents. A workaround recommended by problem management may require a standard change to implement the incident fix.

- **Configuration management** provides information about the service impacted by an incident and the components that make up the service. This can be very valuable in performing triage to determine what component is failing, what support team is most appropriate to address the failure, and how to effectively classify the incident. A mature **configuration management database** (**CMDB**) can link the service to the business process impacted and the user(s) and customer(s) impacted allowing the Service Desk to communicate with information about outages.

- **Capacity management** will be engaged in any incidents that are related to performance issues. Capacity management resources will be called in to assist in the diagnosis of performance concerns, especially when the performance of a service has degraded to the point that it is unusable.

- **Availability management** will be involved in an incident that is unavailable to identify mechanisms that can be used in the future to apply redundancy or automated failover to reduce the unavailability. Availability management also relies on incident data to document and report on availability metrics.

- **Service level management** (**SLM**) uses information provided by incident management to report on the response and restoration commitments that have been agreed to with the customer. SLM provides information to incident management on what the agreed targets are for response and restoration. SLM will use incident data to report on the availability and performance achieved based on SLA commitments. SLM will also identify any major or recurring incidents and work with the customer and service provider to determine what improvement opportunities could be considered and what will be implemented.

- **IT service continuity management** may be invoked as part of the response to a major incident. In some instances, the time needed to restore service from a major incident may exceed the agreed target and require the invocation of your disaster recovery plan as part of the IT service continuity management process. In this instance, the service continuity manager will take over responsibility for the delivery of the service during the declared disaster situation and the incident management process manager will continue to coordinate the resolution of the major incident.

These process relationships represent some of the key interactions with incident management. As previously stated, there are other secondary interactions that are not listed here but are also something that should be considered when standing up incident management or making improvements to it and other processes. In the next section, you will see information about some technology requirements based on the current products available to support incident management.

Technology requirements

Technology has improved the support of ITSM best practices consistently over the last 20 to 30 years. It has especially matured the support of many operational processes including incident management. The following list shows many of the key requirements for the incident management process. You may have additional requirements, but the following list is a sample of what should be expected of any service management tool. The most important thing to remember about selecting any technology is it will not make a poor process better. It is also important to realize how the tool will be used to select one that will be most effective for your needs.

The following is a list of incident management requirements:

- The ability to create, modify, close, or cancel incident records
- The ability to automatically generate a unique record identifier
- Capturing and storing historical data and other incident-related information
- The ability to store and maintain alerting distribution lists by incident type
- The ability to enable automated prioritization, assignment, and escalation of incidents based on categorization
- Supporting escalation both functional and hierarchical, manually or based on business rules
- Supporting input of free text, screen captures, and file attachments to record incident descriptions and resolution activities
- Being able to associate incident records with user and customer data
- Being able to use configurable closure categorization codes on incident closures
- Being able to assign tasks to external service providers
- Being able to allow for multiple types of alerts (email, text) i.e., deadline alerts, reassignment alerts, and inactivity alerts
- Being able to deliver hierarchical notifications about incidents that exceed or will soon exceed the agreed target times based on SLAs or priority
- Being able to collect feedback via a satisfaction survey or other mechanism during incident closures
- Being able to initiate an incident record on behalf of someone else

- Being able to put an incident record on hold and stop the timer for SLA reporting

- The ability to differentiate between an incident and a service request

- A resolved incident record that automatically triggers a notification to the requestor

- An automated incident record closure after a predetermined time after the incident record has been put in a resolved state

- The ability to reopen an incident record in a resolved status

- Automatically establish incident record priority based on impact and urgency

- The ability to search for an incident by various criteria, for instance, an incident-unique identifier, requester name, description, resolver group, and others

- Being able to reassign an incident from one support group to another

- Enabling support teams to quickly and easily see incidents assigned to them and the incident priority

- Enabling managers, supervisors, or team leads to easily view all incidents assigned to their team by priority

- Being able to see a full incident record history clearly and concisely

- A prompt for missing required information before an incident record's closure

As stated earlier, it is very important to understand how you intend to use the technology, define the requirements for the technology, evaluate the current technology to determine what the deficiencies are, and then identify your options for a provider and pick the one that satisfies the most requirements in your list. When defining your requirements, you should consider using the MoSCoW approach. The **MoSCoW approach** suggests classifying your requirements based on the *Must-Have, Should-Have, Could-Have,* or *Would-Like-to-Have* criteria. This allows you to prioritize the requirements and make sure that the Must-Haves and Should-Haves are generally covered by the tool you choose. You should also be careful when defining your requirements; a list that contains mostly Must-Haves will typically limit your choices to one or none.

Summary

In this chapter, you were exposed to the key elements of the incident management process including its purpose and objectives, policies, process terms and definitions, input and output, activities, roles and responsibilities, key process indicators, process integrations, and technology requirements. You were provided with significant details about the process, which should enable you to get started with implementing the process or making improvements to your existing process.

In the next chapter, you will continue to learn about operational processes with problem management. **Problem management** is the process that focuses on eliminating errors in the production environment to enable the organization to improve quality and reduce the impact of unplanned work. You will learn more about what problem management can do in your organization in the next chapter.

7

Problem Management

In this chapter, you will be introduced to the **problem management** capability specifically, and how it's part of formal **service management**. This includes the governance (purpose, objectives, and policies), the execution (the roles and responsibilities, activities, and metrics), and the enablement (accelerating, integrating, and supporting technology) of the capability. This capability enables an organization to learn how to apply various techniques to identify root causes and determine the best permanent solution to resolve them, reducing the impact of known errors and eliminating those errors, and improving the overall quality of the services being delivered.

In this chapter, we're going to cover the following main topics:

- Purpose and objectives
- Policies
- Process terms and definitions
- Process inputs and outputs
- Process activities
- Roles and responsibilities
- Key process indicators
- Process integrations
- Technology requirements

Purpose and objectives

Problem management is the process that is responsible for managing all problems from initiation through to closure.

The purpose of problem management is to manage the life cycle of a problem from the time the problem is raised until the permanent solution to eliminate the error has been applied. Problem management has both a reactive aspect and a proactive aspect. The reactive aspect of problem management involves responding to errors identified through incidents – both recurring and major. The proactive aspect of problem management involves identifying abnormal conditions that have not resulted in an incident but still need attention to determine what is causing the conditions and how to eliminate them. An example of this type of problem analysis would be when a business process is showing poor performance but there do not seem to be any service disruptions and the performance is not bad enough to raise an incident. A problem could be raised to investigate this situation to determine where the error is and what to do about it. Other examples could be applying maintenance releases or program fixes to avoid potential problems from occurring in your environment, as well as using risk management and identified risks to identify possible problem areas and taking corrective action before the risk materializes. These examples represent a few of the ways that proactive problem management can be applied to improve the overall quality and reliability of the services.

A **problem** is defined as the cause or causes of one or more incidents or the cause of abnormal behavior resulting from the utilization of a business or IT service. Problems can be initiated by any stakeholder within the organization or by an external stakeholder. WB Deming stated that the operator or the individual closest to the activities being performed is the best source for identifying where a problem may exist. If this is the case, then any stakeholder could identify an abnormal situation and raise a problem record to be analyzed and resolved if appropriate.

The objectives for problem management include the following:

- Resolving problems to reduce incidents by eliminating errors
- Reducing the negative impact of incidents that cannot be eliminated by facilitating the rapid resolution of incidents by applying workarounds and known errors
- Improving the overall quality of service by eliminating errors permanently
- Improving supplier relationships by providing information to suppliers on problems identified with supplier components or applying permanent solutions provided by suppliers
- Improving visibility and communication about problems, known errors, and permanent solutions
- Preventing incidents by applying proactive problem management to eliminate errors
- Improving user and customer satisfaction by eliminating errors and improving the availability of services

Let's now move on to the policies.

Policies

Policies represent the governance being applied to the problem management process. A policy describes the rules and boundaries being applied to the process to ensure appropriate controls are in place. This ensures consistency and repeatability but also identifies the level of flexibility a practitioner has when executing the process, procedure, or work instruction. In some instances, a policy could be applied to more than one process, and in the case of policies within problem management, this is true. Some of the problem management policies defined will be consistent with the incident management policies, including **categorization**, **prioritization**, **impact**, **urgency**, and **closure**, with only minor variations. Each of these policies will be discussed in more detail with examples in the following sections.

Categorization

Categorization is one of those policies that will be used by other processes (that is, **change management**, **request management**, and **incident management**). Categorization is very important for understanding what service is failing, what configuration items make up the service, and potentially how to respond to and resolve them. Categorization should allow the user to quickly and easily identify what they were doing when the failure occurred and allow the problem management resources to identify all the information available concerning the symptoms of the problem and begin the cause analysis. The categorization scheme will typically be multilevel and will allow you to produce reporting that aligns the service with the business.

A typical categorization scheme might start with the service at the highest level. This would be the service recognized by the customer and user. The next level could be the components of the service, such as a server cluster, storage devices, network, application, and so on. The lowest level could be the configuration item. This is illustrated in the following figure (*Figure 7.1*):

Categorization Scheme

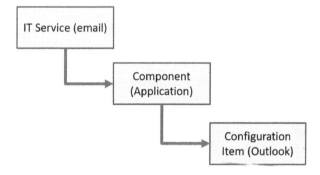

Figure 7.1 – A simple categorization scheme

The preceding figure shows a simple categorization scheme. A similar example in *Figure 7.2* shows a scheme that helps align IT services with business processes. When reporting the impact of a problem on the quality of the service, this scheme allows you to measure the impact on the business process that are affected more easily. It provides the business with a better understanding of how the business was impacted by the error in the service. The benefit of this kind of reporting is transparency and clarity for the business:

Categorization Scheme

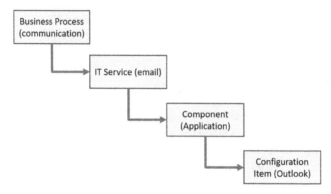

Figure 7.2 – A more complex categorization scheme

A categorization scheme can be very sophisticated but it is always a good idea to keep it straightforward. The more levels, the greater reporting detail can be produced, but it can become very difficult for the staff using the categorization to know how to categorize problems accurately. Your technology capability is also a consideration when attempting to categorize problems. Keeping it simple will help you implement a categorization that will be easy to apply, easy to use, and easy to implement in your technology.

Prioritization

Once you know the categorization of the problem, you must determine the significance of the problem. Prioritization is another key policy that will be used by other processes (that is, change management, incident management, and request management). In the case of problem management, prioritization is used to determine how significant this issue is to the customer and what resources need to be applied to perform root cause analysis and find a permanent solution. Priority allows the problem manager to identify the importance of this issue to the organization and order it with other problems in the queue so that the service provider can ensure that the resources assigned to work on problem cause analysis and resolution are working on those problems that have the most value to the organization. Not all problems need to be resolved or can be resolved, so it is important to focus on those that have the most impact on the business. Prioritization is typically related to two specific factors: impact and urgency. There are instances where other factors should be considered but it makes sense to start with impact and urgency.

Impact and urgency

Impact is defined as the consequences resulting from the service error. It focuses on how significant this error is to the business and what benefits would be achieved by eliminating the error permanently. *Figure 7.3* shows a sample **impact matrix** and the criteria used:

Impact = Degree of failure

Impact Example

Factors	High	Medium	Low
Number of People	Big Group	Small Group	1 Person
Scope	Global	Regional	Local
# of Cis	>10	<10	1
Type of Role	Revenue Role	VIP	Normal

Figure 7.3 – Sample impact criteria matrix

Urgency describes how significant this error is to the business and, consequently, how important it is that you identify the cause or causes and document a permanent solution for the error and get the solution implemented. *Figure 7.4* shows a sample **urgency matrix** and the criteria applied:

Urgency = Time sensitivity in relationship to risk and exposure

Note: These would be based on existing scales: see the following model for an alternative model of establishing High, Medium, and Low

Factors	High	Medium	Low
Revenue Generating	Core	Support	Not Related
Security Classification	Core	Support	Not Related
Brand Exposure	Core	Support	Not Related
Safety Exposure	Core	Support	Not Related

Figure 7.4 – Sample urgency criteria matrix

You could consider developing weighted criteria for urgency and determine what the criteria were and how the weighting would be applied based on the business needs. *Figure 7.5* shows an example using the criteria in *Figure 7.4*:

Incident / Problem/ Change / Release Management

Urgency This model uses a points system to establish a multidimensional view of urgency based on risk

Factors	Points						Total	Weights	WGT*TOT PTS	Comments
	0	1	2	3	4	5				
Revenue Generating	X	1	2	3	4	5	5	100%	5	Scale to measure relationship to revenue generating business process
Security Classification	X	1	X	3	x	5	3	25%	0.75	The range would be indicated of the established security and data sensitivity classification
Brand Exposure	X	x	X	3	4	5	3	100%	3	Media Exposure
Safety Exposure	X	1	2	x	4	5	4	100%	4	Safety classification based on Risk Management model
Total possible points							Total Weighted Points		12.75	

Example Model:	0-5	Low
	6-9	Medium
	>9	High

Figure 7.5 – Sample multidimensional approach to the urgency criteria matrix

The combination of impact and urgency is the primary element involved in determining the priority of an incident, change, problem, or service request. *Figure 7.6* shows a simple matrix for impact and urgency:

Incident / Problem/ Change / Release Management

Impact = Degree of failure

Impact Example

Factors	High	Medium	Low
Number of People	Big Group	Small Group	1 Person
Scope	Global	Regional	Local
# of Cis	>10	<10	1
Type of Role	Revenue Role	VIP	Normal

Urgency = Time sensitivity in relationship to risk and exposure

Note: These would be based on existing scales: see the following model for an alternative model of establishing High, Medium, and Low

Factors	High	Medium	Low
Revenue Generating	Core	Support	Not Related
Security Classification	Core	Support	Not Related
Brand Exposure	Core	Support	Not Related
Safety Exposure	Core	Support	Not Related

Combination of Impact and Urgency Calculates Priority which points to which time-based SLA applies

	High	Medium	Low
High	1	2	3
Medium	2	2	4
Low	3	4	5

Figure 7.6 – Combined impact and urgency to determine the priority matrix

The priority relates to how resources will be applied to the problem analysis and identifying a permanent solution. In the case of problem management, prioritization is different from incident management in that it is not based on a **service-level agreement (SLA)** time commitment; instead, it is more focused on applying a permanent solution and ensuring that any subsequent disruptions to the service do not recur. Once the problem manager has determined what the priority is, they will identify what resources will be allocated to the problem and how much of those resources' time will be allocated to the problem life cycle.

Prioritizing problems is essential to ensure that the problem practitioners assigned to the problem will commit the appropriate attention and effort to analyzing and resolving the error so that it is eliminated and does not recur. An effective prioritization policy ensures that the service provider understands the significance of any identified errors and will allocate the appropriate resources to do so. Moreover, it involves identifying and implementing a cost-effective solution to permanently eliminate the error, improving the overall quality of the service and increasing customer satisfaction.

Another policy to consider is establishing criteria for creating a **problem record**. This policy should define clear guidelines for identifying the situations in which a problem record should be created, as well as specifying the required information to be included in the record. For example, if a major incident is recorded, a problem record would be created once the major incident has been resolved to identify what the root cause or causes were and identify a permanent solution to resolve the root cause(s) identified. Since major incidents result in significant business impact, it is probably something your organization wants to avoid in the future, so it makes sense to initiate a problem record. Another example to consider here is that anyone can raise a problem record but it must include a problem description, the business impact, its frequency of occurrence, the business value of resolving the problem, and more. This particular criterion ensures that the stakeholder submitting the problem record has reviewed the issue and can provide justification for applying resources to resolve the problem. A third criterion for problem record creation could be a top 10 list of incidents. In this case, incident management may provide information about the top 10 incidents recorded for the month or quarter to be considered by problem management. Here, problem management would review the list, identify the top 1-3 recurring incidents, and perform a business case analysis to determine the value of eliminating these recurring incidents. This allows problem management to reduce the number of incidents being handled by the first point of contact and it would improve the quality of the affected services, all while improving customer and user availability and satisfaction. This policy should include the minimum requirements for what gets documented in the problem record. Several elements should be considered when creating problem records, and the choice of technology for recording problems may influence some of these elements. However, at a minimum, the problem record needs to include a problem statement that describes the situation, identifies the deviation from expectations, specifies the business impact, provides measurable information, and avoids assigning blame. The problem statement should be included in the description. All incident information (if incidents exist and are related) should be included in the problem record.

The following table contains sample content for a problem record:

Problem Record Items	
Item	**Description**
The problem's unique identifier	Typically automated as part of the technology
Date and time logged	Typically, an automated date and time stamp is applied by the technology
Problem owner	The problem manager, who is responsible for monitoring and managing the problem through its life cycle
Name of problem initiator	Who requested the problem record be created
Contact information of the initiator	Maybe automated based on the name of the requestor
Short Description	Document the problem statement
Description	Document all the information that can be collected about the problem, including incident information on symptoms, investigation and diagnosis, workarounds used, and more

Problem Record Items	
Item	**Description**
Category of product or service	Document the category of the product or service based on information provided by the requestor.
Sub-category	Typically, the component that might be failing
Service/product	The name of the service or product that failed
Priority of the problem	Prioritization is typically determined automatically based on impact and urgency.
Impact	The impact that the problem has on the business based on information provided in the problem statement
Urgency	How much effort should be applied to this problem based on the business benefit described in the problem statement.
Assign to	Resources assigned to this problem
Investigation and diagnosis	Capture all investigation and diagnosis activities performed as part of root cause analysis.
Workaround(s)	Workaround(s) identified during root cause analysis
Known errors	Document the known error once it has been identified and a workaround or permanent solution has been found.
Resolution description	Capture all activities involved in identifying all possible solutions and documenting the permanent solution or solutions identified.
Resolution date and timestamp	Document when the resolution was completed.
Closure code	What the final disposition of this problem was when it was closed
Closure date and timestamp	The date and time when the permanent solution(s) have been applied and confirmed successful by change management

Table 7.1 – Sample problem record

In many instances, your technology will dictate what is required and optional in the problem record, but a policy should be documented to reflect the expectations for filling out and completing the problem record.

The **problem closure policy** should describe the conditions under which a problem may be closed permanently. According to best practice guidance, a problem should remain open until a permanent solution has been applied, typically through change management. There are instances where identifying a permanent solution may be difficult or too costly to consider applying. In this case, applying a workaround may become the permanent solution and is closed with the appropriate closure code – that is, *closed with a workaround*. In other situations, a problem may be closed because no action will be taken to eliminate the error. It may be because a supplier-owned component is off maintenance and the supplier has chosen not to provide a fix for the error. In other cases, a permanent solution may not have been identified, so the policy will state a closure code such as *closed with no permanent solution*. These are some of the key policies that should be developed, documented, and communicated to all appropriate stakeholders to ensure that the stakeholders understand their responsibilities and realize the expectations when responding to a problem request.

This section described some of the key policies to consider when standing up a problem management process. The next section will define common terms related to problem management.

Process terms and definitions

There are several key terms related to problem management, including **problem**, **root cause(s)**, **known error**, **workaround**, **permanent solution**, and **closure code**. In this section, you will learn about the definitions of these terms.

Problem

A problem is defined as the cause of incidents or abnormal behavior exhibited by a product or service. It could be a situation where the service is working and continues to work but something is going on that cannot be explained. It could be that a major incident has occurred and the service provider has restored the service but the impact was significant enough that the customer does not want it to happen again, so they may request a problem be raised to address the error. It could be an instance where the service desk has identified multiple occurrences of the same incident and the management team wants these incidents eliminated permanently. In many reactive cases, the incident is the driver for a problem record to be initiated. Proactive problem management involves analyzing incident data, performing service-level reviews, getting supplier information, identifying errors during development or testing that are going to be introduced into the production environment, or a customer/user identifying abnormal or unknown behavior that prompts the initiation of a problem. Within your organization, you should clearly define what a problem is and provide examples such as those explained previously so that there is clarity within the organization about what is and what is not a problem.

Root cause

The root cause is defined as the underlying cause or causes of a problem. The root cause is discovered through the application of various techniques in investigation and diagnosis. Although the objective is to discover the single root cause, there can be multiple contributing causes that may dictate resolving more than one root cause. There are a variety of techniques you can apply to perform root cause analysis. These will be discussed later in the *Process activities* section.

Workaround

A workaround is defined as a temporary solution that can be applied to restore the service or component that failed until a permanent solution can be identified and implemented. A workaround should be reviewed each time it is applied to identify any improvements that can be made to improve the effectiveness of the workaround. Workarounds may become the permanent solution for a problem if the actual permanent solution is cost-prohibitive to apply. A workaround is required to document a known error.

Known error

A known error is defined as a problem with a defined root cause or causes with a workaround or permanent solution available. Good practice suggests that a known error can be defined as soon as it makes sense to document it. This suggests that there are cases where a cause is known, but the investigation and diagnosis may not have identified the root cause and continues to work to discover the root. However, it makes sense to mitigate the impact of recurring incidents to document a known cause and the workaround. This enables a single point of contact to identify a recurring incident and apply the workaround to reduce the impact of the incident and restore service faster.

Permanent solution

A permanent solution is a solution that will permanently eliminate the error discovered during root cause analysis or mitigate the impact of recurring incidents. There are instances where the solution(s) that have been defined are cost-prohibitive, are not consistent with the service provider architecture, or the management team is not willing to fund the solution that will permanently eliminate the error. In this case, the permanent solution may be to continue to apply a workaround that consistently reduces the impact of recurring incidents.

Closure code

A closure code is a code that identifies the disposition of the permanent solution for the problem. For instance, the closure code for problem management would include a permanent solution that's been successfully implemented, a workaround to the permanent solution, or a problem that's been canceled. Closure codes for problem management should be documented in a policy.

This section described several common terms related to problem management. The next section will cover the process inputs and outputs for problem management.

Process inputs and outputs

Problems can be created at any time and detected in a variety of ways, such as major incidents, recurring incidents, unexpected behavior from a service, and so on. The following list identifies many of the inputs and outputs for problem management but is not inclusive:

- Incident management data and information
- Triggers from stakeholders
- Supplier information about a potential problem that needs service provider resources
- A stakeholder request to initiate a problem record
- Trend analysis data
- Configuration information
- Information from other processes
- Known error/problem information

The following are examples of incident outputs:

- Change requests
- Permanent solutions implemented
- Known errors
- Workarounds
- Problem symptoms
- Root cause analysis
- Knowledge articles
- Management information

This section looked at the inputs and outputs for problem management. The next section will describe the activities of the problem management process.

Process activities

Problem management is one of the service management processes that has consistent activities for each problem request.

Figure 7.7 shows the flow for problem management:

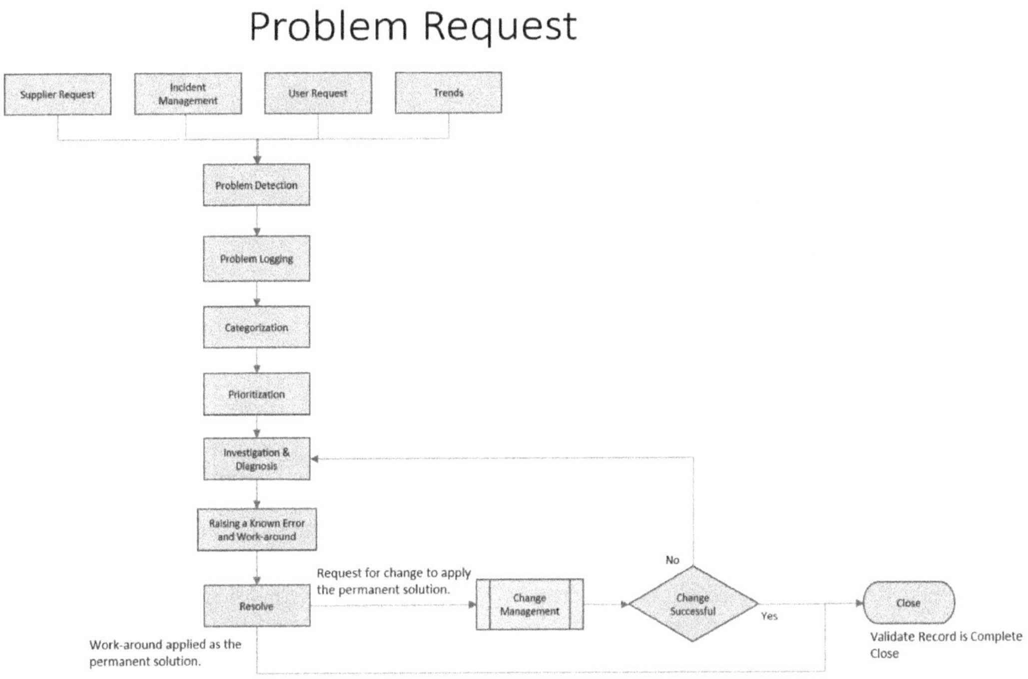

Problem Request

Figure 7.7 – Example problem management process flow

The following subsections will describe what is involved in each of these activities.

Identifying a problem

Identifying a problem can occur in a variety of ways. The inputs described several ways that the service provider may identify that a problem has been raised. Once a problem has been identified, the next step is to log the problem and information about it.

Recording the problem

You should record the problem in the appropriate mechanism created for that purpose. There should be clear guidance on the information that should be recorded about this problem. Information that should be considered when recording the problem includes the following:

- Who initiated the problem
- Who will own the problem
- Problem statement

- Impact of the problem on the business as part of the problem statement
- Urgency describing the effort expected to resolve the problem
- Symptoms of the problem
- Service or services the problem is impacting
- Customers impacted by the problem
- Information about incidents related to the problem and any known errors or workarounds related to the problem

This information will be key for the problem owner to classify and prioritize the problem with the other problems in the queue, as well as identify the appropriate resources to perform root cause analysis as part of the investigation and diagnosis.

Classifying and prioritizing the problem

Classifying and prioritizing the problem is based on several factors. When classifying the problem, identifying the service or services being impacted, the overall impact the problem is having on the customers, and the benefits to be achieved by eliminating the error will be essential for identifying the resources needed to perform investigation and diagnosis. Prioritization is a combination of impact and urgency. The problem priority will be based largely on the impact described in the problem statement and the benefits to the business if this problem were eliminated permanently. Priority in problem management is not for speed like it is in incident management; it is more about its order regarding the other problems in the queue. If this problem has more impact and benefit than existing problems in the queue or those being worked on, then this new problem may take priority over the existing ones. This approach ensures that the limited resources needed to perform problem management activities are always working on those problems that have the most benefit to the business or organization.

Investigation and diagnosis

Once a problem has been classified and prioritized, it is ready for investigation and diagnosis or **root cause analysis**. During this activity, the problem will be investigated based on the available information about recorded incidents, incident details and symptoms (where available), affected services, impacted users, information from the **configuration management database** (**CMDB**), known errors, other problems, technical and specialist knowledge, and knowledge base records. Root cause analysis is performed by a specialist team that has the necessary skills and experience to identify all causes associated with this problem symptoms and then apply various techniques to narrow the causes down to the root cause. It is conceivable that more than one root cause might be identified, but the objective would be to get down to one. A variety of techniques can be leveraged to perform root cause analysis. We will not provide a comprehensive description of all the possible techniques available, but we will provide some examples.

One of the more comprehensive approaches to root cause analysis is the **Kepner-Tregoe approach**. This should be applied to those problems that are very complex and cover a variety of contributing causes or where finding and eliminating the root cause is extremely important to the organization. Kepner-Tregoe defined a specific set of activities to follow to discover the root cause and identify the appropriate solution to resolve it.

A simpler approach could be the **5 Whys**. The 5 Whys uses a why-question approach until the team can no longer answer the why. This approach begins with asking a general why question and continues asking whys to dive deeper into the details of the issue or problem being investigated. Under normal circumstances, experience would suggest that by the time the question has been asked five times, the necessary detail will have been revealed.

Another approach for root cause analysis is **Ishikawa Diagrams** or **fishbone diagrams**. This approach is useful because it provides a visual representation of all the causes and effects involved in the service and provides a means to identify key relationships between the various elements. This helps determine where the fault might be and, potentially, where the solution could be identified.

Probably the most used approach to root cause analysis and the least expensive is **brainstorming**. In brainstorming, you get the appropriate stakeholders in a room and work through all the ideas about what the potential causes are until all ideas have been exhausted and then start throwing out the ones that do not make sense or are not relevant until you get down to the contributing and root causes. Brainstorming tends to be used in combination with many of the different analysis techniques, including **Pain Value Analysis**, **Pareto Analysis**, Ishikawa Diagrams, and even Kepner-Tregoe. These techniques and others can be used to identify root causes.

Raising a known error and a workaround

Raising a known error and a workaround is done by the investigation team during the root cause analysis activities or as part of the **service validation and testing** process when testing new or changed services or components. As the investigation and diagnosis proceed, a workaround may be identified that can be applied to reduce the impact of recurring or similar incidents. In the case of service validation and testing, if an error is identified during testing that is minor or will be deployed to the production environment, the development team should provide a workaround that can be applied to mitigate the impact of this error being introduced into the production environment.

For problems that exist in the production environment, once the investigation and diagnosis team has identified one or more root causes and understands what the error is, they will raise a known error and document that known error in the known error database. As the definition for known error describes, a known error is defined when the root cause has been identified and a workaround or permanent solution is known. In most cases, a known error will be recorded when the error has been discovered and a workaround has been identified. However, best practice would suggest that a known error can be recorded as soon as it becomes useful to do so.

Resolution

The **resolution** of known errors results from a solution team being engaged in reviewing all possible resolutions for the error identified and selecting the one or more that make the most sense. The solution team will brainstorm solutions for the root cause or causes identified and perform an analysis of the cost, the practicality of the solutions, their relevance to the current architecture, and the ability to implement them to determine the best possible solution or solutions to apply. Once the team has determined the best possible solution, a business case will be established to apply the permanent solution. If the permanent solution is going to be applied, the solution team will initiate a request for change to have the solution developed, tested, deployed, and implemented according to change management policies. After the change has been implemented and the post-implementation review has validated the objectives have been achieved, then the problem manager can proceed to the final activity in the process.

In many instances, the permanent solution(s) will be cost-prohibitive or impractical and the decision will be made to apply the workarounds. To close the problem record in this case, the workaround becomes the permanent solution. However, there are instances where the problem record will remain open because the problem owner and stakeholders decide that the permanent solution may become cost-effective or practical and will then be applied to permanently eliminate the root cause.

Closure

Closure is the final activity in the problem management process. Once the change request has been successfully implemented and the objectives have been achieved, the problem owner will validate that the problem record has been updated with all the information involved in the problem investigation and diagnosis, solution discovery, and implementation of the permanent solution. A closure code will be recorded for the problem that indicates how it was closed – that is, a permanent solution has been applied, a workaround is the permanent solution, or it was canceled. Known errors related to this problem should be updated with the disposition of the problem and removed from the known error database before being added to the knowledge base. Once all of this has been completed, the problem record should be formally closed.

Now that we understand the various problem management activities, in the next section, we will describe the roles and responsibilities of a problem management process.

Roles and responsibilities

There are four key roles when it comes to problem management: process owner, process manager, process practitioner, and problem owner. As discussed in *Chapter 5*, there are common responsibilities for every process owner and process manager. There are some key responsibilities that the problem management roles need to consider. For the problem management process owner, this role needs to work very closely with the change, incident, and request process owners so that it can document the policies related to prioritization and categorization. Putting together a consistent policy for prioritization and categorization of service management will be critical for maintaining the relationships between these processes. In addition, the problem management process owner needs to establish the right metrics based on the maturity of the process and the capabilities of the technology to provide the data for the metrics. It will be very important for the process owner to have measures that drive the right behavior and produce metrics that effectively measure the performance of the process.

The problem management process manager is responsible for ensuring that the resources assigned to the problem management process are properly prepared to execute the process efficiently and effectively. It is important to ensure that the practitioners have the necessary tools and resources to be efficient in the day-to-day execution of the process. The problem process manager is responsible for ensuring metrics are captured and reported to the appropriate stakeholders. The problem process manager is responsible for monitoring the execution of the process and identifying opportunities to improve. The process manager is responsible for appointing a problem owner for all problems raised. Periodically, the process manager will review closed problems to assess the contents of the problem records, compliance with the policies, and key process indicators to determine the overall performance of the process execution.

The problem management process practitioners include the problem owner, the diagnosis team, and the solutions team. The problem owner owns the problem(s) assigned to them and will be responsible for managing the life cycle of the problem. They will be the primary focus for communications to stakeholders concerning problems. The problem owner will work with the diagnosis team and the solutions team to ensure progress is made according to the priority of the problem. The problem owner is responsible for validating that all information about the problem life cycle has been recorded in the problem record and will close the problem record when the permanent solution has been deployed.

The diagnosis team is responsible for performing root cause analysis on the problem. They record all activities involved during the investigation and diagnosis. They also identify the root cause(s), workarounds, and known errors, recording these in the problem record or the known error database.

The solutions team identifies and documents all possible solutions and determines the best possible solution based on the analysis of a business case for implementing the permanent solution. The solutions team initiates a request for change to get the permanent solution applied and records all information about the solution's identification activities in the problem record. The solutions team records the results of the change request when the permanent solution has been implemented and deployed.

This section established the roles and responsibilities for problem management. Next, we'll look at the key process indicators.

Key process indicators

The problem management process has several **key process indicators**. These key process indicators should cover the progress of implementing the process across the service provider organization, compliance with the process policies, the effectiveness of producing the process deliverables, and the efficiency of the execution. A balanced set of metrics will ensure that the process is being measured appropriately and the key areas are covered. Some examples of key process indicators are as follows:

- The total number of problems recorded for a specified period as a control
- The number of problems without documentation for root cause analysis and resolution
- The number of problems closed with recurring incidents after the closure
- The time to complete root cause analysis
- The number and percentage of problems opened and closed
- The backlog of problems in the queue
- The number and percentage of workarounds applied to recurring incidents
- The number of known errors added to the known error database

It will be important for the organization to focus on a few key metrics based on where you are in the maturity of your process. It is recommended that one or two metrics per focus area is sufficient to provide guidance on performance and where improvement can be considered. It is also important to monitor the behavior being exhibited as a result of the metrics so that you can identify unintended behavior and make adjustments as appropriate. At some point in your process life cycle, it will be appropriate to set targets for key process indicators, but be careful to ensure that the targets are achievable and realistic so that they do not retard progress. Likewise, monitor the behavior to make sure the targets are driving the right behavior. It is always good to keep in mind that what gets measured gets managed and what you measure is what will be produced.

Now that you understand the key process indicators, the next section will describe the integrations between problem management and other processes.

Process integration

For each process in the best practice frameworks, you will have both primary and secondary relationships and interactions with other processes. Since every process has a relationship with every other process, this section will only cover the primary relationships to key processes. Each process will be described ahead, as well as the key interactions that problem management has with it.

Incident management

Incident management receives information from problem management in the form of problem symptoms, workarounds, known errors, and potential solutions to the incident. Incident management provides information to problem management for recurring incidents, major incidents, a top-10 list of incidents, and the information related to activities involved in investigating, diagnosing, resolving, and restoring incidents.

Change management

Change management provides information to problem management on changes that have been recently implemented that may be the cause of the problem. Problem management will initiate a request for change on any solution that will be deployed to implement a permanent solution or a workaround. Change management will keep problem management informed about the progress of the requests for change initiated by problem management. Problem management will assist change management in identifying errors resulting from failed changes.

Configuration management

Configuration management provides information about the service that's been impacted by the problem and the configuration items that make up the service. This can enable problem management to assess the potential impact of the error and help determine the urgency of the root cause analysis and solution discovery. The **configuration management system** (**CMS**) can be where the **known error database** and problem records reside and can be linked.

Capacity management

Capacity management uses problem management to investigate and diagnose capacity and performance-related errors. Capacity management resources may be called in to assist in the diagnosis of capacity and performance issues. Problem management will provide information to capacity management on the effectiveness of **capacity planning**.

Availability management

Availability management uses data from problem management to assist in making improvements to availability by reducing downtime and improving uptime. Availability management uses problem management to assist in the investigation and diagnosis of availability issues, both reactive and proactive, and to identify possible solutions to improve service availability.

Service-level management

Service-level management (**SLM**) uses information provided by problem management during a **service-level review** with the customer to identify potential areas of concern and initiate a problem record. Problem management provides information about errors that have been eliminated so that SLM can communicate the improvements that have been made to customers. SLM provides information to problem management on the impact of a problem on the customers so that appropriate prioritization can occur.

Financial management

Financial management provides information to problem management on the potential cost of an error to the organization and the proposed cost of solutions being considered. Problem management works with financial management to determine the cost of deploying a proposed solution and perform a business case analysis to determine the viability of the solution(s).

Supplier management

Supplier management is related to problem management and ensures that problems related to a supplier's products are documented and communicated to the supplier in a timely and effective manner. It also is related to the perspective of suppliers being involved in the cause analysis and solution discovery. A supplier may choose to refuse to provide a fix to a known error, which may result in additional risk to the organization in the form of incidents. Problem management needs to communicate with their suppliers when an error has been identified on a supplier component, after which supplier management will perform that communication.

These process relationships represent some of the key interactions with problem management. As previously stated, other secondary interactions are not listed here but are also something that should be considered when you're standing up problem management or making improvements to it and other processes. In the next section, you will learn about some technology requirements based on the current products available to support problem management.

Technology requirements

Technologies have improved the support of ITSM best practices consistently over the last 20-30 years. It has especially matured the support of many operational processes, including problem management. The following list shows many of the key requirements for the problem management process. You may have additional requirements but the following list is an example of what should be expected of any service management tool. The most important thing to remember about selecting any technology is that it will not make a poor process better and it is important to realize how the tool will be used to select the one that will be most effective for your needs.

Here are some of the problem management requirements:

- Providing a means to configure the problem process and category templates
- Creating a unique identifier for the problem record
- Being able to create problem templates
- Preventing problem closure until all tasks are complete
- Ensuring problems can be linked to related incidents and changes

- Providing the capability to assign problem records and known errors to assignment groups

- Displaying historical data on problems and known errors to staff as needed

- Supporting free text, screen captures, and file attachments

- Managing multiple tasks and assignments for a problem

- Enabling the capture of root cause analysis

- Providing search capabilities

It is very important to understand how you intend to use the technology, define the requirements for the technology, evaluate the current technology to determine what the deficiencies are, and then identify your options for a provider and pick the one that satisfies the most requirements in your list. When defining your requirements, you should consider using the **MoSCoW approach**. The MoSCoW approach suggests classifying your requirements based on the *Must-Have*, *Should-Have*, *Could-Have*, or *Would-Like-To-Have* criteria. This allows you to prioritize the requirements and make sure that the Must Haves and Should Haves are generally covered by the tool you choose. You should also be careful when defining your requirements as a list that contains mostly Must Haves will typically limit your choices to one or none.

Summary

In this chapter, you were exposed to the key elements of the problem management process, including its purpose and objectives, policies, process terms and definitions, inputs and outputs, activities, roles and responsibilities, key process indicators, process integrations, and technology requirements. You were provided with significant details about the process, which should enable you to start implementing the process or making improvements to your existing process.

In the next chapter, you will continue to learn about operational processes with change management. Change management is a process that focuses on managing the life cycle of all changes to the production environment to enable the organization to implement planned changes successfully efficiently and effectively. You will learn more about what change management can do in your organization in the next chapter.

8
Change Management

In this chapter, you will be introduced to the **change management** capability specifically, as part of formal **service management**. This includes the governance (the purpose, objectives, and policies), the execution (the roles and responsibilities, activities, and metrics), and the enablement (accelerating, integrating, and supporting technology) of the capability.

In this chapter, we will cover the following main topics:

- The purpose and objectives
- Policies
- Process terms and definitions
- Process inputs and outputs
- Process activities
- Roles and responsibilities
- Key process indicators
- Process integration
- Technology requirements

Purpose and objectives

Change management is the process that is responsible for managing all changes, from initiation through to closure.

The purpose of change management is to manage the life cycle of a change from the time the change is visualized until it has been successfully implemented in the production environment and the business benefits have been achieved. Change management is responsible for the control of all changes to the production environment. Although change management is focused on managing the life cycle of changes being deployed to the production environment, this control can be applied to other environments, including testing, quality assurance, and even various development environments. Change management is also necessary in an **agile** organization where changes are deployed rapidly and frequently; it is still necessary to know what is changing and when those changes are deployed and implemented.

A **change** is defined as a modification to any component, **configuration item** (**CI**), or service that could have a direct or indirect impact on the delivery and support of a service. Changes can have a minor impact, such as the tweaking of parameters on a server to improve performance, or be as significant as introducing a replacement service for the sales management system of an organization. Both of these examples need to be effectively controlled to manage the risk associated with the action and to ensure that the benefits to be delivered are actually achieved. Change management is a control process in best practice, but as with any control process, it is important to realize the appropriate level of control required to manage the risk related to the change.

The objectives for change management include the following:

- Managing the life cycle of all changes

- Protecting services and/or reducing risk from poorly planning a change

- Ensuring that all changes are recorded appropriately

- Ensuring that all changes follow a prescribed procedure for development, testing, deployment, and implementation in a controlled environment

- Ensuring that all changes to configuration items are properly managed

- Communicating the status of changes via a change register

- Performing a post-implementation review of all changes

- Responding to changing business needs

- Ensuring that change benefits are delivered

Policies

Policies represent the governance being applied to the change management process. A policy describes the rules and boundaries being applied to the process to ensure appropriate controls are in place. This ensures consistency and repeatability but also identifies the level of flexibility a practitioner has when executing the process, procedure, or work instruction. In some instances, a policy can be applied to more than one process, and in the case of policies within change management, this is true. Some of the change management policies defined will be consistent with the incident management and problem management policies for categorization. The policies will be discussed in more detail with examples in the following sections.

Categorization

Categorization refers to a policy that will be used by other processes (i.e., **problem management**, **request management**, and **incident management**). Categorization is very important to understand what service will be changed, what CIs make up a service, and potentially, what the impact of a change will be on the identified CIs. Categorization should allow the change requestor to identify quickly and easily what the change will impact and determine the risk related to that change. It is also very important once the change has been implemented to identify any incidents that may occur against the change, enabling the first point of contact to identify what changed and begin the investigation efforts. The categorization scheme allows incident and problem management processes to link their activities to change management and the changes that have been deployed. It can provide evidence of the effectiveness of the change management process, enabling incident management and problem management to perform recovery of an incident or identify the root cause faster. The categorization scheme will typically be multi-level and will allow you to produce reporting that aligns the service to the business.

A typical categorization scheme might start with a service at the highest level. This would be the service recognized by the customer and user. The next level could be the components of the service, such as a server cluster, storage devices, network, or application. The lowest level could be the CI.

This is illustrated in the following figure (*see Figure 8.1*):

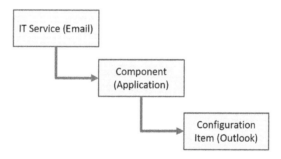

Figure 8.1 – A simple categorization scheme

The preceding figure shows a simple categorization scheme. A similar example in *Figure 8.2* shows a scheme that helps to align IT services with business processes:

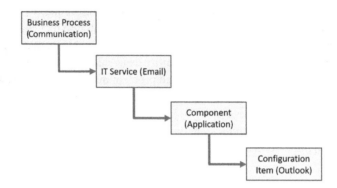

Figure 8.2 – A more complex categorization scheme

When determining the impact of a change on a target component or service, this scheme allows you to measure the impact on the affected business process more easily. It provides the business with a better understanding of how it will be impacted by the change in the service. The benefit of this kind of reporting is transparency and clarity for the business.

A categorization scheme can be very sophisticated, but it is always a good idea to keep it simple and straightforward. The more levels there are, the greater reporting detail can be produced, but it can get very difficult for staff using categorization to know how to categorize changes accurately. Your technology capability is also a consideration when attempting to categorize changes. Keeping it simple will help to implement a categorization that will be easy to apply, easy to use, and easier to implement in your technology.

Prioritization

Prioritization is a key policy for change management because it establishes the degree of control that will be applied to the change. In change management, there are three types of changes described – standard, normal, and emergency. These types relate to the prioritization of a specific change. For each of these types of changes, priority will be described based on the **impact** and **urgency** of the change. So, for any of these types, its impact is determined based on how significant is it to make this change to a business or service provider organization. Urgency involves identifying how important it is to the organization to get the change implemented in a timely manner and whereabouts in the change schedule the change needs to be inserted. You will get more clarity about the change types in the *Process terms and definitions* section. It is important to recognize that for standard changes, impact and urgency help to define for the implementer how fast they can implement the standard change. For normal changes, impact and urgency are much more critical to determining how these changes will be managed. For emergency changes, impact and urgency are valuable to determine the reason the change must be handled as an emergency. Priority allows the change manager to identify the importance of the change and determine the level of control that should be applied to the change. Not all changes require the same level of rigor, so it is essential that the appropriate prioritization is applied to ensure the level of control applied is also appropriate and necessary. Although prioritization is typically related to two factors, impact and urgency, there are instances where other factors should be considered. However, it makes sense to start with impact and urgency.

Impact and urgency

Impact is defined as the impact a change will have on a service or business. It focuses on how significant the change is to the business and what benefits would be achieved by implementing the change.

Figure 8.3 shows a sample impact matrix and the criteria used:

Impact = Degree of failure
Impact Example

Factors	High	Medium	Low
Number of People	Big Group	Small Group	1 Person
Scope	Global	Regional	Local
# of Cis	>10	<10	1
Type of Role	Revenue Role	VIP	Normal

Figure 8.3 – A sample impact criteria matrix

This preceding figure shows the various criteria used to determine the impact that a change could have on an organization.

Urgency describes how significant this change is to a business and, consequently, how important it is that you understand the need to get the change developed, tested, deployed, and implemented to achieve the business benefits.

Figure 8.4 shows a sample urgency matrix and the criteria applied:

Urgency = Time sensitivity in relationship to risk and exposure

Note: These would be based on existing scales: see the following model for an alternative model of establishing High, Medium, and Low

Factors	High	Medium	Low
Revenue Generating	Core	Support	Not Related
Security Classification	Core	Support	Not Related
Brand Exposure	Core	Support	Not Related
Safety Exposure	Core	Support	Not Related

Figure 8.4 – A sample urgency criteria matrix

This preceding matrix describes the criteria that will be used to determine the urgency or speed that this change needs to be completed in. The factors should be defined and agreed with the business. Once the factors are defined and understood, the importance to the business is defined and related to the urgency that the factor and its importance to the business represent.

You could consider developing weighted criteria for urgency and determine, based on the business needs, what the criteria were, and how weighting would be applied.

Figure 8.5 shows an example using the criteria in *Figure 8.4*:

Incident / Problem/ Change / Release Management

Urgency   This model uses a points system to establish a multidimensional view of urgency based on risk

Factors	0	1	2	3	4	5	Total		WGT*TOT PTS	Comments
				Points				Weights		
Revenue Generating	X	1	2	3	4	5	5	100%	5	Scale to measure relationship to revenue generating business process
Security Classification	X	1	X	3	x	5	3	25%	0.75	The range would be indicated of the established security and data sensitivity classification
Brand Exposure	X	x	X	3	4	5	3	100%	3	Media Exposure
Safety Exposure	X	1	2	x	4	5	4	100%	4	Safety classification based on Risk Management model
Total possible points							Total Weighted Points		12.75	

	0-5	Low
Example Model:	6-9	Medium
	>9	High

Figure 8.5 – A sample multidimensional approach to urgency criteria matrix

The combination of impact and urgency is the primary element involved in determining the prioritization of an incident, change, problem, or service request.

Figure 8.6 shows a simple matrix for impact and urgency:

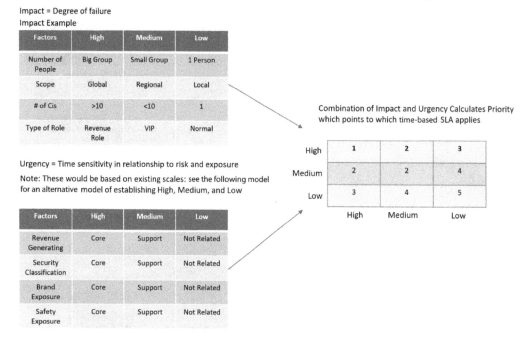

Incident / Problem/ Change / Release Management

Impact = Degree of failure
Impact Example

Factors	High	Medium	Low
Number of People	Big Group	Small Group	1 Person
Scope	Global	Regional	Local
# of Cis	>10	<10	1
Type of Role	Revenue Role	VIP	Normal

Urgency = Time sensitivity in relationship to risk and exposure

Note: These would be based on existing scales: see the following model for an alternative model of establishing High, Medium, and Low

Factors	High	Medium	Low
Revenue Generating	Core	Support	Not Related
Security Classification	Core	Support	Not Related
Brand Exposure	Core	Support	Not Related
Safety Exposure	Core	Support	Not Related

Combination of Impact and Urgency Calculates Priority which points to which time-based SLA applies

	High	Medium	Low
High	1	2	3
Medium	2	2	4
Low	3	4	5

Figure 8.6 – Combined impact and urgency to determine the priority matrix

The priority relates to how resources will be applied to perform the change management activities. In the case of change management, the prioritization is focused on determining the target date to implement the change and where this change fits in the change schedule. Once the change manager has determined what the priority is, they will identify what resources will be allocated to the change and how much of that resource time will be allocated to the change life cycle.

Prioritization of changes is essential to ensure that they are scheduled appropriately, and resources are assigned to ensure that the change is completed on time and within budget. An effective prioritization policy ensures that the service provider understands the significance of the change and will apply the appropriate resources to ensure business needs are met.

Another policy is **establishing criteria** to create a **change record**. This policy will establish clear criteria to determine what situations you would create a change record for and the information that is expected to be in the record. For example, if a major incident is recorded, a change record will be created for the emergency change to apply the fix so that a service can be restored. This policy should describe when and what information needs to be captured for a standard change or a normal change. It is a key element of change management to clearly describe what information must be captured when logging a change, regardless of what type of change it is. Part of this policy will be a statement that all changes must be recorded. This ensures that there will be consequences if an undocumented change is made. Included in this policy should be the minimum requirements for what gets documented in the change record. There are a variety of elements that should be considered, and the technology used to record changes will dictate some of those elements but at a minimum, the change record needs to describe what will change, why the change is necessary, and what the expected results will be. The following table shows an example of change record content:

Change record items	
Item	**Description**
Unique identifier	Typically automated as part of the technology
Date and time logged	Typically, an automated date and time stamp is applied by the technology.
Change owner	The individual that has the responsibility of monitoring and managing the change through its life cycle
Name of change initiator	Who requested the creation of the change record
Contact information for the initiator	Maybe automated, based on the name of the requestor
Short description	Provide brief information about the change.
Description	Document all the information that can be collected about the change, including what CIs will be impacted, the business reason for the change, the benefits to be achieved, how to measure the success of the change, what resources will be needed to develop, test, and implement the change, and any other information that is relevant to assessing the risk and value of making the change.
Type of change	Standard, Normal (minor, significant, or major), or Emergency
Category of the product or service	Document the category of the product or service based on information provided by the requestor.
Sub-category	Typically, the CIs that will be impacted by the change
Service/product	The name of the service or product that will be impacted by the change
Priority of the change	Prioritization is typically determined automatically, based on Impact and Urgency.

Change record items	
Item	**Description**
Impact	The impact that the change has on the business, based on the information provided in the change description
Urgency	How much effort should be applied to this change, based on the business benefit described in the change description
Assign to	Resources assigned to this change
Build activities for the change	Capture the activities that need to be performed to build the change.
Build target date and time	When the build of the change is scheduled to occur
Date and time the build occurred	When the build actually occurred and is completed
Build performed by	What team or teams completed the build activities
Testing activities for the change	Define the activities to be performed to test the change.
Testing target date and time	When the testing is scheduled to occur
Date and time the testing occurred	When the testing actually occurred and completed
Testing performed by	What team or teams performed the testing
Backout/recovery plans	Define how the change will be reverted if it fails and what recovery activities need to occur to restore the environment to the previous state.
Implementation target date and time	When the implementation is scheduled to occur
Date and time the implementation occurred	When the implementation actually occurred and completed
Implementation performed by	What team or teams performed the implementation activities
Criteria for successful implementation of the change	Describe the specific criteria used to validate a successful implementation of the change.
PIR results	Post-implementation results for the change
Closure code	Define the final disposition of the change.
Closure date and time stamp	The date and time at which the change was completed

Table 8.1 – A sample change record

In many instances, your technology will dictate what is required and optional in the change record, but a policy should be documented to reflect the expectations to fill out and complete the change record.

These are some of the key policies that should be developed, documented, and communicated to all appropriate stakeholders to ensure that the stakeholders understand their responsibilities and realize the expectations when responding to a request for change.

Process terms and definitions

There are a number of key terms related to change management, including **change**, **change model**, **standard change**, **normal change**, **emergency change**, and **closure code**. In this section, you will learn the definitions of these terms.

Change

Change is defined as the addition, modification, or removal of anything that could directly or indirectly impact a CI or service. It could be a change to a server or network component. It could be a change to an application. It could be the introduction of a new or significantly changed service. The change must be documented so that there is clear evidence of what occurred, why it was necessary, and potentially, what could be done to recover from the change if it fails. There are three types of change defined as best practices, including standard, normal, and emergency. There have been other types defined in some guidance, but these three are adequate for any change scenario. These three will be defined in more detail in the following subsections.

Change model

A *change model* is a template for a specific instance of a change that recurs frequently and follows a consistent path, but it may have changeable parameters. Change models are used to improve the overall performance of change management. An example of a change model could be the scheduling of a reboot of a server. The service provider might want to regularly schedule a reboot of a server, and the change model could be used to identify the server to be rebooted, the time to execute the reboot, what mechanisms to use to verify a successful reboot of the server, and who is responsible to perform the reboot. The change model ensures that the appropriate information is captured about the reboot and the prescribed steps are followed to perform this activity. You might wonder why this example would be a change. It is a change because the state of the server is changed from an operational state to a rebooted state. If the reboot is successful, the new state is operational, but if the reboot is not successful, then incident management needs to be aware that a reboot was attempted and something went wrong, in order to resolve and restore the server. A more common reason to use a change model is for standard changes. A definition and description of a standard change is next.

Standard change

A *standard change* is defined as a change that is low-risk, happens frequently, is on a pre-authorized list of changes, and has a clear and consistent approach to fulfilling it. Standard changes represent the majority of the operational type of activities that a service provider routinely performs in executing the day-to-day activities of managing components and services (i.e., the server reboot scenario described previously). Standard changes tend to be routine and seldom cause any issues when implemented. They also can result from a service request. An example of a standard change could be the allocation of data access permissions to an employee in the accounting department, as part of a service request to onboard them to the department. A standard change will have less rigor than normal or emergency changes because it is low-risk and has been implemented without constant failure. Using standard changes can streamline the change management activity and provide more time for normal changes. Standard changes are vetted through the normal change procedure before being authorized as a standard change type. All standard changes will reside on a standard change list. If a change does not appear on this list, it cannot be a standard change. There are instances where a standard change may require approvals, but these are typically at a local supervisory level. There are also instances where a standard change can be executed with no additional approval required. Standard changes benefit from change models, allowing the requestor to know what information is required and accelerating the documentation of the standard change. Change models can facilitate the efficiency of recording and executing standard changes.

Normal change

A *normal change* is defined as a change that must be assessed for impact and risk, such as the number of customers impacted, cost, complexity, and service impacted others, and it is not a standard or emergency change. Normal changes represent the changes that may have an impact on the customer organization, and they constitute a level of risk that must be assessed to determine what level of control is required to protect the production environment from disruption or failure. All normal changes must be assessed by a control body. Well practiced, this could be a change control board, a **change advisory board (CAB)**, or a **change management control board**. Whatever you call it, it is a group of stakeholders that has the knowledge, expertise, and authority to review and assess the impact and risk related to the change and can authorize the change to be initiated. Unlike a standard change, a normal change can result in an unexpected impact on the services being delivered, resulting in a negative impact on the organization. It is this characteristic that suggests the need for an effective review and assessment, determining the potential risk of failure and what can be done to mitigate the risk and increase the chance of success. Since the risk of failure can vary based on the change, a normal change can be categorized by degree. A common practice is to categorize normal changes as minor, significant, or major. As described in the policy related to priority, a matrix can establish the criteria for what constitutes minor, significant, and major. A sample matrix for establishing which category to use is shown in *Figure 8.7*:

CHANGE CATEGORY GUIDELINES

STANDARD	MINOR	SIGNIFICANT	MAJOR

LOW	RISK		HIGH
SMALL	CUSTOMERS IMPACTED		LARGE
SHORT	DEVELOPMENT TIME		LONG
ROUTINE	COMPLEXITY		NEW DESIGN
<$15K	<$100K COST	<$200K	>$200K

SIGNIFICANT OR MAJOR BY DEFAULT:
- Business Critical Services
- Major Business Initiatives

Figure 8.7 – Sample change category guidelines

It is the responsibility of the change initiator to determine the category of the initial change, but the **change control board** (CCB) and change manager must review the category and validate that it is correct and change it if necessary. It is also the responsibility of the CCB and change manager to review the backout or remediation plan should the change be unsuccessful, determining its viability through appropriate testing of the change. If a change cannot be backed out of or no remediation plan is available, then the risk associated with the change will be much higher. A normal change is the most common change type after a standard change, and it represents where the majority of work will be performed by an organization when making positive changes to the service provider's environment.

Emergency change

An *emergency change* has all the characteristics of a normal change but must be done quickly to resolve a disruption in service or a potential one to reduce the negative impact on the customer. Emergency changes will still need to be assessed, include some form of backout or remediation plan, and follow the same change activities as a normal change but at an accelerated rate. These changes must be approved by an **emergency change advisory board** (ECAB). The ECAB might delegate its authority during off-shift periods when necessary. Typically, an emergency change is required because a major incident has been logged, and the only way to restore and recover the service is to implement a change. In these cases, it is still important to assess the change that is being developed and implemented to determine the impact and risk, but it needs to be done quickly to minimize the disruption and return the service to normal operation. An emergency change may not have the same level of testing as a normal change, so this must be factored into the risk assessment. Likewise, it may not have a clear backout plan identified because of the accelerated timeline. However, it is important to understand that failure to plan on behalf of the customer or service provider is not a valid reason to apply an emergency change procedure. Changes should always be planned appropriately to minimize the potential for service disruption, and an emergency change should only be used when a disruption has occurred and a change is the only means to restore a service.

Closure code

A *closure code* is a code that identifies the disposition of a change. For instance, the closure code for change management could include the change was successful without a condition, the change was successful with conditions accepted by the customer, and the change was unsuccessful, and backed out. Closure codes for change management should be documented in a policy.

This section provided definitions of the common terms in change management. The following section will describe the input and output of change management.

Process inputs and outputs

Changes can be made at any time and detected in a variety of ways, such as a request for upgrades to hardware or software, adding access for a user, fileshares, or onboarding a new employee. The following lists identify many of the inputs and outputs for change management, but they are not all-inclusive.

These are the change inputs:

- Change requests
- Plans for change development, testing, and implementation
- Configuration information
- Incident information for emergency changes
- Problem solution information for permanent solutions
- Backout plans and remediation information
- Configuration baselines
- Testing information and evaluation results

These are the change outputs:

- Approval or rejection of change requests
- New or updated CIs, services, and information
- Results from a post-implementation review
- A schedule of changes
- Authorizations for change plans
- Updated change records
- Management information

Process activities

Change management is one of the service management processes that has consistent activities for each change request, depending on the change type.

Figure 8.8 shows the flow for change management at its most comprehensive. This describes the flow for a normal or emergency change that poses a significant impact or risk to the business:

Change Request

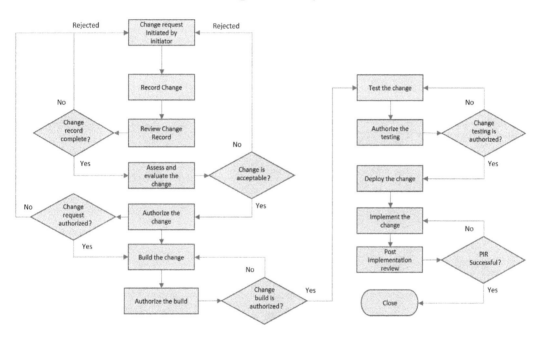

Figure 8.8 – A normal change request process flow

Figure 8.9 shows an example of the flow of a standard change where the risk is known and generally low, the resources necessary to fulfill it are known, and the procedure to implement the change is well understood and typically documented in a change model:

Standard Change Request

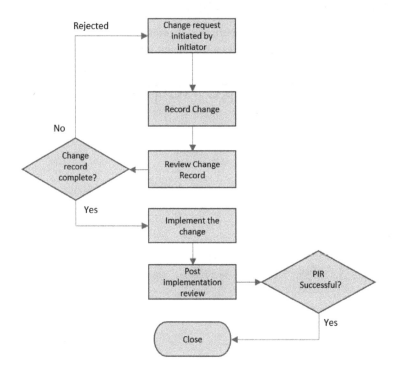

Figure 8.9 – A standard change request process flow

The subsequent subsections describe what is involved in each of the activities described in both process flows.

Initiating a change

Initiating a change occurs when a change initiator begins the change management process. A change can be initiated in a variety of ways, including but not limited to by a supplier, component provider, customer, or employee or due to a service request, incident, problem, and so on. The change initiator must provide as much information as possible about the change so that when the change is reviewed and the assessment and evaluation occur, those teams can effectively and efficiently perform their functions. Some of the key information that should be provided by the change initiator includes the business value from performing the change, the impact and urgency of the change, risk related to the change, the type of change, the expected results to be produced by making the change, and backout/ remediation information if known. Once the change is initiated, it is documented in a change record.

Recording the change

Recording the change can be performed by the change initiator, the service desk, or some other resource. Some of the key information recorded in the change record includes the following:

- Who initiated the change

- The change type

- Who will own the change (typically, a change manager)

- The impact of the change on the business, including the value to the business

- Urgency, describing the effort and importance of completing the change on a specific date

- The CIs that are changed

- A service or services benefiting from the change

- Customers benefiting from the change

- Any information that can accelerate the review, assessment, and evaluation of the change

It is key that the change owner has enough information about the change to facilitate the review, assessment, and evaluation of the change for normal and emergency changes. Standard change records will be reviewed but will typically bypass the assessment and evaluation steps since all standard changes must have been normal before being added to the standard change list.

Reviewing the change record

Reviewing the change record is the activity performed by the change manager to determine whether the change record has been completed with all necessary information. The change manager will review the record and validate that the business need has been established, key dates have been identified, business value has been established, expected outcomes are documented, resources required are defined, a backout plan or remediation strategy is documented, and the record is filled out as comprehensively as possible at this point. The information is necessary for normal and emergency changes to be effectively assessed and evaluated in the next step by the appropriate resources, including the change control team. Ensuring that the necessary information is provided increases the possibility of completing the assessment and evaluation in a timely manner, as well as completing the authorization of the change for subsequent activities. If the change record does not contain the necessary information to proceed, it will be rejected and returned to the change initiator for remedial action.

Assessing and evaluating the change

Once a change record has been reviewed by the change manager, assessing and evaluating the change must occur for all normal and emergency changes. This activity involves knowledgeable resources that can assess the risk of the change in the current environment and evaluate the practicality of the change and the resources needed to achieve the desired results, determining whether the business benefits outweigh the cost of executing the change. There will be a variety of reasons to make changes, but all changes should produce value or reduce/mitigate risk for an organization. If there is no value or benefit to making the change, then it should not be considered for further action. Key resources in the service provider organization will be engaged in performing the assessment and evaluation to determine what resources and efforts will be needed, whether the change can be delivered in the timeframe defined in the change record, and the viability of the change. Key resources in the customer organization will be engaged to provide additional information about the need, benefits, and value of making the change. There can be instances where resources from a third-party supplier will be involved in this activity to provide the necessary information to adequately assess the change, especially in cases where the change was raised by a third-party supplier. Once the change assessment and evaluation have determined the viability and need for the change, they will make a recommendation to approve and authorize it; if not, the change will be rejected and returned to the change initiator.

Authorizing the change

Authorizing the change is the action performed by the CCB. This is a group of managers, staff, and customers/users that will provide the final approval to proceed with the change. As you can see in the process flow in *Figure 8.8*, there can be a number of authorization points in the life cycle of a change. The number of points in the process where these authorizations are required are defined in your organization's policies for change management. The CCB will review all normal and emergency changes to validate that the appropriate controls are in place to protect the production environment from disruptions, resulting from the implementation of the change. It will ensure that the appropriate resources will be allocated for the build, test, deploy, and implement activities. This board will ensure that the risk has been assessed and mitigated, eliminated, or appropriate backout plans are documented. The participants on the CCB will vary from one change to another, based on the board's knowledge, experience, and awareness about the change being approved. It will be necessary to provide the board participants with access to the change records so that they can review the results of the assessment and evaluation before making a decision about the change. If questions about the change exist, the CCB participants should resolve those questions prior to approving the change. Again, your change authorization policy should describe when approval is withheld and what action will be taken with the change request. It is possible that if only one approver has an issue, the change may be authorized, but if the approver is a customer or senior manager, the change may be rejected until the issues identified are resolved to the approver's satisfaction. Only when the change has been authorized by the CCB can the change proceed to the next stage.

For emergency changes, the CCB may require a higher level of management to authorize. This is because emergency changes introduce higher risk, and typically, the change will be accelerated through the various process activities that require a higher level of management authorization. There will be instances in the emergency change flow where testing will be abbreviated since time is an essential element of getting the change implemented. An emergency change is usually executed when a major incident or service disruption has occurred, and the only way to resolve and restore service is to apply the change. This situation requires the service provider and customer to acknowledge the higher risk related to this type of change and be willing to accept the risk. Emergency change procedures can be applied to changes where urgency is essential. Again, it will be necessary to get authorization from more senior leadership to accept the risk related to circumventing or accelerating the normal change process flow.

Standard changes, by definition, are pre-authorized. However, there may be approvals required for these change types. *Pre-authorized* does not necessarily mean *pre-approved*. A standard change will be contained on a standard change list, and the only way a change can be classified as standard is if it appears on the standard change list. This does not preclude the requirement of approvals if certain conditions are defined. One example of this situation would be the addition of a standard device to the environment, such as a new laptop. Because the new laptop may require spending money to acquire it, there may be approval required from the finance department or purchasing department to spend the money. In many instances, providing access to a file share can be automated as a standard change, but it still requires the approval of the file share owner to grant access. Standard changes are pre-authorized but may still require approval to proceed.

Building the change

Building the change begins once the CCB has authorized an activity to proceed. At this point in the process flow, the specialist resources responsible for the building of the change will commence their activities. The builders will gather the resources needed to build the CIs, update or create documentation (i.e., the service provider and user documentation), update or create test plans, develop the backout/remediation mechanisms, verify target dates, develop communications to various stakeholders, and build the implementation plan. Once all build activities have been completed, the change owner will get authorization from the CCB to proceed to the test phase.

Testing the change

Testing the change begins once the CCB has authorized the completion of the build activity and the testing to begin. In this activity, the autonomous testing team will begin testing the build to determine whether it is ready for deployment into the **quality assurance** (**QA**) or production environments. It is always a good idea to have a separate testing group from the build group. This will ensure an unbiased analysis of the results and that the testing is performed based on consistent and repeatable standards. A peer review may be considered acceptable to test the build if operating in an agile environment. The various tests that could be run include unit, functional, user acceptance, integrated, and performance testing. It is important for the testing team to have a clear plan of what it will be testing and what the expected results will be, effectively analyzing whether the build is ready for deployment. If issues are identified during testing that will be introduced into the production environment because the customer is willing to accept the issue, or the function is an infrequently used part of the service, a known error should be documented to reflect the issue so that it can be effectively dealt with if it manifests in the production environment after going live. Once the testing has been completed and the results documented, the CCB will analyze the results and authorize the change to proceed to the next activity.

Deploying the change

The deploying the change activity moves the change from the test environment to the QA or production environment, preparing it for implementation. The deploying the change activity can involve moving the tested change to a QA environment, where additional QA tests are performed to further validate the quality of the build and its readiness for use by customers/employees. This activity is also used to move the quality-assured change into the production environment and prepare it for use by employees. Any stakeholder communication will be conducted to give the stakeholders awareness of the imminent implementation of the change. Any training that must be conducted should be undertaken to prepare users for how their day-to-day routine may change as a result of the introduction of the new build. This is the point where a pilot may be initiated to validate the change in the production environment before providing it to a larger audience. Once deployment into the production environment has occurred, the next activity will complete the implementation of the change and make it available for use by the organization.

Implementing the change

Implementing the change involves completing all communications to the target stakeholders, stabilizing the change in the production environment, providing early life support during the stabilization period, capturing feedback from stakeholders, and monitoring the change in the production environment to determine whether the expected performance and benefits have been achieved. In some cases, where the change impacts a large number of CIs, there may be a need for a detailed implementation plan that may have multiple phases. Each phase will be reviewed, stabilized, and measured to determine the effectiveness of the implementation. It is during the stabilization period, determined by the significance of the change, that the change implementers capture relevant information and data about the results of the change. This information will be key to determining whether the change has been successful and whether it can be closed.

Closing the change

Closing the change is the final activity in the change management process. Part of closing the change is a **post-implementation review** (**PIR**). The PIR is typically performed on all normal and emergency changes. Standard changes will be randomly selected for a PIR to validate that the expected results were achieved. The PIR is conducted after the stabilization period and is typically facilitated by the change manager, with the assistance of the CCB. During the PIR, this group of stakeholders will review all the elements of the change, from authorizing the change through the build, test, deploy, and implement steps. This team analyzes the results achieved at each step, determining whether any adjustments were made by any stakeholder, determining how effective the change was in meeting the expected results, and identifying any deviation from the plans. If there were any deviations, what course of action was taken to resolve them, and what impact, if any, did the deviations have on the results produced? The primary purpose of the PIR is to validate that the customer expectations and benefits have been achieved. If not, what are the consequences of that? The PIR should determine whether the change can be closed as is, should be closed with conditions specified and agreed upon by the customer, or should remain open until all issues have been resolved. The customer/stakeholders are responsible for providing the input needed to determine whether the change will be closed and what its status will be.

Now that you have an understanding of the activities in the change management process, we will explore the variety of roles and responsibilities expected of participants in this process.

Roles and responsibilities

There are many key roles for change management – process owner, process manager, and process practitioner. As we discussed in *Chapter 5*, there are common responsibilities for every process owner and process manager. There are some key responsibilities that the change management roles need to consider. The change management process owner needs to work very closely with the problem, incident, and request management process owners to document the policies related to prioritization and categorization. Putting together a consistent policy for these two elements of service management is critical to maintaining relationships between these processes. In addition, the change management process owner needs to establish the right metrics, based on the maturity of the process and the capabilities of the technology, to provide data for them. It is very important for the process owner to have measures that drive the right behavior and produce metrics that effectively measure the performance of the process.

The change management process manager is responsible for ensuring that the resources assigned to the change management process are properly prepared to execute the process efficiently and effectively. This will ensure that practitioners have the necessary tools and resources to be efficient. The change process manager is responsible for ensuring metrics are captured and reported to the appropriate stakeholders. The process manager is responsible for monitoring the execution of the process and identifying opportunities to improve. The process manager will also be responsible for appointing a change owner to all changes recorded within their responsibility. Periodically, the process manager will review closed changes to assess the content of the change records, compliance with the policies, and key process indicators to determine the overall performance of the process execution.

The change management process practitioners include a number of key roles, described in the following paragraphs.

The change owner will be responsible for managing the life cycle of the change. In many cases, the change owner can be the responsible change manager or an individual within the leadership chain. They will be the primary focus for communications to stakeholders concerning change. The change owner will work with the various teams that are involved in building, testing, deploying, and implementing the change, as well as the team performing the PIR. The change owner is responsible for validating that all information about the change life cycle has been recorded in the change record.

There will be roles for the change build team. Their responsibility is to build the change according to the policies and target environment that the change will be implemented in. The build team will need to coordinate their efforts with the operations staff to ensure that what gets built will work in the operating environment that the change occupies. The build team will take the requirements defined in the change record and ensure that the requirements are fulfilled with the solution built. When the change build is complete, the build team will communicate with the change owner so that they can schedule a review of the results and get authorization to proceed to testing.

The testing team is responsible for all the tests that have been planned for the change build. The testing team is separate from the build team to ensure unbiased analysis of the build results. Although it is preferred to have a separate group perform the testing, in an agile environment, this may be performed by a peer group of the build team. When the testing team receives authorization from the change control board and change owner, it will conduct the planned tests according to the guidelines for each of the tests to be performed. The testing team will document all results from the testing, including any issues that were discovered as well as the successful tests that were performed. The testing team lead will communicate the results to the change owner and other stakeholders for their review. If the review determines a successful test result, the change owner will submit the findings to the CCB for review and authorization to proceed to deployment.

The deployment team is responsible for moving the build from the test environment to a QA or production environment, depending on how your organization chooses to operate. The deployment team will migrate the tested and validated build to the appropriate environment, verifying that the deployment was successful. After completing the deployment, the deployment team will communicate with the change owner, at which point, they will engage the CCB for review and authorization to proceed to implementation.

The implementation team is responsible for making the change available to the customers and users. The implementation team may include various communication activities, training, and early life support during the stabilization period. The implementation team will validate that the change is ready for use in production and confirm utilization by the target users. If a staged implementation is used, the implementation team will monitor the stages and report any issues or feedback as additional stages are implemented. After the stabilization period expires, the implementation team will communicate to the change owner and PIR participants how the implementation went, any issues identified, corrective actions taken, and any existing conditions not resolved. At this point, the change owner and change manager will facilitate a PIR.

The PIR will be conducted by the change manager with participation from customers, users, the change owner, and any other stakeholders as necessary.

Now that we understand the activities involved in executing change management for normal, standard, and emergency changes, the next section will review the key process indicators involved in change management.

Key process indicators

The change management process has a number of key process indicators. These key process indicators should cover the progress of implementing a process across a service provider organization, compliance with the process policies, the effectiveness of producing process deliverables, and the efficiency of the execution. A balanced set of metrics will ensure that the process is measured appropriately and the key areas are covered. Some examples of key process indicators are as follows:

- The total number of changes recorded for a specified period as a control

- The number of changes without documentation at each stage

- The number of changes closed by type and the closure code

- The number of changes by service, group, and CI for a specified period

- The number and percentage of changes completed on schedule

- The number of incidents recorded against a change for a specified period

- The number of incidents recorded where a change was made but no change record was logged

- The accuracy and timeliness of the change schedule

- The number and percentage of emergency changes for a specified period

- The percentage of standard changes for a specified period

It is important for an organization to focus on a few key metrics, based on where it is in the maturity of its process. It is recommended that one or two metrics per focus area is sufficient to provide guidance on performance and where improvement can be considered. It is also important to monitor the behavior that is exhibited as a result of the metrics so that you can identify unintended behavior, making adjustments as appropriate. At some point in your process life cycle, it will be appropriate to set targets for key process indicators, but be careful to ensure that the targets are achievable and realistic so that they do not hinder progress. Likewise, monitor behavior to make sure that the targets drive the right kind of behavior. It is always good to keep in mind that what gets measured gets managed, and what you measure is what will be produced.

Process integration

For each process in a best practice framework, you will have both primary and secondary relationships and interactions with other processes. Since every process has a relationship with every other process, this section will only cover the primary relationships to key processes. Each process will be described in the following list, with the key interactions that change management has with it:

- **Incident management** receives information from change management to link incidents to the change that may have caused the incident(s). Incident management will initiate an emergency change for major incidents when required. Incident management can provide data concerning the effectiveness and success rate of implemented changes. Incident data is used during the PIR to determine whether a change was implemented successfully or not.

- **Problem management** provides information to change management on problems that have been diagnosed, declaring that they are ready to apply a permanent solution. Problem management will initiate a request for change on any solution that will be deployed to implement a permanent solution or a workaround. Change management will keep problem management informed about the progress of the requests for change initiated by problem management. Problem management will assist change management in identifying errors resulting from failed changes.

- **Configuration management** provides information about the service and CIs that will be impacted by the change. This will enable change management to assess the potential impact of the change and assist in determining the overall impact. The **configuration management system (CMS)** relies on change management to manage any changes to CIs.

- **Capacity management** uses change management to implement changes to environments. Capacity management resources are involved with change management to assess the impact changes may have on the demand profiles of the target environments. Capacity management will initiate changes for updates to environments as part of executing the capacity plan.

- **Availability management** will initiate a request for a change to update availability plans and documentation. Availability management will assess changes to determine the impact on agreed availability during a CCB review.

- **IT continuity management** provides information to change management on recovery plans if a continuity situation occurs during a failed change. Typically, this will be part of change management backout/contingency plans if a failure occurs and no other backout means is possible, or the change cannot be backed out effectively.

Every process uses change management to control updates to documentation and changes to the process, procedures, or working instructions. Therefore, all processes have a relationship with change management. The process relationships described reflect some of the key interactions with change management. As previously stated, there are other secondary interactions that are not listed here, but they are also something that should be considered when establishing change management or making improvements to it and other processes. In the next section, we will explore some technology requirements based on the current products available to support change management.

Technology requirements

Technology has improved the support of ITSM best practices consistently over the last 20–30 years. It has especially matured the support of many operational processes, including change management. The following list shows many of the key requirements for the change management process. You may have additional requirements, but the following list is a sample of what should be expected of any service management tool. The most important thing to remember about selecting any technology is that it will not make a poor process better, and it is important to realize how the tool will be used to select one that will be most effective for your needs.

Change management requirements include the following:

- Enabling a mechanism to support a configurable change process and categorization templates
- Offering basic required data fields in a change record
- Enabling a means to document backout procedures, installation directions, and turnover documents as part of the RFC
- Enabling a means to relate incidents and problems resulting from an implemented change
- Enabling role-based approvals, and canceling or rescheduling RFCs
- Enabling the capability to create and reference change models
- Providing a means to edit RFCs based on roles and change status
- Providing the capability to allow multiple approvers and automated routing of approvals
- Providing a way to link RFCs to projects
- Being able to progress RFCs through the authorization and implementation stages and maintaining an accurate record of the progress
- Enabling integration with other operational processes
- Allowing the entry of free-form text, screen captures, file attachments, or other content
- Providing mechanisms to monitor and track the life cycle of a change request

It is very important to understand how you intend to use the technology, define the requirements for the technology, evaluate current technology to determine what the deficiencies are, identify your options for a provider, and then pick the one that satisfies the most requirements on your list. When defining your requirements, you should consider using the **MoSCoW approach**. The MoSCoW approach suggests classifying your requirements based on the *Must-Have, Should-Have, Could-Have,* or *Would-Like-to-Have* criteria. This allows you to prioritize requirements and make sure that the Must-Haves and Should-Haves are generally covered by the tool you choose. You should also be careful when defining your requirements, as a list that contains mostly Must-Haves will typically limit your choices to one or none.

Summary

In this chapter, you were exposed to the key elements of the change management process, including its purpose and objectives, policies, process terms and definitions, inputs and outputs, activities, roles and responsibilities, key process indicators, process integrations, and technology requirements. You were provided with significant details about the process, which should enable you to get started with implementing the process or making improvements to your existing process.

In the next chapter, you will continue to learn about operational processes with **release and deployment management**. Release and deployment management entails the processes that focus on managing the life cycle of releases to the production environment, enabling an organization to implement one or more approved changes successfully as a release. Release and deployment management adds an additional layer of control to change management, ensuring more effective implementation of significant and major changes.

9
Release and Deployment Management

In this chapter, you will be introduced to the release and deployment management capability, both by itself and as part of formal service management. This includes the capability's governance (purpose, objectives, and policies), execution (roles, responsibilities, activities, and metrics), and enablement (acceleration, integration, and supporting technology).

In this chapter, we are going to cover the following main topics:

- Purpose and objectives
- Policies
- Process terms and definitions
- Process input and output
- Process activities
- Roles and responsibilities
- Key process indicators
- Process integrations
- Technology requirements

Purpose and objectives

Release and deployment management are two key processes that are tightly linked to each other and are described together in this chapter.

The purpose of release and deployment management is to manage the life cycle of a release from the time the release is defined, documented, and agreed upon until it is deployed to the target environment and eventually released to the customer, user, and stakeholders. Release and deployment management is responsible for defining what a release is, documenting the release policy, educating the target stakeholders on the release, ensuring that the release is appropriately tested, managing the deployment of the release into various environments, and enabling the release to be used by the target stakeholders. Release and deployment management is focused on managing the life cycle of releases being deployed to the production environment, but this control can be applied to other environments including testing, quality assurance, and even various development environments. Release and deployment management is also necessary in an Agile organization where releases may be deployed rapidly and frequently. It is still necessary to know what is changing as part of the release and when those releases are deployed and implemented.

A **release** is defined as one or more approved changes. The contents of the release must be agreed upon and are defined by a policy for the purpose of clearly establishing what a release will contain and when a release is required. An example of a release could be the combination of a change to an application and any related infrastructure alterations. Another example of a release could be the release of a new major application update. In this case, for a large organization, the service provider may choose to deploy the release in stages. There may be a pilot stage to identify and resolve any issues experienced by the pilot group including deployment issues, integration issues, utilization issues, and so on. This enables the deployment team to resolve the issues in the deployment activities and allows the release team to resolve integration and utilization issues in the next deployment stage. My experience suggests that this staged approach for deploying and releasing large application updates can be very beneficial to reduce the number of incidents and problems related to major updates. Unlike the previous three chapters and the following chapter, release and deployment management is focused on managing a release from the time the approved changes contained in the release have been determined and from when plans for the release and deployment have been defined and agreed upon.

The objectives for release and deployment management include the following:

- Managing the life cycle of all releases
- Ensuring that changes included in the release are approved and ready for deployment
- Ensuring that all releases follow a defined plan for development, testing, deployment, and release to a controlled environment
- Ensuring that all releases are managed according to defined plans and on an agreed schedule
- Communicating with and preparing stakeholders for the deployment and release of the packaged changes (i.e., knowledge sharing, training, communications)
- Ensuring that the expected results of the release are achieved

Policies

Policies represent the governance being applied to the release and deployment management process. A policy describes the rules and boundaries being applied to the process to ensure appropriate controls are in place. This ensures consistency and repeatability but also identifies the level of flexibility a practitioner has when executing the process, procedure, or work instruction. The policies will be discussed in more detail with examples in the following sections.

Release content

Release content is the policy that will define what will be contained in a release. A release can contain a single change, multiple related changes, one or more changes and a related release (often called a release package), and one or more additional releases. Based on the definition of a release, a release must have at least one approved change in it. In some organizations, all changes must be implemented into the production environment through release and deployment management. If this is the case, this policy will be very important to establish what will be contained in the release.

The following figure (*Figure 9.1*) shows an example of what a release or package might look like:

Release and Release Package

Figure 9.1 – Examples of releases and release packages

Figure 9.1 shows three different types of packaging that you could consider in creating a release or release package. For example, Release Package 1 could contain a change to a software component, and Release 1 could be updates to server clusters to accommodate the updated software. Release Package 2 might contain a major release of Windows and a major release of OfficeSuite. You can create a variety of packaging approaches for changes and releases.

A policy defining the *types of releases* should be documented, and the policy should clearly define when each type will be applied. Some examples of release types include **full release**, **delta release**, **package release**, and **emergency release**. These types will be further defined in the *Process terms and definitions* section.

Prioritization

Prioritization for release and deployment management is based on the changes and releases to be contained in the release or release package. Release prioritization will be documented based on the deployment schedule defined by the release and deployment plans. The change information will be a key guide to the target dates for the release or releases and will be documented as part of the release plan.

Establishing criteria for creating a release record

Another policy to consider is establishing criteria for creating a **release record**. This policy would describe the contents of a release record. For example, a release record should identify the contents of the release, the release schedule, the release and deployment plans, the release testing plans, and the resources involved in the release. This policy should describe when and what information needs to be captured for a release.

Release record items	
Item	**Description**
Unique identifier	Typically automated as part of the technology
Date and time logged	Typically, an automated date and timestamp is applied by the technology.
Release owner	The individual that has the responsibility to monitor and manage the release through its life cycle
Short description	Provide brief information about the release.
Description	Document all the information that can be collected about the release including what change(s) or release(s) will be included, benefits to be achieved, how to measure the success of the release, what resources will be needed to develop, test, deploy, and implement the release, and any other information that is relevant to assessing the risk and value of making the release.
Service/product	The name of the service(s) or product(s) that will be impacted by the release
Assign to	Resources assigned this release
Build activities for the release	Capture the activities performed to build the release.
Build target date and time	When the build of the release is scheduled to occur
Date and time build occurred	When the build actually occurred and when it was completed
Build performed by	Which team or teams completed the build activities
Testing activities for the release	Define the activities to be performed to test the release.
Testing target date and time	When the testing is scheduled to occur
Date and time testing occurred	When the testing actually occurred and when it was completed

Release record items	
Item	**Description**
Testing performed by	Which team or teams performed the testing
Backout/recovery plans	Define how the release would be backed out if it fails and what recovery activities would need to occur to restore the environment to the previous state.
Deployment activities for the release	Define the activities to be performed to deploy the release.
Deployment target date and time	When the deployment is scheduled to occur
Date and time deployment occurred	When the deployment actually occurred and when it was completed
Deployment performed by	Which team or teams performed the deployment activities
Criteria for successful deployment of the release	Describe the specific criteria used to validate a successful deployment of the release.
Implementation activities for the release	Define the activities to be performed to implement the release.
Implementation target date(s) and time(s)	Implementation results for the release
Date and time implementation occurred	When the implementation actually occurred and when it was completed
Implementation performed by	Which team or teams performed the implementation activities
Criteria for successful implementation of the release	Describe the specific criteria used to validate a successful implementation of the release.

Table 9.1 – Sample release record content

In many instances, your technology will dictate what is required and optional in the release record, but a policy should be documented to reflect the expectations for filling out and completing the change record. It is also important to keep in mind that the building, testing, deployment, and implementation steps could be iterative, so each time these steps are performed, it should be documented in the release record with appropriate information.

Testing requirements

Testing requirements are another policy to consider, depending on the release contents. All releases will require testing, but the degree and types of testing may vary. What is required should be documented in a policy with appropriate examples. To make sure that all changes within the release will play well together, testing should include, at a minimum, the testing of the release itself. If the release is a package, all elements of the package should have been tested individually but now must be tested as a package to make sure that all elements of the package will work together during deployment and release. Within this policy, testing types should be defined alongside when these different testing types should be applied. Some types of testing would include **integration**, **user acceptance**, **functional**, **performance**, **operational**, etc. A **release test plan** will be documented, and which tests will be applied will be defined in the test plan. The testing of the release itself will be performed by the release management team, but the testing requirements defined in this policy must be performed by an autonomous group selected for that purpose as part of the validation and testing process.

These are some of the key policies that should be developed, documented, and communicated to all appropriate stakeholders to ensure that the stakeholders understand their responsibilities and realize the expectations when managing a release.

Having a better understanding of the policies for release and deployment management, the next section will review some key terms.

Process terms and definitions

There are a number of key terms related to release and deployment management including releases, deployment, transference, retirement, release models, release types, and deployment types. In this section, you will learn the definitions of these terms.

Releases

A **release** is defined as one or more approved changes. A release can be one major change, multiple changes that may or may not have dependencies between them, a change and a release, or two or more releases combined.

Deployment

Deployment refers to the act of moving a release from one environment to another. For example, when development has completed their work on the release, deployment will move the release from the development environment to the test environment, where an independent testing team will perform their activities.

Transference

A **transfer** occurs when one service provider's service is replaced by a different service provider's service. This could be when an organization has decided to replace its current internal **enterprise resource planning (ERP)** system with a cloud-based ERP service.

Retirement

Retirement occurs when a component or service needs to be removed from an environment and is taken out of service. Retirement includes all the activities involved in removing a current component or service from the environment and disposing of it appropriately, along with any documentation or records related to it.

Release model

A **release model** is a template for a specific instance of a release that recurs frequently. It will follow a consistent path but may have varying parameters. Release models are used to improve the overall performance of release and deployment management. An example of a release model could be security releases. Each time patches or new security signatures are identified, a release model could be applied to ensure a consistent and repeatable procedure is followed for rolling out these changes. The release model ensures that the appropriate information about patches or fixes is captured and the prescribed steps are being followed to perform this activity.

Release types

A **release type** is a specific release that an organization can consider creating, building, and deploying. Release types are used for a variety of situations and are further described in the following list:

- A **full release** typically describes a release of the entire component, such as a complete application or a fully functional server cluster

- A **delta release** will normally be part of an application where new functionality is being added, where updates/fixes are being applied, or it will be one server in a cluster of servers

- A **package release**, as briefly described earlier, takes place when a suite of applications are released together as a package, i.e., Microsoft Suite

- An **emergency release** is what it sounds like: a release that needs to be deployed and released quickly to resolve or prevent an issue or disruption in service

Deployment types

Deployment types are different approaches to deploying releases and release packages. The three types include **Big Bang**, **Phased**, or **Pilot** and are described in the following bullet list:

- The Big Bang approach is where all target stakeholders receive the release at the same time. This happens when the new release must be available to all users at once, such as an application that cannot be phased into production.

- A Phased approach takes place when different parts of an organization receive a release at different times. A Phased approach can be beneficial for evaluating the release before deploying it to the entire organization. This approach will typically select a small segment of the user community to roll out the release to, evaluate the results after an agreed period, resolve any issues experienced with the initial group, then roll out the release to the second target group. This iterative approach to deploying and releasing a release package can be very effective in resolving any unexpected issues that may occur during the rollout.

- A Pilot release is an approach that identifies a select user group to receive a release for an agreed period of time. The group then provides feedback on the effectiveness of the release after meeting the agreed requirements. The results of the Pilot approach are reviewed and analyzed to determine whether the release is ready for general distribution. The difference between a Pilot approach and a Phased approach is that with the former, all results are backed out when the agreed timeframe has been reached, and the target audience is returned to the previous state before the Pilot rollout. So, a Phased approach starts with Phase 1, whereas a Pilot is considered to be Phase 0.

Process inputs and outputs

Releases are created when the policy dictates combining one or more changes/releases into a release for deployment into the production environment. The following list identifies many of the inputs for release and deployment management, but it is not all-inclusive:

- Authorized change requests to be included in a release
- Plans for developing, building, testing, deploying, and implementing a release
- Configuration information about the target environments
- Back-out plans and remediation information
- Configuration baselines
- Testing information and evaluation results
- Training and communication plans

The following is a list of release and deployment outputs:

- Approval or rejection of the release
- New or updated CIs, services, and information
- Results from the post-implementation review(s) of the change
- Training and communication
- Schedule for releases
- Authorizations for release and deployment plans
- Updated release records
- Management information

Process activities

Release and deployment management has consistent activities for each release depending on the release type and the testing requirements defined in the release plans.

Figure 9.2 shows the flow for release and deployment management:

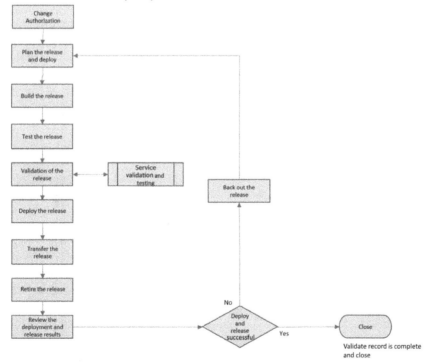

Figure 9.2 – Example of a release and deployment management process flow

The activities defined for release and deployment management include the following:

1. Authorizing the release
2. Planning the release and deployment
3. Building the release
4. Testing the release
5. Validating the release
6. Deploying, transferring, or retiring the release
7. Reviewing the release
8. Closing the release

The subsequent paragraphs describe what is involved in each of the activities described in the process flow.

Change authorization is the trigger that initiates release and deployment management activities. Since a release is made up of one or more approved changes, release and deployment management does not do anything until authorized by change management. Once the authorized change or changes have been identified for a release, then release and deployment management will begin.

The **plan-the-release-and-deploy** stage will begin with identifying the contents of the release. Planning will include the schedule for the release, what resources will be involved in the build, test, and deployment activities, and any training or communications that must occur during the release and deployment efforts. The plan will identify any dependencies between the contents of the release and the order for deploying the release contents. If this release includes the transfer of a component from one entity to another, this will be included in the plan. If this release is retiring any components, this will be identified as part of the plan. The release plan should clearly identify what testing will be conducted and who the testing will be performed by. The plan will describe how the deployment will occur and whether the release about to be deployed will be a Big Bang or a Phased approach. The plan will define whether there will be a Pilot deployment as part of a Phased approach. All of this information is important to include in the overall plan for release and deployment. Now that you have a plan in place for the release, the next step is to build the release.

Building the release takes all of the content that has been defined for this release and builds the release package. The release package will order the content based on any dependencies, develop the scripting for rolling out any applications, configure any infrastructure components that are included, update or create documentation for the components and applications, and develop any training or communication artifacts required. This activity ensures that all elements of the release are built to defined specifications and requirements. Keep in mind that changes are not built as part of the release; the changes are ready to be deployed and released. This activity focuses on building the release that combines the completed changes and any required CIs and components into a deployable release. It will be necessary to ensure that any components used in the release have been appropriately tested prior to including them or that they come from a trusted source that is common in your environment.

Now that you have the changes and components or CIs ready, it's time to put together the release to provide additional control and assurance that what goes into the production environment will cause no harm and will support the expectations of the organization. When the release package has been built, the change authority will review the results of the build activity and approve the move to the testing and validation steps.

Now that the release and all its elements are built, **validation** of the release will begin. Here, you are determining the viability of the release and all of its components. This will typically be performed by an autonomous testing group tasked with performing this step. This team will generally have specific experience and skills in performing the testing and validation activities. The team will have specific skills in documenting and communicating the results produced to the various stakeholders. There will be a variety of testing actions performed by the testing groups, which are described in the following list. This list describes many of the types of testing to be performed. Not all will be done with each release, but all of them will be done on some releases:

- **Release testing** ensures that the release as built is deployable into the target environment
- **Deployment testing** ensures that the deployment scripts will enable effective deployment of the release, installation, commission, or decommission of the release package
- **Operational testing** ensures that the production operation teams are capable of operating the release in the production environment
- **Performance testing** ensures that the release package will meet the agreed SLA targets and commitments
- **User testing** ensures that the users have access to the updated service and can use the service as expected
- **Service validation testing** ensures that the service is working in the target environments

The results of the testing and any defects or errors identified should be documented in the release record. When a defect or error is documented, communicate with appropriate stakeholders to determine whether the release must be halted and returned to the planning step or whether the error or defect is going to be introduced into the production environment as a known error. If the release will be moved forward, the error and the resolution or fix must be documented and logged as a known error and communicated to all support teams. All testing results will be shared with the appropriate change authorization team for evaluation and approval to proceed to the next step.

Deploying, transferring, or retiring is another step to take. The tested and authorized release package will be deployed into the target environment as defined by the release plan. The target environment could be one of quality assurance for further testing and evaluation. The target environment will generally be for production. The deployment could be in a Pilot environment for release to a small targeted user audience for further evaluation. Depending on the type of release and the deployment approach defined in the plan, you could be deployed to the production environment for a specific group of users (a Phased approach) or all the users at the same time (a Big Bang approach). Whatever approach you use, at this point, the release package is being deployed and made available to the target audience for production use.

The release package could be transferred from one service provider to another. For example, you have a service that is currently being provided by XYZ Corp and the decision has been made to transfer this service to ABC Company. In order to ensure a smooth transition from one provider to another, release and deployment management is used to facilitate the transfer and ensure that no disruption in service or degradation in the quality of service is experienced during the transfer.

The release package could be used to retire an existing service being replaced or becoming obsolete. In this instance, it is used to develop a release package containing all of the resources that will be retired, reused, or redeployed. Using release and deployment management for this type of activity ensures that all components that should be retired are appropriately identified, removed from the environment, and disposed of appropriately and sustainably, and that related artifacts are destroyed. Taking advantage of this process can ensure the accuracy of the **configuration management system** (**CMS**) and manage costs by ensuring that only utilized assets are being paid for.

Now that the release is in the production environment, **early life support** (**ELS**) begins. ELS is considered a warranty period where additional resources are allocated to manage the support of the release once it is in the production environment. ELS typically involves expert resources from the development group or Level 2 support teams. These resources sit with the first point of contact (usually virtually) to provide support for the new release while it is being stabilized in the production environment. If any unexpected incidents occur during the stabilization period, these specialized resources can respond more effectively. It also has the advantage of enabling the first point of contact to learn from these specialized resources. The release and deployment plan will dictate what the ELS timeframe is and what the criteria will be for exiting ELS and returning the specialized resources to their normal activities. ELS can be very beneficial for providing support for major releases, improving customer/ user satisfaction, and providing education to first-point-of-contact resources.

Now that the release is in production and stable, **review the deployment and release results**. Here, the change authority is analyzing the post-implementation reviews on all the changes contained in the release. They are looking at the incidents that were identified during the ELS period. They will evaluate the effectiveness of the incident responses and whether there were any serious issues with the release. The change authority will analyze the actual performance of the service in the production environment to see whether the results match what was expected and documented in the validation tests performed earlier in the process flow. If there are issues with the release that cannot be tolerated by the customer, the release will remain open and will return to the release planning activity to identify what failed and how to resolve it. Once the resolution has been identified, the release must go through the subsequent steps to ensure an effective result on the subsequent pass. Once the change authority has performed its due diligence and the customer is satisfied with the results produced, the release and deployment process will proceed to the final step.

Closing the release is the final activity in the release and deployment management process. During the closure of the release, all changes included in the release must have been closed successfully with or without condition. After confirming all changes have been closed, the release owner will ensure that the release record is complete with all pertinent information about the plan(s), building, testing and validation, deployment, and ELS. Once all information about the release is captured, the release owner will confirm authorization from the change authority and close the release.

Now that you have an understanding of the activities in the release and deployment management process, you will get some exposure to the variety of roles and responsibilities expected of participants in this process.

Roles and responsibilities

There are many key roles for release and deployment management, the process owner, the process manager, and the process practitioner. As was discussed in *Chapter 5*, there are common responsibilities for every process owner and process manager. There are some key responsibilities that the release and deployment management roles need to consider.

For the release and deployment management process owner, this role needs to work very closely with the change management process owner to document the policies about when a change must be included in a release because it is the responsibility of change management to authorize the various activities of release and deployment management. Putting together a consistent policy for these two elements of service management will be critical for maintaining the relationships between these processes. In addition, the release and deployment management process owner needs to establish what types of releases will be allowed and when those types will be used. The process owner needs to establish metrics to demonstrate the performance of the process and should be based on the maturity of the process and the capabilities of the technology to provide the data for the metrics.

The release and deployment management process manager is responsible for ensuring that the resources assigned to the process are properly prepared to execute the process efficiently and effectively and to ensure that the practitioners have the necessary tools and resources to be efficient. The release and deployment management process manager is responsible for ensuring metrics are captured and reported to the appropriate stakeholders. The process manager is responsible for monitoring the execution of the process and identifying opportunities to improve. The process manager will be responsible for appointing a release and deployment owner for all releases. Periodically, the process manager will review completed releases to assess the contents of the release records, compliance with the policies, and key process indicators to determine the overall performance of the process execution.

The release and deployment management process practitioners include a number of roles described ahead.

The release and deployment owner will be responsible for managing the life cycle of the release. In many cases, the release owner could be the responsible release and deployment manager or it could be an individual within the leadership chain. They will be the primary focus for communications to stakeholders concerning the release. The release owner will work with various teams that will be involved in building, testing, deploying, and releasing the release package. The release and deployment owner is responsible for validating that all information about the release package has been recorded in the release record.

There will be roles for the release build team. Their responsibility is to build the release package according to the policies, plans, and target environment that the release package will be deployed in. The build team will need to coordinate their efforts with the operations staff to ensure that what gets built will work in the operating environment that the release package will occupy. The build team will take the requirements defined in the release record and ensure that the requirements are fulfilled with the release package. When the release package build is complete, the build team will communicate with the release and deployment owner so the owner can schedule a review of the results and get authorization to proceed to testing.

The service validation and testing team will be responsible for all the tests that have been planned for the release package. The testing team is separate from the build team to ensure unbiased analysis of the testing results. Although it is preferred to have a separate group perform the testing, in an Agile environment, this may be performed by a peer group of the build team. When the testing team receives authorization from the change authority and release owner, they will conduct the planned tests according to the guidelines for each of the tests to be performed. The testing team will document all results from the release package testing, including any issues that were discovered as well as the successful tests that were performed. The testing team lead will communicate the results to the release and deployment owner, change authority, and other stakeholders for their review. If the review determines a successful test result, the release owner will submit the findings to the change authority for authorization to proceed to deployment.

The deployment team is responsible for moving the build from the test environment to a QA or production environment, depending on how your organization chooses to operate. The deployment team will migrate the tested and validated release package to the appropriate environment, verifying that the deployment was successful. After completing the deployment, the deployment team will communicate with the release and deployment owner, and the owner will engage the change authority for review and gain authorization for releasing the service to users.

The release team is responsible for making the release package available to the customers and users. The team will perform a knowledge transfer with the service desk, operations, and support stakeholders to ensure a smooth transition to production. The team may include various communication activities, training, and ELS during the stabilization period. The release team will validate that the release package is ready for use in production and confirm utilization by the target users. If a Phased release is used, the team will monitor the phases and report any issues or feedback as additional phases are implemented.

After the stabilization period expires, the release team will communicate to the release and deployment owner how the release went, any issues identified, corrective actions taken, and any existing conditions not resolved. If this is a Big Bang approach to the release package, the release team will make the release package available to all targeted users and verify the users have access to the service. Once the release is in production and available for use, the release and deployment owner will validate that the release record is complete, inform the change authority, and close the release record.

Key process indicators

The release and deployment management process has a number of key process indicators. These key process indicators should cover the progress of implementing the process across the service provider organization, compliance with the process policies, the effectiveness of producing the process deliverables, and the efficiency of the execution. A balanced set of metrics will ensure that the process is being measured appropriately and the key areas are covered. Some examples of key process indicators include the following:

- The total number of release packages recorded for a specified period as a control
- The number and percentage of releases deployed on time and within budget
- The number of incidents reported against a release
- Customer/user satisfaction with release package results
- The number of known errors identified during the testing of a release package
- The number of release packages by type
- The number and percentage of errors detected after a build

It will be important for the organization to focus on a few key metrics based on where you are in the maturity of your process. It is recommended that one or two metrics per focus area is sufficient to provide guidance on performance and where improvement can be considered. It is also important to monitor the behavior being exhibited as a result of the metrics so that you can identify unintended behavior and make adjustments as appropriate. At some point in your process life cycle, it will be appropriate to set targets for key process indicators. Be careful, however, to ensure that the targets are achievable and realistic so that they do not slow down progress. Likewise, monitor the behavior to make sure the targets are driving the right behavior. It is always good to keep in mind that what gets measured gets managed, and what you measure is what will be produced.

Process integration

For each process in the best practice frameworks, you will have both primary and secondary relationships and interactions with other processes. Since every process has a relationship with every other process, this section will only cover the primary relationships to key processes. Each process will be described in the following sections with the key interactions that release and deployment management has with it.

Incident management

Incident management receives information from release and deployment management about the releases that will be deployed and any known errors that have been identified that may be introduced into the production environment. Incident management will provide release and deployment management with information about incidents that are directly related to a release package. Incident management may provide information about customer/user satisfaction.

Problem management

Problem management receives information from release and deployment management about errors identified during release testing that, for whatever reason, will be introduced into the production environment. This enables problem management to review these errors, perform cause analysis, document the workarounds, and identify permanent solutions that can be scheduled for implementation when appropriate. This could typically be fixes included in the next release.

Change management

Change management provides information to release and deployment management on the changes that will be contained in a specific release and the target schedule for those changes. Change management provides authorization through the change authority to proceed with the various activities defined in the release and deployment management process. Release and deployment management will communicate to change management when specific milestones in the release and deployment process have been reached and when authorization is required to proceed. Change management will provide information on the success or failure of individual changes within a release package after deployment has occurred.

Configuration management

Configuration management provides information about the service(s) and CIs that will be impacted by the release package. This enables release and deployment management to assess the impact of the release package and assist in determining the overall impact. The CMS ensures all appropriate updates to CIs are completed as part of the release and deployment. Configuration management will establish baselines for the Phased deployment of a release package to ensure appropriate backout points if issues with the release package occur.

Service validation and testing

Service validation and **testing** receive the **release package** from release and deployment management. Service validation and testing perform all testing activities required for the release package. Service validation and testing will provide the results of the testing activities to release and deployment management so that authorization to proceed to deployment can be initiated.

Release and deployment management focuses on a few processes indicated previously. There may be other secondary interactions that are not listed here but should be considered when standing up release and deployment management or making improvements to it and other processes. In the next section, you will see information about some technology requirements based on current products available to support release and deployment management.

Technology requirements

Technology has improved the support of ITSM best practices consistently over the last 20 to 30 years. It has especially matured the support of many operational processes including release and deployment management. The following list shows many of the key requirements for the release and deployment management process. You may have additional requirements, but the following list is a sample of what should be expected of any service management tool. The most important thing to remember about selecting any technology is it will not make a poor process better. It is also important to realize how the tool will be used to select the one that will be most effective for your needs.

Release and deployment management requirements include the following:

- Offering release package templates that can be configured to specific requirements
- Basic release record data fields
- The means to document back-out and installation plans in the release record
- The ability to relate post-implementation incidents and problems resulting from a deployed release package
- The ability to provide authorization from the change authority within the release and deployment life cycle
- Providing a mechanism to reference release models enabling linking release packages to projects
- The ability to progress release package authorizations and deployment with an audit trail of these activities
- Allowing for free-form text, screen captures, and file attachments
- Providing a mechanism for monitoring and tracking a release package through its life cycle

It is very important to understand how you intend to use the technology, define the requirements for the technology, evaluate the current technology to determine what the deficiencies are, then identify your options for a provider and pick the one that satisfies the most requirements in your list. When defining your requirements, you should consider using the **MoSCoW approach**. The MoSCoW approach suggests classifying your requirements based on the *Must-Have, Should-Have, Could-Have,* or *Would-Like-to-Have* criteria. This allows you to prioritize the requirements and make sure that the Must-Haves and Should-Haves are generally covered by the tool you choose. You should also be careful when defining your requirements; a list that contains mostly Must-Haves will typically limit your choices to one or none.

Summary

In this chapter, you were exposed to the key elements of the release and deployment management process, including purpose and objectives, policies, process terms and definitions, input and output, activities, roles and responsibilities, key process indicators, process integrations, and technology requirements. You were provided with significant details about what should enable you to get started with implementing the process or making improvements to your existing process.

In the next chapter, you will continue to learn about operational processes with **request management**. Request management is the process that focuses on managing the life cycle of service requests. A **service request** can be characterized as something the requestor does not yet have but would like. This process represents the customer or user asking for new stuff that will help them do their jobs. It is a good thing and should be predictable and clearly defined to enable the service provider to provide a consistent delivery. You will learn more about what request management can do in your organization in the next chapter.

10
Request Management

In this chapter, you will be introduced to the **request management capability** specifically, and as part of formal **service management**. This includes the governance (the purpose, objectives, and policies), the execution (the roles and responsibilities, activities, and metrics), and the enablement (accelerating, integrating, and supporting technology) of the capability.

In this chapter, we are going to cover the following main topics:

- Purpose and objectives
- Policies
- Process terms and definitions
- Process inputs and outputs
- Process activities
- Roles and responsibilities
- Key process indicators
- Process integrations
- Technology requirements

Purpose and objectives

Request management is the process that is responsible for managing all service requests from users, from initiation through to closure.

The purpose of request management is to manage the life cycle of a service request from the time the request is initiated until it has been successfully fulfilled. Request management is responsible for fulfilling all service requests according to the agreed conditions defined in a request model and SLAs.

A **service request** is defined as a user-initiated request for something they do not have today but will need some time in the future to do their job. A service request can be as simple as a request for a password reset or more significant, such as adding a new service to their capability. In all cases, service requests are clearly defined by applying the appropriate request model to identify what actions need to occur to fulfill the request. All service requests will be predefined and documented. Service requests could be requests for information, a new capability, or access to a file share. A service request is not an incident and does not involve a service disruption. A service request may involve a standard change that's necessary to fulfill the service request.

The objectives for request management include the following:

- Manage the life cycle of all service requests
- Ensure that all service requests are recorded appropriately
- Ensure that all service requests follow a defined request model for fulfillment
- Provide a channel for users to request information and log compliments and complaints
- Provide a request catalog describing the service requests a user can initiate
- Ensure that a high volume of requests are fulfilled in the agreed time frame
- Provide communication to the requestor on the status of their service request

Policies

Policies represent the governance being applied to the request management process. A policy describes the rules and boundaries being applied to the process to ensure appropriate controls are in place. This ensures consistency and repeatability but also identifies the level of flexibility a practitioner has when executing the process, procedure, or work instruction. Policies will be discussed in more detail alongside examples in the following subsections.

Generic service request

A policy for a **generic service request** should be developed to establish the agreed response to a service request that has not been received before and is not currently part of the request catalog. A template or request should be developed to show the information necessary to respond to the request and how the request will be handled, the timeline for responding to the request, and where the request will be directed. This policy will provide guidance and set expectations for the customer on how these requests will be handled.

Request authorization

A **request authorization** policy describes how authorization for a request will occur. In most cases, service requests will be pre-authorized based on the request model that has been developed for the request. However, there are instances where additional authorization will be required – that is, funding is needed, new equipment needs to be purchased, and so on. This policy should clearly define how those authorizations will be collected and recorded for approval to proceed with the request and provide an audit trail.

Categorization

Categorization is a policy that is used to help the user identify what service request they need to initiate. Categorization for service requests needs to be easy so that the user can navigate them, quickly identify what they need, and initiate the request. It is typical for the categories to be in user terms so that users can identify the service and what requests can be initiated from the service. The categorization scheme will typically be multilevel and allow you to produce reporting that aligns the service requests with the business processes.

A typical categorization scheme might start with the service or business process at the highest level. This would be the service or business process that's recognized by the customer and user. The next level could describe the requests available for this service. The user could then select the request they want to initiate. This is illustrated in the following figure (*Figure 10.1*):

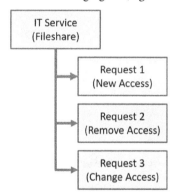

Figure 10.1 – A simple service request

The preceding figure shows a simple categorization scheme for a service where three requests could be initiated for the **Fileshare** service. The example in *Figure 10.2* shows a scheme that helps align with business processes:

Service Request Categorization Scheme

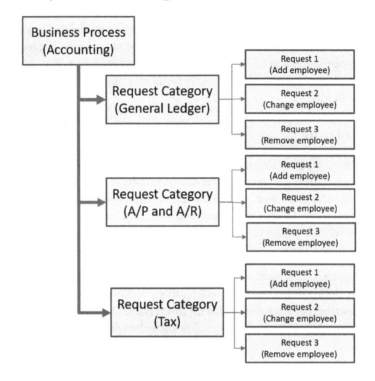

Figure 10.2 – Complex service request

This example shows how a business process can be related to the various activities performed and what requests might be available that a user can ask for. This approach can be very beneficial for users that may not understand IT speak but certainly understand their job and can relate to the business process terms and activities they perform. It can also make it easier for the business to understand when they're providing reporting on what requests were fulfilled and the business processes that were affected.

A categorization scheme can be very sophisticated but it is always a good idea to keep it straightforward. The more levels, the greater reporting detail can be produced, but this can make it very difficult for the users using the categorization to know how to find the request they are looking for. Your technology capability is also a consideration when you're attempting to categorize service requests. Keeping it simple will help you implement a categorization that will be easy to apply, easy to use, and easy to implement in your technology.

Prioritization

A **prioritization** policy may not be necessary for request management because these requests are predefined and have a clearly defined target for fulfillment and are planned activities. This makes establishing a priority for them less necessary. However, if necessary, the same prioritization policy used for change, incident, and problem management can be applied to request management.

Another policy that must be established is for the **request model**. All service requests must have a request model. This policy establishes clear criteria for the information that will be required to establish a service request. This policy should describe when and what information needs to be captured to create a service request and establish the model that will be applied to the service request every time it is selected. The policy should establish the minimum requirements for setting up a request model and it should provide one or more templates that can be applied when a new service request is being considered. The policy should document how a change to an existing request model can be made, as well as remove a request model when the service request is retired. The type of information that's needed to build a request model is shown in the following table:

Request Model Requirements	
Item	**Description**
Unique identifier	Every request model must have a unique identifier that can be applied by the technology.
Date/time created	The documented date and time when the created request model was ready for use
Request model owner	The individual who has the responsibility of managing the request model during its life cycle
Request category	Defines the categorization for the request
Request activities	Documents the steps that the service request must complete to be fulfilled. Documentation is required; optional steps and all information parameters are needed to fulfill the request
Short description	Provides a short description of the service request that can be used in the request catalog
Description	Documents a comprehensive description of what this service request will be used for, what information must be provided by the requestor, what resources will be used to fulfill the request, the normal timeline for the request to be completed, any information about costs, any required approvals to proceed with the request, and any dependencies on other request types.

Table 10.1 – Sample request model content requirements

There should also be a policy for the **request record** that contains some or all of the information mentioned in the following table. Every service request should be recorded so that there is evidence of the work that's been performed and information about what was done. The following table shows the type of information that might be captured for any service request:

Service Request Record	
Item	**Description**
Unique identifier	Typically, this is generated by the technology.
Date/time the request was initiated	The date and time when the service request was initiated, as generated by the technology
Initiator	The individual that initiated the service request
Target time to fulfill	The agreed target time to fulfill this request, as defined in an SLA
Priority	If priority is used, it will be based on impact and urgency, as defined by the initiator and documented in an SLA.
Assign to	Resources assigned to this service request
Request model applied	Describes the request model that was used for this service request
Short description	A short description that's applied by the request model
Resources used	Describes the resources used to fulfill this service request
Status of the service request	Documents the status of the service request as it navigates the request model from requested to fulfilled and closed
Date/time fulfilled	Provides the date and time when the service request was fulfilled. Typically, this is generated by the technology when the status changes to fulfilled.
Related requests	Identifies and documents any related requests (that is, standard changes and other service requests) used to fulfill this service request
Date/time closed	The date and time when the initiator or delegate confirmed fulfillment of the service request and the request can be closed

Table 10.2 – Sample service request record content

In many instances, your technology will dictate what is required and optional in the service request record but a policy should be documented to reflect the expectations for filling out and completing it.

These are some of the key policies that should be developed, documented, and communicated to all appropriate stakeholders to ensure that the stakeholders understand their responsibilities and realize the expectations when responding to a service request.

Process terms and definitions

There are two key terms related to request management: **service request** and **request model**. We'll define them in this section.

Service request

A **service request** is defined as a standard request from a user for information, a new capability, access, or a service. A service request can also be used to enable a customer or user to log feedback on the services being provided or record compliments or complaints about the service. This provides the user or customer with a consistent mechanism for providing information about the perception of a service. All service requests must have a request model defined for them, a clear definition of the resources needed to fulfill the request, and an agreed timeline for satisfying the service request when it's initiated.

Request model

A **request model** is a template for a specific instance of a service request. Request models are used to ensure the efficient and effective fulfillment of a service request. An example of a request model is onboarding a new employee. A variety of activities must be performed by various departments in the organization, one of them being the IT service provider. When a new employee is being onboarded, HR will provide key information about that individual so that IT can identify what resources the employee will need to do their job. In the request model, IT will identify the information needed from HR, capture that information, and initiate the various service requests and standard changes needed to get the equipment, applications, and accesses. IT will then schedule the delivery of the components to the appropriate location at the agreed time so that new employees can be productive as soon as possible. It is important for the requestor – in this case, HR or a manager – to understand the information required and the lead times necessary to effectively satisfy the request for the new employee so that when the individual arrives, all that they need to be productive on the job is available and works. This is just one example of a service request but it is one that almost every organization needs and most organizations struggle with. The request model ensures that the appropriate information is captured and the prescribed steps are being followed to perform this activity.

Process inputs and outputs

Service requests can be created at any time and in a variety of ways. The following list identifies many of the inputs and outputs for request management but they are not inclusive:

- The request inputs are as follows:

    - Service request

    - Request model

    - Configuration information

    - Entitlement information

    - Request catalog

    - Approvals

The request outputs are as follows:

  - Fulfilled requests

  - New or updated CIs, services, and information

  - Survey issued

  - Updated request records

  - Management information

Let's now look at the process activities.

Process activities

Request management activities may vary from one request to another. The activities will be defined in a request model for request management. However, some activities will be consistent for every service request. These are as follows:

- Initiate a request
- Record the request
- Validate the service request
- Determine entitlement
- Authorize the request (if needed)

- Fulfill the request based on the request model

- Confirm that the request has been fulfilled

- Close the request

Figure 10.3 shows the generic flow for request management:

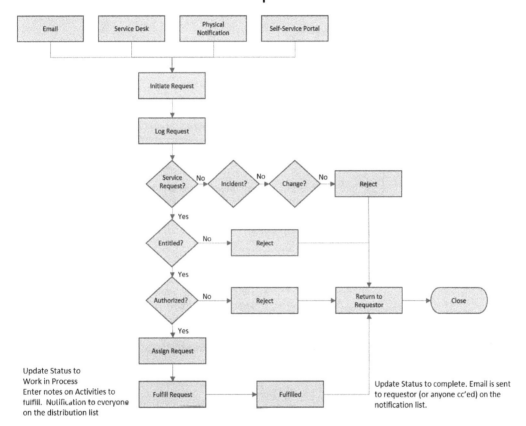

Figure 10.3 – Generic service request process flow

Figure 10.4 shows an example of the flow of an access service request:

Access Service Request

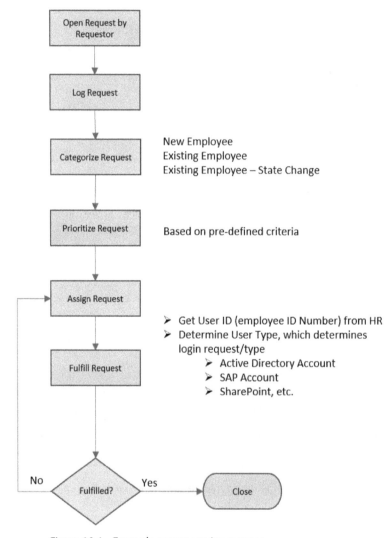

Figure 10.4 – Example access service request

The subsequent sections describe what is involved in each of the activities described in both process flows.

Initiate a request

Initiate a request occurs when a requestor initiates the service request. A request may be initiated in a variety of ways, including via a request to the service desk through a phone call, self-help portal, email, or, in some organizations, a walk-up site. When the request is initiated, the request model should ensure that all the necessary information needed to validate the entitlement and satisfy the request is provided if it's known at the time of the request. There could be instances where additional information will be captured during the request fulfillment, but this will be documented in the request model. Once the request has been initiated, it is logged in a request record.

Log the request

Log the request may be performed by the request initiator or the service desk, or some other resource as appropriate. Some of the key information that's recorded in the request record includes the following:

- Who initiated the request
- The request type and what request model is being applied
- Who will own the request
- Impact (if required)
- Urgency (if required)
- CIs
- Approvers (if required)
- Target time to fulfill
- Any required information documented in the request model

It is key that the request owner has all the information needed to proceed with the remaining activities so that there is no delay in satisfying this request.

Service request

You must determine if the service request is an activity that's been performed to ensure that the request is a service request and not a change, incident, or problem request. If the request is not a service request, then it should be rerouted to the appropriate request type and a notification must be sent to the requestor, identifying that the request was rerouted and will be handled according to the process requirements of the appropriate process flow. The group that validated the request, typically the service desk, should also set expectations with the requestor on when they can expect a resolution for the redirected request. Once the service request has been confirmed as the appropriate request type, it will proceed to the next step to validate that the requestor is entitled to the service being requested.

Entitled

The **Entitled** question is an activity that will validate whether the requestor is entitled to initiate this request. The receiving service provider group, typically the first point of contact or service desk, will assess the request and determine if the requestor is authorized to make the request and receive the results. If this is a service or product that the requestor is entitled to receive, then the service provider will proceed to the next step. If the requestor or their delegate is not entitled to the service or product, then the request will be rejected and the requestor will be notified of the rejection and the reason. Any rejection of a service request must include a reason so that the requestor can resolve the issue if possible.

Authorized

The **Authorized** question determines if the requestor has authorization to satisfy the request. This activity is performed to authorize the requestor so that the service or product request can be fulfilled. It could also be authorization to spend funds on the service or product needed to satisfy the service request. There will always be instances where a service request will need to be authorized by the management team; this step provides the action necessary to satisfy this requirement. However, not all requests will require authorization to proceed, so this step is considered optional, depending on the requirements of the service request. If authorization is required, it should be clearly defined in the request model, and appropriate controls should be put in place to ensure that the authorization is captured before the request is fulfilled. If authorization is required, once it is provided, the request will proceed to the assign request step.

Assign request

The **assign request** step directs the service request to the appropriate fulfiller group(s). This step will notify the fulfillers that a service request has been authorized and can now be fulfilled. There may be multiple steps involved in fulfilling the request and this may require more than one fulfiller group. So, this is an iterative step based on the request model workflow. Once the request has been assigned to the fulfillers, the request moves to the fulfill the request step.

Fulfill the request

The **fulfill the request** step applies the resources, funding, and activities required to satisfy the request. Here, the various service and component provider teams perform the activities necessary to deliver the results expected by the requestor. Fulfilling the request may involve multiple provider groups, multiple components, and appropriate funds, and may involve related request types such as a standard change or another service request. Service requests can be nested and reused based on the need, so one request model could contain other request models as well as a change model for a standard change. This allows the service provider to define requests at a granular level and reuse those for requests that involve many different elements of the service provider organization. This can allow the service provider to define a request model and use it in many different instances.

Fulfilled

Fulfilled begins when the service provider has completed all the activities defined in the request model and the service request is operational for the requestor. In this step, the service provider resources validate that all the resources that are used in satisfying the request are recorded, that all activities defined in the request model have been performed, and that the requestor has received the results that they expected. In the example described earlier, which was onboarding a new employee, the service provider will confirm with HR that the necessary components have been delivered to the new employee, the applications are usable, and that all the needed accesses have been granted or created so that the new employee can begin doing their job. The service provider will confirm that all documentation has been completed successfully and any money spent is within the agreed budget. Once the request model checklist has been completed, the request can proceed to the final step.

Close the request

Close the request is the step in the request management process that finalizes the closure of the request. Typically, this is performed by the first point of contact (service desk). The first point of contact will communicate with the requestor, validating that they can perform the various functions included in the request. The first point of contact will confirm that the request record has been completed with all the required documentation and information relevant to the request. They will initiate a satisfaction survey with the requestor and any other stakeholders as appropriate. In the case of our example, the service provider might send a survey to HR, the hiring manager, and the new employee to determine the level of satisfaction that results from fulfilling the request. The survey results will be included in the request record as evidence of the service provider's performance. After confirming that the service request has been satisfactorily fulfilled, the first point of contact will officially close the service request, sending a notification to all stakeholders that the request has been closed.

Now that you understand the activities involved in the request management process, you will get some exposure to the variety of roles and responsibilities that are expected of participants in this process.

Roles and responsibilities

There are some key roles for request management: process owner, process manager, and process practitioner. As discussed in *Chapter 5*, there are common responsibilities for every process owner and process manager. There are some key responsibilities that the request management roles need to consider. For the request management process owner, this role needs to ensure that policies related to categorization and request models are clearly defined. The process owner will work with other process owners to develop a consistent policy for the categorization scheme. This ensures commonality across all request types and enables linking the request types where necessary. The process owner will document what is expected and required for a request model and develop templates that can be used to facilitate the creation of request models. In addition, the request management process owner needs to establish the right metrics based on the maturity of the process and the capabilities of the technology to provide the data for the metrics. It will be very important for the process owner to have measures that drive the right behavior and produce metrics that effectively measure the performance of the process.

The request management process manager is responsible for ensuring that the resources assigned to the request management process have been prepared to execute the process efficiently and effectively, as well as to ensure that the practitioners have the necessary tools and resources to be efficient. The request process manager is responsible for ensuring metrics are captured and reported to the appropriate stakeholders. The process manager is also responsible for monitoring the execution of the process and identifying opportunities to improve. They will be responsible for appointing a request owner for all requests recorded within their responsibility. This role is also responsible for defining the request models or identifying and assigning the definition of the request model to a practitioner role. Periodically, the process manager will review closed requests to assess the contents of the request records, compliance with the policies, and key process indicators to determine the overall performance of the process execution.

The request management process practitioners have several key roles; let's take a look.

The request owner is responsible for managing the life cycle of the request. In many cases, the request owner could be the responsible request manager or an individual within the leadership chain. They will be the primary focus for communicating with stakeholders concerning the request. The request owner will work with the various teams that will be involved in fulfilling the request. The request owner is responsible for validating that all information about the request life cycle has been recorded in the request record.

The request model owner is responsible for defining the request model and managing the request model from creation to retirement. This role could be performed by the process manager but may also be delegated in larger organizations.

The fulfiller role is responsible for performing all the activities required to satisfy the service request. The fulfiller is anyone in the service provider's organization that is responsible for one or more activities defined in the request model. A fulfiller could be someone in the service provider's organization or it could be a third-party supplier. A fulfiller could be the management team, who is responsible for approving the expenditure of funds for components or authorizing access to an application or file share. Fulfillers perform the activities defined in the request model and record the actions taken during the life cycle of the request. This role is responsible for performing the activities, verifying the expected results were delivered, and documenting what was done. Fulfillers produce and capture the metrics that demonstrate the efficiency and effectiveness of the service request fulfillment. Fulfillers identify where improvements can be applied to make the response to service requests more reliable, efficient, and effective.

Key process indicators

The request management process has several key process indicators. These key process indicators should cover the progress of implementing the process across the service provider organization, compliance with the process policies, the effectiveness of producing the process deliverables, and the efficiency of the execution. A balanced set of metrics will ensure that the process is being measured appropriately and that the key areas are covered. Some examples of key process indicators are as follows:

- Total number of requests recorded for a specified period as a control
- Number of requests per request model for a specified period
- Number and percentage of requests closed within the agreed target by the request model
- Number and percentage of requests logged without a request model
- Mean time to complete requests by the request model for a specified period
- Cost to complete requests by the request model for a specified period

It will be important for the organization to focus on a few key metrics based on where you are in the maturity of your process. It is recommended that one or two metrics per focus area is sufficient to provide guidance on performance and where improvement can be considered. It is also important to monitor the behavior being exhibited as a result of the metrics so that you can identify unintended behavior and make adjustments as appropriate. At some point in your process life cycle, it will be appropriate to set targets for key process indicators, but be careful to ensure that the targets are achievable and realistic so that they do not retard progress. Likewise, monitor the behavior to make sure the targets are driving the right behavior. It is always good to keep in mind that what gets measured gets managed and what you measure is what will be produced.

Process integration

For each process in the best practice frameworks, you will have both primary and secondary relationships and interactions with other processes. Since every process has a relationship with every other process, this section will only cover the primary relationships to key processes. Let's describe each process, along with the key interactions that request management has with them.

Service catalog management

Service catalog management is a key source of information about the service requests that can be logged against a service. The service catalog provides key information about the targets to fulfill the request, what requests are requestable, and any authorizations required.

Incident management

Incident management may ask for a service request to be initiated through request management. In some organizations, service requests are handled through the incident management process. Although this is doable, it is not recommended since incidents represent unplanned work and service requests are planned.

Configuration management

Configuration management provides information about the service and CIs that could be included as part of a service request. This enables request management to identify the service and CIs that may be needed to fulfill the request and it may also identify CIs that need to be added to the CMS.

Capacity management

Capacity management uses request management to identify demand for service requests. This enables capacity management to plan for resources that may be required to fulfill the service requests and ensure appropriate resources are available to respond to the service requests.

Change management

Change management may be involved in a service request via a standard change. There are instances where a service request will require a standard change to be performed to fulfill the service request. Request management will identify the requirement for a standard change in the request model as part of the overall request workflow.

Financial management

Financial management interacts with request management to ensure that the monetary resources that are required to fulfill requests are available and that budgetary information about requests is captured during the **budgeting cycle**.

The process relationships described earlier reflect some of the key interactions with request management. As previously stated, other secondary interactions are not listed here but are also something that should be considered when you're standing up request management or making improvements to it and other processes. In the next section, you will learn about some technology requirements based on current products available to support request management.

Technology requirements

Technologies have improved the support of ITSM best practices consistently over the last 20-30 years. In particular, it has matured the support of many operational processes, including request management. The following list specifies many of the key requirements for the request management process. You may have additional requirements but the following list is a sample of what should be expected of any service management tool. The most important thing to remember about selecting any technology is that it will not make a poor process better and it is important to realize how the tool will be used so that you can select the one that will be most effective for your needs.

Here are some of the technology requirements for request management:

- Enable a variety of workflows to be generated
- The technology will automatically send, receive, and log approvals for requests
- Allow manual override for approvals
- The technology must provide status updates that occur automatically when an activity is completed as part of a workflow
- Provide notifications when request activities are completed to appropriate stakeholders
- The tool must categorize and prioritize requests based on the policy
- Provide a means of creating and applying request models
- Technology should allow linking to other request types and projects
- The tool should monitor and record the progress of requests throughout the request life cycle
- Allow free-form text, screen captures, and file attachments in a request record

It is very important to understand how you intend to use the technology, then define the requirements for the technology, and evaluate the current technology to determine what the deficiencies are. After this, you must identify your options for a provider and pick the one that satisfies the most requirements in your list. When you're defining your requirements, you should consider using the **MoSCoW approach**. The MoSCoW approach suggests classifying your requirements based on the *Must-Have*, *Should-Have*, *Could-Have*, and *Would-Like-to-Have* criteria. This allows you to prioritize the requirements and make sure that the Must Haves and Should Haves are generally covered by the tool you have chosen. You should also be careful when defining your requirements – a list that contains mostly Must-Haves will typically limit your choices to one or none.

Summary

In this chapter, you were exposed to the key elements of the request management process, including its purpose and objectives, policies, process terms and definitions, inputs and outputs, activities, roles and responsibilities, key process indicators, process integrations, and technology requirements. You were provided with significant details about the process, which should enable you to get started with implementing the process or making improvements to your existing process.

In the next chapter, you will continue to learn about **service management processes** by looking at **service catalog management**. Service catalog management focuses on identifying the services a service provider is offering, documenting what the services are, and providing the default and options available for those services. Service catalog management also documents the agreed service requests that can be logged against the documented service, providing clarity about what a customer or user can expect. You will also learn more about what service catalog management can do in your organization.

11
Service Catalog Management

In this chapter, you will be introduced to the **service catalog management** capability specifically, and as part of formal **service management**. This includes the governance (purpose, objectives, and policies), the execution (the roles and responsibilities, activities, and metrics), and the enablement (accelerating, integration, and supporting technology) of the capability.

In this chapter, we are going to cover the following main topics:

- Purpose and objectives
- Policies
- Process terms and definitions
- Process inputs and outputs
- Process activities
- Roles and responsibilities
- Key process indicators
- Process integrations
- Technology requirements

Purpose and objectives

Service catalog management is the process responsible for maintaining a single source of information concerning all operational services and those services that are being prepared for operations. It is the single safe source of all information related to services being offered to customers, provides access to potential customers about the operational services, and identifies how to initiate requests for those services.

Service catalog management is responsible for ensuring that appropriate stakeholders have access to information on all operational services offered by a service provider. It also documents what the customer can expect from the service, which requests are available, and how to initiate the request(s).

A **service** is something a customer or stakeholder needs in order to facilitate the production of one or more outcomes. The **service catalog** is the resource customers use to identify which services are provided by the service provider and how the services will enable the production of business outcomes. A service catalog, like a restaurant menu, provides information that enables customers to make decisions on what they need to fulfill their business needs.

The objectives for service catalog management include the following:

- Manage the content provided in a service catalog
- Ensure that all services defined in the service catalog are accurate and up to date; identify any dependencies between services and any resources needed to deliver the service
- Ensure that access is provided to authorized stakeholders
- Ensure that access to the service catalog is efficient and effective
- Ensure service catalog information is available to other processes as required

Policies

Policies represent the governance being applied to the service catalog management process. A policy describes the rules and boundaries being applied to the process to verify that appropriate controls are in place. This ensures consistency and repeatability but also identifies the level of flexibility a practitioner has when executing the process, procedure, or work instruction. The policies will be discussed in more detail with examples in the following content.

Service portfolio

The **service portfolio** is a policy that documents the criteria that define all services that a service provider offers, is considering offering to their customers, or is retiring and will no longer be offered to customers. It is beyond the scope of this book but it is very important for service catalog management because the service portfolio establishes when a service migrates from the service portfolio to the service catalog. It also describes which type of information will be collected in the service portfolio and the different states for a service portfolio entry. This is important for the service catalog because it is part of the service portfolio. All services, whether new, developing, transitioning, operational, or retired, are contained within the service portfolio. This would suggest that the service catalog is a subset of the service portfolio. Having an integrated policy that describes the rules for the service portfolio will significantly influence what is done when establishing the service catalog management process. It obviously impacts what will be contained in the service catalog. The service portfolio will have an impact on how the service catalog will appear to the approved stakeholder accessing it. This structure should be consistent with what has been described for the operational processes discussed earlier in *Chapters 6, 7,* and *8.*

Service catalog

The service catalog policy will describe the various views that will be required by the different stakeholders that will be accessing it. It will also identify the different service types that could be defined in the service catalog. There will need to be clear definitions of a service and these will be contained in another policy described shortly. The service catalog policy will dictate how each service type will be displayed to the stakeholders, which stakeholder groups have access to the services, and which information will be provided. This policy identifies which information is required in the catalog entry for each type of service documented in the service catalog. Some example views in relation to the service catalog could include **business services**, **IT services**, and **component services**. Following this example, the business services could be viewed by customers wanting to order the service; the business service is made up of IT services. The IT services are viewed by the service provider to identify which IT services make up the business service. The component services would be the various components needed to produce the IT service. This is illustrated in *Figure 11.1*:

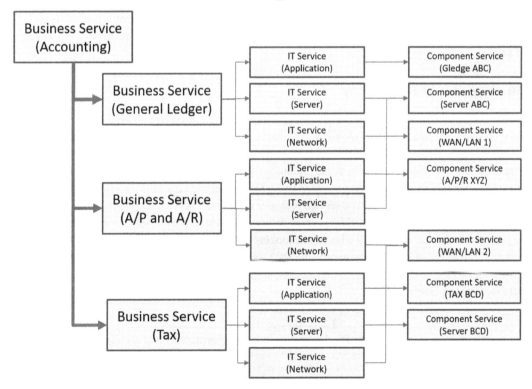

Figure 11.1 – Sample service catalog component view

In the preceding figure, there could be at least two views for the service catalog. The first view would be shared with the customer stakeholders in which they would see only the business services view. The service provider would see all the levels, which would enable them to understand which components and IT services are required for the business and sub-business services. So, if a stakeholder in the **accounting general ledger** has a new employee to add to the **general ledger** service, they could go to the service catalog, find the **accounting business service** and the **general ledger** sub-business service, and select the service request related to adding the new employee to that service. The IT service provider would be able to review the impact that the addition of a new employee to the service would have on the IT services and component services, to ensure that no degradation of service occurred as a result of adding the additional demand, that is, the new employee. This can be very useful when trying to identify the impact on a customer service when a change is being considered or an incident occurs. It will allow both an upstream and downstream analysis of the various elements required to satisfy the demand. For this reason, a consistent categorization scheme can be very important to both the service provider and the customer/user. This makes it much easier to communicate in both directions. Another example of a service catalog is the Amazon website, which has many categories of products and services to offer. When accessing the website, you can select the category you want to search or you can enter a keyword in the search window and a number of offerings will be presented. On the web, in a store, or on paper, all product and service providers categorize their offerings to make it easier for the customer to find what they need. This is one of the key objectives of the service catalog and service catalog management.

The service catalog entry

Another policy to be established is the **service catalog entry**. Each service entered into the service catalog should have consistent and required information described. The information contained in the service catalog should be put in customer-friendly terms that the customer will understand. The various views of the service catalog will offer some guidance on how that information should be presented. If it is customer-facing, it should be presented using terms that the customer can easily understand and use to make decisions. If only the service provider will see the service catalog information, then it can be defined in the service provider's terms. When developing the content for a service catalog entry, it is important to understand who will be looking at the information and how they will use the information. The type of information to consider for a service catalog entry could include the following:

Service Catalog Entry	
Item	Description
Service Owner	The individual or group that is responsible for the service
Service Name	The name of the service as shown in the service catalog
Definition	A brief description of the service
SLAs	The SLAs that apply to this service

Service Catalog Entry	
Item	Description
Default Commitments	The default commitments for response times and minimum levels of service
Business Process(es)	The business process(es) supported by the service
Business Value	How the business benefits from the service and the expected value produced
Provider	The providers involved in delivering and supporting this service
Customers	The customer(s) that use this service
Pricing	The pricing structure for the service if the service provider charges for his/her services
Cost of Service	The various costs associated with this service if the service provider does not charge for the service
Measurements	How the service performance will be measured and reported
Contacts	The contacts for this service responsible for communications and reporting
Offerings	The service requests that can be recorded against this service
Customer/Provider Responsibilities	The expectations of both customer and provider in delivering and supporting this service

Table 11.1 – Service catalog record content

In many instances, your technology will dictate what is required and what is optional in the service catalog record, but a policy should be documented to reflect the expectations for creating and maintaining it.

These are some of the key policies that should be developed, documented, and communicated to all appropriate stakeholders to ensure that the stakeholders understand their responsibilities and realize the expectations when creating a service catalog entry.

Process terms and definitions

There are key terms related to service catalog management; the definitions are as follows:

- **Service catalog**: The service catalog is defined as a structured document, spreadsheet, or data store that describes all the production services offered to customers or services that are ready to be deployed to the customers. The service catalog can have multiple views, usually at least two: the customer-facing view, which customers and users access to determine what the service provider offers, and the supporting service view, which identifies the supporting services needed to deliver the customer-facing services. The service catalog contains the service requests that can be logged against the service. This provides key information to customers about the requests that will be enabled as part of the service. The service catalog is part of the service portfolio.

- **Service**: A service is defined as the means to deliver value to customers by supporting outcomes that the customer wants to achieve. A service can be customer-facing or it can be a supporting service. What constitutes a service is defined and documented by the business and their service providers. A restaurant delivers a service, a meal; there are supporting services: kitchen, wait staff, and management; and the outcome for the customer is a pleasant and satisfying dining experience.

- **Outcome**: The outcome is defined as the results produced by using a product or service. A car is a product used to get the driver and passengers from point A to point B safely. Cars are purchased for a variety of reasons, but the primary outcome is to move people from one place to another.

Process inputs and outputs

Service catalog inputs and outputs are created when a new, modified, or retired service is identified. The following list identifies many of the inputs and outputs for service catalog management but is not all-inclusive:

- Service request for a new service
- Service portfolio information
- Configuration information
- Change requests
- Service catalog information
- Business information
- Feedback from other processes

Here are the service catalog outputs:

- Service catalog updates
- New or updated CIs, services, and information
- Service portfolio updates
- Updated change records
- Management information

Process activities

Service catalog management activities are less linear than other processes since much of the information contained in the catalog is static and does not change significantly over the life of a service. Activities will occur as needed, based on information from the service portfolio. As the service catalog is contained within the service portfolio, the activities performed to manage the service catalog will be initiated as part of the service portfolio management actions.

Figure 11.2 shows the general flow for service catalog management:

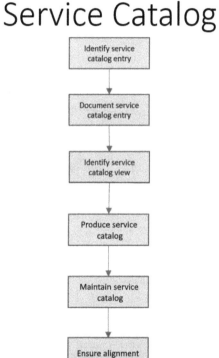

Figure 11.2 – Sample of a service catalog process flow

The following activities focus on the service catalog process:

- Identify services for the service catalog
- Document the services
- Identify service catalog views
- Produce the service catalog
- Maintain the service catalog
- Ensure alignment with the business and the service provider

The activities described in *Figure 11.2* will now be explained further.

Identify a service catalog entry

A service catalog entry occurs in a variety of ways, including a service request from a customer for a new service, a change request from a service provider introducing a new service, a change to an existing service, or the retiring of an obsolete service. The service portfolio management process may provide information on the change in status of a service currently in a development state in the service portfolio. It is important to remember that the service catalog is part of the service portfolio. Once a service catalog entry has been identified, it is necessary to document the service.

Document the service

Documenting the service should be performed by the service owner providing the key information described previously. Here is an example of a template for capturing information relating to a service catalog entry.

Name: *Service name*

Version: 1.0

Last Update: MM/DD/YYYY   **By:**   Service owner

Effective Date: MM/DD/YYYY to MM/DD/YYYY

Description: *Describes the activities that characterize this service.*

- **Key Business Indicators** – *the business functions that these support and the way in which the customer measures success.*

Provider/Product Owner: *organization responsible and accountable for service delivery.*

Consumers: *those who receive the service and produce business results with this.*

Service Level Expectations:

- *Support – describes the service desk and provider roles in supporting the various request types to be recorded against this service, i.e., service desk support is available on a 24/7 basis for this solution, to support the following service request types (Incident, Information, New/Additional Service). All request types must be initiated and logged by the service desk and will follow the standard processes for resolution.*

- *Performance – describes the metric used to report achievement of the agreed level of service performance in business customer terms, i.e., this solution is targeted to provide a page-to-page navigation response for users in 5 seconds or less.*

- *Availability – describes the measure for availability and targets, and how these will be reported.*

- *Cost – describes the cost of the service and how the rate is applied if charge-backs are used, i.e., charging is based on utilization of the service measured by transactions processed per day at $5.00 per transaction.*

Contact: *Service owner name and contact info*

Figure 11.3 – Template for a service catalog entry

The preceding template can be used to gather and validate the information being applied to the service catalog entry. This guarantees accurate information regarding the service and ensures that it is presented using terms easily understood by the business consumers.

Identify the service catalog view

Identifying the service catalog view will determine whether the service is a **customer-facing service** viewed by consumers or whether this is a supporting service only viewable by the service provider organization. It is important to understand who the audience for the service catalog entry will be, so that the terms used and the information provided are appropriate for the viewer. The customer-facing service should be in business terms and the information offered should enable the customer to make a decision about whether this service will satisfy their needs and support the outcomes the customer wants to achieve. A supporting service will be defined in the service provider's terms and will identify the customer-facing services or other supporting services that this service will support. The supporting service should identify the service relationships so that any upstream or downstream relationships are defined and understood.

Produce the service catalog

Producing the service catalog activity will capture the information identified in the previous steps. This step will organize the services according to the prescribed structure defined by the service portfolio and the service catalog management policies. The structure should be easy for consumers and service providers to navigate and find the information needed to make the necessary decisions. The structure of the service catalog can vary depending on the audience using the catalog. Similar to a restaurant menu, which may vary from one restaurant to another, based on the fare offered, a service catalog may have different views for different customer groups. As described previously, Amazon has a service catalog that is dynamic and changes based on the customer's preferences and purchasing behavior. However, Amazon has a basic set of services and pulls from the common pool to provide the customer with a customized view of those products and services. The service catalogs in most technologies are based on the service requests available to the customer to initiate, so the development of the service catalog requires a clear understanding of how your organization will present services to your various stakeholders.

Maintain the service catalog

Maintaining the service catalog is the action needed to manage updates to the catalog. These updates could result from a service request initiated by a customer or a request for change initiated by a customer or the service provider. It is necessary to ensure that any changes/modifications made to the service catalog are documented correctly and vetted using the appropriate process to ensure the accuracy and usability of the service catalog. It is important to remember that the service catalog is used by customers and service providers to make decisions on the services needed to meet customer outcomes and to plan for the effective delivery of services by the service provider.

Ensure alignment

Ensuring alignment is a key step supported by either the business relationship manager and/or the service level manager. In this step, the service catalog manager works with and receives guidance from the business relationship and service level management processes. The two roles in these two processes interact directly with the customers and perform various activities to assess the needs of the customers and to identify what can satisfy these needs in the service catalog. The roles also document how the services are being used by the stakeholders and determine where potential improvements need to be considered, as well as the potential new services that should be added to the service catalog. These two roles ensure that the service catalog content continues to provide value to the customers both strategically and operationally and gives guidance on the content contained in the service catalog. This input is significant in ensuring that the service catalog can continue to be a useful source of information for customers regarding the service provider's services/products.

Now that you have an understanding of the activities in the service catalog management process, you will get some exposure to the variety of roles and responsibilities expected of participants in this process.

Roles and responsibilities

There are key roles within service catalog management, including process owner, process manager, and process practitioner. As discussed in *Chapter 5*, there are common responsibilities for every process owner and process manager. There are some key responsibilities that the service catalog management roles need to consider. With regard to the service catalog management process owner, this role needs to ensure that policies related to a service and the service catalog are clearly defined. The process owner will work with the service portfolio management process owner to develop a consistent policy for the service and the content of the service catalog. The process owner will develop and document templates that can be used to facilitate the creation of service catalog entries. The service catalog management process owner needs to establish the correct metrics based on the maturity of the process and the capabilities of the technology to provide the data for the metrics. It is very important that the process owner has measures that drive the right behavior and produce metrics that effectively measure the performance of the process.

The service catalog management process manager is responsible for ensuring that the resources assigned to the service catalog management process are properly prepared, in order to execute the process efficiently and effectively and to ensure that the practitioners have the necessary tools and resources to be efficient. The service catalog process manager is responsible for ensuring that the metrics are captured and reported to the appropriate stakeholders. The process manager is responsible for monitoring the execution of the process and identifying opportunities to improve. The process manager will appoint a service owner for all service catalog entries recorded within their responsibility. Periodically, the process manager will review the service catalog entries to assess the content of the catalog entries, compliance with the policies, and the key process indicators to determine the overall performance of the process execution.

The service catalog management process practitioner role is the service owner. The service owner will be responsible for managing the life cycle of the service. In many cases, the service owner could be the responsible service level manager or an individual within the leadership chain. They will be the primary focus for communication with the stakeholders concerning the service. The service owner will work with the various teams involved in managing the service. The service owner is responsible for ensuring that all catalog information regarding the service has been recorded in the service catalog entry. The service owner is responsible for all communication with various stakeholders about the service. The service owner will represent the service in internal and external service review meetings. The service owner will ensure updates are made appropriately through the service portfolio management process.

Key process indicators

The service catalog management process has a number of key process indicators. These key process indicators should cover the procedure of implementing the process across the service provider organization, complying with the process policies, and demonstrating effectiveness and efficiency when producing the process deliverables. A balanced set of metrics will ensure that the process is being measured appropriately and that the key areas are covered. Some examples of key process indicators are listed here:

- Percentage of services recorded in the service catalog compared to all services being delivered
- Accuracy of service information contained in the service catalog compared to that which is being delivered
- Percentage of customers that are aware of and use the service catalog
- Customer perception of the accuracy of the information in the service catalog based on survey responses
- Percentage completeness of the supporting services in the service catalog
- Volume of accesses to the service catalog
- Completeness of the service catalog by measuring the number and percentage of incidents related to services in the service catalog

It is important for the organization to focus on a few key metrics based on where you are in the maturity of your process. It is advised that one or two metrics per focus area is sufficient to provide guidance on performance and to identify where improvements can be considered. It is also important to monitor the behavior being exhibited as a result of the metrics, so that you can identify unintended behavior and make adjustments as appropriate. At some point in your process lifecycle, it will be appropriate to set targets for key process indicators, but ensure that the targets are achievable and realistic so that they do not slow progress. Likewise, monitor the behavior to make sure the targets are driving the right behavior. It is always good to remember that what gets measured gets managed, and what you measure is what will be produced.

Process integration

For each process in the best practice frameworks, you will have both primary and secondary relationships and interactions with other processes. Since every process has a relationship with every other process, this section will only cover the primary relationships with key processes. Each process will be described, including the key interactions with service catalog management.

Service portfolio management

Service portfolio management determines the services that will be authorized for delivery to customers, as well as the services included in the service catalog. Service portfolio management defines a service and will work with service catalog management to establish which information will be contained in the service catalog, the various views of the information, and who will have access to it.

Request management

Request management service requests will be reflected in the service catalog entries defining the requests that can be logged against a service. Request management will use the commitments defined in the service catalog to manage and fulfill the service requests.

Configuration management

Configuration management works with service catalog management to ensure that the information needed in the service catalog is appropriately supported by the **configuration management database** (**CMDB**). It also ensures appropriate relationships between the various components that make up the services, and that the relationships between the customers and the users of services are appropriately documented and managed in the **configuration management system** (**CMS**).

Business relationship management

Business relationship management ensures that the services in the service catalog are required by customers and that they will deliver value. Business relationship management works with service catalog management to ensure that the services defined reflect the needs of the business and support the business from a strategic and tactical perspective. Business relationship management assists service catalog management in documenting services in business terms, so customers have a better understanding of what is being offered and delivered. Business relationship management will participate in customer service reviews with service catalog management and service level management.

Service level management

Service level management will be involved with service catalog management to ensure that the service is meeting the operational objectives of the service. Service level management will measure and report on the actual results that have been achieved based on the services in the service catalog. Service level management works with service catalog management to document the agreed levels of service that will be included in the service catalog entries, documenting the targets for default and optional availability, performance, continuity, and security.

Demand management

Demand management along with service portfolio management identifies potential service packaging opportunities and ensures that the service packaging is properly described in the service catalog.

The process relationships described in this section reflect some of the key interactions with service catalog management. As previously stated, there are other secondary interactions that are not listed here but should also be considered when setting up service catalog management or making improvements to it and other processes. In the next section, you will see information regarding certain technology requirements, based on the current products available to support service catalog management.

Technology requirements

Technologies have consistently improved the support of ITSM best practices over the last 20-30 years. This has led, in particular, to the maturing of the support of many processes including service catalog management. The following list shows many of the key requirements for the service catalog management process. You may have additional requirements but the following list is a sample of the expectations of any service management tool. The most important thing to remember when selecting any technology is that it will not make a poor process better. It is also important to realize how the tool will be used to select the technology that will be most effective for your needs.

Service catalog management requirements include the following:

- The technology must offer different views of the service catalog and allow the publishing of various elements of a service catalog entry
- The technology must provide a means of organizing services into logical or hierarchical groupings
- The provision of a mechanism to combine services into service packages that meet customer needs
- Allow a search capability through a variety of attributes and parameters
- Maintenance of the different statuses through a service catalog entry lifecycle
- The technology must provide a means of publishing services, packages, offerings, and pricing
- The tool should provide multiple instances for different departments in an organization

As stated previously, it is very important to understand how you intend to use the technology, define the requirements for the technology, evaluate your current technology to determine the deficiencies, identify your options for a provider, and pick the one that satisfies the most requirements in your list.

When defining your requirements, you should consider using the **MoSCoW approach**. The MoSCoW approach suggests classifying your requirements based on the *Must-Have, Should-Have, Could-Have,* or *Would-Like-to-Have* criteria. This allows you to prioritize the requirements and make sure that the Must Haves and Should Haves are generally covered by the tool you choose. You should also be careful when defining your requirements; a list that contains mostly Must Haves will typically limit your choices to one or none.

Summary

In this chapter, you were exposed to the key elements of the service catalog management process, including purpose and objectives, policies, process terms and definitions, inputs and outputs, activities, roles and responsibilities, key process indicators, process integrations, and technology requirements. You were provided with significant details about the process, which should enable you to get started with implementing the process or making improvements to your existing process.

In the next chapter, you will continue to learn about service management processes with service asset management. Service asset management focuses on identifying the assets used by a service provider to support and deliver services. This process will document which assets are needed, the cost of the assets, characteristics, and lifecycle information. Service asset management documents the key financial information regarding the resources, so the service provider has an understanding of the cost of the components needed to deliver and support the services in the service catalog. This process allows the service provider to understand the cost of services and potentially provides key information on pricing services. You will learn more about what service asset management can do in your organization in the next chapter.

12
Service Asset Management

In this chapter, you will be introduced to the **service asset management** capability specifically, and as part of formal **service management**. This includes the governance (the purpose, objectives, and policies), the execution (the roles and responsibilities, activities, and metrics), and the enablement (accelerating, integrating, and supporting technology) of the capability. In this chapter, we are going to cover the following main topics:

- Purpose and objectives
- Policies
- Process terms and definitions
- Process inputs and outputs
- Process activities
- Roles and responsibilities
- Key process indicators
- Process integrations
- Technology requirements

Purpose and objectives

Service asset management is responsible for maintaining a single source of information about all IT assets used to deliver services to customers, users, and other stakeholders. It is the single safe source of financial information about assets that are used in provisioning IT services being offered to customers. It provides access to information about the financial life cycle of all assets used in IT service provisioning, including receiving, recording, managing, and retiring.

Service asset management is responsible for ensuring financially significant assets are managed throughout their life cycle and that they're disposed of when they expire. It maintains a record of these assets from the time they enter the IT environment until they are retired and disposed of.

A **service asset** is a resource that has agreed financial value and useful life and needs to be managed across the life of the asset. There are two key focuses for service asset management: hardware and software. **Hardware asset management** focuses on the hardware components that make up the infrastructure that applications depend on. **Software asset management**, on the other hand, focuses on the infrastructure software and business applications that must be managed to deliver the IT services customers depend on to produce business outcomes. These activities ensure the effective utilization of software assets and ensure value for money invested in these resources. All service assets will be defined as configuration items but not all configuration items must be service assets. We will look at this in more detail in the next chapter on configuration management.

The objectives for service asset management are as follows:

- Manage the life cycle of all service assets

- Provide management information about service assets

- Meet legal and regulatory requirements for managing software assets

- Ensure effective and efficient use of software assets

- Ensure service assets are properly recorded in an asset management database

- Ensure service assets are retired and disposed of appropriately

- Ensure service asset information is audited periodically for accuracy

Let us now check the policies.

Policies

Policies represent the governance being applied to the service asset management process. A policy describes the rules and boundaries being applied to the process to ensure appropriate controls are in place. This ensures consistency and repeatability but also identifies the level of flexibility a practitioner has when executing the process, procedure, or work instruction. Let's discuss these policies in more detail.

Service asset

The **service asset** policy defines the criteria and characteristics of an asset. This policy identifies the financial value of a service asset. It will establish the agreed value of a resource that will be identified as a service asset. For example, a laptop may be considered a service asset because of the cost to acquire and support it, but a mouse may not be an asset because it is low-cost and readily available at the local office supply store. This policy will also define what information should be captured and recorded for all service assets. In general, this policy should establish the minimum required information about the service asset – that is, **purchase or lease cost, depreciation timeline, lease term, useful life term, residual value, disposal action, sustainability criteria, asset owner, maintenance cost,**

supplier, **unique identifier**, **location**, and more. Software assets will include this information along with licensing information (that is, the total number of licenses, how many are used, and the license term), version levels, release information, and renewal information for the licenses.

Asset class

The **asset class** policy describes the highest level of asset grouping that will be applied. Asset classes identify the high-level groups that will be used to classify assets. Asset classes could include the following:

- Hardware client devices
- Hardware infrastructure
- Software
- Databases

Asset types

Once asset classes have been defined, another policy to define is the **asset types** policy. Asset types represent a subset of an asset class. Asset types are the commonly used names for various hardware and software components. The example types that could be considered include the following:

- Hardware client devices:
  - Workstation/computer
  - Printer
  - Storage device
  - Mobile device
  - Monitor
  - Peripherals
- Hardware infrastructure:
  - Servers
  - Storage
  - Switch
  - Router
  - Peripherals

- Software:

  - Business applications

  - Web-based applications

  - Infrastructure

  - Cloud-based

- Database:

  - Server-based

  - Cloud-based

Hardware asset

A **hardware asset** policy documents the proper management of computer hardware assets in use at your organization. The purpose of having this policy is to reduce cost, eliminate obsolete technology, identify where assets reside, and ensure assets are effectively managed and disposed of in a sustainable way, including addressing the information security of business data and the information contained on these devices. The policy should establish the types of hardware devices that are covered and what is excluded as a hardware asset. For example, desktops, laptops, servers, storage devices, and mobile devices could all be considered hardware assets that should be managed and controlled but employee-owned devices might be excluded. This policy may also establish the responsibilities and authorities of the IT hardware asset manager. This policy will establish the identification requirements for all hardware assets, including tagging, unique identifiers, tracking information, and leasing, purchase, or warranty information. The hardware asset policy should define the various states a hardware asset can occupy – that is, requested, ordered, purchased, received, configured, deployed, production, retiring, retired, and disposed of.

Software assets

A similar policy is established for **software assets**. It guides the effective management of software assets contained in the organization's environment. The purpose of having this policy helps reduce software costs, eliminate obsolete or unused software, identify where software assets are being used, and ensure software assets are effectively managed and disposed of sustainably. The policy should cover all software assets purchased from external resources, downloaded freeware, and software created internally. There should be clear guidance on how to manage any software purchased, including right-to-use documentation, terms of use, reuse, and license management. For freeware, this could include how many instances can be downloaded before it becomes licensable. For internally developed software, this could be where is it used, how many instances are in production, and version control practices. The policy must define what software assets will be excluded from the asset management control, such as software on employee personal devices purchased by the employee with their funds. This policy should describe the responsibilities and authorities of the IT software asset manager. It should also define the various states that a software asset can occupy in its life cycle – that is, requested, ordered, received, configured, developed, tested, deployed, production, recovered, redeployed, reassigned, retiring, retired, and disposed of.

Hardware asset record

A policy should be documented to describe the **hardware asset record**. The following table shows an example of a hardware asset class (hardware) and type (hardware client devices):

	Workstation/Computer	Printer	Storage Device	Mobile Devices	Flatbed Scanners	Peripheral	Monitor	Barcode Scanners
Unique Identifier	X	X	X	X	X	X	X	X
Name/Description	X	X	X	X	X	X	X	X
Install Date	X	X		X	X	X	X	X
Status	X	X		X	X	X	X	X
Historical Data (for example, audit trail)	X	X		X	X	X	X	X
Location	X	X	X	X	X	X	X	X
Asset Owner	X	X	X	X	X	X	X	X
Procured From	X	X	X	X	X	X	X	X
Manufactured By	X	X	X	X	X	X	X	X
Serial Number	X	X	X	X	X	X	X	X
Model Number	X	X	X	X	X	X	X	X
Asset Tag	X	X	X	X	X	X	X	X
Business Division	X	X	X	X	X	X	X	X
Business Department #	X	X	X	X	X	X	X	X
Recipient/End User	X	X	X	X	X	X	X	X

Recipient/End User Department	X	X	X	X	X	X	X	X
Financials	X	X	X	X	X	X	X	X
Service Tag Number	X	X	X	X	X	X	X	X
Vendor Servicing Asset	X	X	X	X	X		X	X
Warranty Start Date	X	X	X	X	X		X	X
Warranty End Date	X	X	X	X	X		X	X
Refresh Life Cycle	X	X	X	X	X	X	X	X
Refresh Year	X			X				

Table 12.1 – Sample hardware asset record

The *Xs* in the preceding table indicate the attributes that are required for each asset type.

Software asset records

A policy for the **software asset record** should be documented. The following table shows an example of the attributes of a software asset:

	Enterprise Business Application	End User Computing	Infrastructure
Unique Identifier	X	X	X
Name/Description	X	X	X
Enterprise Initiative	X	X	X
Install Date	X	X	X
End Date	X	X	X

License Type	X	X	X
Status	X	X	X
Historical Data (for example, audit trail)	X	X	X
Utilities/Tools	X	X	X
Location	X	X	X
Asset Owner	X	X	X
Business Owner	X	X	X
Procured From	X	X	X
Manufactured By	X	X	X
Serviced By	X	X	X
Serial Number	X	X	X
Model Number	X	X	X
Asset Tag	X	X	X
Delivery Method (Web versus Device-Based)	X	X	X
Certificate (Key, Identifier)	X	X	X
OpenSource (Y/N)	X	X	X
OpenSource LIMITATIONS	X	X	X
License SPECIFICATIONS	X	X	X
Vendor Portal	X	X	X
User Class	X	X	X
HR Data	X	X	X
Financials	X	X	X
Contracts	X	X	X

Table 12.2 – Sample software asset record

In the preceding table, all attributes are relevant to all software asset types, so a general policy could define the attributes for all software assets. However, if there is an instance where an attribute does not apply to all, then this table will be necessary to identify those variances.

In many instances, your technology will dictate what is required and optional for the attributes in a hardware or software asset record, such as asset classes and asset definitions, but a policy should be documented to reflect the expectations for creating and maintaining them.

These are some of the key policies that should be developed, documented, and communicated to all appropriate stakeholders to ensure that the stakeholders understand their responsibilities and realize the expectations when creating an asset entry.

Process terms and definitions

There are key terms related to service asset management. Let's take a look at them and define them:

- **Asset**: An asset is defined as any resource or capability. It could be either *capital* assets, as defined by your CFO, or *consumable/expense* assets, as defined by your IT governance group. Assets are controlled by service asset management.

- **Asset record**: An asset record is defined as a set of attributes about an asset. See the examples of asset records in the preceding section.

- **Service asset**: A service asset is defined as any resource or capability that could contribute to the delivery of an IT service.

- **Class**: A class is defined as the highest level a set or collection of similar items may be grouped, such as hardware, software, and so on.

- **Type**: Type is defined as a subset of a class. This is the common name that an asset may be known by, such as computer, printer, server, and so on.

- **Attribute**: An attribute is defined as a characteristic or information about something, such as a hardware or software asset.

Process inputs and outputs

Service asset management's inputs and outputs are created when a new, modified, or retired asset is identified. The following lists identify many of the inputs and outputs for service asset management, but they aren't inclusive:

The following are service asset management inputs:

- A service request for moving, adding, or changing an asset

- RFC for moving, adding, or changing an asset

- Purchase orders for new assets

- Shipping and receiving tickets

- Updates to RFCs

- Audit reports

- Feedback from other processes

The following are service asset management outputs:

- RFCs to dispose of retired assets

- New or updated asset information

- Audit findings

- Management information

Process activities

Service asset management activities involve maintaining a record of all IT assets in use and their financial information. These activities will identify the assets, manage the life cycle of the assets, and ensure that when their useful life has expired, they will be disposed of appropriately and sustainably.

Identifying IT assets

Identifying IT assets occurs when a service request or request for change is initiated to acquire a new IT asset, move or change the IT asset, or retire and dispose of an IT asset. The CFO or IT governance team will have identified what constitutes an IT asset as part of the service asset policy described earlier. When an IT asset is identified, the IT asset manager will capture the appropriate information about the IT asset and record the information in the IT asset database. The information that's recorded is described in the policies for the IT asset record, depending on whether it is a hardware or software asset. Once the IT asset has been recorded, the service request or request for change will proceed to deploy the asset.

Record the IT asset

Record the IT asset involves determining what type of asset it is and what information is required to manage the asset throughout its life cycle. If it is a hardware asset class, the IT asset manager will determine what type of hardware asset it is and capture the information required. If the asset is a software component, the IT asset manager must determine what type of software it is and gather the required information. It is important to understand the difference between assets. Hardware assets will be treated differently than software assets. Knowing and understanding the differences will allow you to capture the appropriate data and record these IT assets properly.

Manage the life cycle

The manage the life cycle activity ensures that the IT asset information is maintained throughout the life of the asset. This involves monitoring the asset as the life of the asset progresses from new to mature to retiring and eventual disposal. During the life cycle of an IT asset, it is the service asset management process role's responsibility to maintain relevant information about the asset, its financial value, its continued utilization and maintenance, the ownership of the asset, where it is, and where it is in its useful life. It is necessary to maintain an accurate and complete record of the asset life cycle so that you can respond to requests for information concerning specific assets. In addition, it is important to be prepared for audit requests when they occur.

Audit the IT assets

Audit the IT assets is the activity that reviews the asset records and validates that the records match what is actually in the IT environments. Audits can be conducted internally or externally. The auditors are looking to determine if the records maintained on the IT assets reflect the IT assets used by the organization. More than one type of audit will be conducted. One example of a hardware audit would entail collecting all the asset records related to client devices and then identifying where those client devices are located, who owns the device, who is using the device, and if the information about the device (that is, memory, storage, peripherals, and so on) are consistent with what is observed when sampling the client devices. Another example related to business software applications might entail a vendor request to identify if the software assets being used are consistent with the licensing. This type of audit is typically described as a "true up" audit. The vendor is seeking to identify whether the licenses that have been purchased are being used and where they are being used. There are instances where organizations have failed to manage the licenses effectively and end up paying a penalty for misuse of the software or there is evidence that the organization has many more licenses than what they have deployed. Both situations are costly to the organization. Whether it is a hardware or software audit, it is important to have accurate information available to facilitate the audit results. An audit can show instances where hardware is coming off of a lease and needs to be returned to the vendor and the maintenance agreement has been terminated. Again, there are numerous examples of organizations that failed to maintain accurate information about their assets and it resulted in unnecessary expense. A periodic internal audit can help identify the potential risk of negative audit findings and resolve them before it becomes a costly issue for the organization. This activity is essential to ensure that the organization is effectively managing its IT assets.

Provide management reporting

The provide management reporting activity involves reporting information about the accuracy of the asset database, the performance of the process, and audit findings. These reports help management make effective decisions about the IT assets being acquired, used, and removed. It provides the accounting organization with information about the cost of IT assets. It also provides information to management about the cost of IT assets, which enables your service provider organization to determine the overall cost of services and when it's appropriate to provide pricing for those services. This reporting can identify exceptions to the policies, assets that are no longer supported, and assets that have reached or exceeded their useful life, potentially putting the organization at risk of failure or service disruption. It can also identify asset areas that need to be refreshed and provide information for budget planning to enable the refresh. Audit findings will provide evidence of the effectiveness of the service asset management process and can help identify areas for improvement. Service asset management reporting will not only provide information about the assets being managed but also information about the efficiency of the process, including information about the IT assets so that audit results can be predicted and costly surprises can be avoided.

Dispose of IT assets

The dispose of IT assets activity ensures IT assets that have reached their end of useful life or have reached the end of their leasing term are disposed of or returned as appropriate. A comprehensive approach to disposing of IT assets is essential to maintaining the security of organizational information assets and protecting the organization from risk. Some potential risks resulting from ineffective disposal activities include data being retrieved from client devices by unauthorized actors, hardware maintenance agreements not being canceled when the hardware is returned, not removing software when licenses expire, and more. It is the responsibility of the IT asset manager to ensure that hardware is scrubbed before disposal and that disposal is performed sustainably and appropriately. Once an IT asset has been disposed of, the IT asset record may be maintained for a certain period before being removed from the IT asset database.

Now that you understand the activities in the service asset management process, you will learn about the variety of roles and responsibilities expected of the participants in this process.

Roles and responsibilities

There are key roles in service asset management, including process owner, process manager, and process practitioner. As discussed in *Chapter 5*, there are common responsibilities for every process owner and process manager. There are some key responsibilities that the service asset management roles need to consider. The service asset management process owner is accountable for ensuring the process meets the needs of the business. The role must be the sponsor for the process, provide design guidance, and ensure changes to the process are managed and improvements are identified and implemented appropriately. The process owner must ensure accurate documentation is maintained about the process and define how the process will be measured for compliance and performance. The service asset management process manager is responsible for ensuring that the resources assigned to the service asset management process are properly prepared to execute the process efficiently and effectively. This role is responsible for the operational management of the process to ensure that the practitioners have the necessary tools and resources to be efficient. The service asset process manager is also responsible for ensuring metrics are captured and reported to the appropriate stakeholders. The process manager is responsible for monitoring the execution of the process and identifying opportunities to improve. Finally, the service asset process manager is responsible for identifying an asset owner for all service assets recorded within their responsibility. Periodically, the process manager will audit service assets to validate the accuracy of the records, compliance with the policies, and key process indicators to determine the overall performance of the process execution.

Let's look at the service asset management process practitioner roles:

- The service asset analyst supports the design (principles and procedures), associated training, and improvement of the process. This role is involved in the audits of the process.

- The service asset librarian is the custodian of the information that's recorded in the asset database. This role assists in audits of the asset database and improvements to the process.

- The service asset owner is responsible for validating that all asset information is accurately recorded in the asset database. The service asset owner is responsible for all communication with various stakeholders about the asset. The service asset owner will represent the asset in internal and external audits. They will also be aware of whether any updates that are made to the assets are appropriate and accurate.

This section covered the key roles and responsibilities of service asset management. The next section will look at and review sample key performance indicators for the service asset management process.

Key process indicators

The service asset management process has several key process indicators. These key process indicators should cover the progress of implementing the process across the service provider's organization, compliance with the process policies, the effectiveness of producing the process deliverables, and the efficiency of the execution. A balanced set of metrics will ensure that the process is being measured appropriately and the key areas are covered. Some examples of key process indicators are as follows:

- IT asset budgets are 90% accurate

- Asset utilization is maintained at or above 50%

- Paid software licenses are 90% utilized

- Asset information is 97% accurate

- Asset audits are at least 95% accurate

It will be important for the organization to focus on a few key metrics based on where you are in the maturity of your process. It is recommended that one or two metrics per focus area is sufficient to provide guidance on performance and where improvement can be considered. It is also important to monitor the behavior being exhibited as a result of the metrics so that you can identify unintended behavior and make adjustments as appropriate. At some point in your process life cycle, it will be appropriate to set targets for key process indicators, but be careful to ensure that the targets are achievable and realistic so that they do not retard progress. Likewise, monitor the behavior to make sure the targets are driving the right behavior. It is always good to keep in mind that what gets measured gets managed and what you measure is what will be produced.

Process integration

For each process in the best practice frameworks, you will have both primary and secondary relationships and interactions with other processes. Since every process has a relationship with every other process, this section will only cover the primary relationships to key processes. Each process will be described in this section, along with the key interactions service asset management has with it.

Supplier management

Supplier management is a key process for service asset management. Suppliers will provide key information about the service assets being deployed by the service provider. This information will be necessary to establish the useful life of the asset, the licensing requirements for software, the maintenance obligations of the supplier, and the cost of the assets. All this information should be captured and recorded as part of the asset management database so that all the service assets can be effectively and efficiently managed.

Service request management

Service request management identifies service assets that will be deployed based on a user request. Service asset management provides information about the availability of assets, especially for redeploying assets or reusing recovered assets.

Configuration management

Configuration management works alongside service asset management to ensure that the information defined in the asset database is consistent with the information contained in the **configuration management database** (**CMDB**). The service asset database is part of the configuration management system.

Change management

Change management documents any changes that occur against an IT asset. Service asset management documents new, changed, or removed assets throughout the change management process.

Financial management

Financial management defines what the criteria for an IT asset will be. The service asset management process gathers financial information from financial management.

The process relationships described earlier reflect some of the key interactions with service asset management. As previously stated, other secondary interactions are not listed here but are also something that should be considered when you're standing up service asset management or making improvements to it and other processes. In the next section, we will learn about some technology requirements based on the current products that are available to support service asset management.

Technology requirements

Technologies have improved the support of ITSM best practices consistently over the last 20-30 years. In particular, it has matured the support of many processes, including service asset management. The following list shows many of the key requirements for the service asset management process. You may have additional requirements but the following list is a sample of what should be expected of any service management tool. The most important thing to remember about selecting any technology is that it will not make a poor process better and it is important to realize how the tool will be used so that you can select the one that will be most effective for your needs.

Here are the technology requirements for service asset management:

- The ability to have PC and non-PC assets related to users, locations, and customers

- The ability to manage assets and asset classes at no additional charge

- The ability to relate parent and child information (that is, an OS on a PC or an application on a PC)

- The ability to provide integration for inventory tools or PC configuration tools, or any tool that provides inventory or asset discovery

- The ability to support the generation of inventory reporting and trending information

- The ability to produce reports for audits

As stated earlier, it is very important to understand how you intend to use the technology, then define the requirements for the technology, evaluate the current technology to determine what the deficiencies are, then identify your options for a provider and pick the one that satisfies the most requirements in your list. When defining your requirements, you should consider using the **MoSCoW approach**. The MoSCoW approach suggests classifying your requirements based on the *Must-Have*, *Should-Have*, *Could-Have*, and *Would-Like-to-Have* criteria. This allows you to prioritize the requirements and make sure that the Must Haves and Should Haves are generally covered by the tool you choose. You should also be careful when defining your requirements – a list that contains mostly Must Haves will typically limit your choices to one or none.

Summary

In this chapter, you were exposed to the key elements of the service asset management process, including its purpose and objectives, policies, process terms and definitions, inputs and outputs, activities, roles and responsibilities, key process indicators, process integrations, and technology requirements. You were provided with significant details about the process, which should enable you to start implementing the process or make improvements to your existing process.

In the next chapter, you will continue to learn about **service management processes** in terms of configuration management. Configuration management focuses on identifying the configuration items a service provider uses to support and deliver services. This process documents what configuration items are used, what services are dependent on the configuration items, the relationships between configuration items, and life cycle information. Configuration management documents the key information about the resources so that the service provider understands the relationships between the components that are needed to deliver and support the services defined in the service catalog. This process allows the service provider to understand what makes up the services and how the services are configured. You will learn more about what configuration management can do in your organization in the next chapter.

13
Configuration Management

In this chapter, you will be introduced to the **configuration management** capability, part of formal **service management**. This includes the governance (the purpose, objectives, and policies), the execution (the roles and responsibilities, activities, and metrics), and the enablement (the accelerating, integrating, and supporting technology) of the capability.

In this chapter, we will cover the following main topics:

- Purpose and objectives
- Policies
- Process terms and definitions
- Process inputs and outputs
- Process activities
- Roles and responsibilities
- Key process indicators
- Process integrations
- Technology requirements

Purpose and objectives

Configuration management is the process responsible for maintaining the single source of information about all components and their relationships, used to deliver services to customers, users, and other stakeholders. It is the single safe source of information about service components and their relationships with each other and the services they support. It provides access to information about the components and how they are used in IT service provision. Configuration Management maintains these relationships and configurations so that you can be more effective in understanding how components are organized to deliver and support IT services.

Configuration management is responsible for ensuring that components, also defined as **configuration items** (**CIs**), are identified, recorded, and managed throughout their life cycle. It will maintain a record of these CIs from the time they enter the IT environment until they are retired and disposed of.

A CI is a resource that is part of an IT service and contributes to the value delivered to stakeholders. A CI can be many different things and differs from an asset, in that a CI can be an asset but not all of them are assets. A CI can be hardware, software, data, a service, a business process, or anything that contributes to the delivery and support of an IT service, and the relationship to the service needs to be managed.

The objectives for Configuration Management include the following:

- Managing the life cycle of all CIs
- Managing the relationships between CIs
- Providing management information about CIs
- Ensuring CIs are properly recorded in **configuration management databases** (**CMDBs**)
- Ensuring CIs are retired and removed from the CMDBs appropriately
- Ensuring CI information is audited periodically for accuracy
- Providing CI information and relationship information to all other Service Management processes

Policies

Policies represent the governance that is applied to the Configuration Management process. A policy describes the rules and boundaries that are applied to the process to ensure appropriate controls are in place. This ensures consistency and repeatability but also identifies the level of flexibility a practitioner has when executing the process, procedure, or work instruction. Policies will be discussed in more detail with examples in the following subsections.

Configuration item

A CI policy defines the criteria and attributes of a CI. This policy establishes what a CI is and the information about it to be collected and maintained. For example, every CI will have at least one relationship with another one. Every CI must fall under **change management** control. In general, this policy should establish the minimum required information about a CI – that is, relationships, where it is used, the services supported, its owner, its unique identifier, and so on.

Configuration management

The **configuration management** policy establishes the governance for this process. Industry standards such as what is defined by the **International Organization of Standards** (**ISO**) stress that information systems (e.g., general support systems, and major and minor applications) must document and assess the potential impact that proposed system changes may have on the operational processes and security posture of a system. IT industry best practices recognize Configuration management as an essential aspect of effective system management. Configuration management is a critical control process to ensure the integrity, security, and reliability of information systems. This policy should apply to all IT activities and CIs. IT must meet or exceed all requirements governing configuration management and change management processes affecting CIs. IT must document, implement, and maintain these processes, including the following:

- Documenting and maintaining the **configuration baselines** that apply to **deployed systems**
- Managing and tracking all configurations and related documentation changes
- Maintaining the integrity, availability, and maintainability of the systems
- Planning to ensure the ability to reverse a deployment or implementation when required

This policy will document the requirements to ensure that all changes to CIs are recorded – that is, the installation of patches to hardware, software, firmware, and documentation. It must include appropriate industry best practices for roles and responsibilities, standardized methods, processes, and procedures. The policy should establish a **Configuration Control Board** (**CCB**) to ensure that the overarching intention and policies of configuration management are applied across the service management life cycle. The policy must enforce the utilization of the CMDB and the tracking of relevant information about CIs and their attributes, baselines, documentation, changes, and relationships.

CI class

A **CI class** policy documents the classes that are defined for configuration management. CI classes represent the highest level that a set or collection of similar items can be grouped together, such as the following:

- Hardware
- Software
- Network
- Database
- Business application
- Service

CI types

A similar policy is established for **CI types**. This policy identifies the subsets of each CI class. CI types are a subset of each CI class, and the configuration item class policy should include this information, or a similar policy should be established:

- Hardware:
  - Workstation/computer
  - Printer
  - Mobile device
  - Flatbed scanner
  - Peripheral
  - Monitor
  - Barcode scanner
  - Chassis
  - Storage device
  - Switch
  - Router
  - Wireless access point
  - Server
- Network:
  - **Content delivery network (CDN)**
  - Endpoint group
  - **Internet service provider (ISP)**
  - Wi-Fi
- Database:
  - Catalog
  - Instance

- Software:

    - Enterprise business application

    - Open source

    - End user computing

    - Infrastructure management

    - IoT

- Application:

    - Internal

    - External

- Service:

    - Business (e.g., SaaS)

    - Technical

    - Application (e.g., websites)

Hardware CI record

A policy for **hardware CI record** defines the information that will be collected for each CI. In many instances, there may be information differences between each class or type of CI. The following table describes the common attributes of CIs:

CI attributes	Description
Unique identifier	This is an identifier that is applied automatically by the technology used to manage the CIs.
CI name/description	The name the CI is known by and a description of the CI
Install date	Identifies when the CI was installed and is available for production use
Status	Identifies the current state of the CI, such as *testing, deployed, production, retiring, disposed*
Historical data (e.g., an audit trail)	Provides an audit trail of all changes applied to this CI, including who made the change, when it was performed, and the state
Location	Where the CI is currently located
CI owner	Identifies the individual or group that owns and is responsible for the CI.

CI attributes	Description
Relationships	Identifies what other CIs this CI is related to. The CI could be related to one or more CIs, but every CI must have at least one relationship with another one
Serial number	Identifies the serial number of the CI
Model number	Identifies the model number of the CI

Table 13.1 – A sample hardware CI record

The preceding table could be expanded to identify specific attributes for a specific class and type of CI.

Software CI records

A policy for **software CI records** should be documented. The following table describes an example of the attributes of a software CI:

CI attributes	Description
Unique identifier	This is an identifier that is applied automatically by the technology used to manage the CIs
Name/description	The name the CI is known by and a description of the CI
Install date	Identifies when the CI was installed and available for production use
Status	Identifies the current state of the CI such as testing, deployed, production, retiring, disposed
Historical data (e.g., an audit trail)	Provides an audit trail of all changes applied to this CI including who made the change, when it was performed, and state
Location	Where the CI is currently located
CI owner	Identifies the individual or group that owns and is responsible for the CI
Version	The version identifier for the software CI
Release	The release that this software is a part of
Relationships	Identifies what other CIs this CI is related to. The CI could be related to one or more CIs, but every CI must have at least one relationship with another one

Table 13.2 – A sample software CI record

In this table, all attributes are relevant to all software CI types, so a general policy could define the attributes for all software CIs.

In many instances, your technology will dictate what is required and optional for the attributes in a CI record, but a policy should be documented to reflect the expectations and create and maintain them.

These are some of the key policies that should be developed, documented, and communicated to all appropriate stakeholders to ensure that they understand their responsibilities and realize the expectations when creating an asset entry.

Process terms and definitions

There are key terms related to configuration management; the definitions are as follows:

- **Configuration management system**: This is the logical entity containing the CMDBs and other information sources to manage data and information about the operational environments.

- **CMDB**: This is the repository where CIs and their attributes are recorded and maintained. An organization may have one or more CMDBs containing CIs.

- **CI**: A CI is defined as a service component that must be managed to deliver an IT service. CIs are under the control of change management.

- **CI record**: A CI record is defined as a set of attributes about a CI. See the examples of CI records in the preceding section.

- **Class**: A class is defined as the highest level that a set or collection of similar items can be grouped together, such as hardware or software.

- **Type**: A type is defined as a subset of a class. It is the common name that an asset may be known as, such as a computer, printer, or server.

- **Attribute**: An attribute is defined as the characteristic or information about something, such as a hardware or software asset.

Let's now check the process inputs and outputs.

Process inputs and outputs

Configuration management inputs and outputs are created when a new, modified, or retired CI is identified. The following list identifies many of the inputs and outputs for configuration management, but it doesn't include all of them:

- A service request to move, add, or change a CI

- **Request for change (RFC)** documents the actions involved to move, add, or change a CI

- Updates to RFCs

- Audit reports

- Feedback from other processes

Configuration management outputs:

- Completed updates from RFCs

- New or updated CI information

- Visual representations of the structure of CIs

- Audit findings

- Information provided to other processes

- Management information

Process activities

Configuration management activities involve maintaining a record of all CIs in use and their relationship information. These activities will identify the CIs used in the provision of IT services to business customers/users, manage the life cycle of the CIs, and ensure that when their useful life has expired, they will be removed from the CMDB.

Identification

Identification involves identifying all components required to deliver and support services. It also includes the identification of the relationships between components and the services these components enable. The components and services are CIs, and the relationships reflect how the CIs are organized to deliver the services. The identification of the services and the business processes supported by the services will also be considered CIs because the relationship between services and business processes is important to manage the provision of a service. Another aspect of this activity is the identification of the CI configurations. This involves documenting how a server is configured or a software component is set up as part of the attributes of the CI. This activity will capture the attribute information for each CI and the relationships between the various CIs. *Figure 13.1* shows an example of an IT service hierarchy. The IT service is a CI that contains child CIs. This hierarchy describes the various component CIs required to support the IT service being delivered.

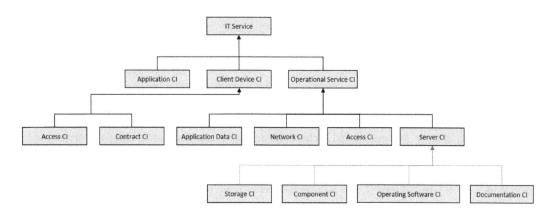

Figure 13.1 – An example hierarchy of configuration items for an IT service

Once the CI and its relationships have been recorded, any changes will be applied as part of a service request or request for change.

Control

Control involves managing the CIs throughout their life cycle. Without appropriate controls in place, CIs will quickly become out of date and will no longer reflect what the actual environment represents. All CIs must fall under change management control. Change management will document the changes that are made to CIs in the production environment, and configuration management will apply the changes to the CIs. No CI should be added, deleted, or modified without evidence of an RFC or service request. Control will ensure that all software versioning and hardware components will always match what is used in the production environment. It will ensure that the information that other processes rely on (i.e., incident management, change management, and problem management) will always have reliable information to use when performing their tasks. For example, incident management will use information from configuration management to identify what service and components may be impacted during a disruption in service. It may also provide information about the business process impacted and what customers/users are affected by the outage. It allows the service desk to communicate to the appropriate stakeholders about the outage. Control must be appropriately applied so that other service management processes can rely on the information. Part of the control activity is keeping track of the various states a CI will occupy through its life cycle. The next activity will keep track of the various states of a CI.

Status accounting

Status accounting ensures that the various states of a CI are always maintained and managed throughout the life cycle. This activity is responsible to define the states of a CI and update the state as the CI progresses through its life cycle. For example, a software CI may progress through various states in its lifecycle, including development, tested, released, deployed, production, and ultimately retired, and status accounting will ensure that each transition from one state to the next is properly recorded. Proper recording of state changes should include the date and time the state change occurred and who was responsible for it. The CI record will maintain an audit trail of the state changes for reporting purposes. Status accounting will provide reporting data on status changes for other processes and periodic audits. All CIs will have status accounting performed, and these states will be controlled through change management.

Verification

Verification is the activity that reviews the CI records and validates that the records match what is actually in the IT environments. Verification will be performed on a periodic basis to validate that the contents of the CMDBs match the current environments. Typically, this would happen on a monthly basis for most CIs in the CMDB. The verification activity validates that the changes that occurred during a specified period are reflected in the CMDB. This verification demonstrates that change management functions appropriately and that no changes to CIs were made without the appropriate documented RFCs. Verification is also the precursor to an official audit. Audits can be conducted internally or externally. An internal audit is typically performed before an external audit is scheduled. This allows an organization to resolve any potential audit findings by an external auditor before the audit occurs. These audits are performed to verify that the organization is managing its resources appropriately. Audits provide evidence that the organization follows its policies and procedures and that the records maintained are accurate. A typical audit of the CMDB will select a group of CIs and review the records to validate that the state changes are accurate, that there is an audit trail for the changes that have been made, and that there is a change record showing the state changes that were applied. The verification activity ensures that the organization performs its due diligence in maintaining accurate information about its environment.

Now that you have an understanding of the activities in the configuration management process, we will explore the variety of roles and responsibilities expected of participants in this process.

Roles and responsibilities

There are key roles for configuration management, including process owner, process manager, and process practitioner. As we discussed in *Chapter 5*, there are common responsibilities for every process owner and process manager. There are some key responsibilities that the configuration management roles need to consider. The configuration management process owner is accountable for ensuring the process meets the needs of the business. The role must be the sponsor for the process, provide design guidance, and ensure changes to the process are managed and improvements are identified and implemented appropriately. The process owner will ensure accurate documentation is maintained on the process and define how the process will be measured for compliance and performance.

The configuration management process manager is responsible for ensuring that the resources assigned to the process are properly prepared to execute the process efficiently and effectively. This role is responsible for the operational management of the process. To ensure that the practitioners have the necessary tools and resources to be efficient. The configuration management process manager is responsible for ensuring that metrics are captured and reported to the appropriate stakeholders. The process manager is responsible for monitoring the execution of the process and identifying opportunities to improve. The configuration management process manager is responsible for identifying a configuration owner for all CIs recorded within their responsibility. Periodically, the process manager will audit CIs to validate the accuracy of the records, compliance with the policies, and key process indicators to determine the overall performance of the process execution.

The configuration management process practitioner roles include the following.

The CMDB data architect is responsible to evaluate the configuration management systems for efficiency and effectiveness. This role proposes and agrees on standards, practices, and procedures for configuration management. The CMDB data architect proposes and agrees on the interfaces with other ITSM processes. They provide architectural direction for the design of the CMDBs. This role is also responsible for creating the CMDB libraries.

The CMBD application architect is responsible for identifying and maintaining the CMDB tools. This role will provide integration to other ITSM tools and data stores. It will also ensure compliance with ITSM standards and practices.

The CMDB librarian is responsible for implementing and enforcing the scheme for configuration management. They will create the CMDBs. This role is responsible for updating and maintaining CIs and providing CI information to other ITSM processes. The CMDB librarian will create and maintain baselines at the request of other ITSM processes – that is, release and deployment management or change management.

The CI owner is responsible for validating that all CI information is accurately recorded in the CMDB. The CI owner is responsible for all communication with various stakeholders about a CI. The CI owner will represent the CI in internal and external audits. The CI owner will be aware of any updates made to the CI and ensure that the updates are appropriate and accurate.

Key process indicators

Configuration management process has a number of key process indicators. These key process indicators should cover the progress of implementing a process across the service provider organization, compliance with the process policies, the effectiveness of producing the process deliverables, and the efficiency of the execution. A balanced set of metrics will ensure that the process is measured appropriately and the key areas are covered. Some examples of key process indicators are as follows:

- The number and percentage of IT services with comprehensive relationships documented
- The number and percentage of hardware devices recorded in the CMDB
- The number and percentage of software applications recorded in the CMDB
- The number and percentage of databases recorded in the CMDB
- Faster resolution of incidents
- More efficient and effective change impact assessment
- The number and percentage of CIs without a relationship (also known as orphan CIs)

It is important for the organization to focus on a few key metrics based on where you are in the maturity of your process. It is recommended that one or two metrics per focus area is sufficient to provide guidance on performance and where improvements can be considered. It is also important to monitor the behavior that is exhibited as a result of the metrics so that you can identify unintended behavior and make adjustments as appropriate. At some point in your process life cycle, it will be appropriate to set targets for key process indicators, but be careful to ensure that the targets are achievable and realistic so that they do not hinder progress. Likewise, monitor behavior to make sure that the targets drive the right behavior. It is always good to keep in mind that what gets measured gets managed and what you measure is what will be produced.

Process integration

For each process in the best practice frameworks, you will have both primary and secondary relationships and interactions with other processes. Since every process has a relationship with every other process (this is especially true of configuration management), this section will only cover the primary relationships to key processes. Each process is described in the following list, along with the key interactions that configuration management has with it:

- **Service asset management** is tightly integrated with configuration management in that many of the assets recorded in an asset management database will also be CIs in the CMDB. Service asset management and configuration management have to work together to ensure any redundant information between these two repositories is limited and that there is a valid business reason for any replication. These two processes depend on each other to ensure valid data and information is maintained consistently across both repositories.

- **Change management** has a key relationship with configuration management because all changes to CIs are made through the change management process. The changes that are made are documented via a request for a change, and configuration management actually implements the change, documenting what was done and that it was done. Configuration management provides the necessary information to change management about the impact of potential changes to related CIs and configurations. This is key for change management, since all changes must be assessed before being authorized to proceed.

- **Release and deployment management** depends on configuration management to capture baselines between the various stages of a release. Configuration management will create a baseline before release and deployment management moves from test to production if an issue arises, so there will always be a safe source baseline to fall back to. Configuration management also provides release and deployment management with information about the CIs that will be impacted by the release.

- **Incident management** relies on configuration management for a view of the CIs that might be impacted by the disruption in service and, potentially, where to look for a failing component. Incident management uses the information provided to accelerate the diagnosis and resolution of an incident and service restoration. This can provide tremendous value to a business by improving availability and reducing downtime.

- **Problem management** uses configuration management information to assist in the diagnosis of a root cause and to help in identifying failing components. Configuration management can provide information about similar CIs that could also fail, allowing problem management to proactively deal with potential failures before they disrupt services.

- **IT service continuity management** uses configuration management information to identify potential components that could be reallocated to facilitate recovery during a disaster event. The CMDB information can also be used to identify areas of vulnerability and potential resources to recover.

- **Availability management** uses configuration management data to identify single points of failure and, potentially, how to resolve them, improving the overall availability and reliability of services.

The process relationships described here reflect some of the key interactions with configuration management. As previously stated, there are other secondary interactions that are not listed here, but they should be considered when establishing configuration management or making improvements to it and other processes. In the following section, you will see information about some technology requirements based on current products available to support configuration management.

Technology requirements

Technologies have improved the support of ITSM best practices consistently over the last 20–30 years. It has especially matured the support of many processes, including configuration management. The following list shows many of the key requirements for the configuration management process. You may have additional requirements, but the following list is a sample of what should be expected of any service management tool. The most important thing to remember about selecting any technology is that it will not make a poor process better, and it is important to realize how the tool will be used and to select the one that will be most effective for your needs.

Configuration management requirements include the following:

- The ability to integrate multiple data repositories
- The ability to support multiple CI types
- The ability to support multiple relationship types – that is, hierarchical or networked
- The ability to maintain multiple relationships for each CI
- The ability to support various attributes by CI type
- Providing mechanisms to report on CIs, query the CMDBs, and present dashboard views
- The ability to automatically validate required data by CI type
- The ability to automatically update state changes as a CI matures
- Providing multiple means of updating CIs
- Providing discovery and population mechanisms

As stated earlier, it is very important to understand how you intend to use the technology, then define the requirements for the technology, evaluate the current technology to determine what the deficiencies are, identify your options for a provider, and pick the one that satisfies the most requirements in your list. When defining your requirements, you should consider using the **MoSCoW approach**. The MoSCoW approach suggests classifying your requirements based on the *Must-Have, Should-Have, Could-Have,* or *Would-Like-to-Have* criteria. This allows you to prioritize the requirements and make sure that the Must Haves and Should Haves are generally covered by the tool you choose. You should also be careful when defining your requirements; a list that contains mostly Must-Haves will typically limit your choices to one or none.

Summary

In this chapter, we explored the key elements of the configuration management process, including the purpose and objectives, policies, process terms and definitions, inputs and outputs, activities, roles and responsibilities, key process indicators, process integrations, and technology requirements. You were provided with significant details about the process, which should enable you to get started with implementing the process or making improvements to your existing process.

In the next chapter, you will continue to learn about **service management processes** with **business relationship management**. Business relationship management focuses on the customer and what is important to them, how they determine value, what outcomes they want to achieve, and what services you provide that satisfy those outcomes and deliver value. This process will capture key information from the customer to assist in the alignment of IT services to the customer's needs. Business relationship management builds and maintains a positive relationship between the customer and the service provider. This process allows the service provider to understand what is important, why it is important, and how to satisfy the needs of the business. You will learn more about what business relationship management can do in your organization in the next chapter.

14
Business Relationship Management

In this chapter, the reader will be introduced to the **business relationship management** (**BRM**) capability specifically, and in the context of a formal **service management** program. This includes the concept, governance (purpose, objectives, and policies), execution (the roles and responsibilities, activities, and metrics), and enablement (accelerating, integrating, and supporting technology) of the capability.

In this chapter, the following main topics are covered:

- BRM concept
- BRM purpose and objectives
- BRM policies
- Key BRM concepts, terms, and definitions
- BRM inputs and outputs
- Basic BRM activities
- BRM roles and responsibilities
- BRM key capability indicators
- BRM integrations with other capabilities, processes, and practices
- BRM technology considerations

BRM concept

Throughout this book, the words *process*, *practice*, and *capability* have been used, and largely interchangeably. A commonality across all three is the presence of **activities**—things that have to be done with a consistent approach and, in many cases, in a particular sequence. The same is true for BRM. When speaking of BRM, consider it from two perspectives: as a role and as a capability.

With respect to a role, a person could be assigned to carry out related activities, whereas a capability, for instance, has more to do with how an organization uses the concept to further an organization's strategy. It is not unusual to see BRM represented as a department (capability) with a number of BRMs (roles) assigned to different parts of the business. This chapter provides a fundamental understanding of the subject. As the many BRM pundits would support, there is an entire body of knowledge and associated publications, amounting to hundreds of pages, on this subject.

BRM purpose and objectives

In terms of a formal service management capability, the real intent of BRM is to manage the **life cycle** of the relationship with its business partners and, ultimately, to be considered a critical stakeholder in any **business unit** (**BU**). For example, do the other parts of the company consider the IT **service provider** (**SP**) to be a critical relationship to how they run their part of the business day to day? Life cycle, in this case, means establishing, maintaining, and improving relationships. Consider that most companies cannot conduct their business without the help of IT, making IT and the IT SP a critical aspect of business operations. Having the role and capability of BRM in place, and accepted, positions IT as a (critical) partner within the overall company.

It is generally accepted that the IT SP desires to be considered as a partner with the other parts of the business it provides services or products for. For many, though, this is much easier said than done. Service management plays a critical role here. The IT SP will likely not be considered a partner with other key areas of the business without first proving its ability to consistently provide the products and services it is chartered to do. In essence, an IT SP's ability to sell the concept of BRM to its business partners will likely suffer without having established a formal service management capability. This largely explains why, for many years, the phrase *IT and the business* has been used as if the IT SP were not part of the same overall organization.

The earlier use of the word *activities* is directly related to the concept of a partner, where the implication is that at least two sides are engaged together in an activity. This requires a level of trust that must be in place in order to effectively complete the activity. Why would a business partner want to *partner* with the IT SP to explore additional ways of working together if IT hasn't proven it can consistently and successfully provide value in the products and services delivered—the very essence of formal service management?

The objectives for BRM include understanding the following:

- Key business partner stakeholders, including the decision makers and decision influencers, and what they value
- Which products and services from the IT SP are most directly connected to business partner stakeholder value, and the current state of provisioning—from both the business partner and IT perspectives

- Overall business strategy and objectives

- Key business partner stakeholder needs and requirements, current and future

- The stakeholder ecosystem, including the internal and external stakeholders involved in the provision of IT products and services

- Emerging technologies that might help further the achievement of value for key business partner stakeholders

BRM policies

Appropriate governance is a key aspect of success for any initiative or practice and applies significantly to a formal service management capability. **Governance** is inclusive of management, measurement, and assurance, as there has to be some way of knowing where we are on the journey, whatever that journey is. In the case of BRM, the importance of related policies as a means of providing direction and control, is as critical to the success as having a formal service management practice in place, as mentioned earlier. For instance, it is long known that accountability without authority limits the chance for long-term success. Given that the BRM role is intended to operate at a strategic (preferred) and tactical level, how and where should a BRM be positioned on an organization chart? Policies should be in place to speak to that. Policies are considered to be rules of engagement, describing boundaries being applied to the process to ensure appropriate controls are in place, ensuring consistency and repeatability but also identifying the level of flexibility in place. For instance, under what conditions would a BRM say *no* to a key business partner stakeholder on behalf of the IT SP? By the same token, under what conditions would a BRM say *yes* to a key business partner stakeholder? The following list lays out key policies that ought to be in place in order to support the BRM role and capability:

- BRM should be sponsored at a high leadership level within the organization as appropriate. This includes the *C-level*, whether the IT SP or otherwise (BRM can be sponsored at an organizational change level or so-called *business side*). For the purposes of this book/chapter, the BRM is part of the IT SP.

- The BRM role operates within an established BRM capability, with all BRMs reporting to a single executive accountable for the BRM capability.

- The BRM role is a key participant in **service portfolio management** (**SPM**), participating alongside both key business partners and SP stakeholders in the management of strategic and/ or tactical demand, acting as a formal channel for **demand capture**.

- The BRM role will work with key business partner stakeholders on **idea documents**, associated business cases, and funding models for strategic and tactical requests. Idea documents are directly related to the term *ideation*, where someone believes an enhancement or innovation will provide value to the organization.

- BRM-related staff will conduct and review assessments that speak to the state of BRM from the view of key business partner stakeholders. This includes the use of targeted assessments, surveys, scheduled interviews, and focus groups. The intention is to understand how well the IT SP is meeting the expectations of its consumers.

Key BRM concepts, terms, and definitions

Along with the many concepts, terms, and definitions already shared throughout this book, there are other key terms related to BRM, including the following definitions:

- **Agreement**: An agreement is defined as a documented set of expectations between the customer and the SP. It should document the agreed-upon performance and responsibilities of the parties involved in the use of the product or service. Part of the role of the BRM is to be part of the negotiation of expectations associated with products and services. Although a BRM is not accountable for the development and publishing of a **service-level agreement** (**SLA**) (as discussed in *Chapter 15*), the BRM is consulted and informed along the journey of its development and production, from negotiation through to sign-off. Policy may dictate the BRM provides the sign-off on behalf of the IT SP.

- **Business partner**: The business partner is representative of the primary audience for the BRM role. Referred to throughout this chapter as a key business partner stakeholder, this is an entity the BRM strikes an alliance with, from the point of establishing a relationship with them, through to maintaining and improving this over time.

- **Demand**: Demand is defined as the incoming request for the use of IT SP time and resources toward the delivery of customer value or outcomes. At a BRM level, this demand would be typically categorized as strategic or tactical. Think of the simple economic concept of supply and demand, where demand is generated by key business partner stakeholders and countered with the time and resources (supply) to meet that demand. The BRM plays a key role in **demand management**. The BRM role should always have a perspective on the incoming demand from the part of the business they are most closely associated with.

- **Value**: Value represents the perspective of the key business partner stakeholder and is expressed as strategic, financial, economic, operational, or technical (also referred to as how the consumer perceives the importance, benefit, or worth of something). As a BRM, the role demands that the specific view of the customer is considered and represented in the product or service from the IT SP.

- **Outcome**: An outcome is defined as the results produced by using a product or service. The question to be answered is *What is intended to be achieved?* As a BRM, and from a key business partner stakeholder perspective, it ought to be very clear what part of the business the specific product or service supports; this is oftentimes referred to as the **business outcome**.

BRM inputs and outputs

Given the general description of BRM so far, along with the policies shared, a window is provided into the required inputs needed to be effective. These inputs enable the performance of the activities conducted and discussed in the very next section of this chapter. Anyone in the role of BRM must recognize the importance of having access to the following artifacts and resources, as they are ingredients for a successful BRM capability:

- **Business strategy**: Artifacts related to the business strategy speak to what the organization says it values going forward, at least for the current and next fiscal year, allowing the BRM to assess the IT SP capability to enable and support the business (for example, the corresponding IT strategic plan). Understanding what is valued is a key aspect here, as the BRM role has to understand and be able to parse the information and develop and manage respective plans to help develop, maintain, and improve the related products and services to ensure value is realized.

- **Customer and IT service portfolio information, including the latest demand-related requests**: Access to this information will help the BRM understand the linkage between the two areas, but also the related assets, needed resources, current initiatives, associated funding, prioritization, and risks involved in realizing the value from the respective portfolios. The respective view afforded to the BRM is perhaps the most critical in understanding whether the relationship between the product or service provided is in line with the associated revenue and value being realized and in line with expectations.

- **SLAs**: As previously stated in this chapter, in the *Key BRM concepts, terms, and definitions* section, the BRM ought to be a key resource, exhibiting a consultative role in the development and production of SLAs, specifically as part of negotiating and assurance that the expectations of both the customer and provider are fairly represented. SLAs also position the BRM to then assess the level of performance against those expectations.

- **Emerging technology related to business partner objectives**: Improvements, innovations, and disruptors represent a key aspect of the performance of a BRM. It tells the key business partner stakeholders that their IT SP seeks to find more effective and efficient approaches that go beyond the current state of how business is conducted, whether or not there are current concerns. It also speaks to the potential for the BRM role to lead the discussion around business strategy going forward. BRM is largely concerned with being respected as a strategic partner within the organization, beyond being just an SP.

- **Complaints, compliments, and escalations**: This information, though likely operational in nature, provides some insight into the quality of the current relationship between the SP and key business partner stakeholders. The BRM could then use this information to formulate an approach on how best to move forward.

Though inputs are critical, the value of BRM is in what is created, and acknowledged, on the back end, as that is where value is realized for all involved. As stated earlier in this chapter, in the *Key BRM concepts, terms, and definitions* section, value ought to be presented to stakeholders based on what that stakeholder values, which can be subject to change over time. Value realization is what will sustain and market the IT SP's BRM capability and the BRM role. Consider the following outputs:

- **A clear understanding of the perception of BRM**: Resulting in information, achieved through assessments, surveys, and interviews, that speaks to the current status of the relationships and the next steps. A related factor is the ability of the BRM role to improve or mature its own capability.

- **A clear understanding between the business portfolio and supporting IT portfolio**: Allowing a synchronization between where the SP is dedicating resources and what the key business partner stakeholder expects. There is the implication that there should be a proper level of negotiation of what value will be realized and when it is projected to occur, along with how it will be achieved and what the target measures providing evidence are. These target measures are often expressed as **objectives and key results (OKRs)** and **key performance indicators (KPIs)**.

- **Prioritized synchronization between business requirements and what constitutes value**: Related to portfolio management, and the concept of parsing different value types of services (for example, what is *must have*, *like to have*, and beyond). In essence, this relates to how the spend is allocated, while understanding the level of risk involved. Synchronization implies that both the customer groups and the IT SP are in agreement on approach and prioritization. It represents a team effort, where both sides are moving forward as a partnership.

- **Business case development**: As far as the BRM area goes, if a business case for an initiative is being produced (or given the go-ahead), the implication is that the assigned BRM and business partner have worked closely together and considered the viability to seek approval for the initiative. More specifically, they collaborated on the risks, viability, and potential value that could be realized. This entire scenario speaks to the quality of the relationship, serving as an indicator of the value of BRM.

Basic BRM activities

The word *activities* was mentioned from the very outset of this chapter. Activities are simply time-consuming things that are done. In the context of formal service management, BRM has the overarching activity to perform all those tasks that, together, provide a bi-directional conduit between the SP and its business customers. This goes well beyond being just a *supplier* of services. The following diagram represents a basic interpretation of the BRM role, which acts as the intermediary between provided services and the specific services utilized by a particular business partner, each with its own unique business processes:

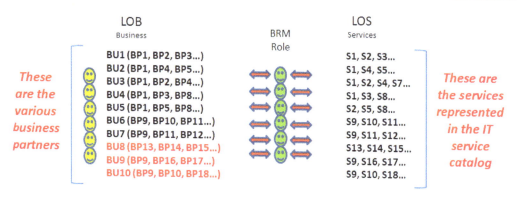

Figure 14.1 – Interpretation of the BRM role

Note that all of the services would be reflected in a **service catalog**. Also, note that some business partners are reflected in black while others are in red. This is intended to represent that the IT SP provides services not only to the business partners that generate revenue for the company but also to those other SPs that service the same audience as the IT SP (oft referred to as **shared services**)—for example, human resources, finance, facilities, and so on. **LOB** represents **line of business**, while **LOS** represents **line of service**. The point is that the services are required to help generate desired results for consumers of the service.

The following also represent key activities of BRM:

- Establishing a relationship

- Managing the life cycle of the relationship

- Reviewing performance

- Transitioning from an SP

Establishing a relationship

The beginning of the relationship life cycle involves an initiating action with the target customer (key business partner stakeholder), where the primary aim is to establish the intent for engaging an interaction going forward. Remember, as part of the policy, BRM is sponsored at the executive level, and the BRM role is intended to be in place, with BRMs assigned across the varying BUs. The assigned BRM should have the skills and competencies required to perform the BRM role, requiring not only formal education but also the necessary mentoring and coaching. This is especially true for the resource that is new to the role. Note the previously described inputs, including overall business knowledge, provider knowledge, and the various artifacts. These are key aspects of the role, as they are helpful in building initial trust with the target customer. The more the assigned BRM role knows about the target customer and their respective part of the company, the better chance for success in building the relationship long term. The groundwork needs to have been laid with the target customer, where they have been informed of the BRM capability of the SP, as well as the potential resource fulfilling the role of BRM assigned to them. As discussed earlier as part of the *BRM purpose and objectives* section of this chapter, the IT SP needs to have built some level of credibility in providing the expected level of service to present the best chance for getting BRM in place. It will be difficult to garner success initially if the SP's reputation is less than effective. Some organizations have realized that a poor service management reputation is a barrier to success for BRM.

Managing the life cycle of the relationship

Initial and continual assessment of the BRM capability and BRM role is critical. A number of questions need to be answered (assessed) here, as follows:

- What is the SP's capability to meet the needs of the customer?
- What is the maturity level of the BRM capability?
- What is the maturity (competency) level of each BRM role?
- What is the business partner's appetite for the IT SP capability?

Though each of these questions is related, there are also specific tools and approaches available to determine the level and performance of each. Continual assessment keeps attention on the long-term viability of BRM at the organization. Assessments are also valuable in their relationship with the measurement and assurance aspects of governance. It is important to remember the objective of establishing and increasing the value of the IT SP, with BRM perhaps the biggest driver in making that happen. The goal of the IT SP is to go well beyond just being a supplier of products and services to the rest of the organization. It is far better to be considered a partner than a supplier.

The life-cycle approach further implies that the BRM is involved in the following aspects:

- Strategy development (business and IT), where the BRM role has input to both, given their knowledge of the business partner's area as well as the capabilities of the IT SP
- Product and service planning, and associated design and development, where the BRM role understands the requirements and watches and informs on progressions and status along the way
- Release and deployment, and testing and assurance, where the BRM role watches and informs on results and readiness toward realization of the requirements
- Product/service delivery and operations, where the BRM role watches and informs on the realization of the requirements and expectations of both the business partner and the IT SP
- Continual improvement, where the BRM role, in its knowledge of business strategy and emerging technologies, identifies opportunities to improve, innovate, or even progressively disrupt the current state of executing products/services

Reviewing performance

If value is not visible, it follows that value is in question! In terms of BRM capability and the BRM role, remember that the BRM largely represents the IT SP for the rest of the business and, therefore, has to have knowledge of overall performance (of the IT SP). Also remember that, technically, the BRM capability is part of the IT SP. In reviewing performance, we are seeking to understand how well the IT SP is positioning the business to meet its strategic objectives. Formal service management represents an integration across all practices, processes, and capabilities. BRM is highly dependent on the activities of **service catalog management** (**SCM**; previous chapter) and **service level management** (**SLM**; next chapter) to assist with performance review. SCM makes it clear which products and services the IT SP provides, while SLM makes clear the agreed expectations for those products and services, articulated through SLAs.

The BRM role should participate in continual reviews (some level of frequency, annually at least) called out in a formal SLA; these formal reviews are scheduled and include other IT SP stakeholders, such as product owners and service owners. The business partner, with whom the BRM role has a direct relationship, is also part of these continual reviews and, in some cases, might be represented by the BRM. Remember that the BRM role has a bi-directional aspect to it (as depicted in *Figure 14.1*). As part of these reviews, the desired result is to understand the state of the relationship and how the IT SP is performing. There should be a published agenda, and there should be published minutes (circulated accordingly) that speak to actions taken and decisions made. The BRM is expected to understand which IT SP resource is deemed to take ownership of any agreed further actions and decisions. This approach drives further understanding that the BRM is involved, but not necessarily accountable or responsible for executing the action.

Transitioning from an SP

In the event it becomes necessary to move away from an existing IT SP, the BRM role should be highly involved in the transition. It starts with the business partner providing a notification of intent to discontinue the use of the IT SP, for which there could be multiple reasons (for example, no further need for the capability, replacement of the provider, poor performance, and so on). The most important consideration is for the BRM to be sure of and trap critical knowledge and information, understand the extent of activities underway, and have significant involvement in managing the transition of the customer to the new provider.

To this point, it has been illustrated that the BRM capability is intended to be strategic in nature, though there are tactical aspects, and there could be some operational considerations. We have seen the importance of the SP performing at a level of consistency with products and services offered, as a prerequisite for the BRM capability to be introduced and sustained within an organization. SLM, discussed in the next chapter, is a key capability that works closely with BRM. It makes sense to now specifically look at the role of the BRM.

BRM roles and responsibilities

At the beginning of this chapter, in the *BRM policies* section, we stated that *accountability without authority does not work*. Now that the high-level activities of BRM have been spoken to, the natural follow-on is to understand which roles are involved in the performance of those activities. Remember that the BRM role is intended to have a high level of authority, actually having the ability to say yes or no to a business partner, while representing the IT SP. Also, remember that BRM is a capability and BRM is a role, where there would be the overarching capability in governing how BRM is approached at the organization, and then within that, having multiple resources in the role of a BRM. It makes sense to mention the concept of **RACI** here, as it is a tool that is designed to break out who is **Responsible** for an activity, versus **Accountable** for an activity, versus who is **Consulted** in an activity, and, lastly, who is **Informed** on an activity. Though not providing a RACI chart here for BRM, the following is a line of thinking of how the BRM roles and responsibilities are spoken to, specifically as it relates to the BRM capability and the BRM role:

- **BRM capability**: For the purposes of this book and, specifically, this chapter, this role represents the senior executive resource that is accountable for the success of BRM within an organization. Ideally, this executive fully understands BRM, including the ability to coach and mentor resources assigned to the role of BRM. It could also be very likely that this resource once operated as a BRM, bringing background and experience. It is important that this role is knowledgeable of all of the input artifacts previously discussed, especially as many of them tend to evolve over time (for example, business strategy, IT strategy, and so on). With this being defined as an executive role within the organization, it follows that there would be collaboration and integration with the executive team, regularly participating in activities at that level. This role is also critical to selling the value of BRM to the organization.

- **BRM role**: The key responsibility of a BRM is to operate at a strategic and tactical level with their assigned key business partner stakeholder. This includes establishing, managing, and improving the relationship, representing a life-cycle approach to relationship management. Since this role is largely about people interacting, it is not enough to just understand the inputs needed for the role (as discussed earlier). Having skills and competencies around culture is also key (organizational change management). In fact, as part of the evolution for bringing BRM into the organization, it could actually be initiated (and reported to) a change management initiative, and later moved under the IT SP. Performing this role well also means that there are likely no surprises—from either the business partner side or the IT SP side.

Remember the importance of integration within and across process capabilities in a formal service management capability. So, within the BRM capability, there is integration between the policies, activities, and roles. All facets are intended to be connected. This is also the very essence of **systems thinking**, the subject of *Chapter 4*.

BRM key capability indicators

Targets largely represent a goal to be achieved, while **indicators** help the audience understand how much of a target has been achieved. For instance, a performance target for a restaurant might be that all meals are served to customers within 30 minutes of placing their order (representing the goal). The indicator (also known as a KPI), computed based on the actual data (metrics), might say that 80% of the meals ordered were delivered within 30 minutes (meaning the target goal was not accomplished). From a high-level perspective, BRM has generic targets, sometimes referred to as OKRs or **critical success factors** (**CSFs**), that speak to how well the BRM capability or role is performing. These data points become validation points on whether a preferred level of maintaining BRM performance is being achieved or identifying opportunities for improvement or innovation. Whether tracking as OKRs or CSFs, there should be a direct connection to the policies and objectives of the BRM capability. It is always important to understand, with supportive data, how well the IT SP is meeting the needs of the business, and if not, why not. CSFs for BRM include the following:

- **OKR**: Collaboration and trust between the business partner and BRM role:

  - **Related KPI**: Percentage increase/decrease in customer satisfaction scores and business partner feedback

  - **Related KPI**: Percentage increase/decrease in communications between the business partner and BRM

- **OKR**: Ability to identify variation in demand from the business partner's objectives potentially impacting requirements and expectations of IT SP products and services:

  - **Related KPI**: The percentage reduction/increase in changes affecting the business partner environment without prior knowledge or agreement (note: this represents a business partner view)

- **OKR**: Ability to identify changes in the business partner environment that could potentially impact IT products/services provided:

  - **Related KPI**: The percentage increase/decrease in the need to perform urgent changes to IT products/services (**note**: this represents an IT service provider view)

Any organization needs to focus on a few key metrics based on where you are in the maturity of BRM. It is recommended that one or two metrics per focus area is sufficient to provide guidance on performance and where improvement or innovation can be considered. At some point in the BRM life cycle, it will be appropriate to set targets for key indicators, but be careful to ensure that the targets are **SMART (specific, measurable, achievable, realistic, and timely)** so that they do not retard progress. Likewise, monitor the behavior to make sure the targets are driving the right behavior. Remember—it is always good to keep in mind that what gets measured gets managed, and what is measured is what will be produced.

BRM integration with other capabilities, processes, and practices

As previously stated in the chapter and throughout this book, for any specific capability (for example, SCM, SLM, BRM, and so on) as part of a formal service management capability, there are both primary and secondary relationships and interactions. This section will only cover the primary relationships and integrations with other key areas with the BRM capability. Ahead, each is described in its key interactions with BRM:

- **Demand management**: Demand management, along with portfolio management, identifies potential service packaging opportunities and ensures that the service packaging is properly described in the service catalog and represents the evolving needs of business partners. BRM plays a significant role in demand management, especially as it relates to specific business partner needs, for which there is an assigned BRM. Demand management is also strongly aligned with capacity management (not specifically covered in this publication), in that there are trends identified in the use of any service over the course of its lifetime. For instance, during normal customer business cycles (time of day, time of week, time of month, and time of year), the use of the service is consumed differently. These are known as **patterns of business activity (PBAs)**. It is important for the BRM role to understand these patterns.

- **Portfolio and resource management**: Portfolio and resource management is strategic in nature. With BRM as an intentional channel to capture strategic demand, it assists this capability in its role of planning and forecasting the use of resources (for example, assets, funding, and decisioning) to deliver value and business outcomes. SPM has a key role in defining what a service is and will work with SCM to establish what information will be contained in the service catalog, the various views of the information, and who will have access to it.

- **SLM**: SLM will be involved with BRM to ensure that the product or service is meeting the operational objectives of the service. SLM will measure and report on the actual results that have been achieved for the services in the service catalog. SLM works with BRM to proactively document the agreed levels of service that will be provided to business partners, then also participate downstream in continual reviews of the performance of the services.

- **SCM**: SCM ensures that the services in the service catalog are what customers need and deliver value. BRM works with SCM to ensure that the services defined reflect the needs of the business and support the business from a strategic and tactical perspective. BRM assists SCM in documenting services in business terms so that customers have a better understanding of which IT products and services help generate the business processes and business outcomes they seek.

- **Request management**: Request management can serve as an audit trail and channel for incoming requests from business partners. Some of these requests could be for non-standard services or even brand-new product or service offerings. It is another avenue for the BRM to become aware of incoming business partner needs.

The preceding list is not an exhaustive one. As previously stated, there are other secondary interactions that are not listed here but are also something that should be considered when standing up BRM.

BRM technology considerations

BRM is far more about relationships than it is about technology. That said, it is the other capabilities and their respective use of technology that support the BRM capability and BRM role. For example, and as previously discussed in this chapter, the need for the BRM to have access to the service catalog and the BRM roles to have access to business partner-specific SLA is paramount to a BRM role's ability to carry out its responsibilities. Both the IT service catalog and SLA performance metrics likely reside on technologies managed by those other capabilities.

BRM does conduct, as earlier discussed, assessments to better understand the various aspects of the capability. Many of these assessments are conducted through the use of templates used as part of interviews and scoring aspects. These templates are more technology-specific to the BRM arena. Tools or technology used for this purpose tend to be simpler in nature.

Customer relationship management (CRM) platforms can be useful, as they can serve as an audit trail for customer interaction, communications, and related data. The CRM platform could also be used to trap recordings (with business partner permission), chat capability, email, agreements, or even BRM notes related to the customer. There can also be an integration between the CRM platform and the service management platform.

Summary

In this chapter, BRM was introduced as both a role and a capability, with success grounded in the established reputation of the IT SP. An SP that has established a formal service management capability represents the best chance for success with BRM, as it creates a willingness of the key business partner stakeholders to explore a broader relationship. Also discussed was the life-cycle approach with BRM, including the aspects of establishing, maintaining, and improving relationships over time.

In the next chapter, SLM is discussed. There is a strong relationship between BRM, the service catalog, and SLM. BRM represents the products and services in the catalog to those key business partner stakeholders at a strategic and tactical level. In fact, BRM is a key influence on this catalog overall, as BRM should always know the value perspective on service catalog entries, whether it is an emerging service (to meet new demand), an existing service (serving current demand), or being retired (subsided demand). Remember that the BRM can only be successful over the life cycle of the relationship if the IT SP consistently performs product and service delivery, which is a primary aspect of SLM. Remember that none of these processes, practices, or capabilities are intended to be standalone. Success is grounded in the ability to have integration across them.

15
Service Level Management

In this chapter, you will be introduced to **service level management**, both by itself and as part of formal **service management**. This includes the capability's governance (purpose, objectives, and policies), execution (roles, responsibilities, activities, and metrics), and enablement (acceleration, integration, and supporting technology).

You learned about the role business relationship management plays in managing the relationship between the service provider and the customer at a strategic and tactical level. Service level management gives you an understanding of the operational relationship between a service provider and their customers and users. **Service level management**, or **SLM**, establishes the operational conditions under which a service provider will deliver a service to a customer and how that commitment will be measured and reported.

In this chapter, we are going to cover the following main topics:

- Purpose and objectives
- Policies
- Process terms and definitions
- Process input and output
- Process activities
- Roles and responsibilities
- Key process indicators
- Process integrations
- Technology requirements

Purpose and objectives

SLM is the process responsible for maintaining an operational relationship between a service provider and their customers and other stakeholders. It is the process that focuses on the service provider's ability to deliver services based on agreed commitments documented in **service level agreements (SLAs)** and supported by **operational level agreements (OLAs)** and **supplier contracts**.

The purpose of the SLM process is to maintain and improve the quality of an IT service through defining, agreeing, documenting, and reviewing the levels of the service. IT services are defined in business terms that are easily understood by the customer. Agreements are made with IT service providers and customers to specify the service level, scope, and quality of service to be provided. Where appropriate, agreements are made to improve the service provided based on changing business conditions and to use as a basis for improving the relationship between the IT service and its customers.

The objectives of SLM include the following:

- Reducing the gap between customer expectations and service delivery

- Defining IT services in association with business relationship management in business terms and placing them in a **service catalog** for customer access

- Documenting the components of services within the service catalog by utilizing OLAs and supplier contracts

- Creating accurate and measurable SLAs and agreeing with customers

- Creating and maintaining reports and metrics on service achievement and using the data to align IT services with customers' business goals

- Ensuring that ownership for each IT service is defined and documented

- Communicating, setting, and managing customer/stakeholder expectations on service delivery

- Delivering commitments documented in SLAs, OLAs, and supplier contracts

Policies

Policies represent the governance applied to the SLM process. A policy describes the rules and boundaries applied to the process to ensure that the appropriate controls are in place. This ensures consistency and repeatability but also identifies the level of flexibility a practitioner has when executing the process, procedure, or work instruction. Policies will be discussed in more detail with examples later in this chapter.

Service levels

Service levels are policies that describe the different levels of service that will be offered in your organization. These service offerings represent differing levels of service that a customer can agree to pay for and receive. Service levels to consider could be mission-critical, high availability, or standard.

There are a number of examples of differing service levels in common services used by different people and organizations. For example, a car dealership may offer a premium level of service for an additional cost, such as offering transportation, bumping you to the top of the queue, or washing and waxing your vehicle. Cell phone providers have long offered additional benefits if you are willing to pay a higher price for the service, such as higher data limits, unlimited international travel, and others. SLAs are an internal document between the service provider and their internal customers, so it is important to establish the levels of service that you will provide because every service has a cost related to it, and the cost should be commensurate with the benefit or value produced for the organization and the impact if that service is disrupted during service hours. Service levels recognize the importance of a service to the business and ensure appropriate resources are allocated to deliver and support it.

SLAs and OLAs

Service level agreement and operational level agreement policies establish the governance for these key artifacts (SLAs, OLAs). SLAs and OLAs are written agreements that document the commitments that a service provider is making either to their customers or as a supporting document to enable the service. SLAs document the conditions under which service will be delivered to the internal customer. OLAs underpin SLAs and describe the commitments being made by the internal component providers. The internal component providers document what they are capable of delivering to support the service level commitments. This enables SLAs to document what is possible and to communicate with the customer what will be delivered based on what the customer is willing to pay or what the organization is willing to fund. These two types of agreements, along with supplier contracts, establish the level of service that can be offered to the customer. A diagram showing a sample of the relationships between SLAs, OLAs, and supplier contracts is shown in *Figure 15.1*:

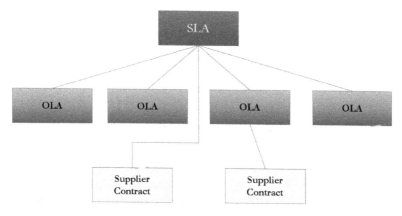

Figure 15.1 – Service Agreements Cascade

A sample SLA is provided in *Appendix A*.

Service level reporting

A **service level reporting** policy describes the expectations for communicating service level results to customers and service provider leadership. In this policy, you describe the frequency of providing service level reports on SLA and OLA performance to management, customers, and other stakeholders as appropriate. The policy should describe the type of reporting that will be provided and the metrics for key performance factors, such as availability, security, and performance. The reporting should identify disruptions in customer-facing services and their duration, impact, and remediation. It should also provide information on any improvement activities being considered or undertaken to reduce or eliminate disruption.

Service level requirements

The **service level requirements (SLR)** document defines the business customer's requirements for the service solution being offered or developed by the service provider. The business relationship manager works with the service level manager to communicate the business outcomes and benefits the customer expects to realize. The service level manager will then work with the customer to document the service level requirements and then engage with the various component providers and suppliers to determine how the service level requirements will be met by existing or new services. A sample of an SLR document is provided in *Appendix B*.

The preceding policies are some of the key policies that should be developed, documented, and communicated to all appropriate stakeholders to ensure that they understand their responsibilities and realize what is expected when creating a service entry.

Process terms and definitions

There are key terms related to SLM:

- **Service level agreement (SLA)**: An SLA is defined as an agreement between the customer and the service provider within the same organization. The agreement will document the service, how it is measured, what the customer and service provider are responsible for, and the business processes that are fulfilled.

- **Operational level agreement (OLA)**: An OLA is defined as an agreement with a component provider within the service provider organization that describes the performance and availability capabilities that could be offered for a service. It describes the commitments made by component providers to support the SLA targets.

- **Underpinning contract**: An underpinning contract is defined as a contract between the internal service provider and their external suppliers. The underpinning contract should align with and support OLA and SLA targets. Also described in this chapter as the supplier contract.

- **Service level requirements (SLRs)**: The SLRs are the requirements the business customer needs the service to fulfill.

Process input and output

SLM input and output are created when an agreement or underpinning contract is added, changed, or removed. The following list identifies most, but not all, of the inputs for SLM:

- Service requests for new or changed SLA

- Updates to OLAs or underpinning contracts

- SLRs

- Information from the service catalog and service portfolio

- Information from other processes

- Financial information

Here are some examples of SLM outputs:

- Updated or new SLAs, OLAs, or underpinning contracts

- Updates to SLRs

- Updates to the service catalog and service portfolio

- Information provided to other processes

- The following are examples of management information:

  - Service performance reporting

  - Availability dashboard

  - Incidents logged and resolved for the service

Process activities

SLM activities involve capturing information about the needs of the business and creating, maintaining, and managing the documents related to delivering and supporting IT services. SLM maintains an operational relationship with the business customer and monitors, measures, and reports on the delivery and support of IT services to meet business needs and deliver business value. The activities defined here will capture the information necessary to meet business needs and ensure that the service provider is meeting those needs as efficiently and effectively as possible. The activities for SLM include the following:

- Planning

- Defining requirements

- Negotiating

- Agreeing

- Monitoring

- Reviewing and reporting

- Improving

Figure 15.2 shows the high-level process flow for SLM:

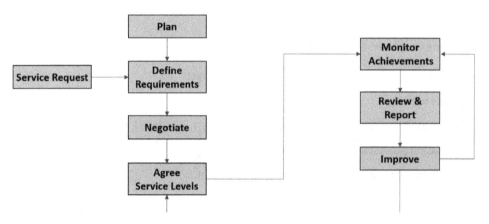

Figure 15.2 – The SLM process flow

As the flow in the preceding chart indicates, the planning activity happens infrequently based on updates to the approach for performing SLM. Some of these activities occur on a periodic basis when a new service or a change to an existing service is requested as in defining the requirements, negotiating, and agreeing, while monitoring, reviewing and reporting, and improving take place in an ongoing fashion. Each of the activities will be further described presently.

Planning

Planning refers to developing the approach your organization will apply when establishing services and the mechanisms and tools that will be used to develop your agreements. In this activity, the templates that will be used for the SLAs and OLAs will be documented. The reporting structure and frequency options will be established. Policies related to the process activities will be worked out with the process owner. Information requirements to enable the development of the SLAs and OLAs will be developed and agreed upon. The planning step enables the organization to ensure a consistent and repeatable approach to creating the key artifacts for this process. Planning typically occurs when standing up the SLM process but will be repeated when an opportunity to improve the process is identified so that the impact of the improvement can be assessed and appropriate updates to the process can be implemented. Once a clear approach to SLM has been determined, the operational execution of the process will begin.

Defining the requirements

Defining the requirements is the activity initiated when the customer, BRM, or SLM requests a new service or updates to an existing service. In this step, the service level manager will begin by identifying the requirements needed to fulfill the customer's business outcomes. Once the requirements are known, documented, and agreed upon between the customer and the service provider, the service level manager will review the requirements to determine whether the requirements can be satisfied by existing services contained in the service catalog. It may be that an existing service can be modified to meet the requirements or a new service needs to be created. If the requirements can be satisfied by an existing service, the service level manager will verify whether the current service provider resources are adequate to handle the increased demand for the target service. If changes are required to the existing service, the service level manager will work with the service provider to determine what additional resources may be required to satisfy the changes identified. If it is a new service, then the service level manager will work with the service provider to determine what resources will be needed and whether those resources will be added to the environment or if there is sufficient current capability to address the new service requirements.

An example of defining requirements might be a restaurant experience. As the diner, you would review the menu and determine what you want to eat. You would share that information with the server. Once there is clarity about the service requirements and demand, the service level manager moves to the next step in the process.

Negotiating

The negotiating step involves presenting the service to the customer and appropriate stakeholders and documenting what options there are and any costs associated with those options. In this step, the service level manager, business relationship manager, and the customer will review the agreed requirements and the proposed service solution to fulfill the requirements. In negotiations, the BRM, SLM, and customer determine what the best option is based on the cost/price the customer is comfortable with. This is where the customer will be presented with potential options for availability, performance, continuity, response and resolution times, and security.

In this step, the service level manager will document the capabilities of the service provider, the expectations for the customer, and their users for the service. There may be multiple iterations of this step as the service provider and customer work to come to a mutually beneficial understanding. Continuing with the restaurant example, you might negotiate with the server about potential special needs, such as gluten-free bread or the temperature of the steak you are ordering. When the customer and the service provider have come to an understanding of what the service will provide, the next step consummates the relationship.

Agreeing

In the agreement step, the customer and the service provider representative (the service level manager or management signatory) will sign the SLA agreement. There should be agreement on the OLAs aligned to the SLA prior to signing the SLA. Any underpinning contracts will have been signed and aligned with the OLA or SLA that they support. Copies of the agreements and contracts are provided to the various stakeholders, including the customer, business relationship manager, service level manager, component groups, and suppliers. Continuing with the restaurant example, now that you and the server have completed the negotiation of your requirements, you and the server agree, which results in the server carrying your request back to the kitchen where the chef and their helpers will prepare your meal and deliver it to your table. Once the agreements and underpinning contracts are in place, the service is available for the customer's users to start using the service.

Monitoring

At this point, the monitoring step begins. This step involves monitoring the various components and services to ensure that the commitments and targets established in the SLA, OLA, and underpinning contracts are being met. Monitoring includes capturing the appropriate metrics defined in the agreements and contracts, identifying disruptions in service, documenting the disruptions in incident management, identifying areas where improvements can be made, and identifying errors that should be corrected. In the restaurant example, the server might come by periodically to make sure your dining experience is satisfactory. The server might keep your drinks filled, ask you whether the steak is prepared appropriately, and ask whether there are any other issues with the food that was delivered. If anything is wrong, the server will take appropriate corrective action to resolve the issue, and if necessary, bring a manager in to help with the resolution. Periodically, the results of monitoring are used in the next step to communicate with the customer and other stakeholders.

Reviewing and reporting

The reviewing and reporting step is where the service level manager will provide information to the customer about how effective the service provider was in delivering the service. The reports that will be delivered to the customer and the frequency will have been documented in the SLA. Typically, monthly service level reports will be delivered to the customer showing the results of meeting the agreed targets defined in the SLAs. The report will provide information about how well the availability and performance targets were met, whether there were any incidents logged, and how effective the recovery of the service was. The report will document the resolution times, whether the targets were breached, and the potential business impact of those breaches. If penalties are involved, the report will define what the consequences of the penalties will be. If incentives were fulfilled, this will be included in the report as well. In this step, a sitdown with the customer will occur quarterly, semi-annually, or annually (at a minimum) to review the SLA and service provider performance. During these reviews, the service level manager, business relationship manager, and the customer will review the results fulfilled by the service. They will assess the effectiveness of the service in meeting the needs of the customer, seek any opportunities to improve, identify any updates to the SLA capability, and take action to eliminate service disruption. This is an opportunity for the service provider to validate that the service is still meeting the customer's needs and check what updates/improvements need to be considered.

At this point in our restaurant example, the server is stopping by at the end of the meal to inquire about the diner's satisfaction with the meal experience. Was the service satisfactory? Was the meal gratifying? Were there any issues that need to be addressed? This is the diner's last opportunity to express their pleasure or displeasure with the dining experience. If the diner had a poor experience, they may be offered the meal for free or at a reduced cost. If the experience was a positive one, the diner might agree to post a positive review on Yelp.

Improving

After the review and report step, the final activity in this process is to improve. Gathering feedback from the customer and various stakeholders, the service provider will identify improvement opportunities and determine which of those has the most value and benefit for the customer. As part of the review, the service level manager and business relationship manager gather intelligence from the customer about where they might find significant improvements. The service provider will assess these improvement opportunities, determine what the cost/benefit is, and develop a business case for making the improvements. Once the business case is made and the improvements are identified, the service provider will create a plan to implement the improvements.

In the restaurant example, the restaurant manager may review incident reports to determine whether there is a difference between what customers think is a rare steak and what the chef thinks is rare. The restaurant manager may choose to update the menu to describe what a rare steak is so there is less chance of dissatisfaction with the temperature of the steak.

Now that you have an understanding of the activities in the SLM process, you will get some exposure to the variety of roles and responsibilities expected of participants in this process.

Roles and responsibilities

There are key roles for SLM, including the process owner, process manager, and process practitioner. As was discussed in *Chapter 5*, there are common responsibilities for every process owner and process manager. The SLM process owner is accountable for ensuring the process meets the needs of the business. The role must be the sponsor for the process, providing design guidance, ensuring changes to the process are managed, and identifying and implementing any improvements implemented appropriately. The process owner will ensure accurate documentation is maintained on the process and define how the process will be measured for compliance and performance.

The SLM process manager is responsible for ensuring that the resources assigned to the process are properly prepared to execute the process efficiently and effectively. This role is responsible for the operational management of the process to ensure that the practitioners have the necessary tools and resources to be efficient. The SLM process manager is responsible for ensuring metrics are captured and reported to the appropriate stakeholders. The process manager is responsible for monitoring the execution of the process and identifying opportunities to improve. The SLM process manager will be responsible for identifying a service owner for all services within their responsibility. Periodically, the process manager will audit services, validate the accuracy of the records, look over compliance with the policies, and observe key process indicators to determine the overall performance of the process execution.

The SLA manager is responsible for the following:

- Providing input to the service level manager and other process managers for ongoing process improvements, including metrics and policies, that reflect best practices, technology improvements, and lessons learned

- Understanding the customer's business and how IT contributes to the delivery of their product or service

- Understanding key performance indicators and business impact related to an IT service

- Translating business requirements into IT capabilities that satisfy business requirements

- Establishing OLAs for IT infrastructure and applications that support SLAs

- Having a full understanding of the IT service provider's capabilities

- Recommending process improvements

- Working with IT service providers to develop **service improvement plans (SIPs)** to improve SLA performance

- Managing SLA commitments and achievement

- Negotiating, agreeing, and maintaining SLAs

- Reporting on SLA compliance metrics:

  - Identifying reported incidents that impact the SLA

  - Completing SLA metrics reporting

  - Maintaining OLA-SLA relationships

  - Analyzing and reviewing service performance against the SLAs and OLAs

  - Reporting service achievements to the customer, service owner, and BRM

- Conducting a formal SLA review at least annually with the service owner and customer (or as defined in the SLA)

- Participating on the change advisory board where SLA impact may occur

The OLA analyst is responsible for the following:

- Determining OLA targets

- Maintaining the OLA

- Ensuring compliance with OLA standards

- Providing feedback and improvement opportunities to the SLM manager

- Reviewing underpinning contracts with external suppliers and OLAs to ensure alignment

- Communicating any service gaps to the SLM manager

- Identifying and documenting key OLA metrics

- Reporting metrics to the SLM manager

The OLA owner is responsible for the following:

- Owning one or more components within the service provider and being held accountable for them

- Assigning OLA analysts to the component provider group

- Reviewing OLAs to ensure that key support, performance, and availability metrics are included

- Assigning responsibility for the collection and distribution of key metrics to appropriate service level managers and service owners

- Progressing OLA development activities to agreed targets

- Having a clear understanding of component capabilities to effectively communicate gaps and related costs to achieve identified SLRs

The IT service owner owns one or more IT services and is accountable for those services.

This section covered the roles and responsibilities suggested for the SLM process. Many of the roles, as in other processes, could be filled by one person in a small organization or multiple people in larger organizations.

Key process indicators

SLM processes have a number of key process indicators. These key process indicators should cover the progress of implementing the process across the service provider organization, compliance with the process policies, effectiveness of producing the process deliverables, and the efficiency of the execution. A balanced set of metrics will ensure that the process is being measured appropriately and the key areas are covered. Here are some examples of key process indicators:

- The number and percentage of IT services covered by an SLA

- The number and percentage of SLAs supported by OLAs

- The number and percentage of SLAs within agreed targets

- The number of scheduled SLA reviews performed with the customer

- Time from SLR agreement to SLA signing

- The number and percentage of OLAs within agreed targets

It is important for your organization to focus on a few key metrics based on where you are in the maturity of your process. It is recommended that one or two metrics per focus area is sufficient to provide guidance on performance and where improvement can be considered. It is also important to monitor the behavior being exhibited as a result of the metrics so that you can identify unintended behavior and make adjustments as appropriate. At some point in your process life cycle, it will be appropriate to set targets for key process indicators, but be careful to ensure that the targets are achievable and realistic so that they do not slow progress. Likewise, monitor the behavior to make sure the targets are driving the right behavior. It is always good to keep in mind that what gets measured gets managed and what you measure is what will be produced.

Process integration

For each process in the best practice frameworks, you will have both primary and secondary relationships and interactions with other processes. Since every process has a relationship with every other process, this section will only cover the primary relationships to key processes. Each process will be described ahead with the key interactions that SLM has with it.

Financial management

Financial management provides financial information to the service level manager so the cost of service can be identified and appropriate pricing is established. If an organization chooses to charge for its services, financial management will provide the billing for the service(s), and the SLM manager will deliver the bill to the customer. This is intentional because the SLM manager maintains the relationship with the customer and can explain any questions related to the bill.

Availability management

Availability management provides availability options for the various components that make up a service. This information is used by the SLM manager to document the different levels of availability that could be offered as part of a service. Availability management will also monitor and report on the actual availability achieved for the services provided to customers. The SLM manager will use the information to produce periodic reports for the customer showing what was achieved against the targets that were agreed in the SLA.

Incident management

Incident management is the best source of information about the business impact a customer may have experienced during the agreed uptime for the service. The SLM manager can use the incident information to identify the business impacts of an outage and validate the availability of the service against availability management reporting. There are instances where an outage may not impact the business availability of the service so incident data can be very valuable for reporting purposes. An example of an incident not impacting the customer could be when an individual server in a cluster fails. While it is still an incident, the service is still available to the customer. The SLM manager will also use incident information to identify potential areas for improvement.

Capacity management

Capacity management provides performance options for the infrastructure and application components of SLM. SLM uses this information to define options for a service and to negotiate with the customer the most desirable option based on the business need or willingness to pay. Capacity management monitors the components and provides performance data used for service level reporting.

Information security management

Information security management provides information to SLM on security requirements for users. This is used by SLM to document the security requirements for users and to set expectations with the customer on potential impacts if these conditions are not met.

IT service continuity management

IT service continuity management provides information to SLM on **recovery time objectives** (**RTOs**) and **recovery point objectives** (**RPOs**) that will appear in the SLA. This information is significant in the development of an SLA and enables the service level manager to set expectations for the level of service delivered during a significant disruption in service, also known as a disaster situation.

Business relationship management

Business relationship management (**BRM**) maintains the strategic relationship with the customer and must work with the SLM manager to ensure an understanding of current services being delivered to the customer and potential new services or changes to existing services resulting from changes in the customer's strategic plans. The BRM manager participates in the service review meetings to assist the customer in understanding what is being presented and to answer any questions about the service. BRM can assist SLM in translating business requirements into SLRs. BRM and SLM must maintain a tight relationship to ensure a single voice is delivered to the customer.

The process relationships described previously reflect some of the key interactions with SLM. As previously stated, there are secondary interactions that are not listed here but are also something that should be considered when standing up SLM or making improvements to it and other processes. In the next section, you will see information about some technology requirements based on current products available to support SLM.

Technology requirements

Technology has improved the support of ITSM best practices consistently over the last 20 to 30 years. It has especially matured the support of many processes including SLM. The following list shows many of the key requirements for the SLM process. You may have additional requirements, but the list is a sample of what should be expected of any service management tool. The most important things to remember about selecting any technology is that it will not make a poor process better and that you need to select the one that will be most effective for your needs.

SLM requirements include the following:

- The capability to store SLAs, OLAs, and underpinning contracts
- Being able to associate SLAs to business groups so that impact can be determined if a service is performing to below-agreed-upon levels
- Being able to maintain historical data and information on services such as SLA/OLA results produced for each service
- Being able to organize services into logical groupings or hierarchical structures used to build services in business-relevant packages or offerings

- Being able to document severity definitions for SLAs

- Being able to report on SLA results achieved versus SLA targets

- Being able to identify alerts/notifications when service delivery is approaching and/or exceeding an SLA target

As stated earlier, it is very important to understand how you intend to use the technology, define the requirements for the technology, evaluate the current technology to determine what the deficiencies are, then identify your options for a provider and pick the one that satisfies the most requirements in your list. When defining your requirements, you should consider using the MoSCoW approach. The **MoSCoW approach** suggests classifying your requirements based on the *Must-Have*, *Should-Have*, *Could-Have*, or *Would-Like-to-Have* criteria. This allows you to prioritize the requirements and make sure that the Must-Haves and Should-Haves are generally covered by the tool you choose. You should also be careful when defining your requirements; a list that contains mostly Must-Haves will typically limit your choices to one or none.

Summary

In this chapter, you were exposed to the key elements of the SLM process including purpose and objectives, policies, process terms and definitions, input and output, activities, roles and responsibilities, key process indicators, process integrations, and technology requirements. You were provided with significant details about the process that should enable you to get started with implementing the process or making improvements to your existing process.

This is the final chapter for discussing processes. In subsequent chapters, you will learn some practical lessons and information that you can use in standing up a service management capability in your organization. The next chapter speaks to using **continual improvement** as a pragmatic approach to starting or sustaining a service management practice.

Part 3:
How to Apply a Pragmatic, Customized Service Management Capability

Part 3 describes many key elements to practically implement a service management capability, customized to an organization's business needs in a sustainable and repeatable approach.

This part has the following chapters:

- *Chapter 16, Pragmatic Application of Service Management*
- *Chapter 17, Implementing a Successful Service Management Capability with Key Artifacts*
- *Chapter 18, Reviewing Critical Success Factors for Service Management Capability*
- *Chapter 19, Realizing CSFs for Service Management Implementation*
- *Chapter 20, Sustaining a Service Management Practice*
- *Appendix A, SLA Template*
- *Appendix B, SLR Template*

16
Pragmatic Application of Service Management

In this chapter, we will explore the nature of **continual improvement**. There are a variety of organizations and individuals that have described what continual improvement is and how to be successful in applying it to large strategic initiatives and incremental operational improvements. This discussion will look at the activities involved in continual improvement with the intent of explaining the reasoning and value of applying this approach to establishing and executing a **service management** initiative. It will help you understand the necessity of following a consistent and repeatable approach to initiating and sustaining a service management program.

In this chapter, we are going to cover the following main topics:

- Delving into the vision, mission, goals, and objectives
- Understanding assessment and desired state
- Exploring planning and execution
- Comprehending measures and reports
- Examining rinse and repeat, or do it again and again...

Delving into the vision, mission, goals, and objectives

In implementing a service management capability, it is important to apply a consistent and effective approach that enables the IT service provider organization to align with the overall business direction. The business' direction is defined and expressed in the vision (what the organization is about and who they are), mission (how the organization acts and deals with its various stakeholders), goals (what the organization is attempting to achieve in this planning cycle), and objectives (the detailed targets to produce). This is useful when you're undertaking any significant or incremental improvement and can be applied whenever clarity is required about where to start and where the effort is going. Let's discuss the incremental steps for executing a continual improvement effort.

Documenting the starting point for continual improvement

The starting point for continual improvement is understanding and documenting the vision, mission, goals, and objectives for the initiative or effort you intend to undertake. This will allow you to determine what it is that you intend to align with to make improvements. It is important to understand what it is that you will be looking at to understand how you can effectively align your efforts with what is important to your business or organization. In the case of this book, it is the initiative to implement or improve a formal service management capability.

The purpose of establishing a vision for the service management effort is to ensure that the activities and improvements that will be achieved are appropriately aligned with what is significant to the business. If there is a lack of understanding regarding the reason the action you're undertaking is important to the business, the overall value of the effort will or may be compromised, resulting in a lack of perceived value.

To determine the vision aligned with the overall business needs, it is important to understand the business continuity plan, business strategy, and IT strategy. The business continuity plan identifies the **vital business functions** (**VBFs**) the organization must support to be successful. A **business impact analysis** identifies the critical components of the business that support business demand. *Figure 16.1* shows some of the key elements involved in determining the vision, mission, goals, and objectives based on the organization's key artifacts:

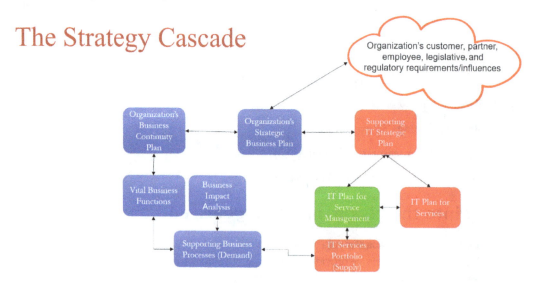

Figure 16.1 – The Strategy Cascade

This cascade applies to any type of organization, whether it be for-profit or non-profit, healthcare, finance, manufacturing, academia, government, or military. Understanding what is important to the business will enable you to understand how the current services are being applied and what you can do to improve the overall value of the services you provide. It is also critical that you align the goals and objectives of the service management initiative with the **IT strategy** to effectively develop an **IT service management strategy**. This cascade from vision to measurements ensures alignment from vision to results. The first activity of continual improvement is determining the vision, mission, goals, and objectives in the cascade. These elements of the strategy for your service management initiative are essential to achieving benefits and value.

Once you understand the vision, mission, goals, and objectives, you will develop **critical success factors (CSFs)** and **key performance indicators (KPIs)** in subsequent activities. Knowing the vision, mission, goals, and objectives prepares you so that you can continue developing your continual improvement plan and deliverables.

Understanding assessment and desired state

Once you understand the vision, mission, goals, and objectives, you must determine the current state of the area you are targeting.

It is important to get a clear understanding of the current state of the service management initiative. Here, you are attempting to determine where the organization is, relative to the defined objectives for the initiative, what in the current state is good, and what potentially needs to be changed to achieve the objectives. These objectives represent the desired state that the organization wants to achieve. Once the current state has been established, you need to document a baseline. This baseline can then be used to demonstrate that progress has been achieved by comparing the results being produced to the baseline current state.

There are a variety of methods for performing a current state assessment. Some of these include the following:

- SWOT analysis
- Benchmarking
- Maturity assessments

Each of these has value and can be used singly or together. Let's look at each of these to see how they could be applied to understand the current state environment.

Strengths, Weaknesses, Opportunities, and Threats (SWOT) analysis is a brainstorming technique that's used to assess an organization's internal and external environments with the desired state in mind. Strengths and weaknesses look at the internal characteristics of the organization's ability to plan and deliver the intended future state. Strengths look at those characteristics within the community or team that support and/or enable the team to achieve the desired state. Weaknesses look at the characteristics within the community or team that will prevent or retard the ability to achieve the desired future state. Opportunities and threats represent those characteristics outside of the organization's planning and delivering the intended future state. Opportunities reflect those characteristics outside of the community or team that can be leveraged to improve or support the achievement of the future state. Threats are those characteristics outside the community or team that will prevent or raise risks so that the desired future state can be achieved.

A facilitator would walk key participants through an exercise to identify the strengths and weaknesses within the group that is charged with delivering the improvements or changes needed to achieve the desired state. Strengths are those areas of the group that should be leveraged and reinforced while weaknesses need to be reduced or mitigated to improve the overall success of the initiative. The facilitator will also walk the key participants through a review of the opportunities and threats outside of the group that could assist in them achieving the desired state or pose risks to achieving the desired state.

Establishing a SWOT analysis can provide you with tremendous information on the current state of the environment, as well as help you identify what will help you achieve the desired state and what could prevent you from achieving it. A simple example of a SWOT analysis result is shown in *Figure 16.2*:

Strengths

- Willingness to put in the time to complete requests/demand/projects
- The ability to communicate effectively with customers and co-workers
- A lot of talent and expertise in a wide range of topics
- Excellent and knowledgeable technicians/resources (smart, big picture thinking, analytical, soft skills)
- Candor
- Enthusiasm for getting started

Weaknesses

- We are not good at rewarding and recognizing individuals
- Talent and skills are being underutilized
- Tools and technology are inadequate or outdated to support the automation capability required
- Lack of understanding about how individual roles contribute to the bigger picture
- Lack of accountability ('The Five Dysfunctions of a Team' by Lencioni)
- Shadow IT

Opportunities

- Promoting our service and resources to the business
- Leveraging external resources for education and SM guidance
- Leveraging technologies
- More effective compliance with legal and regulatory requirements
- Leverage best practices – use and apply best practices to accelerate the implementation of process capability
- More effective communication with external stakeholders

Threats

- Lack of process
- Economy and the impact on budget-related decisions
- Outsourcing
- Competition
- Security – threats from external sources
- New technology

Figure 16.2 – Sample SWOT analysis

Along with the SWOT analysis, a review of the **assumptions** and **risks** should be considered. An assumption is a statement that's presumed to be true without clear evidence to support it. In our experience, assumptions are used in a wide variety of situations to enable organizations to plan and make decisions where there is a degree of uncertainty. Risk is an uncertainty that's related to an event or events that could prevent the organization from achieving its objectives. This provides some context to the SWOT analysis, allowing the organization to understand what assumptions will influence the results of the SWOT and any risks that should be considered and potentially mitigated to improve the overall success of your initiative. *Figure 16.3* shows some examples of assumptions and risks that have been captured during our practice:

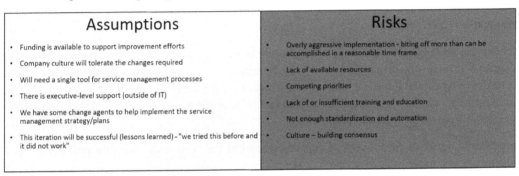

Figure 16.3 — Sample assumptions and risks

Benchmarking is a technique that's used to compare one organization's capabilities with another similar organization or a best practice or standard. Typically performed by a third party, benchmarking can leverage the experience of a consultancy to identify where improvements can be made. Benchmarking can focus on a variety of elements within the organization. Benchmarking can focus on the efficiency of the organization, how cost-effective the service that's being delivered is compared to best-in-class providers, and whether it makes sense for the organization to provide best-in-class or something less. It can focus solely on the processes your organization executes or it can look at processes and technology. The ultimate focus for benchmarking could include processes, technology, and the organization, where all these elements are considered in determining your organization's capabilities. The benchmarking approach helps you determine where your organization is compared to another organization that provides similar services or products and is of a similar size. It can also be used to compare your organization's capabilities with a recognized standard or best practice.

Capability Maturity Model Integration (CMMI) is a technique for establishing the maturity of a process or capability. It can be used to perform benchmarking and allows an organization to establish a maturity for its current state in the form of a numerical value. **Controlled Objectives for Information and Related Technology (COBIT)** is a best practice framework for determining the governance and control of an organization and can be used to assess the maturity of an organization's ability to effectively manage and control its service management capability. Both CMMI and COBIT are owned and managed by **Information Systems Audit and Control Association (ISACA)**, a global association that offers information and guidance on governance, control, risk, security, and audit/assurance. You can read more about them at `www.isaca.org`.

The purpose of an assessment is to help the organization identify where improvements are most beneficial.

First and foremost, it enables your organization to effectively monitor and manage the progress of the improvements. It can allow you to benchmark your capabilities against similar organizations and identify how effective your improvements make your business. Finally, in some instances, applying the assessment can result in a certification of your capability, such as an **International Standards Organization (ISO)** certificate.

It focuses on measuring the maturity of your organization's capability to execute the practices or processes across the organization's service value system. There will be specific criteria that must be met to allow you to establish the level of maturity that the organization has achieved and, potentially, what improvements could be considered in your future state. It is a comprehensive assessment of the organization's service management capabilities.

Once there is clarity about the current state and a baseline has been established, the next activity is to document and finalize the desired future state.

This activity focuses on what it is you want to accomplish in a specified time frame. Typical strategic planning windows are limited to a 12-24-month period. Establishing this limit tends to ensure a reasonable planning window and recognizes the fast pace of change within the organization. Understanding that things can change allows you to establish some improvement opportunities that can be accomplished in short, medium, or longer-term windows while ensuring that quick wins can be identified and delivered to generate enthusiasm and momentum for continuing improvements. It is important to ensure that the desired state is realistic and achievable given the resources available within the time frame described. To set that future desired state, one approach to performing this activity is to engage an objective facilitator so that they can lead the team through a brainstorming session to gather the elements that will make up the desired state view. This exercise could result in the identification of key practices that need attention in the desired state or governance controls that should be implemented to improve efficiency or effectiveness. It can ensure key members of the initiative can be heard and their contributions captured so that the most comprehensive and achievable strategy can be developed. The result of this activity will be a roadmap that can be used to plan the subsequent activities in continual improvement. This roadmap is also a visual that will be used to communicate what the desired future state will be. *Figure 16.4* shows a sample service management roadmap:

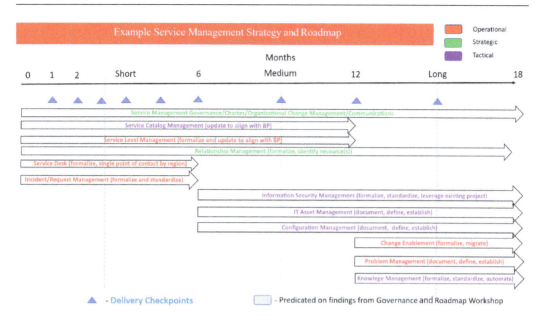

Figure 16.4 — Sample service management roadmap

This example illustrates the activities that need to be considered in establishing the desired future state and shows the checkpoints where progress should be analyzed and reported. It also shows the strategic, tactical, and operational elements covered by the strategy.

Along with setting the realistic desired future state, you will need to establish some clear measurable targets that will provide a guide for the planning necessary to move the organization from the current state to the desired future state. For example, if you are going to implement a formal incident management practice and you are not sure all incidents are being recorded, you might identify the number of incidents currently being recorded as a baseline and set a target to increase the number of incidents by a certain percentage in a 6-month time frame. If you were implementing a formal change enablement practice, you might measure the volume of change types – that is, how many standard, normal, and emergency changes were processed in the previous 6 months. For each practice you decide to include in your roadmap, some form of measurement should be described, measured, and reported on.

The resulting activities and improvements will produce the guidance needed to identify and document what needs to be done to accomplish the targets. Understanding this roadmap enables you to be more effective in the planning activities that follow.

Exploring planning and execution

Once clarity about the current and future states has been defined and documented, it is time to develop the plan.

Your leadership team needs to determine what the organization can invest in to make the necessary improvements to achieve the future state. This will help you determine what improvements to make and the approach to managing those improvements:

- Do we need to establish a multi-generational program to cover the short, medium, and long-term projects that will be initiated to manage the improvements that are being identified?

- Are there existing programs or projects or initiatives that can be leveraged to accelerate some of the benefits the improvements will deliver?

It is appropriate to consider the current state's capabilities when developing the plans for the changes that must be made to achieve the desired future state. SWOT analysis or benchmarking activities will provide significant input in determining what can be leveraged in the current state and what will need to be changed. Taking advantage of the positive things you are doing in the current environment can allow improvement benefits to be achieved faster and without *reinventing the wheel*. It will also reinforce the value of using current capabilities as a starting point for making the improvements needed to achieve a future state.

The overall program should include a diverse set of projects that cover **short-term objectives** (those that will deliver benefit and value in 3-6 months); **medium-term objectives** (those produced in 6-12 months); and **long-term objectives** (those produced in 12 months or more). Although it may sound like this would take a minimum of 3 months to deliver value, applying **Agile methodology** to the service management program will enable your organization to deliver value in 2- or 4-week sprints. You will be able to continually deliver value while maintaining a view of the overall objectives defined in the future state and aligning with the overall vision of the service management program.

At this point, you should have identified multiple projects or activities that you will include in your strategy. These projects should include short, medium, and long-term objectives covering strategic, tactical, and operational needs. It is valuable to have a diverse mix of projects to cover as many service management capabilities as is reasonable given the available resources and funding. This also ensures that quick wins can be delivered to establish value and benefit for the initiative and generate enthusiasm for the effort.

A **critical success factor** will communicate what will be done across the organization and then convey these quick wins and successes when they're achieved to raise awareness about what was accomplished. Included in that message should be what benefit the audience should see from it. As part of the **organizational change management (OCM)** effort, it will be necessary to develop and deliver communications to the various stakeholders about what you intend to do and the value this effort can have for the organization and various stakeholders. This will enable the service management initiative to achieve visibility across the organization and potentially identify where support and resistance may occur. It will allow you to leverage the supporting communities and manage the areas of resistance.

Now that you know what you are going to do, it is time to take action and execute the plan(s).

This is where you will be executing the projects and implementing the improvements that have been identified through the vision, mission, goals, and objectives defined previously. The first step to take here is to charter the program that will contain the projects you will be executing to deliver value. As you work through these projects, producing results, you will be measuring those results, documenting the successes, identifying where the effort may have not produced the results expected, and documenting challenges and opportunities along the way. Again, if an Agile approach is desired, identifying the results produced at the end of each sprint will be important to delivering value in the form of a minimum viable product while still maintaining a clear focus on the objectives defined for your short, medium, and long-term activities.

As action proceeds, course adjustments may be necessary. If something in the vision, mission, goals, or objectives changes, then it is appropriate to revisit any of the previous steps to identify what changed, if there is an impact on the existing planned activities, and what that impact will be. If necessary, it is reasonable to consider stopping a planned activity and starting a project that may be more aligned with the business changes. Likewise, if the metrics are difficult to capture or do not reflect the results expected, then a course adjustment may be required. It will be important to select a set of balanced metrics that can be captured and reflect the actual results being produced. Focus on a limited number of key metrics that can help communicate the benefits and value being delivered by the improvement projects.

Comprehending measures and reports

You are now ready to compare the results produced and the measures captured to the desired state targets defined earlier. Here, you are validating that what you intended to deliver has been delivered and to what degree.

At this point, you must compare the actual results produced to the targets established in the future state definition. Each time an objective is accomplished, communication should be crafted and delivered to the appropriate stakeholders. Reporting should provide evidence indicating how well you did in meeting the targets that were established and what benefits have resulted. Your reporting should also identify what challenges were encountered and how those challenges were overcome. You should also be prepared to identify any roadblocks that occurred and how those were overcome. If there are still issues, identify what those are and who needs to be involved in helping to overcome them or at least mitigate the impact on the service management effort. If you're using an Agile approach, each sprint should include communication with the stakeholders showing how well the minimum viable product has been received, how it is being utilized, and its alignment with the overall goals and objectives of the program.

It is important to recognize the significance of having a clear OCM plan for the reporting aspect of this step. The importance of an effective organizational change plan cannot be overstated when ensuring the overall success of the service management initiative. Every win that's achieved in the program should have a communication related to it and be delivered to the different stakeholder groups. As part of the OCM effort, identifying each stakeholder group, what is important to them, the best approach for communicating with them, and the best resource to deliver the message is critical. It is important to understand who those stakeholder groups are and what is important to them so that your communications can be targeted at the audience and a clear message delivered. You should also consider having a checkpoint for communication periodically throughout the implementation of your roadmap to deliver status updates to the various stakeholder groups. This helps stakeholders see the progress that is being made, what quick wins have been achieved, and how the overall program is proceeding. Each time a project or improvement is completed, a celebration should be considered to reward the participants involved in the effort and bring awareness across the organization to the accomplishments that have been produced.

As you approach the end of the 12-24-month period for this iteration of the service management initiative, you should take stock of how successful you were with this iteration and what should be considered for the next iteration – what you have been executing is continual improvement, so it will soon be time to begin planning for the next set of improvements.

Examining rinse and repeat, or do it again and again...

Now that the service management program iteration is nearing its end of term, what happens next? You should begin planning for the next cycle of improvements.

It is key for any organization starting the formal service management journey to understand it is never over; it is a continual improvement path. As we come to the end of one cycle, we prepare for the next cycle by repeating the activities of continual improvement. Just as Rome was not built in a day, a formal service management capability does not happen in 1 or 2 years. In one instance, the journey continued for 10 years and was still ongoing beyond that. As you have seen in previous chapters, there are several practices in service management. It will take time and resources to gain competency in all these practices. Most organizations implementing a service management capability will be able to do 3-4 practices in a 6-12-month time frame. With that in mind, a long-term view has to be considered when embarking on the service management path.

Once one iteration is nearing completion, it is time to start planning for the next iteration, which requires repeating the continual improvement approach. Here, you will look at what was accomplished in the iteration that was just completed, what was successful, what wasn't successful, what challenges have been identified that you want to consider in the next iteration, and what has changed as a result of the projects that have been completed.

Then, you will review the vision, mission, goals, and objectives to determine if anything has changed and how it might affect the new desired state. You will review the current state to see how it has changed based on what was achieved in the previous iteration and then define the new desired state. Once the new desired state has been documented and targets set, it will be time to plan the next set of improvements and execute them.

Continual improvement is intended to be continual, repeatable, and consistent in its execution. In our experience, this approach is a critical success factor for a service management initiative and has consistently produced excellent results for those organizations that have used it.

Summary

In this chapter, you learned about continual improvement and how this enables an organization to effectively understand what is needed to produce an effective service management capability. We covered analyzing and documenting the vision, mission, goals, and objectives of the organization so that you can align your program with what is important to the business. We then reviewed the current state to understand what is good to keep, what needs to be discarded, and what needs to change. After, we looked at the desired state and defined the differences between the desired and current state to establish what needs to change and what measurable targets will be set. Once we had defined the current and desired state, we identified the projects that would be initiated to achieve the desired state. We then took action to implement the improvements we'd identified. As these improvements progressed and results were produced, we measured those results against the targets to see how effective our results were. After completing the improvements, we maintained momentum by performing continual improvement over and over again.

In the next chapter, *Implementing a Successful Service Management Capability with Key Artifacts*, we will review the key artifacts that are necessary to successfully implement service management practices, including, but not limited to, roles and responsibilities, value streams and processes, organizational change management, metrics and measures, and reporting.

17
Implementing a Successful Service Management Capability with Key Artifacts

In this chapter, we will review key artifacts for a successful implementation of a service management practice. These key elements of a service management capability will enable your organization to be more efficient and effective in managing the organizational capability that is key to becoming a valued service provider. As we discussed in the previous chapter, this chapter reflects the elements of continual improvement of an overall program that increases an organization's potential for success. The artifacts that will be discussed in this chapter include the following:

- Roles and responsibilities
- Value streams and process artifacts
- Organizational change management
- Metrics and measures
- Reporting

Roles and responsibilities

In understanding the implementation of best practices, it is essential to understand the key roles necessary to achieve positive results and the responsibilities and accountabilities for those roles. The following diagram, *Figure 17.1*, identifies some of the key roles needed in establishing a **service management** capability:

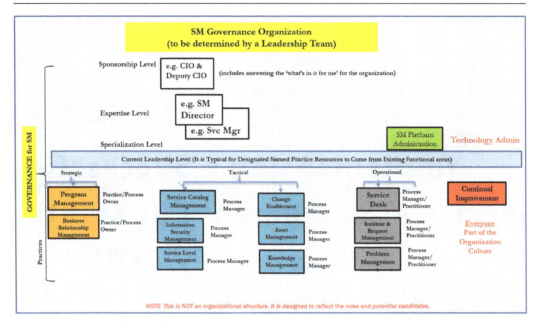

Figure 17.1 – A service management governance organization

First and foremost, this is not intended to be an organizational structure or plan. It is illustrative of the roles necessary to successfully implement a service management capability. It describes the levels of governance involved in implementing and sustaining a service management program. If you remember the foundation information presented in *Chapter 6* through *Chapter 15*, governance is one of the **service value system (SVS)** elements and represents the controls, policies, and rules that will be applied to ensure an effective and efficient application of service management principles. As you can see, *Figure 17.1* shows the **sponsorship level**, **expertise level**, and **specialization level**. The following paragraphs will describe each level in more detail.

At the sponsorship level, a senior leader must be accountable for the guidance and commitment to making the improvements identified in the strategy defined in the **continual improvement approach** exercise that was just completed. The senior leader (perhaps the **chief information officer (CIO)** or a designated senior manager) must have the authority to drive the organization in the direction defined in the strategy and make the changes necessary to achieve the defined objectives. The sponsor must be an example for the organization in practicing the behaviors expected from the organization as they move from their current to future state. They must also be visible and vocal in their commitment to fulfilling the objectives defined in the strategy. The sponsor will be the primary voice for setting expectations within the IT organization, to the customers, and to other stakeholder groups impacted by the change.

An example of this kind of support can be seen in one CIO's continuing communication within the organization, describing service management as *table stakes*, a term used in gambling to describe the amount necessary to even be in the game. This CIO not only shared this perspective with his organization frequently but took advantage of instances where the practices were not being followed to make the point that not following the practices was not acceptable behavior and would not be tolerated. This CIO also helped communicate to a variety of stakeholders the importance of service management as an organizational capability. He built a coalition of sponsorships by engaging the leadership chain in advocating for the service management initiative. Finally, he made it a requirement to include a service management-focused objective in each person's performance targets. This is the sponsor's role, and it is absolutely necessary to achieve success.

At the expertise level, you are identifying the individual (described as the service manager) that will provide guidance on best practices and help define the practices and methods that will be applied to achieve the stated objectives. This individual will typically be a senior leader or architect that understands the best practice, the organization and its culture, the current state of the service management capability, and who has a clear understanding of the future desired state. This role will manage the **service management office (SMO)**, which is the organizational element responsible for the development, deployment, and management of the service management capability. The service manager must have a solid understanding of the practices contained in the service management strategy from a best-practice perspective as well as the current state of capability. This enables the service manager to guide the practice/process owners and practice/process managers in implementing their individual practices and processes.

The service manager must also work with the sponsor to ensure that the **service management program** stays on the right track. This role has the responsibility to raise any challenges, issues, or concerns identified during the program to the sponsor, such as receiving their guidance on how best to address and/or mitigate the impact on the program. The service manager is responsible for the results produced by the service management initiative and is accountable to the sponsor for the objectives being met. This role is a key voice in the **organizational change management (OCM)** effort and will assist in developing and delivering communications concerning the progress of the service management program and reporting the results achieved.

The specialization level is focused on three roles: owner, manager, and practitioner. These roles are responsible and accountable for the individual practices and processes they will be guiding and executing. As you can see in *Figure 17.1*, the strategic focus is primarily on the owner of a practice or process. The manager focuses on the tactical and operational elements of a practice or process. The practitioner is executing the practice or process at an operational level. These roles require considerable focus and attention in the initial definition, development, deployment, and execution of a new or improved practice and process. The typical smaller organization may have one individual fulfilling these roles for one or more practices. In larger organizations, one individual may be fulfilling one of the roles and another individual may fulfill the other roles for a specific practice. It is our experience that these roles should be filled by staff resources that have the time and focus to fulfill the responsibilities instead of a manager or supervisor.

There are a variety of best practices, standards, and methodologies that offer guidance on the accountabilities and responsibilities of these roles. Generally speaking, they are all pretty consistent when describing the activities performed. Although I refer to practices in the following descriptions, these same accountabilities and responsibilities apply to processes within the practices.

This is what the practice/process owner will be accountable or responsible for:

- Defining the process strategy
- Working with various stakeholders to design the process
- Acting as the practice sponsor
- Making sure there is adequate documentation in place
- Ensuring that policies are defined and enforced
- Ensuring changes to the process are appropriately managed
- Performing periodic audits of the practice
- Reviewing the practice strategy as needed to address changing business conditions (at least annually)
- Participating in communicating information and education about the practice
- Working with other process owners
- Making sure that process objectives and outcomes are achieved
- Identifying opportunities to improve the efficiency and effectiveness of the practice

This is what the practice/process manager will be accountable or responsible for:

- Engaging with and assisting in establishing the practice and following the direction provided by the practice owner
- Making sure that all activities of the practice are followed according to defined policies
- Assigning resources to various practitioner roles and managing resources assigned to the practice
- Working with various stakeholders in executing the practice's activities
- Monitoring the performance of the practice
- Providing performance reports to appropriate stakeholders
- Identifying improvement opportunities and implementing improvements as appropriate

This is what the practice/process practitioner will be responsible for:

- Executing one or more practice activities
- Working with stakeholders to ensure effective output

- Ensuring that correct input, output, and interfaces are effectively applied

- Creating data and information about the practice activities performed

- Identifying and sharing improvement opportunities with the practice manager

It is everyone's responsibility in the organization to identify, document, and raise opportunities to improve the practices and processes. The practice managers and practitioners are the most valuable resources for identifying where practices and processes can be improved since these resources are the most closely involved in the day-to-day activities being performed.

Although *Figure 17.1* does not describe an organizational structure, it does describe key roles that must be assigned and responsibilities/accountabilities fulfilled to ensure success in a service management program.

In this section, we described the key responsibilities for many roles involved in developing and executing a service management capability including the management team, leaders, staff, and the specific roles responsible and accountable for the processes being executed. It will be critical for your organization to understand what is expected of all resources in the service provider organization to be successful in delivering and supporting services.

Value streams and process artifacts

Value streams represent the flow of work for a specific type of demand generated by a user or customer. For example, a value stream could start with a request to a restaurant hostess for an appetizer. The request is delivered to the kitchen, and the chef pulls the ingredients needed for the appetizer, prepares the dish, completes the preparation, and notifies the hostess that it is ready. The hostess delivers it to the table, and the customer consumes it. The value results from the customer getting satisfaction from consuming the appetizer. Value streams are a visual representation of what happens from the time a **request** or **transaction** is received until it is fulfilled by the service provider. **Value stream mapping** is an activity performed by the service provider organization to visualize the requests and transactions you support in delivering a product or service to your users and customers. A value stream map reflects the high-level (macro) steps taken to generate a desired output (e.g., value).

These steps can be a subset of a larger value stream. For example, an assembly plant could have multiple assembly lines, with each subsequent assembly line leveraging the output of the previous assembly line as input, while also creating an output from the executed steps within it:

- Any assembly line could be a value stream in and of itself

- A subset of sequential steps in that assembly line could also be considered a value stream (there is an optimal number of steps desired for a value stream – few enough to facilitate an improvement, but not too many that it takes too long to implement that improvement)

A process is a set of related or highly connected activities:

- Associated with a particular value stream step and creating a micro-level view of the activities required to complete the macro-level step

- Without the process-related work, the step in the value stream is not complete

The following illustration, *Figure 17.2*, shows an example of a value stream:

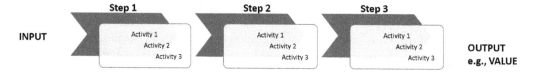

Figure 17.2 – Value streams and processes

This illustrates the value of having both value streams and processes:

- **Value stream maps** show the major activities in a value stream:

  - Macro-level

  - Represent a strategic direction (why and where)

  - Requires leadership involvement

- **Process maps** trace the sequence of activities for a single process:

  - Micro-level

  - Identify tactical improvements (how)

  - Heavy employee involvement

Value stream mapping is very important for understanding the elements involved in performing work and all the interactions that are involved in producing the output that supports a business's outcomes. Value stream mapping can be very beneficial in helping to identify waste in a flow and improving the overall efficiency and effectiveness of the work.

To perform value stream mapping, you will need to gather the appropriate resources from the business, IT, suppliers, and other stakeholders that may have information to share about the work being mapped. There are a variety of techniques that can be applied to capture the knowledge of the participants, such as **brainstorming**. Creating a value stream map conceptually requires just a few simple considerations:

- **Subject matter experts** (**SMEs**) for the value stream identified for improvement (e.g., multi-departmental, product/service, process, etc.). These SMEs are there to brainstorm the current state, then interrogate it for improvement opportunities.

- A blank wall for collaboration (using a roll of butcher paper enables the ability to "roll it up" after the exercise is completed).

- Post-it note pads (allowing flexibility to move/adjust steps and activities).

An illustration of brainstorming is shown in *Figure 17.3*:

Figure 17.3 – A brainstorming exercise

In *Figure 17.3*, you see participants mapping the activities involved in satisfying a business process output. Each person is involved in describing their understanding of what is happening, what the input and output are for their step or activity, what comes before and after it, and who is involved in collecting the input and producing the output. Once all the information is collected, an analysis of the interactions, timeline, lead times, and resources are performed. The idea here is to document the current state and then determine what could be improved or adjusted to make the flow more efficient and effective. Value stream mapping is a technique related to the quality management method called **Lean**. Lean was developed to identify and eliminate waste in a process or system. Value stream mapping is instrumental in helping to identify where waste or delay exists and determining if it can be removed or reduced. It has multiple uses as part of a formal service management capability. Two prevalent areas are the service desk, which deals with incidents, and service requests. These two value streams, though both managed by the service desk, represent different steps to meet the required result (e.g., output):

- The steps associated with managing an incident (largely involving detecting and subsequent actions to resolve)

- The steps associated with fulfilling a request (largely involving detecting and fulfilling)

An example of a value stream map is in *Figure 17.4*. This is a simple picture of a value stream showing the activities being performed for an incident request and a service request:

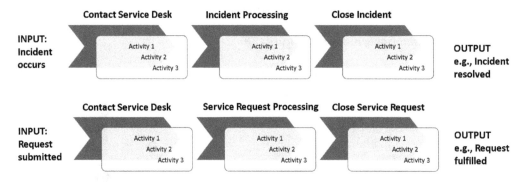

Figure 17.4 – An incident and a request to fulfill a value stream

As indicated in the figure, value stream mapping has a wide variety of uses and can be applied to any workflow that needs to be reviewed and potentially improved.

A value stream as illustrated earlier in *Figure 17.2* may involve multiple processes. A process focuses on the detailed level of work. Processes describe the input, activities, and output for work that must be performed. A process model helps to understand the elements involved in a process, which was illustrated in *Chapter 5*.

Process model

A model shows the key factors involved in creating a process. There are three key areas for consideration in creating a process. These include **process control**, **process** (specifically, its execution), and **process enablers**.

In process control, you define the process owner, the individual accountable and responsible to see that the process is defined and documented according to the business needs and policies. Process objectives are defined here to ensure an understanding of what is expected for this process and how the process will be measured to determine performance. Performance, in this case, includes not only compliance with the policies of the process, but also efficiency and effectiveness in executing the process. In this block, you will establish policies or rules related to the management and execution of the process.

Policies should establish clear rules for governing the process, consequences for non-compliance, elements of the process (e.g., prioritization of changes or impact and urgency for incidents), and how the process will be measured and managed. Process metrics will be defined keeping in mind the level of maturity for the process. The more mature the process, the more sophisticated the metrics can be. For example, initially, you may only be measuring that all incidents are being recorded. However, once this process becomes more mature and stable, you may choose to measure the resolution times for incidents.

All of these elements described here will be included in the process documentation developed and produced to ensure an understanding of the expectations for the process and how it will be executed. Finally, in the process control block, there is a need to ensure that a feedback loop is provided for the users and receivers of the process output so that you can identify any issues, challenges, risks, or opportunities encountered during the execution of the process. This feedback is a key input to identifying waste in the process and improvements that can make the process more efficient and effective.

In the process block, you will define the process activities. Here, you establish the activities that will be performed under various conditions and define the flow of the input and output from one activity to another. Here, you will also define the cascade from value streams to processes to procedures to working instructions, as illustrated in the following figure:

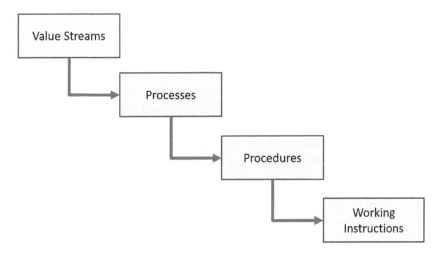

Figure 17.5 – The value streams to working instructions cascade

As stated earlier in this section, processes are defined at a micro-level compared to a value stream. A process provides a high-level definition of the activities that could be executed for any work instance of the process. A **procedure** defines a common instance of a process execution. For example, if you are executing a standard change, you would have a specific procedure for performing that standard change as part of executing the change management process. **Working instructions** describe how to perform the procedure using your technology platform. Working instructions tend to be very specific and are detailed instructions on how to do something. An example of this might be when you log an incident record, the working instruction describes what kind of information is required in the description field, and what parameters can be applied to determine priority based on impact and urgency.

Process roles will vary from one process to another. The roles for each process must be defined and the accountabilities and responsibilities documented in the process block. This ensures that individual practitioners understand what the expectations are for them when executing the process, procedure, or working instruction. It also clearly defines the specific responsibilities of this process for each role defined. Earlier, we spoke about some generic roles for service management, but in this area of the process model, it is specific to a process. Finally, a method for reviewing the results of the process execution and identifying improvement opportunities will come from this process control block. Here, you will describe the timing for the reviews, the approach for the reviews, and where the improvement opportunities will be documented, prioritized, and actioned.

In the process enablers' block, you are looking at the resources and capabilities available to support and enable the execution and performance of the process. Here, you are reviewing the capabilities of the individuals that will be executing the process to ensure they are well-prepared to perform their functions. You will be looking at your technology platforms to determine how effective they are in supporting the execution of the process. Does the technology improve the capability to execute, or are there deficiencies that could hinder the execution? For example, does the technology you are using enable users to quickly and easily initiate a service request? Does that service request ensure that all the appropriate information has been captured and validated before allowing the submission of the request? If not, what must change in the platform to enable users to facilitate the fulfillment of a service request? The more effective your technology is in enabling the processes, the more reliable your results will be, and the happier your users and customers will be.

Having discussed the importance of documenting the value streams and processes, now we will talk about the importance of developing effective communications with all the stakeholders that may be involved in applying the value streams and processes to effectively and efficiently meet the needs of the business and deliver value to all the stakeholders.

Organizational change management

What is **organizational change management** (**OCM**)? OCM is the approach that an organization uses to engage its stakeholders and communicate the changes the organization intends to make. When stakeholders do not understand the changes that are being proposed, they may feel threatened and resist the change. OCM is intended to effectively reduce fear and resistance by providing information and knowledge about the change and the benefits that each stakeholder group will experience. In a nutshell, it is about preparing the various stakeholders of an organization for changes the organization is making to improve or increase its value or capability. For service management, this can be a critical success factor, because the changes implemented as a result of a service management initiative are changing the way people work. This requires changes in people's behavior, and that can be a significant challenge. No matter how bad your current state might be, moving to a future state is going to involve changing something that people are comfortable with, and people will potentially resist the new way of doing things.

How can you effectively manage the human element of change? First off, you must understand who your stakeholders are and what is important to them. This involves stakeholder management. There are a variety of artifacts and techniques that can be applied to identify who the stakeholders are, what impact/influence they could have on the changes intended, and what is important to them. *Figure 17.6* shows one example of the types of elements you might look at to identify what is important to the stakeholders and potentially how they would influence and support or resist the service management effort:

Stakeholders	Strategy	Finance Resources	Relationship	Governance	Security Regulatory
CIO/CLT	●	●		●	
CITO	●	●		●	●
COO	●	●	●	●	
SM Director	●	●	●	●	●
SM Manager	●	●	●	●	●
Service Desk	●		●		
Tier 2/3	●		●		●
Customer/Agency	●	●	●	●	
Agency Staff	●		●		
Process Owner Process Manager Process Practitioner	●	●	●	●	●

Figure 17.6 – The stakeholder interest chart

The stakeholder interest chart intends to develop an understanding of what the various stakeholders value and how the initiative could support the stakeholders' interests. It also helps the program team to develop communications that reinforce the elements of the program that will resonate with the specific stakeholder group. One of the techniques used to identify and determine the significance of a stakeholder group is a **stakeholder power matrix**. An example of a stakeholder power matrix criteria is shown in *Figure 17.7*:

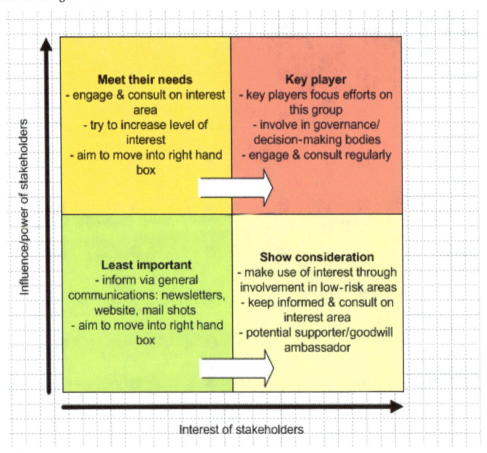

Figure 17.7 – Criteria for stakeholder influence/power

An example of how *Figure 17.7* could be used is shown in *Figure 17.8*, which shows various stakeholders and where they are positioned in the matrix:

Legend:
1. CIO/CLT
2. CITO
3. COO
4. SM Director
5. SM Manager
6. Service Desk
7. Tier 2/3
8. Customer/Agency
9. Agency/Staff
10. Process Roles

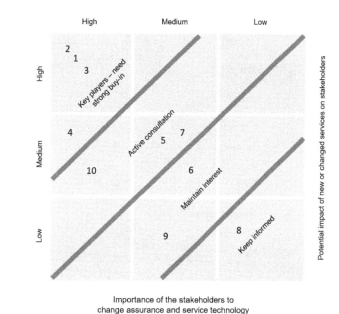

Figure 17.8 – The stakeholder power matrix

Once the stakeholders have been identified and once it is known what is significant about them, it will be important to understand where they are now and where they need to be to achieve the objectives of the program. In order to do this, we must build a stakeholder chart showing the current and future state. *Figure 17.9* is an example of what this chart would look like for the various stakeholders that have been identified. The *O* symbol indicates where the stakeholder is now, and the *X* symbol indicates where the stakeholder needs to be:

Key players	Not committed	No resistance	Helps it happen	Makes it happen
CIO/CLT	O ——————————————————————→			X
CITO				OX
COO				OX
SM Director				OX
SM Manager			OX	
Service Desk			OX	
Tier 2/3			OX	
Customer/Agencies		OX		
Agency/Staff		OX		
Process Roles				OX

Figure 17.9 – Where stakeholders are and where they need to be

Now that there is some understanding of who the stakeholders are, what is important to them, where they are now, and where they need to be, you can begin to develop a communication strategy and plan for how you will manage the stakeholders during the service management program. It will be important to focus the communications to the appropriate audience when communicating with the various stakeholders. In order to do this, the communication plan should identify the key message for each group, how that message should be delivered, how often should you communicate with that group, and who should deliver the message. As with any effort like this, there should be key metrics to identify how effective the communication is in delivering the message. Your metrics should determine if the message being heard is the message you intended to be delivered.

A key element of the communication plan is establishing methods for gathering feedback from the various audiences you deliver your communications to. The feedback loops will help to determine if the message was heard, if the expectations set are being met, and if the actions being requested are being taken by those audiences. In every communication, it should be clear to the audience what you as the communicator expect them to take away from the communication and, if action is expected, that it is being fulfilled. A sample communication plan is shared in *Figure 17.10*. It can be used to develop the necessary talking points, the audience, the delivery method, and the frequency for a service management OCM plan:

Communications Plan
Template

Program/Project: Service
Management Initiative

Target Audience	Objectives	Message	Delivery Method	Frequency	Responsible Resource(s)	Delivery Date(s)	Delivered by	Feedback
C-suite	Inform	Significance of the SM initiative	Face to Face	Quarterly	CIO and Program Lead	2nd Tuesday of each quarter		
IT Management and Staff	Inform/Set Expectations	Provide information about the SM initiative and set expectations on what each stakeholder group within IT is responsible for.	Lunch and learns/email	Monthly	Managers/Supervisors	1st Wednesday of each month		

Figure 17.10 – A template for a stakeholder communication plan

The importance of OCM cannot be understated. Changing the way people work requires communication to help them understand what is in it for them, why the organization needs to change, how will things be better once the changes have been implemented, and what the consequences/risks are if they don't make the changes. These key messages will help people understand what needs to happen and why. It will help them accept the changes and, in many instances, can encourage them to actively participate in the changes as change agents. Without this, people will resist, and people only resist change when they do not understand it.

Metrics and measures

When it comes to the assessment of the success or failure of a service management program, identifying, capturing, and analyzing the metrics and measures is an essential element of the overall program. Each process included in the program will need to be measured to identify how effective it is being executed according to the objectives and policies that were defined as part of the strategy. There are a variety of resources to identify metrics and measures that can be leveraged to determine the performance of a process, service, or resource. As your organization matures, additional or alternate measures may be considered to better align with the business outcomes.

It is important to review your current metrics to assess how effective they are in driving behavior. Remember the old adage: *what gets measured gets managed*. This suggests that measures influence the behavior of practitioners and can potentially drive the wrong behavior. For example, if service desk agents are being measured on the number of incidents closed by them, a savvy agent will attempt to pull the incidents that are quick and easy to resolve so they can increase their numbers. This may leave the more difficult issues for the less experienced agents to deal with, resulting in an increased time to resolve problems and a number of dissatisfied users.

Look at the current metrics as a starting point for deciding what to measure, why you are measuring it, how effective that measure is in producing the desired behavior, and how easy is it to capture the results. It is also important to understand how the measures are demonstrating the overall capability of your organization in producing the desired results. When trying to decide what to measure, collect those that are actionable and provide clear evidence of what is being produced. An example of **incident management** might be measuring the resolution times for critical incidents to determine how effective you are in classifying the incidents correctly and resolving them within the agreed timeframe established. This will provide evidence that the service desk can quickly establish the importance of this incident, classify it correctly so that it is routed to the proper resolution team, and that the resolution is being deployed within the timeframe committed to as part of a **service level agreement** (**SLA**).

Metrics and measures will drive the behavior of those being measured, but they are also instrumental in identifying where improvements can be made and in communicating to various stakeholders how your IT organization is performing. As you identify and document what you will measure, keep in mind that you will need to efficiently communicate how well the organization is doing in meeting its commitments and objectives. This is known as *reporting*.

Reporting

Reporting is the mechanism you use to communicate the level of performance achieved by the service management program in meeting the business needs. As was discussed earlier in this chapter, communication is an essential element of an overall service management strategy, and reporting is one area of that communication.

Reporting includes describing how well the projects included in the service management program are doing in meeting the goals and objectives defined. In this case, you might be communicating the measures produced by the project in meeting the targets that were set for that project. You would be answering the question, *did we meet, exceed, or miss the targets that were set?* This reporting enables the project team to provide evidence to the stakeholders so that the leadership can assess the relative success or failure of the project. The frequency and format for the reporting would be documented as part of the OCM communication plan described earlier.

There will be reporting needed frequently for the results being produced, by the measures being captured on the delivery, and support of the IT services you provide. This reporting establishes how well the IT organization is doing in managing the services you are responsible for and how well you are meeting the commitments made either implicitly or explicitly. For example, if SLAs are in place, you provide a monthly report showing how well you performed in meeting the commitments and targets established by the SLA. As part of a service review, you are sharing information about what incidents occurred, how effectively they were handled, what changes were made to improve the service, whether or not the performance targets were met, and if not, what is being done to ensure they will be met in the future.

Reporting is the culmination of what your IT organization has done to support the business and to apply technology to enable the business to achieve its goals and objectives. The end result is better customer satisfaction and higher profitability or greater achievement of the organization's mission.

Summary

In this chapter, you were introduced to the roles and responsibilities that are key to delivering and managing a service management program and services. You received information about value streams and processes to help you understand the importance of knowing what it is you do, how it is done, and the interactions necessary to fulfill customer needs. You were also exposed to the key artifacts of a process by reviewing the process model and what is involved in establishing a formal process capability. We reviewed the OCM strategy and plans and discussed the significance of communication in increasing the overall potential for success in implementing service management. We looked at the elements of metrics and measures to ensure that what gets measured will produce the behavior and results that enable you to communicate how well the service provider is doing in meeting the needs of the organization.

These are all key areas that require the attention of the service management organization to enable the service provider to be successful and provide value to their customer, users, and stakeholders. In the next chapter, you will see information related to the critical success factors needed to produce an effective service management capability.

18
Reviewing Critical Success Factors for Service Management Capability

In this chapter, we will review the **critical success factors** (CSFs) to initiate and sustain a service management capability, including leadership commitment and the difference between commitment and support, governance to ensure compliance and control, accountability and authority to fulfill expectations, and quick wins to generate enthusiasm and maintain momentum.

In this chapter, we will cover the following main topics:

- Understanding commitment or support
- Ensuring compliance and control with governance
- The importance of accountability and authority
- Benefiting from quick wins

Understanding commitment or support

In any major endeavor, commitment and support are key elements. How do we determine whether to be committed or simply supportive of the endeavor? It is important to define what these terms mean in the context of **service management**. **Commitment** is the characteristic of leadership and organization that executes their day-to-day activities even when it is uncomfortable or difficult to do so. Commitment is about doing the right thing the right way when the pressure is on. **Support** is a characteristic of leadership and organization that suggests *do as I say*. It is that characteristic that indicates leadership supports you when things are going well and the actions taken deliver consistent results for your stakeholders. However, support can sometimes be limited when the pressure is on to get something done and the right way is not necessarily the easiest or most expeditious way.

There are a variety of examples that show the difference between commitment and support. There is an analogy concerning chickens and pigs when talking about their contributions to breakfast. Chickens contribute eggs for breakfast; the chicken lays the egg, the farmer collects the egg, and the chicken gets fed so they can lay more eggs. However, a pig must give up their existence to contribute ham and bacon to breakfast. In this scenario, *a chicken supports breakfast, but the pig is committed.*

How would this manifest itself in a business environment? Let us look at some examples. You are asked to make a change to a software component for an important service. The normal and expected process is to plan the change, develop the change, test the change, schedule the change, and then make the change. However, the customer may apply pressure on your supervisor to implement the change before the end of the week. It is Tuesday, and the normal lead time for this type of change is two weeks. Your supervisor says, *"Ignore the two weeks; get this implemented on Friday this week."* You know that this significantly increases the risk of failure, but it is your supervisor and you want to be customer-focused, so you do it. At the water cooler during the week, you share your experience with your colleagues. They walk away thinking that the message concerning the importance of following the **change management** process policies is not that important. On Monday, after your change has been implemented with limited testing and little documentation, it fails. You are scrambling to fix the error that was introduced, your supervisor is frustrated with you for making the error, and the customer is mad because the service is not working.

The previous example shows how supervision says they support the policies and rules related to a process, but when the pressure is on and a customer demands a deviation from the norm, they ignore the prescribed approach and force the shortcut to fail. There are many examples where taking the shortcut or circumventing the prescribed approach has resulted in errors, rework, and dissatisfied customers and users.

What does commitment look like in the previous scenario? Your supervisor would have communicated to the leadership chain that this request violates the agreed conditions for this type of change and that by ignoring the policy, there is a greater risk of causing a failure and service outage. The IT leadership would discuss the situation with the customer, determine the business significance of the need for the change, and come to an agreement about the approach for this request. There will always be a need for exceptions to the policies defined for a practice, but it is important to limit those exceptions and only apply an exception when there is a solid business case. It is good to remember that *failure to plan on your part is not an emergency on my part.*

As we discussed in the previous chapter, **OCM** is key to communicating with the various stakeholders. Your leadership can show support for the service management initiative and execution by communicating internally and externally the importance of following the policies and procedures for the practices. The leadership can show commitment by ensuring that the policies and procedures are followed in the majority of situations and that exceptions are limited. Another example of commitment is requiring individual and organizational objectives for service management. In one organization, incident response/resolution for priority one incidents was defined as one of the incentive compensation factors. In this case, bonuses were tied to the effectiveness of the IT organization in responding to mission-critical incidents in the agreed timeframe.

Another example of commitment to service management is holding the leadership chain accountable for following the policies defined for the practices. In one case, a **CIO** challenged the leadership chain by stating that not following the change management process was unacceptable and that there would be consequences if a deviation from the agreed procedure was discovered. This scenario was prompted by an extended outage that resulted from a failed change that did not follow the agreed procedure and was not documented, so it took considerably longer to discover the implemented change and correct the error. The CIO stated in no uncertain terms that this would not be tolerated, and the consequences could be significant to all involved, from the top of the leadership chain all the way down to the staff member making the change.

It is important to have both support and commitment for the service management efforts. Support takes the form of communication on what you should be doing and how. It manifests itself in the form of alignment, from the top of the leadership chain to the staff executing the practices. Commitment is essential when there is pressure to deviate from the agreed approach for the practices and processes being executed. Commitment will ensure that you do what is right according to the policies and rules that have been defined and agreed upon by the leadership and stakeholders, which describes the next discussion point – governance.

Ensuring compliance and control with governance

In the previous topic, there were multiple references to policies and rules. **Governance** defines the policies and rules that will control how an organization acts in delivering and supporting its services. Governance is key in managing the practices and services that are used to support business customers and stakeholders. Governance is defined as the means by which an organization is directed and controlled. Without policies and rules to govern the development, implementation, and execution of processes, it is difficult to be consistent or repeatable. This results in inconsistency and unreliable outcomes affecting stakeholder satisfaction and value.

The key activities involved in establishing governance include *evaluate*, *direct*, and *monitor*, as described in the following figure:

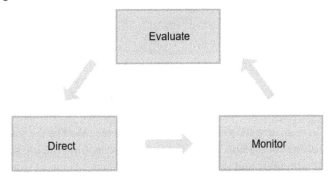

Figure 18.1 – Governance activities

Evaluate involves continual analysis of an organization's performance in the context of the internal and external environments. It also involves reviewing strategies to assess the effectiveness and success of achieving the organization's goals and objectives.

Direct involves the effective communication of a strategy, policies, and plans. It involves ensuring that guidelines are established to enable compliance with governance.

Monitor is the activity that reviews the results to ensure compliance with governance and, where deviations occur, identify what actions need to be taken. It also provides information on the effectiveness of controls, enabling improvements to be considered.

There is a continual loop through these activities as part of the establishment, enforcement, and maintenance of the governance policies and rules necessary to conduct effective service management.

Governors and managers have distinct roles – governors establish governance, while managers ensure compliance and performance in line with it. The following figure shows the role managers play in governance:

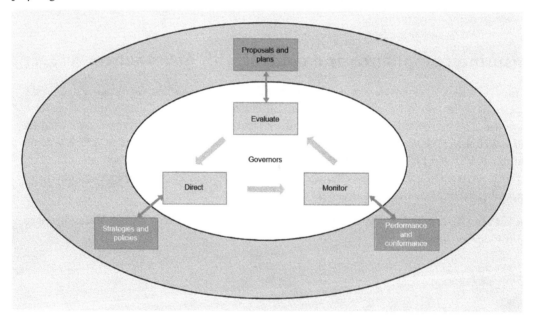

Figure 18.2 – Managers' roles in governance

Managers are involved in evaluating the proposals and plans that are raised by the governors. Managers will be involved in directing their teams to understand strategies and policies, so they can ensure that their teams comply with them and execute them appropriately. Managers will then monitor the performance of their teams to ensure compliance with the policies and rules established by the governors.

The organizational relationship between governors or a board of directors and managers is illustrated in the following figure:

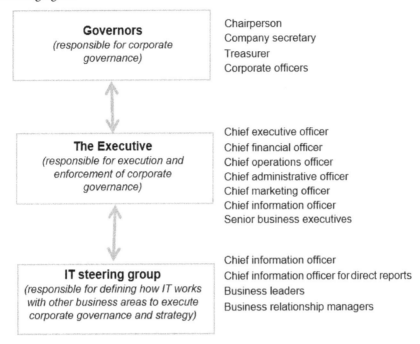

Figure 18.3 – Governance structure

One of the key elements of IT governance is the **IT steering group**. This entity is responsible for taking the guidance provided by the governors and ensuring that IT strategies and plans are appropriately aligned to the governance defined. This is not an organizational structure; instead, it describes the organizational elements that must be involved between governors and managers to set up and manage an effective governance capability.

Policies, **strategies**, and **plans** are key components of an overall governance approach. Policies establish the rules and controls that will be applied to ensure that an organization behaves in a way that is consistent with its culture. A policy such as *no fighting will be tolerated and will result in immediate dismissal* establishes an expectation for the employees of the organization and the consequences for violating the policy. Every practice developed, implemented, and executed requires policies to be defined to exercise the appropriate control for that practice and process. For example, an **incident management** policy could define the requirement that all incidents must be recorded. In this instance, the leadership tells the IT organization that a record of any request defined as an incident must be recorded in whatever platform or technology is used for this purpose. This ensures that the activities related to an incident are documented and the consumption of resources is captured. The term *"must"* in a policy statement should always be considered to reduce ambiguity and ensure that employees understand the expectations. When creating a policy, it is necessary to define what the requirements are for the policy, what controls will be established to maintain compliance, and what the consequences are for violating the policy – just like driving 5 miles over the speed limit may not result in a ticket, driving 10 miles over may get you a ticket, and driving 15 miles over may get your license suspended for reckless driving. A policy without consequences is unenforceable and will result in people ignoring the policy or violating it.

Strategies and plans are key to documenting where an organization is going and what the expectations are for the stakeholders. As you saw earlier in this book and repeated in *Figure 18.4*, the **strategy cascade** helps to document the responsibilities of the various levels of the organization:

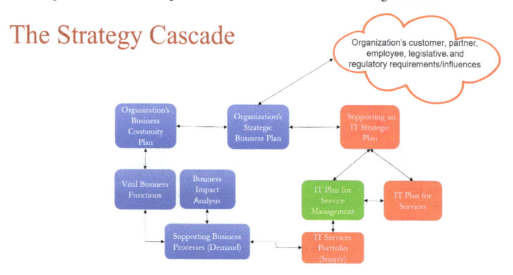

Figure 18.4 – The strategy cascade

Likewise, the diagram in *Figure 18.3* shows the cascade from governors to executive to IT management, illustrating the development of policies, strategies, and plans.

Governance is necessary to establish the controls an organization will apply to ensure that the various stakeholders will behave consistently and appropriately. Without governance, an organization may not produce the value its stakeholders expect. It also could result in unexpected outcomes that could jeopardize the organization's viability and success. Governance is the responsibility of the governors and is enforced by the executive. As illustrated in *Figure 18.4*, IT must align its governance with the overall governance of the business; otherwise, IT will not be able to ensure its ability to meet the business needs.

The importance of accountability and authority

Earlier in the book, there was a discussion about **Responsible, Accountable, Consulted, and Informed (RACI)**. When talking about Accountable, it is valuable to understand what this means. Accountable is about establishing the individual who will ensure that the expected results are produced and that those results meet the needs of an organization. It is important to establish who in the organization is accountable for the delivery of the services. Would your CIO be the person ultimately accountable for the efficient and effective delivery of IT services? The answer to that question would typically be a resounding yes. When developing a **RACI matrix**, one of the key validation points is to ensure that one and only one role or individual is accountable for the defined activity. If more than one role or individual is accountable, then no one is accountable. In the previous CIO example, yes, the CIO is ultimately accountable for the delivery of service, but the CIO may delegate the accountability for one or more services to a subordinate. When this happens, the CIO also delegates authority to the subordinate to do what is necessary to fulfill the conditions of the service. This is a critical consideration when delegating accountability because accountability without authority will not be effective. What is authority? It is granting the accountable individual the right to do what is needed to fulfill the assignment they have been given within the agreed policies.

As you saw in *Chapter 17*, roles and responsibilities were described for the process owner, process manager, and process practitioner. In the description of those roles, there were statements describing what the roles were accountable for. The process owner is accountable for the process, so this role must ensure that the process is clearly defined, documented, and implemented according to its governance. The process manager is accountable for the day-to-day execution of the process, ensuring that the results being produced are consistent with the overall objectives of the process. These two roles must be given the authority needed to effectively deliver on the objectives of the process within the agreed governance established for it. Without the authority to establish the practice/process according to the governance defined, these roles will not be effective, and the practice/process will not produce the expected results.

Benefiting from quick wins

What is a **quick win**? A quick win, also described as low-hanging fruit, is an effort that can be performed in a fairly short period of time, maybe two to six sprints or one to six months. It can be done by a small team, such as a staff of two to five. It tends to be a low-cost improvement. It is typically something that an organization can easily recognize as an opportunity to improve. Quick wins are valuable in that they tend to generate enthusiasm for an initiative because they produce results very quickly. They tend to be very recognizable as something that delivers benefits and can be implemented with little effort and resources. They allow a bigger initiative to show progress toward a larger goal or objective. Quick wins allow the organization to see improvements without significant investment in time, money, or resources. In *Chapter 16*, there was a review of the continual improvement activities, which can be used by smaller groups within the organization to identify and execute quick wins.

What would a quick win look like? For incident management, a quick win could be to ensure that all incidents are recorded. In this instance, the service desk deals with many incident requests, but they do not record all of them. This results in a lack of the necessary evidence in the form of an incident record to show the volume of incidents being processed. The service desk needs more resources, but it does not have the information necessary to justify the additional resources because there is no record of the incidents being handled. By ensuring that all incidents are logged, management will have the necessary evidence to show the need for additional resources to meet their agreed response time commitments when dealing with the incident volume.

Another example of a quick win is applying **problem management** to a top 10 list of incidents. This instance would involve reviewing the list of top 10 incidents and applying problem management techniques to identify the root cause of, say, items 1 and 2 on the list to determine a permanent solution to the errors identified. This provides an opportunity to eliminate repeating incidents for items 1 and 2 and improve the users' performance by increasing the availability of the services related to those incidents.

Whenever developing a strategy as part of continual improvement, always identify some quick wins that allow a team to generate enthusiasm for the effort, establish benefits and progress for the initiative, and show value.

Summary

In this chapter, you learned about the difference between commitment and support, understanding which stakeholders need to be committed and which ones you need support from. It is extremely important to recognize that in any major effort, commitment across the management chain is absolutely essential for success. Likewise, having the support of all the stakeholders will significantly improve the potential for success of any initiative, large or small and anywhere in between. You learned about governance and the importance of clearly establishing policies and controls that will dictate the expected behavior exhibited by an organization's stakeholders. You learned about the concept of accountability and how significant it is to establish the roles and individuals that will be accountable for the processes and services being delivered by the organization. In addition, you now understand the importance of allocating authority to a role or individual that is accountable so that they can fulfill the requirements of a process or service. Finally, quick wins were explored, along with their characteristics and some examples. The importance of having quick wins as part of a major initiative can improve the potential for success by delivering benefits and value faster.

These are all key areas that require the attention of a service management organization to make the service provider successful and provide value to their customers, users, and stakeholders. In the next chapter, you will see information related to the **CSFs** needed to execute an effective service management strategy.

19
Realizing CSFs for Service Management Implementation

In this chapter, you will be introduced to the **critical success factors** (**CSFs**) that will increase an organization's ability to successfully implement a **service management** program. CSFs play a crucial role in determining the success of a service management initiative. They help to comprehend the various approaches to establishing a benchmark for the improvements that are made during the implementation of a service management capability. CSFs are responsible for identifying and monitoring the metrics that showcase the progress made in achieving the objectives outlined in the service management implementation plans. Furthermore, CSFs understand the importance of managing the speed at which changes are introduced in order to effectively implement a service management program. They also possess the knowledge of the resources, both human and financial, that are required to ensure steady progress in the implementation of a service management program. Lastly, CSFs identify the necessary capabilities and technologies needed to support and enable the successful implementation of a service management capability.

In this chapter, we will cover the following main topics:

- Setting a baseline
- Measuring and monitoring progress
- Establishing a pace for change
- Allocating the necessary resources
- Identifying and implementing tools and technology

Setting a baseline

When establishing a service management program, one of the key challenges for the program team is communicating value and benefits to the senior leadership. This program, like all major efforts, requires a commitment of resources and people to make it happen. It also requires an organization to make changes to the way you do things. In order to effectively communicate the benefits of the program, there must be a means to measure progress and **return on investment** (**ROI**). To demonstrate progress and ROI, there must be an understanding of where the organization starts from. The term used to define that starting point is a **baseline**.

Baselines need to be captured when a program starts and as reporting is conducted, comparing the results of the program changes to the starting point or baseline. As the program progresses and reporting occurs, baselines are updated to reflect the new current state, so as more change is completed, the benefits can be shared with the management team and other stakeholders.

There can be a variety of baselines applied, including the following:

- Process baselines showing the current state of the process capability and measures:

    - **Incident management**: Incident resolution success or recovery times

    - **Problem management**: The root cause analysis success rate

    - **Change management**: The percentage of emergency changes compared to normal changes

    - **Configuration management**: The accuracy of the **CIs** on the **CMDB**

    - **Asset management**: The accuracy of the asset database compared to the actual inventory of assets

    - **Service level management**: The percentage of service-level commitments made compared to all service-level agreement commitments

- Monetary baselines:

    - IT budget

    - Cost of services

    - Program budget

    - Project budgets versus actual budgets

- Service provision baselines:

    - Customer/user satisfaction numbers

It is essential to capture one or more baselines for the service management program to have something to measure your results against, showing the improvements that have been achieved and the benefits that have been realized. In some instances, you may not have made a measurable improvement, but this too can be valuable to help identify areas where additional attention is required or the improvement objectives were not achievable or realistic. As you proceed in the journey, establishing a baseline before continuing down a path is a necessary requirement to show how the program provides value to an organization.

Measuring and monitoring progress

As a baseline establishes where you are in your journey, it is also important to show progress in meeting the objectives of your initiative. When showing progress, the metrics you defined in your project and program plans should have intermediate reports that demonstrate the implementation effort moves toward the future state targets. Here, you show the various stakeholders that the efforts and investments being made in the program actually produce tangible and intangible results.

Showing interim results that have been achieved helps stakeholders continue to be engaged. It ensures that the stakeholders and leadership understand that progress is being made toward the objectives and what that progress reflects. It also helps to identify where issues or challenges have occurred and the possible remedies that can be introduced to mitigate the impact of those challenges. It ensures that the benefits realized are regularly communicated and celebrated by an organization.

By effectively communicating the progress of the service management initiative, you will be able to sustain interest in what is produced, maintain engagement across an organization, and provide evidence that the objectives are delivered. You can also demonstrate the achievement of ROI.

Progress will ensure that milestones in the program and projects are acknowledged and the results produced for the milestones are documented and reported to the appropriate stakeholders.

Establishing a pace for change

As with any significant change in an organization, it is important to manage the pace of the changes that are introduced. An organization and its stakeholders can only accommodate so much change in the way they do things. In developing a program roadmap and identifying the projects that will be executed, you will need to understand how much change you will introduce and what can be absorbed. A key factor in being able to manage change is the effectiveness of your OCM efforts. Helping stakeholders understand the benefits they will see as a result of changes will help them accommodate more change.

A key element of managing the pace of change requires an understanding of the culture of your organization and how change is introduced and managed. You should answer the following questions about your organization:

- How has change been introduced in the past?

- How effective is OCM across the organization in raising awareness of organizational changes?

- Who are the key stakeholders that must be the change agents?

- How effective have similar changes been received and implemented in the past?

In answering these and other questions, you should get a sense of how fast and to what degree your organization is capable of accommodating the changes that will result from a service management program. Service management programs are largely a **culture change** more than they are a **technical change**. The organization must be effectively prepared for what will happen. Knowing how your organization can deal with a change will dictate the speed by which it will happen.

An example of how an organization's culture reflects the pace of change can be demonstrated through the following scenario. A service management architect was enjoying lunch at work and was approached by a senior manager. The manager expressed some concerns with the pace of the service management program. His question was, *"Why is this taking so long?"* The architect suggested to the senior manager that if the leadership team would consider taking their foot off the brake and applying it to the accelerator, things could proceed at a faster pace. In this scenario, the culture of the organization was to delegate the responsibility for implementing the service management program to lower levels of the organization, but it did not provide the authority to actually make the necessary decisions to move at the desired speed.

Recognizing the significance of a company's culture and the amount of organizational change that your stakeholders can accommodate is extremely valuable in establishing the pace of your implementation and what you can accomplish.

Allocating the necessary resources

Resources are a fundamental necessity for any undertaking. In this case, there are a variety of resources needed. You obviously have the human resources and financial resources necessary to accomplish the objectives of your service management program. There is also the need for tool resources, which will be described in the next section.

In order to be successful in implementing a service management capability, you will need the following roles filled:

- **Program and project managers**: These individuals will manage the program and projects that are included in your roadmap to deliver the changes necessary and achieve the organizational objectives.

- **Process owners**: As we described in the previous chapters, each process in your program will require a process owner to be accountable for the process and ensure that the process objectives and results are delivered.

- **Process managers**: These individuals are accountable to ensure the day-to-day operational elements of a process are delivered.

- **Process practitioners**: These individuals in an organization are responsible for executing one or more activities in a process.

- **Leadership**: This includes management and the architecture resources that will lead the efforts. These roles will be accountable and responsible for providing the governance and guidance necessary to achieve the goals and objectives defined for the program.

- **Customers and users**: These resources need to contribute to the implementation of many of the processes you will consider in your program because they will be impacted by the changes being made and benefit from the improvements. Their involvement increases the potential for success.

- **Suppliers**: These resources might be engaged to assist in defining the service management program, such as consultants to provide guidance on developing a roadmap or performing current state assessments before defining it. These resources can also contribute to identifying the best technology for your organization, based on your level of maturity and specific requirements. Suppliers also need to contribute to the execution of the processes you intend to implement, thus better aligning your organization with those external providers that support your delivery and support of services.

There are other stakeholders you will want to consider, but the preceding list is a very good starting point.

Financial resources will be necessary to accomplish the service management objectives. First, there is the cost of human resources to consider. There is a requirement to invest in training and education for the key participants in a program. There is a need to spend on communication mechanisms, such as the development of a roadshow, a lunch and learn, or a website. Funding could be included to support celebrations when a significant result has been achieved or a major milestone has been reached. It is important for your success in implementing the service management program to have adequate funding for the objectives an organization wants to achieve.

Another critical resource to consider is tools, which we will explore in the next section.

Identifying and implementing tools and technology

Service management activities benefit from having the right tools and technology. Some of these tools include artifacts produced during planning sessions, architecture diagrams, process design documents, standards documentation, analysis documents, roadmaps, and assessment results. Some of these tools are technology platforms to support executing working instructions and delivering services.

There are tools needed to manage a program and projects that will be identified as part of your roadmap. These tools could include the following:

- Project management software or spreadsheet software
- Architecture design software
- Process design software
- Assessment tools such as a benchmarking approach
- Metrics and measurement tools

Tools are needed for **organizational change management** activities. These tools could include the following:

- Stakeholder mapping documents
- A stakeholder power matrix
- A stakeholder commitment chart
- Communication plans

There will be process tools needed, such as the following:

- A policy document repository
- Process design tools
- Storage locations for the following:
  - Process flow diagrams
  - Procedure documentation
  - Working instructions
  - Standards and practices

You need technology to execute processes efficiently and effectively and capture the results produced. You should consider a technology platform that will integrate as many processes as possible. You should also give strong consideration to the existing technologies you use and how effective they are in supporting the improvements you will produce with the service management program.

You will want to document the requirements for your future state and compare that to the existing technology. This review should identify any gaps in the current technology and, potentially, how those gaps will be addressed, either with an upgrade to your current technology or a replacement.

Once you know what your requirements are, categorize them using the **MoSCoW approach**. The MoSCoW approach suggests classifying your requirements based on the *Must-Have, Should-Have, Could-Have*, or *Would-Like-to-Have* criteria. Once the requirements have been appropriately categorized, you can effectively identify the best solution to fulfill them.

Summary

In this chapter, you were given guidance on the importance of setting baselines for a variety of key elements of the service management program. You reviewed the need to establish a baseline that can be used to compare what has been achieved against a known starting point. We explored the importance of identifying and communicating progress on an initiative to various stakeholders. We also explored managing the pace of change that your organization can accommodate to improve the possibility of achieving success. You reviewed information on the resources needed to accomplish a program, including people, money, and tools. This chapter wrapped up by describing some of the tools and technology necessary to support delivering the key elements of a service management program.

There are many examples of organizations that failed to understand the significance of each of these elements of a service management program and did not achieve the intended results. Every organization must consider each of these areas when considering a service management program; otherwise, they risk spending time and resources to not deliver the results expected.

In the final chapter, you will learn more about sustaining the service management practice through **continual improvement**, by maintaining ongoing commitment from your leadership and maturing processes as you add additional ones. We will also offer some final thoughts on what organizations have done to be successful and what challenges result in failures.

20

Sustaining a Service Management Practice

In this chapter, we will discuss *sustaining a service management practice*. We will describe the importance of continual improvement, management commitment, and monitoring, measuring, and reporting on managing the service management program while continuing to mature the existing capabilities. At the same time, we will introduce new or formalize existing capabilities to ensure continued benefit and value.

Throughout this chapter, you will learn about ensuring your continuing attention to maturing the service management capability. You will gain a deep understanding of the importance of establishing a structure and key resources to lead the service management practice beyond its initial implementation. This includes establishing a **service management office** and a **continual improvement** team with an appropriate budget. Furthermore, you will learn how to develop an approach to assess the maturity of your existing formalized capabilities and identify the next set of practices to formalize or introduce into the service management environment. To enrich your learning experience, we will document several final lessons learned from early adopters and successful implementations across a variety of business, academia, finance, and government entities. These insights will provide you with valuable knowledge and perspectives, enabling you to enhance your service management capability effectively.

This chapter will address the following key subjects:

- Why do formal service management initiatives fail?
- Why do formal service management programs succeed?
- Maturing and incrementally adding capabilities
- Final tips on this book

Why do formal service management initiatives fail?

Whether an organization refers to its formal **service management** capability as a **service management office (SMO)**, a **service management center of excellence**, a **service management center of expertise**, or a **service management practice (SMP)**, the value is in the outcomes that are created for the overall organization. The importance of the name is grounded in the implication that the IT service provider has dedicated resources in place that focus on generating value for all of the stakeholders involved. Consider the following *it* statements:

- It is initiating and managing (maintaining) the formal service management capability, both of which are key aspects of success

- It is said that not learning from the past is a recipe for failure going forward

- It is said that resting on your laurels (past accomplishments) is not moving forward

So, what are the barriers to success associated with initiating and sustaining a formal service management capability? The following perspectives speak to common reasons formal service management initiatives and programs are not successful:

- **The value provided is not visible**: Though many organizations made significant investments (money, time, and people) in service management initiatives in the late nineties and the next 10 to 15 years after, there arose an inability to further justify that expense. The initiative/program began to be perceived as bureaucratic, rigorous, and slow, preventing products and services from getting to market quicker. Further, many began to liken service management to the **waterfall approach**, which is used to get application enhancements to production. During this same time frame, the market started to see the emergence and adoption of **agile approaches**, where the advertised ability to get products and services to market quicker got the attention of key decision-makers. Although Agile thinking and the idea of improving quality, cost-efficiency, and time to market are clear benefits, these attributes still represent the ideas of managing services. Much of service management, from the very beginning, is in the interpretation of the content, as there is clear evidence of Agile language in place. Admittedly, the technology platforms, like always, evolved, affording the ability to further the application of service management concepts (and related frameworks). Any enhancements to the ability to improve products and services, as well as increase value for customers, ought to be considered part of service management. Both **systems thinking** and **design thinking**, discussed back in *Chapters 3* and *4*, are examples of the need to combine disciplines to create value for stakeholders.

- **Organizations tend to be reflections of their leadership**: Formal service management is a capability, meaning that it represents the involvement of the entire IT service provider, strong leadership for the initiative, and, later, the program, requires an executive presence. Lack or loss of executive sponsorship has proven to be a barrier to the success of the program and, in many cases, has resulted in the loss of gains previously achieved. This includes the sponsor leaving the organization or even moving to a different part of the organization. In some cases, the incoming leader may not believe in the capability or may want to introduce another capability (or framework) they perceive would bring more value to the overall organization. In some cases, this has been done as a result of ignorance. Done well, service management ought to afford the new sponsor a continued approach to add value to the IT service provider and formal service management, where they can leverage (or continue) the work and accomplishments already realized – that is, they can leverage the value that has already been realized to produce further value. It is not a matter of replacing one discipline or framework with another, but more converging multiples since one is typically never enough. There are typically *pockets of excellence* in each of the varying frameworks and capabilities.

- **Lack of service management governance**: Formal service management does not happen by mere suggestion. Without a governing body and an associated roadmap that speaks to what the program is to accomplish, even with initial momentum, there is a strong chance of failure. Formal service management is not something that an organization gets done, but more of a journey that is never completed. As part of a formal service management program, the governing body and associated roadmap must include strategic, tactical, and operational elements. It must also be representative of the stakeholders impacted by the program. Always consider that the strategic and tactical elements take longer to come to fruition, while the operational elements should produce immediate value. Focusing on just one of any of the three lends itself to failing to produce value for the other two, and the associated stakeholders. For instance, focusing on just incidents and service requests for users (both of which are operational) without focusing on **service-level management** and **business relationship management** (tactical and strategic, respectively) will hurt customers and senior leaders in the long term. As part of governance, there also has to be some level of assurance, through defined measurements trapped at some regular interval, that the service management capability is providing value (or remediation is needed).

- **Technical debt**: Technical debt can apply to people, just like it traditionally does with equipment or computing infrastructure (servers, storage, and so on). As it relates to the people performing specific service management roles (service desk, service owners, business relationship managers, and so on), a lack of service management skills and competencies results in the failure of the program (eventually). There needs to be expertise well beyond fundamental knowledge, especially in the case of service management leadership, core processes, and related technology platforms. This is not confined to book knowledge as these roles must also be able to interpret overall business and IT service provider strategies, the organization's culture, and their intersection with service management. Regarding the supporting technology platform (or even multiple tools) for service management, they are often blamed for the preferred results not being realized. The effectiveness of supporting technology, regardless of its cost, depends on its understanding of the organization's business and how well the responsible roles comprehend the processes it enables.

- **Existing attitudes and behaviors**: Culture is a significant factor in the success of service management programs. The IT service provider within an organization likely wants to be respected as a business partner, but this will not likely occur unless that provider can demonstrate consistent delivery of products and services. The very notion of formal service management is to provide value to customers in the form of products and services. A lack of understanding of the various stakeholders, their interests, their influences, and what they value will surely result in failure in the long term, even if there is early success with the program. Going into a service management initiative without a full and proper understanding of the current and desired state will lead to implementing or improving those processes and capabilities that fall short of the value users and customers desire. Replicating what another organization's approach was is also a risky proposition as strategy and culture tend not to be the same across two organizations, even if both are in the same line of business.

Understanding the barriers to success for a formal service management program is a key aspect of avoiding these pitfalls. Underestimating the effort it will take to be successful, including any of the five perspectives presented, will have a negative impact eventually, if not sooner. There is a prescriptive approach to avoiding these pitfalls.

Why do formal service management initiatives succeed?

Just like potential pitfalls are faced as part of a formal service management capability, there are also ingredients for success associated with initiating and sustaining the capability. These ingredients include the following:

- Governance
- Strategy
- Culture
- Skills and competencies
- Service management technology
- Ongoing improvement

All of these factors could also be associated with a lack of success. It is not unusual for success and failure to be associated with the same aspects since risks to success are very often reflected as a lack of an ingredient.

Having a formal service management capability requires a serious intent, including executive sponsorship (**governance**) and a pragmatic plan (**strategy**). Key inputs include the overall business strategy, the IT strategy, and, ideally, an up-to-date **business continuity plan** (**BCP**). From these inputs, the key outputs to be realized are the governing body and a roadmap focused on the initial areas of service management. So, how do we get to these outputs?

Remember that the whole idea of service management is to improve results for stakeholders, thereby increasing the value provided by the IT service provider in the form of products and services. While leveraging the key inputs, the IT service provider's current and existing **strengths**, **weaknesses**, **opportunities**, and **threats** against that landscape – also known as **SWOT analysis** – should be determined. The results of this analysis start to dictate what areas of focus (for service management) make the most sense and in what order these areas of focus should occur. Since recommendations are to be made from this analysis, the most appropriate stakeholders must be involved. Along with these stakeholders, and the suggested key inputs, other artifacts might be considered for review, including the following:

- Existing portfolio of services and any related plans

- Current initiatives, which may be identified as part of the strategy documents

- Organization charts

- Existing policies

- Existing procedures

- Specific service management artifacts (for example, incident records, change records, service-level agreements, and more)

- Screenshots from existing tools

- Existing management reports and metrics

All of these inputs should be carefully considered as they will have an impact on the output service management roadmap. A formal workshop should be conducted that includes the key stakeholders, primarily from the IT service provider (if prudent, business consumer stakeholders could also participate), as identified by the facilitator. However, the IT service provider may not have the best resource (yet) to facilitate such a workshop. In this case, the sponsor should enlist the help of an external provider that brings this acumen. In that very first meeting, the initial discussion is not only to help everyone know why they have been asked to participate but to also level-set the audience on the concept of service management. It is better to present the workshop to everyone participating as an opportunity (and potentially a privilege) to be part of making IT a better service provider for the organization. It is also important to let the group know that, together, they represent the internal knowledge of the service provider, so who better to assess the strengths, weaknesses, opportunities, and threats?

Post the workshop, an analysis is conducted of the findings from the workshop, but this must occur by resources with a profound understanding of service management. Consider that the data analyzed results in specific recommendations, prioritized, that are reflected in a roadmap view. This roadmap includes those areas of service management that should be pursued initially. The following swim lane diagram (*Figure 20.1*) is an example of a rolling *18-month service management strategy*:

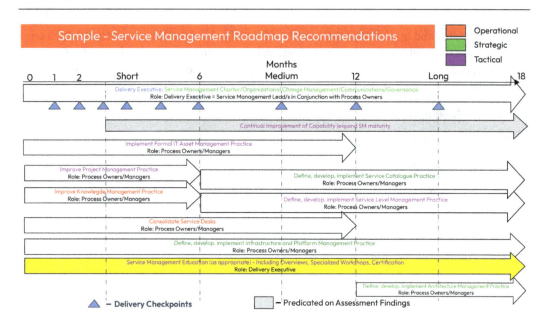

Figure 20.1 – Sample service management roadmap

Figure 20.2 shows a 6-month extract of the 18-month view:

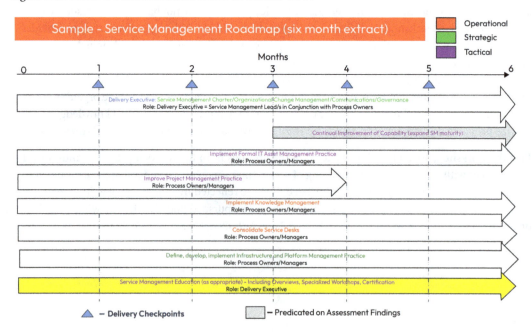

Figure 20.2 – Sample service management roadmap (extract)

Note that there are strategic, tactical, and operational aspects. Also, note that there are checkpoints (data points) that are calculated in 30 to 45 increments, allowing the formal service management capability to understand the levels of progress being made. These data points were previously discussed as **critical success factors** in *Chapters 18* and *19*.

Another part of the post-workshop data analysis is establishing the governing body for formal service management. *Figure 20.3* reflects an organization chart for the governing body:

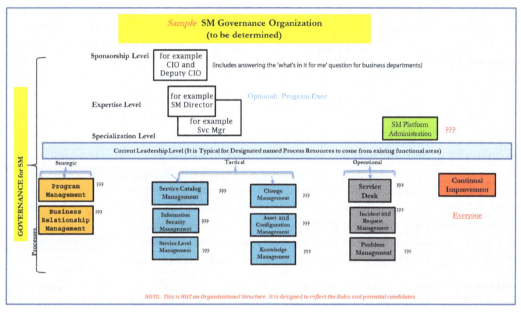

Figure 20.3 – Sample service management governing body

Note the three levels within the governing body:

- **Sponsorship**: Typically, this is the **CIO** or an executive within the IT service provider. This role is not expected to have expert knowledge of service management but does have the authority to sponsor and the ability to speak about the importance and value of formal service management for the business.

- **Expertise**: This role, especially in the beginning, could be an internal or external provider. This role understands service management at an overall and detailed level. For an external resource, note the mention of the *delivery executive* at the top of the swim lane diagram. For an internal resource, the *service manager*, *service management lead*, or similar role makes sense. In essence, this role shares accountability (with the sponsor) and owns responsibility for the formal service management capability. Some organizations have realized the need to hire a resource specifically for this role.

- **Specialization**: This relates to those specific areas that are called out on the swim lane diagram. These roles require far more than a fundamental understanding of the specific process, and how that process integrates with the other processes and associated technology platforms. These resources should have elevated skill and competency, not only for the role for which they are responsible but also some knowledge of other processes. These specialization resources will likely emerge from the existing IT service provider organization, and based on who is best qualified and available.

Between the *swim lane diagrams* and the *governing body diagram*, the areas of governance and service management strategy are covered, but this is not the end game for this area. In observing the swim lane diagram, note the mention of a **service management charter** and **service management education**. Chartering the program makes it official, and presents the implication of the program being ongoing and having specific associated projects and disciplines like any program would have. Presuming that there is also the equivalent of a **project management office** (**PMO**) within the organization, that could be a great resource to assist in developing the charter.

The current IT strategy and portfolio would likely speak to *current and future initiatives*. These cannot be ignored when establishing or maintaining a formal service management capability. These very initiatives may prove to be advantageous to the service management roadmap, especially if they are highly related to a process that was identified as part of the analysis, leading to the roadmap that was created earlier. For instance, if there is an initiative around **asset management**, why not pair the formal implementation or improvement of the asset management process as part of that initiative? It just makes sense, and the business case justification has already been presented.

Initial and ongoing service management education is also key, specifically the *skills and competencies* needed. To build and sustain a formal service management capability, the entire service provider team must have some level of exposure to service management. For some, a 2- to 4-hour overview is enough. For others, formal certification education is appropriate; for a smaller percentage (that is, process owners), more in-depth education is needed (required). It is not unusual to provide some level of service management education for business customers of the IT service provider, but this must be done carefully and with the use of common business language versus IT technical terminology. In addition, most formal service management capabilities recognize that external service providers should also know about service management. Imagine an organization that has outsourced its **service desk** at level one, and that provider has no formal knowledge of service management best practices.

It is likely that the IT service provider already has supporting **service management technology** platform(s) in place. As part of the analysis of strengths, weaknesses, opportunities, and threats, where did the technology land? If considered a strength and an opportunity, it would be leveraged to bring the roadmap to life. If a weakness or a threat, the business case is not likely built to justify bringing in a different solution as it has likely proven that the existing tools won't meet the requirements or produce the desired results. In the case where the existing technology is deemed to be a strength or an opportunity, bear in mind that the existing platform administration has been set up and managed as best it can, independent of an overarching formal service management governance and roadmap.

Now that these are available, the service provider can expect that the platform will become even more of an enabler. Just because an IT service provider has best-in-class supporting technology does not mean there is a best-in-class formal service management capability. Many times, the tools are blamed for other important work that has not been done. These related technologies are only as good as what they know about the business of the overall organization.

Lastly, and discussed as part of the pitfalls to success, **culture** plays a key role. It doesn't matter how well the roadmap is laid out and the governance organization is set up if human resources are not on board, typically evidenced by attitudes and behaviors. Education is not only about learning concepts – it is also about why the subject matter is important personally, professionally, and organization-wide. Most put this subject in the area of **organizational change management** (**OCM**). A related term is *adoption enablement*. All organizations are different, even those in the same line of business, if for no other reason than their culture. The words *stakeholders* and *culture* have been used consistently throughout this book as they go hand in hand. As discussed in previous chapters, it is important to identify the stakeholders and understand their values. Additionally, it is crucial to determine the organization's capacity to handle change, often referred to as change appetite. It is equally important to recognize the threshold beyond which change becomes overwhelming, known as change fatigue. The success or failure of initiating and/or sustaining formal service management is also about understanding the culture of the organization. Any major initiative should have a strong OCM aspect since the absence of that introduces a pitfall to overall success. This means the need for periodic measurement that's aligned with significant changes and appropriate communications. These measurements can be conducted by internal or external providers. Communications, through multiple mediums as appropriate, should be managed internally by appropriate delivery resources, customized to the situation, and at defined intervals. Examples of mediums are town halls, brown bag lunches, surveys, and team meetings.

To summarize, organizations make a significant investment in people, time, and technology related to establishing and maintaining a formal service management capability. Without executive sponsorship, coupled with a continual improvement culture, the value of the capability will diminish. This work is never done, given the many factors that can have an impact (for example, change in leadership, change in business demand, change in business strategy, change in legislative and regulatory requirements, and more). Vigilance is key.

Maturing and incrementally adding capabilities

Previously in this chapter, we covered the service management roadmap and provided an example. It happened to be an 18-month view, broken down into 6-month increments, and we understood various performance checkpoints (of 30 to 60 days). In reality, the efforts continue beyond 18 months. By the end of the first 6-month interval, an additional 6 months should be added to reflect the 18-month lookahead. Ideally, the same group that was involved in creating the first roadmap would also be involved in creating the subsequent 6-month additions. This is an indicator of maintaining the formal service management capability. The trapped data is an indicator of the value being provided by the capability with continued governance in place. It is also practical for new process owners to be introduced, and existing process owners might move to a different process, whether existing or newly added, creating continuity within the governing body. This involves analyzing the same artifacts that were used initially, even if they have likely evolved. This can be considered a steady state of the formal service management capability.

Even though the roadmap speaks to continued education and continued improvement, don't forget the concept of technical debt. The service management resources should continue to improve skillsets and competencies, furthering the adoption of systems thinking and design thinking, as discussed in *Chapters 3* and *4*. There are always simulations, skill-up events, user groups, hack-a-thons, and conferences. There are also continued specialized learning and certification classes. Doing these activities allows continued evolution of the service management capability and prevents resting on your laurels. Change is constant. If change is not happening, then standing still is in place. Standing still is not moving forward – in fact, some believe that standing still is moving backward.

Summary – final tips on this book

In establishing a formal service management capability, organizations make a conscious, significant effort and dedicate themselves to governance, formalizing the capability, and putting a significant investment into funding and people. This chapter speaks to the attributes required to produce value for the entire stakeholder ecosystem (for example, internal and external providers, business partners, and other stakeholders). A continual perspective on the health of a formal service management capability should yield self-sustaining momentum and further satisfy its purpose.

The entirety of this book was broken down into three major areas:

- **The importance of service management**: Understanding that service management serves as a structure from which other complementary frameworks, methods, movements, and standards can be harmonized to provide value for customers in the form of desired outcomes (products and services).

- **Essential service management processes**: These are key processes that are considered to be essential to a formal service management capability. They are not exhaustive but represent fundamental aspects that any IT service provider should consider. These processes are typically incorporated in any service management framework, methodology, or standard that is adopted.

- **Pragmatic application of service management**: This describes many key elements to the practical implementation of a service management capability, customized to the organization's business needs in a sustainable and repeatable manner.

Essentially, this book has been about helping you understand what formal service management is (with a bit of history), the fundamental aspects of it (essential processes), and providing a pragmatic approach to initiating and sustaining the capability. Although there has been significant mention of IT, this book has been about becoming the best service provider you can be, meaning that many of the concepts discussed can be attributed to any service provider. For example, as referenced in early chapters, a restaurant is another type of service provider and has to deal with many of the essential processes covered in *Chapters 5* through *15*.

Bear in mind that being a great service provider may be a prerequisite to other aspirations. In *Chapter 14*, **business relationship management** (**BRM**) was discussed as a process. There is a much broader curriculum for BRM than what was discussed in that chapter. Further learning would yield that, to be respected in the BRM role, the service provider has to first prove it is consistent when delivering products and services before it can be respected as a partner. It is also known that some IT service providers are taking a lead role in helping the overall organization define its business strategy. This can't occur without the IT service provider demonstrating a consistent level of service and also having a mature BRM capability in place and a solid understanding of governance. In *Chapters 3* and *4*, when we talked about design thinking and systems thinking, the overall takeaway was the advantage of understanding various frameworks, methods, and standards since this is key to being a great service provider. Even though an overall company may have an internal IT service provider, it is also likely true that the overall organization is a service provider itself. Who better to learn from than an internal business unit with a mature understanding of service management?

Appendix A
SLA Template

Appendix A provides a sample template for a **service level agreement** (**SLA**). This template can be used to create an SLA for a customer, describing the services being offered or can be modified to provide **operational level agreement** (**OLA**) information about supporting services to an SLA. *Chapter 15* provides additional information about creating and using SLAs and OLAs.

Here is the sample template:

Service Level Agreement (SLA) for [IT Service]

between

_____

[IT Service Provider Name]

and

[Customer Name]

Effective Date: [##/##/##]

Table of Contents

Document Revision History/Release Notes

Procedure Name	Service Level Agreement (SLA) Template
Original Author	

Version	Date	Author Role	Revision Notes

1.0 Introduction

1.1 Parties to the Agreement

This agreement describes the relationship and commitment between [**Service Provider**] and [**Customer**] with regard to the use and support of the IT service solution:

- For the purposes of this agreement, "service user" refers to connectivity and usage by the customer's users
- General terms and definitions (linked below)

1.2 Changes and Version Control

- Current version number
- When and why changed, authorization
- Copy holders

1.3 Definitions

1.3.1 Specific Terms

1.3.2 External References

An ITSM Glossary of Terms link can be placed here.

1.3.3 Relationship to Other Documents

1.3.4 Service Catalog

2.0 IT Service Description

2.1 Description of Service

- Overview in terms understood by the customer or prospect of the functions supported and benefits provided by the service

2.2 Exclusions

- Specific functionality not provided, geographic regions where unavailable, prospects not served

2.3 Service-Specific Terminology

- Acronyms and definitions (specific to the service)

2.4 Roles and Responsibilities

- Bulleted list of roles and responsibilities

3.0 IT Service Availability

- Hours of operation, end-to-end perspective.
- When is this service available?
- What are the capabilities of this service for differentiated service levels?
- Uptime/downtime, change management schedules.

4.0 IT Service Continuity

- Recovery time objective target.
- Recovery point objective target.
- How is service continuity sustained in case of various degrees of disruption to service? That is, will there be changes in performance or availability targets? Will a suspension of service request processing be enforced until normal service has been restored?

5.0 IT Service Performance

- Demand/throughput based on vital business functions.
- How should this service perform?
- Response times.

6.0 IT Service Support

- Details timeliness of response to service request, incidents, and priority schemes
- How/when do I get support for this service? (Support hours, contact procedures (on and off shift))
- Incident management procedures

6.1 Support Procedures

- What are the procedures one would follow to contact support?

7.0 Financial

- Basis for charging for service use (pricing)

8.0 Service Level Reporting

- How is this service measured?

- Who is responsible for communicating these metrics?

- How does one measure this service's availability? Who should the information be reported to, and how often?

Responsible Party	Scorecard Metrics	Distribution	Month	YTD	Future Metric

9.0 Service Credits

- Basis for recompense in case of serious service breach or reward if higher than agreed service levels delivered

10.0 Service Improvement Program

- Methods by which to introduce measurable improvements within this service

11.0 Review Policy and Schedule

This Agreement is valid from the [**Effective Date**] outlined herein. The Agreement should be reviewed at a minimum once per fiscal year; however, in the absence of a review during any period, the current Agreement will remain in effect.

The [**Service Level Manager**] (Document Owner) is responsible for facilitating regular reviews of this document. Contents of this document may be amended as required, provided mutual agreement is obtained and communicated to all affected parties. The Component Provider will incorporate all subsequent revisions and obtain mutual agreements/approvals as required.

Service Level Manager: [**Document Owner**]

Review Period: [**Review Period**] e.g. "Annually" or "Quarterly"

Previous Review Date: [**Last or Previous Review Date**]

Next Review Date: [**Next Review Date**]

12.0 Agreement and Signatories

Service Level Manager – [Name Goes Here]   [Date Signed]

Customer – [Name Goes Here]   [Date Signed]

Appendix B
SLR Template

Appendix B provides a sample template for a **service level requirements** (**SLR**) document. This template is described in *Chapter 15* and provides information about identifying key requirements for developing SLAs and OLAs.

Here is the template:

IT Service:_____

Interview questions

Processes

1. Which key business activities or processes are the most important for the customer's business?

    This is to help understand the relationship between the business process and the IT service. The answer to this question will define high-impact incidents for this particular customer. These key business activities or processes must be aligned with business importance levels.

    Process involvement: All ITSM processes

    Option:

    What key business activities or processes does the IT service support?

    - List business processes and activities here

    - Other business areas impacted

2. Do your key business activities or processes have dependencies on any others?

    Determine significant upstream or downstream effects of an outage. Are there impacts on other business groups?

    - Prioritize the importance of each function and each dependency

    Process involvement: All ITSM processes

3.   What are the hours and days of operation for the customer's key business activities or processes supported by the IT service?

- What are the key critical hours? For example, 8:00 am – 4:00 pm.

- If there is a peak time(s), what is it? For example, 2:00 pm – 4:00 pm.

- If there are critical calendar dates, what are they? For example, beginning of each month due to increased business or customer demand.

- Is the operation seven days per week?

- What holidays are observed and what is the impact on business processes?

  - All national holidays

  - Some national holidays – list dates:

  - Non-national holidays – list dates:

  - None

Are there any scheduled shutdown periods?

Process involvement: Availability/capacity/ITSCM/service desk

4.   For the key business activities supported by the IT service, are there any seasonal variations?

- Spikes – list timeframes:

- Downturns – list timeframes:

- None

Process involvement: Availability/capacity

5.   At any given time, what is the maximum number of users using the IT service? For example:

- 0-10 – timeframe:

- 10-50 – timeframe:

- 50-150 – timeframe:

- 150 – 300 – timeframe:

- 300 – 750 – timeframe:

- 750 – 1,250 – timeframe:

- >1,250 – timeframe:

Process involvement: Availability/service desk/capacity

6.   How many business transactions are performed on a daily basis that utilize the IT service?

- <50
- 50 – 500
- 501 – 1,000
- 1,001 – 5,000
- >5,001

Process involvement: Capacity

7.   Are there any security restrictions for the IT service?

- Regulatory
- Other – explain:

Process involvement: Availability/information security

Impacts on business

1.   How long can the IT service supporting key business activities or processes be unavailable or performing poorly before it has a *minor* impact on the business?

- < 1 hour
- 1 hour
- 4 hours
- 8 hours
- 24 hours
- Other – explain
- Unknown

How long can the IT service supporting key business activities or processes be unavailable or performing poorly before it has a *major* impact on the business?

- < 1 hour
- 1 hour
- 4 hours
- 8 hours
- 24 hours
- > 24 hours

- Other – explain

- Unknown

Measurement = RTO

Process involvement: Availability/ITSCM

2. Do the customer's key business activities or processes have workarounds or contingency plans in place for when the IT service is unavailable? Please explain.

    What is the maximum length of time business can be conducted in a contingency situation?

    - < 4 hours

    - 4 – 8 hours

    - 8 – 16 hours

    - 16 – 24 hours

    - > 24 hours – 3 days

    - > 3 days – 5 days

    - > 5 days

    - Other – explain

    Process involvement: Availability/ITSCM

3. For the IT service supporting key business activities or processes, what is the financial impact:

    - Of a degradation of service during a critical or peak time?

    - Of a degradation of service during a non-critical time?

    - Due to service being unavailable during a critical or peak time?

    - Due to service being unavailable during a non-critical time?

    Moreover, at what point, and in what timeframe, does a degradation of service for the IT service supporting the business become an availability issue?

    Need financial information. Looking for tangibles and intangibles. Dollar impact at a given timeframe. Are there any legal, contractual, or regulatory impacts? What is the timeframe/trigger for penalties?

    Process involvement: Availability/incident/ITSCM/financial/SLM

Communications

1. What are the expectations for IT in regard to communications in the event of degradation of service and/or a service outage of the IT service?

    - What frequency?

        - Hourly

        - Every 4 hours

        - Every 8 hours

        - Other (explain):

    - Who (for example, the incident manager, IT manager, business coordinator, business relationship manager, or service level manager) would expect to receive these communications? Please provide name(s), contact info, and position.

    Process involvement: Service desk

2. What are the expectations for IT in regard to the communication of scheduled changes (planned changes) to the IT service?

    - What is the lead time?

        - One week

        - Two weeks

        - Four weeks

        - > Four weeks

        - Other (explain):

    - Who is to receive these communications? Please provide name(s), contact, and position.

    Process involvement: Change/service desk

3. What is the acceptable frequency and timing for implementing changes to the production environment for the IT service?

    - Frequency for maintenance releases:

        - Weekly

        - Monthly

        - Quarterly

- Annually
- Other (explain):
- Frequency for major releases:
  - Monthly
  - Quarterly
  - Annually
  - Other (explain):
- Best timing for implementation:
  - Certain day of week:
  - Certain day of month:
  - Certain month:
- Best time of day for implementation.
- Is there a position within the organization/business that should be a part of the implementation team, responsible for testing, approval for implementation, and implementation checkout?

  Process involvement: Change/release and deployment

Growing the business

It is possible that the following information should be solicited on a scheduled basis to satisfy capacity requirements of the business activities for the IT service, regardless of SLA review frequency.

1. Are there any growth activities currently happening that impact the IT service? Please specify.

   Process involvement: Capacity/SLM/BRM

2. Are there any growth initiatives planned for the future that could impact the IT service?

   Short term and long term. Additional customers; additional volume; new product; new technology, etc.

   Process involvement: Capacity/SLM/BRM

Service levels

1. Are there any current/pending issues with the specific IT service in this questionnaire? Please be specific:

   - What are the pain points?

   - How long were key business activities affected?

   - What were the impacts of the issue?

   - Has normal operation been resumed?

   - How long did it take to return to normal?

   Process involvement: ITSCM/SLM/BRM

2. How often should a review of the service being delivered be conducted for the IT service?

   - Monthly

   - Quarterly

   - Semi-annually

   - Annually

   - Other (specify):

   - Who should be included in the review process (name, contact info, and position)?

   - What information in terms of reporting for performance, availability, etc., should be delivered during the review? Please specify.

   Process involvement: SLM/BRM

Index

U

V

W

www.packtpub.com

Subscribe to our online digital library for full access to over 7,000 books and videos, as well as industry leading tools to help you plan your personal development and advance your career. For more information, please visit our website.

Why subscribe?

- Spend less time learning and more time coding with practical eBooks and Videos from over 4,000 industry professionals

- Improve your learning with Skill Plans built especially for you

- Get a free eBook or video every month

- Fully searchable for easy access to vital information

- Copy and paste, print, and bookmark content

Did you know that Packt offers eBook versions of every book published, with PDF and ePub files available? You can upgrade to the eBook version at packtpub.com and as a print book customer, you are entitled to a discount on the eBook copy. Get in touch with us at customercare@packtpub.com for more details.

At www.packtpub.com, you can also read a collection of free technical articles, sign up for a range of free newsletters, and receive exclusive discounts and offers on Packt books and eBooks.

Other Books You May Enjoy

If you enjoyed this book, you may be interested in these other books by Packt:

ServiceNow for Architects and Project Leaders

Roy Justus | David Zhao

ISBN: 978-1-80324-529-4

- Understand the key drivers of value in ServiceNow implementation
- Structure your ServiceNow programs for successful delivery
- Discover methods and tools for securely using ServiceNow
- Set up a multi-instance environment with best practices and patterns
- Architect and lead the deployment of AI capabilities in ServiceNow
- Build innovative experiences using NLU, virtual agents and the Now Experience Framework

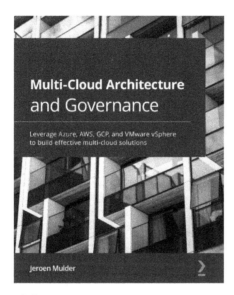

Multi-Cloud Architecture and Governance

Jeroen Mulder

ISBN: 978-1-80020-319-8

- Get to grips with the core functions of multiple cloud platforms

- Deploy, automate, and secure different cloud solutions

- Design network strategy and get to grips with identity and access management for multi-cloud

- Design a landing zone spanning multiple cloud platforms

- Use automation, monitoring, and management tools for multi-cloud

- Understand multi-cloud management with the principles of BaseOps, FinOps, SecOps, and DevOps

- Define multi-cloud security policies and use cloud security tools

- Test, integrate, deploy, and release using multi-cloud CI/CD pipelines

Packt is searching for authors like you

If you're interested in becoming an author for Packt, please visit authors.packtpub.com and apply today. We have worked with thousands of developers and tech professionals, just like you, to help them share their insight with the global tech community. You can make a general application, apply for a specific hot topic that we are recruiting an author for, or submit your own idea.

Share Your Thoughts

Now you've finished *A Practical Guide to Service Management*, we'd love to hear your thoughts! Scan the QR code below to go straight to the Amazon review page for this book and share your feedback or leave a review on the site that you purchased it from.

https://packt.link/r/1804612502

Your review is important to us and the tech community and will help us make sure we're delivering excellent quality content.

Download a free PDF copy of this book

Thanks for purchasing this book!

Do you like to read on the go but are unable to carry your print books everywhere? Is your eBook purchase not compatible with the device of your choice?

Don't worry, now with every Packt book you get a DRM-free PDF version of that book at no cost.

Read anywhere, any place, on any device. Search, copy, and paste code from your favorite technical books directly into your application.

The perks don't stop there, you can get exclusive access to discounts, newsletters, and great free content in your inbox daily

Follow these simple steps to get the benefits:

1. Scan the QR code or visit the link below

https://packt.link/free-ebook/9781804612507

2. Submit your proof of purchase
3. That's it! We'll send your free PDF and other benefits to your email directly

About the Author

Anand Balachandran Pillai is an Engineering and Technology professional with over 18 years of experience in the software industry in Product Engineering, Software Design and Architecture and Research. He has a Bachelor's degree in Mechanical Engineering from the Indian Institute of Technology, Madras.

He has worked at companies such as Yahoo!, McAfee, and Infosys in the roles of Lead Engineer and Architect in product development teams, to build new products.

His interests lie in Software Performace Engineering, High Scalability Architectures, Security and open source communities. He often works with startups in lead technical or consulting role.

He is the founder of the Bangalore Python Users Group and a Fellow of the Python Software Foundation (PSF).

Anand is currently working as Senior Architect of Yegii Inc.

Dedicated to friends & family

Credits

Author
Anand Balachandran Pillai

Reviewer
Mike Driscoll

Commissioning Editor
Aaron Lazar

Acquisition Editor
Vinay Argekar

Content Development Editor
Rohit Kumar Singh

Technical Editors
Leena Patil
Vibhuti Gawde

Copy Editor
Sonia Mathur

Project Coordinator
Vaidehi Sawant

Proofreader
Safis Editing

Indexer
Mariammal Chettiyar

Graphics
Abhinash Sahu

Production Coordinator
Arvindkumar Gupta

Software Architecture with Python

Copyright © 2017 Packt Publishing

First published: April 2017

Production reference: 2060619

Published by Packt Publishing Ltd.
Livery Place
35 Livery Street
Birmingham B3 2PB, UK.

ISBN 978-1-78646-852-9

www.packtpub.com

Software Architecture with Python

Design and architect highly scalable, robust, clean, and high performance applications in Python

Anand Balachandran Pillai

BIRMINGHAM - MUMBAI

About the Reviewer

Mike Driscoll has been programming in Python since 2006. He enjoys writing about Python in his blog, `http://www.blog.pythonlibrary.org/`. He has coauthored the Core Python refcard for DZone. He has also worked as a technical reviewer for *Python 3 Object Oriented Programming*, *Python 2.6 Graphics Cookbook*, *Tkinter GUI Application Development Hotshot*, and several other book. He recently wrote the book Python 101 and is working on his next book.

> I would like to thank my beautiful wife, Evangeline, for always supporting me and my friends and family for all that they do to help me. And I would like to thank Jesus Christ for saving me.

www.PacktPub.com

For support files and downloads related to your book, please visit www.PacktPub.com.

Did you know that Packt offers eBook versions of every book published, with PDF and ePub files available? You can upgrade to the eBook version at www.PacktPub.com and as a print book customer, you are entitled to a discount on the eBook copy. Get in touch with us at service@packtpub.com for more details.

At www.PacktPub.com, you can also read a collection of free technical articles, sign up for a range of free newsletters and receive exclusive discounts and offers on Packt books and eBooks.

https://www.packtpub.com/mapt

Get the most in-demand software skills with Mapt. Mapt gives you full access to all Packt books and video courses, as well as industry-leading tools to help you plan your personal development and advance your career.

Customer Feedback

Thanks for purchasing this Packt book. At Packt, quality is at the heart of our editorial process. To help us improve, please leave us an honest review on this book's Amazon page at https://www.amazon.com/dp/1786468522.

If you'd like to join our team of regular reviewers, you can e-mail us at customerreviews@packtpub.com. We award our regular reviewers with free eBooks and videos in exchange for their valuable feedback. Help us be relentless in improving our products!

Table of Contents

Preface

Software architecture, or creating a blueprint design for a particular software application, is not a walk in the park. The two biggest challenges in software architecture are keeping the architecture in sync, first with the requirements as they are uncovered or evolve, and next with the implementation as it gets built and evolves.

Filled with examples and use cases, this guide takes a direct approach to helping you with everything it takes to become a successful software architect. This book will help you understand the ins and outs of Python so that you can architect and design highly scalable, robust, clean, and performant applications in Python.

What this book covers

Chapter 1, *Principles of Software Architecture*, introduces the topic of software architecture, giving you a brief on architectural quality attributes and the general principles behind them. This will enable you to have strong fundamentals in software architectural principles and foundational attributes.

Chapter 2, *Writing Modifiable and Readable Code*, covers developmental architectural quality attributes, namely, modifiability and readability. It will help you gain an understanding of the architectural quality attribute of maintainability and tactics of writing code in Python to test your applications.

Chapter 3, *Testability – Writing Testable Code*, helps you understand the architectural quality attribute of testability and how to architect Python applications for testability. You will also learn about various aspects of testability and software testing and the different libraries and modules available in Python to write testable applications.

Chapter 4, *Good Performance is Rewarding!*, covers the performance aspects of writing Python code. You will be equipped with the knowledge of performance as a quality attribute in architecture and when to optimize for performance. You will learn when to optimize for performance in the SDLC.

Chapter 5, Writing Applications that Scale, talks about the importance of writing scalable applications. It discusses different ways to achieve of application scalability and discusses scalability techniques using Python. You will also learn about theoretical aspects of scalability and the best practices in the industry.

Chapter 6, Security – Writing Secure Code, discusses the security aspect of architecture and teaches you best practices and techniques of writing applications that are secure. You will understand the different security issues to watch out for and to and to architecture applications in Python that are secure from the ground up.

Chapter 7, Design Patterns in Python, gives you an overview of design patterns in Python from a pragmatic programmer's perspective, with brief theoretical background of each pattern. You will gain knowledge of design patterns in Python that are actually useful to pragmatic programmer.

Chapter 8, Python Architectural Patterns, introduces you to the modern architectural patterns in Python from a high-level perspective while giving examples of Python libraries and frameworks to realize the approaches of these patterns to solve high-level architecture problems.

Chapter 9, Deploying Python Applications, covers the aspect of easily deploying your code on remote environments or on the cloud using Python the right way.

Chapter 10, Techniques for Debugging, covers some of the debugging techniques for Python code — from the simplest, strategically placed print statement to logging and system call tracing which will be very handy to the programmer and also help the system architect to guide his team.

What you need for this book

To run most of the code samples shown in this book, you need to have Python 3 installed on your system. The other prerequisites are mentioned at the respective instances.

Who this book is for

This book is for experienced Python developers who are aspiring to become the architects of enterprise-grade applications or software architects who would like to leverage Python to create effective blueprints of applications.

Conventions

In this book, you will find a number of text styles that distinguish between different kinds of information. Here are some examples of these styles and an explanation of their meaning.

Code words in text, database table names, folder names, filenames, file extensions, pathnames, dummy URLs, user input, and Twitter handles are shown as follows: "We can include other contexts through the use of the `include` directive."

A block of code is set as follows:

```python
class PrototypeFactory(Borg):
    """ A Prototype factory/registry class """

    def __init__(self):
        """ Initializer """

        self._registry = {}

    def register(self, instance):
        """ Register a given instance """

        self._registry[instance.__class__] = instance

    def clone(self, klass):
        """ Return clone given class """

        instance = self._registry.get(klass)
        if instance == None:
            print('Error:',klass,'not registered')
        else:
            return instance.clone()
```

When we wish to draw your attention to a particular part of a code block, the relevant lines or items are set in bold:

```
[default]
exten => s,1,Dial(Zap/1|30)
exten => s,2,Voicemail(u100)
exten => s,102,Voicemail(b100)
exten => i,1,Voicemail(s0)
```

Any command-line input or output is written as follows:

```
>>> import hash_stream
>>> hash_stream.hash_stream(open('hash_stream.py'))
'30fbc7890bc950a0be4eaa60e1fee9a1'
```

New terms and **important words** are shown in bold. Words that you see on the screen, for example, in menus or dialog boxes, appear in the text like this: "Clicking the **Next** button moves you to the next screen."

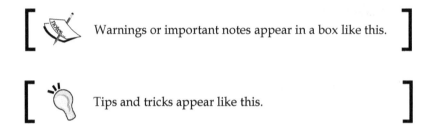

Warnings or important notes appear in a box like this.

Tips and tricks appear like this.

Reader feedback

Feedback from our readers is always welcome. Let us know what you think about this book—what you liked or disliked. Reader feedback is important for us as it helps us develop titles that you will really get the most out of.

To send us general feedback, simply e-mail feedback@packtpub.com, and mention the book's title in the subject of your message.

If there is a topic that you have expertise in and you are interested in either writing or contributing to a book, see our author guide at www.packtpub.com/authors.

Customer support

Now that you are the proud owner of a Packt book, we have a number of things to help you to get the most from your purchase.

Downloading the example code

You can download the example code files for this book from your account at http://www.packtpub.com. If you purchased this book elsewhere, you can visit http://www.packtpub.com/support and register to have the files e-mailed directly to you.

You can download the code files by following these steps:

1. Log in or register to our website using your e-mail address and password.
2. Hover the mouse pointer on the **SUPPORT** tab at the top.
3. Click on **Code Downloads & Errata**.
4. Enter the name of the book in the **Search** box.
5. Select the book for which you're looking to download the code files.
6. Choose from the drop-down menu where you purchased this book from.
7. Click on **Code Download**.

You can also download the code files by clicking on the **Code Files** button on the book's webpage at the Packt Publishing website. This page can be accessed by entering the book's name in the **Search** box. Please note that you need to be logged in to your Packt account.

Once the file is downloaded, please make sure that you unzip or extract the folder using the latest version of:

- WinRAR / 7-Zip for Windows
- Zipeg / iZip / UnRarX for Mac
- 7-Zip / PeaZip for Linux

The code bundle for the book is also hosted on GitHub at `https://github.com/PacktPublishing/Software-Architecture-with-Python`. We also have other code bundles from our rich catalog of books and videos available at `https://github.com/PacktPublishing/`. Check them out!

Downloading the color images of this book

We also provide you with a PDF file that has color images of the screenshots/ diagrams used in this book. The color images will help you better understand the changes in the output. You can download this file from `https://www.packtpub.com/sites/default/files/downloads/SoftwareArchitecturewithPython_ColorImages.pdf`.

Errata

Although we have taken every care to ensure the accuracy of our content, mistakes do happen. If you find a mistake in one of our books—maybe a mistake in the text or the code—we would be grateful if you could report this to us. By doing so, you can save other readers from frustration and help us improve subsequent versions of this book. If you find any errata, please report them by visiting http://www.packtpub.com/submit-errata, selecting your book, clicking on the **Errata Submission Form** link, and entering the details of your errata. Once your errata are verified, your submission will be accepted and the errata will be uploaded to our website or added to any list of existing errata under the Errata section of that title.

To view the previously submitted errata, go to https://www.packtpub.com/books/content/support and enter the name of the book in the search field. The required information will appear under the **Errata** section.

Piracy

Piracy of copyrighted material on the Internet is an ongoing problem across all media. At Packt, we take the protection of our copyright and licenses very seriously. If you come across any illegal copies of our works in any form on the Internet, please provide us with the location address or website name immediately so that we can pursue a remedy.

Please contact us at copyright@packtpub.com with a link to the suspected pirated material.

We appreciate your help in protecting our authors and our ability to bring you valuable content.

Questions

If you have a problem with any aspect of this book, you can contact us at questions@packtpub.com, and we will do our best to address the problem.

1
Principles of Software Architecture

This is a book on Python. At the same time, it is a book about software architecture and its various attributes, which are involved in a software development life cycle.

In order for you to understand and combine both aspects, which is essential to get maximum value from this book, it is important to grasp the fundamentals of software architecture, the themes and concepts related to it, and the various quality attributes of software architecture.

A number of software engineers, taking on senior roles in their organizations, often get very different interpretations of the definitions of software design and architecture, and the roles they play in building testable, maintainable, scalable, secure, and functional software.

Though there is a lot of literature in the field, which is available both in conventional book form and on the internet; very often, the practitioners among us get a confusing picture of these very important concepts. This is often due to the pressures involved in *learning the technology* rather than learning the fundamental design and architectural principles underlying the use of technology in building systems. This is a common practice in software development organizations, where the pressures of delivering working code often overpowers and eclipses everything else.

A book such as this one, strives to transcend the middle path in bridging the rather esoteric aspects of software development related to its architectural quality attributes to the mundane details of building software using programming languages, libraries, and frameworks—in this case, using Python and its developer ecosystem.

The role of this introductory chapter is to demystify these concepts, and explain them in very clear terms to the reader to prepare his/her for the path towards understanding the rest of this book. Hopefully, by the end of this book, the concepts and their practical details will represent a coherent body of knowledge to the reader.

We will now get started on this path without any further ado, roughly fitting this chapter into the following sections:

- Defining software architecture
- Software architecture versus design
- Aspects of software architecture
- Characteristics of software architecture
- Why is software architecture important?
- System versus Enterprise Architecture
- Architectural quality attributes
  - Modifiability
  - Testability
  - Scalability/performance
  - Security
  - Deployability

Defining software architecture

There are various definitions of software architecture in the literature concerning the topic. A simple definition is given as follows:

Software architecture is a description of the subsystems or components of a software system, and the relationships between them.

The following is a more formal definition, from the **Recommended Practice for Architectural Description of Software-Intensive Systems (IEEE)** technology:

> *"Architecture is the fundamental organization of a system embodied in its components, their relationships to each other, and to the environment, and the principles guiding its design and evolution."*

It is possible to get umpteen such definitions of software architecture if one spends some time searching on the web. The wordings might differ, but all the definitions refer to some core, fundamental aspects underlying software architecture.

Software architecture versus design

In the experience of the author, this question of the software architecture of a system versus its design seems to pop up quite often, in both online as well as offline forums. Hence, let us take a moment to understand this aspect.

Though both terms are often used interchangeably, the rough distinction of architecture versus design can be summarized as follows:

- Architecture covers the higher level structures and interactions in a system. It is concerned with those questions that entail decision making about the *skeleton* of the system, involving not only its functional but also its organizational, technical, business, and quality attributes.

- Design is all about the organization of parts or components of the system and the subsystems involved in making the system. The problems here are typically closer to the code or modules in question, such as these:

    ◦ Which modules to split code into? How to organize them?

    ◦ Which classes (or modules) to assign the different functionalities to?

    ◦ Which design pattern should I use for class "C"?

    ◦ How do my objects interact at runtime? What are the messages passed, and how is the interaction organized?

Software architecture is about the design of the entire system, whereas, software design is mostly about the details, typically at the implementation level of the various subsystems and components that make up those subsystems.

In other words, the word *design* comes up in both contexts, however, with the distinction that the former is at a much higher abstraction and at a larger scope than the latter.

There is a rich body of knowledge available for both software architecture and design, namely, **architectural patterns and design patterns** respectively. We will discuss both these topics in later chapters of this book.

Aspects of software architecture

In both the formal IEEE definition and the rather informal definition given earlier, we find some common, recurring themes. It is important to understand them in order to take our discussion on software architecture further:

- **System**: A system is a collection of components organized in specific ways to achieve a specific functionality. A software system is a collection of such software components. A system can often be subgrouped into subsystems.

- **Structure**: A structure is a set of elements that are grouped or organized together according to a guiding rule or principle. The elements can be software or hardware systems. A software architecture can exhibit various levels of structures depending on the observer's context.

- **Environment**: The environment is the context or circumstances in which a software system is built, which has a direct influence on its architecture. Such contexts can be technical, business, professional, operational, and so on.

- **Stakeholder**: A stakeholder is a person or groups of persons, who has an interest or concern in the system and its success. Examples of stakeholders are the architect, development team, customer, project manager, marketing team, and others.

Now that you have understood some of the core aspects of software architecture, let us briefly list some of its characteristics.

Characteristics of software architecture

All software architectures exhibit a common set of characteristics. Let us look at some of the most important ones here.

An architecture defines a structure

An architecture of a system is best represented as structural details of the system. It is a common practice for practitioners to draw the system architecture as a structural component or class diagram in order to represent the relationships between the subsystems.

For example, the following architecture diagram describes the backend of an application that reads from a tiered database system, which is loaded using an ETL process:

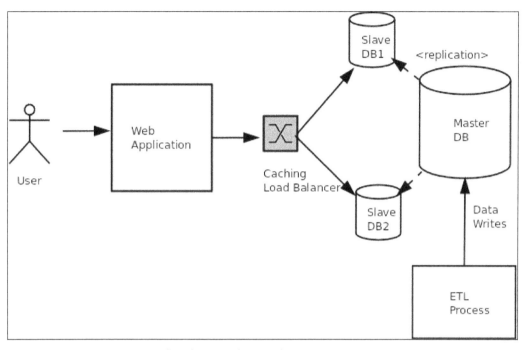

Example architecture diagram showing system structure

Structures provide insight into architectures, and provide a unique perspective to analyze the architecture with respect to its quality attributes.

Some examples are as follows:

- The runtime structures, in terms of the objects created at runtime, and how they interact often determine the deployment architecture. The deployment architecture is strongly connected to the quality attributes of scalability, performance, security, and interoperability.

- The module structures, in terms of how the code is broken down and organized into modules and packages for task breakdown, often has a direct bearing on the maintainability and modifiability (extensibility) of a system. This is explained as follows:

  - Code which is organized with a view to extensibility would often keep the parent classes in separate well-defined packages with proper documentation and configuration, which are then easily extensible by external modules, without the need to resolve too many dependencies.

  - Code which is dependent on external or third-party developers (libraries, frameworks, and the like) would often provide setup or deployment steps, which manually or automatically pull in these dependencies from external sources. Such code would also provide documentation (README, INSTALL, and so on) which clearly documents these steps.

An architecture picks a core set of elements

A well-defined architecture clearly captures only the core set of structural elements required to build the core functionality of the system, and which have a lasting effect on the system. It does not set out to document everything about every component of the system.

For example, an architect describing the architecture of a user interacting with a web server for browsing web pages — a typical client/server architecture — would focus mainly on two components: the user's browser (client) and the remote web server (server), which form the core elements of the system.

The system may have other components such as multiple caching proxies in the path from the server to the client, or a remote cache on the server which speeds up web page delivery. However, this is not the focus of the architecture description.

An architecture captures early design decisions

This is a corollary to the characteristics described previously. The decisions that help an architect to focus on some core elements of the system (and their interactions) are a result of the early design decisions about a system. Thus, these decisions play a major role in further development of the system due to their initial weight.

For example, an architect may make the following early design decisions after careful analysis of the requirements for a system:

- The system will be deployed only on Linux 64-bit servers, since this satisfies the client requirement and performance constraints

- The system will use HTTP as the protocol for implementing backend APIs

- The system will try to use HTTPS for APIs that transfer sensitive data from the backend to frontend using encryption certificates of 2,048 bits or higher

- The programming language for the system would be Python for the backend, and Python or Ruby for the frontend

The first decision freezes the deployment choices of the system to a large extent to a specific OS and system architecture. The next two decisions have a lot of weight in implementing the backend APIs. The last decision freezes the programming language choices for the system.

Early design decisions need to be arrived at after careful analysis of the requirements and matching them with the constraints—such as organizational, technical, people, and time constraints.

An architecture manages stakeholder requirements

A system is designed and built, ultimately, at the behest of its stakeholders. However, it is not possible to address each stakeholder requirement to its fullest due to an often contradictory nature of such requirements. Following are some examples:

- The marketing team is concerned with having a full-featured software application, whereas, the developer team is concerned with *feature creep* and performance issues when adding a lot of features.

- The system architect is concerned with using the latest technology to scale out his/her deployments to the cloud, while the project manager is concerned about the impact such technology deployments will have on his/her budget. The end user is concerned about correct functionality, performance, security, usability, and reliability, while the development organization (architect, development team, and managers) is concerned with delivering all these qualities while keeping the project on schedule and within budget.

- A good architecture tries its best to balance out these requirements by making trade-offs, and delivering a system with good quality attributes while keeping the people and resource costs within limits.

- An architecture also provides a common language among the stakeholders, which allows them to communicate efficiently via expressing these constraints, and helping the architect zero-in on an architecture that best captures these requirements and their trade-offs.

An architecture influences the organizational structure

The system structures an architecture describes, quite often have a direct mapping to the structure of the teams that build those systems.

For example, an architecture may have a data access layer which describes a set of services that read and write large sets of data — it is natural that such a system gets functionally assigned to the database team, which already has the required skill sets.

Since the architecture of a system is its best description of the top-down structures, it is also often used as the basis for the task-breakdown structures. Thus, software architecture often has a direct bearing on the organizational structures that build it:

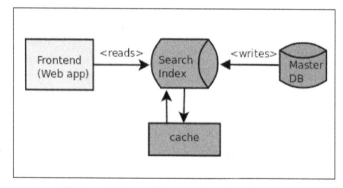

System architecture for a search web application

The following diagram shows the mapping to the team structure which would be building this application:

Frontend Team — Data Indexing Team — Database Team

An architecture is influenced by its environment

An environment imposes outside constraints or limits within which an architecture must function. In the literature, these are often called *architecture in context* [Ref: Bass, Kazman]. Some examples are as follows:

- **Quality attribute requirements**: In modern day web applications, it is very common to specify the scalability and availability requirements of the application as an early technical constraint, and capture it in the architecture. This is an example of a technical context from a business perspective.

- **Standards conformance**: In some organizations where there is often a large set of governing standards for software, especially those in the banking, insurance, and health-care domains, these get added to the early constraints of the architecture. This is an example of an external technical context.

- **Organizational constraints**: It is common to see that organizations which either have an experience with a certain architectural style or a set of teams operating with certain programming environments which impose such a style (J2EE is a good example), prefer to adopt similar architectures for future projects as a way to reduce costs and ensure productivity due to current investments in such architectures and related skills. This is an example of an internal business context.

- **Professional context**: An architect's set of choices for a system's architecture, aside from these outside contexts, is mostly shaped from his/her set of unique experiences. It is common for an architect to continue using a set of architectural choices that he/she has had the most success with in his/her past, for new projects.

Architecture choices also arise from one's own education and professional training, and also from the influence of one's professional peers.

An architecture documents the system

Every system has an architecture, whether it is officially documented or not. However, properly documented architectures can function as an effective documentation for the system. Since an architecture captures the system's initial requirements, constraints, and stakeholder trade-offs, it is a good practice to document it properly. The documentation can be used as a basis for training later on. It also helps in continued stakeholder communication, and for subsequent iterations of the architecture based on changing requirements.

The simplest way to document an architecture is to create diagrams for the different aspects of the system and organizational architecture such as Component Architecture, Deployment Architecture, Communication Architecture, and the Team or Enterprise Architecture.

Other data that can be captured early include the system requirements, constraints, early design decisions, and rationale for those decisions.

An architecture often conforms to a pattern

Most architectures conform to certain sets of styles which have had a lot of success in practice. These are referred to as architectural patterns. Examples of such patterns are client-server, pipes and filters, data-based architectures, and others. When an architect chooses an existing pattern, he/she gets to refer to and reuse a lot of existing use cases and examples related to such patterns. In modern day architectures, the job of the architect comes down to mixing and matching existing sets of such readily available patterns to solve the problem at hand.

For example, the following diagram shows an example of a client-server architecture:

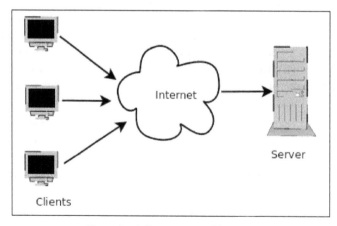

Example of client-server architecture

The following diagram describes another common architecture pattern, namely, the pipes and filters architecture for processing streams of data:

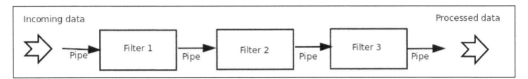

Example of pipe and filters architecture

We will see examples of architectural patterns later in this book.

Importance of software architecture

So far, we have discussed the fundamental principles of software architecture, and also seen some of its characteristics. These sections, of course, assumed that software architecture is important, and is a critical step of the software development process.

It is time to play devil's advocate, and look back at software architecture and ask some existential questions about it as follows:

- Why software architecture?
- Why is software architecture important?
- Why not build a system without a formal software architecture?

Let us take a look at the critical insights that software architecture provides, which would otherwise be missing from an informal software development process. We are only focusing on the technical or developmental aspects of the system in the following table:

Aspect	Insight/Impact	Examples
Architecture selects quality attributes to be optimized for a system.	Aspects such as scalability, availability, modifiability, security, and so on of a system depend on early decisions and trade-offs while selecting an architecture. You often trade one attribute in favor of another.	A system that is optimized for scalability must be developed using a decentralized architecture where elements are not tightly coupled. For example: microservices, brokers.

Aspect	Insight/Impact	Examples
Architecture facilitates early prototyping.	Defining an architecture allows the development organization to try and build early prototypes, which gives valuable insights into how the system would behave without having to build the complete system top down.	Many organizations build out quick prototypes of services — typically, by building only the external APIs of these services and mocking the rest of the behavior. This allows for early integration tests and figuring out interaction issues in the architecture early on.
Architecture allows a system to be built component-wise.	Having a well-defined architecture allows the reuse and assembly of existing, readily available components to achieve the functionality without having to implement everything from scratch.	Libraries or frameworks which provide ready-to-use building blocks for services. For example: web application frameworks such as Django/RoR, and task distribution frameworks such as Celery.
Architecture helps to manage changes to the system.	An architecture allows the architect to scope out changes to the system in terms of components that are affected and those which are not. This helps to keep system changes to a minimum when implementing new features, performance fixes, and so on.	A performance fix for database reads to a system would need changes only to the DB and Data Access Layer (DAL) if the architecture is implemented correctly. It need not touch the application code at all. For example, this is how most modern web frameworks are built.

There are a number of other aspects which are related to the business context of a system, into which architecture provides valuable insights. However, since this is a book mostly on the technical aspects of software architecture, we have limited our discussion to the ones given in the preceding table.

Now, let us take on the second question:

Why not build a system without a formal software architecture?

If you've been following the arguments so far thoroughly, it is not very difficult to see the answer for it. It can, however, be summarized in the following few statements:

- Every system *has* an architecture, whether it is documented or not
- Documenting an architecture makes it formal, allowing it to be shared among stakeholders, making change management and iterative development possible
- All the other benefits and characteristics of software architecture are ready to be taken advantage of when you have a formal architecture defined and documented
- You may be still able to work and build a functional system without a formal architecture, but it would not produce a system which is extensible and modifiable, and would most likely produce a system with a set of quality attributes quite far away from the original requirements

System versus enterprise architecture

You may have heard the term *architect* used in a few contexts. The following job *roles* or *titles* are pretty common in the software industry for architects:

- The Technical architect
- The Security architect
- The Information architect
- The Infrastructure architect

You also may have heard the term *System architect*, perhaps the term *Enterprise architect*, and maybe, *Solution architect* also. The interesting question is: *What do these people do?*

Let us try and find the answer to this question.

An Enterprise architect looks at the overall business and organizational strategies for an organization, and applies architecture principles and practices to guide the organization through the business, information, process, and technology changes necessary to execute their strategies. The Enterprise architect usually has a higher strategy focus and a lower technology focus. The other architect roles take care of their own subsystems and processes. For example:

- **The Technical architect**: The Technical architect is concerned with the core technology (hardware/software/network) used in an organization. A Security architect creates or tunes the security strategy used in applications to fit the organization's information security goals. An Information architect comes up with architectural solutions to make information available to/from applications in a way that facilitates the organization's business goals.

  These specific architectural roles are all concerned with their own systems and subsystems. So, each of these roles is a System architect role.

  These architects help the Enterprise architect to understand the smaller picture of each of the business domain they are responsible for, which helps the Enterprise architect to get information that will aid him in formulating business and organizational strategies.

- **The System architect**: A System architect usually has a higher technology focus and a lower strategy focus. It is a practice in some service-oriented software organizations to have a Solution architect, who combines the different systems to create a solution for a specific client. In such cases, the different architect roles are often combined into one, depending on the size of the organization, and the specific time and cost requirements of the project.

- **The Solution architect**: A Solution architect typically straddles the middle position when it comes to strategy versus technology focus and organizational versus project scope.

The following schematic diagram depicts the different layers in an organization–
Technology, **Application**, **Data**, **People**, **Process**, and **Business**, and makes the focus
area of the architect roles very clear:

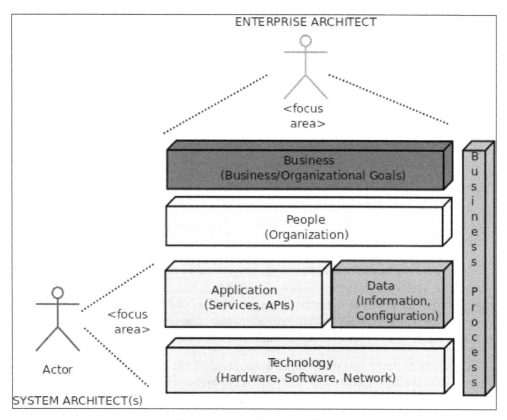

Enterprise versus System architects

Let's discuss the preceding diagram a bit to understand the picture it lays out.

The System architect is pictured on the bottom-left side of the diagram, looking at
the system components of the enterprise. His/her focus is on the applications that
power the enterprise, their data, and the hardware and software stack powering the
applications.

The Enterprise architect, on the other hand, is pictured on the top, having a top-down view of the enterprise including the business goals and the people, and not just the underlying systems that power the organization. The vertical stack of business processes connect the technical components that power the organization with its people and business components. These processes are defined by the Enterprise architect in discussion with the other stakeholders.

Now that you have understood the picture behind Enterprise and System architecture, let us take a look at some formal definitions:

> *"Enterprise Architecture is a conceptual blueprint that defines the structure and behavior of an organization. It determines how the organization's structure, processes, personnel and flow of information is aligned to its core goals to efficiently achieve its current and future objectives."*

> *"A system architecture is the fundamental organization of a system, represented by its structural and behavioral views. The structure is determined by the components of the system and the behavior by the relationships between them and their interaction with external systems."*

An Enterprise architect is concerned with how the different elements in an organization and their interplay is tuned towards achieving the goals of the organization in an efficient manner. In this work, he/she needs the support of not just the technical architects in the organization, but also people managing the organization, such as project managers and human resource professionals.

A Systems architect, on the other hand, is worried about how the core system architecture maps to the software and hardware architecture, and the various details of human interactions with the components in the system. His/her concern never arises above the boundaries defined by the system and its interactions.

The following diagram depicts the different focus areas and scopes of the different architect roles that we've discussed so far:

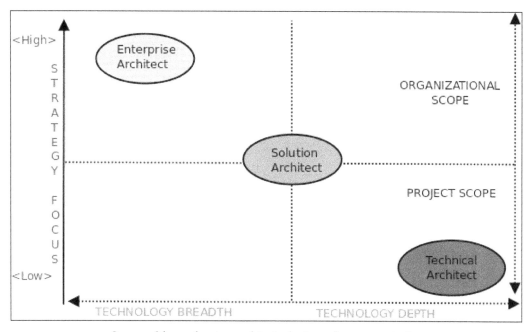

Scope and focus of various architect roles in a software organization

Architectural quality attributes

Let us now focus on an aspect which forms the main topic for the rest of this book–Architectural Quality Attributes.

In a previous section, we discussed how an architecture balances and optimizes stakeholder requirements. We also saw some examples of contradicting stakeholder requirements, which an architect seeks to balance, by choosing an architecture which does the necessary trade-offs.

The term **quality attribute** has been used to loosely define some of these aspects that an architecture makes trade-offs for. It is now the time to formally define what an Architectural Quality Attribute is:

> *"A quality attribute is a measurable and testable property of a system which can be used to evaluate the performance of a system within its prescribed environment with respect to its non-functional aspects"*

There are a number of aspects that fit this general definition of an architectural quality attribute. However, for the rest of this book, we will be focusing on the following quality attributes:

- Modifiability
- Testability
- Scalability and performance
- Availability
- Security
- Deployability

Modifiability

Many studies show that about 80% of the cost of a typical software system occurs after the initial development and deployment. This shows how important modifiability is to a system's initial architecture.

Modifiability can be defined as the ease with which changes can be made to a system, and the flexibility with which the system adjusts to the changes. It is an important quality attribute, as almost every software system changes over its lifetime — to fix issues, for adding new features, for performance improvements, and so on.

From an architect's perspective, the interest in modifiability is about the following:

- **Difficulty**: The ease with which changes can be made to a system
- **Cost**: In terms of time and resources required to make the changes
- **Risks**: Any risk associated with making changes to the system

Now, what kind of changes are we talking about here? Is it changes to code, changes to deployment, or changes to the entire architecture?

The answer is: it can be at *any* level.

From an architecture perspective, these changes can generally be captured at the following three levels:

1. **Local**: A local change only affects a specific element. The element can be a piece of code such as a function, a class, a module, or a configuration element such as an XML or JSON file. The change *does not cascade* to any neighboring element or to the rest of the system. Local changes are the easiest to make, and the least risky of all. The changes can usually be quickly validated with local unit tests.

2. **Non-local**: These changes involve more than one element. The examples are as follows:

    ◦   Modifying a database schema, which then needs to cascade into the model class representing that schema in the application code

    ◦   Adding a new configuration parameter in a JSON file, which then needs to be processed by the parser parsing the file and/or the application(s) using the parameter

    Non-local changes are more difficult to make than local changes, require careful analysis, and wherever possible, integration tests to avoid code regressions.

3. **Global**: These changes either involve architectural changes from top down, or changes to elements at the global level, which cascade down to a significant part of the software system. The examples are as follows:

    ◦   Changing a system's architecture from RESTful to messaging (SOAP, XML-RPC, and others) based web services

    ◦   Changing a web application controller from Django to an Angular-js based component

    ◦   A performance change requirement which needs all data to be preloaded at the frontend to avoid any inline model API calls for an online news application

    These changes are the riskiest, and also the costliest, in terms of resources, time and money. An architect needs to carefully vet the different scenarios that may arise from the change, and get his/her team to model them via integration tests. Mocks can be very useful in these kinds of large-scale changes.

The following table shows the relationship between **Cost** and **Risk** for the different levels of system modifiability:

Level	Cost	Risk
Local	Low	Low
Non-local	Medium	Medium
Global	High	High

Modifiability at the code level is also directly related to its readability:

> *"The more readable a code is, the more modifiable it is. Modifiability of a code goes down in proportion to its readability."*

The modifiability aspect is also related to the maintainability of the code. A code module which has its elements very tightly coupled would yield to modification much less than a module which has a loosely coupled elements — this is the **Coupling** aspect of modifiability.

Similarly, a class or module which does not define its role and responsibilities clearly would be more difficult to modify than another one which has well-defined responsibility and functionality. This aspect is called **Cohesion** of a software module.

The following table shows the relation between **Cohesion**, **Coupling**, and **Modifiability** for an imaginary module A. Assume that the coupling is from this module to another module B:

Cohesion	Coupling	Modifiability
Low	High	Low
Low	Low	Medium
High	High	Medium
High	Low	High

It is pretty clear from the preceding table that having higher Cohesion and lower Coupling is the best scenario for the modifiability of a code module.

Other factors that affect modifiability are as follows:

- **Size of a module (number of lines of code)**: Modifiability decreases when size increases.
- **Number of team members working on a module**: Generally, a module becomes less modifiable when a larger number of team members work on the module due to the complexities in merging and maintaining a uniform code base.
- **External third-party dependencies of a module**: The larger the number of external third-party dependencies, the more difficult it is to modify the module. This can be thought of as an extension of the coupling aspect of a module.
- **Wrong use of the module API**: If there are other modules which make use of the private data of a module rather than (correctly) using its public API, it is more difficult to modify the module. It is important to ensure proper usage standards of modules in your organization to avoid such scenarios. This can be thought of as an extreme case of tight **Coupling**.

Testability

Testability refers to how much a software system is amenable to demonstrating its faults through testing. Testability can also be thought of as how much a software system *hides* its faults from end users and system integration tests — the more testable a system is, the less it is able to hide its faults.

Testability is also related to how predictable a software system's behavior is. The more predictable a system, the more it allows for repeatable tests, and for developing standard test suites based on a set of input data or criteria. Unpredictable systems are much less amenable to any kind of testing, or, in extreme case, not testable at all.

In software testing, you try to control a system's behavior by, typically, sending it a set of known inputs, and then observing the system for a set of known outputs. Both of these combine to form a testcase. A test suite or test harness, typically, consists of many such test cases.

Test assertions are the techniques that are used to fail a test case when the output of the element under the test does not match the expected output for the given input. These assertions are usually manually coded at specific steps in the test execution stage to check the data values at different steps of the testcase:

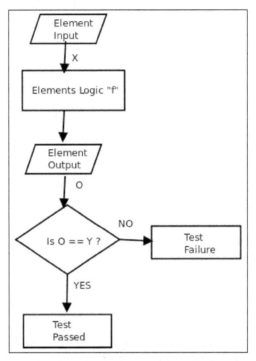

Representative flowchart of a simple unit test case for function f('X') = 'Y'

The preceding diagram shows an example of a representative flowchart for a testable function "**f**" for a sample input "**X**" with expected output "**Y**".

In order to recreate the session or state at the time of a failure, the *record/playback* strategy is often used. This employs specialized software (such as Selenium), which records all user actions that led to a specific fault, and saves it as a testcase. The test is reproduced by replaying the testcase using the same software which tries to simulate the same testcase; this is done by repeating the same set and order of UI actions.

Testability is also related to the complexity of code in a way very similar to modifiability. A system becomes more testable when parts of it can be isolated and made to work independent of the rest of the system. In other words, a system with low coupling is more testable than a system with high coupling.

Another aspect of testability, which is related to the predictability mentioned earlier, is to reduce non-determinism. When writing test suites, we need to isolate the elements that are to be tested from other parts of the system which have a tendency to behave unpredictably so that the tested element's behavior becomes predictable.

An example is a multi-threaded system, which responds to events raised in other parts of the system. The entire system is probably quite unpredictable, and not amenable to repeated testing. Instead, one needs to separate the events subsystem, and possibly, mock its behavior so that those inputs can be controlled, and the subsystem which receives the events becomes predictable and hence, testable.

The following schematic diagram explains the relationship between the testability and predictability of a system to the **Coupling** and **Cohesion** between its components:

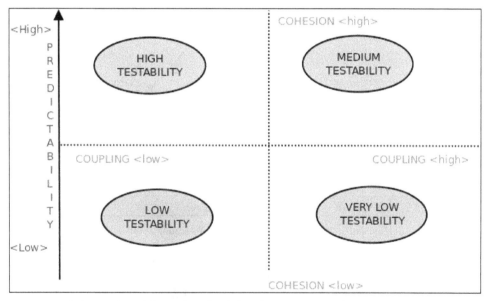

Relation of testability and predictability of a system to coupling and cohesion

Scalability

Modern-day web applications are all about *scaling up*. If you are part of any modern-day software organization, it is very likely that you have heard about or worked on an application that is written for the cloud, which is able to scale up elastically on demand.

Scalability of a system is its capacity to accommodate increasing workload on demand while keeping its performance within acceptable limits.

Scalability in the context of a software system, typically, falls into two categories, which are as follows:

- **Horizontal scalability**: Horizontal scalability implies scaling out/in a software system by adding more computing nodes to it. Advances in cluster computing in the last decade have given rise to the advent of commercial horizontally scalable **elastic** systems as services on the web. A well-known example is Amazon Web Services. In horizontally scalable systems, typically, data and/or computation is done on units or nodes, which are, usually, virtual machines running on commodity systems known as virtual private servers (VPS). The scalability is achieved "n" times by adding n or more nodes to the system, typically fronted by a load balancer. Scaling out means expanding the scalability by adding more nodes, and scaling in means reducing the scalability by removing existing nodes:

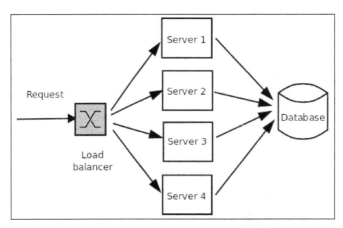

Example deployment architecture showing horizontally scaling a web application server

- **Vertical scalability**: Vertical scalability involves adding or removing resources from a single node in a system. This is usually done by adding or removing CPUs or RAM (memory) from a single virtual server in a cluster. The former is called scaling up, and the latter, scaling down. Another kind of scaling up is increasing the capacity of an existing software process in the system – typically, by augmenting its processing power. This is usually done by increasing the number of processes or threads available to an application. Some examples are as follows:
    - Increasing the capacity of an Nginx server process by increasing its number of worker processes
    - Increasing the capacity of a PostgreSQL server by increasing its number of maximum connections

Performance

Performance of a system is related to its scalability. Performance of a system can be defined as follows:

> *"Performance of a computer system is the amount of work accomplished by a system using a given unit of computing resource. Higher the work/unit ratio, higher the performance."*

The unit of computing resource to measure performance can be one of the following:

- **Response time**: How much time a function or any unit of execution takes to execute in terms of real time (user time) and clock time (CPU time).

- **Latency**: How much time it takes for a system to get its stimulation, and then provide a response. An example is the time it takes for the request-response loop of a web application to complete, measured from the end-user perspective.

- **Throughput**: The rate at which a system processes its information. A system which has higher performance would usually have a higher throughput, and correspondingly higher scalability. An example is the throughput of an e-commerce website measured as the number of transactions completed per minute.

Performance is closely tied to scalability, especially, vertical scalability. A system that has excellent performance with respect to its memory management would easily scale up vertically by adding more RAM.

Similarly, a system that has multi-threaded workload characteristics and is written optimally for a multicore CPU, would scale up by adding more CPU cores.

Horizontal scalability is thought of as having no direct connection to the performance of a system within its own compute node. However, if a system is written in a way that it doesn't utilize the network effectively, thereby producing network latency issues, it may have a problem scaling horizontally effectively, as the time spent on network latency would offset any gain in scalability obtained by distributing the work.

Some dynamic programming languages such as Python have built-in scalability issues when it comes to scaling up vertically. For example, the **Global Interpreter Lock (GIL)** of Python (CPython) prevents it from making full use of the available CPU cores for computing by multiple threads.

Availability

Availability refers to the property of readiness of a software system to carry out its operations when the need arises.

Availability of a system is closely related to its reliability. The more reliable a system is, the more available it is.

Another factor which modifies availability is the ability of a system to recover from faults. A system may be very reliable, but if the system is unable to recover either from complete or partial failures of its subsystems, then it may not be able to guarantee availability. This aspect is called **recovery**.

The availability of a system can be defined as follows:

> *"Availability of a system is the degree to which the system is in a fully operable state to carry out its functionality when it is called or invoked at random."*

Mathematically, this can be expressed as follows:

Availability = $MTBF/(MTBF + MTTR)$

Take a look at the following terms used in the preceding formula:

- **MTBF**: Mean time between failures
- **MTTR**: Mean time to repair

This is often called the **mission capable rate** of a system.

Techniques for **Availability** are closely tied to recovery techniques. This is due to the fact that a system can never be 100% available. Instead, one needs to plan for faults and strategies to recover from faults, which directly determines the availability. These techniques can be classified as follows:

- **Fault detection**: The ability to detect faults and take action helps to avert situations where a system or parts of a system become unavailable completely. Fault detection typically involves steps such as monitoring, heartbeat, and ping/echo messages, which are sent to the nodes in a system, and the response measured to calculate if the nodes are alive, dead, or are in the process of failing.

- **Fault recovery**: Once a fault is detected, the next step is to prepare the system to recover from the fault and bring it to a state where the system can be considered available. Typical tactics used here include Hot/Warm Spares (Active/Passive redundancy), Rollback, Graceful Degradation, and Retry.

- **Fault prevention**: This approach uses active methods to anticipate and prevent faults from occurring so that the system does not have a chance to go to recovery.

Availability of a system is closely tied to the consistency of its data via the CAP theorem which places a theoretical limit on the trade-offs a system can make with respect to consistency versus availability in the event of a network partition. The CAP theorem states that a system can choose between being consistent or being available — typically leading to two broad types of systems, namely, CP (consistent and tolerant to network failures) and AP (available and tolerant to network failures).

Availability is also tied to the system's scalability tactics, performance metrics, and its security. For example, a system that is highly horizontally scalable would have a very high availability, since it allows the load balancer to determine inactive nodes and take them out of the configuration pretty quickly.

A system which, instead, tries to scale up may have to monitor its performance metrics carefully. The system may have availability issues even when the node on which the system is fully available if the software processes are squeezed for system resources, such as CPU time or memory. This is where performance measurements become critical, and the system's load factor needs to be monitored and optimized.

With the increasing popularity of web applications and distributed computing, security is also an aspect that affects availability. It is possible for a malicious hacker to launch remote denial of service attacks on your servers, and if the system is not made foolproof against such attacks, it can lead to a condition where the system becomes unavailable or only partially available.

Security

Security, in the software domain, can be defined as the degree of ability of a system to avoid damage to its data and logic from unauthenticated access, while continuing to provide services to other systems and roles that are properly authenticated.

A security crisis or attack occurs when a system is intentionally compromised with a view to gaining illegal access to it in order to compromise its services, copy, or modify its data, or deny access to its legitimate users.

In modern software systems, the users are tied to specific roles which have exclusive rights to different parts of the system. For example, a typical web application with a database may define the following roles:

- **user**: End user of the system with login and access to his/her private data
- **dbadmin**: Database administrator, who can view, modify, or delete all database data
- **reports**: Report admin, who has admin rights only to those parts of database and code that deal with report generation
- **admin**: Superuser, who has edit rights to the complete system

This way of allocating system control via user roles is called **access control**. Access control works by associating a user role with certain system privileges, thereby decoupling the actual user login from the rights granted by these privileges.

This principle is the **Authorization** technique of security.

Another aspect of security is with respect to transactions where each person must validate the actual identity of the other. Public key cryptography, message signing, and so on are common techniques used here. For example, when you sign an e-mail with your GPG or PGP key, you are validating yourself — *The sender of this message is really me, Mr. A* — to your friend Mr. B on the other side of the e-mail. This principle is the **Authentication** technique of security.

The other aspects of security are as follows:

- **Integrity**: These techniques are used to ensure that data or information is not tampered with in anyway on its way to the end user. Examples are message hashing, CRC Checksum, and others.
- **Origin**: These techniques are used to assure the end receiver that the origin of the data is exactly the same as where it is purporting to be from. Examples of this are SPF, Sender-ID (for e-mail), Public Key Certificates and Chains (for websites using SSL), and others.
- **Authenticity**: These are the techniques which combine both the Integrity and Origin of a message into one. This ensures that the author of a message cannot deny the contents of the message as well as its origin (himself/herself). This typically uses **Digital Certificate Mechanisms**.

Deployability

Deployability is one of those quality attributes which is not fundamental to the software. However, in this book, we are interested in this aspect, because it plays a critical role in many aspects of the ecosystem in the Python programming language and its usefulness to the programmer.

Deployability is the degree of ease with which software can be taken from the development to the production environment. It is more of a function of the technical environment, module structures, and programming runtime/languages used in building a system, and has nothing to do with the actual logic or code of the system.

The following are some factors that determine deployability:

- **Module structures**: If your system has its code organized into well-defined modules/projects which compartmentalize the system into easily deployable subunits, the deployment is much easier. On the other hand, if the code is organized into a monolithic project with a single setup step, it would be hard to deploy the code into a multiple node cluster.

- **Production versus development environment**: Having a production environment which is very similar to the structure of the development environment makes deployment an easy task. When the environments are similar, the same set of scripts and toolchains that are used by the developers/DevOps team can be used to deploy the system to a development server as well as a production server with minor changes — mostly in the configuration.

- **Development ecosystem support**: Having a mature tool-chain support for your system runtime, which allows configurations such as dependencies to be automatically established and satisfied, increases deployability. Programming languages such as Python are rich in this kind of support in its development ecosystem, with a rich array of tools available for the DevOps professional to take advantage of.

- **Standardized configuration**: It is a good idea to keep your configuration structures (files, database tables, and others) the same for both developer and production environments. The actual objects or filenames can be different, but if the configuration structures vary widely across both the environments, deployability decreases, as extra work is required to map the configuration of the environment to its structures.

- **Standardized infrastructure:** It is a well-known fact that keeping your deployments to a homogeneous or standardized set of infrastructure greatly aids deployability. For example, if you standardize your frontend application to run on 4 GB RAM, Debian-based 64-bit Linux VPS, then it is easy to automate deployment of such nodes—either using a script, or by using elastic compute approaches of providers such as Amazon—and to keep a standard set of scripts across both development and production environments. On the other hand, if your production deployment consists of heterogeneous infrastructure, say, a mix of Windows and Linux servers with varying capacities and resource specifications, the work typically doubles for each type of infrastructure decreasing deployability.

- **Use of containers:** The user of container software, popularized by the advent of technology such as Docker and Vagrant built on top of Linux containers, has become a recent trend in deploying software on servers. The use of containers allows you to standardize your software, and makes deployability easier by reducing the amount of overhead required to start/stop the nodes, as containers don't come with the overhead of a full virtual machine. This is an interesting trend to watch for.

Summary

In this chapter, we learned about software architecture. We saw the different aspects of software architecture, and learned that every architecture comprises a system, which has a structure working in an environment for its stakeholders. We briefly looked at how software architecture differs from software design.

We went on to look at various characteristics of software architecture such as how a software architecture defines a structure, picks a core set of elements, and connects stakeholders.

We then addressed the important question of the importance of software architecture to an organization, and why it is a good idea to have a formal software architecture defined for your software systems.

The distinction of different roles of architects in an organization was discussed next. We saw the various roles system architects play in an organization, and how an Enterprise architect's focus is different from that of the System architect. The focus of strategy and technology breadth versus technology depth was clarified with illustrations.

We then discussed the elements of the main theme of this book — Architectural Quality Attributes. We defined what a quality attribute is, and then looked, in quite some detail, at the quality attributes of Modifiability, Testability, Scalability/Performance, Security, and Deployability. While going into the details of these attributes, we discussed their definitions, techniques, and how they relate to each other.

With this chapter serving as the base, we are now ready to take on these quality attributes, and then discuss in detail the various tactics and techniques to achieve them using the Python programming language. That forms the rest of this book.

In the next chapter, we'll start with one of the very first quality attributes we discussed in this chapter, namely, Modifiability and its associated attribute, Readability.

2
Writing Modifiable and Readable Code

In the first chapter, we discussed the various aspects of software architecture and covered some definitions of the terms involved. We looked at the different aspects of software architecture that an architect should be concerned with. Toward the end of the chapter, we discussed the various architectural quality attributes that an architect should focus on when building a system. We went in some detail into each of these attributes and looked at some definitions and various concerns that should be kept in mind when architecting a system for achieving these attributes.

From this chapter onward, we will focus on each of these quality attributes one by one, and discuss them in detail, per chapter. We will delve deep into an attribute — such as its various factors, techniques to achieve it, aspects to keep in mind when programming toward it, and so on. Since our focus in this book is on Python and its ecosystem, we will also look at various code examples and third-party software support that Python provides for achieving and maintaining these quality attributes.

The focus of this chapter is on the quality attribute of modifiability.

This chapter will cover the following topics:

- What is modifiability?
- Aspects related to modifiability
- Understanding readability
- Fundamentals of modifiability — cohesion and coupling
- Exploring strategies for modifiability
- Metrics — tools for static analysis
- Refactoring code

What is modifiability?

The architectural quality attribute of modifiability can be defined as follows:

> *Modifiability is the degree of ease with which changes can be made to a system, and the flexibility with which the system adapts to such changes.*

We discussed various aspects of modifiability in the first chapter, such as **cohesion**, **coupling**, and others. We will dig a little bit deeper into these aspects in this chapter with some examples. However, before we dig deeper, it might be a good idea to take a look at the big picture of how modifiability fits in with the other quality attributes that are related to it.

Aspects related to modifiability

We have already seen some aspects of modifiability in the previous chapter. Let's discuss this a bit further and look at some of the related quality attributes that are closely related to modifiability:

- **Readability**: Readability can be defined as the ease with which a program's logic can be followed and understood. Readable software is code that has been written in a specific style, following guidelines typically adopted for the programming language used, and whose logic uses the features provided by the language in a concise, clear way.

- **Modularity**: Modularity means that the software system is written in well-encapsulated modules, which do very specific, well-documented functions. In other words, modular code provides programmer friendly APIs to the rest of the system. Modifiability is closely connected to reusability.

- **Reusability**: This measures the number of parts of a software system, including code, tools, designs, and others, that can be reused in other parts of the system with zero or very little modifications. A good design would emphasize reusability from the beginning. Reusability is embodied in the DRY principle of software development.

- **Maintainability**: Maintainability of a software is the ease and efficiency with which the system can be updated and kept working in a useful state by its intended stakeholders. Maintainability is a metric, which encompasses the aspects of modifiability, readability, modularity and testability.

In this chapter, we are going to go deep into the readability, reusability, and modularity aspects. We will look at these one by one from the context of the Python programming language. We will start with readability first.

Understanding readability

The readability of a software system is closely tied to its modifiability. Well-written, well-documented code, keeping up with standard or adopted practices for the programming language, tends to produce simple, concise code that is easy to read and modify.

Readability is not only related to the aspect of following good coding guidelines, but it also ties up to how clear the logic is, how much the code uses standard features of the language, how modular the functions are, and so on.

In fact, we can summarize the different aspects of readability as follows:

- **Well-written**: A piece of code is well-written if it uses simple syntax and well-known features and idioms of the language, if the logic is clear and concise, and if it uses variables, functions, and class/module names meaningfully, that is, they express what they do.

- **Well-documented**: Documentation usually refers to the inline comments in the code. A well-documented piece of code tells what it does, what its input arguments are, and what is its return value (if any) along with the logic or algorithm, in some detail. It also documents any external library or API usage and configuration required for running the code either inline or in separate files.

- **Well-formatted**: Most programming languages, especially the open source languages like Python, developed over the internet via distributed but closely-knit programming communities, tend to have well-documented style guidelines. A piece of code that keeps up with these guidelines on aspects such as indentation and formatting will tend to be more readable than something that doesn't.

Lack of readability affects modifiability, and hence, maintainability of the code, thereby incurring ever-increasing costs for the organization in terms of resources — mainly people and time — in maintaining the system in a useful state.

Python and readability

Python is a language that has been designed from the ground-up for readability. To borrow a line from the well-known Zen of Python, we can say:

Readability counts

The Zen of Python is a set of 20 principles that influence the design of the Python programming language, 19 of which have been written down. You can see the Zen of Python by opening the Python interpreter prompt and typing this:

```
>>>import this
```

Python, as a language, emphasizes readability. It achieves this by clear, concise keywords, which mimic their English language counterparts, using minimal operators, and using the following philosophy:

There should be one – and preferably only one – obvious way to do it.

For example, here is one way to iterate through a sequence in Python while also printing its index:

```
for idx in range(len(seq)):
    item = seq[idx]
    print(idx, '=>', item)
```

However, a more common idiom used in Python is the enumerate() helper for iterators, which returns a two tuple of (idx, item) for each item in the sequence:

```
for idx, item in enumerate(seq):
    print(idx, '=>', item)
```

In many other programming languages such as C++ or Java, the first version would be considered with the same merit as the second version. However, in Python, there are certain idioms of writing code that keep up with the language's principles – the Zen – than certain others.

In this case, the second version is closer to the way Python programmers would write code to solve the problem. The first way would be considered less Pythonic than the second one.

The term "Pythonic" is something you would commonly encounter when interacting with the Python community. It means that the code not just solves the problem, but follows the conventions and idioms the Python community generally follows, and uses the language in the way it is intended to be used.

The definition of Pythonic is subjective, but you can think of it as Python code keeping up with the Zen of Python, or in general, following well-known idiomatic programming practices adopted by the community.

Python, by its design principles and clean syntax, makes writing readable code easy. However, it is a common trap for programmers migrating to Python from other more pedantic and less-idiomatic languages to write Python code in a less Pythonic way.

It is important for a Python programmer to understand this aspect early so that you tend to write more idiomatic or Pythonic code as you get used to the language more and more. You can be more productive with Python in the long term if you familiarize yourself with its coding principles and idioms than otherwise.

Readability – antipatterns

Python, in general, encourages and facilitates writing readable code. However, it would be, of course, very unrealistic to say that any code written in Python is highly readable. Even with all of its readability DNA, Python also has its fair share of difficult-to-read, badly written, or unreadable code as can be evident by spending some time scanning through some of the public, open source code written in Python on the web.

There are certain practices that tend to produce difficult-to-read or unreadable code in a programming language. These can be thought of as antipatterns, which are a bane, not just in programming with Python, but in any programming language:

- **Code with little or no comments**: Lack of code comments is often the primary reason for producing code that is unreadable. More often than not, programmers don't do a very good job of documenting their thoughts, which led to a particular implementation, in code. When the same code is read by another programmer or by the same programmer a few months later (this happens quite a lot!), it is not easy to figure out why the specific implementation approach was followed. This makes it difficult to reason about the pros and cons of an alternate approach.

  This also makes taking decisions on modifying the code – perhaps for a customer fix – difficult, and in general, affects code modifiability in the long term. The commenting of code is often an indicator of the discipline and rigor of the programmer who wrote the code and of the organization in enforcing such practices.

- **Code that breaks best practices of the language**: Best practices of a programming language typically evolve from years of experience in using the language by a community of developers, and the efficient feedback that it generates. They capture the best way of putting the programming language to good use to solve problems, and typically, capture the idioms and common patterns for using the language.

For example, in Python, the Zen can be considered as a shining torch to its best practices and the set of common programming idioms adopted by the community.

Often, programmers who are either inexperienced or those who migrate from other programming languages or environments tend to produce code that is not in keeping with these practices, and hence, end up writing code that is low on readability.

- **Programming antipatterns**: There are a large number of coding or programming antipatterns, which tend to produce difficult-to-read, and hence, difficult-to-maintain code. Here are some of the well-known ones:
    - **Spaghetti code**: This is a piece of code with no discernible structure or control-flow. It is typically produced by following complex logic with a lot of unconditional jumps and unstructured exception handling, badly written concurrent code and so on.
    - **Big ball of mud**: This is a system with pieces of code that show no overall structure or goal. Big ball of mud typically consists of many pieces of spaghetti code and is usually a sign of code that has been worked on by multiple people, patched-up multiple times with little or zero documentation.
    - **Copy-Paste programming**: Often produced in organizations where expediency of delivery is favored over thoughtful design, copy/paste coding produces long, repetitive chunks of code, which essentially do the same thing again and again with minor modifications. This leads to code-bloat and, in the long term, the code becomes unmaintainable.

        A similar antipattern is *cargo-cult programming*, where programmers follows the same design or programming pattern over and over again without a thought to whether it fits the specific scenarios or problems that they are trying to solve.
    - **Ego programming**: Ego programming is where a programmer — often an experienced one — favors their personal style over the documented best practices or the organizational style of coding. This sometimes creates code that is cryptic and difficult to read for the other — usually, younger or less-experienced programmers. An example is the tendency to use functional programming constructs in Python to write everything as a one-liner.

Coding antipatterns can be circumvented by adopting practices of structured programming in your organization, and by enforcing the use of coding guidelines and best practices.

The following are some antipatterns that are specific to Python:

- **Mixed indentation**: Python uses indentation to separate blocks of code, as it lacks braces or other syntactical constructs of languages such as C/C++ or Java, which separate code blocks. However, we need to be careful when indenting code in Python. A common antipattern is where people mix both tabs (the `\t` character) and spaces in their Python code. This can be fixed by using editors that always use either tabs or spaces to indent code.

    Python comes with built-in modules such as `tabnanny`, which can be used to check your code for indentation issues.

- **Mixing string literal types**: Python provides three different ways to create string literals: either by using the single quote (`'`), the double quote (`"`), or Python's own special triple quote (`'''` or `"""`). Code that mixes these three types of literals in the same block of code or functional unit becomes more difficult to read.

- **Overuse of functional constructs**: Python, being a mixed paradigm language, provides support for functional programming via its lambda keyword and its `map()`, `reduce()`, and `filter()` functions. However, sometimes, experienced programmers or programmers coming from a background of functional programming to Python overuse these constructs, producing code that is too cryptic and, hence, unreadable to other programmers.

Techniques for readability

Now that we have a good knowledge on what helps readability of code, let's look at the approaches that we can adopt in order to improve the readability of code in Python.

Document your code

A simple and effective way to improve the readability of your code is to document what it does. Documentation is important for readability and long term modifiability of your code.

Code documentation can be categorized as follows:

- **Inline documentation**: The programmer documents their code by using code comments, function documentation, module documentation, and others as part of the code itself. This is the most effective and useful type of code documentation.

- **External documentation**: These are additional documentation captured in separate files, which usually document aspects such as usage of code, code changes, install steps, deployment, and the like. Examples are the README, INSTALL, or CHANGELOG files usually found with open source projects keeping up with the GNU build principles.

- **User manuals**: These are formal documents, usually by a dedicated person or team, using pictures and text that is usually targeted toward users of the system. Such documentation is usually prepared and delivered toward the end of a software project when the product is stable and is ready to ship. We are not concerned with this type of documentation in our discussion here.

Python is a language that is designed for smart inline code documentation from the ground up. In Python, inline documentation can be done at the following levels:

- **Code comments**: This is the text inline with code, prefixed by the hash (#) character. They can be used liberally inside your code explaining what each step of the code does.

  Here is an example:

```
# This loop performs a network fetch of the URL, retrying up to 3
# times in case of errors. In case the URL can't be fetched,
# an error is returned.

# Initialize all state
count, ntries, result, error = 0, 3, None, None
while count < ntries:
    try:
        # NOTE: We are using an explicit   timeout of 30s here
        result = requests.get(url, timeout=30)
    except Exception as error:
        print('Caught exception', error, 'trying again after a
            while')
      # increment count
      count += 1
      # sleep 1 second every time
      time.sleep(1)

    if result == None:
```

```
    print("Error, could not fetch URL",url)
    # Return a tuple of (<return code>, <lasterror>)
    return (2, error)


# Return data of URL
    return result.content
```

Notice the liberal use of comments even in places it may be deemed superfluous. We will look at some general rules of thumb in commenting your code later.

- **The docstring function**: Python provides a simple way to document what a function does by using a string literal just below the function definition. This can be done by using any of the three styles of string literals.

Here is an example:

```
def fetch_url(url, ntries=3, timeout=30):
    " Fetch a given url and return its contents "

    # This loop performs a network fetch of the URL, retrying
    # up to
    # 3 times in case of errors. In case the URL can't be
    # fetched,
    # an error is returned.

    # Initialize all state
    count, result, error = 0, None, None
    while count < ntries:
        try:
            result = requests.get(url, timeout=timeout)
        except Exception as error:
            print('Caught exception', error, 'trying again
                    after a while')
            # increment count
            count += 1
            # sleep 1 second every time
            time.sleep(1)

    if result == None:
        print("Error, could not fetch URL",url)
    # Return a tuple of (<return code>, <lasterror>)
    return (2, error)

    # Return data of URL
    return result.content
```

The function docstring is the line that says *fetch a given URL and return its contents*. However, though it is useful, the usage is limited, since it only says what the function does and doesn't explain its parameters. Here is an improved version:

```
def fetch_url(url, ntries=3, timeout=30):
    """ Fetch a given url and return its contents.

    @params
        url - The URL to be fetched.
        ntries - The maximum number of retries.
        timeout - Timout per call in seconds.

    @returns
        On success - Contents of URL.
        On failure - (error_code, last_error)
    """

    # This loop performs a network fetch of the URL,
    # retrying up to
    # 'ntries' times in case of errors. In case the URL
    # can't be fetched, an error is returned.

    # Initialize all state
    count, result, error = 0, None, None
    while count < ntries:
        try:
            result = requests.get(url, timeout=timeout)
        except Exception as error:
            print('Caught exception', error, 'trying again
                    after a while')
            # increment count
            count += 1
            # sleep 1 second every time
            time.sleep(1)

    if result == None:
        print("Error, could not fetch URL",url)
        # Return a tuple of (<return code>, <lasterror>)
        return (2, error)

    # Return data of the URL
    return result.content
```

In the preceding code, the function usage has become much clearer to the programmer. Note that such extended documentation would usually span more than one line, and hence, it is a good idea to always use triple quotes with your function docstrings.

- **Class docstrings**: These work just like a function docstring except that they provide documentation for a class directly. This is provided just below the class keyword defining the class.

Here is an example:

```
class UrlFetcher(object):
    """ Implements the steps of fetching a URL.

        Main methods:
        fetch - Fetches the URL.
        get - Return the URLs data.
    """

    def __init__(self, url, timeout=30, ntries=3, headers={}):
        """ Initializer.
        @params
            url - URL to fetch.
            timeout - Timeout per connection (seconds).
            ntries - Max number of retries.
            headers - Optional request headers.
        """
        self.url = url
        self.timeout = timeout
        self.ntries = retries
        self.headers = headers
        # Enapsulated result object
        self.result = result

    def fetch(self):
        """ Fetch the URL and save the result """

        # This loop performs a network fetch of the URL,
          # retrying
        # up to 'ntries' times in case of errors.

        count, result, error = 0, None, None
        while count < self.ntries:
```

```
        try:
            result = requests.get(self.url,
                                    timeout=self.timeout,
                                    headers = self.headers)
        except Exception as error:
            print('Caught exception', error, 'trying again
                    after a while')
            # increment count
            count += 1
            # sleep 1 second every time
            time.sleep(1)

    if result != None:
        # Save result
        self.result = result

def get(self):
    """ Return the data for the URL """

    if self.result != None:
        return self.result.content
```

See how the class docstring defines some of the main methods of the class. This is a very useful practice, as it gives the programmer useful information at the top level without having to go and inspect each function's documentation separately.

- **Module docstrings**: Module docstrings capture information at the module level, usually about the functionality of the module and some detail about what each member of the module (function, class, and others) does. The syntax is the same as the class or function docstring. The information is usually captured at the top of the module, before any code.

A module documentation can also capture any specific external dependencies of a module:

```
"""
    urlhelper - Utility classes and functions to work with URLs.

    Members:

        # UrlFetcher - A class which encapsulates action of
        # fetching content of a URL.
```

```
        # get_web_url - Converts URLs so they can be used on the
        # web.
        # get_domain - Returns the domain (site) of the URL.
"""

import urllib

def get_domain(url):
    """ Return the domain name (site) for the URL"""

    urlp = urllib.parse.urlparse(url)
    return urlp.netloc

def get_web_url(url, default='http'):
    """ Make a URL useful for fetch requests
    -  Prefix network scheme in front of it if not present already
    """

    urlp = urllib.parse.urlparse(url)
    if urlp.scheme == '' and urlp.netloc == '':
            # No scheme, prefix default
      return default + '://' + url

    return url

class UrlFetcher(object):
      """ Implements the steps of fetching a URL.

        Main methods:
        fetch - Fetches the URL.
        get - Return the URLs data.
      """

      def __init__(self, url, timeout=30, ntries=3, headers={}):
          """ Initializer.
          @params
              url - URL to fetch.
              timeout - Timeout per connection (seconds).
              ntries - Max number of retries.
              headers - Optional request headers.
          """
          self.url = url
          self.timeout = timeout
          self.ntries = retries
```

```
            self.headers = headers
            # Enapsulated result object
            self.result = result

    def fetch(self):
        """ Fetch the URL and save the result """

        # This loop performs a network fetch of the URL, retrying
        # up to 'ntries' times in case of errors.

        count, result, error = 0, None, None
        while count < self.ntries:
            try:
                result = requests.get(self.url,
                                      timeout=self.timeout,
                                      headers = self.headers)
            except Exception as error:
                print('Caught exception', error, 'trying again
                      after a while')
                # increment count
                count += 1
                # sleep 1 second every time
                time.sleep(1)

        if result != None:
            # Save result
            self.result = result

    def get(self):
        """ Return the data for the URL """

        if self.result != None:
            return self.result.content
```

Follow coding and style guidelines

Most programming languages have a relatively well-known set of coding and/or style guidelines. These are either developed over many years of use as a convention, or come as a result of discussions in the online community of that programming language. C/C++ is a good example of the former, and Python is a good example of the latter.

It is also a common practice for companies to specify their own guidelines—mostly, by adopting existing standard guidelines and customizing them for the company's own specific development environment and requirements.

For Python, there is a clear set of coding style guidelines published by the Python programming community. This guideline, known as PEP-8, is available online as part of the **Python Enhancement Proposal** (**PEP**) set of documents.

 You can find PEP-8 at the following URL: `https://www.python.org/dev/peps/pep-0008/`.

PEP-8 was first created in 2001 and has undergone multiple revisions since then. The primary author is the creator of Python, Guido Van Rossum, with input from Barry Warsaw and Nick Coghlan.

PEP-8 was created by adapting Guido's original *Python Style Guide* essay with additions from Barry's style guide.

We will not go deep into PEP-8 in this book, as the goal of this section is not to teach you PEP-8. However, we will discuss the general principles underlying PEP-8.

The philosophy underlying PEP-8 can be summarized as follows:

- Code is read more than it is written. Hence, providing a guideline would make code more readable and make it consistent across a full spectrum of Python code.
- Consistency within a project is important. However, consistency within a module or package is more important. Consistency within a unit of code—such as class or function is the most important.

- Know when to ignore a guideline. For example, this may happen if adopting the guideline makes your code less readable, breaks the surrounding code, or breaks backward compatibility of the code. Study examples, and choose what is best.

- If a guideline is not directly applicable or useful for your organization, customize it. If you have any doubts about a guideline, get clarification by asking the Python community.

Review and refactor code

Code requires maintenance. Unmaintained code that is used in production can become a problem if not tended to periodically.

Periodically scheduled reviews of code can be very useful in keeping the code readable and in good health aiding modifiability and maintainability. Code that is central to a system or an application in production tends to get a lot of quick-fixes over time, as it is customized or enhanced for different use cases or patched for issues. It is observed that programmers generally don't document such quick fixes, as the situations demand expedite testing and deployment over good engineering practices such as documentation.

Over time, such patches can accumulate, thereby causing code-bloat and creating future engineering debts for the team, which can become a costly affair. The solution is periodical reviews.

Reviews should be done with engineers who are familiar with the application, but ideally, who are not working on the same code. This gives the code a fresh set of eyes, which is often useful in detecting bugs that the original author(s) may have overlooked. It is a good idea to get large changes reviewed by a couple of reviewers who are experienced developers.

This can be combined with the general refactoring of code to improve implementation, reduce coupling, or increase cohesion.

Commenting the code

We are coming toward the end of our discussions on readability of code, and it is a good time to introduce some general rules of thumb to follow when writing code comments. These can be listed as follows:

- Comments should be descriptive, and should explain the code. A comment that simply repeats what is obvious from the function name is not very useful.

  Here is an example. Both of the following codes show the same implementation of a **Root-Mean-Squared** (**RMS**) velocity calculation, but the second version has a much more useful docstring than the first:

  ```
  def rms(varray=[]):
      """ RMS velocity """

      squares = map(lambda x: x*x, varray)
      return pow(sum(squares), 0.5)


  def rms(varray=[]):
      """ Root mean squared velocity. Returns
      square root of sum of squares of velocities """

      squares = map(lambda x: x*x, varray)
      return pow(sum(squares), 0.5)
  ```

- Code comments should be written in the block we are commenting on, rather than as follows:

  ```
  # This code calculates the sum of squares of velocities
  squares = map(lambda x: x*x, varray)
  ```

  The preceding version is much clearer than the following version, which uses comments below the code:

  ```
  squares = map(lambda x: x*x, varray)
  # The above code calculates the sum of squares of velocities
  ```

- Inline comments should be used as little as possible. This is because it is very easy to get these confused as part of the code itself, especially if the separating comment character is accidentally deleted, causing bugs:

```
squares = map(lambda x: x*x, varray)    # Calculate squares of
velocities
```

- Try to avoid comments that are superfluous and add little value:

```
# The following code iterates through odd numbers
for num in nums:
    # Skip if number is odd
    if num % 2 == 0: continue
```

The second comment in the last piece of code adds little value and can be omitted.

Fundamentals of modifiability – cohesion and coupling

Let's now get back to the main topic of modifiability and discuss the two fundamental aspects that affect modifiability of code—namely, cohesion and coupling.

We've already discussed these concepts briefly in the first chapter. Let's do a quick review here.

Cohesion refers to how tightly the responsibilities of a module are related to each other. A module that performs a specific task or group of related tasks has high cohesion. A module in which a lot of functionality is dumped without a thought as to the core functionality would have low cohesion.

Coupling is the degree to which the functionality of two modules, A and B, are related. Two modules are strongly coupled if their functionality overlaps strongly at the code level—in terms of function or method calls. Any changes in module A would probably require changes in module B.

Strong coupling is always prohibitory for modifiability, as it increases the cost of maintaining the code base. Code which aims to increase modifiability should aim for high cohesion and low coupling.

We will analyze cohesion and coupling in the following subsections with some examples.

Measuring cohesion and coupling

Let's look at a simple example of two modules to figure out how we can measure coupling and cohesion quantitatively. The following is the code for module A, which purportedly implements functions that operate with a series (array) of numbers:

```
"" Module A (a.py) - Provides functions that operate on series of
numbers """

def squares(narray):
    """ Return array of squares of numbers """
    return pow_n(array, 2)

def cubes(narray):
    """ Return array of cubes of numbers """
    return pow_n(narray, 3)

def pow_n(narray, n):
    """ Return array of numbers raised to arbitrary power n each """
    return [pow(x, n) for x in narray]

def frequency(string, word):
    """ Find the frequency of occurrences of word in string
    as percentage """

    word_l = word.lower()
    string_l = string.lower()

    # Words in string
    words = string_l.split()
    count = w.count(word_l)

    # Return frequency as percentage
    return 100.0*count/len(words)
```

Next is the listing of module B:

```
""" Module B (b.py) - Provides functions implementing some statistical
methods """

import a

def rms(narray):
```

```
    """ Return root mean square of array of numbers"""
    return pow(sum(a.squares(narray)), 0.5)

def mean(array):
    """ Return mean of an array of numbers """
    return 1.0*sum(array)/len(array)

def variance(array):
    """ Return variance of an array of numbers """

    # Square of variation from mean
    avg = mean(array)
    array_d = [(x - avg) for x in array]
    variance = sum(a.squares(array_d))
    return variance

def standard_deviation(array):
    """ Return standard deviation of an array of numbers """

    # S.D is square root of variance
    return pow(variance(array), 0.5)
```

Let's do an analysis of the functions in module A and B. Here is the report:

Module	Core functions	Unrelated functions	Function dependencies
B	4	0	3 x 1 = 3
A	3	1	0

This has four functions that can be explained as follows:

- Module B has four functions, all of them dealing with the core functionality. There are no unrelated functions in this module. Module B has `100%` cohesion.

- Module A has four functions, three of which are related to its core functionality, but the last one (frequency) isn't. This gives module A approximately 75% cohesion.

- Three of the module B functions depend on one function in module A, namely, squares. This makes module B strongly coupled to module A. Coupling at function level is 75% from module B → A.

- Module A doesn't depend on any functionality of module B. Module A will work independent of module B. Coupling from module A → B is zero.

Let's now look at how we can improve the cohesion of module A. In this case, it is as simple as dropping the last function, which doesn't really belong there. It could be dropped out entirely or moved to another module.

Here is the rewritten module A code, now with 100% cohesion with respect to its responsibilities:

```
""" Module A (a.py) - Implement functions that operate on series of
numbers """

def squares(narray):
    """ Return array of squares of numbers """
    return pow_n(array, 2)

def cubes(narray):
    """ Return array of cubes of numbers """
    return pow_n(narray, 3)

def pow_n(narray, n):
    """ Return array of numbers raised to arbitrary power n each """
    return [pow(x, n) for x in narray]
```

Let's now analyze the quality of coupling from module B→ A and look at the risk factors of modifiability of code in B with respect to code in A, which are as follows:

- The three functions in B depend on just one function in module A.
- The function is named *squares*, which accepts an array and returns each of its member *squared*.
- The function signature (API) is simple, so chances of changing the function signature in the future is less.
- There is no two-way coupling in the system. The dependency is only from the direction B → A.

In other words, even though there is strong coupling from B to A, it is good coupling and doesn't affect the modifiability of the system in any way at all.

Let's now look at another example.

Measuring cohesion and coupling – string and text processing

Let's consider a different use case now, an example with modules that do a lot of string and text processing:

```
""" Module A (a.py) - Provides string processing functions """
import b

def ntimes(string, char):
    """ Return number of times character 'char'
    occurs in string """

    return string.count(char)

def common_words(text1, text2):
    """ Return common words across text1 and text2"""

    # A text is a collection of strings split using newlines
    strings1 = text1.split("\n")
    strings2 = text2.split("\n")

    common = []
    for string1 in strings1:
        for string2 in strings2:
            common += b.common(string1, string2)

    # Drop duplicates
    return list(set(common))
```

Next is the listing of module B, which is as follows:

```
""" Module B (b.py) - Provides text processing functions to user """

import a

def common(string1, string2):
    """ Return common words across strings1 1 & 2 """

    s1 = set(string1.lower().split())
    s2 = set(string2.lower().split())
    return s1.intersection(s2)
```

```
def common_words(text1, text2):
    """ Return common words across two input files """

    lines1 = open(filename1).read()
    lines2 = open(filename2).read()

    return a.common_words(lines1, lines2)
```

Let's go through the coupling and cohesion analysis of these modules, given in following table:

Module	Core functions	Unrelated functions	Function dependencies
B	2	0	1 x 1 = 1
A	2	0	1 x 1 = 1

Here is an explanation of these numbers in the table:

- Module A and B have two functions each, each of them dealing with the core functionality. Modules A and B both have 100% cohesion.
- One function of module A is dependent on one function of module B. Similarly, one function of module B is dependent on one function of module A. There is strong coupling from A→ B and from B → A. In other words, the coupling is bidirectional.

Bidirectional coupling between two modules ties their modifiability to each other very strongly. Any changes in module A will quickly cascade to behavior of module B and vice versa. In other words, this is bad coupling.

Exploring strategies for modifiability

Now that we have seen some examples of good and bad coupling and cohesion, let's get to the strategies and approaches that a software architect can adopt to improve the modifiability of the software system.

Providing explicit interfaces

A module should mark a set of functions, classes, or methods as the **interface** it provides to external code. This can be thought of as the API of this module. Any external code that uses this API would become a client to the module.

Methods or functions that the module considers internal to its function, and which do not make up its API, should either be explicitly made private to the module or should be documented as such.

In Python, which doesn't provide variable access scope for functions or class methods, this can be done by conventions such as prefixing the function name with a single or double underscore, thereby signaling to potential clients that these functions are internal and shouldn't be referred to from outside.

Reducing two-way dependencies

As seen in the examples earlier, coupling between two software modules is manageable if the coupling direction is one-way. However, bidirectional coupling creates very strong linkages between modules, which can complicate the usage of the modules and increase their maintenance costs.

In Python, which uses reference-based garbage collection, this may also create cryptic referential loops for variables and objects, thereby making garbage collection difficult.

Bidirectional dependencies can be broken by refactoring the code in such a way that a module always uses the other one and not vice versa. In other words, encapsulate all related functions in the same module.

Here are our modules A and B of the earlier example, rewritten to break their bidirectional dependency:

```python
""" Module A (a.py) - Provides string processing functions """

def ntimes(string, char):
    """ Return number of times character 'char'
    occurs in string """

    return string.count(char)

def common(string1, string2):
    """ Return common words across strings1 1 & 2 """

    s1 = set(string1.lower().split())
    s2 = set(string2.lower().split())
    return s1.intersection(s2)

def common_words(text1, text2):
    """ Return common words across text1 and text2"""
```

```
# A text is a collection of strings split using newlines
strings1 = text1.split("\n")
strings2 = text2.split("\n")

common_w = []
for string1 in strings1:
    for string2 in strings2:
        common_w += common(string1, string2)

return list(set(common_w))
```

Next is the listing of module B:

```
""" Module B (b.py) - Provides text processing functions to user """

import a

def common_words(filename1, filename2):
  """ Return common words across two input files """

  lines1 = open(filename1).read()
  lines2 = open(filename2).read()

  return a.common_words(lines1, lines2)
```

We achieved this by simply moving the common function, which picks common words from two strings from module B to A. This is an example of refactoring to improve modifiability.

Abstract common services

Usage of helper modules that abstract common functions and methods can reduce coupling between two modules and increase their cohesion. For example, in the first example, module A acts as a helper module for module B.

Helper modules can be thought of as intermediaries or mediators, which abstract common services for other modules so that the dependent code is all available in one place without duplication. They can also help modules to increase their cohesion by moving out unwanted or unrelated functions.

Using inheritance techniques

When we find similar code or functionality occurring in classes, it might be a good time to refactor them so as to create class hierarchies so that common code is shared by virtue of inheritance.

Let's take a look at the following example:

```
""" Module textrank - Rank text files in order of degree of a specific
word frequency. """

import operator

class TextRank(object):
    """ Accept text files as inputs and rank them in
    terms of how much a word occurs in them """

    def __init__(self, word, *filenames):
        self.word = word.strip().lower()
        self.filenames = filenames

    def rank(self):
        """ Rank the files. A tuple is returned with
        (filename, #occur) in decreasing order of
        occurences """

        occurs = []

        for fpath in self.filenames:
            data = open(fpath).read()
            words = map(lambda x: x.lower().strip(), data.split())
            # Filter empty words
            count = words.count(self.word)
            occurs.append((fpath, count))

        # Return in sorted order
        return sorted(occurs, key=operator.itemgetter(1),
                    reverse=True)
```

Here is another module, `urlrank`, which performs the same function on URLs:

```
""" Module urlrank - Rank URLs in order of degree of a specific
word frequency """
import operator
```

```
import operator
import requests

class UrlRank(object):
    """ Accept URLs as inputs and rank them in
    terms of how much a word occurs in them """

    def __init__(self, word, *urls):
        self.word = word.strip().lower()
        self.urls = urls

    def rank(self):
        """ Rank the URLs. A tuple is returned with
        (url, #occur) in decreasing order of
        occurences """

        occurs = []

        for url in self.urls:
            data = requests.get(url).content
            words = map(lambda x: x.lower().strip(), data.split())
            # Filter empty words
            count = words.count(self.word)
            occurs.append((url, count))

        # Return in sorted order
        return sorted(occurs, key=operator.itemgetter(1),
                      reverse=True)
```

Both these modules perform similar functions of ranking a set of input data in terms of how much a given keyword appears in them. Over time, these classes could develop a lot of similar functionality, and the organization could end up with a lot of duplicate code, reducing modifiability.

We can use inheritance to help us here to abstract away the common logic in a parent class. Here is the parent class named RankBase, which accomplishes this by abstracting all common code as part of its API:

```
""" Module rankbase - Logic for ranking text using degree of word
frequency """

import operator

class RankBase(object):
```

```
""" Accept text data as inputs and rank them in
terms of how much a word occurs in them """

def __init__(self, word):
    self.word = word.strip().lower()

def rank(self, *texts):
    """ Rank input data. A tuple is returned with
    (idx, #occur) in decreasing order of
    occurences """

    occurs = {}

    for idx,text in enumerate(texts):
        words = map(lambda x: x.lower().strip(), text.split())
        count = words.count(self.word)
        occurs[idx] = count

    # Return dictionary
    return occurs

def sort(self, occurs):
    """ Return the ranking data in sorted order """

    return sorted(occurs, key=operator.itemgetter(1),
                    reverse=True)
```

We now have the `textrank` and `urlrank` modules rewritten to take advantage of the logic in the parent class:

```
""" Module textrank - Rank text files in order of degree of a specific
word frequency. """

import operator
from rankbase import RankBase

class TextRank(object):
    """ Accept text files as inputs and rank them in
    terms of how much a word occurs in them """

    def __init__(self, word, *filenames):
        self.word = word.strip().lower()
        self.filenames = filenames

    def rank(self):
```

```
""" Rank the files. A tuple is returned with
(filename, #occur) in decreasing order of
occurences """

texts = map(lambda x: open(x).read(), self.filenames)
occurs = super(TextRank, self).rank(*texts)
# Convert to filename list
occurs = [(self.filenames[x],y) for x,y in occurs.items()]

return self.sort(occurs)
```

Here is the modified listing for the urlrank module:

```
""" Module urlrank - Rank URLs in order of degree of a specific word
frequency """

import requests
from rankbase import RankBase

class UrlRank(RankBase):
    """ Accept URLs as inputs and rank them in
    terms of how much a word occurs in them """

def __init__(self, word, *urls):
    self.word = word.strip().lower()
    self.urls = urls

def rank(self):
    """ Rank the URLs. A tuple is returned with
    (url, #occur) in decreasing order of
    occurences"""

    texts = map(lambda x: requests.get(x).content, self.urls)
    # Rank using a call to parent class's 'rank' method
    occurs = super(UrlRank, self).rank(*texts)
    # Convert to URLs list
    occurs = [(self.urls[x],y) for x,y in occurs.items()]

    return self.sort(occurs)
```

Not only has refactoring reduced the size of the code in each module, but it has also resulted in improved modifiability of the classes by abstracting the common code to a parent class which can be developed independently.

Using late binding techniques

Late binding refers to the practice of postponing the binding of values to parameters as late as possible in the order of execution of a code. Late binding allows the programmer to defer the factors that influence code execution, and hence the results of execution and performance of the code, to a later time by making use of multiple techniques.

Some late-binding techniques that can be used are as follows:

- **Plugin mechanisms**: Rather than statically binding modules together, which increases coupling, this technique uses values resolved at runtime to load plugins that execute a specific dependent code. Plugins can be Python modules whose names are fetched during computations done at runtime or via IDs or variable names loaded from database queries or from configuration files.

- **Brokers/registry lookup services**: Some services can be completely deferred to brokers, which look up the service names from a registry on demand, and call them dynamically and return results. An example may be a currency exchange service, which accepts a specific currency transformation as input (say USDINR), and looks up and configures a service for it dynamically at runtime, thereby requiring only the same code to execute on the system at all times. Since there is no dependent code on the system that varies with the input, the system remains immune from any changes required if the logic for the transformation changes, as it is deferred to an external service.

- **Notification services**: Publish/subscribe mechanisms, which notify subscribers when the value of an object changes or when an event is published, can be useful to decouple systems from a volatile parameter and its value. Rather than tracking changes to such variables/objects internally, which may need a lot of dependent code and structures, such systems keep their clients immune to the changes in the system that affect and trigger the objects' internal behavior, but bind them only to an external API, which simply notifies the clients of the changed value.

- **Deployment time binding**: By keeping the variable values associated to names or IDs in configuration files, we can defer object/variable binding to deployment time. The values are bound at startup by the software system once it loads its configuration files, which can then invoke specific paths in the code that creates appropriate objects.

  This approach can be combined with object-oriented patterns such as factories, which create the required object at runtime given the name or ID, hence keeping the clients that are dependent on these objects immune from any internal changes, increasing their modifiability.

- **Using creational patterns**: Creational design patterns such as factory or builder, which abstract the task of creating of an object from the details of creating it, are ideal for separation of concerns for client modules that don't want their code to be modified when the code for creation of a dependent object changes.

  These approaches, when combined with deployment/configuration time or dynamic binding (using lookup services), can greatly increase the flexibility of a system and aid its modifiability.

We will look at examples of Python patterns in a later chapter in this book.

Metrics – tools for static analysis

Static code analysis tools can provide a rich summary of information on the static properties of your code, which can provide insights into aspects such as complexity and modifiability/readability of the code.

Python has a lot of third-party tool support, which helps in measuring the static aspects of Python code such as these:

- Conformance to coding standards such as PEP-8
- Code complexity metrics such as the McCabe metric
- Errors in code such as syntax errors, indentation issues, missing imports, variable overwrites, and others
- Logic issues in code
- Code smells

The following are some of the most popular tools in the Python ecosystem that can perform such static analysis:

- **Pylint**: Pylint is a static checker for Python code, which can detect a range of coding errors, code smells, and style errors. Pylint uses a style close to PEP-8. The newer versions of Pylint also provide statistics about code complexity and can print reports. Pylint requires the code to be executed before checking it. You can refer to http://pylint.org.

- **Pyflakes**: Pyflakes is a more recent project than Pylint. It differs from Pylint in that it need not execute the code before checking it for errors. Pyflakes does not check for coding style errors and only performs logic checks in code. You can refer to https://launchpad.net/pyflakes.

- **McCabe**: It is a script that checks and prints a report on the McCabe complexity of your code. You can refer to `https://pypi.python.org/pypi/mccabe`.

- **Pycodestyle**: Pycodestyle is a tool that checks your Python code against some of the PEP-8 guidelines. This tool was earlier called PEP-8. Refer to `https://github.com/PyCQA/pycodestyle`.

- **Flake8**: Flake8 is a wrapper around the Pyflakes, McCabe, and pycodestyle tools and can perform a number of checks including the ones provided by these tools. Refer to `https://gitlab.com/pycqa/flake8/`.

What are code smells?

Code smells are surface symptoms of deeper problems with your code. They usually indicate problems with the design, which can cause bugs in the future or negatively impact development of the particular piece of code.

Code smells are not bugs themselves, but they are patterns that indicate that the approach to solving problems adopted in the code is not right and should be fixed by refactoring.

Some of the common code smells are as follows:

At the class level, there are the following:

- **God object**: A class that tries to do too many things. In short, this class lacks any kind of cohesion.

- **Constant class**: A class that's nothing but a collection of constants, which is used elsewhere, and hence, should not ideally belong here.

- **Refused bequest**: A class that doesn't honor the contract of the base class, and hence, breaks the substitution principle of inheritance.

- **Freeloader**: A class with too few functions that do almost nothing and add little value.

- **Feature envy**: A class that is excessively dependent on methods of another class, indicating high coupling.

At the method/function level, there are the following:

- **Long method**: A method or function that has grown too big and complex.

- **Parameter creep**: This is when there are too many parameters for a function or method. This makes the callability and testability of the function difficult.

- **Cyclomatic complexity**: This is a function or method with too many branches or loops, which creates a convoluted logic that is difficult to follow and can cause subtle bugs. Such a function should be refactored and broken down to multiple functions, or the logic rewritten to avoid too much branching.

- **Overly long or short identifiers**: A function that uses either overly long or overly short variable names so that their purpose is not clear from their names. The same is applicable to the function name as well.

A related antipattern to code smell is design smell, which are the surface symptoms in the design of a system that indicate underlying deeper problems in the architecture.

Cyclomatic complexity – the McCabe metric

Cyclomatic complexity is a measure of complexity of a computer program. It is computed as the number of linearly independent paths through the program's source code from start to finish.

For a piece of code with no branches at all, such as the one given next, the Cyclomatic complexity would be 1, as there is just one path through the code:

```
""" Module power.py """

def power(x, y):
    """ Return power of x to y """
    return x^y
```

A piece of code with two branches, like the following one, will have a complexity of 2:

```
""" Module factorial.py """

def factorial(n):
    """ Return factorial of n """
    if n == 0:
        return 1
    else:
        return n*factorial(n-1)
```

The use of Cyclomatic complexity as a metric using the control graph of a code was developed by Thomas J. McCabe in 1976. Hence, it is also called McCabe complexity or the **McCabe index**.

To measure the metric, the control graph can be pictured as a directed graph, where the nodes represent the blocks of the program and edges represent control flow from one block to another.

With respect to the control graph of a program, the McCabe complexity can be expressed as follows:

$$M = E - N + 2P$$

In the preceding equation, we have the following:

- E => Number of edges in the graph
- N => Number of nodes in the graph
- P => Number of connected components in the graph

In Python, the `mccabe` package, written by Ned Batcheldor, can be used to measure a program's Cyclomatic complexity. It can be used as a standalone module or as a plugin to programs such as Flake8 or Pylint.

For example, here is how we measure the Cyclomatic complexity of the two code pieces given earlier:

```
                        Chapter 2: Modifiability                      —  +  ✕
(arch) $ python -m mccabe --min 1 power.py
1:1: 'power' 1
(arch) $
(arch) $ python -m mccabe --min 1 factorial.py
1:1: 'factorial' 2
(arch) $ ▮
```

McCabe metrics for some sample Python programs

The `-min` argument tells the `mccabe` module to start measuring and reporting from the given McCabe index.

Testing for metrics

Let's now try a few of the aforementioned tools and use them on an example module to find out what kind of information these tools report.

The purpose of the following sections is not to teach you the usage of these tools or their command-line options — these can be picked up via the tool's documentation. Instead, the purpose is to explore the depth and richness of information that these tools provide with respect to the style, logic, and other issues with the code.

For purposes of this testing, the following contrived module example has been used. It is written purposefully with a lot of coding errors, style errors, and coding smells.

Since the tools we are using lists errors by line numbers, the code has been presented with numbered lines so that it is easy to follow the output of the tools back to the code:

```
1    """
2    Module metrictest.py
3
4    Metric example - Module which is used as a testbed for static
     checkers.
5    This is a mix of different functions and classes doing
     different things.
6
7    """
8    import random
9
10   def fn(x, y):
11       """ A function which performs a sum """
12       return x + y
13
14   def find_optimal_route_to_my_office_from_home(start_time,
15                                                 expected_time,
16                                                 favorite_route='SBS1K',
17                                                 favorite_option='bus'):
18
19
20       d = (expected_time - start_time).total_seconds()/60.0
21
22       if d<=30:
23           return 'car'
24
25       # If d>30 but <45, first drive then take metro
26       if d>30 and d<45:
27           return ('car', 'metro')
28
29       # If d>45 there are a combination of options
```

```
30        if d>45:
31            if d<60:
32                # First volvo,then connecting bus
33                return ('bus:335E','bus:connector')
34            elif d>80:
35                # Might as well go by normal bus
36                return random.choice(('bus:330','bus:331',':'.
                        join((favorite_option,
37                            favorite_route))))
38            elif d>90:
39                # Relax and choose favorite route
40                return ':'.join((favorite_option,
41                            favorite_route))
42
43
44  class C(object):
45      """ A class which does almost nothing """
46
47      def __init__(self, x,y):
48          self.x = x
49          self.y = y
50
51      def f(self):
52          pass
53
54      def g(self, x, y):
55
56          if self.x>x:
57              return self.x+self.y
58          elif x>self.x:
59              return x+ self.y
60
61  class D(C):
62      """ D class """
63
64      def __init__(self, x):
65          self.x = x
66
67      def f(self, x,y):
68          if x>y:
69              return x-y
70          else:
```

```
71              return x+y
72
73     def g(self, y):
74
75         if self.x>y:
76             return self.x+y
77         else:
78             return y-self.x
```

Running static checkers

Let's see what Pylint has to say about our rather horrible-looking piece of test code.

```
$ pylint -reports=n metrictest.py
```

 Pylint prints a lot of styling errors, but the purpose of this example being to focus on logic issues and code smells, the log is shown only starting from these reports.

Here is the detailed output captured in two screenshots:

```
                        Chapter 2: Modifiability                    _ + x
(arch) $ pylint --reports=n metrictest.py
************* Module metrictest
C: 22, 0: Exactly one space required around comparison
        if d<=30:
            ^^ (bad-whitespace)
C: 24, 0: Exactly one space required around comparison
        elif d<45:
              ^ (bad-whitespace)
C: 26, 0: Exactly one space required around comparison
        elif d<60:
              ^ (bad-whitespace)
C: 28, 0: Exactly one space required after comma
          return ('bus:335E','bus:connector')
                            ^ (bad-whitespace)
C: 29, 0: Exactly one space required around comparison
        elif d>80:
              ^ (bad-whitespace)
C: 31, 0: Exactly one space required after comma
          return random.choice(('bus:330','bus:331',':'.join((favorite_option,
                                         ^ (bad-whitespace)
C: 31, 0: Exactly one space required after comma
          return random.choice(('bus:330','bus:331',':'.join((favorite_option,
                                                    ^ (bad-whitespace)
C: 32, 0: Wrong continued indentation (remove 4 spaces).
                                                favorite_route))))
```

Pylint output for metric test program (page 1)

Take a look at the screenshot of the next page of the report:

```
Chapter 2: Modifiability                              – + x
File Edit View Search Terminal Help
C: 11, 0: Invalid function name "fn" (invalid-name)
C: 11, 0: Invalid argument name "x" (invalid-name)
C: 11, 0: Invalid argument name "y" (invalid-name)
W: 15, 4: Unreachable code (unreachable)
C: 15, 4: Invalid function name "find_optimal_route_to_my_office_from_home" (invalid-name)
C: 15, 4: Missing function docstring (missing-docstring)
C: 21, 8: Invalid variable name "d" (invalid-name)
E: 32,19: Undefined variable 'random' (undefined-variable)
W: 15, 4: Unused variable 'find_optimal_route_to_my_office_from_home' (unused-variable)
C: 39, 0: Invalid class name "C" (invalid-name)
C: 43, 8: Invalid attribute name "x" (invalid-name)
C: 44, 8: Invalid attribute name "y" (invalid-name)
C: 46, 4: Invalid method name "f" (invalid-name)
C: 46, 4: Missing method docstring (missing-docstring)
C: 49, 4: Invalid method name "g" (invalid-name)
C: 49, 4: Invalid argument name "x" (invalid-name)
C: 49, 4: Invalid argument name "y" (invalid-name)
C: 49, 4: Missing method docstring (missing-docstring)
W: 49,19: Unused argument 'y' (unused-argument)
C: 56, 0: Invalid class name "D" (invalid-name)
W: 59, 4: __init__ method from base class 'C' is not called (super-init-not-called)
W: 62, 4: Arguments number differs from overridden 'f' method (arguments-differ)
W: 68, 4: Arguments number differs from overridden 'g' method (arguments-differ)
C: 75, 0: Invalid argument name "a" (invalid-name)
C: 75, 0: Invalid argument name "b" (invalid-name)
C: 75, 0: Missing function docstring (missing-docstring)
E: 77,15: Undefined variable 'c' (undefined-variable)
W:  9, 0: Unused import sys (unused-import)
```

Pylint output for metric test program (page 2)

Let's focus on those very interesting last 10-20 lines of the Pylint report, skipping the earlier styling and convention warnings.

Here are the errors, classified into a table. We have skipped similar occurrences to keep the table short:

Error	Occurrences	Explanation	Type of Code Smell
Invalid function name	The fn function	The name fn is too short to explain what the function does	Too short identifier
Invalid variable name	The x and y variables of the fn function, f	The names x and y too short to indicate what the variables represent	Too short identifier

Error	Occurrences	Explanation	Type of Code Smell
Invalid function name	Function name, `find_optimal_route_to_my_office_from_home`	The function name is too long	Too long identifier
Invalid variable name	The d variable of function, `find_optimal...`	The name d too short to indicate what the variable represents	Too short identifier
Invalid class name	Class C	The name C doesn't tell anything about the class	Too short identifier
Invalid method name	Class C: Method f	The name f too short to explain what it does	Too short identifier
Invalid __init__ method	Class D: Method __init__	Doesn't call base class __init__	Breaks contract with base Class
Arguments of f differ in class D from class C	Class D: Method f	Method signature breaks contract with base class signature	Refused bequest
Arguments of g differ in class D from class C	Class D: Method g	Method signature breaks contract with base class signature	Refused bequest

As you can see, Pylint has detected a number of code smells, which we discussed in the previous section. Some of the most interesting ones are how it detected the absurdly long function name and how the subclass D breaks the contract with the base class, C, in its __init__ method and other methods.

Let's see what `flake8` has to tell us about our code. We will run it in order to report the statistics and summary of error counts:

```
$  flake8 --statistics --count metrictest.py
```

The preceding command gives the following output:

```
                            Chapter 2: Modifiability                            _ + x
File  Edit  View  Search  Terminal  Help
$ flake8 --statistics --count metrictest.py
metrictest.py:8:1: F401 'sys' imported but unused
metrictest.py:10:1: E302 expected 2 blank lines, found 1
metrictest.py:22:13: E225 missing whitespace around operator
metrictest.py:24:15: E225 missing whitespace around operator
metrictest.py:26:15: E225 missing whitespace around operator
metrictest.py:28:31: E231 missing whitespace after ','
metrictest.py:29:15: E225 missing whitespace around operator
metrictest.py:31:20: F821 undefined name 'random'
metrictest.py:31:44: E231 missing whitespace after ','
metrictest.py:31:54: E231 missing whitespace after ','
metrictest.py:32:69: E127 continuation line over-indented for visual indent
metrictest.py:37:1: W293 blank line contains whitespace
metrictest.py:41:25: E231 missing whitespace after ','
metrictest.py:44:1: W293 blank line contains whitespace
metrictest.py:50:18: E225 missing whitespace around operator
metrictest.py:52:15: E225 missing whitespace around operator
metrictest.py:53:21: E225 missing whitespace around operator
metrictest.py:55:1: E302 expected 2 blank lines, found 1
metrictest.py:61:18: E231 missing whitespace after ','
metrictest.py:62:13: E225 missing whitespace around operator
metrictest.py:69:18: E225 missing whitespace around operator
metrictest.py:74:1: E302 expected 2 blank lines, found 1
metrictest.py:75:9: E225 missing whitespace around operator
metrictest.py:76:16: F821 undefined name 'c'
1        E127 continuation line over-indented for visual indent
10       E225 missing whitespace around operator
5        E231 missing whitespace after ','
3        E302 expected 2 blank lines, found 1
1        F401 'sys' imported but unused
2        F821 undefined name 'c'
2        W293 blank line contains whitespace
24
```

Flake8 static check output of the metrictest program

As you would've expected from a tool that is written to mostly follow PEP-8 conventions, the errors reported are all styling and convention errors. These errors are useful to improve the readability of the code and make it follow closer to the style guidelines of PEP-8.

 You can get more information about the PEP-8 tests by passing the –show-pep8 option to Flake8.

It is a good time to now check the complexity of our code. First, we will use mccabe directly and then call it via Flake8:

```
Chapter 2: Modifiability                                    _  +  x
(arch) $ python -m mccabe --min 3 metrictest.py
54:1: 'C.g' 3
14:1: 'find_optimal_route_to_my_office_from_home' 7
(arch) $ ▮
```

mccabe complexity of metric test program

As expected, the complexity of the office-route function is too high, as it has too many branches and sub-branches.

As flake8 prints too many styling errors, we will grep specifically for the report on complexity:

```
Chapter 2: Modifiability                                    _  +  x
(arch) $ flake8 --max-complexity 3 metrictest.py | grep complex
metrictest.py:14:1: C901 'find_optimal_route_to_my_office_from_home' is too compl
ex (7)
(arch) $ ▮
```

mccabe complexity of metric test program as reported by flake8

As expected, Flake8 reports the find_optimal_route_to_my_office_from_home function as too complex.

 There is a way to run mccabe as a plugin from Pylint as well, but since it involves some configuration steps, we will not cover it here.

As a last step, let's run `pyflakes` on the code:

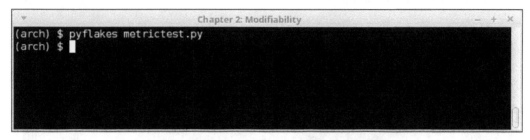

Static analysis output of pyflakes on the metric test code

There is no output! So, Pyflakes finds no issues with the code. The reason is that Pyflakes is a basic checker that does not report anything beyond the obvious syntax and logic errors, unused imports, missing variable names, and the like.

Let's add some errors into our code and rerun Pyflakes. Here is the adjusted code with line numbers:

```
1   """
2   Module metrictest.py
3
4   Metric example - Module which is used as a testbed for static
    checkers.
5   This is a mix of different functions and classes doing
    different things.
6
7   """
8   import sys
9
10  def fn(x, y):
11      """ A function which performs a sum """
12      return x + y
13
14  def find_optimal_route_to_my_office_from_home(start_time,
15                                      expected_time,
16                                      favorite_route='SBS1K',
17                                      favorite_option='bus'):
18
19
20      d = (expected_time - start_time).total_seconds()/60.0
21
22      if d<=30:
```

```
23          return 'car'
24
25      # If d>30 but <45, first drive then take metro
26      if d>30 and d<45:
27          return ('car', 'metro')
28
29      # If d>45 there are a combination of options
30      if d>45:
31          if d<60:
32              # First volvo,then connecting bus
33              return ('bus:335E','bus:connector')
34          elif d>80:
35              # Might as well go by normal bus
36              return random.choice(('bus:330','bus:331',':'.
                    join((favorite_option,
37                      favorite_route))))
38          elif d>90:
39              # Relax and choose favorite route
40              return ':'.join((favorite_option,
41                      favorite_route))
42
43
44  class C(object):
45      """ A class which does almost nothing """
46
47      def __init__(self, x,y):
48          self.x = x
49          self.y = y
50
51      def f(self):
52          pass
53
54      def g(self, x, y):
55
56          if self.x>x:
57              return self.x+self.y
58          elif x>self.x:
59              return x+ self.y
60
61  class D(C):
62      """ D class """
63
64      def __init__(self, x):
```

```
65              self.x = x
66
67         def f(self, x,y):
68             if x>y:
69                 return x-y
70             else:
71                 return x+y
72
73         def g(self, y):
74
75             if self.x>y:
76                 return self.x+y
77             else:
78                 return y-self.x
79
80   def myfunc(a, b):
81       if a>b:
82           return c
83       else:
84           return a
```

Take a look at the following output:

```
                        Chapter 2: Modifiability                  — + x
(arch) $ pyflakes metrictest.py
metrictest.py:8: 'sys' imported but unused
metrictest.py:36: undefined name 'random'
metrictest.py:82: undefined name 'c'
(arch) $
```

Static analysis output of pyflakes on the metric test code, after modifications

Pyflakes now returns some useful information in terms of a missing name (random), unused import (sys), and an undefined name (the c variable in the newly introduced function, myfunc). So it does perform some useful static analysis on the code. For example, the information on the missing and undefined names is useful to fix obvious bugs in the preceding code.

It is a good idea to run Pylint and/or Pyflakes on your code to report and figure out logic and syntax errors after the code is written. To run Pylint to report only errors, use the -E option. To run Pyflakes, just follow the preceding example.

Refactoring code

Now that we have seen how static checkers can be used to report a wide range of errors and issues in our Python code, let's do a simple exercise of refactoring our code. We will take our poorly written metric test module as the use case (the first version of it) and perform a few refactoring steps.

Here are the rough guidelines to follow when refactoring software:

1. **Fix complex code first**: This will get a lot of code out of the way as typically, when a complex piece of code is refactored, we end up reducing the number of lines of code. This overall improves the code quality and reduces code smells. You may be creating new functions or classes here, so it always helps to perform this step first.

2. **Do an analysis of the code**: It is a good idea to run the complexity checkers at this step and see how the overall complexity of the code — class/module or functions — has been reduced. If not, iterate again.

3. **Fix code smells next**: Fix any issue with code smells — class, function, or module — next. This gets your code into a much better shape and improves the overall semantics.

4. **Run checkers**: Run checkers such as Pylint on the code now, and get a report on the code smells. Ideally, they should be close to zero or reduced very much from the original.

5. **Fix low-hanging fruits**: Fix low-hanging fruits, such as code style and convention errors, last. This is because, in the process of refactoring, when trying to reduce complexity and code smells, you typically would introduce or delete a lot of code. So, it doesn't make sense to try and improve the code convention issues at earlier stages.

6. **Perform a final check using the tools**: You can run Pylint for code smells, Flake8 for PEP-8 conventions, and Pyflakes for catching the logic, syntax, and missing variable issues.

Here is a step-by-step demonstration of fixing our metric test module using this approach in the next section.

Refactoring code – fixing complexity

Most of the complexity is in the office route function, so let's try and fix it. Here is the rewritten version (showing only that function here):

```python
def find_optimal_route_to_my_office_from_home(start_time,
                                              expected_time,
                                              favorite_route='SBS1K',
                                              favorite_option='bus'):

    d = (expected_time - start_time).total_seconds()/60.0

    if d<=30:
        return 'car'
    elif d<45:
        return ('car', 'metro')
    elif d<60:
        # First volvo,then connecting bus
        return ('bus:335E','bus:connector')
    elif d>80:
        # Might as well go by normal bus
        return random.choice(('bus:330','bus:331',':'.
                              join((favorite_option,
                                    favorite_route))))
    # Relax and choose favorite route
    return ':'.join((favorite_option, favorite_route))
```

In the preceding rewrite, we got rid of the redundant if...else conditions. Let's check the complexity now:

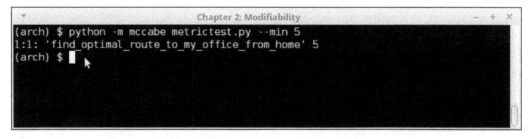

mccabe metric of metric test program after refactoring step 1

We were able to reduce the complexity from 7 to 5. Can we do better?

In the following piece of code, the code is rewritten to use ranges of values as keys, and the corresponding return value as values. This simplifies our code a lot. Also, the earlier default return at the end would never have got picked, so it is removed now, hence getting rid of a branch and reducing complexity by one. The code has become much simpler:

```
def find_optimal_route_to_my_office_from_home(start_time,
                                              expected_time,
                                              favorite_route='SBS1K',
                                              favorite_option='bus'):

    # If I am very late, always drive.
    d = (expected_time - start_time).total_seconds()/60.0
    options = { range(0,30): 'car',
    range(30, 45): ('car','metro'),
    range(45, 60): ('bus:335E','bus:connector') }


if d<80:
# Pick the range it falls into
for drange in options:
    if d in drange:
    return drange[d]

    # Might as well go by normal bus
    return random.choice(('bus:330','bus:331',':'.join((favorite_
                          option, favorite_route)))))
```

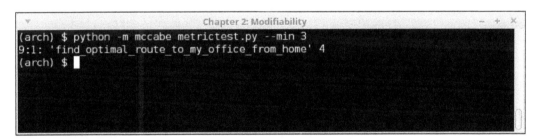

```
(arch) $ python -m mccabe metrictest.py --min 3
9:1: 'find_optimal_route_to_my_office_from_home' 4
(arch) $
```

mccabe metric of metric test program after refactoring step #2

The complexity of the function is now reduced to 4, which is manageable.

Refactoring code – fixing code smells

The next step is to fix code smells. Thankfully, we have a very good list from the previous analysis, so this is not too difficult. Mostly, we need to change function names and variable names and fix the contracts from child class to parent class.

Here is the code with all of the fixes:

```python
""" Module metrictest.py - testing static quality metrics of Python
code """

import random

def sum_fn(xnum, ynum):
    """ A function which performs a sum """

    return xnum + ynum

def find_optimal_route(start_time,
                       expected_time,
                       favorite_route='SBS1K',
                       favorite_option='bus'):
    """ Find optimal route for me to go from home to office """

    # Time difference in minutes - inputs must be datetime instances
    tdiff = (expected_time - start_time).total_seconds()/60.0

    options = {range(0, 30): 'car',
               range(30, 45): ('car', 'metro'),
               range(45, 60): ('bus:335E', 'bus:connector')}


    if tdiff < 80:
        # Pick the range it falls into
        for drange in options:
            if tdiff in drange:
                return drange[tdiff]

    # Might as well go by normal bus
    return random.choice(('bus:330', 'bus:331',
                          ':'.join((favorite_option,
                                    favorite_route))))


class MiscClassC(object):
```

```
    """ A miscellaneous class with some utility methods """

    def __init__(self, xnum, ynum):
        self.xnum = xnum
        self.ynum = ynum

    def compare_and_sum(self, xnum=0, ynum=0):
        """ Compare local and argument variables
        and perform some sums """

        if self.xnum > xnum:
            return self.xnum + self.ynum
        else:
            return xnum + self.ynum

class MiscClassD(MiscClassC):
    """ Sub-class of MiscClassC overriding some methods """

    def __init__(self, xnum, ynum=0):
        super(MiscClassD, self).__init__(xnum, ynum)

    def some_func(self, xnum, ynum):
        """ A function which does summing """

        if xnum > ynum:
            return xnum - ynum
        else:
            return xnum + ynum

    def compare_and_sum(self, xnum=0, ynum=0):
        """ Compare local and argument variables
        and perform some sums """

        if self.xnum > ynum:
            return self.xnum + ynum
        else:
            return ynum - self.xnum
```

Let's run Pylint on this code and see what it outputs this time:

```
Chapter 2: Modifiability                                    − + ×
(arch) $ pylint --reports=n metrictest.py
************* Module metrictest
W: 42,38: Unused argument 'ynum' (unused-argument)
R: 35, 0: Too few public methods (1/2) (too-few-public-methods)
R: 57, 4: Method could be a function (no-self-use)
This option 'required-attributes' will be removed in Pylint 2.0This option 'ignor
e-iface-methods' will be removed in Pylint 2.0(arch) $ ■
```

Pylint output of refactored metric test program

You see that the number of code smells has boiled down to near zero except a complaint of lack of `public` methods, and the insight that the `some_func` method of the `MiscClassD` class can be a function, as it does not use any attributes of the class.

> We have invoked Pylint with the `–reports=n` option in order to avoid Pylint printing its summary report, as it would make the entire output too long to display here. These reports can be enabled by calling Pylint without any argument.

Refactoring code – fixing styling and coding issues

Now that we have fixed the major code issues, the next step is to fix code style and convention errors. However, in order to shorten the number of steps and the amount of code to be printed in this book for this exercise, this was already merged along with the last step, as you may have guessed from the output of Pylint.

Except for a few whitespace warnings, all of the issues are fixed.

This completes our Refactoring exercise.

Summary

In this chapter, we looked at the architectural quality attribute of modifiability and its various aspects. We discussed readability in some detail, including the readability antipatterns along with a few coding antipatterns.

We looked at various techniques for improving readability of code and understood the different aspects of commenting of code such as function, class and module docstrings. We also looked at PEP-8, the official coding convention guideline for Python.

We then looked at some rules of thumb for code comments and went on to discuss the fundamentals of modifiability, namely, coupling and cohesion of code. We looked at different cases of coupling and cohesion with a few examples. We then went on to discuss the strategies of improving modifiability of code such as providing explicit interfaces or APIs, avoiding two-way dependencies, abstracting common services to helper modules, and using inheritance techniques. We looked at an example where we refactored a class hierarchy via inheritance to abstract away common code and to improve the modifiability of the system.

Toward the end, we listed the different tools, providing static code metrics in Python such as Pylint, Flake8, Pyflakes, and others. We learned about McCabe Cyclomatic complexity with the help of a few examples. We also learned what code smells are and performed a refactoring exercise to improve the quality of the piece of code in stages.

In the next chapter, we'll discuss another important quality attribute of software architecture, namely, testability.

3
Testability – Writing Testable Code

In the previous chapter, we covered a very important architectural attribute of software, namely, modifiability, and its related aspects. In this chapter, the topic is a closely related quality attribute: **testability** of software.

We briefly covered testability in the first chapter of this book, where we understood what testability is, and how it relates to the complexity of the code. In this chapter, we will look into the different aspects of software testability in detail.

Software testing by itself has developed into a large field with its own standards and unique set of tools and processes. The focus of this chapter is not to cover the formal aspects of software testing. Instead, what we will strive to do here is to understand software testing from an architectural perspective and understand its relation to the other quality attributes and, in the second half of this chapter, discuss the Python tools and libraries relevant to our discussion on software testing using Python.

We will cover the following topics in this chapter:

- Understanding testability
- White-box testing principles
- Test-driven development
- TDD with palindromes

Understanding testability

Testability can be defined as follows:

> *"The degree of ease with which a software system exposes its faults through execution-based testing".*

A software system with a high level of testability provides a high degree of exposure of its faults through testing, thereby giving the developers higher accessibility to the system's issues and allowing them to find and fix bugs faster. A less testable system, on the other hand, would make it difficult for developers to figure out issues with it and can often lead to unexpected failures in production.

Testability is, hence, an important aspect in ensuring the quality, stability, and predictability of the software system in production.

Software testability and related attributes

A software system is testable if it gives up (exposes) its faults easily to the tester. Not only that, the system should behave in a predictable way for the tester to develop useful tests. An unpredictable system would give varying output variables to fixed input at varying times, hence, is not testable (or very useful for that matter!).

More than unpredictability, complex or chaotic systems are also less amenable to testing. For example, a system whose behavior varies wildly across a spectrum under load doesn't make a good candidate for load testing. Hence, deterministic behavior is also important to assure the testability of a system.

Another aspect is the amount of control that the tester has on the substructures of the system. In order to design meaningful tests, a system should be easily identifiable to subsystems with their well-defined APIs, for which tests can be written. A software system that is complex and doesn't provide easy access to its subsystems, by definition, becomes much less testable than the one which does.

This means that systems that are more structurally complex are more difficult to test than ones that aren't.

Let's list this in an easy-to-read table:

Determinism	Complexity	Testability
High	Low	High
Low	High	Low

Testability – architectural aspects

Software testing generally implies that the software artifact being tested is being assessed for its functionality. However, in practical software testing, functionality is just one of the aspects that can fail. Testing implies assessing the software for other quality attributes such as performance, security, and robustness.

Due to these different aspects of testing, software testability is usually grouped at different levels. We will take a look at these from the point of view of software architecture.

Here is a brief listing of the different aspects that usually fall under software testing:

- **Functional testing**: This involves testing the software for verifying its functionality. A unit of software passes its functional test if it behaves exactly the way it is supposed to as per its development specifications. Functional testing is usually of two types:

    ◦ **White-box testing**: These are usually tests implemented by the developers, who have visibility into the software code, themselves. The units being tested here are the individual functions, methods, classes, or modules that make up the software rather than the end user functionality. The most basic form of white-box testing is **unit testing**. Other types are **integration testing** and **system testing**.

    ◦ **Black-box testing**: This type of testing is usually performed by someone who is outside the development team. The tests have no visibility into the software code, and treat the entire system like a black box. Black-box testing tests the end user functionality of the system without bothering about its internal details. Such tests are usually performed by dedicated testing or QA engineers. However, nowadays, a lot of black-box tests on web-based applications can be automated by using testing frameworks such as Selenium.

    Other than functional testing, there are a lot of testing methodologies that are used to assess the various architectural quality attributes of a system. We will discuss these next.

- **Performance testing**: Tests that measure how a software performs with respect to its responsiveness and robustness (stability) under high workloads come within this category. Performance tests are usually categorized into the following:

    ○ **Load testing**: These are tests that assess how a system performs under a certain specific load, either in terms of the number of concurrent users, input data, or transactions.

    ○ **Stress testing**: This tests the robustness and response of the system when some inputs present a sudden or high rate of growth and go to extreme limits. Stress tests typically tend to test the system slightly beyond its prescribed design limits. A variation of stress testing is running the system under a certain specified load for extended periods of time and measuring its responsiveness and stability.

    ○ **Scalability testing**: Measure how much the system can scale out or scale up when the load is increased. For example, if a system is configured to use a cloud service, this can test the horizontal scalability – as in how the system auto scales to a certain number of nodes upon increased load or vertical scalability – in terms of the degree of utilization of CPU cores and/or RAM of the system.

- **Security testing**: Tests that verify the system's security fall into this category. For web-based applications, this usually involves verifying authorization of roles by checking that a given login or role can only perform a specified set of actions and nothing more (or less). Other tests that fall under security would be to verify proper access to data or static files to make sure that all sensitive data of an application is protected by proper authorization via logins.

- **Usability testing**: Usability testing involves testing how much the user interface of a system is easy to use, is intuitive, and understandable by its end users. Usability testing is usually done via target groups comprising selected people who fall into the definition of the intended audience or end users of the system.

- **Installation testing**: For software that is shipped to the customer's location and is installed there, installation testing is important. This tests and verifies that all of the steps involved in building and/or installing the software at the customer's end work as expected. If the development hardware differs from the customer's, then the testing also involves verifying the steps and components in the end user's hardware. Apart from a regular software installation, installation testing is also important when delivering software updates, partial upgrades, and so on.

- **Accessibility testing**: Accessibility, from a software standpoint, refers to the degree of usability and inclusion of a software system towards end users with disabilities. This is usually done by incorporating support for accessibility tools in the system, and designing the user interface by using accessible design principles. A number of standards and guidelines have been developed over the years, which allow organizations to develop software with a view to making the software accessible to such an audience. Examples are the **Web Content Accessibility Guidelines (WCAG)** of W3C, Section 508 of the Government of USA, and the like.

  Accessibility testing aims to assess the accessibility of software with respect to these standards, wherever applicable.

There are various other types of software testing, which involves different approaches, and are invoked at various phases of software development, such as regression testing, acceptance testing, alpha or beta testing, and so on.

However, since our focus of discussion is on the architectural aspects of software testing, we will limit our attention to the topics mentioned in the previous list.

Testability – strategies

We saw in a previous section how testability varies according to the complexity and determinism of the software system under testing.

Being able to isolate and control the artifacts that are being tested is critical to software testing. Separation of concerns on the system being tested, as in being able to test components independently and without too much external dependency, is key to this.

Let's look at the strategies that the software architect can employ in order to make sure that the components he/she is subjecting to tests provide predictable and deterministic behavior, which will provide valid and useful test results.

Reduce system complexity

As mentioned earlier, a complex system has lower testability. The system complexity can be reduced by techniques such as splitting systems into subsystems, providing well-defined APIs for systems to be tested, and so on. Here is a list of these techniques in some detail:

- **Reducing coupling**: This is to isolate components so that coupling is reduced in the system. Inter-component dependencies should be well defined, and if possible, documented.

- **Increasing cohesion**: This is to increase cohesion of modules, that is, to make sure that a particular module or class performs only a well-defined set of functions.

- **Providing well-defined interfaces**: Try to provide well-defined interfaces for getting/setting the state of the components and classes involved. For example, getters and setters allow us to provide specific methods for getting and setting the value of a class's attributes. A reset method allows to set the internal state of an object to its state at the time of creation. In Python, this can be done by defining properties.

- **Reducing class complexity**: This means to reduce the number of classes a class derives from. A metric called **Response For Class (RFC)** is a set of methods of a class C, plus the methods on other classes called by the methods of class C. It is suggested to keep the RFC of a class in manageable limits, usually not more than 50 for small- to medium-sized systems.

Improving predictability

We saw that having a deterministic behavior is very important to design tests that provide predictable results, and hence, can be used to build a test harness for repeatable testing. Here are some strategies to improve the predictability of the code under test:

- **Correct exception handling**: Missing or improperly-written exception handlers is one of the main reasons for bugs and thence, unpredictable behavior in software systems. It is important to find out places in the code where exceptions can occur and then handle errors. Most of the time, exceptions occur when a code interacts with an external resource such as performing a database query, fetching a URL, waiting on a shared mutex, and the like.

- **Infinite loops and/or blocked wait**: When writing loops that depend on specific conditions such as availability of an external resource, or getting an handle to or data from a shared resource, say a shared mutex or queue, it is important to make sure that there are always safe exit or break conditions provided in the code. Otherwise, the code can get stuck in infinite loops that never break or on never-ending blocked waits on resources causing bugs that are hard to troubleshoot and fix.

- **Logic that is time dependent**: When implementing logic that is dependent on certain times of the day (hours or specific weekdays), make sure that the code works in a predictable fashion. When testing such code, we often need to isolate such dependencies by using mocks or stubs.

- **Concurrency**: When writing code that uses concurrent methods such as multiple threads and/or processes, it is important to make sure that the system logic is not dependent on threads or processes starting in any specific order. The system state should be initialized in a clean and repeatable way via well-defined functions or methods that allow the system behavior to be repeatable, and hence, testable.

- **Memory management**: A very common reason for software errors and unpredictability is incorrect usage and mismanagement of memory. In modern runtimes with dynamic memory management, such as Python, Java, or Ruby, this is less of a problem. However, memory leaks and unreleased memory leading to bloated software are still very much a reality in modern software systems.

It is important to analyze and be able to predict the maximum memory usage of your software system so that you allocate enough memory for it and run it on the right hardware. Also, software should be periodically evaluated and tested for memory leaks and better memory management, and any major issues should be addressed and fixed.

Control and isolate external dependencies

Tests usually have some sort of external dependency. For example, a test may need to load/save data to/from a database. Another may depend on the test running on specific times of the day. A third may require fetching data from a URL on the web.

However, having external dependencies usually complicates a test scenario. This is because external dependencies are usually not within the control of the test designer. In the aforementioned cases, the database may be in another data center, the connection may fail, or the website may not respond within the configured time or may give a 50X error.

Isolating such external dependencies is very important in designing and writing repeatable tests. The following are a few techniques for the same:

- **Data sources**: Most realistic tests require data of some form. More often than not, data is read from a database. However, a database being an external dependency cannot be relied upon. The following are a few techniques to control data source dependencies:

  ° Using local files instead of a database: Quite often, test files with prefilled data can be used instead of querying a database. Such files could be text, JSON, CSV, or YAML files. Usually, such files are used with mock or stub objects.

- ○ Using an in-memory database: Rather than connecting to a real database, a small in-memory database could be used. A good example is the SQLite DB, a file or memory-based database which implements a good, but minimal, subset of SQL.

- ○ Using a test database: If the test really requires a database, the operation can use a test database that uses **transactions**. The database is set up in the `setUp()` method of the test case, and rolled back in the `tearDown()` method so that no real data remains at the end of the operation.

- **Resource virtualization**: In order to control the behavior of resources that are outside the system, we can virtualize them, that is, build a version of these resources that mimic their APIs, but not the internal implementation. Some common techniques for resource virtualization are as follows:

  - ○ **Stubs**: Stubs provide standard (canned) responses to function calls made during a test. A `Stub()` function replaces the details of the function it replaces, only returning the response as required.

    For example, here is a function that returns `data` for a given URL:

    ```
    import hashlib
    import requests


    def get_url_data(url):
        """ Return data for a URL """

        # Return data while saving the data in a file
        # which is a hash of the URL
        data = requests.get(url).content
        # Save it in a filename
        filename = hashlib.md5(url).hexdigest()
        open(filename, 'w').write(data)
        return data
    ```

And the following is the stub that replaces it, which internalizes the external dependency of the URL:

```
import os

def get_url_data_stub(url):
    """ Stub function replacing get_url_data """

    # No actual web request is made, instead
    # the file is opened and data returned
```

```
filename = hashlib.md5(url).hexdigest()
if os.path.isfile(filename):
    return open(filename).read()
```

A more common way to write such a function is to combine both the original request and the file cache in the same code. The URL is requested just once — the first time the function is called — and in subsequent requests, the data from the file cache is returned:

```
def get_url_data(url):
    """ Return data for a URL """

    # First check for cached file - if so return its
    # contents. Note that we are not checking for
    # age of the file - so content may be stale.
    filename = hashlib.md5(url).hexdigest()
    if os.path.isfile(filename):
        return open(filename).read()

    # First time - so fetch the URL and write to the
    # file. In subsequent calls, the file contents will
    # be returned.
    data = requests.get(url).content
    open(filename, 'w').write(data)

    return data
```

- ° **Mocks**: Mocks fake the API of the real-world objects they replace. We program mock objects directly in the test by setting expectations — in terms of the type and order of the arguments the functions will expect and the responses they will return. Later, the expectations can be optionally verified in a verification step.

We will see examples of writing unit test via mocks with Python later.

The main difference between mocks and stubs is that a stub implements just enough behavior for the object under test to execute the test. A mock usually goes beyond by also verifying that the object under test calls the mock as expected — for example, in terms of number and order of arguments.

When using a mock object, part of the test involves verifying that the mock was used correctly. In other words, both mocks and stubs answer the question, *What is the result?*, but mocks also answer the question, *How has the result been achieved?*

○ **Fakes**: Fake objects have working implementations, but fall short of production usage because they have some limitations. A Fake object provides a very lightweight implementation, which goes beyond just stubbing the object.

For example, here is a Fake object that implements a very minimal logging, mimicking the API of the Logger object of the Python's logging module:

```python
import logging

class FakeLogger(object):
    """ A class that fakes the interface of the
    logging.Logger object in a minimalistic fashion """

    def __init__(self):
        self.lvl = logging.INFO

    def setLevel(self, level):
        """ Set the logging level """
        self.lvl = level

    def _log(self, msg, *args):
        """ Perform the actual logging """

        # Since this is a fake object - no actual logging is
        # done.
        # Instead the message is simply printed to standard
        # output.

        print (msg, end=' ')
        for arg in args:
            print(arg, end=' ')
        print()

    def info(self, msg, *args):
        """ Log at info level """
        if self.lvl<=logging.INFO:
            return self._log(msg, *args)

    def debug(self, msg, *args):
        """ Log at debug level """
```

```
        if self.lvl<=logging.DEBUG:
            return self._log(msg, *args)

    def warning(self, msg, *args):
        """ Log at warning level """
        if self.lvl<=logging.WARNING:
            return self._log(msg, *args)

    def error(self, msg, *args):
        """ Log at error level """
        if self.lvl<=logging.ERROR:
            return self._log(msg, *args)

    def critical(self, msg, *args):
        """ Log at critical level """
        if self.lvl<=logging.CRITICAL:
            return self._log(msg, *args)
```

The FakeLogger class in the preceding code implements some main methods of the logging.Logger class, which it is trying to fake.

It is ideal as a fake object for replacing the Logger object for implementing tests.

White-box testing principles

From a software architecture perspective, one of the most important steps of testing is at the time the software is developed. The behavior or functionality of a software, which is apparent only to its end users, is an artifact of the implementation details of the software.

Hence, it follows that a system that is tested early and tested often has a higher likelihood to produce a testable and robust system, which provides the required functionality to the end user in a satisfactory manner.

The best way, therefore, to start implementing testing principles is right from the source, that is, where the software is written, and by the developers. Since the source code is visible to the developer, this testing is often called white-box testing.

So, how do we make sure that we can follow the correct testing principles, and perform due diligence while the software is getting developed? Let's take a look at the different types of testing that are involved during the development stage before the software ends up in front of the customer.

Unit testing

Unit testing is the most fundamental type of testing performed by developers. A unit test applies the most basic unit of software code—typically, functions or class methods—by using executable assertions, which check the output of the unit being tested against an expected outcome.

In Python, support for unit testing is provided by the `unittest` module in the standard library.

The unit test module provides the following high-level objects:

- **Test cases**: The `unittest` module provides the `TestCase` class, which provides support for test cases. A new test case class can be set up by inheriting from this class and setting up the test methods. Each test method will implement unit tests by checking the response against an expected outcome.

- **Test fixtures**: Test fixtures represent any setup or preparation required for one or more tests followed by any cleanup actions. For example, this may involve creating temporary or in-memory databases, starting a server, creating a directory tree, and the like. In the `unittest` module, support for fixtures is provided by the `setUp()` and `tearDown()` methods of the `TestCase` class and the associated class and module methods of the `TestSuite` class.

- **Test suites**: A test suite is an aggregation of related test cases. A test suite can also contain other test suites. A test suite allows to group test cases that perform functionally similar tests on a software system, and whose results should be read or analyzed together. The `unittest` module provides support for test suites through the `TestSuite` class.

- **Test runners**: A test runner is an object that manages and runs the test cases, and provides the results to the tester. A test runner can use a text interface or a GUI.

- **Test results**: Test result classes manage the test result output shown to the tester. Test results summarize the number of successful, failed, and erred-out test cases. In the `unittest` module, this is implemented by the `TestResult` class with a concrete, default implementation of the `TextTestResult` class.

Other modules that provide support for Unit testing in Python are `nose` (nose2) and `py.test`. We will discuss each of these briefly in the following sections.

Unit testing in action

Let's take a specific unit-testing task and then try to build a few test cases and test suites. Since the `unittest` module is the most popular, and available by default in the Python standard library, we will start with it first.

For our test purposes, we will create a class that has a few methods, which are used for date/time conversions.

The following code shows our class:

```python
""" Module datetime helper - Contains the class DateTimeHelper
providing some helpful methods for working with date and datetime
objects """

import datetime
class DateTimeHelper(object):
    """ A class which provides some convenient date/time
    conversion and utility methods """

    def today(self):
        """ Return today's datetime """
        return datetime.datetime.now()

    def date(self):
        """ Return today's date in the form of DD/MM/YYYY """
        return self.today().strftime("%d/%m/%Y")

    def weekday(self):
        """ Return the full week day for today """
        return self.today().strftime("%A")

    def us_to_indian(self, date):
        """ Convert a U.S style date i.e mm/dd/yy to Indian style
            dd/mm/yyyy """

        # Split it
        mm,dd,yy = date.split('/')
        yy = int(yy)
        # Check if year is >16, else add 2000 to it
        if yy<=16: yy += 2000
        # Create a date object from it
```

```
date_obj = datetime.date(year=yy, month=int(mm), day=int(dd))
# Retur it in correct format
return date_obj.strftime("%d/%m/%Y")
```

Our `DateTimeHelper` class has a few methods, which are as follows:

- `date`: Returns the day's timestamp in the dd/mm/yyyy format
- `weekday`: Returns the day's weekday, for example, Sunday, Monday, and so on
- `us_to_indian`: Converts a US date format (mm/dd/yy(yy)) into the Indian format (dd/mm/yyyy)

Here is a `unittest` `TestCase` class, which implements a test for the last method:

```
""" Module test_datetimehelper -  Unit test module for testing
datetimehelper module """

import unittest
import datetimehelper

class DateTimeHelperTestCase(unittest.TestCase):
    """ Unit-test testcase class for DateTimeHelper class """

    def setUp(self):
        print("Setting up...")
        self.obj = datetimehelper.DateTimeHelper()

    def test_us_india_conversion(self):
        """ Test us=>india date format conversion """

        # Test a few dates
        d1 = '08/12/16'
        d2 = '07/11/2014'
        d3 = '04/29/00'
        self.assertEqual(self.obj.us_to_indian(d1), '12/08/2016')
        self.assertEqual(self.obj.us_to_indian(d2), '11/07/2014')
        self.assertEqual(self.obj.us_to_indian(d3), '29/04/2000')

if __name__ == "__main__":
    unittest.main()
```

Note that, in the main part of the test case code, we just invoke `unittest.main()`. This automatically figures out the test cases in the module, and executes them. The following screenshot shows the output of the test run:

```
(env) anand@ubuntu-pro-book:~/Documents/ArchitectureBook/code/chap3$ python3 test_datetimehelper.py
Setting up...
.
-------------------------------------------------------------
Ran 1 test in 0.000s

OK
(env) anand@ubuntu-pro-book:~/Documents/ArchitectureBook/code/chap3$
```

Output of the unit-test case for the datetimehelper module—version #1

As we can see from the output, this simple test case passes.

Extending our unit test case

You may have noted that the first version of the unit test case for the `datetimehelper` module contained a test only for one method, namely, the method that converts the US date format in to the Indian one.

However, what about the other two methods? Shouldn't we write unit tests for them too?

The problem with the other two methods is that they get data from today's date. In other words, the output is dependent on the exact day that the code is run. Hence, it is not possible to write a specific test case for them by feeding in a date value and expecting the result to match an outcome as the code is time dependent. We need a way to control this external dependency.

This is where mocking comes to our rescue. Remember that we discussed mock objects as a way to control external dependencies. We can use the patching support of the `unittest.mock` library, and patch the method that returns today's date to return a date that we control. This way, we are able to test the methods that depend on it.

Here is the modified test case with support added for the two methods using this technique:

```
""" Module test_datetimehelper -  Unit test module for testing
datetimehelper module """

import unittest
import datetime
import datetimehelper
```

```python
from unittest.mock import patch

class DateTimeHelperTestCase(unittest.TestCase):
    """ Unit-test testcase class for DateTimeHelper class """

    def setUp(self):
        self.obj = datetimehelper.DateTimeHelper()

    def test_date(self):
        """ Test date() method """

        # Put a specific date to test
        my_date = datetime.datetime(year=2016, month=8, day=16)

        # Patch the 'today' method with a specific return value
        with patch.object(self.obj, 'today', return_value=my_date):
            response = self.obj.date()
            self.assertEqual(response, '16/08/2016')

    def test_weekday(self):
        """ Test weekday() method """

        # Put a specific date to test
        my_date = datetime.datetime(year=2016, month=8, day=21)

        # Patch the 'today' method with a specific return value
        with patch.object(self.obj, 'today', return_value=my_date):
            response = self.obj.weekday()
            self.assertEqual(response, 'Sunday')

    def test_us_india_conversion(self):
        """ Test us=>india date format conversion """

        # Test a few dates
        d1 = '08/12/16'
        d2 = '07/11/2014'
        d3 = '04/29/00'
        self.assertEqual(self.obj.us_to_indian(d1), '12/08/2016')
        self.assertEqual(self.obj.us_to_indian(d2), '11/07/2014')
        self.assertEqual(self.obj.us_to_indian(d3), '29/04/2000')

if __name__ == "__main__":
    unittest.main()
```

As you can see, we have patched the `today` method to return a specific date in the two test methods. This allows us to control the method's output and, in turn, compare the result with a specific outcome.

Here is the new output of the test case:

```
(env) anand@ubuntu-pro-book:~/Documents/ArchitectureBook/code/chap3$ python3 test_datetimehelper.py
...
---------------------------------------------------------------
Ran 3 tests in 0.001s

OK
(env) anand@ubuntu-pro-book:~/Documents/ArchitectureBook/code/chap3$ █
```

Output of the unit-test case for datetimehelper module with two more tests—version #2

unittest.main is a convenience function on the `unittest` module, which makes it easy to load a set of test cases automatically from a module and run them.

To find out more details of what is happening when the tests are run, we can make the test runner show more information by increasing the verbosity. This can be done either by passing the `verbosity` argument to `unittest.main` or by passing the `-v` option on the command line as follows:

```
(env) anand@ubuntu-pro-book:~/Documents/ArchitectureBook/code/chap3$ python3 test_datetimehelper.py -v
test_date (__main__.DateTimeHelperTestCase)
Test date() method ... ok
test_us_india_conversion (__main__.DateTimeHelperTestCase)
Test us=>india date format conversion ... ok
test_weekday (__main__.DateTimeHelperTestCase)
Test weekday() method ... ok

---------------------------------------------------------------
Ran 3 tests in 0.001s

OK
```

Producing verbose output from the unit-test case by passing the -v argument

Nosing around with nose2

There are other unit-testing modules in Python that are not part of the standard library, but are available as third-party packages. We will look at the first one named `nose`. The most recent version (at the time of writing) is version 2, and the library has been renamed as `nose2`.

The nose2 package can be installed by using the Python package installer, pip:

```
$ pip install nose2
```

Running nose2 is very simple. It automatically detects Python test cases to run in the folder that it is run from by looking for classes derived from unittest.TestCase and functions starting with test.

In the case of our datetimehelper test case, nose2 picks it up automatically. Simply run it from the folder containing the module. Here is the test output:

```
(env) anand@ubuntu-pro-book:~/Documents/ArchitectureBook/code/chap3$ nose2
...
----------------------------------------------------------------------
Ran 3 tests in 0.001s

OK
```

Running unit tests using nose2

The preceding output doesn't, however, report anything, since, by default, nose2 runs quietly. We can turn on some reporting of tests by using the verbose option (-v):

```
(env) anand@ubuntu-pro-book:~/Documents/ArchitectureBook/code/chap3$ nose2 -v
test_date (test_datetimehelper.DateTimeHelperTestCase)
Test date() method ... ok
test_us_india_conversion (test_datetimehelper.DateTimeHelperTestCase)
Test us=>india date format conversion ... ok
test_weekday (test_datetimehelper.DateTimeHelperTestCase)
Test weekday() method ... ok

----------------------------------------------------------------------
Ran 3 tests in 0.001s

OK
```

Running unit-tests using nose2 with verbose output

nose2 also supports reporting code coverage by using plugins. We will look at code coverage in a later section.

Testing with py.test

The py.test package, commonly known as pytest, is a full-featured, mature testing framework for Python. Like nose2, py.test also supports test discovery by looking for files starting with certain patterns.

The `py.test` can also be installed with `pip`:

```
$ pip install pytest
```

Like `nose2`, test execution with pytest is also easy. Simply run the `pytest` executable in the folder containing the test cases:

```
(env) anand@ubuntu-pro-book:~/Documents/ArchitectureBook/code/chap3$ pytest
=============================== test session starts ================================
platform linux -- Python 3.5.2, pytest-3.0.0, py-1.4.31, pluggy-0.3.1
rootdir: /home/anand/Documents/ArchitectureBook/code/chap3, inifile:
collected 3 items

test_datetimehelper.py ...

============================ 3 passed in 0.02 seconds =============================
```

Test discovery and execution with py.test

Like nose2, `pytest` also comes with its own plugin support, the most useful among them being the code coverage plugin. We will see examples in a later section.

It is to be noted that pytest doesn't require test cases to be derived formally from the `unittest.TestCase` module. `pytest` automatically discovers tests from any modules containing classes prefixed with `Test` or from functions prefixed with `test_`.

For example, here is a new test case without any dependency on the `unittest` module but with the test case class derived from `object`, the most base type in Python. The new module is called `test_datetimehelper_object`:

```python
""" Module test_datetimehelper_object - Simple test case with test
class derived from object """

import datetimehelper

class TestDateTimeHelper(object):

    def test_us_india_conversion(self):
        """ Test us=>india date format conversion """

        obj = datetimehelper.DateTimeHelper()
        assert obj.us_to_indian('1/1/1') == '01/01/2001'
```

Note how this class has zero dependency on the `unittest` module and defines no fixtures. Here is the output of running `pytest` on the folder now:

```
(env) anand@ubuntu-pro-book:~/Documents/ArchitectureBook/code/chap3$ py.test -v
============================ test session starts ============================
platform linux -- Python 3.5.2, pytest-3.0.0, py-1.4.31, pluggy-0.3.1 -- /home/anand/arch3/env/bin/python3
cachedir: .cache
rootdir: /home/anand/Documents/ArchitectureBook/code/chap3, inifile:
plugins: cov-2.3.1
collected 4 items

test_datetimehelper.py::DateTimeHelperTestCase::test_date PASSED
test_datetimehelper.py::DateTimeHelperTestCase::test_us_india_conversion PASSED
test_datetimehelper.py::DateTimeHelperTestCase::test_weekday PASSED
test_datetimehelper2.py::TestDateTimeHelper::test_us_india_conversion PASSED
============================ 4 passed in 0.02 seconds ============================
```

Test case discovery and execution without the unittest module support using py.test

The `py.test` has picked up the test case in this module and executed it automatically as the output shows.

`nose2` also has similar capabilities to pick up such test cases. The following screenshot shows the output of `nose2` with the new test case defined:

```
(env) anand@ubuntu-pro-book:~/Documents/ArchitectureBook/code/chap3$ nose2 -v
test_date (test_datetimehelper.DateTimeHelperTestCase)
Test date() method ... ok
test_us_india_conversion (test_datetimehelper.DateTimeHelperTestCase)
Test us=>india date format conversion ... ok
test_weekday (test_datetimehelper.DateTimeHelperTestCase)
Test weekday() method ... ok
test_datetimehelper2.TestDateTimeHelper.test_us_india_conversion ... ok

----------------------------------------------------------------------
Ran 4 tests in 0.001s

OK
```

Test case discovery and execution without the unittest module support using nose2

The preceding output shows that the new test has been picked up and executed.

The `unittest` module, `nose2`, and `py.test` packages provide a lot of support for developing and implementing test cases, fixtures, and test suites in a very flexible and customizable manner. Discussing all of the multitude of options of these tools is beyond the scope of this chapter, as our focus is on getting to know these tools to understand how we can use them to satisfy the architectural quality attribute of testability.

So, at this point, we will go on to the next major topic in unit testing, that of **code coverage**. We will look at these three tools, namely, `unittest`, `nose2`, and `pytest`, and see how they allow the architect to help his/her developers and testers find information about the code coverage in their unit tests.

Code coverage

Code coverage is measured as the degree to which the source code under test is covered by a specific test suite. Ideally, test suites should aim for higher code coverage, as this would expose a larger percentage of the source code to tests and help to uncover bugs.

Code coverage metrics are reported typically as a percentage of **Lines of Code** (**LOC**) or a percentage of the subroutines (functions) covered by a test suite.

Let's now look at different tools support for measuring code coverage. We will continue to use our test example (`datetimehelper`) for these illustrations too.

Measuring coverage using coverage.py

`coverage.py` is a third-party Python module, which works with test suites and cases written with the `unittest` module, and reports their code coverage.

`coverage.py` can be installed, like other tools shown here so far, using pip:

```
$ pip install coverage
```

This last command installs the coverage application, which is used to run and report code coverages.

Coverage.py has two stages: first, where it runs a piece of source code and collects coverage information, and next, where it reports the coverage data.

To run `coverage.py`, use the following syntax:

```
$ coverage run <source file1> <source file 2> ...
```

Once the run is complete, report the coverage using this command:

```
$ coverage report -m
```

For example, here is the output with our test modules:

```
(env) anand@ubuntu-pro-book:~/Documents/ArchitectureBook/code/chap3$ coverage run test_datetimehelper.py
...
----------------------------------------------------------------------
Ran 3 tests in 0.001s

OK
(env) anand@ubuntu-pro-book:~/Documents/ArchitectureBook/code/chap3$ coverage report -m
Name                      Stmts   Miss  Cover   Missing
---------------------------------------------------------
datetimehelper.py            14      1    93%   9
test_datetimehelper.py       26      0   100%
---------------------------------------------------------
TOTAL                        40      1    98%
```

Test coverage report for the datetimehelper module using coverage.py coverage.py reports that our tests cover 93% of the code in the datetimehelper module, which is pretty good code coverage. (You can ignore the report on the test module itself.)

Measuring coverage using nose2

The nose2 package comes with plugin support for code coverage. This is not installed by default. To install the code coverage plugin for nose2, use this command:

```
$ pip install cov-core
```

Now, nose2 can be run with the code coverage option to run the test cases and to report coverage in one shot. This can be done as follows:

```
$ nose2 -v -C
```

> Behind the scenes, cov-core makes use of coverage.py to get its work done, so the metric report of coverage by both coverage.py and nose2 is the same.

Here is the output of running test coverage using nose2:

```
(env) anand@ubuntu-pro-book:~/Documents/ArchitectureBook/code/chap3$ nose2 -v -C
test_date (test_datetimehelper.DateTimeHelperTestCase)
Test date() method ... ok
test_us_india_conversion (test_datetimehelper.DateTimeHelperTestCase)
Test us=>india date format conversion ... ok
test_weekday (test_datetimehelper.DateTimeHelperTestCase)
Test weekday() method ... ok
test_datetimehelper2.TestDateTimeHelper.test_us_india_conversion ... ok


----------------------------------------------------------------------
Ran 4 tests in 0.002s

OK
---------- coverage: platform linux, python 3.5.2-final-0 -----------
Name                        Stmts   Miss  Cover
-----------------------------------------------
datetimehelper.py              14      1    93%
test_datetimehelper.py         26      1    96%
test_datetimehelper2.py         5      0   100%
-----------------------------------------------
TOTAL                          45      2    96%
```

Test coverage report for the datetimehelper module using nose2

By default, the coverage report is written to the console. To produce other forms of output, the –coverage-report option can be used. For example, --coverage-report html will write the coverage report in the HTML format to a subfolder named htmlcov:

```
(env) anand@ubuntu-pro-book:~/Documents/ArchitectureBook/code/chap3$ nose2 -C --coverage-report html
....
------------------------------------------------------------
Ran 4 tests in 0.002s

OK
----------- coverage: platform linux, python 3.5.2-final-0 -----------
coverage HTML written to dir htmlcov
```

Producing HTML coverage output using nose2

Here is how the HTML output looks in the browser:

HTML coverage report as viewed in the browser

Measuring coverage using pytest

pytest also comes with its own coverage plugin for reporting code coverage. Like nose2, it utilizes coverage.py behind the scenes to get the work done.

To provide support for code coverage for py.test, the pytest-cov package needs to be installed as follows:

```
$ pip install pytest-cov
```

To report code coverage of test cases in the current folder, use the following command:

```
$ pytest –cov
```

Here is a sample output of pytest code coverage:

```
(env) anand@ubuntu-pro-book:~/Documents/ArchitectureBook/code/chap3$ pytest --cov .
============================ test session starts =============================
platform linux -- Python 3.5.2, pytest-3.0.0, py-1.4.31, pluggy-0.3.1
rootdir: /home/anand/Documents/ArchitectureBook/code/chap3, inifile:
plugins: cov-2.3.1
collected 4 items

test_datetimehelper.py ...
test_datetimehelper2.py .

----------- coverage: platform linux, python 3.5.2-final-0 -----------
Name                     Stmts   Miss  Cover
----------------------------------------------
datetimehelper.py           14      1    93%
test_datetimehelper.py      26      1    96%
test_datetimehelper2.py      5      0   100%
----------------------------------------------
TOTAL                       45      2    96%

========================= 4 passed in 0.04 seconds =========================
```

Running code coverage for current folder using py.test

Mocking things up

We saw an example of using the patch support of `unittest.mock` in our test example earlier. However, the mock support provided by `unittest` is even more powerful than this, so let's look at one more example to understand its power and applicability in writing unit tests.

For the purpose of this illustration, we will consider a class that performs a keyword search on a large dataset and returns the results ordered by weightage. Assume that the dataset is stored in a database, and the results are returned as a list of (sentence, relevance) tuples, where sentence is the original string with a match for the keyword, and relevance is its hit weightage in the result set.

Here is the code:

```
"""
Module textsearcher - Contains class TextSearcher for performing
search on a database and returning results
"""

import operator

class TextSearcher(object):
    """ A class which performs a text search and returns results """

    def __init__(self, db):
```

```
        """ Initializer - keyword and database object """

        self.cache = False
        self.cache_dict = {}
        self.db = db
        self.db.connect()

    def setup(self, cache=False, max_items=500):
        """ Setup parameters such as caching """

        self.cache = cache
        # Call configure on the db
        self.db.configure(max_items=max_items)

    def get_results(self, keyword, num=10):
        """ Query keyword on db and get results for given keyword """

        # If results in cache return from there
        if keyword in self.cache_dict:
            print ('From cache')
            return self.cache_dict[keyword]

        results = self.db.query(keyword)
        # Results are list of (string, weightage) tuples
        results = sorted(results, key=operator.itemgetter(1),
                reverse=True)[:num]
        # Cache it
        if self.cache:
            self.cache_dict[keyword] = results

        return results
```

The class has the following three methods:

- `__init__`: This is the initializer; it accepts an object that acts as a handle to the data source (database). It also initializes a few attributes and connects to the database

- `setup`: It sets up the searcher and configures the database object

- `get_results`: It performs a search using the data source (database) and returns the results for a given keyword

We now want to implement a unit test case for this searcher. Since the database is an external dependency, we will virtualize the database object by mocking it. We will test only the searcher's logic, callable signatures, and return data.

We will develop this program step by step so that each step of mocking is clear to you. We will use a Python interactive interpreter session for the same.

First, let's get the mandatory imports:

```
>>> from unittest.mock import Mock, MagicMock
>>> import textsearcher
>>> import operator
```

Since we want to mock the DB, the first step is to do that exactly:

```
>>> db = Mock()
```

Now let's create the `searcher` object. We are not going to mock this, as we need to test the calling signature and the return value of its methods:

```
>>> searcher = textsearcher.TextSearcher(db)
```

At this point, the database object has been passed to the __init__ method of `searcher`, and `connect` has been called on it. Let's verify this expectation:

```
>>> db.connect.assert_called_with()
```

No issues, so the assertion has succeeded! Let's now set up `searcher`:

```
>>> searcher.setup(cache=True, max_items=100)
```

Looking at the code of the `TextSearcher` class, we realize that the preceding call should have called `configure` on the database object with the `max_items` parameter set to the value `100`. Let's verify this:

```
>>> searcher.db.configure.assert_called_with(max_items=100)
<Mock name='mock.configure_assert_called_with()' id='139637252379648'>
```

Bravo! Finally, let's try and test the logic of the `get_results` method. Since our database is a mock object, it won't be able to do any actual query, so we pass some canned results to its `query` method, effectively mocking it:

```
>>> canned_results = [('Python is wonderful', 0.4),
...                   ('I like Python',0.8),
...                   ('Python is easy', 0.5),
...                   ('Python can be learnt in an afternoon!',
0.3)]
>>> db.query = MagicMock(return_value=canned_results)
```

Now we set up the keyword and the number of results and call `get_results` using these parameters:

```
>>> keyword, num = 'python', 3
>>> data = searcher.get_results(python, num=num)
```

Let's inspect the data:

```
>>> data
[('I like Python', 0.8), ('Python is easy', 0.5), ('Python is
wonderful', 0.4)]
```

It looks good! In the next step, we verify that `get_results` has indeed called `query` with the given keyword:

```
>>> searcher.db.query.assert_called_with(keyword)
```

Finally, we verify that the data returned has been sorted right and truncated to the number of results (num) value we passed:

```
>>> results = sorted(canned_results, key=operator.itemgetter(1),
reverse=True)[:num]
>>> assert data == results
True
```

All good! The example shows how to use mock support in the `unittest` module in order to mock an external dependency and effectively virtualize it, while at the same time testing the program's logic, control flow, callable arguments, and return values.

Here is a test module combining all of these tests into a single test module and the output of `nose2` on it:

```
"""
Module test_textsearch - Unittest case with mocks for textsearch
module
"""

from unittest.mock import Mock, MagicMock
import textsearcher
import operator

def test_search():
```

```
""" Test search via a mock """

# Mock the database object
db = Mock()
searcher = textsearcher.TextSearcher(db)
# Verify connect has been called with no arguments
db.connect.assert_called_with()
# Setup searcher
searcher.setup(cache=True, max_items=100)
# Verify configure called on db with correct parameter
searcher.db.configure.assert_called_with(max_items=100)

canned_results = [('Python is wonderful', 0.4),
                  ('I like Python',0.8),
                  ('Python is easy', 0.5),
                  ('Python can be learnt in an afternoon!', 0.3)]
db.query = MagicMock(return_value=canned_results)

# Mock the results data
keyword, num = 'python', 3
data = searcher.get_results(keyword,num=num)
searcher.db.query.assert_called_with(keyword)

# Verify data
results = sorted(canned_results, key=operator.itemgetter(1),
         reverse=True)[:num]
assert data == results
```

Here is the output of `nose2` on this test case:

```
(env) anand@ubuntu-pro-book:~/Documents/ArchitectureBook/code/chap3$ nose2 -v test_textsearch
test_textsearch.transplant_class.<locals>.C (test_search)
Test search via a mock ... ok

----------------------------------------------------------------------
Ran 1 test in 0.001s

OK
(env) anand@ubuntu-pro-book:~/Documents/ArchitectureBook/code/chap3$
```

Running testsearcher test-case using nose2

For good measure, let's also look at the coverage of our mock test example, the `test_textsearch` module, using the py.test coverage plugin:

```
(env) anand@ubuntu-pro-book:~/Documents/ArchitectureBook/code/chap3$ pytest --cov textsearcher
================================ test session starts ================================
platform linux -- Python 3.5.2, pytest-3.0.0, py-1.4.31, pluggy-0.3.1
rootdir: /home/anand/Documents/ArchitectureBook/code/chap3, inifile:
plugins: cov-2.3.1
collected 5 items

test_datetimehelper.py ...
test_datetimehelper2.py .
test_textsearch.py .

----------- coverage: platform linux, python 3.5.2-final-0 -----------
Name                Stmts   Miss  Cover
--------------------------------------
textsearcher.py        19      2    89%

============================ 5 passed in 0.04 seconds ============================
```

Measuring coverage of the textsearcher module via test_textsearch test case using py.test

So our mock test has a coverage of `89%`, missing just two statements out of 20. Not bad!

Tests inline in documentation – doctests

Python has unique support for another form of inline code tests, which are commonly called **doctests**. These are inline unit tests in a function, class, or module documentation, which add a lot of value by combining code and tests in one place without having to develop or maintain separate test suites.

The `doctest` module works by looking for pieces of text in code documentation that look like Python strings, and executing those sessions to verify that they work exactly as found. Any test failures are reported on the console.

Let's look at a code example to see this in action. The following piece of code implements the simple factorial function by using an iterative approach:

```
"""
Module factorial - Demonstrating an example of writing doctests
"""

import functools
import operator

def factorial(n):
```

```
    """ Factorial of a number.

    >>> factorial(0)
    1
    >>> factorial(1)
    1
    >>> factorial(5)
    120
    >>> factorial(10)
    3628800


    """


    return functools.reduce(operator.mul, range(1,n+1))

if __name__ == "__main__":
    import doctest
    doctest.testmod(verbose=True)
```

Let's look at the output of executing this module:

```
(env) anand@ubuntu-pro-book:~/Documents/ArchitectureBook/code/chap3$ python3 factorial.py
**********************************************************************
File "factorial.py", line 13, in __main__.factorial
Failed example:
    factorial(0)
Exception raised:
    Traceback (most recent call last):
      File "/usr/lib/python3.5/doctest.py", line 1321, in __run
        compileflags, 1), test.globs)
      File "<doctest __main__.factorial[3]>", line 1, in <module>
        factorial(0)
      File "factorial.py", line 17, in factorial
        return functools.reduce(operator.mul, range(1,n+1))
    TypeError: reduce() of empty sequence with no initial value
**********************************************************************
1 items had failures:
    1 of   4 in __main__.factorial
***Test Failed*** 1 failures.
```

Output of doctest for the factorial module

The doctest reports that one out of four tests failed.

A quick scan of the output tells us that we forgot to code in the special case to compute the factorial for zero. The error occurs because the code tries to compute range(1, 1), which raises an exception with reduce.

The code can be easily rewritten to fix this. Here is the modified code:

```
"""
Module factorial - Demonstrating an example of writing doctests
"""

import functools
import operator

def factorial(n):
    """ Factorial of a number.

    >>> factorial(0)
    1
    >>> factorial(1)
    1
    >>> factorial(5)
    120
    >>> factorial(10)
    3628800
    """

    # Handle 0 as a special case
    if n == 0:
        return 1

    return functools.reduce(operator.mul, range(1,n+1))

if __name__ == "__main__":
    import doctest
    doctest.testmod(verbose=True)
```

The next screenshot shows the fresh output of executing the module now:

```
(env) anand@ubuntu-pro-book:~/Documents/ArchitectureBook/code/chap3$ python3 factorial.py
Trying:
    factorial(1)
Expecting:
    1
ok
Trying:
    factorial(5)
Expecting:
    120
ok
Trying:
    factorial(10)
Expecting:
    3628800
ok
Trying:
    factorial(0)
Expecting:
    1
ok
1 items had no tests:
    __main__
1 items passed all tests:
    4 tests in __main__.factorial
4 tests in 2 items.
4 passed and 0 failed.
Test passed.
(env) anand@ubuntu-pro-book:~/Documents/ArchitectureBook/code/chap3$
```

Output of doctest for the factorial module after the fix

Now all of the tests pass.

 We turned on the verbose option of the doctest module's `testmod` function in this example in order to show the details of the tests. Without this option, doctest would be silent if all of the tests passed, producing no output.

The `doctest` module is very versatile. Rather than just Python code, it can also load Python interactive sessions from sources such as text files and execute them as tests.

The `doctest` module examines all docstrings including function, class, and module docstrings to search for Python interactive sessions.

 The `pytest` package comes with built-in support for doctests. To allow `pytest` to discover and run doctests in the current folder, use the following command:

```
$ pytest –doctest-modules
```

Integration tests

Unit tests, though very useful to discover and fix bugs during white-box testing early on in the software development life cycle, aren't enough by themselves. A software system is fully functional only if the different components work together in expected ways in order to deliver the required functionality to the end user, satisfying the pre-defined architectural quality attributes. This is where integration tests assume importance.

The purpose of integration tests is to verify the functional, performance, and other quality requirements on the different functional subsystems of a software system, which act as a logical unit, providing certain functionality. Such subsystems deliver some piece of functionality through the cumulative action of their individual units. Though each component may have defined its own unit test, it is also important to verify the combined functionality of the system by writing integration tests.

Integration tests are usually written after unit testing is completed and before validation testing is done.

It would be instructional to list down the advantages provided by integration tests at this point, as this could be useful for any software architect who is at a phase where he/she has designed and implemented his/her unit tests for the different components:

- **Testing component interoperability**: Each unit in a functional subsystem could be written by different programmers. Though each programmer is aware of how this component should perform, and may have written unit tests for the same, the entire system may have issues working in unison, as there could be errors or misunderstanding in the integration points where components talk to each other. Integration testing would reveal such mistakes.

- **Testing for system requirement modifications**: The requirements may have changed during the time of implementation. These updated requirements may not have been unit tested, hence, an integration test becomes very useful to reveal issues. Also, some parts of the system may not have implemented the requirements correctly, which can also be revealed by an appropriate integration test.

- **Testing external dependencies and APIs**: Software components these days use a lot of third-party APIs, which are usually mocked or stubbed during unit tests. Only an integration test would reveal how these APIs would perform and expose any issues either in the calling convention, response data, or performance with them.

- **Debugging hardware issues**: Integration tests are helpful in getting information about any hardware problems, and debugging such tests gives the developer(s) data about whether an update or change in the hardware configuration is required.

- **Uncovering exceptions in code paths**: Integration tests can also help developers figure out exceptions that they may not have handled in their code, as unit tests wouldn't have executed paths or conditions which raised such errors. Higher code coverage can identify and fix a lot of such issues. However, a good integration test combining known code paths for each functionality with high coverage is a good formula for making sure most potential errors that may occur during usage are uncovered and executed during testing.

There are three approaches to writing integration tests. These are as follows:

- **Bottom-up**: In this approach, components at the lower level are tested first, and these test results are used to integrate tests of the higher-level components in the chain. The process repeats until we reach the top of the hierarchy of the components with respect to the control flow. In this approach, critical modules at the top of the hierarchy may be tested inadequately.

  If the top-level components are under development, drivers may be required to simulate (mock) them:

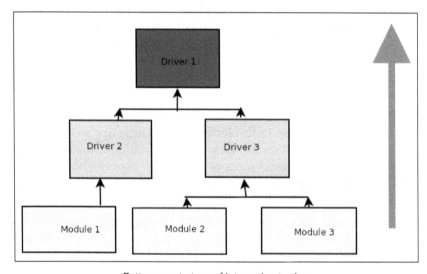

Bottom-up strategy of integration testing

- **Top-down**: Test development and testing happens top-down, following the workflow in the software system. Hence, components at the top level of the hierarchy are tested first and the lower-level modules are tested last. In this approach, critical modules are tested on priority, so we can identify major design or development flaws first and fix them. However, lower-level modules may be tested inadequately.

  Lower-level modules can be replaced by stubs which mock their functionality. Early prototypes are possible in this approach, as lower-level module logic can be stubbed out:

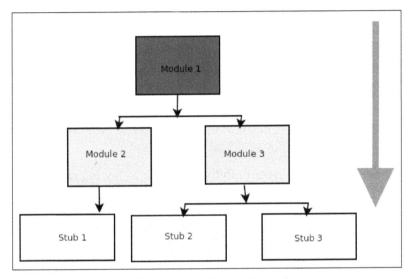

Top-down strategy of integration testing

- **Big-bang**: This is the approach is one where all of the components are integrated and tested at the very end of development. Since the integration tests come at the end, this approach saves time for development. However, this may not give enough time to test critical modules, as there may not be enough time to spend equally on all of the components.

There is no specific software for general integration testing. A certain class of applications, such as web frameworks, define their own specific integration test frameworks. For example, some web frameworks such as Django, Pyramid, and Flask have some specific testing frameworks developed by their own communities.

Another example is the popular WebTest framework, which is useful for automated testing of the Python WSGI applications. A detailed discussion of such frameworks is outside the scope of this chapter and this book.

Test automation

There are a number of tools on the internet that are useful for automating integration testing of software applications. We will take a quick look at some of the popular ones here.

Test automation using Selenium WebDriver

Selenium has been a popular choice for automating integration, regression, and validation tests for a number of software applications. Selenium is free and open source and comes with support for most popular web browser engines.

In Selenium, the primary object is a **web driver**, which is a stateful object on the client side, representing a browser. The web driver can be programmed to visit URLs, perform actions (such as clicking, filling forms, and submitting forms), effectively replacing the human test subject, who usually performs these steps manually.

Selenium provides client driver support for most popular programming languages and runtimes.

To install the Selenium WebDriver in Python, use the following command:

```
$ pip install selenium
```

We will look at a small example that uses Selenium along with pytest in order to implement a small automation test, which will test the Python website (http://www.python.org) for some simple test cases.

Here is our test code. The module is named selenium_testcase.py:

```
"""
Module selenium_testcase - Example of implementing an automated UI
test using selenium framework
"""

from selenium import webdriver
import pytest
import contextlib

@contextlib.contextmanager
@pytest.fixture(scope='session')
def setup():
    driver = webdriver.Firefox()
    yield driver
```

```
        driver.quit()

    def test_python_dotorg():
        """ Test details of python.org website URLs """

        with setup() as driver:
            driver.get('http://www.python.org')
            # Some tests
            assert driver.title == 'Welcome to Python.org'
            # Find out the 'Community' link
            comm_elem = driver.find_elements_by_link_text('Community')[0]
            # Get the URL
            comm_url = comm_elem.get_attribute('href')
            # Visit it
            print ('Community URL=>',comm_url)
            driver.get(comm_url)
            # Assert its title
            assert driver.title == 'Our Community | Python.org'
            assert comm_url == 'https://www.python.org/community/'
```

Before running the preceding example and showing the output, let's inspect the functions a bit:

- The setUp function is a test fixture, which sets up the main object required for our test, that is, the Selenium WebDriver for Firefox. We convert the setUp function in to a context manager by decorating it with the contextmanager decorator from the contextlib module. At the end of the setUp function, the driver exits, since its quit method is called.

- In the test_python_dot_org test function, we set up a rather simple, contrived test for visiting the main Python website URL and checking its title via an assertion. We load the URL for the Python community by locating it on the main page and then visit this URL. We finally assert its title and URL before ending our tests.

Let's see the program in action. We will specifically ask pytest to load only this module and run it. The command line for this is as follows:

```
$ pytest -s selenium_testcase.py
```

The Selenium driver will launch the browser (Firefox) and open a window automatically, visiting the Python website URL while running the tests. The console output for the test is shown in the following screenshot:

```
(env) anand@ubuntu-pro-book:~/Documents/ArchitectureBook/code/chap3$ pytest -s selenium_testcase.py
========================================= test session starts =========================================
platform linux -- Python 3.5.2, pytest-3.0.0, py-1.4.31, pluggy-0.3.1
rootdir: /home/anand/Documents/ArchitectureBook/code/chap3, inifile:
plugins: cov-2.3.1
collected 1 items

selenium_testcase.py Community URL=> https://www.python.org/community/
.
========================================= 1 passed in 16.35 seconds ====================================
```

Console output of a simple Selenium test case on the Python programming language website

Selenium can be used for more complex test cases, as it provides a number of methods for inspecting the HTML of pages, locating elements, and interacting with them. There are also plugins for Selenium, which can execute the JavaScript content of the pages to make the testing support complex interactions via JavaScript (such as AJAX requests).

Selenium can also be run on the server. It provides support for remote clients via its remote driver support. Browsers are instantiated on the server (typically, using virtual X sessions), whereas, the tests can be run and controlled from client machines via the network.

Test-driven development

Test-Driven Development (TDD) is an agile practice of software development, which uses a very short development cycle, where code is written to satisfy an incremental test case.

In TDD, a functional requirement is mapped to a specific test case. Code is written to pass the first test case. Any new requirement is added as a new test case. Code is refactored to support the new test case. The process continues till the code is able to support the entire spectrum of user functionality.

The steps in TDD are as follows:

1. Define a few starting test cases as a specification for the program.
2. Write code to make the early test cases pass.
3. Add a new test case defining new functionality.
4. Run all of the tests and see whether the new test fails or passes.
5. If the new test fails, write some code for the test to pass.

6. Run the tests again.

7. Repeat steps 4 to 6 till the new test passes.

8. Repeat steps 3 to 7 to add a new functionality via test cases.

In TDD, the focus is on keeping everything simple, including the unit test cases and the new code that is added to support the test cases. TDD practitioners believe that writing tests upfront allows the developer to understand the product requirements better, allowing a focus on software quality from the very beginning of the development lifecycle.

In TDD, often, a final refactoring step is also done after many tests have been added to the system in order to make sure no coding smells or antipatterns are introduced and to maintain code readability and maintainability.

There is no specific software for TDD, rather, it is a methodology and process for software development. Most of the time, TDD uses unit tests, so the toolchain support is mostly the `unittest` module and the related packages that we've discussed in this chapter.

TDD with palindromes

Let's understand TDD as discussed earlier with a simple example of developing a program in Python that checks whether an input string is a palindrome.

 A palindrome is a string that reads the same in both directions. For example, *bob*, *rotator*, and *Malayalam* are palindromes. So is the sentence, *Madam, I'm Adam* when you get rid of the punctuation marks.

Let us follow the steps of TDD. Initially, we need a test case that defines the basic specification of the program. Our first version of the test code looks like this:

```
"""
Module test_palindrome - TDD for palindrome module
"""

import palindrome

def test_basic():
    """ Basic test for palindrome """

    # True positives
    for test in ('Rotator','bob','madam','mAlAyAlam', '1'):
```

```
        assert palindrome.is_palindrome(test)==True

    # True negatives
    for test in ('xyz','elephant', 'Country'):
        assert palindrome.is_palindrome(test)==False
```

Note that the preceding code not only gives us a specification for the program in terms of its early functionality, but also gives a function name and signature — in terms of the argument and return value. We can list down the requirements for the first version by looking at the test:

- The function is named is_palindrome. It should accept a string and return True if it is a palindrome and False otherwise. The function sits in the palindrome module.

- The function should treat strings as case-insensitive.

With these specifications, here is our first version of the palindrome module:

```
def is_palindrome(in_string):
    """ Returns True whether in_string is palindrome, False otherwise
    """

    # Case insensitive
    in_string = in_string.lower()
    # Check if string is same as in reverse
    return in_string == in_string[-1::-1]
```

Let's check whether this passes our test. We will run py.test on the test module to verify this:

```
(env) $ py.test -s test_palindrome.py
========================= test session starts =========================
platform linux -- Python 3.5.2, pytest-3.0.7, py-1.4.33, pluggy-0.4.0
rootdir: /home/user/programs/chap3, inifile:
plugins: cov-2.4.0
collected 1 items

test_palindrome.py .

========================= 1 passed in 0.02 seconds =========================
(env) $ 
```

Test output of test_palindrome.py version #1

As you can see in the last image, the basic test passes; so, we've got a first version of the palindrome module, which works and passes its tests.

Now as per the TDD step, let's go to step 3 and add a new test case. This adds a check for testing palindrome strings with spaces. Here is the new test module with this extra test:

```python
"""
Module test_palindrome - TDD for palindrome module
"""

import palindrome

def test_basic():
    """ Basic test for palindrome """

    # True positives
    for test in ('Rotator','bob','madam','mAlAyAlam', '1'):
        assert palindrome.is_palindrome(test)==True

    # True negatives
    for test in ('xyz','elephant', 'Country'):
        assert palindrome.is_palindrome(test)==False

def test_with_spaces():
    """ Testing palindrome strings with extra spaces """

    # True positives
    for test in ('Able was I ere I saw Elba',
                 'Madam Im Adam',
                 'Step on no pets',
                 'Top spot'):
        assert palindrome.is_palindrome(test)==True

    # True negatives
    for test in ('Top post','Wonderful fool','Wild Imagination'):
        assert palindrome.is_palindrome(test)==False
```

Let's run the updated test and see the results:

```
                                    Chapter 3: Testability                          — + x
(env) $ py.test -s test_palindrome.py
=================================== test session starts ===================================
platform linux -- Python 3.5.2, pytest-3.0.7, py-1.4.33, pluggy-0.4.0
rootdir: /home/user/programs/chap3, inifile:
plugins: cov-2.4.0
collected 2 items

test_palindrome.py .F

===================================== FAILURES =====================================
_____ test_with_spaces _____

    def test_with_spaces():
        """ Testing palindrome strings with extra spaces """

        # True positives
        for test in ('Able was I ere I saw Elba',
                    'Madam Im Adam',
                    'Step on no pets',
                    'Top spot'):
>           assert palindrome.is_palindrome(test)==True
E           AssertionError: assert False == True
E            +  where False = <function is_palindrome at 0x7fd856207488>('Madam Im Adam')
E            +    where <function is_palindrome at 0x7fd856207488> = palindrome.is_palindrome

test_palindrome.py:28: AssertionError
=========================== 1 failed, 1 passed in 0.07 seconds ===========================
(env) $ ▌
```

Test output of test_palindrome.py version #2

The test fails, because the code is not enabled to process palindrome strings with spaces in them. So let's do as TDD step 5 says and write some code to make this test pass.

Since it is clear we need to ignore spaces, a quick fix is to purge all spaces from the input string. Here is the modified `palindrome` module with this simple fix:

```python
"""
Module palindrome - Returns whether an input string is palindrome or
not
"""

import re

def is_palindrome(in_string):
    """ Returns True whether in_string is palindrome, False otherwise
    """

    # Case insensitive
    in_string = in_string.lower()
    # Purge spaces
    in_string = re.sub('\s+','', in_string)
    # Check if string is same as in reverse
    return in_string == in_string[-1::-1]
```

Let's now repeat step 4 of TDD to see whether the updated code makes the test pass:

```
                                     Chapter 3: Testability                          -  +  x
(env) $ py.test -s test_palindrome.py -v
============================== test session starts ==============================
platform linux -- Python 3.5.2, pytest-3.0.7, py-1.4.33, pluggy-0.4.0 -- /home/anand/py3/env/bin/python
3
cachedir: .cache
rootdir: /home/user/programs/chap3, inifile:
plugins: cov-2.4.0
collected 2 items

test_palindrome.py::test_basic PASSED
test_palindrome.py::test_with_spaces PASSED

============================== 2 passed in 0.01 seconds ==============================
(env) $ ▉
```

Console output of test_palindrome.py version #2, after code updates

Surely, the code passes the test now!

What we just saw was an instance of TDD with one update cycle for implementing a module in Python, which checks strings for palindromes. In a similar way, we can keep adding tests and keep updating the code as per step 8 of TDD, thereby adding new functionality while maintaining the updated tests naturally via the process.

We conclude this section with the final version of our palindrome test case, which adds a test case for checking for strings with extra punctuation marks:

```python
"""
Module test_palindrome - TDD for palindrome module
"""

import palindrome

def test_basic():
    """ Basic test for palindrome """

    # True positives
    for test in ('Rotator','bob','madam','mAlAyAlam', '1'):
        assert palindrome.is_palindrome(test)==True

    # True negatives
    for test in ('xyz','elephant', 'Country'):
        assert palindrome.is_palindrome(test)==False

def test_with_spaces():
```

```
    """ Testing palindrome strings with extra spaces """

    # True positives
    for test in ('Able was I ere I saw Elba',
                 'Madam Im Adam',
                 'Step on no pets',
                 'Top spot'):
        assert palindrome.is_palindrome(test)==True

    # True negatives
    for test in ('Top post','Wonderful fool','Wild Imagination'):
        assert palindrome.is_palindrome(test)==False


def test_with_punctuations():
    """ Testing palindrome strings with extra punctuations """

    # True positives
    for test in ('Able was I, ere I saw Elba',
                 "Madam I'm Adam",
                 'Step on no pets.',
                 'Top spot!'):
        assert palindrome.is_palindrome(test)==True

    # True negatives
    for test in ('Top . post','Wonderful-fool','Wild Imagination!!'):
        assert palindrome.is_palindrome(test)==False
```

And here is the updated `palindrome` module that makes this test pass:

```
"""

Module palindrome - Returns whether an input string is palindrome or
not
"""

import re
from string import punctuation

def is_palindrome(in_string):
    """ Returns True whether in_string is palindrome, False otherwise
    """

    # Case insensitive
    in_string = in_string.lower()
```

```
# Purge spaces
in_string = re.sub('\s+','', in_string)
# Purge all punctuations
in_string = re.sub('[' + re.escape(punctuation) + ']+', '',
            in_string)
# Check if string is same as in reverse
return in_string == in_string[-1::-1]
```

Let's inspect the final output of the `test_palindrome` module on the console:

```
                        Chapter 3: Testability                    - + x
(env) $ py.test -s test_palindrome.py -v
========================== test session starts ===========================
platform linux -- Python 3.5.2, pytest-3.0.7, py-1.4.33, pluggy-0.4.0 -- /home/anand/py3/env/bin/python
3
cachedir: .cache
rootdir: /home/user/programs/chap3, inifile:
plugins: cov-2.4.0
collected 3 items

test_palindrome.py::test_basic PASSED
test_palindrome.py::test_with_spaces PASSED
test_palindrome.py::test_with_punctuations PASSED

========================= 3 passed in 0.03 seconds =========================
(env) $
```

Console output of test_palindrome.py version #3, with matching code updates

Summary

In this chapter, we revisited the definition of testability and its related architectural quality aspects, such as complexity and determinism. We looked at the different architectural aspects that are tested and got an understanding of the type of tests that are usually performed by the software testing process.

We then discussed the various strategies for improving the testability of software, and looked at techniques to reduce system complexity and improve predictability and to control and manage external dependencies. Along the way, we learned the different ways to virtualize and manage external dependencies, such as fakes, mocks and stubs, by way of examples.

We then looked at unit testing and its various aspects mainly from the perspective of the Python `unittest` module. We saw an example by using a `datetime` helper class, and explained how to write effective unit tests—a simple example followed by an interesting example of patching functions using the mock library of `unittest`.

We then introduced, and learned quite a bit about, the two other well-known testing frameworks in Python, namely, nose2 and py.test. Next, we discussed the very important aspect of code coverage and saw examples of measuring code coverage using the coverage.py package directly, and by using it via plugins of nose2 and pytest.

In the next section, we sketched an example of a textsearch class for using advanced mock objects, where we mocked its external dependency and wrote a unit test case. We went on to discuss the Python doctest support of embedding tests in the documentation of classes, modules, methods, and functions via the doctest module while looking at examples.

The next topic was integration tests, where we discussed the different aspects and advantages of integration tests, and looked at the three different ways in which tests can be integrated in a software organization. Test automation via Selenium was discussed next with an example of automating a couple of tests on the Python language website using Selenium and py.test.

We ended this chapter with a quick overview of TDD, and discussed an example of writing a program for detecting palindromes in Python using TDD principles, where we developed the program using tests in a step-by-step fashion.

In the next chapter, we will look at one of the most critical quality attribute of architecture when developing software — namely, performance.

4
Good Performance is Rewarding!

Performance is one of the cornerstones of modern-day software applications. Every day we interact with high-performing computing systems in many different ways, as part of our work and our leisure.

When you book an airline ticket from one of the travel sites on the web, you are interacting with a high-performance system that carries out hundreds of such transactions at any given time. When you transfer money to someone or pay your credit card bill online via an internet banking transaction, you are interacting with a high performance and high throughput transactional system. Similarly, when you play online games on your mobile phone and interact with other players, again there is a network of servers built for high concurrency and low latency that is receiving input from you and thousands of other players, performing computations at the backend and sending data to you — all with reasonable and quiet efficiency.

Modern day web applications that serve millions of users concurrently became possible with the advent of high-speed internet and huge drops in the price and performance ratio of hardware. Performance is still a key quality attribute of modern day software architecture and writing high-performing and scalable software still continues to be something of a difficult art. You may write an application which ticks all the boxes of functionality and other quality attributes, but if it fails its performance tests, then it cannot be moved to production.

In this chapter and the next, we focus on two aspects of writing software with high throughput — namely performance and scalability. In this chapter, the focus is on performance, the various aspects of it, how to measure it, the performance of various data structures, and when to choose what — with the focus on Python.

The topics we will be discussing in this chapter roughly fall under the following sections:

- Defining performance
- Software performance engineering
- Types of performance-testing tool
- Performance complexity and the Big O notation:
    - Measuring performance
    - Finding performance complexity using graphs
    - Improving performance
- Profiling:
    - Deterministic profiling
    - `cProfile` and `profile`
    - Third-party profilers
- Other tools:
    - Objgraph
    - Pympler
- Programming for performance — data structures:
    - Lists
    - Dictionaries
    - Sets
    - Tuples
- High performance containers — the collections module:
    - `deque`
    - `defaultdict`
    - `OrderedDict`
    - `Counter`
    - `ChainMap`
    - `namedtuple`
- Probabilistic data structures — bloom filters

What is performance?

The performance of a software system can be broadly defined as:

The degree to which the system is able to meet its throughput and/or latency requirements in terms of the number of transactions per second or time taken for a single transaction.

We've already taken an overview of measuring performance in the introductory chapter. Performance can be measured either in terms of response time/latency or in terms of throughput. The former is the time it takes for the application to complete a request/response loop on average. The latter is the rate at which the system processes its input in terms of the number of requests or transactions successfully completed per minute.

The performance of a system is a function of its software and of its hardware capabilities. A badly written piece of software could still be made to perform better by scaling the hardware — for example, the amount of RAM.

Similarly, a piece of software can be made to work better on existing hardware by increasing its performance — for example, by rewriting routines or functions to be more efficient in terms of time or memory, or by modifying the architecture.

However, the right type of performance engineering is the one where the software is tuned for the hardware in an optimal fashion so that software scales linearly or better with respect to the available hardware.

Software performance engineering

Software performance engineering includes all the activities of software engineering and analysis applied during the **Software Development Life Cycle (SDLC)** and is directed towards meeting performance requirements.

In conventional software engineering, performance testing and feedback are done usually towards the end of the SDLC. This approach is purely measurement-based and waits for the system to be developed before applying tests and diagnostics and tuning the system based on the results.

Another more formal model named **Software Performance Engineering (SPE)**, itself develops performance models early in the SDLC and uses results from the models to modify the software design and architecture to meet performance requirements in multiple iterations.

In this approach, both performance as a non-functional requirement and software development meeting its functional requirement go hand in hand. There is a specific **Performance Engineering Life Cycle (PELC)** that parallels the steps in the SDLC. At every step, starting from the design and architecture all the way to deployment, feedback between both the life cycles is used to iteratively improve the software quality:

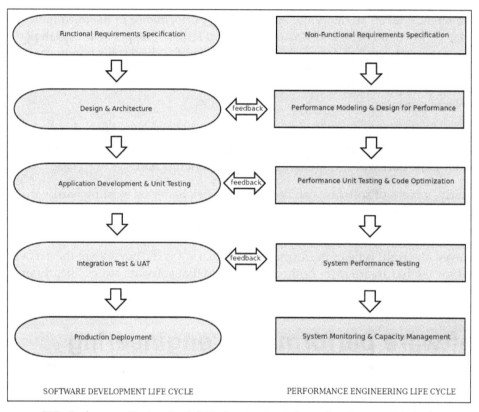

SPE—Performance Engineering Life Cycle mirroring Software Development Life Cycle

In both approaches, performance testing and diagnostics are important, followed by tuning the design/architecture or the code based on the results obtained. Hence performance testing and measurement tools play an important role in this step.

Performance testing and measurement tools

These tools fall under two broad categories—namely, the ones used for performance testing and diagnostics, and the ones used for performance metrics gathering and instrumentation.

Performance testing and diagnostic tools can be classified further as follows:

- **Stress-testing tools**: These tools are used to supply workload to the system under test, simulating peak workloads in production. These tools can be configured to send a continuous stream of input to the application to simulate high stress or to periodically send a burst of very high traffic—much exceeding even peak stress—to test the robustness of the system. These tools are also called **load generators**. Examples of common stress testing tools used for web application testing include **httpperf**, **ApacheBench**, **LoadRunner**, **Apache JMeter**, and **Locust**. Another class of tools involves those that actually record real user traffic and then replay it via the network to simulate real user load. For example, the popular network packet capturing and monitoring tool, **Wireshark** and its console cousin program, `tcpdump`, can be used to do this. We won't be discussing these tools in this chapter as they are general-purpose and examples of usage for them can be found in abundance on the web.

- **Monitoring tools**: These tools work with the application code to generate performance metrics such as the time and memory taken for functions to execute, the number of function calls made per request-response loop, the average and peak times spent on each function, and so on.

- **Instrumentation tools**: Instrumentation tools trace metrics, such as the time and memory required for each computing step, and also track events, such as exceptions in code, covering such details as the module/function/line number where the exception occurred, the timestamp of the event, and the environment of the application (environment variables, application configuration parameters, user information, system information, and so on). Often external instrumentation tools are used in modern web-application programming systems to capture and analyze such data in detail.

- **Code or application profiling tools**: These tools generate statistics about functions, their frequency of duration of calls, and the time spent on each function call. This is a kind of dynamic program analysis. It allows the programmer to find critical sections of code where the most time is spent, allowing them to optimize those sections. Optimization without profiling is not advised as the programmer may end up optimizing the wrong code, thereby not surfacing the intended benefits up to the application.

Most programming languages come with their own set of instrumentation and profiling tools. In Python, a set of tools in the standard library (such as the `profile` and `cProfile` modules) do this—this is supplemented by a rich ecosystem of third-party tools. We will discuss these tools in the coming sections.

Performance complexity

It would be helpful to spend some time discussing what we mean by the performance complexity of code before we jump into code examples in Python and discuss tools to measure and optimize performance.

The performance complexity of a routine or function is defined in terms of how they respond to changes in the input size typically in terms of the time spent in executing the code.

This is usually represented by the so-called Big-O notation which belongs to a family of notations called the **Bachmann–Landau notation or asymptotic** notation.

The letter O is used as the rate of growth of a function with respect to input size—also called the **order** of the function.

Commonly used Big-O notations or function orders are shown in the following table in order of increasing complexity:

#	Order	Complexity	Example
1	$O(1)$	Constant	Looking for a key in a constant lookup table such as a HashMap or dictionary in Python
2	$O(log (n))$	Logarithmic	Searching for an item in a sorted array with a binary search. All operations on a heapq in Python
3	$O(n)$	Linear	Searching an item in an array (list in Python) by traversing it
4	$O(n*k)$	Linear	Worst-case complexity of Radix sort
5	$O(n * log (n))$	n log-star n	Worst-case complexity in a mergesort or heapsort algorithm
6	$O(n^2)$	Quadratic	Simple sorting algorithms such as bubblesort, insertion sort, and selection sort. Worst-case complexity on some sorting algorithms such as quicksort, shellsort, and so on

#	Order	Complexity	Example
7	$O(2^n)$	Exponential	Trying to break a password of size n using brute force, solving the travelling salesman problem using dynamic programming
8	$O(n!)$	Factorial	Generating all partitions of a set

Table 1: Common Big-O notations for function orders with respect to input size "n"

When implementing a routine or algorithm accepting an input of a certain size n, the programmer ideally should aim for implementing it in an order that falls in the first five. Anything which is of the order of $O(n)$ or $O(n* log(n))$ or lesser indicates reasonable to good performance.

Algorithms with an order of $O(n^2)$ can usually be optimized to work at a lower order. We will see some examples of this in the sections in the following diagram.

The following diagram shows how each of these orders grow with respect to n:

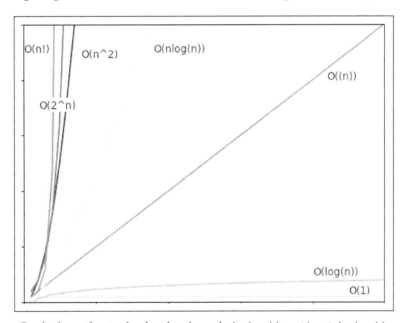

Graph of growth rate of each order of complexity (y axis) w.r.t input size (x axis)

Measuring performance

Now that we've had an overview of what performance complexity is and also of performance testing and measurement tools, let us take an actual look at the various ways of measuring performance complexity with Python.

One of the simplest time measurements can be done by using the `time` command of a POSIX/Linux system.

This is done by using the following command line:

```
$ time <command>
```

For example, here is a screenshot of the time it takes to fetch a very popular page from the web:

```
                         anand@ubuntu-pro-book: /home/user/programs

  File  Edit  View  Search  Terminal  Help
$ time wget http://www.google.com -O /dev/null
--2016-12-28 16:59:27--  http://www.google.com/
Resolving www.google.com (www.google.com)... 216.58.197.36, 2404:6800:4007:807::2004
Connecting to www.google.com (www.google.com)|216.58.197.36|:80... connected.
HTTP request sent, awaiting response... 302 Found
Location: http://www.google.co.in/?gfe_rd=cr&ei=F6JjWITaLeeK8Qfvj7OQBg [following]
--2016-12-28 16:59:27--  http://www.google.co.in/?gfe_rd=cr&ei=F6JjWITaLeeK8Qfvj7OQBg
Resolving www.google.co.in (www.google.co.in)... 216.58.197.35, 2404:6800:4007:807::2003
Connecting to www.google.co.in (www.google.co.in)|216.58.197.35|:80... connected.
HTTP request sent, awaiting response... 200 OK
Length: unspecified [text/html]
Saving to: '/dev/null'

/dev/null                   [ <=>                        ]  12.14K  --.-KB/s    in 0.004s

2016-12-28 16:59:27 (2.80 MB/s) - '/dev/null' saved [12429]


real    0m0.121s
user    0m0.004s
sys     0m0.008s
$
```

Output of the time command on fetching a web page from the internet via wget

See that it shows three classes of time output, namely `real`, `user`, and `sys`. It is important to know the distinction between these three so let us look at them briefly:

- `real`: Real time is the actual wall-clock time that elapsed for the operation. This is the time of the operation from start to finish. It will include any time the process sleeps or spends blocked—such as time taken for I/O to complete.

- `User`: User time is the amount of actual CPU time spent within the process in user mode (outside the kernel). Any sleep time or time spent in waiting such as I/O doesn't add to the user time.

- `Sys`: System time is the amount of CPU time spent on executing system calls within the kernel for the program. This counts only those functions that execute in kernel space such as privileged system calls. It doesn't count any system calls that execute in user space (which is counted in `User`).

The total CPU time spent by a process is `user` + `sys` time. The real or wall-clock time is the time mostly measured by simple time counters.

Measuring time using a context manager

In Python, it is not very difficult to write a simple function that serves as a context manager for blocks of code whose execution time you want to measure.

But first we need a program whose performance we can measure.

Take a look at the following steps to learn how to use a context manager for measuring time:

1. Let us write a program that calculates the common elements between two sequences as a test program. Here is the code:

```
def common_items(seq1, seq2):
    """ Find common items between two sequences """

    common = []
    for item in seq1:
        if item in seq2:
            common.append(item)

    return common
```

2. Let us write a simple context-manager timer to time this code. For timing we will use `perf_counter` of the `time` module, which gives the time to the most precise resolution for short durations:

```
from time import perf_counter as timer_func
from contextlib import contextmanager

@contextmanager
def timer():
    """ A simple timing function for routines """

    try:
        start = timer_func()
        yield
    except Exception as e:
        print(e)
        raise
    finally:
        end = timer_func()
        print ('Time spent=>',1000.0*(end - start),'ms.')
```

3. Let us time the function for some simple input data. For this a `test` function is useful that generates random data, given an input size:

```
def test(n):
    """ Generate test data for numerical lists given input size
    """

    a1=random.sample(range(0, 2*n), n)
    a2=random.sample(range(0, 2*n), n)

    return a1, a2
```

Here is the output of the `timer` method on the `test` function on the Python interactive interpreter:

```
>>> with timer() as t:
... common = common_items(*test(100))
... Time spent=> 2.0268699999999864 ms.
```

4. In fact both test data generation and testing can be combined in the same function to make it easy to test and generate data for a range of input sizes:

```
def test(n, func):
    """ Generate test data and perform test on a given function
    """

    a1=random.sample(range(0, 2*n), n)
    a2=random.sample(range(0, 2*n), n)

    with timer() as t:
        result = func(a1, a2)
```

5. Now let us measure the time taken for different ranges of input sizes in the Python interactive console:

```
>>> test(100, common_items)
    Time spent=> 0.6799279999999963 ms.
>>> test(200, common_items)
    Time spent=> 2.7455590000000085 ms.
>>> test(400, common_items)
    Time spent=> 11.440810000000024 ms.
>>> test(500, common_items)
    Time spent=> 16.83928100000001 ms.
>>> test(800, common_items)
    Time spent=> 21.15130400000004 ms.
>>> test(1000, common_items)
    Time spent=> 13.200749999999983 ms.
```

Oops, the time spent for 1000 items is less than that for 800! How's that possible? Let's try again:

```
>>> test(800, common_items)
    Time spent=> 8.328282999999992 ms.
>>> test(1000, common_items)
    Time spent=> 34.85899500000001 ms.
```

Now the time spent for 800 items seems to be lesser than that for 400 and 500. And time spent for 1000 items has increased to more than twice what it was before.

The reason is that our input data is random, which means it will sometimes have a lot of common items — which takes more time — and sometimes have much fewer. Hence on subsequent calls the time taken can show a range of values.

In other words, our timing function is useful to get a rough picture, but not very useful when it comes to getting the true statistical measure of time taken for program execution, which is more important.

6. For this we need to run the timer many times and take an average. This is somewhat similar to the **amortized** analysis of algorithms, which takes into account both the lower end and upper end of the time taken for executing algorithms and gives the programmer a realistic estimate of the average time spent.

Python comes with such a module, which helps to perform such timing analysis, in its standard library, namely the `timeit` module. Let us look at this module in the next section.

Timing code using the timeit module

The `timeit` module in the Python standard library allows the programmer to measure the time taken to execute small code snippets. The code snippets can be a Python statement, an expression, or a function.

The simplest way to use the `timeit` module is to execute it as a module in the Python command line.

For example, here is timing data for some simple Python inline code measuring the performance of a list comprehension calculating squares of numbers in a range:

```
$ python3 -m timeit '[x*x for x in range(100)]'
100000 loops, best of 3: 5.5 usec per loop
```

```
$ python3 -m timeit '[x*x for x in range(1000)]'
10000 loops, best of 3: 56.5 usec per loop
```

```
$ python3 -m timeit '[x*x for x in range(10000)]'
1000 loops, best of 3: 623 usec per loop
```

The result shows the time taken for execution of the code snippet. When run on the command line, the `timeit` module automatically determines the number of cycles to run the code and also calculates the average time spent in a single execution.

The results show that the statement we are executing is linear or O(n) as a range of size 100 takes 5.5 usec and that of 1,000 takes 56.5 usec or about 10 times its time. A usec — or microsecond — is 1 millionth of a second or 1*10-6 seconds.

Here is how to use the `timeit` module on the Python interpreter in a similar manner:

```
>>> 1000000.0*timeit.timeit('[x*x for x in range(100)]',
number=100000)/100000.0
6.007622049946804

>>> 1000000.0*timeit.timeit('[x*x for x in range(1000)]',
number=10000)/10000.0
58.761584300373215
```

Observe that when used in this way, the programmer has to pass the correct number of iterations as the `number` argument and, to average, has to divide by the same number. The multiplication by `1000000` is to convert the time to microseconds (usec).

The `timeit` module uses a `Timer` class behind the scenes. The class can be made use of directly as well as for finer control.

When using this class, `timeit` becomes a method of the instance of the class to which the number of cycles is passed as an argument.

The `Timer` class constructor also accepts an optional `setup` argument, which sets up the code for the `Timer` class. This can contain statements for importing the module that contains the function, setting up globals, and so on. It accepts multiple statements separated by semi-colons.

Measuring the performance of our code using timeit

Let us rewrite our `test` function to test the common items between two sequences. Now that we are going to use the `timeit` module, we can remove the context manager timer from the code. We will also hardcode the call to `common_items` in the function.

We also need to create the random input outside the test function otherwise the time taken for it will add to the test function's time and corrupt our results.

Hence we need to move the variables out as globals in the module and write a `setup` function, which will generate the data for us as a first step.

Our rewritten `test` function looks like this:

```
def test():
    """ Testing the common_items function """

    common = common_items(a1, a2)
```

The `setup` function with the global variables looks like this:

```
# Global lists for storing test data
a1, a2 = [], []

def setup(n):
    """ Setup data for test function """

    global a1, a2
    a1=random.sample(range(0, 2*n), n)
    a2=random.sample(range(0, 2*n), n)
```

Let's assume the module containing both the `test` and `common_items` functions is named `common_items.py`.

The timer test can now be run as follows:

```
>>> t=timeit.Timer('test()', 'from common_items import test,setup;
setup(100)')
>>> 1000000.0*t.timeit(number=10000)/10000
116.58759460115107
```

So the time taken for a range of `100` numbers is around 117 usec (0.12 microseconds) on average.

Executing it now for a few other ranges of input sizes gives the following output:

```
>>> t=timeit.Timer('test()','from common_items import test,setup;
setup(200)')
>>> 1000000.0*t.timeit(number=10000)/10000
```

```
482.8089299000567

>>> t=timeit.Timer('test()','from common_items import test,setup;
setup(400)')
>>> 1000000.0*t.timeit(number=10000)/10000
1919.577144399227

>>> t=timeit.Timer('test()','from common_items import test,setup;
setup(800)')
>>> 1000000.0*t.timeit(number=1000)/1000
7822.607815993251

>>> t=timeit.Timer('test()','from common_items import test,setup;
setup(1000)')
>>> 1000000.0*t.timeit(number=1000)/1000
12394.932234004957
```

So the maximum time taken for this test run is 12.4 microseconds for an input size of `1000` items.

Finding out time complexity – graphs

Is it possible to find out from these results what the time-performance complexity of our function is? Let us try plotting it in a graph and see the results.

The `matplotlib` library is very useful in plotting graphs in Python for any type of input data. We just need the following simple piece of code for this to work:

```python
import matplotlib.pyplot as plt

def plot(xdata, ydata):
    """ Plot a range of ydata (on y-axis) against xdata (on x-axis)
    """

    plt.plot(xdata, ydata)
    plt.show()
```

The preceding code gives you the following output:

```
This is our x data.
>>> xdata = [100, 200, 400, 800, 1000]
This is the corresponding y data.
>>> ydata = [117,483,1920,7823,12395]
>>> plot(xdata, ydata)
```

Take a look at the following graph:

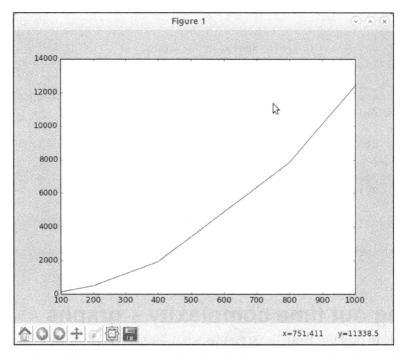

Plot of the input range versus time taken for the common_items function

This is clearly not linear, yet of course not quadratic (in comparison with the figure on Big-O notations). Let us try and plot a graph of O(n*log(n)) superimposed on the current plot to see if there's a match.

Since we now need two series of ydata, we need another slightly modified function:

```python
def plot_many(xdata, ydatas):
    """ Plot a sequence of ydatas (on y-axis) against xdata
    (on x-axis) """

    for ydata in ydatas:
        plt.plot(xdata, ydata)
    plt.show()
```

The preceding code gives you the following output:

```python
>>> ydata2=map(lambda x: x*math.log(x, 2), input)

>>> plot_many(xdata, [ydata2, ydata])
```

You get the following graph:

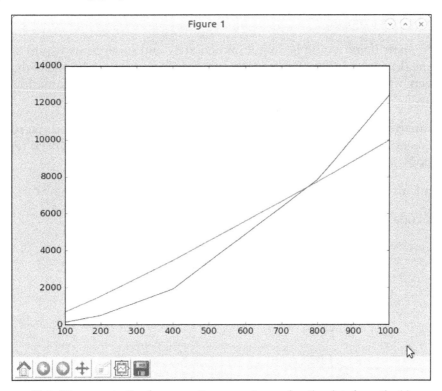

Plot of time complexity of common_items superimposed on the plot of y = x*log(x)

The superimposed plot shows that the function is a close match for the n*log(n) order, if not exactly the same. So our current implementation's complexity seems to be roughly O(n*log(n)).

Now that we've done the performance analysis, let us see if we can rewrite our routine to perform better.

Here is the current code:

```python
def common_items(seq1, seq2):
    """ Find common items between two sequences """

    common = []
    for item in seq1:
        if item in seq2:
            common.append(item)

    return common
```

The routine first does a pass over an outer `for` loop (of size n) and does a check in a sequence (also of size n) for the item. Now the second search is also of time complexity n on average.

However, some items would be found immediately and some items would take linear time (k) where 1<k<n. On average, the distribution would be somewhere in between, which is why the code has an average complexity approximating O(n*log(n)).

A quick analysis will tell you that the inner search can be avoided by converting the outer sequence to a dictionary, setting values to 1. The inner search will be replaced with a loop on the second sequence that increments values by 1.

In the end, all common items will have a value greater than 1 in the new dictionary.

The new code is as follows:

```python
def common_items(seq1, seq2):
    """ Find common items between two sequences, version 2.0 """

    seq_dict1 = {item:1 for item in seq1}

    for item in seq2:
        try:
            seq_dict1[item] += 1
        except KeyError:
            pass

    # Common items will have value > 1
    return [item[0] for item in seq_dict1.items() if item[1]>1]
```

With this change, the timer gives the following updated results:

```
>>> t=timeit.Timer('test()','from common_items import test,setup;
setup(100)')
>>> 1000000.0*t.timeit(number=10000)/10000
35.777671200048644

>>> t=timeit.Timer('test()','from common_items import test,setup;
setup(200)')
>>> 1000000.0*t.timeit(number=10000)/10000
65.20369809877593

>>> t=timeit.Timer('test()','from common_items import test,setup;
setup(400)')
>>> 1000000.0*t.timeit(number=10000)/10000
```

```
139.67061050061602

>>> t=timeit.Timer('test()','from common_items import test,setup;
setup(800)')
>>> 1000000.0*t.timeit(number=10000)/10000
287.0645995993982

>>> t=timeit.Timer('test()','from common_items import test,setup;
setup(1000)')
>>> 1000000.0*t.timeit(number=10000)/10000
357.764518300246
```

Let us plot this and superimpose it on an O(n) graph:

```
>>> input=[100,200,400,800,1000]
>>> ydata=[36,65,140,287,358]

# Note that ydata2 is same as input as we are superimposing with y = x
# graph
>>> ydata2=input
>>> plot.plot_many(xdata, [ydata, ydata2])
```

Let's take a look at the following graph:

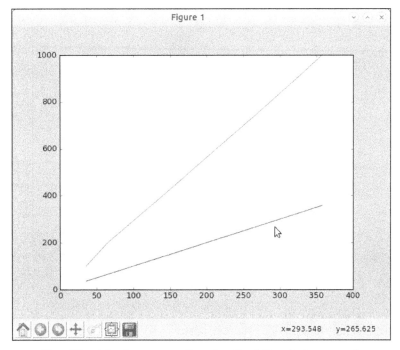

Plot of time taken by common_items function (v2) against y = x graph

The upper green line is the reference **y** = **x** graph and the lower blue line is the plot of the time taken by our new function. It is pretty obvious that the time complexity is now linear or O(n).

However, there seems to be a constant factor here as the slopes of the two lines are different. From a quick calculation one can compute this factor as roughly 0.35.

After applying this change, you will get the following output:

```
>>> input=[100,200,400,800,1000]
>>> ydata=[36,65,140,287,358]

# Adjust ydata2 with the constant factor
>>> ydata2=map(lambda x: 0.35*x, input)
>>> plot.plot_many(xdata, [ydata, ydata2])
```

The output can be seen in the following graph as follows:

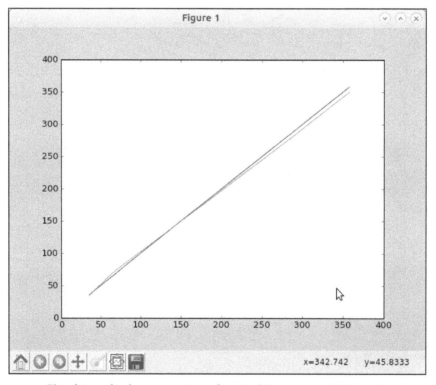

Plot of time taken by common_items function (v2) against y = 0.35*x graph

You can see that the plots pretty much superimpose on each other. So our function is now performing at O(c*n) where c ~= 0.35.

Another implementation of the `common_items` function is to convert both sequences to sets and return their intersection. It would be an interesting exercise for the reader to make this change, time it, and plot the graphs to determine the time complexity.

Measuring CPU time with timeit

The `Timer` module by default uses the `perf_counter` function of the `time` module as the default `timer` function. As mentioned earlier, this function returns the wall-clock time spent to the maximum precision for small time durations, hence it will include any sleep time, time spent for I/O, and so on.

This can be made clear by adding a little sleep time to our test function as follows:

```
def test():
    """ Testing the common_items function using a given input size """

    sleep(0.01)
    common = common_items(a1, a2)
```

The preceding code will give you the following output:

```
>>> t=timeit.Timer('test()','from common_items import test,setup;
setup(100)')
>>> 1000000.0*t.timeit(number=100)/100
10545.260819926625
```

The time jumped by as much as 300 times since we are sleeping `0.01` seconds (10 milliseconds) upon every invocation, so the actual time spent on the code is now determined almost completely by the sleep time as the result shows `10545.260819926625` microseconds (or about 10 milliseconds).

Sometimes you may have such sleep times and other blocking or wait times but you want to measure only the actual CPU time taken by the function. To use this, the `Timer` object can be created using the `process_time` function of the `time` module as the `timer` function.

This can be done by passing in a `timer` argument when you create the `Timer` object:

```
>>> from time import process_time
>>> t=timeit.Timer('test()','from common_items import
test,setup;setup(100)', timer=process_time)
>>> 1000000.0*t.timeit(number=100)/100
345.22438
```

If you now increase the sleep time by a factor of, say, 10, the testing time increases by that factor, but the return value of the timer remains the same.

For example, here is the result when sleeping for 1 second. The output comes after about 100 seconds (since we are iterating `100` times), but notice that the return value (time spent per invocation) doesn't change:

```
>>> t=timeit.Timer('test()','from common_items import
test,setup;setup(100)', timer=process_time)
>>> 1000000.0*t.timeit(number=100)/100
369.8039100000002
```

Let us move on to profiling next.

Profiling

In this section, we will discuss profilers and take a deep look at the modules in the Python standard library, which provides support for deterministic profiling. We will also look at third-party libraries that provide support for profiling such as `line_profiler` and `memory_profiler`.

Deterministic profiling

Deterministic profiling means that all function calls, function returns, and exception events are monitored, and precise timings are made for the intervals between these events. Another type of profiling, namely **statistical profiling**, randomly samples the instruction pointer and deduces where time is being spent—but this may not be very accurate.

Python, being an interpreted language, already has a certain overhead in terms of metadata kept by the interpreter. Most deterministic profiling tools make use of this information and hence only add very little extra processing overhead for most applications. Hence deterministic profiling in Python is not a very expensive operation.

Profiling with cProfile and profile

The `profile` and `cProfile` modules provide support for deterministic profiling in the Python standard library. The `profile` module is purely written in Python. The `cProfile` module is a C extension that mimics the interface of the `profile` module but adds lesser overhead to it when compared to `profile`.

Both modules report statistics that are converted into reportable results using the `pstats` module.

We will use the following code, which is a prime number iterator, in order to show our examples using the `profile` modules:

```python
class Prime(object):
    """ A prime number iterator for first 'n' primes """

    def __init__(self, n):
        self.n = n
        self.count = 0
        self.value = 0

    def __iter__(self):
        return self

    def __next__(self):
        """ Return next item in iterator """

        if self.count == self.n:
            raise StopIteration("end of iteration")
        return self.compute()

    def is_prime(self):
        """ Whether current value is prime ? """

        vroot = int(self.value ** 0.5) + 1
        for i in range(3, vroot):
            if self.value % i == 0:
                return False
        return True

    def compute(self):
        """ Compute next prime """

        # Second time, reset value
        if self.count == 1:
            self.value = 1

        while True:
            self.value += 2

            if self.is_prime():
```

```
                    self.count += 1
                    break

            return self.value
```

The prime number iterator generates the first n prime numbers given the value of n:

```
>>> for p in Prime(5):
...  print(p)
...
2
3
5
7
11
```

To profile this code, we just need to pass the code to be executed as a string to the run method of profile or cProfile module. In the following examples, we will be using the cProfile module:

```
anand@ubuntu-pro-book: /home/user/programs/chap4
File  Edit  View  Search  Terminal  Help
>>> cProfile.run("list(primes.Prime(100))")
         477 function calls in 0.004 seconds

   Ordered by: standard name

   ncalls  tottime  percall  cumtime  percall filename:lineno(function)
        1    0.000    0.000    0.004    0.004 <string>:1(<module>)
        1    0.000    0.000    0.000    0.000 primes.py:25(__init__)
        1    0.000    0.000    0.000    0.000 primes.py:30(__iter__)
      101    0.000    0.000    0.003    0.000 primes.py:33(__next__)
      271    0.003    0.000    0.003    0.000 primes.py:40(is_prime)
      100    0.001    0.000    0.003    0.000 primes.py:49(compute)
        1    0.000    0.000    0.004    0.004 {built-in method builtins.exec}
        1    0.000    0.000    0.000    0.000 {method 'disable' of '_lsprof.Profiler' objects}


>>>
```

Profiling output of the prime iterator function for the first 100 primes

See how the profiler reports its output. The output is ordered into six columns as follows:

- `ncalls`: The number of calls per function
- `tottime`: The total time spent in the call
- `percall`: The `percall` time (quotient of `tottime`/`ncalls`)
- `cumtime`: The cumulative time in this function plus any child function
- `percall`: Another `percall` column (the quotient of `cumtime`/number of primitive calls)
- `filename: lineno(function)`: The filename and line number of the function call

In this case, our function took 4 microseconds to complete with most of that time (3 microseconds) being spent inside the is_prime method, which also dominates the number of calls at 271.

Here are the outputs of the profiler at n = 1000 and 10000 respectively:

Profiling output of the prime iterator function for the first 1,000 primes

Take a look at the following additional output:

```
                              anand@ubuntu-pro-book: /home/user/programs/chap4                    ⌄ ^ ×
 File  Edit  View  Search  Terminal  Help
>>> cProfile.run("list(primes.Prime(10000))")
         72371 function calls in 0.458 seconds

   Ordered by: standard name

   ncalls  tottime  percall  cumtime  percall filename:lineno(function)
        1    0.006    0.006    0.458    0.458 <string>:1(<module>)
        1    0.000    0.000    0.000    0.000 primes.py:25(__init__)
        1    0.000    0.000    0.000    0.000 primes.py:30(__iter__)
    10001    0.006    0.000    0.452    0.000 primes.py:33(__next__)
    52365    0.417    0.000    0.417    0.000 primes.py:40(is_prime)
    10000    0.028    0.000    0.445    0.000 primes.py:49(compute)
        1    0.000    0.000    0.458    0.458 {built-in method builtins.exec}
        1    0.000    0.000    0.000    0.000 {method 'disable' of '_lsprof.Profiler' objects}


>>> ▮
```

Profiling output of the Prime iterator function for the first 10,000 primes

As you can see, at n=1000 it took about 0.043 seconds (43 microseconds) and at n=10000 it took 0.458 seconds (458 microseconds). Our Prime iterator seems to be performing at an order close to O(n).

As usual, most of that time is spent in is_primes. Is there a way to reduce that time?

At this point, let us analyze the code.

Prime number iterator class – performance tweaks

A quick analysis of the code tells us that inside is_prime we are dividing the value by every number in the range from 3 to the successor of the square root of the value.

This contains many even numbers as well—we are doing unnecessary computation, which we can avoid by dividing only by the odd numbers.

The modified is_prime method is as follows:

```
def is_prime(self):
    """ Whether current value is prime ? """

    vroot = int(self.value ** 0.5) + 1
    for i in range(3, vroot, 2):
        if self.value % i == 0:
            return False
    return True
```

With this, the profile for n=1000 and n=10000 looks as follows.

The following is the output of the profiler for n = 1000:

```
anand@ubuntu-pro-book: /home/user/programs/chap4
File  Edit  View  Search  Terminal  Help
>>> cProfile.run("list(primes.Prime(1000))")
         5966 function calls in 0.038 seconds

   Ordered by: standard name

   ncalls  tottime  percall  cumtime  percall filename:lineno(function)
        1    0.001    0.001    0.038    0.038 <string>:1(<module>)
        1    0.000    0.000    0.000    0.000 primes.py:25(__init__)
        1    0.000    0.000    0.000    0.000 primes.py:30(__iter__)
     1001    0.002    0.000    0.037    0.000 primes.py:33(__next__)
     3960    0.029    0.000    0.029    0.000 primes.py:40(is_prime)
     1000    0.006    0.000    0.035    0.000 primes.py:49(compute)
        1    0.000    0.000    0.038    0.038 {built-in method builtins.exec}
        1    0.000    0.000    0.000    0.000 {method 'disable' of '_lsprof.Profiler' objects}

>>> █
```

Profiling output of the Prime iterator function for the first 1,000 primes with tweaked code

The following is the output of the profiler for n = 10000:

```
anand@ubuntu-pro-book: /home/user/programs/chap4
File  Edit  View  Search  Terminal  Help
>>> cProfile.run("list(primes.Prime(10000))")
         72371 function calls in 0.232 seconds

   Ordered by: standard name

   ncalls  tottime  percall  cumtime  percall filename:lineno(function)
        1    0.003    0.003    0.232    0.232 <string>:1(<module>)
        1    0.000    0.000    0.000    0.000 primes.py:25(__init__)
        1    0.000    0.000    0.000    0.000 primes.py:30(__iter__)
    10001    0.005    0.000    0.228    0.000 primes.py:33(__next__)
    52365    0.202    0.000    0.202    0.000 primes.py:40(is_prime)
    10000    0.022    0.000    0.224    0.000 primes.py:49(compute)
        1    0.000    0.000    0.232    0.232 {built-in method builtins.exec}
        1    0.000    0.000    0.000    0.000 {method 'disable' of '_lsprof.Profiler' objects}

>>> █
```

Profiling output of the Prime iterator function for the first 10,000 primes with tweaked code

You can see that, at 1000, the time has dropped a bit (43 microseconds to 38 microseconds) but at 10000, there is nearly a 50% drop from 458 microseconds to 232 microseconds. At this point, the function is performing better than O(n).

Profiling – collecting and reporting statistics

The way we used cProfile in the example earlier, it ran and reported the statistics directly. Another way to use the module is to pass a filename argument to which it writes the statistics, which can later be loaded and interpreted by the pstats module.

We modify the code as follows:

```
>>> cProfile.run("list(primes.Prime(100))", filename='prime.stats')
```

By doing this, the stats, instead of getting printed out, are saved to the file named prime.stats.

Here is how to parse the statistics using the pstats module and print the results ordered by the number of calls:

```
                        anand@ubuntu-pro-book: /home/user/programs/chap4        ⌄ ⌃ ⌂ ×
 File  Edit  View  Search  Terminal  Help
>>> pstats.Stats('prime.stats').sort_stats('ncalls').print_stats()
Thu Dec 29 06:34:39 2016    prime.stats

        577 function calls in 0.002 seconds

  Ordered by: call count

  ncalls  tottime  percall  cumtime  percall filename:lineno(function)
     271    0.001    0.000    0.001    0.000 /home/user/programs/chap4/primes.py:41(is_prime)
     101    0.000    0.000    0.002    0.000 /home/user/programs/chap4/primes.py:34(__next__)
     100    0.000    0.000    0.000    0.000 {method 'append' of 'list' objects}
     100    0.000    0.000    0.001    0.000 /home/user/programs/chap4/primes.py:51(compute)
       1    0.000    0.000    0.000    0.000 /home/user/programs/chap4/primes.py:31(__iter__)
       1    0.000    0.000    0.002    0.002 <string>:1(<module>)
       1    0.000    0.000    0.000    0.000 /home/user/programs/chap4/primes.py:25(__init__)
       1    0.000    0.000    0.002    0.002 {built-in method builtins.exec}
       1    0.000    0.000    0.000    0.000 {method 'disable' of '_lsprof.Profiler' objects}


<pstats.Stats object at 0x7f5b97262da0>
>>> ▮
```

Parsing and printing saved profile results using the pstats module

The pstats module allows sorting the profile results by a number of headers such as total time (tottime), number of primitive calls (pcalls), cumulative time (cumtime), and so on. You can see from the output of pstats again that most of the processing in terms of number of calls are being spent in the is_prime method, as we are sorting the output by 'ncalls' or the number of function calls.

The Stats class of the pstats module returns a reference to itself after every operation. This is a very useful aspect of some Python classes and allows us to write compact one-line code by chaining method calls.

Another useful method of the `Stats` object is to find out the callee/caller relationship. This can be done by using the `print_callers` method instead of `print_stats`. Here is the output from our current statistics:

```
anand@ubuntu-pro-book: /home/user/programs/chap4
File  Edit  View  Search  Terminal  Help
>>> pstats.Stats('prime.stats').sort_stats('pcalls').print_callers()
   Ordered by: primitive call count

Function                                        was called by...
                                                  ncalls  tottime  cumtime
/home/user/programs/chap4/primes.py:41(is_prime)  <-     271     0.001     0.001  /home/user/programs/chap
4/primes.py:51(compute)
/home/user/programs/chap4/primes.py:34(__next__)  <-     101     0.000     0.002  <string>:1(<module>)
{method 'append' of 'list' objects}               <-     100     0.000     0.000  /home/user/programs/chap
4/primes.py:51(compute)
/home/user/programs/chap4/primes.py:51(compute)   <-     100     0.000     0.001  /home/user/programs/chap
4/primes.py:34(__next__)
/home/user/programs/chap4/primes.py:31(__iter__)  <-       1     0.000     0.000  <string>:1(<module>)
<string>:1(<module>)                              <-       1     0.000     0.002  {built-in method builtin
s.exec}
/home/user/programs/chap4/primes.py:25(__init__)  <-       1     0.000     0.000  <string>:1(<module>)
{built-in method builtins.exec}                   <-
{method 'disable' of '_lsprof.Profiler' objects}  <-


<pstats.Stats object at 0x7f5b9907e550>
>>> 
```

Printing callee/caller relationships ordered by primitive calls using the pstats module

Third-party profilers

The Python ecosystem comes with a plethora of third-party modules for solving most problems. This is true in the case of profilers as well. In this section, we will take a quick look at a few popular third-party profiler applications contributed by developers in the Python community.

Line profiler

Line profiler is a profiler application developed by Robert Kern for performing line-by-line profiling of Python applications. It is written in Cython, an optimizing static compiler for Python that reduces the overhead of profiling.

Line profiler can be installed via `pip` as follows:

```
$ pip3 install line_profiler
```

As opposed to the profiling modules in Python, which profile functions, line profiler is able to profile code line by line, thus providing more granular statistics.

Line profiler comes with a script called `kernprof.py` that makes it easy to profile code using line profiler. One needs only to decorate the functions that need to be profiled with the `@profile` decorator when using `kernprof`.

For example, we realized that most of the time in our prime number iterator was being spent in the `is_prime` method. However, line profiler allows us to go into more detail and find which lines of those functions take the most time.

To do this, just decorate the method with the `@profile` decorator:

```
@profile
def is_prime(self):
    """ Whether current value is prime ? """

    vroot = int(self.value ** 0.5) + 1
    for i in range(3, vroot, 2):
        if self.value % i == 0:
            return False
    return True
```

Since `kernprof` accepts a script as an argument, we need to add some code to invoke the prime number iterator. To do that, we can append the following at the end of the `primes.py` module:

```
# Invoke the code.
if __name__ == "__main__":
    l=list(Prime(1000))
```

Now, run it with line profiler as follows:

```
$ kernprof -l -v primes.py
```

By passing `-v` to the `kernprof` script, we tell it to display the profile results in addition to saving them.

Here is the output:

```
                              anand@ubuntu-pro-book: /home/user/programs/chap4
 File  Edit  View  Search  Terminal  Help
$ kernprof -l -v primes.py
Wrote profile results to primes.py.lprof
Timer unit: 1e-06 s

Total time: 0.04177 s
File: primes.py
Function: is_prime at line 40

Line #      Hits         Time  Per Hit   % Time  Line Contents
==============================================================
    40                                           @profile
    41                                           def is_prime(self):
    42                                               """ Whether current value is prime ? """
    43
    44      3960         3339      0.8      8.0       vroot = int(self.value ** 0.5) + 1
    45     41579        17141      0.4     41.0       for i in range(3, vroot, 2):
    46     40579        19821      0.5     47.5           if self.value % i == 0:
    47      2960         1072      0.4      2.6               return False
    48      1000          397      0.4      1.0       return True

$
```

Line profiler results from profiling the `is_prime` method using n = 1000

Line profiler tells us that the majority of the time—close to 90% of the total time spent in the method—is spent in the first two lines: the `for` loop and the reminder check.

This tells us that, if ever we want to optimize this method, we need to concentrate on these two aspects.

Memory profiler

Memory profiler is a profiler similar to line profiler in that it profiles Python code line by line. However, instead of profiling the time taken in each line of code, it profiles lines by memory consumption.

Memory profiler can be installed the same way as line profiler:

```
$ pip3 install memory_profiler
```

Once installed, memory for lines can be printed by decorating the function with the `@profile` decorator in a similar way to line profiler.

Here is a simple example:

```
# mem_profile_example.py
@profile
def squares(n):
    return [x*x for x in range(1, n+1)]


squares(1000)
```

Here's how to run this:

```
                        anand@ubuntu-pro-book: /home/user/programs/chap4
 File  Edit  View  Search  Terminal  Help
$ python3 -m memory_profiler mem_profile_example.py
Filename: mem_profile_example.py

Line #    Mem usage    Increment   Line Contents
================================================
     1    31.559 MiB    0.000 MiB   @profile
     2                              def squares(n):
     3    31.559 MiB    0.000 MiB       return [x*x for x in range(1, n+1)]


$
```

Memory profiler profiling a list comprehension of squares of the first 1,000 numbers

Memory profiler shows memory increments line by line. In this case, there is almost no increment for the line containing the number of squares (the list comprehension) as the numbers are rather small. The total memory usage remains what it was at the beginning: about 32 MB.

What happens if we change the value of n to 1,000,000? This can be done by rewriting the last line of the code as follows:

```
squares(100000)
```

```
                        anand@ubuntu-pro-book: /home/user/programs/chap4
 File  Edit  View  Search  Terminal  Help
$ python3 -m memory_profiler mem_profile_example.py
Filename: mem_profile_example.py

Line #    Mem usage    Increment   Line Contents
================================================
     1    31.418 MiB    0.000 MiB   @profile
     2                              def squares(n):
     3    70.027 MiB   38.609 MiB       return [x*x for x in range(1, n+1)]


$
```

Memory profiler profiling a list comprehension of squares of the first 1,000,000 numbers

Now you can see that there is a clear memory increment of about 39 MB for the list comprehension calculating the squares, with a total final memory usage of about 70 MB.

To demonstrate the real usefulness of memory profiler, let us look at another example.

This involves finding the strings from a sequence that are subsequences of any of the strings present in another sequence, generally containing larger strings.

Substring (subsequence) problem

Let us say you have a sequence containing the following strings:

```
>>> seq1 = ["capital","wisdom","material","category","wonder"]
```

And say there is another sequence as follows:

```
>>> seq2 = ["cap","mat","go","won","to","man"]
```

The problem is to find the strings in `seq2` that are substrings—as is found anywhere contiguously in any of the strings in `seq1`:

In this case, the answer is as follows:

```
>>> sub=["cap","mat","go","won"]
```

This can be solved using a brute-force search—checking for each string one by one in each of the parent strings as follows:

```
def sub_string_brute(seq1, seq2):
    """ Sub-string by brute force """

    subs = []
    for item in seq2:
        for parent in seq1:
            if item in parent:
                subs.append(item)

    return subs
```

However, a quick analysis will tell you that the time complexity of this function scales rather badly as the size of the sequences increase. Since every step needs iteration through two sequences and then a search in each string in the first sequence, the average performance would be O(n1*n2), where n1, n2 are the sizes of the sequences respectively.

Here are the results of some tests of this function with input sizes (both sequences of the same size) of random strings varying from length 2 to 10:

Input size	Time taken
100	450 usec
1000	52 microseconds
10000	5.4 seconds

Table 2: Input size versus time taken for subsequence solution via brute force

The results indicate the performance is almost exactly $O(n^2)$.

Is there a way to rewrite the function to be more performance-efficient? This approach is captured in the following `sub_string` function:

```
def slices(s, n):
    return map(''.join, zip(*(s[i:] for i in range(n))))


def sub_string(seq1, seq2):
    """ Return sub-strings from seq2 which are part of strings in seq1
    """

    # Create all slices of lengths in a given range
    min_l, max_l = min(map(len, seq2)), max(map(len, seq2))
    sequences = {}

    for i in range(min_l, max_l+1):
        for string in seq1:
          # Create all sub sequences of given length i
          sequences.update({}.fromkeys(slices(string, i)))

    subs = []
    for item in seq2:
        if item in sequences:
            subs.append(item)

    return subs
```

In this approach, we pre-compute all the substrings of a size range from the strings in `seq1` and store it in a dictionary. Then it is a matter of going through the strings in `seq2` and checking if they are in this dictionary and if so adding them to a list.

To optimize the calculation, we only compute strings whose size is in the range of the minimum and maximum length of the strings in `seq2`.

As with almost all solutions to performance issues, this one trades space for time. By pre-computing all the substrings, we are expending more space in memory but this eases the computation time.

The test code looks like this:

```
import random
import string

seq1, seq2 = [], []

def random_strings(n, N):
    """ Create N random strings in range of 4..n and append
    to global sequences seq1, seq2 """

    global seq1, seq2
    for i in range(N):
        seq1.append(''.join(random.sample(string.ascii_lowercase,
                                random.randrange(4, n))))

    for i in range(N):
        seq2.append(''.join(random.sample(string.ascii_lowercase,
                                random.randrange(2, n/2))))

def test(N):
    random_strings(10, N)
    subs=sub_string(seq1, seq2)

def test2():
    # random_strings has to be called before this
    subs=sub_string(seq1, seq2)
```

Here are the timing results of this function using the `timeit` module:

```
>>> t=timeit.Timer('test2()',setup='from sub_string import test2,
random_
strings;random_strings(10, 100)')
>>> 1000000*t.timeit(number=10000)/10000.0
1081.6103347984608
>>> t=timeit.Timer('test2()',setup='from sub_string import test2,
random_
strings;random_strings(10, 1000)')
>>> 1000000*t.timeit(number=1000)/1000.0
11974.320339999394
```

```
>>> t=timeit.Timer('test2()',setup='from sub_string import test2,
random_
strings;random_strings(10, 10000)')
>>> 1000000*t.timeit(number=100)/100.0124718.30968977883
124718.30968977883
>>> t=timeit.Timer('test2()',setup='from sub_string import test2,
random_
strings;random_strings(10, 100000)')
>>> 1000000*t.timeit(number=100)/100.0
1261111.164370086
```

Here are the summarized results for this test:

Input size	Time taken
100	1.08 microseconds
1000	11.97 microseconds
10000	0.12 microseconds
100000	1.26 seconds

Table 3: Input size versus time taken for optimized sub-sequence solution using pre-computed strings

A quick calculation tells us that the algorithm is now performing at O(n). Pretty good!

But this is at the expense of memory in terms of the pre-computed strings. We can get an estimate of this by invoking memory profiler.

Here is the decorated function for doing this:

```
@profile
def sub_string(seq1, seq2):
    """ Return sub-strings from seq2 which are part of strings in seq1
    """

    # Create all slices of lengths in a given range
    min_l, max_l = min(map(len, seq2)), max(map(len, seq2))
    sequences = {}

    for i in range(min_l, max_l+1):
        for string in seq1:
            sequences.update({}.fromkeys(slices(string, i)))

    subs = []
    for item in seq2:
        if item in sequences:
            subs.append(item)
```

The test function would now be as follows:

```
def test(N):
    random_strings(10, N)
    subs = sub_string(seq1, seq2)
```

Let's test this for the sequence of sizes 1,000 and 10,000 respectively.

Here is the result for an input size of 1,000:

```
anand@ubuntu-pro-book: /home/user/programs/chap4
File  Edit  View  Search  Terminal  Help
$ python3 -m memory_profiler sub_string.py
Filename: sub_string.py

Line #    Mem usage    Increment   Line Contents
================================================
    24    31.352 MiB   0.000 MiB   @profile
    25                             def sub_string(seq1, seq2):
    26                                 """ Return sub-strings from seq2 which are in seq1 """
    27
    28                                 # E.g: seq1 = ['introduction','discipline','animation']
    29                                 # seq2 = ['in','on','is','mat','ton']
    30                                 # Result = ['in','on','mat','is']
    31
    32                                 # Create all slices of lengths in a given range
    33    31.352 MiB   0.000 MiB       min_l, max_l = min(map(len, seq2)), max(map(len, seq2))
    34    31.352 MiB   0.000 MiB       sequences = {}
    35
    36    32.797 MiB   1.445 MiB       for i in range(min_l, max_l+1):
    37    32.797 MiB   0.000 MiB           for string in seq1:
    38    32.797 MiB   0.000 MiB               sequences.update({}.fromkeys(slices(string, i)))
    39
    40    32.797 MiB   0.000 MiB       subs = []
    41    32.797 MiB   0.000 MiB       for item in seq2:
    42    32.797 MiB   0.000 MiB           if item in sequences:
    43    32.797 MiB  -0.000 MiB               subs.append(item)
    44
    45    32.797 MiB   0.000 MiB       return subs
```

Memory profiler results for testing sub-strings of sequences of size 1,000

And here is the result for an input size of 10,000:

```
                          anand@ubuntu-pro-book: /home/user/programs/chap4

 File  Edit  View  Search  Terminal  Help
$ python3 -m memory_profiler sub_string.py
Filename: sub_string.py

Line #    Mem usage    Increment   Line Contents
================================================
    24    32.523 MiB    0.000 MiB   @profile
    25                              def sub_string(seq1, seq2):
    26                                  """ Return sub-strings from seq2 which are in seq1 """
    27
    28                                  # E.g: seq1 = ['introduction','discipline','animation']
    29                                  # seq2 = ['in','on','is','mat','ton']
    30                                  # Result = ['in','on','mat','is']
    31
    32                                  # Create all slices of lengths in a given range
    33    32.523 MiB    0.000 MiB       min_l, max_l = min(map(len, seq2)), max(map(len, seq2))
    34    32.523 MiB    0.000 MiB       sequences = {}
    35
    36    38.770 MiB    6.246 MiB       for i in range(min_l, max_l+1):
    37    38.770 MiB    0.000 MiB           for string in seq1:
    38    38.770 MiB    0.000 MiB               sequences.update({}.fromkeys(slices(string, i)))
    39
    40    38.770 MiB    0.000 MiB       subs = []
    41    38.770 MiB    0.000 MiB       for item in seq2:
    42    38.770 MiB    0.000 MiB           if item in sequences:
    43    38.770 MiB    0.000 MiB               subs.append(item)
    44
    45    38.770 MiB    0.000 MiB       return subs
```

Memory profiler results for testing sub-strings of sequences of size 10,000

For the sequence of size of 1,000, the memory usage increased by a paltry 1.4 MB. For the sequence of size 10,000 it increased by 6.2 MB. Clearly, these are not very significant numbers.

So the test with memory profiler makes it clear that our algorithm, while being efficient on time performance, is also memory-efficient.

Other tools

In this section, we will discuss a few more tools that will aid the programmer in debugging memory leaks and also enable them to visualize their objects and their relations.

objgraph

objgraph (**object graph**) is a Python object visualization tool that makes use of the graphviz package to draw object reference graphs.

It is not a profiling or instrumentation tool but can be used along with such tools to visualize object trees and references in complex programs while hunting for elusive memory leaks. It allows you to find out references to objects to figure out what references are keeping an object alive.

As with almost everything in the Python world, it is installable via `pip`:

```
$ pip3 install objgraph
```

However objgraph is really useful only if it can generate graphs. Hence we need to install the `graphviz` package and the `xdot` tool.

In a Debian/Ubuntu system, you will install this as follows:

```
$ sudo apt install graphviz xdot -y
```

Let's look at a simple example of using `objgraph` to find out hidden references:

```python
import objgraph

class MyRefClass(object):
    pass

ref=MyRefClass()
class C(object):pass

c_objects=[]
for i in range(100):
    c=C()
    c.ref=ref
    c_objects.append(c)

import pdb; pdb.set_trace()
```

We have a class named `MyRefClass` with a single instances `ref` that is referred to by 100 instances of the class `C` created in a `for` loop. These are references that may cause memory leaks. Let us see how `objgraph` allows us to identify them.

When this piece of code is executed, it stops at the debugger (`pdb`):

```
$ python3 objgraph_example.py
--Return--
[0] > /home/user/programs/chap4/objgraph_example.py(15)<module>()->None
-> import pdb; pdb.set_trace()
```

```
(Pdb++) objgraph.show_backrefs(ref, max_depth=2, too_many=2,
filename='refs.png')
```

```
Graph written to /tmp/objgraph-xxhaqwxl.dot (6 nodes)
```

```
Image generated as refs.png
```

 The left side of the image has been cropped to show only the relevant part.

Next is the diagram generated by `objgraph`:

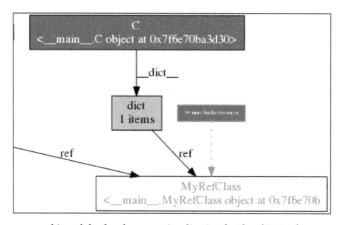

objgraph back references visualization for the object ref

The red box in the preceding diagram says **99 more references**, which means that it is showing one instance of class **C** and informing us there are 99 more like it— totaling to 100 instances of C, that refer to the single object **ref**.

In a complex program where we are unable to track object references that cause memory leaks, such reference graphs can be put to good use by the programmer.

Pympler

Pympler is a tool that can be used to monitor and measure the memory usage of objects in a Python application. It works on both Python 2.x and 3.x. It can be installed using `pip` as follows:

```
$ pip3 install pympler
```

The documentation of `pympler` is rather lacking. However, it's well-known use is to track objects and print their actual memory usage via its `asizeof` module.

The following is our `sub_string` function modified to print the memory usage of the sequences dictionary (where it stores all the generated substrings):

```
from pympler import asizeof

def sub_string(seq1, seq2):
    """ Return sub-strings from seq2 which are part of strings in seq1
    """


    # Create all slices of lengths in a given range
    min_l, max_l = min(map(len, seq2)), max(map(len, seq2))
    sequences = {}

    for i in range(min_l, max_l+1):
        for string in seq1:
            sequences.update({}.fromkeys(slices(string, i)))

    subs = []
    for item in seq2:
        if item in sequences:
            subs.append(item)
    print('Memory usage',asizeof.asized(sequences).format())

    return subs
```

When running this for a sequence size of 10,000:

```
$ python3 sub_string.py
Memory usage {'awg': None, 'qlbo': None, 'gvap': No....te':
                        None, 'luwr':
                        None, 'ipat': None}
size=5874384
flat=3145824
```

The memory size of `5870408` bytes (or around 5.6 MB) is in line with what memory profiler reported (around 6 MB)

Pympler also comes with a package called muppy which allows us to keep track of all objects in a program. This can be summarized with the `summary` package to print out the summary of memory usage of all objects (classified according to their types) in an application.

Here is a report of our `sub_string` module run with n =10,000. To do this, the execution part has to be modified as follows:

```
if __name__ == "__main__":
    from pympler import summary
    from pympler import muppy
    test(10000)
    all_objects = muppy.get_objects()
    sum1 = summary.summarize(all_objects)
    summary.print_(sum1)
```

The following shows the output that `pympler` summarizes at the end of the program:

```
                                           anand@ubuntu-pro-book: /home/user/programs/chap4
 File  Edit  View  Search  Terminal  Help
 $ python3 sub_string.py
 Memory usage {'gra': None, 'usrq': None, 'slx': Non....gj': None, 'yzfp': None, 'egfa': None} size=588
 7488 flat=3145824
                               types |  # objects |   total size
 ==================================== | ========== | ============
                      <class 'str |       30048 |      2.14 MB
                     <class 'dict |        1540 |      1.19 MB
                     <class 'type |         462 |    458.64 KB
                     <class 'code |        3067 |    431.45 KB
                     <class 'list |         413 |    229.49 KB
                      <class 'set |         363 |    139.91 KB
        <class 'wrapper_descriptor |        1106 |     86.41 KB
                    <class 'tuple |        1266 |     83.86 KB
                   <class 'weakref |         975 |     76.17 KB
   <class 'builtin_function_or_method |       920 |     64.69 KB
        <class 'method_descriptor |         828 |     58.22 KB
              <class 'abc.ABCMeta |          51 |     48.13 KB
                      <class 'int |        1489 |     41.66 KB
           <class 'getset_descriptor |        504 |     35.44 KB
                 <class 'frozenset |          42 |     27.94 KB
 $
```

Summary of memory usage classified by object type by pympler

Programming for performance – data structures

We've looked at the definition of performance, measuring performance complexity, and the different tools for measuring program performance. We've also gained insights by profiling code for statistics, memory usage, and so on.

We also saw a couple of examples of program optimization to improve the time performance of the code.

In this section, we will take a look at common Python data structures and discuss what their best and worst performance scenarios are and also discuss some situations of where they are an ideal fit and where they may not be the best choice.

Mutable containers – lists, dictionaries, and sets

Lists, dictionaries, and sets are the most popular and useful mutable containers in Python.

Lists are appropriate for object access via a known index. Dictionaries provide a near-constant time lookup for objects with known keys. Sets are useful to keep groups of items while dropping duplicates and finding their difference, intersection, union, and so on in near-linear time.

Let us look at each of these in turn.

Lists

Lists provide a near constant time O(1) order for the following operations:

- `get(index)` via the `[]` operator
- The `append(item)` via the `.append` method

However, lists perform badly (`O(n)`) in the following cases:

- Seeking an item via the `in` operator
- Inserting at an index via the `.insert` method

A list is ideal in the following cases:

- If you need a mutable store to keep different types or classes of items (heterogeneous).
- If your search of objects involves getting the item by a known index.
- If you don't have a lot of lookups via searching the list (**item in list**).
- If any of your elements are non-hashable. Dictionaries and sets require their entries to be hashable. So in this case, you almost default to using a list.

If you have a huge list—of, say, more than 100,000 items—and you keep finding that you search it for elements via the `in` operator, you should replace it with a dictionary.

Similarly, if you find that you keep inserting to a list instead of appending to it most of the time, you can think of replacing the list with `deque` from the `collections` module.

Dictionaries

Dictionaries provide a constant time order for:

- Setting an item via a key
- Getting an item via a key
- Deleting an item via a key

However, dictionaries take slightly more memory than lists for the same data. A dictionary is useful in the following situations:

- You don't care about the insertion order of the elements
- You don't have duplicate elements in terms of keys

A dictionary is also ideal where you load a lot of data uniquely indexed by keys from a source (database or disk) in the beginning of the application and need quick access to them — in other words, a lot of random reads as against fewer writes or updates.

Sets

The usage scenario of sets lies somewhere between lists and dictionaries. Sets are in implementation closer to dictionaries in Python — since they are unordered, don't support duplicate elements, and provide near O(1) time access to items via keys. They are kind of similar to lists in that they support the pop operation (even if they don't allow index access!).

Sets are usually used in Python as intermediate data structures for processing other containers — for operations such as dropping duplicates, finding common items across two containers, and so on.

Since the order of set operations is exactly the same as that of a dictionary, you can use them for most cases where a dictionary needs to be used, except that no value is associated to the key.

Examples include:

- Keeping heterogeneous, unordered data from another collection while dropping duplicates
- Processing intermediate data in an application for a specific purpose — such as finding common elements, combining unique elements across multiple containers, dropping duplicates, and so on

Immutable containers – tuples

Tuples are an immutable version of lists in Python. Since they are unchangeable after creation, they don't support any of the methods of list modification such as insert, append, and so on.

Tuples have the same time complexity as when using the index and search (via **item in tuple**) as lists. However, they take much less memory overhead when compared to lists; the interpreter optimizes them more as they are immutable.

Hence tuples can be used whenever there are use cases for reading, returning, or creating a container of data that is not going to be changed but requires iteration. Some examples are as follows:

- Row-wise data loaded from a data store that is going to have read-only access. For example, results from a DB query, processed rows from reading a CSV file, and so on.

- A constant set of values that needs iteration over and over again. For example, a list of configuration parameters loaded from a configuration file.

- When returning more than one value from a function. In this case, unless one explicitly returns a list, Python always returns a tuple by default.

- When a mutable container needs to be a dictionary key. For example, when a list or set needs to be associated to a value as a dictionary key, the quick way is to convert it to a tuple.

High performance containers – the collections module

The collection module supplies high performance alternatives to the built-in default container types in Python, namely `list`, `set`, `dict`, and `tuple`.

We will briefly look at the following container types in the collections module:

- `deque`: An alternative to a list container supporting fast insertions and pops at either ends

- `defaultdict`: A sub-class of `dict` that provides factory functions for types to provide missing values

- `OrderedDict`: A sub-class of `dict` that remembers the order of insertion of keys

- `Counter`: A `dict` sub-class for keeping count and statistics of hashable types

- `ChainMap`: A class with a dictionary-like interface for keeping track of multiple mappings
- `namedtuple`: A type for creating tuple-like classes with named fields

deque

A deque or *double ended queue* is like a list but supports nearly constant (O(1)) time appends and pops from either side as opposed to a list, which has an O(n) cost for pops and inserts at the left.

Deques also support operations such as rotation for moving `k` elements from back to front and reverse with an average performance of O(k). This is often slightly faster than the similar operation in lists, which involves slicing and appending:

```
def rotate_seq1(seq1, n):
    """ Rotate a list left by n """
    # E.g: rotate([1,2,3,4,5], 2) => [4,5,1,2,3]

    k = len(seq1) - n
    return seq1[k:] + seq1[:k]

def rotate_seq2(seq1, n):
    """ Rotate a list left by n using deque """

    d = deque(seq1)
    d.rotate(n)
    return d
```

By a simple `timeit` measurement, you should find that deques have a slight performance edge over lists (about 10-15%), in the above example.

defaultdict

Default dicts are `dict` sub-classes that use type factories to provide default values to dictionary keys.

A common problem one encounters in Python when looping over a list of items and trying to increment a dictionary count is that there may not be any existing entry for the item.

For example, if one is trying to count the number of occurrences of a word in a piece of text:

```
counts = {}
for word in text.split():
    word = word.lower().strip()
    try:
        counts[word] += 1
    except KeyError:
        counts[word] = 1
```

We are forced to write code like the preceding or a variation of it.

Another example is when grouping objects according to a key using a specific condition, for example, trying to group all strings with the same length to a dictionary:

```
cities = ['Jakarta','Delhi','Newyork','Bonn','Kolkata','Bangalore','S
eoul']
cities_len = {}
for city in cities:
  clen = len(city)
  # First create entry
  if clen not in cities_len:
    cities_len[clen] = []
  cities_len[clen].append(city)
```

A `defaultdict` container solves these problems elegantly by defining a type factory to supply the default argument for any key that is not yet present in the dictionary. The default factory type supports any of the default types and defaults to None.

For each type, its empty value is the default value. This means:

```
0 → default value for integers
[] → default value for lists
'' → default value for strings
{} → default value for dictionaries
```

The word-count code can then be rewritten as follows:

```
counts = defautldict(int)
for word in text.split():
    word = word.lower().strip()
    # Value is set to 0 and incremented by 1 in one go
    counts[word] += 1
```

Similarly, for the code which groups strings by their length we can write this:

```
cities = ['Jakarta','Delhi','Newyork','Bonn','Kolkata','Bangalore','S
eoul']
cities_len = defaultdict(list)
for city in cities:
    # Empty list is created as value and appended to in one go
    cities_len[len(city)].append(city)
```

OrderedDict

OrderedDict is a sub-class of dict that remembers the order of the insertion of entries. It kind of behaves as a dictionary and list hybrid. It behaves like a mapping type but also has list-like behavior in remembering the insertion order plus supporting methods such as popitem to remove the last or first entry.

Here is an example:

```
>>> cities = ['Jakarta','Delhi','Newyork','Bonn','Kolkata',
'Bangalore','Seoul']
>>> cities_dict = dict.fromkeys(cities)
>>> cities_dict
{'Kolkata': None, 'Newyork': None, 'Seoul': None, 'Jakarta': None,
'Delhi': None, 'Bonn': None, 'Bangalore': None}

# Ordered dictionary
>>> cities_odict = OrderedDict.fromkeys(cities)
>>> cities_odict
OrderedDict([('Jakarta', None), ('Delhi', None), ('Newyork', None),
('Bonn', None), ('Kolkata', None), ('Bangalore', None), ('Seoul',
None)])
>>> cities_odict.popitem()
('Seoul', None)
>>> cities_odict.popitem(last=False)
('Jakarta', None)
```

You can compare and contrast how the dictionary changes the order around and how the OrderedDict container keeps the original order.

This allows for a few recipes using the OrderedDict container.

Dropping duplicates from a container without losing the order

Let us modify the cities list to include duplicates:

```
>>> cities = ['Jakarta','Delhi','Newyork','Bonn','Kolkata',
              'Bangalore','Bonn','Seoul','Delhi','Jakarta','Mumbai']
>>> cities_odict = OrderedDict.fromkeys(cities)
>>> print(cities_odict.keys())
odict_keys(['Jakarta', 'Delhi', 'Newyork', 'Bonn', 'Kolkata',
            'Bangalore', 'Seoul', 'Mumbai'])
```

See how the duplicates are dropped but the order is preserved.

Implementing a Least Recently Used (LRU) cache dictionary

An LRU cache gives preference to entries that are recently used (accessed) and drops those entries that are least used. This is a common caching algorithm used in HTTP caching servers such as Squid and in places where one needs to keep a limited size container that keeps recently accessed items preferentially over others.

Here we make use of the behavior of `OrderedDict`: when an existing key is removed and re-added, it is added at the end (the right side):

```
class LRU(OrderedDict):
    """ Least recently used cache dictionary """

    def __init__(self, size=10):
        self.size = size

    def set(self, key):
        # If key is there delete and reinsert so
        # it moves to end.
        if key in self:
            del self[key]

        self[key] = 1
        if len(self)>self.size:
            # Pop from left
            self.popitem(last=False)
```

Here is a demonstration:

```
>>> d=LRU(size=5)
>>> d.set('bangalore')
>>> d.set('chennai')
>>> d.set('mumbai')
>>> d.set('bangalore')
>>> d.set('kolkata')
>>> d.set('delhi')
>>> d.set('chennai')

>>> len(d)
5
>>> d.set('kochi')
>>> d
LRU([('bangalore', 1), ('chennai', 1), ('kolkata', 1), ('delhi', 1),
('kochi', 1)])
```

Since a key mumbai was set first and never set again, it became the leftmost one and got dropped off.

Notice how the next candidate to drop off is bangalore, followed by chennai. This is because chennai was set once more after bangalore was set.

Counter

A counter is a subclass of a dictionary to keep a count of hashable objects. Elements are stored as dictionary keys and their counts get stored as the values. The Counter class is a parallel for multisets in languages such as C++ or Bag in languages such as Smalltalk.

A counter is a natural choice for keeping the frequency of items encountered when processing any container. For example, a counter can be used to keep the frequency of words when parsing text or the frequency of characters when parsing words.

For example, both of the following code snippets perform the same operation but the counter one is less verbose and compact.

They both return the most common 10 words from the text of the famous Sherlock Holmes Novel, *The Hound of Baskervilles* from its Gutenberg version online:

- Using the `defaultdict` container in the following code:

```
import requests, operator
    text=requests.get('https://www.gutenberg.org/
files/2852/2852-0.txt').text
    freq=defaultdict(int)
    for word in text.split():
        if len(word.strip())==0: continue
        freq[word.lower()] += 1
        print(sorted(freq.items(), key=operator.itemgetter(1),
reverse=True) [:10])
```

- Using the `Counter` class in the following code:

```
import requests
text = requests.get('https://www.gutenberg.org/files/2852/2852-0.
txt').text
freq = Counter(filter(None, map(lambda x:x.lower().strip(), text.
split())))
print(freq.most_common(10))
```

ChainMap

A `ChainMap` is a dictionary-like class that groups multiple dictionaries or similar mapping data structures together to create a single view that is updateable.

All of the usual dictionary methods are supported. Lookups search successive maps until a key is found.

The `ChainMap` class is a more recent addition to Python, having been added in Python 3.3.

When you have a scenario where you keep updating keys from a source dictionary to a target dictionary over and over again, a `ChainMap` class can work in your favor in terms of performance, especially if the number of updates is large.

Here are some practical uses of a `ChainMap`:

- A programmer can keep the GET and POST arguments of a web framework in separate dictionaries and keep the configuration updated via a single `ChainMap`.

- Keeping multilayered configuration overrides in applications.

- Iterating over multiple dictionaries as a view when there are no overlapping keys.

- A `ChainMap` class keeps the previous mappings in its maps attribute. However, when you update a dictionary with mappings from another dictionary, the original dictionary state is lost. Here is a simple demonstration:

```
>>> d1={i:i for i in range(100)}
>>> d2={i:i*i for i in range(100) if i%2}
>>> c=ChainMap(d1,d2)
# Older value accessible via chainmap
>>> c[5]
5
>>> c.maps[0][5]
5
# Update d1
>>> d1.update(d2)
# Older values also got updated
>>> c[5]
25
>>> c.maps[0][5]
25
```

namedtuple

A `namedtuple` is like a class with fixed fields. Fields are accessible via attribute lookups like a normal class but are also indexable. The entire namedtuple is also iterable like a container. In other words, a namedtuple behaves like a class and a tuple combined in one:

```
>>> Employee = namedtuple('Employee', 'name, age, gender, title, department')
>>> Employee
<class '__main__.Employee'>
```

Let's create an instance of Employee:

```
>>> jack = Employee('Jack',25,'M','Programmer','Engineering')
>>> print(jack)
Employee(name='Jack', age=25, gender='M', title='Programmer',
department='Engineering')
```

We can iterate over the fields of the instance, as if it is an iterator:

```
>>> for field in jack:
... print(field)
...
Jack
25
M
Programmer
Engineering
```

Once created, the `namedtuple` instance, like a tuple, is read-only:

```
>>> jack.age=32
Traceback (most recent call last):
  File "<stdin>", line 1, in <module>
AttributeError: can't set attribute
```

To update values, the `_replace` method can be used. It returns a new instance with the specified keyword arguments replaced with new values:

```
>>> jack._replace(age=32)
Employee(name='Jack', age=32, gender='M', title='Programmer',
department='Engineering')
```

A namedtuple is much more memory-efficient when compared to a class which has the same fields. Hence a namedtuple is very useful in the following scenarios:

- A large amount of data needs to be loaded as read-only with keys and values from a store. Examples are loading columns and values via a DB query or loading data from a large CSV file.

- When a lot of instances of a class need to be created but not many write or set operations need to be done on the attributes. Instead of creating class instances, `namedtuple` instances can be created to save on memory.

- The `_make` method can be used to load an existing iterable that supplies fields in the same order to return a `namedtuple` instance. For example, if there is an `employees.csv` file with the columns name, age, gender, title, and department in that order, we can load them all into a container of `namedtuples` using the following command line:

```
employees = map(Employee._make, csv.reader(open('employees.csv')))
```

Probabilistic data structures – bloom filters

Before we conclude our discussion on the container data types in Python, let us take a look at an important probabilistic data structure named **Bloom Filter**. Bloom filter implementations in Python behave like containers, but they are probabilistic in nature.

A bloom filter is a sparse data structure that allows us to test for the presence of an element in the set. However, we can only positively be sure of whether an element is not there in the set—that is, we can assert only for true negatives. When a bloom filter tells us an element is there in the set, it might be there—in other words, there is a non-zero probability that the element may actually be missing.

Bloom filters are usually implemented as bit vectors. They work in a similar way to a Python dictionary in that they use hash functions. However, unlike dictionaries, bloom filters don't store the actual elements themselves. Also elements, once added, cannot be removed from a bloom filter.

Bloom filters are used when the amount of source data implies an unconventionally large amount of memory if we store all of it without hash collisions.

In Python, the `pybloom` package provides a simple bloom filter implementation (however, at the time of writing, it doesn't support Python 3.x, so the examples here are shown in Python 2.7.x):

```
$ pip install pybloom
```

Let us write a program to read and index words from the text of The Hound of Baskervilles, which was the example we used in the discussion of the Counter data structure, but this time using a bloom filter:

```
# bloom_example.py
from pybloom import BloomFilter
import requests

f=BloomFilter(capacity=100000, error_rate=0.01)
```

```
text=requests.get('https://www.gutenberg.org/files/2852/2852-0.txt').
text

for word in text.split():
    word = word.lower().strip()
    f.add(word)

print len(f)
print len(text.split())
for w in ('holmes','watson','hound','moor','queen'):
    print 'Found',w,w in f
```

Executing this, we get the following output:

```
$ python bloomtest.py
9403
62154
Found holmes True
Found watson True
Found moor True
Found queen False
```

> The words holmes, watson, hound, and moor are some of the most
> common in the story of *The Hound of Baskervilles*, so it is reassuring
> that the bloom filter finds these words. On the other hand, the word
> queen never appears in the text so the bloom filter is correct on that
> fact (true negative). The number of the words in the text is 62,154, out
> of which only 9,403 got indexed in the filter.

Let us try and measure the memory usage of the bloom filter as opposed to the
Counter. For that we will rely on memory profiler.

For this test, we will rewrite the code using the Counter class as follows:

```
# counter_hound.py
import requests
from collections import Counter

@profile
def hound():
    text=requests.get('https://www.gutenberg.org/files/2852/2852-0.
txt').text
    c = Counter()
```

```
        words = [word.lower().strip() for word in text.split()]
        c.update(words)

    if __name__ == "__main__":
        hound()
```

And the one using the bloom filter as follows:

```
# bloom_hound.py
from pybloom import BloomFilter
import requests

@profile
def hound():
    f=BloomFilter(capacity=100000, error_rate=0.01)
    text=requests.get('https://www.gutenberg.org/files/2852/2852-0.
txt').text

    for word in text.split():
        word = word.lower().strip()
        f.add(word)

    if __name__ == "__main__":
        hound()
```

Here is the output from running the memory profiler for the first one:

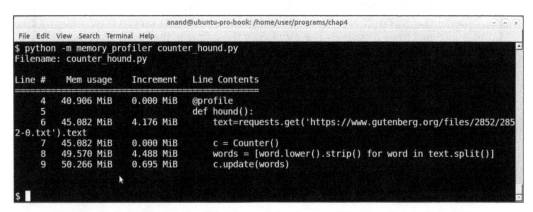

Memory usage by the Counter object when parsing the text of The Hound of the Baskervilles

The following result is for the second one:

```
                         anand@ubuntu-pro-book: /home/user/programs/chap4        ⌄ ⌃ ✕
 File  Edit  View  Search  Terminal  Help
$ python -m memory_profiler bloom_hound.py
Filename: bloom_hound.py

Line #    Mem usage    Increment   Line Contents
================================================
     4    40.996 MiB    0.000 MiB   @profile
     5                              def hound():
     6    41.160 MiB    0.164 MiB       f=BloomFilter(capacity=100000, error_rate=0.01)
     7    45.621 MiB    4.461 MiB       text=requests.get('https://www.gutenberg.org/files/2852/285
2-0.txt').text
     8
     9    49.742 MiB    4.121 MiB       for word in text.split():
    10    49.742 MiB    0.000 MiB           word = word.lower().strip()
    11    49.742 MiB    0.000 MiB           f.add(word)
```

Memory usage by the Bloom filter for parsing text of The Hound of the Baskervilles

The final memory usage is roughly the same at about 50 MB each. In the case of the Counter, nearly no memory is used when the Counter class is created but close to 0.7 MB is used when words are added to the counter.

However, there is a distinct difference in the memory growth pattern between both these data structures.

In the case of the bloom filter, an initial memory of 0.16 MB is allotted to it upon creation. The addition of the words seems to add nearly no memory to the filter and hence to the program.

So when should we use a bloom filter as opposed to, say, a dictionary or set in Python? Here are some general principles and real-world usage scenarios:

- When you are fine with not storing the actual element itself but only interested in the presence (or absence) of the element. In other words, where your application use case relies more on checking the absence of data than its presence.

- When the size of your input data is so large that storing each and every item in a deterministic data structure (as a dictionary or hashtable) in memory is not feasible. A bloom filter takes much less data in memory as opposed to a deterministic data structure.

- When you are fine with a certain well-defined error rate of *false positives* with your dataset—let us say this is 5% out of 1,000,000 pieces of data—you can configure a bloom filter for this specific error rate and get a data hit rate that will satisfy your requirements.

Some real-world examples of using bloom filters are as follows:

- **Security testing**: Storing data for malicious URLs in browsers, for example
- **Bio-informatics**: Testing the presence of a certain pattern (a k-mer) in a genome
- To avoid storing URLs with just one hit in a distributed web-caching infrastructure

Summary

This chapter was all about performance. At the start of the chapter, we discussed performance and SPE. We looked at the two categories of performance testing and diagnostic tools—namely, stress-testing tools and profiling/instrumentation tools.

We then discussed what performance complexity really means in terms of the Big-O notation and discussed briefly the common time orders of functions. We looked at the time taken by functions to execute and learned the three classes of time usage—namely real, user, and sys in POSIX systems.

We moved on to measuring performance and time in the next section—starting with a simple context manager timer and moving on to more accurate measurements using the timeit module. We measured the time taken for certain algorithms for a range of input sizes. By plotting the time taken against the input size and superimposing it on the standard time complexity graphs, we were able to get a visual understanding of the performance complexity of functions. We optimized the common item problem from its O(n*log(n)) performance to O(n) and the plotted graphs of time usage confirmed this.

We then started our discussion on profiling code and saw some examples of profiling using the cProfile module. The example we chose was a prime number iterator returning the first n primes performing at O(n). Using the profiled data, we optimized the code a bit, making it perform better than O(n). We briefly discussed the pstats module and used its Stats class to read profile data and produce custom reports ordered by a number of available data fields. We discussed two other third-party profilers—the liner_profiler and the memory_profiler, which profile code line by line—and discussed the problem of finding sub-sequences among two sequences of strings, writing an optimized version of them, and measuring its time and memory usage using these profilers.

Among other tools, we discussed objgraph and pympler—the former as a visualization tool to find relations and references between objects, helping to explore memory leaks, and the latter as a tool to monitor and report the memory usage of objects in the code and provide summaries.

In the last section on Python containers, we looked at the best and worst use case scenarios of standard Python containers—such as list, dict, set, and tuple. We then studied high performance container classes in the collections module—`deque`, `defaultdict`, `OrderedDict`, `Counter`, `Chainmap`, and `namedtuple`, with examples and recipes for each. Specifically, we saw how to create an LRU cache very naturally using `OrderedDict`.

Towards the end of the chapter, we discussed a special data structure called the bloom filter, which is very useful as a probabilistic data structure to report true negatives with certainty and true positives within a pre-defined error rate.

In the next chapter, we will discuss a close cousin of performance, scalability, where we will look at the techniques of writing scalable applications and the details of writing scalable and concurrent programs in Python.

5
Writing Applications that Scale

Imagine the checkout counter of a supermarket on a Saturday evening, the usual rush-hour time. It is common to see long queues of people waiting to check out with their purchases. What could a store manager do to reduce the rush and waiting time?

A typical manager would try a few approaches, including telling those manning the checkout counters to pick up their speed, and to try and redistribute people to different queues so that each queue roughly has the same waiting time. In other words, they would manage the current load with available resources by *optimizing the performance* of the existing resources.

However, if the store has existing counters that are not in operation—and enough people at hand to manage them—the manager could enable those counters, and move people to these new counters. In other words, they would add resources to the store to *scale* the operation.

Software systems, too, scale in a similar way. An existing software application can be scaled by adding compute resources to it.

When the system scales by either adding or making better use of resources inside a compute node, such as CPU or RAM, it is said to *scale vertically* or *scale up*. On the other hand, when a system scales by adding more compute nodes to it, such as a creating a load-balanced cluster of servers, it is said to *scale horizontally* or *scale out*.

The degree to which a software system is able to scale when compute resources are added is called its *scalability*. Scalability is measured in terms of how much the system's performance characteristics, such as throughput or latency, improve with respect to the addition of resources. For example, if a system doubles its capacity by doubling the number of servers, it is scaling linearly.

Increasing the concurrency of a system often increases its scalability. In the supermarket example given earlier, the manager is able to scale out his operations by opening additional counters. In other words, they increase the amount of concurrent processing done in their store. Concurrency is the amount of work that gets done simultaneously in a system.

In this chapter, we look at the different techniques of scaling a software application with Python.

We will be following the approximate sketch of the following topics in our discussion in this chapter:

- Scalability and performance
- Concurrency
    - Concurrency and parallelism
    - Concurrency in Python – multithreading
        - Thumbnail generator
        - Thumbnail generator – producer/consumer architecture
        - Thumbnail generator – program end condition
        - Thumbnail generator – resource constraint using locks
        - Thumbnail generator – resource constraint using semaphores
        - Resource constraint – semaphore versus lock
        - Thumbnail generator – URL rate controller using conditions
        - Multi-threading – Python and GIL
    - Concurrency in Python – multiprocessing:
        - A primality checker
        - Sorting disk files
        - Sorting disk files – using a counter
        - Sorting disk files – using multiprocessing
    - Multi-threading versus multiprocessing
    - Concurrency in Python – Asynchronous execution
        - Pre-emptive versus co-operative multitasking
        - asyncio in Python

- ◦ Waiting for future – `async` and `await`
- ◦ Concurrent futures – high-level concurrent processing
- ◦ Concurrency options - how to choose

- Parallel processing libraries:
    - ◦ joblib
    - ◦ PyMP
        - ◦ Fractals – the Mandelbrot set
        - ◦ Fractals – scaling the Mandelbrot set implementation

- Scaling for the web:
    - ◦ Scaling workflows – message queues and task queues
    - ◦ Celery – a distributed task queue

        The Mandelbrot set - Using Celery

    - ◦ Serving Python on the web – WSGI

        uWSGI – WSGI middleware on steroids

        Gunicorn – unicorn for WSGI

        Gunicorn versus uWSGI

- Scalability architectures:
    - ◦ Vertical scalability architectures
    - ◦ Horizontal scalability architectures

Scalability and performance

How do we measure the scalability of a system? Let's take an example, and see how this is done.

Let's say our application is a simple report generation system for employees. It is able to load employee data from a database, and generate a variety of reports in bulk, such as pay slips, tax deduction reports, employee leave reports, and more.

The system is able to generate 120 reports per minute — this is the *throughput* or *capacity* of the system expressed as the number of successfully completed operations in a given unit of time. Let's say the time it takes to generate a report at the server side (latency) is roughly 2 seconds.

Let's say the architect decides to scale up the system by doubling the RAM on its server.

Once this is done, a test shows that the system is able to increase its throughput to 180 reports per minute. The latency remains the same at 2 seconds.

So, at this point, the system has scaled *close to linear* in terms of the memory added. The scalability of the system expressed in terms of throughput increase is as follows:

Scalability (throughput) = *180/120 = 1.5X*

As a second step, the architect decides to double the number of servers on the backend — all with the same memory. After this step, it's found that the system's performance throughput has now increased to 350 reports per minute. The scalability achieved by this step is given as follows:

Scalability (throughput) = *350/180 = 1.9X*

The system has now responded much better with a close to linear increase in scalability.

After further analysis, the architect finds that by rewriting the code that was processing reports on the server to run in multiple processes instead of a single process, he is able to reduce the processing time at the server, and hence, the latency of each request by roughly 1 second per request at peak time. The latency has now gone down from 2 seconds to 1 second.

The system's performance with respect to latency has become better as follows:

Performance (latency): *X = 2/1 = 2X*

How does this improve scalability? Since the time taken to process each request is less now, the system overall will be able to respond to similar loads at a faster rate than what it was able to earlier. With the exact same resources, the system's throughput performance, and hence, scalability has increased assuming other factors remain the same.

Let's summarize what we've discussed so far, as follows:

1. In the first step, the architect increased the throughput of a single system by scaling it up by adding extra memory as a resource, which increased the overall scalability of the system. In other words, he scaled the performance of a single system by *scaling up*, which boosted the overall performance of the whole system.

2. In the second step, he added more nodes to the system, and hence, its ability to perform work concurrently, and found that the system responded well by rewarding him with a near-linear scalability factor. In other words, he increased the throughput of the system by scaling its resource capacity. Thus, he increased scalability of the system by *scaling out*, that is, by adding more compute nodes.

3. In the third step, he made a critical fix by running a computation in more than one process. In other words, he increased the *concurrency* of a single system by dividing the computation into more than one part. He found that this increased the performance characteristic of the application by reducing its *latency*, potentially setting up the application to handle workloads better at high stress.

We find that there is a relationship between scalability, performance, concurrency, and latency. This can be explained as follows:

1. When the performance of one of the components in a system goes up, generally the performance of the overall system goes up.

2. When an application scales in a single machine by increasing its concurrency, it has the potential to improve performance, and hence, the net scalability of the system in deployment.

3. When a system reduces its performance time, or its latency, at the server, it positively contributes to scalability.

We have captured these relationships in the following table:

Concurrency	Latency	Performance	Scalability
High	Low	High	High
High	High	Variable	Variable
Low	High	Poor	Poor

An ideal system is one that has good concurrency and low latency; such a system has high performance, and would respond better to scaling up and/or scaling out.

A system with high concurrency, but also high latency, would have variable characteristics — its performance, and hence, scalability would be potentially very sensitive to other factors such as current system load, network congestion, geographical distribution of compute resources and requests, and so on.

A system with low concurrency and high latency is the worst case—it would be difficult to scale such a system, as it has poor performance characteristics. The latency and concurrency issues should be addressed before the architect decides to scale the system horizontally or vertically.

Scalability is always described in terms of variation in performance throughput.

Concurrency

A system's concurrency is the degree to which the system is able to perform work simultaneously instead of sequentially. An application written to be concurrent in general, can execute more units of work in a given time than one which is written to be sequential or serial.

When we make a serial application concurrent, we make the application better utilize the existing compute resources in the system—CPU and/or RAM—at a given time. Concurrency, in other words, is the cheapest way of making an application scale inside a machine in terms of the cost of compute resources.

Concurrency can be achieved using different techniques. The common ones include the following:

- **Multithreading**: The simplest form of concurrency is to rewrite the application to perform parallel tasks in different threads. A thread is the simplest sequence of programming instructions that can be performed by a CPU. A program can consist of any number of threads. By distributing tasks to multiple threads, a program can execute more work simultaneously. All threads run inside the same process.

- **Multiprocessing**: Another way to concurrently scale up a program is to run it in multiple processes instead of a single process. Multiprocessing involves more overhead than multithreading in terms of message passing and shared memory. However, programs that perform a lot of CPU-intensive computations can benefit more from multiple processes than multiple threads.

- **Asynchronous Processing**: In this technique, operations are performed asynchronously with no specific ordering of tasks with respect to time. Asynchronous processing usually picks tasks from a queue of tasks, and schedules them to execute at a future time, often receiving the results in callback functions or special future objects. Asynchronous processing usually happens in a single thread.

There are other forms of concurrent computing, but in this chapter, we will focus our attention on only these three.

Python, especially Python 3, has built-in support for all these types of concurrent computing techniques in its standard library. For example, it supports multi-threading via its `threading` module, and multiple processes via its `multiprocessing` module. Asynchronous execution support is available via the *asyncio* module. A form of concurrent processing that combines asynchronous execution with threads and processes is available via the `concurrent.futures` module.

In the coming sections we will take a look at each of these in turn with sufficient examples.

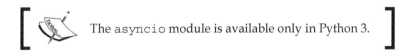 The `asyncio` module is available only in Python 3.

Concurrency versus parallelism

We will take a brief look at the concept of concurrency and its close cousin, namely parallelism.

Both concurrency and parallelism are about executing work simultaneously rather than sequentially. However, in concurrency, the two tasks need not be executed at the exact same time; instead, they just need to be scheduled to be executed simultaneously. Parallelism, on the other hand, requires that both the tasks execute together at a given moment in time.

To take a real-life example, let's say you are painting two exterior walls of your house. You have employed just one painter, and you find that he is taking a lot more time than you thought. You can solve the problem in these two ways:

1. Instruct the painter to paint a few coats on one wall before switching to the next wall, and doing the same there. Assuming he is efficient, he will work on both the walls simultaneously (though not at the same time), and achieve the same degree of finish on both walls for a given time. This is a *concurrent* solution.
2. Employ one more painter. Instruct the first painter to paint the first wall, and the second painter to paint the second wall. This is a *parallel* solution.

Two threads performing bytecode computations in a single core CPU do not exactly perform parallel computation, as the CPU can accommodate only one thread at a time. However, they are concurrent from a programmer's perspective, since the CPU scheduler performs fast switching in and out of the threads so that they appear to run in parallel.

However, on a multi-core CPU, two threads can perform parallel computations at any given time in its different cores. This is true parallelism.

Parallel computation requires that the computation resources increase at least linearly with respect to its scale. Concurrent computation can be achieved by using the techniques of multitasking, where work is scheduled and executed in batches, making better use of existing resources.

> In this chapter, we will use the term *concurrent* uniformly to indicate both types of execution. In some places, it may indicate concurrent processing in the traditional way, and in some others, it may indicate true parallel processing. Use the context to disambiguate.

Concurrency in Python – multithreading

We will start our discussion of concurrent techniques in Python with multithreading.

Python supports multiple threads in programming via its *threading* module. The threading module exposes a `Thread` class, which encapsulates a thread of execution. Along with this, it also exposes the following synchronization primitives:

- A `Lock` object, which is useful for synchronized protected access to share resources, and its cousin `RLock`
- A `Condition` object, which is useful for threads to synchronize while waiting for arbitrary conditions
- An `Event` object, which provides a basic signaling mechanism between threads
- A `Semaphore` object, which allows synchronized access to limited resources
- A `Barrier` object, which allows a fixed set of threads to wait for each other, synchronize to a particular state, and proceed

Thread objects in Python can be combined with the synchronized `Queue` class in the queue module for implementing thread-safe producer/consumer workflows.

Thumbnail generator

Let's start our discussion of multi-threading in Python with the example of a program used to generate thumbnails of image URLs.

In the example, we are using **Pillow**, a fork of the **Python Imaging Library (PIL)** to perform this operation:

```
# thumbnail_converter.py
from PIL import Image
import urllib.request

def thumbnail_image(url, size=(64, 64), format='.png'):
    """ Save thumbnail of an image URL """

    im = Image.open(urllib.request.urlopen(url))
    # filename is last part of the URL minus extension + '.format'
    pieces = url.split('/')
    filename = ''.join((pieces[-2],'_',pieces[-1].split('.')[0],'_
thumb',format))
    im.thumbnail(size, Image.ANTIALIAS)
    im.save(filename)
    print('Saved',filename)
```

The preceding code works very well for single URLs.

Let's say we want to convert five image URLs to their thumbnails:

```
img_urls = ['https://dummyimage.com/256x256/000/fff.jpg',
            'https://dummyimage.com/320x240/fff/00.jpg',
            'https://dummyimage.com/640x480/ccc/aaa.jpg',
            'https://dummyimage.com/128x128/ddd/eee.jpg',
            'https://dummyimage.com/720x720/111/222.jpg']
for url in img_urls:
    thumbnail_image(urls)
```

Let's see how such a function performs with respect to time taken in the following screenshot:

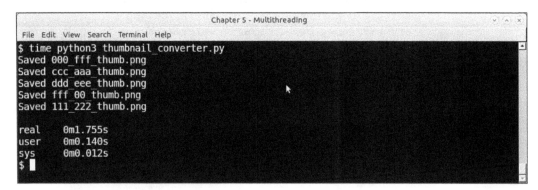

Response time of serial thumbnail converter for 5 URLs

The function took approximately 1.7 seconds per URL.

Let's now scale the program to multiple threads so we can perform the conversions concurrently. Here is the rewritten code to run each conversion in its own thread:

```
import threading

for url in img_urls:
    t=threading.Thread(target=thumbnail_image,args=(url,))
    t.start()
```

The timing that this last program now gives is shown in this screenshot:

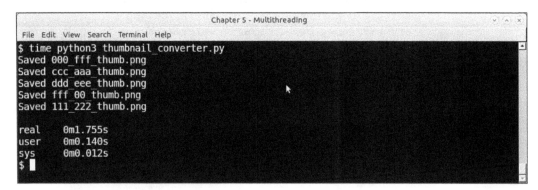

Response time of threaded thumbnail converter for 5 URLs

With this change, the program returns in 1.76 seconds, almost equal to the time taken by a single URL in serial execution before. In other words, the program has now linearly scaled with respect to the number of threads. Note that, we had to make no change to the function itself to get this scalability boost.

Thumbnail generator – producer/consumer architecture

In the previous example, we saw a set of image URLs being processed by a thumbnail generator function concurrently by using multiple threads. With the use of multiple threads, we were able to achieve near linear scalability as compared to serial execution.

However, in real life, rather than processing a fixed list of URLs, it is more common for the URL data to be produced by some kind of URL producer. It could be fetching this data from a database, a **comma separated value** (**CSV**) file or from a TCP socket for example.

In such a scenario, creating one thread per URL would be a tremendous waste of resources. It takes a certain overhead to create a thread in the system. We need some way to reuse the threads we create.

For such systems that involve a certain set of threads producing data and another set of threads consuming or processing data, the producer/consumer model is an ideal fit. Such a system has the following features:

1. Producers are a specialized class of workers (threads) producing the data. They may receive the data from a specific source(s), or generate the data themselves.

2. Producers add the data to a shared synchronized queue. In Python, this queue is provided by the `Queue` class in the aptly named `queue` module.

3. Another set of specialized class of workers, namely consumers, wait on the queue to get (consume) the data. Once they get the data, they process it and produce the results.

4. The program comes to an end when the producers stop generating data and the consumers are starved of data. Techniques like timeouts, polling, or poison pills can be used to achieve this. When this happens, all threads exit, and the program completes.

We have rewritten our thumbnail generator to a producer consumer architecture. The resulting code is given next. Since this is a bit detailed, we will discuss each class one by one.

First, let's look at the imports—these are pretty self-explanatory:

```
# thumbnail_pc.py
import threading
import time
import string
import random
import urllib.request
from PIL import Image
from queue import Queue
```

Next is the code for the producer class:

```
class ThumbnailURL_Generator(threading.Thread):
    """ Worker class that generates image URLs """

    def __init__(self, queue, sleep_time=1,):
        self.sleep_time = sleep_time
        self.queue = queue
        # A flag for stopping
        self.flag = True
        # choice of sizes
        self._sizes = (240,320,360,480,600,720)
        # URL scheme
        self.url_template = 'https://dummyimage.com/%s/%s/%s.jpg'
        threading.Thread.__init__(self, name='producer')

    def __str__(self):
        return 'Producer'

    def get_size(self):
        return '%dx%d' % (random.choice(self._sizes),
                          random.choice(self._sizes))

    def get_color(self):
        return ''.join(random.sample(string.hexdigits[:-6], 3))

    def run(self):
        """ Main thread function """

        while self.flag:
            # generate image URLs of random sizes and fg/bg colors
            url = self.url_template % (self.get_size(),
                                       self.get_color(),
                                       self.get_color())
```

```
# Add to queue
print(self,'Put',url)
self.queue.put(url)
time.sleep(self.sleep_time)


    def stop(self):
        """ Stop the thread """

        self.flag = False
```

Let's analyze the producer class code:

1. The class is named `ThumbnailURL_Generator`. It generates the URLs (by using the service of a website named `http://dummyimage.com`) of different sizes, foreground, and background colors. It inherits from the `threading.Thread` class.

2. It has a `run` method, which goes in a loop, generates a random image URL, and pushes it to the shared queue. Every time, the thread sleeps for a fixed time, as configured by the `sleep_time` parameter.

3. The class exposes a `stop` method, which sets the internal flag to `False` causing the loop to break and the thread to finish its processing. This can be called externally by another thread, typically, the main thread.

Now we have the URL consumer class that consumes the thumbnail URLs and creates the thumbnails:

```
class ThumbnailURL_Consumer(threading.Thread):
    """ Worker class that consumes URLs and generates thumbnails """

    def __init__(self, queue):
        self.queue = queue
        self.flag = True
        threading.Thread.__init__(self, name='consumer')

    def __str__(self):
        return 'Consumer'

    def thumbnail_image(self, url, size=(64,64), format='.png'):
        """ Save image thumbnails, given a URL """

        im=Image.open(urllib.request.urlopen(url))
```

```
        # filename is last part of URL minus extension + '.format'
        filename = url.split('/')[-1].split('.')[0] + '_thumb' +
format
        im.thumbnail(size, Image.ANTIALIAS)
        im.save(filename)
        print(self,'Saved',filename)

    def run(self):
        """ Main thread function """

        while self.flag:
            url = self.queue.get()
            print(self,'Got',url)
            self.thumbnail_image(url)

    def stop(self):
        """ Stop the thread """

        self.flag = False
```

Here's the analysis of the consumer class:

1. The class is named `ThumbnailURL_Consumer`, as it consumes URLs from the queue, and creates thumbnail images of them.

2. The `run` method of this class goes in a loop, gets a URL from the queue, and converts it to a thumbnail by passing it to the `thumbnail_image` method. (Note that this code is exactly the same as that of the `thumbnail_image` function we created earlier.)

3. The `stop` method is very similar, checking for a stop flag every time in the loop, and ending once the flag has been unset.

Here is the main part of the code—setting up a couple of producers and consumers each, and running them:

```
q = Queue(maxsize=200)
producers, consumers = [], []

for i in range(2):
    t = ThumbnailURL_Generator(q)
    producers.append(t)
    t.start()

for i in range(2):
    t = ThumbnailURL_Consumer(q)
    consumers.append(t)
    t.start()
```

Here is a screenshot of the program in action:

```
Chapter 5 - Multithreading                              ⌄ ⌃ ×
File  Edit  View  Search  Terminal  Help
Producer Put https://dummyimage.com/240x600/4c8/1d0.jpg
Producer Put https://dummyimage.com/240x240/18d/c05.jpg
Consumer Got https://dummyimage.com/240x600/4c8/1d0.jpg
Consumer Got https://dummyimage.com/240x240/18d/c05.jpg
Producer Put https://dummyimage.com/320x600/e41/58d.jpg
Producer Put https://dummyimage.com/360x720/9c0/b39.jpg
Consumer Saved 1d0_thumb.png
Consumer Got https://dummyimage.com/320x600/e41/58d.jpg
Consumer Saved c05_thumb.png
Consumer Got https://dummyimage.com/360x720/9c0/b39.jpg
Producer Put https://dummyimage.com/600x480/b9d/8e5.jpg
Producer Put https://dummyimage.com/360x600/62a/fc9.jpg
Producer Put https://dummyimage.com/320x240/eb7/c9b.jpg
Producer Put https://dummyimage.com/360x320/a90/340.jpg
Consumer Saved b39_thumb.png
Consumer Got https://dummyimage.com/600x480/b9d/8e5.jpg
Consumer Saved 58d_thumb.png
Consumer Got https://dummyimage.com/360x600/62a/fc9.jpg
Producer Put https://dummyimage.com/240x320/4f7/036.jpg
Producer Put https://dummyimage.com/480x720/8d9/d03.jpg
```

Running the thumbnail producer/consumer program with 4 threads, 2 of each type

In the above program, since the producers keep generating random data without any end, the consumers will keep consuming it without any end. Our program has no proper end condition.

Hence, this program will keep running until the network requests are denied or timed out or the disk space of the machine runs out because of thumbnails.

However, a program solving a real world problem should end in some way that is predictable.

This could be due to a number of external constraints

- It could be a timeout introduced where the consumers wait for data for a certain maximum time, and then exit if no data is available during that time. This, for example, can be configured as a timeout in the get method of the queue.

- Another technique would be to signal program end after a certain number of resources are consumed or created. In this program, for example, it could be a fixed limit to the number of thumbnails created.

In the following section, we will see how to enforce such resource limits by using threading synchronization primitives such as Locks and Semaphores.

You may have observed that we start a thread using its `start` method, though the overridden method in the Thread subclass is `run`. This is because, in the parent `Thread` class, the `start` method sets up some state, and then calls the `run` method internally. This is the right way to call the thread's run method. It should never be called directly.

Thumbnail generator – resource constraint using locks

In this section, we will see how to modify the program using a `Lock`, a synchronization primitive to implement a counter that will limit the number of images created as a way to end the program.

Lock objects in Python allows exclusive access by threads to a shared resource.

The pseudo-code would be as follows:

```
try:
  lock.acquire()
  # Do some modification on a shared, mutable resource
  mutable_object.modify()
finally:
  lock.release()
```

However, Lock objects support context-managers via the with statement, so this is more commonly written as follows:

```
with lock:
  mutable_object.modify()
```

To implement a fixed number of images per run, our code needs to be supported to add a counter. However, since multiple threads would check and increment this counter, it needs to be synchronized via a `Lock` object.

This is our first implementation of the resource counter class using Locks.

```
class ThumbnailImageSaver(object):
    """ Class which saves URLs to thumbnail images and keeps a counter
    """

    def __init__(self, limit=10):
        self.limit = limit
        self.lock = threading.Lock()
        self.counter = {}

    def thumbnail_image(self, url, size=(64,64), format='.png'):
        """ Save image thumbnails, given a URL """

        im=Image.open(urllib.request.urlopen(url))
        # filename is last two parts of URL minus extension +
'.format'
        pieces = url.split('/')
        filename = ''.join((pieces[-2],'_',pieces[-1].split('.')[0],'_
thumb',format))
        im.thumbnail(size, Image.ANTIALIAS)
        im.save(filename)
        print('Saved',filename)
        self.counter[filename] = 1
        return True

    def save(self, url):
        """ Save a URL as thumbnail """

        with self.lock:
            if len(self.counter)>=self.limit:
                return False
            self.thumbnail_image(url)
            print('Count=>',len(self.counter))
            return True
```

Since this modifies the consumer class as well, it makes sense to discuss both changes together. Here is the modified consumer class to accommodate the extra counter needed to keep track of the images:

```
class ThumbnailURL_Consumer(threading.Thread):
    """ Worker class that consumes URLs and generates thumbnails """

    def __init__(self, queue, saver):
        self.queue = queue
```

```python
        self.flag = True
        self.saver = saver
        # Internal id
        self._id = uuid.uuid4().hex
        threading.Thread.__init__(self, name='Consumer-'+ self._id)

    def __str__(self):
        return 'Consumer-' + self._id

    def run(self):
        """ Main thread function """

        while self.flag:
            url = self.queue.get()
            print(self,'Got',url)
            if not self.saver.save(url):
                # Limit reached, break out
                print(self, 'Set limit reached, quitting')
                break

    def stop(self):
        """ Stop the thread """

        self.flag = False
```

Let's analyze both of these classes. First, we'll look at the new class,
ThumbnailImageSaver:

1. This class derives from the object. In other words, it is not a Thread. It is not
   meant to be one.

2. It initializes a lock object and a counter dictionary in its initializer method.
   The lock is for synchronizing access to the counter by threads. It also accepts
   a limit parameter equal to the number of images it should save.

3. The thumbnail_image method moves to here from the consumer class. It is
   called from a save method, which encloses the call in a synchronized context
   using the lock.

4. The save method first checks if the count has crossed the configured limit;
   when this happens, the method returns False. Otherwise, the image is saved
   with a call to thumbnail_image, and the image filename is added to the
   counter, effectively incrementing the count.

Next, we'll consider the modified `ThumbnailURL_Consumer` class:

1. The class's initializer is modified to accept an instance of the `ThumbnailImageSaver` as a `saver` argument. The rest of the arguments remain the same.

2. The `thumbnail_image` method no longer exists in this class, as it is moved to the new class.

3. The `run` method is much simplified. It makes a call to the `save` method of the saver instance. If it returns `False`, it means the limit has been reached, the loop breaks, and the consumer thread exits.

4. We have also modified the `__str__` method to return a unique ID per thread, which is set in the initializer using the `uuid` module. This helps to debug threads in a real-life example.

The calling code also changes a bit, as it needs to set up the new object, and configure the consumer threads with it:

```
q = Queue(maxsize=2000)
# Create an instance of the saver object
saver = ThumbnailImageSaver(limit=100)

    producers, consumers = [], []
    for i in range(3):
        t = ThumbnailURL_Generator(q)
        producers.append(t)
        t.start()

    for i in range(5):
        t = ThumbnailURL_Consumer(q, saver)
        consumers.append(t)
        t.start()

    for t in consumers:
        t.join()
        print('Joined', t, flush=True)

    # To make sure producers don't block on a full queue
    while not q.empty():
        item=q.get()

    for t in producers:
        t.stop()
        print('Stopped',t, flush=True)

    print('Total number of PNG images',len(glob.glob('*.png')))
```

The following are the main points to be noted here:

1. We create an instance of the new `ThumbnailImageSaver` class, and pass it on to the consumer threads when creating them.

2. We wait on consumers first. Note that, the main thread doesn't call `stop`, but `join` on them. This is because the consumers exit automatically when the limit is reached, so the main thread should just wait for them to stop.

3. We stop the producers after the consumers exit—explicitly so—since they would otherwise keep working forever, since there is no condition for the producers to exit.

We use a dictionary instead of an integer as because of the nature of the data.

Since the images are randomly generated, there is a minor chance of one image URL being the same as another one created previously, causing the filenames to clash. Using a dictionary takes care of such possible duplicates.

The following screenshot shows a run of the program with a limit of 100 images. Note that we can only show the last few lines of the console log, since it produces a lot of output:

```
Chapter 5 - Multithreading                                        ⌄ ⌃ ✕
File  Edit  View  Search  Terminal  Help
Producer-27f794680560473f939b0bd1fae5166f Put https://dummyimage.com/480x720/372/35f.jpg
Producer-8e2aa45e1ec14693939ec5b87a45429b Put https://dummyimage.com/320x360/e2f/d71.jpg
Producer-0ac969637a5c4b95af4f9d30638b42da Put https://dummyimage.com/720x480/754/e14.jpg
Producer-27f794680560473f939b0bd1fae5166f Put https://dummyimage.com/720x720/815/d3b.jpg
Producer-8e2aa45e1ec14693939ec5b87a45429b Put https://dummyimage.com/320x360/4b5/f02.jpg
Saved da4_fde_thumb.png
Count=> 100
Consumer-2df279565d52400985500148e402da08 Got https://dummyimage.com/600x480/38a/316.jpg
Consumer-71399ff8d7504ef49ac104c6cdab6ec3 Set limit reached, quitting
Consumer-d597bdfebe58452bb84f526ead921b64 Set limit reached, quitting
Joined Consumer-71399ff8d7504ef49ac104c6cdab6ec3
Consumer-c845a8d36fe543fd9945345a7a1e67fb Set limit reached, quitting
Consumer-2df279565d52400985500148e402da08 Set limit reached, quitting
Joined Consumer-c845a8d36fe543fd9945345a7a1e67fb
Joined Consumer-d597bdfebe58452bb84f526ead921b64
Joined Consumer-2df279565d52400985500148e402da08
Stopped Producer-0ac969637a5c4b95af4f9d30638b42da
Stopped Producer-27f794680560473f939b0bd1fae5166f
Stopped Producer-8e2aa45e1ec14693939ec5b87a45429b
Total number of PNG images 100
$
```

Run of the thumbnail generator program with a limit of 100 images using a Lock

You can configure this program with any limit of the images, and it will always fetch exactly the same count—nothing more or less.

In the next section, we will familiarize ourselves with another synchronization primitive, namely *semaphore,* and learn how to implement a resource limiting class in a similar way using the semaphore.

Thumbnail generator – resource constraint using semaphores

Locks aren't the only way to implement synchronization constraints and write logic on top of them in order to limit resources used/generated by a system.

A semaphore, one of the oldest synchronization primitives in computer science, is ideally suited for such use cases.

A semaphore is initialized with a value greater than zero:

1. When a thread calls acquire on a semaphore that has a positive internal value, the value gets decremented by one, and the thread continues on its way.

2. When another thread calls release on the semaphore, the value is incremented by 1.

3. Any thread calling acquire once the value has reached zero is blocked on the semaphore until it is woken up by another thread calling release.

Due to this behavior, a semaphore is perfectly suited for implementing a fixed limit on shared resources.

In the following code example, we will implement another class for resource limiting our thumbnail generator program, this time using a semaphore:

```
class ThumbnailImageSemaSaver(object):
    """ Class which keeps an exact counter of saved images
    and restricts the total count using a semaphore """

    def __init__(self, limit = 10):
        self.limit = limit
        self.counter = threading.BoundedSemaphore(value=limit)
        self.count = 0

    def acquire(self):
        # Acquire counter, if limit is exhausted, it
        # returns False
        return self.counter.acquire(blocking=False)

    def release(self):
```

```
        # Release counter, incrementing count
        return self.counter.release()

    def thumbnail_image(self, url, size=(64,64), format='.png'):
        """ Save image thumbnails, given a URL """

        im=Image.open(urllib.request.urlopen(url))
        # filename is last two parts of URL minus extension +
'.format'
        pieces = url.split('/')
        filename = ''.join((pieces[-2],'_',pieces[-1].split('.')
[0],format))
        try:
            im.thumbnail(size, Image.ANTIALIAS)
            im.save(filename)
            print('Saved',filename)
            self.count += 1
        except Exception as e:
            print('Error saving URL',url,e)
            # Image can't be counted, increment semaphore
            self.release()

        return True

    def save(self, url):
        """ Save a URL as thumbnail """

        if self.acquire():
            self.thumbnail_image(url)
            return True
        else:
            print('Semaphore limit reached, returning False')
            return False
```

Since the new semaphore-based class keeps the exact same interface as the previous lock-based class—with a save method—there is no need to change any code on the consumer!

Only the calling code needs to be changed.

This line in the previous code initialized the ThumbnailImageSaver instance:

```
saver = ThumbnailImageSaver(limit=100)
```

The preceding line needs to be replaced with the following one:

```
saver = ThumbnailImageSemaSaver(limit=100)
```

The rest of the code remains exactly the same.

Let's quickly discuss the new class using the semaphore before seeing this code in action:

1. The `acquire` and `release` methods are simple wrappers over the same methods on the semaphore.

2. We initialize the semaphore with a value equal to the image limit in the initializer.

3. In the save method, we call the `acquire` method. If the semaphore's limit is reached, it will return `False`. Otherwise, the thread saves the image and returns `True`. In the former case, the calling thread quits.

 The internal count attribute of this class is only there for debugging. It doesn't add anything to the logic of limiting images.

This class behaves in a way similar way to the previous one, and limits resources exactly. The following is an example with a limit of 200 images:

```
                        Chapter 5 - Multithreading
 File  Edit  View  Search  Terminal  Help
Consumer-275279a36ff049c38c77b506c5fa4010 Got https://dummyimage.com/720x360/47e/76b.jpg
Semaphore limit reached, returning False
Consumer-275279a36ff049c38c77b506c5fa4010 Set limit reached, quitting
Producer-cac6092edbbf40fa89ebdb530f1afc40 Put https://dummyimage.com/480x720/172/1fe.jpg
Producer-cc88bd03b49b43348aa3d6128869aea4 Put https://dummyimage.com/320x320/2f1/75c.jpg
Producer-b6fa5b443b8045e792278b4c49c6037f Put https://dummyimage.com/720x360/eab/570.jpg
Saved f96_3d0.png
Consumer-8b3103b9076640b1a4387b6cdc81f7c7 Got https://dummyimage.com/360x320/5be/567.jpg
Semaphore limit reached, returning False
Consumer-8b3103b9076640b1a4387b6cdc81f7c7 Set limit reached, quitting
Joined Consumer-8b3103b9076640b1a4387b6cdc81f7c7
Joined Consumer-275279a36ff049c38c77b506c5fa4010
Joined Consumer-ef6c97e1618744c9af41cc31c70552da
Joined Consumer-92460417f9984080bea7417159a9112b
Producer-cac6092edbbf40fa89ebdb530f1afc40 Put https://dummyimage.com/240x320/4fb/bc5.jpg
Producer-b6fa5b443b8045e792278b4c49c6037f Put https://dummyimage.com/360x320/792/491.jpg
Stopped Producer-cc88bd03b49b43348aa3d6128869aea4
Stopped Producer-cac6092edbbf40fa89ebdb530f1afc40
Stopped Producer-b6fa5b443b8045e792278b4c49c6037f
Total number of PNG images 200
$
```

Run of the thumbnail generator program with a limit of 200 images using a Semaphore

Resource constraint – semaphore versus lock

We saw two competing versions of implementing a fixed resource constraint in the previous two examples—one using `Lock` and another using `Semaphore`.

The differences between the two versions are as follows:

1. The version using Lock protects all the code that modifies the resource—in this case, checking the counter, saving the thumbnail, and incrementing the counter—to make sure that there are no data inconsistencies.

2. The Semaphore version is implemented more like a gate—a door that is open while the count is below the limit, and through which any number of threads can pass, and that only closes when the limit is reached. In other words, it doesn't mutually exclude threads from calling the thumbnail saving function.

Hence, the effect is that the semaphore version would be faster than the version using Lock.

How much faster? The following timing example for a run of 100 images gives an idea.

This screenshot shows the time it takes for the Lock version to save 100 images:

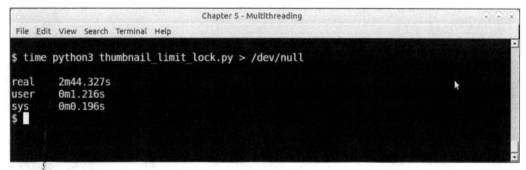

Timing the run of the thumbnail generator program—the Lock version—for 100 images

The following screenshot shows the time for the semaphore version to save a similar number:

Chapter 5 - Multithreading

```
$ time python3 thumbnail_limit_sema.py > /dev/null

real    0m43.206s
user    0m1.256s
sys     0m0.220s
$
```

Timing the run of the thumbnail generator program—the semaphore version—for 100 images

By a quick calculation you can see that the semaphore version is about 4 times faster than the lock version for the same logic. In other words, it *scales 4 times better*.

Thumbnail generator – URL rate controller using conditions

In this section, we will briefly see the application of another important synchronization primitive in threading, namely the Condition object.

First, we will get a real life example of using a Condition object. We will implement a throttler for our thumbnail generator to manage the rate of URL generation.

In the producer/consumer systems in real life, the following three kinds of scenario can occur with respect to the rate of data production and consumption:

1. Producers produce data at a faster pace than consumers can consume. This causes the consumers to always play catch up with the producers. Excess data by the producers can accumulate in the queue, which causes the queue to consume a higher memory and CPU usage in every loop causing the program to slow down.

2. Consumers consume data at a faster rate than producers. This causes the consumers to always wait on the queue—for data. This, in itself, is not a problem as long as the producers don't lag too much. In the worst case, this leads to half of the system, that is, the consumers, remaining idle, while the other half – the producers—try to keep up with the demand.

3. Both producers and consumers work at nearly the same pace keeping the queue size within limits. This is the ideal scenario.

There are many ways to solve this problem. Some of them are as follows:

1. **Queue with a fixed size**: Producers would be forced to wait until data is consumed by a consumer once the queue size limit is reached. However this would almost always keep the queue full.

2. **Provide the workers with timeouts plus other responsibilities**: Rather than remain blocked on the queue, producers and/or consumers can use a timeout to wait on the queue. When they time out they can either sleep or perform some other responsibilities before coming back and waiting on the queue.

3. **Dynamically configure the number of workers**: This is an approach where the worker pool size automatically increases or decreases upon demand. If one class of workers is ahead, the system will launch just the required number of workers of the opposite class to keep the balance.

4. **Adjust the data generation rate**: In this approach, we statically or dynamically adjust the data generation rate by the producers. For example, the system can be configured to produce data at a fixed rate, say, 50 URLs in a minute or it can calculate the rate of consumption by the consumers, and adjust the data production rate of the producers dynamically to keep things in balance.

In the following example, we will implement the last approach — to limit the production rate of URLs to a fixed limit using `Condition` objects.

A `Condition` object is a sophisticated synchronization primitive that comes with an implicit built-in lock. It can wait on an arbitrary condition till it becomes true. The moment the thread calls `wait` on the condition, the internal lock is released, but the thread itself becomes blocked:

```
cond = threading.Condition()
# In thread #1
with cond:
    while not some_condition_is_satisfied():
        # this thread is now blocked
        cond.wait()
```

Now, another thread can wake up this preceding thread by setting the condition to True, and then calling `notify` or `notify_all` on the condition object. At this point, the preceding blocked thread is woken up, and continues on its way:

```
# In thread #2
with cond:
    # Condition is satisfied
```

```
if some_condition_is_satisfied():
    # Notify all threads waiting on the condition
    cond.notify_all()
```

Here is our new class namely `ThumbnailURLController` which implements the rate control of URL production using a condition object.

```
class ThumbnailURLController(threading.Thread):
    """ A rate limiting controller thread for URLs using conditions
    """

    def __init__(self, rate_limit=0, nthreads=0):
        # Configured rate limit
        self.rate_limit = rate_limit
        # Number of producer threads
        self.nthreads = nthreads
        self.count = 0
        self.start_t = time.time()
        self.flag = True
        self.cond = threading.Condition()
        threading.Thread.__init__(self)

    def increment(self):
        # Increment count of URLs
        self.count += 1

    def calc_rate(self):
        rate = 60.0*self.count/(time.time() - self.start_t)
        return rate

    def run(self):
        while self.flag:
            rate = self.calc_rate()
            if rate<=self.rate_limit:
                with self.cond:
                    # print('Notifying all...')
                    self.cond.notify_all()

    def stop(self):
        self.flag = False

    def throttle(self, thread):
        """ Throttle threads to manage rate """
        # Current total rate
        rate = self.calc_rate()
```

```
print('Current Rate',rate)
# If rate > limit, add more sleep time to thread
diff = abs(rate - self.rate_limit)
sleep_diff = diff/(self.nthreads*60.0)

if rate>self.rate_limit:
    # Adjust threads sleep_time
    thread.sleep_time += sleep_diff
    # Hold this thread till rate settles down with a 5% error
    with self.cond:
        print('Controller, rate is high, sleep more
by',rate,sleep_diff)
        while self.calc_rate() > self.rate_limit:
            self.cond.wait()
elif rate<self.rate_limit:
    print('Controller, rate is low, sleep less by',rate,sleep_
diff)
    # Decrease sleep time
    sleep_time = thread.sleep_time
    sleep_time -= sleep_diff
    # If this goes off < zero, make it zero
    thread.sleep_time = max(0, sleep_time)
```

Let's discuss the preceding code before we discuss the changes in the producer class that will make use of this class:

1. The class is an instance of `Thread`, so it runs in its own thread of execution. It also holds a `Condition` object.

2. It has a `calc_rate` method, which calculates the rate of generation of URLs by keeping a counter and using timestamps.

3. In the `run` method, the rate is checked. If it's below the configured limit, the condition object notifies all threads waiting on it.

4. Most importantly, it implements a `throttle` method. This method uses the current rate, calculated via `calc_rate`, and uses it to throttle and adjust the sleep times of the producers. It mainly does these two things:

    1. If the rate is more than the configured limit, it causes the calling thread to wait on the condition object until the rate levels off. It also calculates an extra sleep time that the thread should sleep in its loop to adjust the rate to the required level.

    2. If the rate is less than the configured limit, then the thread needs to work faster and produce more data, so it calculates the sleep difference and lowers the sleep limit accordingly.

Here is the code of the producer class to incorporate the changes:

```python
class ThumbnailURL_Generator(threading.Thread):
    """ Worker class that generates image URLs and supports throttling
        via an external controller """

    def __init__(self, queue, controller=None, sleep_time=1):
        self.sleep_time = sleep_time
        self.queue = queue
        # A flag for stopping
        self.flag = True
        # sizes
        self._sizes = (240,320,360,480,600,720)
        # URL scheme
        self.url_template = 'https://dummyimage.com/%s/%s/%s.jpg'
        # Rate controller
        self.controller = controller
        # Internal id
        self._id = uuid.uuid4().hex
        threading.Thread.__init__(self, name='Producer-'+ self._id)

    def __str__(self):
        return 'Producer-'+self._id

    def get_size(self):
        return '%dx%d' % (random.choice(self._sizes),
                          random.choice(self._sizes))

    def get_color(self):
        return ''.join(random.sample(string.hexdigits[:-6], 3))

    def run(self):
        """ Main thread function """

        while self.flag:
            # generate image URLs of random sizes and fg/bg colors
            url = self.url_template % (self.get_size(),
                                       self.get_color(),
                                       self.get_color())
            # Add to queue
            print(self,'Put',url)
            self.queue.put(url)
            self.controller.increment()
```

```
                # Throttle after putting a few images
                if self.controller.count>5:
                    self.controller.throttle(self)

                time.sleep(self.sleep_time)

        def stop(self):
            """ Stop the thread """

            self.flag = False
```

Let's see how the preceding code works:

1. The class now accepts an additional controller object in its initializer. This is the instance of the controller class given earlier.

2. After putting a URL, it increments the count on the controller. Once the count reaches a minimum limit (set as 5 to avoid early throttling of the producers), it calls `throttle` on the controller, passing itself as the argument.

The calling code also needs quite a few changes. The modified code is shown as follows:

```
q = Queue(maxsize=2000)
# The controller needs to be configured with exact number of
# producers
controller = ThumbnailURLController(rate_limit=50, nthreads=3)
saver = ThumbnailImageSemaSaver(limit=200)

controller.start()

producers, consumers = [], []
for i in range(3):
    t = ThumbnailURL_Generator(q, controller)
    producers.append(t)
    t.start()

for i in range(5):
    t = ThumbnailURL_Consumer(q, saver)
    consumers.append(t)
    t.start()

for t in consumers:
    t.join()
```

```
        print('Joined', t, flush=True)

    # To make sure producers dont block on a full queue
    while not q.empty():
        item=q.get()
    controller.stop()

    for t in producers:
        t.stop()
        print('Stopped',t, flush=True)



    print('Total number of PNG images',len(glob.glob('*.png')))
```

The main changes here are the ones listed next:

1. The controller object is created with the exact number of producers that will be created. This helps the correct calculation of sleep time per thread.

2. The producer threads, themselves, are passed the instance of the controller in their initializer.

3. The controller is started as a thread before all other threads.

Here is a run of the program configured with 200 images at the rate of 50 images per minute. We show two images of the running program's output, one at the beginning of the program and one towards the end.

Starting the thumbnail program with URL rate controller—at 50 URLs per minute

You will find that, when the program starts, it almost immediately slows down, and nearly comes to a halt, since the original rate is high. What happens here is that the producers call on the `throttle` method, and since the rate is high, they all get blocked on the condition object.

After a few seconds, the rate comes down to the prescribed limit, since no URLs are generated. This is detected by the controller in its loop, and it calls `notify_all` on the threads, waking them up.

After a while you will see that the rate is getting settled around the set limit of 50 URLs per minute.

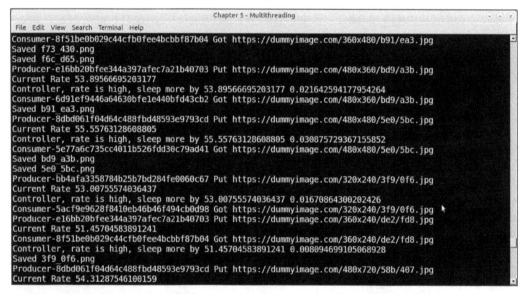

The thumbnail program with URL rate controller 5-6 seconds after start

Towards the end of the program, you will see that the rate has almost settled to the exact limit:

```
                        Chapter 5 - Multithreading                          ˅ ^ x
File Edit View Search Terminal Help
Consumer-c2a30ea8d7494631a8203f5c90abea50 Got https://dummyimage.com/320x240/92f/f1c.jpg
Semaphore limit reached, returning False
Consumer-c2a30ea8d7494631a8203f5c90abea50 Set limit reached, quitting
Producer-ace34b3fc9644cd0a5760373db9aa0fa Put https://dummyimage.com/720x480/0a1/c69.jpg
Current Rate 50.15528364068437
Consumer-e0c93e3825df407a9d452b993eedd7ca Got https://dummyimage.com/720x480/0a1/c69.jpg
Controller, rate is high, sleep more by 50.15528364068437 0.0008626868926909263
Semaphore limit reached, returning False
Consumer-e0c93e3825df407a9d452b993eedd7ca Set limit reached, quitting
Producer-198415b202dc4b979d68d423c6ba0f16 Put https://dummyimage.com/360x720/7ad/6f4.jpg
Current Rate 50.08487818479042
Controller, rate is high, sleep more by 50.08487818479042 0.00047154547105788446
Consumer-d82287478e0d4a07afa4085b0a666160 Got https://dummyimage.com/360x720/7ad/6f4.jpg
Semaphore limit reached, returning False
Consumer-d82287478e0d4a07afa4085b0a666160 Set limit reached, quitting
Joined Consumer-d82287478e0d4a07afa4085b0a666160
Joined Consumer-1cbb1331c886469abd9892b5219abb9e
Joined Consumer-e0c93e3825df407a9d452b993eedd7ca
Joined Consumer-c2a30ea8d7494631a8203f5c90abea50
Stopping controller
Stopping producers...
Stopped Producer-198415b202dc4b979d68d423c6ba0f16
Stopped Producer-bd2baedf319e45298bc320a1346a46c6
Stopped Producer-ace34b3fc9644cd0a5760373db9aa0fa
Total number of PNG images 200
```

The thumbnail program with URL rate controller towards the end

We are coming towards the end of our discussion on threading primitives and how to use them in improving the concurrency of your programs and in implementing shared resource constraints and controls.

Before we conclude, we will look at an aspect of Python threads which prevents multi-threaded programs from making full use of the CPU in Python – namely the GIL or Global Interpreter Lock.

Multithreading – Python and GIL

In Python there is, a global lock that prevents multiple threads from executing native bytecode at once. This lock is required, since the memory management of CPython (the native implementation of Python) is not thread-safe.

This lock is called **Global Interpreter Lock** or just **GIL**.

Python cannot execute bytecode operations concurrently on CPUs due to the GIL. Hence, Python becomes almost unsuitable for the following cases:

- When the program depends on a number of heavy bytecode operations, which it wants to run concurrently

- When the program uses multithreading to utilize the full power of multiple CPU cores on a single machine

I/O calls and long-running operations typically occur outside the GIL. Therefore, multithreading is efficient in Python only when it involves some amount of I/O or such operations – such as image processing.

In such cases, scaling your program to concurrently scale beyond a single process becomes a handy approach. Python makes this possible via its `multiprocessing` module, which is our next topic of discussion.

Concurrency in Python – multiprocessing

The Python standard library provides a multiprocessing module, which allows a programmer to write programs that scale concurrently using multiple processes instead of threads.

Since multiprocessing scales computation across multiple processes, it effectively removes any issues with the GIL in Python. Programs can make use of multiple CPU cores efficiently using this module.

The main class exposed by this module is the `Process` class, the analog to the `Thread` class in the threading module. It also provides a number of synchronization primitives, which are almost exact counterparts of their cousins in the threading module.

We will get started by using an example using the `Pool` object provided by this module. It allows a function to execute in parallel over multiple inputs using processes.

A primality checker

The following function is a simple checker function for primality, that is, whether the input number is prime or not:

```
def is_prime(n):
    """ Check for input number primality """

    for i in range(3, int(n**0.5+1), 2):
```

```
        if n % i == 0:
            print(n,'is not prime')
            return False

    print(n,'is prime')
    return True
```

The following is a threaded class that uses this last function to check numbers from a queue for primality:

```
# prime_thread.py
import threading

class PrimeChecker(threading.Thread):
    """ Thread class for primality checking """

    def __init__(self, queue):
        self.queue = queue
        self.flag = True
        threading.Thread.__init__(self)

    def run(self):

        while self.flag:
            try:
                n = self.queue.get(timeout=1)
                is_prime(n)
            except Empty:
                break
```

We will test it with 1,000 large prime numbers. In order to save space for the list represented here, what we've done is to take 10 of these numbers and multiply the list with 100:

```
numbers = [1297337, 1116281, 104395303, 472882027, 533000389,
           817504243, 982451653, 112272535095293, 115280095190773,
           1099726899285419]*100

q = Queue(1000)

for n in numbers:
    q.put(n)

threads = []
for i in range(4):
```

```
          t = PrimeChecker(q)
          threads.append(t)
          t.start()

      for t in threads:
          t.join()
```

We've used four threads for this test. Let's see how the program performs, in the following screenshot:

Primality checker of 1,000 numbers using a pool of 4 threads

Now, here is the equivalent code using the multiprocessing `Pool` object:

```
      numbers = [1297337, 1116281, 104395303, 472882027, 533000389,
                  817504243, 982451653, 112272535095293, 115280095190773,
                  1099726899285419]*100
      pool = multiprocessing.Pool(4)
      pool.map(is_prime, numbers)
```

The following screenshot shows its performance over the same set of numbers:

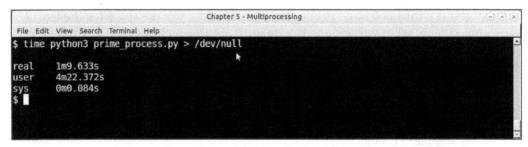

Primality checker of 1,000 numbers using a multiprocessing Pool of 4 processes

We learn the following by comparing these numbers:

1. The real time, that is, the wall clock time spent by the process pool version at 1 minute 9.6 seconds (69.6 seconds) is nearly 50% lesser than that of the thread pool version at 2 minute 12 seconds (132 seconds).

2. However, notice that the user time — that is, the time spent inside the CPU for user code — for the process pool version at 4 minute 22 seconds (262 seconds) is nearly two times more than that of the thread pool version at 2 minutes 12 seconds (132 seconds).

3. The real and user CPU time of the thread pool version is exactly the same at 2 minutes 12 seconds. This is a clear indication that the threaded version was able to execute effectively, only in one of the CPU cores.

This means that the process pool version was able to better make use of all the CPU cores, since, for the 50% of the real time of the thread pool version, it was able to make use of the CPU time twice over.

Hence, the real performance boost in terms of CPU time/real time for the two programs is as follows:

1. Threaded version → 132 seconds/132 seconds = 1

2. Process version → 262 seconds/69.6 seconds = 3.76 ~= 4

The real performance ratio of the process version to the threaded version is, hence, given as follows:

$4/1 = 4$

The machine on which the program was executed has a four-core CPU. This clearly shows that the multiprocess version of the code was able to utilize all the four cores of the CPU nearly equally.

This is because the threaded version is being restricted by the GIL, whereas the process version has no such restriction and can freely make use of all the cores.

In the next section, let's move on to a more involved problem — that of sorting disk-based files.

Sorting disk files

Imagine you have hundreds of thousands of files on the disk, each containing a certain fixed number of integers in a given range. Let's say we need the files to be sorted and merged into a single file.

If we decide to load all this data into memory, it will need large amounts of RAM. Let's do a quick calculation for a million files, each containing around 100 integers in the range of 1 to 10,000 for a total of 100,000,000 or 100 million integers.

Let's assume each of the files is loaded as a list of integers from the disk—we will ignore string processing, and the like for the time being.

Using `sys.getsizeof`, we can get a rough calculation going:

```
>>> sys.getsizeof([100000]*1000)*100000/(1024.0*1024.0)
769.04296875
```

So, the entire data will take close to 800 MB if loaded into memory at once. Now this may not look like a large memory footprint at first, but the larger the list, the more system resources it takes to sort it in memory as one large list.

Here is the simplest code for sorting of all the integers present in the disk files after loading them into memory:

```python
# sort_in_memory.py
import sys

all_lists = []

for i in range(int(sys.argv[1])):
    num_list = map(int, open('numbers/numbers_%d.txt' %
i).readlines())
    all_lists += num_list

print('Length of list',len(all_lists))
print('Sorting...')
all_lists.sort()
open('sorted_nums.txt','w').writelines('\n'.join(map(str, all_lists))
+ '\n')
print('Sorted')
```

This preceding code loads a certain number of files from the disk, each containing 100 integers in the range 1 to 10,000. It reads each file, maps it to a list of integers, and adds each list to a cumulative list. Finally, the list is sorted and written to a file.

The following table shows the time taken to sort a certain number of disk files:

Number of files (n)	Time taken for sorting
1000	17.4 seconds
10000	101 seconds
100000	138 seconds
1000000	NA

As you can see, the time taken scales pretty reasonably—less than *O(n)*. However, this is one problem where more than the time, it is the space—in terms of memory and operations on it—that matters.

For example, in the machine that was used to conduct the test, an 8 -GB RAM, 4-core CPU laptop with 64-bit Linux, the test with a million numbers didn't finish. Instead, it caused the system to hang, so it was not completed.

Sorting disk files – using a counter

If you look at the data, you find that there is an aspect that allows us to treat the problem as more about space than time. This is the observation that the integers are in a fixed range with a maximum limit of 10,000.

Hence, instead of loading all the data as separate lists and merging them, one can use a data structure like a counter.

Here is the basic idea of how this works:

1. Initialize a data structure—a counter, where each integer starts from 1… 10,000 the maximum entry is initialized to zero.

2. Load each file and convert the data to a list. For any number found in the list, increment its count in the counter data structure initialized in Step 1.

3. Finally, loop through the counter, and output each number with a count greater than zero *so many times*, and save the output to a file. The output is your merged and sorted single file:

```python
# sort_counter.py
import sys
import collections

MAXINT = 100000

def sort():
    """ Sort files on disk by using a counter """
```

```
counter = collections.defaultdict(int)
for i in range(int(sys.argv[1])):
filename = 'numbers/numbers_%d.txt' % i
for n in open(filename):
counter[n] += 1
print('Sorting...')

with open('sorted_nums.txt','w') as fp:
for i in range(1, MAXINT+1):
    count = counter.get(str(i) + '\n', 0)
if count>0:
fp.write((str(i)+'\n')*count)

print('Sorted')
```

In the preceding code, we use a `defaultdict` from the collections module as the counter. Whenever we encounter an integer, we increment its count. In the end, the counter is looped through, and each item is output as many times as it was found.

The sort and merge happen due to the way we have converted the problem from one of sorting integers to one of keeping a count and outputting in a naturally sorted order.

The following table summarizes the time taken for the sorting of numbers against the size of the input – in terms of number of disk files:

Number of files (n)	Time taken for sorting
1000	16.5 seconds
10000	83 seconds
100000	86 seconds
1000000	359 seconds

Though the performance for the smallest case – that of 1,000 files is similar to that for the in-memory sort, the performance becomes better as the size of the input increases. This code also manages to finish the sorting of a million files or 100 million integers - in about 5m 59s.

In timing measurements for processes that read files, there is always the effect of buffer caches in the kernel. You will find that running the same performance test successively shows a tremendous improvement, as Linux caches the contents of the files in its buffer cache. Hence, subsequent tests for the same input size should be done after clearing the buffer cache. In Linux, this can be done by the following command:

```
$ echo 3 > /proc/sys/vm/drop_caches
```

In our tests for successive numbers, we *don't* reset the buffer caches as shown before. This means that runs for higher numbers enjoy a performance boost from the caches created during the previous runs. However, since this is done uniformly for each test, the results are comparable. The cache is reset before starting the test suite for a specific algorithm.

This algorithm also requires much less memory, since, for each run, the memory requirements are *the same* since we are using an array of integers up to MAXINT and just incrementing the count.

Here is the memory usage of the sort in-memory program for 100,000 files using the memory_profiler, which we have encountered in the previous chapter.

```
                        Chapter 5 - Multiprocessing

File  Edit  View  Search  Terminal  Help
$ python3 -m memory_profiler sort_in_memory.py 100000
Length of list 10000000
Sorting...
Sorted
Filename: sort_in_memory.py

Line #    Mem usage    Increment   Line Contents
================================================
     5    31.328 MiB    0.000 MiB   @profile
     6                              def sort():
     7    31.328 MiB    0.000 MiB       all_lists = []
     8
     9   447.043 MiB  415.715 MiB       for i in range(int(sys.argv[1])):
    10   447.043 MiB    0.000 MiB           num_list = map(int, open('numbers/numbers_%d.txt
' % i).readlines())
    11   447.043 MiB    0.000 MiB           all_lists += num_list
    12
    13   447.043 MiB    0.000 MiB       print('Length of list',len(all_lists))
    14   447.043 MiB    0.000 MiB       print('Sorting...')
    15   456.887 MiB    9.844 MiB       all_lists.sort()
    16   465.199 MiB    8.312 MiB       open('sorted_nums.txt','w').writelines('\n'.join(map
(str, all_lists)) + '\n')
    17   465.199 MiB    0.000 MiB       print('Sorted')
```

Memory usage of in-memory sort program for an input of 100,000 files

The following screenshot shows the memory usage for the sort counter for the same number of files:

```
                                    Chapter 5 - Multiprocessing
 File  Edit  View  Search  Terminal  Help
$ python3 -m memory_profiler sort_counter.py 100000
Sorting...
Sorted
Filename: sort_counter.py

Line #    Mem usage    Increment   Line Contents
================================================
     7    31.305 MiB    0.000 MiB   @profile
     8                              def sort():
     9
    10    31.305 MiB    0.000 MiB       counter = collections.defaultdict(int)
    11
    12    69.836 MiB   38.531 MiB       for i in range(int(sys.argv[1])):
    13    69.836 MiB    0.000 MiB           num_list = map(int, open('numbers/numbers_%d.txt' % i
).readlines())
    14    69.836 MiB    0.000 MiB           for n in num_list:
    15    69.836 MiB    0.000 MiB               counter[n] += 1
    16
    17
    18    69.836 MiB    0.000 MiB       print('Sorting...')
    19    69.836 MiB    0.000 MiB       with open('sorted_nums.txt','w') as fp:
    20    69.836 MiB    0.000 MiB           for i in range(1, MAXINT+1):
    21    69.836 MiB    0.000 MiB               count = counter.get(i, 0)
    22    69.836 MiB    0.000 MiB               if count>0:
    23    69.836 MiB    0.000 MiB                   fp.write((str(i)+'\n')*count)
    24    69.836 MiB    0.000 MiB       print('Sorted')
```

Memory usage of counter sort program for an input of 100,000 files

The memory usage of the in-memory sort program at 465 MB is more than six times that of the counter sort program at 70 MB. Also note, that the sorting operation itself takes extra memory of nearly 10 MB in the in-memory version.

Sorting disk files – using multiprocessing

In this section, we rewrite the counter sorting program using multiple processes. The approach is to scale the processing input files for more than one process by splitting the list of file paths to a pool of processes – and planning to take advantage of the resulting data parallelism.

Here is the rewrite of the code:

```python
# sort_counter_mp.py
import sys
import time
import collections
from multiprocessing import Pool

MAXINT = 100000

def sorter(filenames):
```

```
    """ Sorter process sorting files using a counter """

    counter = collections.defaultdict(int)

    for filename in filenames:
for i in open(filename):
counter[i] += 1

return counter

def batch_files(pool_size, limit):
""" Create batches of files to process by a multiprocessing Pool """
batch_size = limit // pool_size

filenames = []

for i in range(pool_size):
batch = []
for j in range(i*batch_size, (i+1)*batch_size):
filename = 'numbers/numbers_%d.txt' % j
batch.append(filename)

filenames.append(batch)

return filenames

def sort_files(pool_size, filenames):
""" Sort files by batches using a multiprocessing Pool """

with Pool(pool_size) as pool:
counters = pool.map(sorter, filenames)
with open('sorted_nums.txt','w') as fp:
for i in range(1, MAXINT+1):
count = sum([x.get(str(i)+'\n',0) for x in counters])
if count>0:
fp.write((str(i)+'\n')*count)
print('Sorted')
if __name__ == "__main__":
limit = int(sys.argv[1])
pool_size = 4
filenames = batch_files(pool_size, limit)
sort_files(pool_size,
```

It is exactly the same code as earlier with the following changes:

1. Instead of processing all the files as a single list, the filenames are put in batches, with batches equaling the size of the pool.

2. We use a sorter function, which accepts the list of filenames, processes them, and returns a dictionary with the counts.

3. The counts are summed for each integer in the range from 1 to MAXINT, and so many numbers are written to the sorted file.

The following table shows the data for processing a different number of files for pool sizes of 2 and 4 respectively:

Number of files (n)	Pool size	Time taken for sorting
1,000	2	18 seconds
	4	20 seconds
10,000	2	92 seconds
	4	77 seconds
100,000	2	96 seconds
	4	86 seconds
1,000,000	2	350 seconds
	4	329 seconds

The numbers tell an interesting story:

1. The multiple process version one with 4 processes (equal to number of cores in the machine) has better numbers overall when compared to the one with 2 processes and the single process one.

2. However, the multiple-process version doesn't seem to offer much of a performance benefit when compared to the single-process version. The performance numbers are very similar and any improvement is within bounds of error and variation. For example, for 1 million number input the multiple process with 4 processes has just an 8% improvement over the single-process one.

3. This is because the bottleneck here is the processing time it takes to load the files into memory — in file I/O — not the computation (sorting), as the sorting is just an increment in the counter. Hence the single process version is pretty efficient as it is able to load all the file data in the same address space. The multiple-process ones are able to improve this a bit by loading the files in multiple address spaces, but not by a lot.

This example shows that, in situations where there is not much computation done but the bottleneck is disk or file I/O, the impact of scaling by multiprocessing is much less.

Multithreading versus multiprocessing

Now that we have come to the end of our discussion on multiprocessing, it is a good time to compare and contrast the scenarios where one needs to choose between scaling using threads in a single process or using multiple processes in Python.

Here are some guidelines.

Use multithreading in the following cases:

1. The program needs to maintain a lot of shared states, especially mutable ones. A lot of the standard data structures in Python, such as lists, dictionaries, and others, are thread-safe, so it costs much less to maintain a mutable shared state using threads than via processes.

2. The program needs to keep a low memory foot-print.

3. The program spends a lot of time doing I/O. Since the GIL is released by threads doing I/O, it doesn't affect the time taken by the threads to perform I/O.

4. The program doesn't have a lot of data-parallel operations which it can scale across multiple processes

Use multiprocessing in these scenarios:

*   The program performs a lot of CPU-bound heavy computing such as byte-code operations, number crunching, and the like on reasonably large inputs.

*   The program has inputs which can be parallelized into chunks and whose results can be combined afterwards – in other words, the input of the program yields well to data-parallel computations.

*   The program doesn't have any limitations on memory usage, and you are on a modern machine with a multicore CPU and large enough RAM.

*   There is not much shared mutable state between processes that need to be synchronized – this can slow down the system, and offset any benefits gained from multiple processes.

*   Your program is not heavily dependent on I/O – file or disk I/O or socket I/O.

Concurrecy in Python – Asynchronous Execution

We have seen two different ways to perform concurrent execution using multiple threads and multiple processes. We saw different examples of using threads and their synchronization primitives. We also saw a couple of examples using multi-processing with slightly varied outcomes.

Apart from these two ways to do concurrent programming, another common technique is that of asynchronous programming or asynchronous I/O.

In an asynchronous model of execution, tasks are picked to be executed from a queue of tasks by a scheduler, which executes these tasks in an interleaved manner. There is no guarantee that the tasks will be executed in any specific order. The order of execution of tasks depends upon how much processing time a task is willing to *yield* to another task in the queue. Put in other words, asynchronous execution happens through co-operative multitasking.

Asynchronous execution usually happens in a single thread. This means no true data parallelism or true parallel execution can happen. Instead, the model only provides a semblance of parallelism.

As execution happens out of order, asynchronous systems need a way to return the results of function execution to the callers. This usually happens with *callbacks*, which are functions to be called when the results are ready or using special objects that receive the results, often called *futures*.

Python 3 provides support for this kind of execution via its *asyncio* module using coroutines. Before we go on to discuss this, we will spend some time understanding pre-emptive multitasking versus cooperative multitasking, and how we can implement a simple cooperative multitasking scheduler in Python using generators.

Pre-emptive versus cooperative multitasking

The programs we wrote earlier using multiple threads were examples of concurrency. However, we didn't have to worry about how and when the operating system chose to run the thread — we just had to prepare the threads (or processes), provide the target function, and execute them. The scheduling is taken care of by the operating system.

Every few ticks of the CPU clock, the operating system pre-empts a running thread, and replaces it with another one in a particular core. This can happen due to different reasons, but the programmer doesn't have to worry about the details. He just creates the threads, sets them up with the data they need to process, uses the correct synchronization primitives, and starts them. The operating system does the rest including switching and scheduling.

This is how almost all modern operating systems work. It guarantees each thread a fair share of the execution time, all other things being equal. This is known as **pre-emptive multitasking**.

There is another type of scheduling which is the opposite of pre-emptive multitasking. This is called as co-operative multitasking, where the operating system plays no role in deciding the priority and execution of competing threads or processes. Instead, a process or thread willingly yields control for another process or thread to run. Alternatively, a thread can replace another thread which is idling (sleeping) or waiting for I/O.

This is the technique used in the asynchronous model of concurrent execution using co-routines. A function, while waiting for data, say a call on the network that is yet to return, can yield control for another function or task to run.

Before we go to discuss actual co-routines using `asyncio` let's write our own co-operative multitasking scheduler using simple Python generators. It is not very difficult to do this as you can see below.

```python
# generator_tasks.py
import random
import time
import collections
import threading

def number_generator(n):
    """ A co-routine that generates numbers in range 1..n """

    for i in range(1, n+1):
        yield i

def square_mapper(numbers):
    """ A co-routine task for converting numbers to squares """

    for n in numbers:
        yield n*n

def prime_filter(numbers):
```

```
    """ A co-routine which yields prime numbers """

    primes = []
    for n in numbers:
        if n % 2 == 0: continue
        flag = True
        for i in range(3, int(n**0.5+1), 2):
            if n % i == 0:
                flag = False
                break

        if flag:
            yield n

def scheduler(tasks, runs=10000):
    """ Basic task scheduler for co-routines """

    results = collections.defaultdict(list)

    for i in range(runs):
        for t in tasks:
            print('Switching to task',t.__name__)
            try:
                result = t.__next__()
                print('Result=>',result)
                results[t.__name__].append(result)
            except StopIteration:
                break

    return results
```

Let's analyze the preceding code:

- We have four functions — three generators, since they use the `yield` keyword to return the data, and a scheduler, which runs a certain set of tasks

- The `square_mapper` function accepts an iterator, which returns integers iterating through it, and yields the squares of the members

- The `prime_filter` function accepts a similar iterator, and filters out numbers that are not prime, yielding only prime numbers

- The `number_generator` function acts as the input iterator to both these functions, providing them with an input stream of integers

Let's now look at the calling code which ties all the four functions together.

```
import sys

tasks = []
start = time.clock()

limit = int(sys.argv[1])

# Append sqare_mapper tasks to list of tasks
tasks.append(square_mapper(number_generator(limit)))
# Append prime_filter tasks to list of tasks
tasks.append(prime_filter(number_generator(limit)))

results = scheduler(tasks, runs=limit)
print('Last prime=>',results['prime_filter'][-1])
end = time.clock()
print('Time taken=>',end-start)
```

Here is an analysis of the calling code:

- The number generator is initialized with a count, which is received via the command-line argument. It is passed to the `square_mapper` function. The combined function is added as a task to the `tasks` list.

- A similar operation is performed for the `prime_filter` function.

- The `scheduler` method is run by passing the task list to it, which it runs by iterating through a `for` loop, running each task one after another. The results are appended to a dictionary using the function's name as the key, and returned at the end of execution.

- We print the last prime number's value to verify correct execution, and also the time taken for the scheduler to process.

Let's see the output of our simple cooperative multitasking scheduler for a limit of 10. This allows us to capture all the input in a single command window, as seen in the following screenshot:

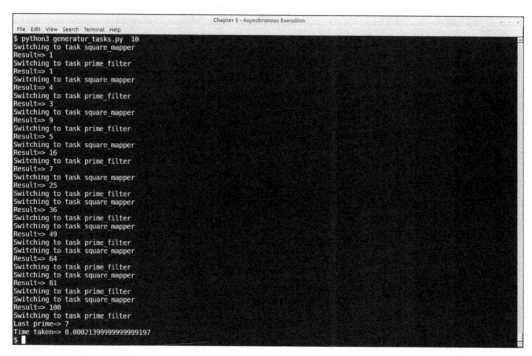

Output of the simple co-operative multitasking program example for an input of 10

Let's analyze the output:

1. The output of the `square_mapper` and `prime_filter` functions alternates on the console. This is because the scheduler switches between them in the `for` loop. Each of the functions are co-routines (generators) so they *yield* execution – that is the control is passed from one function to the next – and vice-versa. This allows both functions to run concurrently, while maintaining state and producing output.

2. Since we used generators here, they provide a natural way of generating the result plus yielding control in one go, using the *yield* keyword.

The asyncio module in Python

The `asyncio` module in Python provides support for writing concurrent, single-threaded programs using co-routines. It is available only in Python 3.

A co-routine using the `asyncio` module is one that uses either of the following approaches:

- Using the `async def` statement for defining functions
- Being decorated using the `@asyncio.coroutine` expression

Generator-based co-routines use the second technique, and they yield from expressions.

Co-routines created using the first technique typically use the `await <future>` expression to wait for the future to be completed.

Co-routines are scheduled for execution using an `event` loop, which connects the objects and schedules them as tasks. Different types of event loop are provided for different operating systems.

The following code rewrites our earlier example of a simple cooperative multitasking scheduler to use the `asyncio` module:

```python
# asyncio_tasks.py
import asyncio

def number_generator(m, n):
    """ A number generator co-routine in range(m...n+1) """
    yield from range(m, n+1)

async prime_filter(m, n):
    """ Prime number co-routine """

    primes = []
    for i in number_generator(m, n):
        if i % 2 == 0: continue
        flag = True

        for j in range(3, int(i**0.5+1), 2):
            if i % j == 0:
                flag = False
                break

        if flag:
```

```
print('Prime=>',i)
primes.append(i)

# At this point the co-routine suspends execution
# so that another co-routine can be scheduled
await asyncio.sleep(1.0)
return tuple(primes)

async def square_mapper(m, n):
""" Square mapper co-routine """
squares = []

for i in number_generator(m, n):
print('Square=>',i*i)
squares.append(i*i)
# At this point the co-routine suspends execution
# so that another co-routine can be scheduled
await asyncio.sleep(1.0)
return squares

def print_result(future):
print('Result=>',future.result())
```

Here is how the preceding code works:

1. The `number_generator` function is a co-routine that yields from the sub-generator `range(m, n+1)`, which is an iterator. This allows this co-routine to be called in other co-routines.

2. The `square_mapper` function is a co-routine of the first type using the `async def` keyword. It returns a list of squares using numbers from the number generator.

3. The `prime_filter` function is of the same type. It also uses the number generator, and appends prime numbers to a list and returns it.

4. Both co-routines yield to the other by sleeping, using the *asyncio.sleep* function and waiting on it. This allows both co-routines to work concurrently in an interleaved fashion.

Here is the calling code with the event loop and the rest of the plumbing:

```
loop = asyncio.get_event_loop()
future = asyncio.gather(prime_filter(10, 50), square_mapper(10, 50))
future.add_done_callback(print_result)
loop.run_until_complete(future)

loop.close()
```

Here is the output of the program. Observe how the results of each of the tasks is being printed in an interleaved fashion.

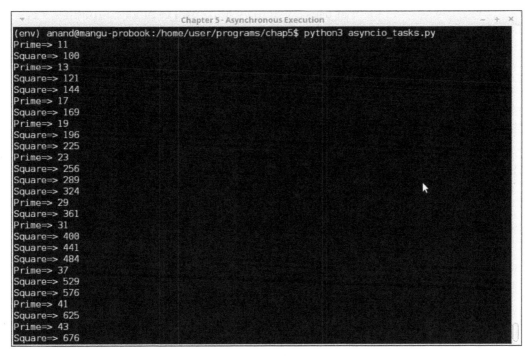

```
Chapter 5 - Asynchronous Execution                          – + ×
(env) anand@mangu-probook:/home/user/programs/chap5$ python3 asyncio_tasks.py
Prime=> 11
Square=> 100
Prime=> 13
Square=> 121
Square=> 144
Prime=> 17
Square=> 169
Prime=> 19
Square=> 196
Square=> 225
Prime=> 23
Square=> 256
Square=> 289
Square=> 324
Prime=> 29
Square=> 361
Prime=> 31
Square=> 400
Square=> 441
Square=> 484
Prime=> 37
Square=> 529
Square=> 576
Prime=> 41
Square=> 625
Prime=> 43
Square=> 676
```

Result of executing the asyncio task calculating prime numbers and squares

Let's analyze how the preceding code worked line by line, while following a top-to-bottom approach:

1. We first get an asyncio event `loop` using the `factory` function `asyncio.get_event_loop`. This returns the default event loop implementation for the operating system.

2. We set up an asyncio `future` object by using the `gather` method of the module. This method is used to aggregate results from a set of co-routines or futures passed as its argument. We pass both the `prime_filter` and the `square_mapper` to it.

3. A callback is added to the `future` object—the `print_result` function. It will be automatically called once the future's execution is completed.

4. The loop is run until the future's execution is completed. At this point, the callback is called and it prints the result. Note how the output appears interleaved—as each task yields to the other one using the *sleep* function of the asyncio module.

5. The loop is closed and terminates is operation.

Waiting for a future – async and await

We discussed how one could wait for data from a future inside a co-routine using await. We saw an example that uses await to yield control to other co-routines. Let's now look at an example that waits for I/O completion on a future, which returns data from the web.

For this example, you need the `aiohttp` module which provides an HTTP client and server to work with the asyncio module and supports futures. We also need the `async_timeout` module which allows timeouts on asynchronous co-routines. Both these modules can be installed using pip.

Here is the code — this is a co-routine that fetches a URL using a timeout and awaits the future, that is, the result of the operation:

```
# async_http.py
import asyncio
import aiohttp
import async_timeout

@asyncio.coroutine
def fetch_page(session, url, timeout=60):
""" Asynchronous URL fetcher """

with async_timeout.timeout(timeout):
response = session.get(url)
return response
```

The following is the calling code with the event loop:

```
loop = asyncio.get_event_loop()
urls = ('http://www.google.com',
        'http://www.yahoo.com',
        'http://www.facebook.com',
        'http://www.reddit.com',
        'http://www.twitter.com')

session = aiohttp.ClientSession(loop=loop)
tasks = map(lambda x: fetch_page(session, x), urls)
# Wait for tasks
done, pending = loop.run_until_complete(asyncio.wait(tasks,
                                            timeout=120))
loop.close()

for future in done:
```

```
response = future.result()
print(response)
response.close()
session.close()

loop.close()
```

What are we doing in the preceding code?

1. We create an event loop and a list of URLs to be fetched. We also create an instance of `aiohttp ClientSession` object which is a helper for fetching URLs.

2. We create a map of tasks by mapping the `fetch_page` function to each of the URLs. The session object is passed as first argument to the `fetch_page` function.

3. The tasks are passed to the wait method of `asyncio` with a timeout of `120` seconds.

4. The loop is run until complete. It returns two sets of futures — `done` and `pending`.

5. We iterate through the future that is done, and print the response by fetching it using the `result` method of the `future`.

You can see the result of the operation (the first few lines, as many lines are output) in the following screenshot:

Output of program doing an async fetch of URLs for 5 URLs

As you can see, we are able to print the responses in terms of a simple summary. How about processing the response to get more details about it such as the actual response text, the content length, status code, and so on?

The function below parses a list of *done* futures — waiting for the response data via *await* on the *read* method of the response. This returns the data for each response asynchronously:

```
async def parse_response(futures):
""" Parse responses of fetch """
for future in futures:
response = future.result()
data = await response.text()
        print('Response for URL',response.url,'=>', response.status,
len(data))
        response.close()
```

The details of the `response` object — the final URL, status code, and length of data — are output by this method for each response before closing the response.

We only need to add one more processing step on the list of completed responses for this to work:

```
session = aiohttp.ClientSession(loop=loop)
# Wait for futures
tasks = map(lambda x: fetch_page(session, x), urls)
done, pending = loop.run_until_complete(asyncio.wait(tasks,
                                          timeout=300))

# One more processing step to parse responses of futures
loop.run_until_complete(parse_response(done))

session.close()
loop.close()
```

Note how we chain the co-routines together. The final link in the chain is the `parse_response` co-routine, which processes the list of done futures before the loop ends.

The following screenshot shows the output of the program:

```
                          Chapter 5 - Asynchronous Execution                    v  ^  x
 File  Edit  View  Search  Terminal  Help
$ python3 async_fetch_url2.py
Response for URL https://twitter.com/ => 200 296219
Response for URL http://www.google.co.in/?gfe_rd=cr&ei=zcZ7WMrDLNTFuATnqbrADQ => 200 12390
Response for URL https://in.yahoo.com/?p=us => 200 380341
Response for URL https://www.reddit.com/ => 200 138933
Response for URL https://www.facebook.com/ => 200 147941
$ █
```

Output of program doing fetching and response processing of 5 URLs asynchronously

A lot of complex programming can be done using the `asyncio` module. One can wait for futures, cancel their execution, and run `asyncio` operations from multiple threads. A full discussion is beyond the scope of this chapter.

We will move on to another model for executing concurrent tasks in Python, namely the `concurrent.futures` module.

Concurrent futures – high-level concurrent processing

The `concurrent.futures` module provides high-level concurrent processing using either threads or processes, while asynchronously returning data using future objects.

It provides an executor interface which exposes mainly two methods, which are as follows:

- `submit`: Submits a callable to be executed asynchronously, returning a `future` object representing the execution of the callable.

- `map`: Maps a callable to a set of iterables, scheduling the execution asynchronously in the `future` object. However, this method returns the results of processing directly instead of returning a list of futures.

There are two concrete implementations of the executor interface: `ThreadPoolExecutor` executes the callable in a pool of threads, and `ProcessPoolExecutor` does so in a pool of processes.

Here is a simple example of a `future` object that calculates the factorial of a set of integers asynchronously:

```
from concurrent.futures import ThreadPoolExecutor, as_completed
import functools
import operator

def factorial(n):
    return functools.reduce(operator.mul, [i for i in range(1, n+1)])

with ThreadPoolExecutor(max_workers=2) as executor:
    future_map = {executor.submit(factorial, n): n for n in range(10,
21)}
    for future in as_completed(future_map):
        num = future_map[future]
        print('Factorial of',num,'is',future.result())
```

The following is a detailed explanation of the preceding code:

- The `factorial` function computes the factorial of a given number iteratively by using `functools.reduce` and the multiplication operator

- We create an executor with two workers, and submit the numbers (from 10 to 20) to it via its `submit` method

- The submission is done via a dictionary comprehension, returning a dictionary with the future as the key and the number as the value

- We iterate through the completed futures, which have been computed, using the `as_completed` method of the `concurrent.futures` module

- The result is printed by fetching the future's result via the `result` method

When executed, the program prints its output, rather in order, as shown in the next screenshot:

```
Chapter 5 - Asynchronous Execution
File  Edit  View  Search  Terminal  Help
$ python3 concurrent_factorial.py
Factorial of 10 is 3628800
Factorial of 11 is 39916800
Factorial of 12 is 479001600
Factorial of 13 is 6227020800
Factorial of 14 is 87178291200
Factorial of 15 is 1307674368000
Factorial of 16 is 20922789888000
Factorial of 17 is 355687428096000
Factorial of 18 is 6402373705728000
Factorial of 19 is 121645100408832000
Factorial of 20 is 2432902008176640000
$
```

Output of concurrent futures factorial program

Disk thumbnail generator

In our earlier discussion of threads, we used the example of the generation of thumbnails for random images from the Web to demonstrate how to work with threads, and process information.

In this example, we will do something similar. Here, rather than processing random image URLs from the Web, we will load images from disk, and convert them to thumbnails using the `concurrent.futures` function.

We will reuse our thumbnail creation function from before. On top of that, we will add concurrent processing.

First, here are the imports:

```
import os
import sys
import mimetypes
from concurrent.futures import ThreadPoolExecutor,
ProcessPoolExecutor, as_completed
```

Here is our familiar thumbnail creation function:

```
def thumbnail_image(filename, size=(64,64), format='.png'):
    """ Convert image thumbnails, given a filename """

    try:
        im=Image.open(filename)
        im.thumbnail(size, Image.ANTIALIAS)

        basename = os.path.basename(filename)
        thumb_filename = os.path.join('thumbs',
            basename.rsplit('.')[0] + '_thumb.png')
        im.save(thumb_filename)
        print('Saved',thumb_filename)
        return True

    except Exception as e:
        print('Error converting file',filename)
        return False
```

We will process images from a specific folder — in this case, the `Pictures` subdirectory of the `home` folder. To process this, we will need an iterator that yields image filenames. We have written one next with the help of the `os.walk` function:

```
def directory_walker(start_dir):
    """ Walk a directory and generate list of valid images """

    for root,dirs,files in os.walk(os.path.expanduser(start_dir)):
        for f in files:
            filename = os.path.join(root,f)
            # Only process if it's a type of image
            file_type = mimetypes.guess_type(filename.lower())[0]
            if file_type != None and file_type.startswith('image/'):
                yield filename
```

As you can see, the preceding function is a generator.

Here is the main calling code, which sets up an executor and runs it over the folder:

```
root_dir = os.path.expanduser('~/Pictures/')
if '--process' in sys.argv:
    executor = ProcessPoolExecutor(max_workers=10)
else:
    executor = ThreadPoolExecutor(max_workers=10)

with executor:
    future_map = {executor.submit(thumbnail_image, filename):
    filename for filename in directory_walker(root_dir)}
    for future in as_completed(future_map):
        num = future_map[future]
        status = future.result()
        if status:
            print('Thumbnail of',future_map[future],'saved')
```

The preceding code uses the same technique of submitting arguments to a function asynchronously, saving the resultant futures in a dictionary and then processing the result as and when the futures are finished, in a loop.

To change the executor to use processes, one simply needs to replace ThreadPoolExecutor with ProcessPoolExecutor; the rest of the code remains the same. We have provided a simple command-line flag, --process, to make this easy.

Here is an output of a sample run of the program using both thread and process pools on the ~/Pictures folder — generating around 2000+ images in roughly the same time.

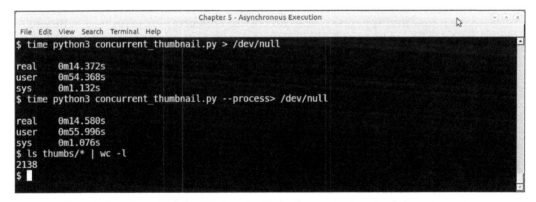

Output of concurrent futures disk thumbnail program — using thread and process executor

Concurrency options – how to choose?

We are at the end of our discussion of concurrency techniques in Python. We discussed threads, processes, asynchronous I/O, and concurrent futures. Naturally, a question arises — when to pick what?

This question has been already answered for the choice between threads and processes, where the decision is mostly influenced by the GIL.

Here are some rough guidelines for picking your concurrency options.

- **Concurrent futures versus multiprocessing:** Concurrent futures provide an elegant way to parallelize your tasks using either a thread or process pool executor. Hence, it is ideal if the underlying application has similar scalability metrics with either threads or processes, since it's very easy to switch from one to the other as we've seen in a previous example. Concurrent futures can be chosen also when the result of the operation needn't be immediately available. Concurrent futures is a good option when the data can be finely parallelized and the operation can be executed asynchronously, and when the operations involve simple callables without requiring complex synchronization techniques.

  Multiprocessing should be chosen if the concurrent execution is more complex, and not just based on data parallelism, but has aspects like synchronization, shared memory, and so on. For example, if the program requires processes, synchronization primitives, and IPC, the only way to truly scale up then, is to write a concurrent program using the primitives provided by the multiprocessing module.

  Similarly when your multithreaded logic involves simple parallelization of data across multiple tasks, one can choose concurrent futures with a thread pool. However if there is a lot of shared state to be managed with complex thread synchronization objects — one has to use thread objects and switch to multiple threads using `threading` module to get finer control of the state.

- **Asynchronous I/O vs threaded concurrency:** When your program doesn't need true concurrency (parallelism), but is dependent more on asynchronous processing and callbacks, then `asyncio` is the way to go. Asyncio is a good choice when there are lot of waits or sleep cycles involved in the application, such as waiting for user input, waiting for I/O, and so on, and one needs to take advantage of such wait or sleep times by yielding to other tasks via co-routines. Asyncio is not suitable for CPU-heavy concurrent processing, or for tasks involving true data parallelism.

AsyncIO seems to be suitable for request-response loops, where a lot of I/O happens – so its good for writing web application servers which do not have real-time data requirements.

You can use the points just listed as rough guidelines when deciding on the correct concurrency package for your applications.

Parallel processing libraries

Apart from the standard library modules that we've discussed so far, Python is also rich in its ecosystem of third-party libraries, which support parallel processing in **symmetric multi-processing** (**SMP**) or multi-core systems.

We will take a look at a couple of such packages, that are somewhat distinct and present some interesting features.

Joblib

`joblib` is a package that provides a wrapper over multiprocessing to execute code in loops in parallel. The code is written as a generator expression, and interpreted to execute in parallel over CPU cores using multiprocessing modules behind the scenes.

For example, take the following code which calculates square roots for first 10 numbers:

```
>>> [i ** 0.5 for i in range(1, 11)]
[1.0, 1.4142135623730951, 1.7320508075688772, 2.0, 2.23606797749979,
2.449489742783178, 2.6457513110645907, 2.8284271247461903, 3.0,
3.1622776601683795]
```

This preceding code can be converted to run on two CPU cores by the following:

```
>>> import math
>>> from joblib import Parallel, delayed
    [1.0, 1.4142135623730951, 1.7320508075688772, 2.0,
     2.23606797749979, 2.449489742783178, 2.6457513110645907,
     2.8284271247461903, 3.0, 3.1622776601683795]
```

Here is another example: this is our primality checker that we had written earlier to run using multiprocessing, rewritten to use the `joblib` package:

```python
# prime_joblib.py
from joblib import Parallel, delayed

def is_prime(n):
    """ Check for input number primality """

    for i in range(3, int(n**0.5+1), 2):
        if n % i == 0:
            print(n,'is not prime')
            return False

    print(n,'is prime')
    return True

if __name__ == "__main__":
    numbers = [1297337, 1116281, 104395303, 472882027, 533000389,
               817504243, 982451653, 112272535095293, 115280095190773,
               1099726899285419]*100
    Parallel(n_jobs=10)(delayed(is_prime)(i) for i in numbers)
```

If you execute and time the preceding code, you will find the performance metrics very similar to that of the version using multiprocessing.

PyMP

`OpenMP` is an open API, which supports shared memory multiprocessing in C/C++ and Fortran. It uses special work-sharing constructs such as pragmas (special instructions to compilers) indicating how to split work among threads or processes.

For example, the following C code using the `OpenMP` API indicates that the array should be initialized in parallel using multiple threads:

```c
int parallel(int argc, char **argv)
{
    int array[100000];

    #pragma omp parallel for
    for (int i = 0; i < 100000; i++) {
array[i] = i * i;
    }

    return 0;
}
```

PyMP is inspired by the idea behind OpenMP, but uses the fork system call to parallelize code executing in expressions such as for loops across processes. For this, PyMP also provides support for shared data structures such as lists and dictionaries, and also provides a wrapper for numpy arrays.

We will look at an interesting and exotic example — that of fractals — to illustrate how PyMP can be used to parallelize code and obtain performance improvement.

 NOTE: The PyPI package for PyMP is named pymp-pypi so make sure you use this name when trying to install it via pip. Also note that it doesn't do a good job of pulling its dependencies such as numpy, so these have to be installed separately.

Fractals – the Mandelbrot set

The following is the code listing of a very popular class of complex numbers, which when plotted, produces very interesting fractal geometries, namely, the **Mandelbrot set**:

```
# mandelbrot.py
import sys
import argparse
from PIL import Image

def mandelbrot_calc_row(y, w, h, image, max_iteration = 1000):
    """ Calculate one row of the Mandelbrot set with size wxh """

    y0 = y * (2/float(h)) - 1 # rescale to -1 to 1

    for x in range(w):
        x0 = x * (3.5/float(w)) - 2.5 # rescale to -2.5 to 1

        i, z = 0, 0 + 0j
        c = complex(x0, y0)
        while abs(z) < 2 and i < max_iteration:
            z = z**2 + c
            i += 1

        # Color scheme is that of Julia sets
        color = (i % 8 * 32, i % 16 * 16, i % 32 * 8)
```

```
                image.putpixel((x, y), color)


def mandelbrot_calc_set(w, h, max_iteration=10000, output='mandelbrot.
png'):
    """ Calculate a mandelbrot set given the width, height and
    maximum number of iterations """

    image = Image.new("RGB", (w, h))

    for y in range(h):
        mandelbrot_calc_row(y, w, h, image, max_iteration)

    image.save(output, "PNG")

if __name__ == "__main__":
    parser = argparse.ArgumentParser(prog='mandelbrot',
description='Mandelbrot fractal generator')
    parser.add_argument('-W','--width',help='Width of the
image',type=int, default=640)
    parser.add_argument('-H','--height',help='Height of the
image',type=int, default=480)
    parser.add_argument('-n','--niter',help='Number of
iterations',type=int, default=1000)
    parser.add_argument('-o','--output',help='Name of output image
file',default='mandelbrot.png')

    args = parser.parse_args()
    print('Creating Mandelbrot set with size %(width)sx%(height)s,
#iterations=%(niter)s' % args.__dict__)
    mandelbrot_calc_set(args.width, args.height, max_iteration=args.
niter, output=args.output)
```

The preceding code calculates a Mandelbrot set using a certain number of c and a variable geometry (*width x height*). It is complete with argument parsing to produce fractal images of varying geometries, and supports different iterations.

For simplicity's sake, and for producing rather more beautiful pics than what Mandelbrot usually does, the code takes some liberties, and uses the color scheme of a related fractal class, namely, Julia sets.

How does it work ? Here is an explanation of the code .

1. The `mandelbrot_calc_row` function calculates a row of the Mandelbrot set for a certain value of the y coordinate for a certain number of maximum iterations. The pixel color values for the entire row, from 0 to width w for the x coordinate, is calculated. The pixel values are put into the `Image` object that is passed to this function.

2. The `mandelbrot_calc_set` function calls the `mandelbrot_calc_row` function for all values of the y coordinate ranging from 0 to the height h of the image. An `Image` object (via the **Pillow library**) is created for the given geometry (*width x height*), and filled with pixel values. Finally, we save this image to a file, and we've got our fractal!

Without further ado, let's see the code in action.

Here is the image that our Mandelbrot program produces for the default number of iterations namely 1000.

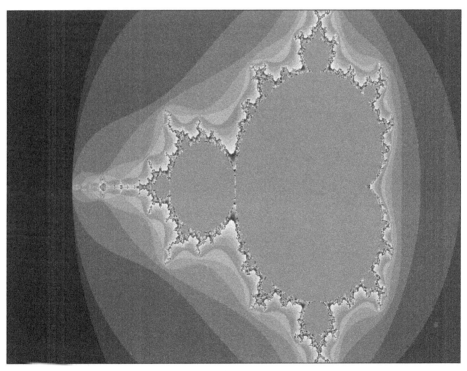

Mandelbrot set fractal image for 1,000 iterations

Here is the time it takes to create this image.

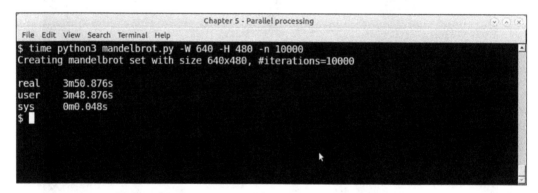

Timing of single process Mandelbrot program — for 1,000 iterations

However, if you increase the number of iterations — the single process version slows down quite a bit. Here is the output when we increase the number of iterations by 10X — for 10,000 iterations:

```
Chapter 5 - Parallel processing
File  Edit  View  Search  Terminal  Help
$ time python3 mandelbrot.py -W 640 -H 480 -n 10000
Creating mandelbrot set with size 640x480, #iterations=10000

real    3m50.876s
user    3m48.876s
sys     0m0.048s
$
```

Timing of single process Mandelbrot program — for 10,000 iterations

If we look at the code, we can see that there is an outer for loop in the `mandelbrot_calc_set` function, which sets things in motion. It calls `mandelbrot_calc_row` for each row of the image ranging from `0` to the height of the function, varied by the y coordinate.

Since each invocation of the `mandelbrot_calc_row` function calculates one row of the image, it naturally fits into a data parallel problem, and can be parallelized sufficiently easily.

In the next section, we will see how to do this using PyMP.

Fractals – scaling the Mandelbrot set implementation

We will use PyMP to parallelize the outer for loop across many processes in a rewrite of the previous simple implementation of the Mandelbrot set, to take advantage of the inherent data parallelism in the solution.

Here is the PyMP version of the two functions of the Mandelbrot program. The rest of the code remains the same.

```python
# mandelbrot_mp.py
import sys
from PIL import Image
import pymp
import argparse


def mandelbrot_calc_row(y, w, h, image_rows, max_iteration = 1000):
    """ Calculate one row of the mandelbrot set with size wxh """

    y0 = y * (2/float(h)) - 1 # rescale to -1 to 1

    for x in range(w):
        x0 = x * (3.5/float(w)) - 2.5 # rescale to -2.5 to 1

        i, z = 0, 0 + 0j
        c = complex(x0, y0)
        while abs(z) < 2 and i < max_iteration:
            z = z**2 + c
            i += 1

        color = (i % 8 * 32, i % 16 * 16, i % 32 * 8)
        image_rows[y*w + x] = color


def mandelbrot_calc_set(w, h, max_iteration=10000, output='mandelbrot_
mp.png'):
    """ Calculate a mandelbrot set given the width, height and
    maximum number of iterations """

    image = Image.new("RGB", (w, h))
    image_rows = pymp.shared.dict()

    with pymp.Parallel(4) as p:
```

```
        for y in p.range(0, h):
            mandelbrot_calc_row(y, w, h, image_rows, max_iteration)

    for i in range(w*h):
        x,y = i % w, i // w
        image.putpixel((x,y), image_rows[i])

    image.save(output, "PNG")
    print('Saved to',output)
```

The rewrite mainly involved converting the code to one that builds the Mandelbrot image line by line, each line of data being computed separately and in a way that it can be computed in parallel—in a separate process.

- In the single process version, we put the pixel values directly in the image in the mandelbrot_calc_row function. However, since the new code executes this function in parallel processes, we cannot modify the image data in it directly. Instead, the new code passes a shared dictionary to the function, and it sets the pixel color values in it using the location as key and the pixel RGB value as value.

- A new shared data structure—a shared dictionary—is hence added to the mandelbrot_calc_set function, which is finally iterated over, and the pixel data, filled, in the Image object, which is then saved to the final output.

- We use four PyMP parallel processes, as the machine has four CPU cores, using a with context and enclosing the outer for loop inside it. This causes the code to execute in parallel in four cores, each core calculating approximately 25% of the rows. The final data is written to the image in the main process.

Here is the result timing of the PyMP version of the code:

Timing of parallel process Mandelbrot program using PyMP—for 10000 iterations

The program is about 33% faster in real time. In terms of CPU usage, you can see that the PyMP version has a higher ratio of user CPU time to real CPU time, indicating a higher usage of the CPU by the processes than the single process version.

We can write an even more efficient version of the program by avoiding the shared data structure image_rows which is used to keep the pixel values of the image. This version however uses that to show the features of PyMP. The code archives of this book contain two more versions of the program — one that uses multiprocessing and another that uses PyMP without the shared dictionary.

This is the output fractal image produced by this run of the program:

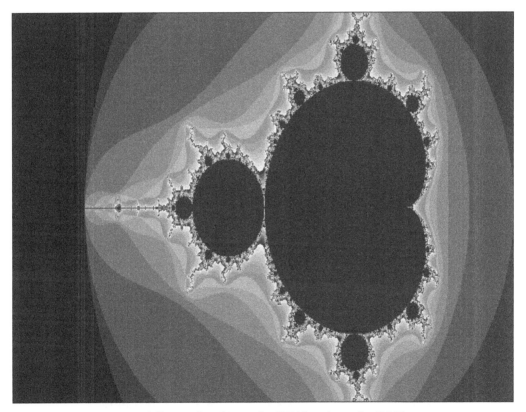

Mandelbrot set fractal image for 10000 iterations using PyMP

You can observe that the colors are different, and this image provides more detail and a finer structure than the previous one due to the increased number of iterations.

Scaling for the web

So far, all the scalability and concurrency techniques we discussed were involved with scalability within the confines of a single server or machine—in other words, scaling up. In real world, applications also scale by scaling out, that is, by spreading their computation over multiple machines. This is how most real-world web applications run and scale at present.

We will look at a few techniques, scaling out an application in terms of scaling communications/workflows, scaling computation, and horizontal scaling using different protocols.

Scaling workflows – message queues and task queues

One important aspect of scalability is to reducing coupling between systems. When two systems are tightly coupled, they prevent each other from scaling beyond a certain limit.

For example, a code written serially, where data and computation is tied into the same function, prevents the program from taking advantage of the existing resources like multiple CPU cores. When the same program is rewritten to use multiple threads (or processes) and a message passing system like a queue in between, we find it scales well to multiple CPUs. We've seen such examples aplenty in our concurrency discussion.

In a much similar way, systems over the Web scale better when they are decoupled. The classic example is the client/server architecture of the Web itself, where clients interact via well-known RestFUL protocols like HTTP, with servers located in different places across the world.

Message queues are systems that allow applications to communicate in a decoupled manner by sending messages to each other. The applications typically run in different machines or servers connected to the Internet, and communicate via queuing protocols.

One can think of a message queue as a scaled-up version of the multi-threaded synchronized queue, with applications on different machines replacing the threads, and a shared, distributed queue replacing the simple in-process queue.

Message queues carry packets of data called messages, which are delivered from the **Sending Applications** to the **Receiving Applications**. Most **Message Queues** provide **store and forward** semantics, where the message is stored on the queue till the receiver is available to process the message.

Here is a simple schematic model of a **Message Queue**:

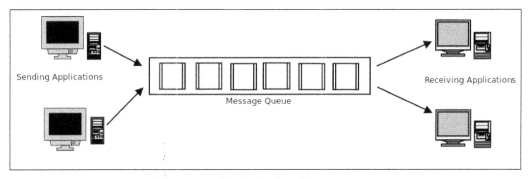

> Schematic model of a distributed message queue

The most popular and standardized implementation of a message queue or **message-oriented middleware (MoM)** is the **Advanced Message Queuing Protocol (AMQP)**. AMQP provides features such as queuing, routing, reliable delivery, and security. The origins of AMQP are in the financial industry, where reliable and secure message delivery semantics are of critical importance.

The most popular implementations of AMQP (version 1.0) are Apache Active MQ, RabbitMQ, and Apache Qpid.

RabbitMQ is a MoM written in Erlang. It provides libraries in many languages including Python. In RabbitMQ, a message is always delivered via exchanges via routing keys which indicate the queues to which the message should be delivered.

We won't be discussing RabbitMQ in this section anymore, but will move on to a related, but slightly different, middleware with a varying focus, namely, Celery.

Celery – a distributed task queue

Celery is a distributed task queue written in Python, which works using distributed messages. Each execution unit in celery is called a **task**. A task can be executed concurrently on one or more servers using processes called **workers**. By default, Celery achieves this using `multiprocessing`, but it can also use other backends such as gevent, for example.

Tasks can be executed synchronously or asynchronously with results available in the future, like objects. Also, task results can be stored in storage backend such as Redis, databases, or in files.

Celery differs from message queues in that the basic unit in celery is an executable task—a callable in Python—rather than just a message.

Celery, however, can be made to work with message queues. In fact, the default broker for passing messages in celery is RabbitMQ, the popular implementation of AMQP. Celery can also work with Redis as the broker backend.

Since Celery takes a task, and scales it over multiple workers, over multiple servers, it is suited to problems involving data parallelism as well as computational scaling. Celery can accept messages from a queue and distribute it over multiple machines as tasks for implementing a distributed e-mail delivery system, for example, and achieve horizontal scalability. Or, it can take a single function and perform parallel data computation by splitting the data over multiple processes, achieving parallel data processing.

In the following example, we will take our Mandelbrot fractal program and, rewrite it to work with Celery. We will try to scale the program by performing data parallelism, in terms of computing the rows of the Mandelbrot set over multiple celery workers—in a similar way to what we did with PyMP.

The Mandelbrot set using Celery

For implementing a program to take advantage of Celery, it needs to be implemented as a task. This is not as difficult as it sounds. Mostly, it just involves preparing an instance of the celery app with a chosen broker backend, and decorating the callable we want to parallelize—using the special decorator `@app.task` where *app* is an instance of Celery.

We will look at this program listing step by step, since it involves a few new things. The software requirements for this session are as follows:

- Celery

- An AMQP backend; RabbitMQ is preferred

- Redis as a result storage backend

First we will provide the listing for the Mandelbrot tasks module:

```python
# mandelbrot_tasks.py
from celery import Celery

app = Celery('tasks', broker='pyamqp://guest@localhost//',
             backend='redis://localhost')


@app.task
def mandelbrot_calc_row(y, w, h, max_iteration = 1000):
    """ Calculate one row of the mandelbrot set with size w x h """

    y0 = y * (2/float(h)) - 1 # rescale to -1 to 1

    image_rows = {}
    for x in range(w):
        x0 = x * (3.5/float(w)) - 2.5 # rescale to -2.5 to 1

        i, z = 0, 0 + 0j
        c = complex(x0, y0)
        while abs(z) < 2 and i < max_iteration:
            z = z**2 + c
            i += 1

        color = (i % 8 * 32, i % 16 * 16, i % 32 * 8)
        image_rows[y*w + x] = color

    return image_rows
```

Let's analyze the preceding code:

- We first do the imports required for Celery. This requires importing the `Celery` class from the `celery` module.

- We prepare an instance of the `Celery` class as the Celery app using AMQP as the message broker and Redis as the result backend. The AMQP configuration will use whatever AMQP MoM is available on the system. (In this case, it is RabbitMQ.)

- We have a modified version of `mandelbrot_calc_row`. In the `PyMP` version, the `image_rows` dictionary was passed as an argument to the function. Here, the function calculates it locally and returns a value. We will use this return value at the receiving side to create our image.

- We decorated the function using `@app.task`, where app is the `Celery` instance. This makes it ready to be executed as a Celery task by the Celery workers.

Next is the main program, which calls the task for a range of `y` input values and creates the image:

```python
# celery_mandelbrot.py
import argparse
from celery import group
from PIL import Image
from mandelbrot_tasks import mandelbrot_calc_row

def mandelbrot_main(w, h, max_iterations=1000,
output='mandelbrot_celery.png'):
    """ Main function for mandelbrot program with celery """

    # Create a job - a group of tasks
    job = group([mandelbrot_calc_row.s(y, w, h, max_iterations) for y
in range(h)])
    # Call it asynchronously
    result = job.apply_async()

    image = Image.new('RGB', (w, h))

    for image_rows in result.join():
        for k,v in image_rows.items():
            k = int(k)
            v = tuple(map(int, v))
```

```
            x,y = k % args.width, k // args.width
            image.putpixel((x,y), v)

    image.save(output, 'PNG')
    print('Saved to',output)
```

The argument parser is the same, so is not reproduced here.

This last bit of code introduces some new concepts in Celery, so needs some explanation. Let's analyze the code in some detail:

1. The `mandelbrot_main` function is similar to the previous `mandelbrot_calc_set` function in its arguments.

2. This function sets up a group of tasks, each performing `mandelbrot_calc_row` execution on a given y input over the entire range of y inputs from 0 to the height of the image. It uses the `group` object of Celery to do this. A group is a set of tasks which can be executed together.

3. The tasks are executed by calling the `apply_async` function on the group. This executes the tasks asynchronously in the background in multiple workers. We get an async `result` object in return — the tasks are not completed yet.

4. We then wait on this result object by calling `join` on it, which returns the results — the rows of the image as a dictionary from each single execution of the `mandelbrot_calc_row` task. We loop through this, and do integer conversions for the values, since Celery returns data as strings, and put the pixel values in the image.

5. Finally, the image is saved in the output file.

So, how does Celery execute the tasks? This needs the Celery program to run, processing the tasks module with a certain number of workers. Here is how we start it in this case:

```
Chapter 5 - Parallel processing
File  Edit  View  Search  Terminal  Tabs  Help
Chapter 5 - Parallel processing          ×  anand@ubuntu-pro-book: /home/user/programs/chap5
$ celery -A mandelbrot_tasks worker -c 4 --loglevel info

 -------------- celery@ubuntu-pro-book v4.0.2 (latentcall)
---- **** -----
--- * *** * -- Linux-4.4.0-57-generic-x86_64-with-Ubuntu-16.04-xenial 2017-01-17 01:55:05
-- * - **** ---
- ** ---------- [config]
- ** ---------- .> app:         tasks:0x7fee7c7e84e0
- ** ---------- .> transport:   amqp://guest:**@localhost:5672//
- ** ---------- .> results:     redis://localhost/
- *** --- * --- .> concurrency: 4 (prefork)
-- ******* ---- .> task events: OFF (enable -E to monitor tasks in this worker)
--- ***** -----
 -------------- [queues]
               .> celery               exchange=celery(direct) key=celery


[tasks]
  . mandelbrot_tasks.mandelbrot_calc_row

[2017-01-17 01:55:05,511: INFO/MainProcess] Connected to amqp://guest:**@127.0.0.1:5672//
[2017-01-17 01:55:05,519: INFO/MainProcess] mingle: searching for neighbors
[2017-01-17 01:55:06,540: INFO/MainProcess] mingle: all alone
[2017-01-17 01:55:06,583: INFO/MainProcess] celery@ubuntu-pro-book ready.
```

Celery console — workers starting up with the Mandelbrot task as target

The command starts Celery with tasks loaded from the module `mandelbrot_tasks.py` with a set of 4 worker processes. Since the machine has 4 CPU cores, we have chosen this as the concurrency.

Note that Celery will automatically default the workers to the number of cores if not specifically configured.

The program ran under 15 seconds, twice as fast in as the single-process version, and also the `PyMP` version.

If you observe the Celery console, you will find a lot of messages getting echoed, since we configured Celery with the INFO log level. All these are info messages with data on the tasks and their results:

The following screenshot shows the result of the run for 10000 iterations. This performance is slightly better than that of the similar run by the PyMP version earlier, by around 20 seconds:

Celery Mandelbrot program for a set of 10000 iterations.

Celery is used in production systems in many organizations. It has plugins for some of the more popular Python web application frameworks. For example, Celery supports Django out-of-the-box with some basic plumbing and configuration. There are also extension modules such as django-celery-results, which allow the programmer to use the Django ORM as a Celery results backend.

It is beyond the scope of this chapter and book to discuss this in detail, so the reader is advised to refer to the documentation available on this on the Celery project website.

Serving with Python on the Web – WSGI

Web Server Gateway Interface (WSGI) is a specification for a standard interface between Python web application frameworks and web servers.

In the early days of Python web applications, there was a problem connecting web application frameworks to web servers, since there was no common standard. Python web applications were designed to work with one of the existing standards of CGI, FastCGI, or mod_python (Apache). This meant that an application written to work with one web server might not be able to work with another. In other words, interoperability between the uniform application and web server was missing.

WSGI solved this problem by specifying a simple, but uniform, interface between servers and web application frameworks to allow for portable web application development.

WSGI specifies two sides: the server (or gateway) side, and the application or framework side. A WSGI request gets processed as follows:

- The server side executes the application, providing it with an environment and a callback function

- The application processes the request, and returns the response to the server using the provided callback function

Here is a schematic diagram showing the interaction between a web server and web application using WSGI:

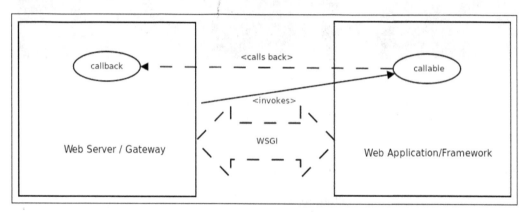

Schematic diagram showing WSGI protocol interaction

The following is the simplest function that is compatible with the application or framework side of WSGI:

```python
def simple_app(environ, start_response):
    """Simplest possible application object"""

    status = '200 OK'
    response_headers = [('Content-type', 'text/plain')]
    start_response(status, response_headers)
    return ['Hello world!\n']
```

The preceding function can be explained as follows:

1. The `environ` variable is a dictionary of environment variables passed from the server to the application as defined by the **Common Gateway Interface (CGI)** specification. WSGI makes a few of these environment variables mandatory in its specification.

2. The `start_response` is a callable provided as a callback from the server side to the application side, to start response processing on the server side. It must take two positional arguments. The first should be a status string with an integer status code, and the second, a list of (`header_name`, `header_value`), tuples describing the HTTP response header.

For more details, the reader can refer to the WSGI specification v1.0.1, which is published on the Python language website as PEP 3333.

Python Enhancement Proposal (PEP) is a design document on the Web, that describes a new feature or feature suggestion for Python, or provides information to the Python community about an existing feature. The Python community uses PEPs as a standard process for describing, discussing, and adopting new features and enhancements to the Python programming language and its standard library.

WSGI middleware components are software that implement both sides of the specification, and hence, provide capabilities such as the following:

• Load balancing of multiple requests from a server to an application
• Remote processing of requests by forwarding requests and responses over a network
• Multi-tenancy or co-hosting of multiple servers and/or applications in the same process
• URL-based routing of requests to different application objects

The middleware sits in between the server and application. It forwards requests from server to the application and responses from application to the server.

There are a number of WSGI middleware an architect can choose from. We will briefly look at two of the most popular ones, namely, uWSGI and Gunicorn.

uWSGI – WSGI middleware on steroids

uWSGI is an open source project and application, which aims to build a full stack for hosting services. The WSGI of the uWSGI project stems from the fact that the WSGI interface plugin for Python was the first one developed in the project.

Apart from WSGI, the uWSGI project also supports **Perl Webserver Gateway Interface (PSGI)** for Perl web applications, and the rack web server interface for Ruby web applications. It also provides gateways, load balancers, and routers for requests and responses. The Emperor plugin of uWSGI provides management and monitoring of multiple uWSGI deployments of your production system across servers.

The components of uWSGI can run in preforked, threaded, asynchronous. or green-thread/co-routine modes.

uWSGI also comes with a fast and in-memory caching framework, which allows the responses of the web applications to be stored in multiple caches on the uWSGI server. The cache can also be backed with a persistence store such as a file. Apart from a multitude of other things, uWSGI also supports virtualenv based deployments in Python.

uWSGI also provides a native protocol that is used by the uWSGI server. uWSGI version 1.9 also adds native support for the web sockets.

Here is a typical example of a uWSGI configuration file:

```
[uwsgi]

# the base directory (full path)
chdir           = /home/user/my-django-app/
# Django's wsgi file
module          = app.wsgi
# the virtualenv (full path)
home            = /home/user/django-virtualenv/
# process-related settings
master          = true
# maximum number of worker processes
processes       = 10
# the socket
socket          = /home/user/my-django-app/myapp.sock
# clear environment on exit
vacuum          = true
```

A typical deployment architecture with uWSGI looks like that depicted in the following diagram. In this case, the web server is Nginx, and the web application framework is Django. uWSGI is deployed in a reverse-proxy configuration with Nginx, forwarding requests and responses between Nginx and Django:

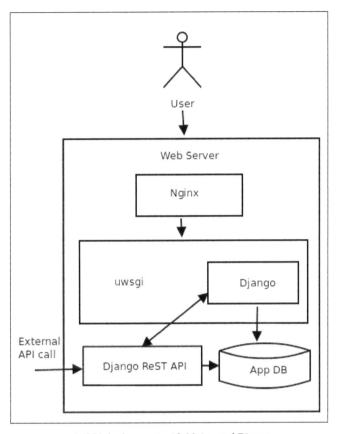

uWSGI deployment with Nginx and Django

 The Nginx web server supports a native implementation of the uWSGI protocol since version 0.8.40. There is also a proxy module support for uWSGI in Apache named `mod_proxy_uwsgi`.

uWSGI is an ideal choice for Python web application production deployments where one needs a good balance of customization with high performance and features. It is the swiss-army knife of components for WSGI web application deployments.

Gunicorn – unicorn for WSGI

The Gunicorn project is another popular WSGI middleware implementation, which is open source. It uses a preforked model, and is a ported version from the unicorn project of Ruby. There are different worker types in Gunicorn, like uWSGI supporting synchronous and asynchronous handling of requests. The asynchronous workers make use of the Greenlet library which is built on top of gevent.

There is a master process in Gunicorn that runs an event loop, processing and reacting to various signals. The master manages the workers, and the workers process the requests, and send responses.

Gunicorn versus uWSGI

Here are a few guidelines when choosing whether to go with Gunicorn or uWSGI for your Python web application deployments:

- For simple application deployments which don't need a lot of customization, Gunicorn is a good choice. uWSGI has a bigger learning curve when compared to Gunicorn, and it takes a while to get used to. The defaults in Gunicorn work pretty well for most deployments.

- If your deployment is homogenously Python, then Gunicorn is a good choice. On the other hand, uWSGI allows you to perform heterogeneous deployments due to its support for other stacks such as PSGI and Rack.

- If you want a more full-featured WSGI middleware, which is heavily customizable, then uWSGI is a safe bet. For example, uWSGI makes Python virtualenv-based deployments simple, whereas, Gunicorn doesn't natively support virtualenv; instead, Gunicorn itself has to be deployed in the virtual environment.

- Since Nginx supports uWSGI natively, it is very commonly deployed along with Nginx on production systems. Hence, if you use Nginx, and want a full-featured and highly customizable WSGI middleware with caching, uWSGI is the default choice.

- With respect to performance, both Gunicorn and uWSGI score similarly on different benchmarks published on the web.

Scalability architectures

As discussed, a system can scale vertically, or horizontally, or both. In this section, we will briefly look at a few of the architectures that an architect can choose from when deploying his systems to production to take advantage of the scalability options.

Vertical scalability architectures

Vertical scalability techniques come in the following two flavors:

- **Adding more resources to an existing system**: This could mean adding more RAM to a physical or virtual machine, adding more vCPUs to a virtual machine or VPS, and so on. However, none of these options are dynamic, as they require stopping, reconfiguring, and restarting the instance.

- **Making better use of existing resources in the system**: We have spent a lot of this chapter discussing this approach. This is when an application is rewritten to make use of the existing resources, such as multiple CPU cores, and more effectively by concurrency techniques such as threading, multiple processes, and/or asynchronous processing. This approach scales dynamically, since no new resource is added to the system, and hence, there is no need for a stop/start.

Horizontal scalability architectures

Horizontal scalability involves a number of techniques that an architect can add to his tool box, and pick and choose from. They include the ones listed next:

- **Active redundancy**: This is the simplest technique of scaling out, which involves adding multiple, homogenous processing nodes to a system typically fronted with a load balancer. This is a common practice for scaling out web application server deployments. Multiple nodes make sure that, even if one or a few of the systems fail, the remaining systems continue to carry out request processing, ensuring no downtime for your application.

  In a redundant system, all the nodes are actively in operation, though only one or a few of them may be responding to requests at a specific time.

- **Hot standby**: A hot standby (hot spare) is a technique used to switch to a system that is ready to server requests, but is not active until the moment the main system goes down. A hot spare is in many ways exactly similar to the main node(s) that is serving the application. In the event of a critical failure, the load balancer is configured to switch to the hot spare.

The hot spare itself may be a set of redundant nodes instead of just a single node. Combining redundant systems with a hot spare ensures maximum reliability and failover.

> A variation of a hot standby is a software standby, which provides a mode in the application that switches the system to a minimum **Quality of Service (QoS)** instead of offering the full feature at extreme load. An example is a web application that switches to the read-only mode under high loads, serving most users but not allowing writes.

- **Read replicas**: The response of a system that is dependent on read-heavy operations on a database can be improved by adding read-replicas of the database. Read replicas are essentially database nodes that provide hot backups (online backups), which constantly sync from the main database node. Read replicas, at a given point in time, may not be exactly consistent with the main database node, but they provide eventual consistency with SLA guarantees.

  Cloud service providers such as Amazon make their RDS database service available with a choice of read replicas. Such replicas can be distributed geographically closer to your active user locations to ensure less response time and failover in case the master node goes down, or doesn't respond.

  Read replicas basically offer your system a kind of data redundancy.

- **Blue-green deployments**: This is a technique where two separate systems (labeled `blue` and `green` in the literature) are run side by side. At any given moment, only one of the systems is active and is serving requests. For example, blue is *active*, green is *idle*.

  When preparing a new deployment, it is done on the idle system. Once the system is ready, the load balancer is switched to the idle system (green), and away from the active system (blue). At this point, green is active, and blue is idle. The positions are reversed again in the next switch.

  Blue-green deployments, if done correctly, ensure zero to minimum downtime of your production applications.

- **Failure monitoring and/or restart**: A failure monitor is a system that detects failure of critical components — software or hardware — of your deployments, and either notifies you, and/or takes steps to mitigate the downtime.

  For example, you can install a monitoring application on your server that detects when a critical component, say, a Celery or RabbitMQ server, goes down, sends an e-mail to the DevOps contact, and also tries to restart the daemon.

Heartbeat monitoring is another technique where a software actively sends pings or heartbeats to a monitoring software or hardware, which could be in the same machine or another server. The monitor will detect the downtime of the system if it fails to send the heartbeat after a certain interval, and could then inform and/or try to restart the component.

Nagios is an example of a common production monitoring server, usually deployed in a separate environment, and monitors your deployment servers. Other examples of system-switch monitors and restart components are **Monit** and **Supervisord**.

Apart from these techniques, the following best practices should be followed when performing system deployments to ensure scalability, availability, and redundancy/failover:

- **Cache it**: Use caches, and, if possible, distributed caches, in your system as much as possible. Caches can be of various types. The simplest possible cache is caching static resources on the **content delivery network (CDN)** of your application service provider. Such a cache ensures geographic distribution of resources closer to your users, which reduces response, and hence, page-load times.

  A second kind of cache is your application's cache, where it caches responses and database query results. Memcached and Redis are commonly used for these scenarios, and they provide distributed deployments, typically, in master/slave modes. Such caches should be used to load and cache most commonly requested content from your application with proper expiry times to ensure that the data is not too stale.

  Effective and well-designed caches minimize system load, and avoid multiple, redundant operations that can artificially increase load on a system and decrease performance:

- **Decouple**: As much as possible, decouple your components to take advantage of the shared geography of your network. For example, a message queue may be used to decouple components in an application that need to publish and subscribe data instead of using a local database or sockets in the same machine. When you decouple, you automatically introduce redundancy and data backup to your system, since the new components you add for decoupling—message queues, task queues, and distributed caches—typically come with their own stateful storage and clustering.

  The added complexity of decoupling is the configuration of the extra systems. However, in this day and age, with most systems being able to perform auto configuration or provide simple web-based configurations, this is not an issue.

You can refer to literature for application architectures that provide effective decoupling, such as observer patterns, mediators, and other such middleware:

- **Gracefully degrade**: Rather than being unable to answer a request and providing timeouts, arm your systems with graceful degradation behaviors. For example, a write-heavy web application can switch to the read-only mode under heavy load when it finds that the database node is not responding. Another example is when a system which provides heavy, JS-dependent dynamic web pages could switch to a similar static page under heavy loads on the server when the JS middleware is not responding well.

  Graceful degradation can be configured on the application itself, or on the load balancers, or both. It is a good idea to prepare your application itself to provide a gracefully downgraded behavior, and configure the load balancer to switch to that route under heavy loads.

- **Keep data close to the code:** A golden rule of performance-strong software is to provide data closer to where the computation is. For example, if your application is making 50 SQL queries to load data from a remote database for every request, then you are not doing this correctly.

  Providing data close to the computation reduces data access and transport times, and hence, processing times, decreasing latency in your application, and making it more scalable.

  There are different techniques for this: caching, as discussed earlier, is a favored technique. Another one is to split your database to a local and remote one, where most of the reads happen from the local read replica, and writes (which can take time) happen to a remote write master. Note that local, in this sense, may not mean the same machine, but typically, the same data center, sharing the same subnet if possible.

  Also, common configurations can be loaded from an on-disk database like SQLite or local JSON files, reducing the time it takes for preparing the application instances.

  Another technique is to not store any transactional state in the application tier or the frontend, but to move the state closer to the backend where the computation is. Since this makes all application server nodes equal in terms of not having any intermediate state, it also allows you to front them with a load-balancer, and provide a redundant cluster of equals, any of which can serve a given request.

- **Design according to SLAs**: It is very important for an architect to understand the guarantees that the application provides to its users, and design the deployment architecture accordingly.

The CAP theorem ensures that, if a network partition in a distributed system fails, the system can guarantee only one of consistency or availability at a given time. This groups distributed systems into two common types, namely, CP and AP systems.

Most web applications in today's world are AP. They ensure availability, but data is only eventually consistent, which means they will serve stale data to users in case one of the systems in the network partition, say the master DB node, fails.

On the other hand, a number of businesses such as banking, finance, and healthcare need to ensure consistent data, even if there is a network partition failure. These are CP systems. The data in such systems should never be stale, so, in case of a choice between availability and consistent data, they will choose the latter.

The choice of software components, application architecture, and the final deployment architecture are influenced by these constraints. For example, an AP system can work with NoSQL databases which guarantee eventual consistent behavior. It can make better use of caches. A CP system, on the other hand, may need ACID guarantees provided by **Relational Database Systems (RDBMs)**.

Summary

In this chapter, we reused a lot of ideas and concepts that you learned in the previous chapter on performance.

We started with a definition of scalability, and looked at its relationship with other aspects like concurrency, latency, and performance. We briefly compared and contrasted concurrency and its close cousin, parallelism.

We then went on to discuss various concurrency techniques in Python with detailed examples and performance comparisons. We used a thumbnail generator with random URLs from the Web as an example to illustrate the various techniques of implementing concurrency using multi-threading in Python. You also learned and saw an example of the producer/consumer pattern, and, using a couple of examples, learned how to implement resource constraints and limits using synchronization primitives.

Next we discussed how to scale applications using multiprocessing and saw a couple of examples using the `multiprocessing` module—such as a primality checker which showed us the effects of `GIL` on multiple threads in Python and a disk file sorting program which showed the limits of multiprocessing when it comes to scaling programs using a lot disk I/O .

We looked at asynchronous processing as the next technique of concurrency. We saw a generator based co-operative multitasking scheduler and also its counterpart using `asyncio`. We saw a couple of examples using asyncio and learned how to perform URL fetches using the aiohttp module asynchronously. The section on concurrent processing compared and contrasted concurrent futures with other options on concurrency in Python while sketching out a couple of examples.

We used Mandelbrot fractals as an example to show how to implement data parallel programs and showed an example of using `PyMP` to scale a Mandelbrot fractal program across multiple processes and hence multiple cores.

Next we went on to discuss how to scale your programs out on the Web. We briefly discussed the theoretical aspect of message queues and task queues. We looked at Celery, the Python task queue library, and rewrote the Mandelbrot program to scale using Celery workers, and did performance comparisons.

WSGI, Python's way of serving web applications over web servers, was the next topic of discussion. We discussed the WSGI specification, and compared and contrasted two popular WSGI middleware, namely, uWSGI and Gunicorn.

Towards the end of the chapter, we discussed scalability architectures, and looked at the different options of scaling vertically and horizontally on the Web. We also discussed some best practices an architect should follow while designing, implementing, and deploying distributed applications on the web for achieving high scalability.

In the next chapter, we discuss the issue of security in software architecture and discuss aspects of security the architect should be aware of and strategies for making your applications secure.

6
Security – Writing Secure Code

Security of software applications (or lack of it) has been attracting a lot of importance in the past few years in the industry and the media. It seems that every other day, we hear about an instance or two of malicious hackers causing massive data breaches in software systems in different parts of the world, and causing millions of dollars worth of losses. The victims are either government departments, financial institutions, firms handling sensitive customer data such as passwords, credit cards, and so on.

Software security and secure coding has assumed more importance than ever due to the unprecedented amounts of data being shared across software and hardware systems—the explosion of smart personal technologies such as smart phones, smart watches, smart music players, and other smart systems has aided this immense traffic of data across the Internet in a big way. With the advent of IPv6 and expected large scale adoption of **IoT** devices (**Internet of Things**) in the next few years, the amount of data is only going to increase exponentially.

As we discussed in the first chapter, security is an important aspect of software architecture. Apart from architecting systems with secure principles, architects should also try to imbibe their team with secure coding principles to minimize security pitfalls in the code written by them.

In this chapter, we will look at the principles of architecting secure systems, and also look at tips and techniques for writing secure code in Python.

The topics we will be discussing can be summed up in the following list:

- Information security architecture
- Secure coding
- Common security vulnerabilities
- Is Python secure?
  - Reading input
  - Evaluating arbitrary input
  - Overflow errors
  - Serializing objects
  - Security issues with web applications
- Strategies for Security – Python
- Secure coding strategies

Information security architecture

A secure architecture involves creating a system that is able to provide access to data and information to authorized people and systems while preventing any unauthorized access. Creating an architecture for information security for your systems involves the following aspects:

- **Confidentiality**: A set of rules or procedures that restricts the envelope of access to information in the system. Confidentiality ensures that data is not exposed to unauthorized access or modification.

- **Integrity**: Integrity is the property of the system which ensures that the information channels are trustworthy and reliable and that the system is free from external manipulations. In other words, integrity ensures the data can be trusted as it flows through the system across its components.

- **Availability**: Property that the system will ensure a level of service to its authorized users according to its **Service Level Agreements (SLAs)**. Availability ensures that the system will not deny service to its authorized users.

The three aspects of confidentiality, integrity, and availability, often called the CIA triad form the corner stones of building an information security architecture for your system.

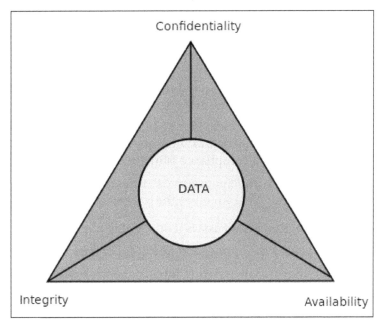

CIA triad of information security architecture

These aspects are aided by other characteristics, such as the following:

- **Authentication**: This verifies the identity of the participants of a transaction, and ensures that they are actually those who they purport to be. Examples are digital certificates used in e-mail, public keys used to log in to systems, and the like.

- **Authorization**: This gives rights to a specific user/role to perform a specific task or groups of related tasks. Authorization ensures that certain groups of users are tied to certain roles, which limit their access and modification rights in the system.

- **Non-reputability**: This refers to security techniques that guarantee that users involved in a transaction cannot later deny that the transaction happened. For example, a sender of an e-mail cannot later deny that they had sent the e-mail; a recipient of a bank funds transfer cannot later deny that they received the money, and so on.

Secure coding

Secure coding is the practice of software development that guards programs against security vulnerabilities, and makes it resistant to malicious attacks right from program design to implementation. It is about writing code that is inherently secure, as opposed to thinking of security as a layer which is added on later.

The philosophies behind secure coding include the following:

- Security is an aspect to be considered right from the design and development of a program or application; it is not an afterthought.

- Security requirements should be identified early in the development cycle, and these should be propagated to subsequent stages of development of the system to make sure that compliance is maintained.

- Use threat modeling to anticipate security threats to the system from the beginning. Threat modeling involves the following:

    1. Identifying important assets (code/data)
    2. Decomposing the application into components
    3. Identifying and categorizing threats to each asset or component
    4. Ranking the threats based on an established risk model
    5. Developing threat mitigation strategies

The practice or strategies of secure coding include the following main tasks:

1. **Definition of areas of interest of the application**: Identify important assets in code/data of the application which are critical and need to be secured.

2. **Analysis of software architecture**: Analyze the software architecture for obvious security flaws. Secure interaction between components in order to help ensure data confidentiality and integrity. Ensure confidential data is protected via proper authentication and authorization techniques. Ensure availability is built into the architecture from the ground up.

3. **Review of implementation details**: Review the code using secure coding techniques. Ensure peer review is done with a view to finding security holes. Provide feedback to the developer and make sure the required changes are made.

4. **Verification of logic and syntax**: Review code logic and syntax to ensure there are no obvious loopholes in the implementation. Make sure programming is done keeping with in commonly available secure coding guidelines of the programming language/platform.

5. **Whitebox/Unit Testing**: The developer unit tests his code with security tests apart from tests ensuring functionality. Mock data and/or APIs can be used to virtualize third party data/API required for testing.

6. **Blackbox Testing**: The application is tested by an experienced QA engineer who looks for security loopholes such as unauthorized access to data, pathways accidentally exposing code and or data, weak passwords or hashes etc. The testing reports are fed back the stakeholders including the architect to make sure the loopholes identified are fixed.

Common security vulnerabilities

So what are the common security vulnerabilities, a professional programmer today should be prepared to face and mitigate during the course of their career? Looking at the available literature, these can be organized into a few specific categories:

- **Overflow errors**: These include the popular and often abused **buffer overflow** errors, and the lesser known but still vulnerable **arithmetic or integer overflow** errors:
    - **Buffer overflow**: Buffer overflows are produced by programming errors that allow an application to write past the end or beginning of a buffer. Buffer overflows allow attackers to take control of systems by gaining access to the applications stack or heap memory by carefully crafted attack data.
    - **Integer or arithmetic overflow**: These errors occur when an arithmetic or mathematical operation on integers produces a result that is too large for the maximum size of the type used to store it.

    Integer overflows can create security vulnerabilities if they are not properly handled. In programming languages supporting signed and unsigned integers, overflows can cause the data to wrap and produce negative numbers, allowing the attacker with a result similar to buffer overflows to gain access to heap or stack memory outside the program execution limits.

- **Unvalidated/Improperly validated input**: A very common security issue with modern web applications, unvalidated input can cause major vulnerabilities, where attackers can trick a program into accepting malicious input such as code data or system commands, which, when executed, can compromise a system. A system that aims to mitigate this type of attack should have filters to check and remove content that is malicious, and only accept data that is reasonable and safe to the system.

  Common subtypes of this type of attack include SQL injections, Server-Side Template Injections, **Cross-Site-Scripting** (**XSS**), and Shell Execution Exploits.

  Modern web application frameworks are vulnerable to this kind of attack due to use of HTML templates which mix code and data, but many of them have standard mitigation procedures such as escaping or filtering of input.

- **Improper access control**: Modern day applications should define separate roles for their classes of users, such as regular users, and those with special privileges, such as superusers or administrators. When an application fails to do this or does it incorrectly, it can expose routes (URLs) or workflows (series of actions specified by specific URLs containing attack vectors), which can either expose sensitive data to attackers, or, in the worst case, allow an attacker to compromise and take control of the system.

- **Cryptography issues**: Simply ensuring that access control is in place is not enough for hardening and securing a system. Instead, the level and strength of security should be verified and ascertained; otherwise, your system can still be hacked or compromised. Some examples are as follows:

  ○ **HTTP instead of HTTPS**: When implementing RESTFul web services, make sure you favor HTTPS (SSL/TLS) over HTTP. In HTTP, all communication is in plain text between the client and server, and can be easily captured by passive network sniffers or carefully crafted packet capture software or devices installed in routers.

    Projects like letsencrypt have made life easy for system administrators for procuring and updating free SSL certificates, so securing your servers using SSL/TLS is easier these days than ever before.

° **Insecure authentication**: Prefer secure authentication techniques on a web server over insecure ones. For example, prefer HTTP Digest authentication to Basic authentication on web servers, as, in the latter, passwords are sent in the clear. Similarly, use **Kerberos** authentication in a large shared network over less secure alternatives such as **Lightweight Directory Access Protocol (LDAP)** or **NT LAN Manager (NTLM)**.

° **Use of weak passwords**: Easy-to-guess or default/trivial passwords are the bane of many modern-day web applications.

° **Reuse of secure hashes/secret keys**: Secure hashes or secret keys are usually specific to an application or project and should never be reused across applications. Whenever required, generate fresh hashes and or keys.

° **Weak encryption techniques**: Ciphers used in encrypting communication, either on the server (SSL certificates) or personal computers (GPG/PGP keys), should use high-grade security – of at least 2048 bits and use peer-reviewed and crypto-safe algorithms.

° **Weak hashing techniques**: Just as in ciphers, hashing techniques used to keep secrets and salts of sensitive data such as passwords, should be careful in choosing strong algorithms. For example, if one is writing an application that requires hashes to be computed and stored today, they would be better off using the SHA-1 or SHA-2 algorithms rather than the weaker MD5.

° **Invalid or expired certificates/keys**: Web masters often forget to keep their SSL certificates updated, and this can become a big problem, compromising the security of their web servers, as invalid certificates offer no protection. Similarly, personal keys such as GPG or PGP public/private key pairs used for e-mail communication should be kept updated.

° **Password enabled SSH**: SSH access to remote systems using clear text passwords is a security hole. Disable password-based access and only enable access via authorized SSH keys for specific users only. Disable remote root SSH access.

- **Information leak**: A lot of web servers systems—mostly due to open configuration, or misconfiguration, or due to lack of validation of inputs—can reveal a lot of information about themselves to an attacker. Some examples are as follows:

  ○ **Server meta information**: Many web servers leak information about themselves via their 404 pages, and sometimes, via their landing pages. Here is an example:

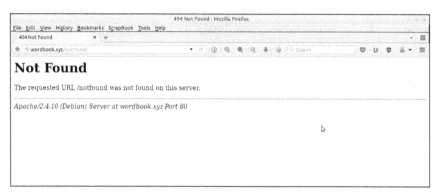

404 page of a web server exposing server meta information

By simply requesting for a non-existing page, we came to know that the site seen in the preceding screenshot runs Apache version 2.4.10 on a Debian Server. For a crafty attacker, this is often information enough to try out specific attacks for that particular web-server/OS combination.

  ○ **Open index pages**: Many websites don't protect their directory pages, and leave them open for world access. This screenshot shows an example:

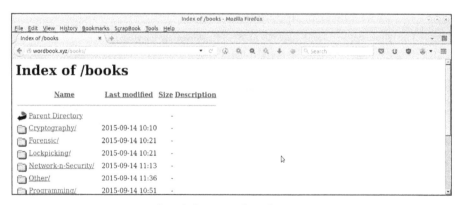

Open index page of a web server

Open ports: It is a common error to provide world-access to an application's ports running on remote web servers instead of limiting access to them by specific IP addresses or security groups by using firewalls – such as *iptables*. A similar error is to allow a service to run on 0.0.0.0 (all IP addresses on the server) for a service which is only consumed on the localhost. This makes it easy for attackers to scan for such ports using network reconnaissance tools such as `nmap/hping3`, and the like, and plan their attack.

- **Open access to files/folders/databases**: A very poor practice is to provide open or world access to application configuration files, log files, process ID files, and other artifacts so that any logged-in user can access and obtain information from these files. Instead, such files should be part of security policies to ensure that only specific roles with the required privileges have access to the files.

- **Race conditions**: A race condition exists when a program has two or more actors trying to access a certain resource, but the output depends on the correct order of access, which cannot be ensured. An example is two threads trying to increment a numerical value in shared memory without proper synchronization.

  Crafty attackers can take advantage of the situation to insert malicious code, change a filename, or sometimes, take advantage of small time gaps in the processing of code to interfere with the sequence of operations.

- **System clock drifts**: This is the phenomena on where the system or local clock time on a server slowly drifts away from the reference time due to improper or missing synchronization. Over time, the clock drift can cause serious security flaws such as error in SSL certificate validation, which can be exploited by highly sophisticated techniques like *timing attacks* where an attacker tries to take control over the system by analyzing the time taken to execute cryptographic algorithms. Time synchronization protocols like NTP can be used to mitigate this.

- **Insecure file/folder operations**: Programmers often make assumptions about the ownership, location, or attributes of a file or folder that might not be true in practice. This can result in conditions where a security flaw can occur or where we may not detect tampering with the system. Some examples are as follows:

  - Failing to check results after a write operation, assuming it succeeded
  - Assuming local file paths are always local files (whereas, they might be symbolic links to system files for which the application may not have access)

- ◦ Improperly using sudo in executing system commands, which, if not done correctly, can cause loopholes, which can be used to gain root access of the system

- ◦ Generous use of permissions on shared files or folders, for example, turning on all the execute bits of a program which should be limited to a group, or open home folders which can be read by any logged in user

- ◦ Using unsafe serialization and deserialization of code or data objects

It is beyond the scope of this chapter to visit each and every type of vulnerability in this list. However, we will make an earnest attempt to review and explain the common classes of software vulnerabilities that affect Python, and some of its web frameworks in the coming section.

Is Python secure?

Python is a very readable language with simple syntax, and typically, one clearly stated way to do things. It comes with a set of well-tested and compact standard library modules. All of this seems to indicate that Python should be a very secure language.

But is it so?

Let's look at a few examples in Python, and try to analyze the security aspect of Python and its standard libraries.

For the purposes of usefulness, we will demonstrate the code examples shown in this section using both Python 2.x and Python 3.x versions. This is because a number of security vulnerabilities that are present in Python 2.x versions are fixed in the recent 3.x versions. However, since many Python developers are still using some form or the other of Python 2.x, the code examples would be useful to them, and also illustrate the importance of migrating to Python 3.x.

All examples are executed on a machine running the Linux (Ubuntu 16.0), x86_64 architecture:

```
$ python3
Python 3.5.2 (default, Jul  5 2016, 12:43:10)
[GCC 5.4.0 20160609] on linux
Type "help", "copyright", "credits" or "license" for more information.
>>> import sys
>>> print (sys.version)
3.5.2 (default, Jul  5 2016, 12:43:10)
[GCC 5.4.0 20160609]
```

```
$ python2
Python 2.7.12 (default, Jul  1 2016, 15:12:24)
[GCC 5.4.0 20160609] on linux2
Type "help", "copyright", "credits" or "license" for more information.
>>> import sys
>>> print sys.version
2.7.12 (default, Jul  1 2016, 15:12:24)
[GCC 5.4.0 20160609]
```

> Python 3.x version used for these examples are Python 3.5.2,
> and the Python 2.x version used is Python 2.7.12. All examples
> are executed on a machine running the Linux (Ubuntu 16.0),
> 64 bit x86 architecture.
>
> Most of the examples will use one version of code, which will
> run both in Python 2.x and Python 3.x. In cases where this is
> not possible, two versions of the code will be listed.

Reading input

Let's look at this program that is a simple guessing game. It reads a number from the
standard input, and compares it with a random number. If it matches, the user wins,
otherwise, the user has to try again:

```
# guessing.py
import random

# Some global password information which is hard-coded
passwords={"joe": "world123",
           "jane": "hello123"}

def game():
    """A guessing game """

    # Use 'input' to read the standard input
    value=input("Please enter your guess (between 1 and 10): ")
    print("Entered value is",value)
```

```
        if value == random.randrange(1, 10):
            print("You won!")
        else:
            print("Try again")

    if __name__ == "__main__":
        game()
```

The preceding code is simple, except that it has some sensitive global data, which is the passwords of some users in the system. In a realistic example, these could be populated by some other functions, which read the passwords and cache them in memory.

Let's try the program with some standard inputs. We will initially run it with Python 2.7, as follows:

```
$ python2 guessing.py
Please enter your guess (between 1 and 10): 6
('Entered value is', 6)
Try again

$ python2 guessing.py
Please enter your guess (between 1 and 10): 8
('Entered value is', 8)
You won!
```

Now, let's try a "non-standard" input:

```
$ python2 guessing.py
Please enter your guess (between 1 and 10): passwords
('Entered value is', {'jane': 'hello123', 'joe': 'world123'})
Try again
```

Note how the preceding run exposed the global password data!

The problem is that in Python 2, the input value is evaluated as an expression without doing any check, and when it is printed, the expression prints its value. In this case, it happens to match a global variable, so its value is printed out.

Now let's look at this one:

```
$ python2 guessing.py
Please enter your guess (between 1 and 10): globals()
('Entered value is', {'passwords': {'jane': 'hello123',
'joe' : 'world123'}, '__builtins__': <module '__builtin__' (built-
in)>,
 '__file__': 'guessing.py', 'random':
```

```
<module 'random' from '/usr/lib/python2.7/random.pyc'>,
 '__package__': None, 'game':
<function game at 0x7f6ef9c65d70>,
 '__name__': '__main__', '__doc__': None})
Try again
```

Now, not only has it exposed the passwords, it has exposed the complete global variables in the code including the passwords. Even if there were no sensitive data in the program, a hacker using this approach can reveal valuable information about the program such as variable names, function names, packages used, and so on.

What is the fix for this? For Python 2, one solution is to replace input, which evaluates its contents by passing directly to eval, with raw_input, which doesn't evaluate the contents. Since raw_input doesn't return a number, it needs to be converted to the target type. (This can be done by casting the return data to an int.) The following code does not only that, but also adds an exception handler for the type conversion for extra safety:

```python
# guessing_fix.py
import random

passwords={"joe": "world123",
           "jane": "hello123"}

def game():
    value=raw_input("Please enter your guess (between 1 and 10): ")
    try:
        value=int(value)
    except TypeError:
        print ('Wrong type entered, try again',value)
        return

    print("Entered value is",value)
    if value == random.randrange(1, 10):
        print("You won!")
    else:
        print("Try again")

if __name__ == "__main__":
    game()
```

Let's see how this version fixes the security hole in evaluating inputs

```
$ python2 guessing_fix.py
Please enter your guess (between 1 and 10): 9
('Entered value is', 9)
Try again

$ python2 guessing_fix.py
Please enter your guess (between1 and 10): 2
('Entered value is', 2)
You won!

$ python2 guessing_fix.py
Please enter your guess (between 1 and 10): passwords
(Wrong type entered, try again =>, passwords)

$ python2 guessing_fix.py
Please enter your guess (between 1 and 10): globals()
(Wrong type entered, try again =>, globals())
```

The new program is now much more secure than the first version.

This problem is not there in Python 3.x as the following illustration shows. (We are using the original version to run this.)

```
$ python3 guessing.py
Please enter your guess (between 1 and 10): passwords
Entered value is passwords
Try again

$ python3 guessing.py
Please enter your guess (between 1 and 10): globals()
Entered value is globals()
Try again
```

Evaluating arbitrary input

The eval function in Python is very powerful, but it is also dangerous, since it allows one to pass arbitrary strings to it, which can evaluate to potentially dangerous code or commands.

Let's look at this rather silly piece of code as a test program to see what `eval` can do:

```python
# test_eval.py
import sys
import os

def run_code(string):
    """ Evaluate the passed string as code """

    try:
        eval(string, {})
    except Exception as e:
        print(repr(e))

if __name__ == "__main__":
    run_code(sys.argv[1])
```

Let's assume a scenario where an attacker is trying to exploit this piece of code to find out the contents of the directory where the application is running. (For the time being, you can assume the attacker can run this code via a web application, but hasn't got direct access to the machine itself.)

Let's assume the attacker tries to list the contents of the current folder:

```
$ python2 test_eval.py "os.system('ls -a')"
NameError("name 'os' is not defined",)
```

This preceding attack doesn't work, because `eval` takes a second argument, which provides the global values to use during evaluation. Since, in our code, we are passing this second argument as an empty dictionary, we get the error, as Python is unable to resolve the `os` name.

So does this mean, `eval` is safe? No it's not. Let's see why.

What happens when we pass the following input to the code?

```
$ python2 test_eval.py "__import__('os').system('ls -a')"
.   guessing_fix.py  test_eval.py     test_input.py
..  guessing.py      test_format.py   test_io.py
```

We can see that we are still able to coax `eval` to do our bidding by using the built-in function `__import__`.

The reason why this works is because names such as __import__ are available in the default built-in __builtins__ global. We can deny eval this by specifically passing this as an empty dictionary via the second argument. Here is the modified version:

```
# test_eval.py
import sys
import os


def run_code(string):
    """ Evaluate the passed string as code """

    try:
        # Pass __builtins__ dictionary as empty
        eval(string, {'__builtins__':{}})
    except Exception as e:
        print(repr(e))

if __name__ == "__main__":
    run_code(sys.argv[1])
```

Now the attacker is not able to exploit via the built-in __import__:

```
$ python2 test_eval.py "__import__('os').system('ls -a')"
NameError("name '__import__' is not defined",)
```

However, this doesn't still make eval any safer, as it is open to slightly longer, but clever attacks. Here is one such attack:

```
$ python2 test_eval.py "(lambda f=(lambda x: [c for c in [].__
class__.__bases__[0].__subclasses__() if c.__name__ == x][0]):
f('function')(f('code')(0,0,0,0,'BOOM',(), (),(),'','',0,''),{})())())"
Segmentation fault (core dumped)
```

We are able to core dump the Python interpreter with a rather obscure looking piece of malicious code. How did this happen ?

Here is a somewhat detailed explanation of the steps.

First, let's consider this:

```
>>> [].__class__.__bases__[0]
<type 'object'>
```

This is nothing but the base-class object. Since we don't have access to the built-ins, this is an indirect way to get access to it.

Next, the following line of code loads all the sub-classes of `object` currently loaded in the Python interpreter:

```
>>> [c for c in [].__class__.__bases__[0].__subclasses__()]
```

Among them, what we want is the `code` object type. This can be accessed by checking the name of the item via the `__name__` attribute:

```
>>> [c for c in [].__class__.__bases__[0].__subclasses__() if c.__name__ == 'code']
```

Here is the same achieved by using an anonymous `lambda` function:

```
>>> (lambda x: [c for c in [].__class__.__bases__[0].__subclasses__()
if c.__name__ == x])('code')
[<type 'code'>]
```

Next, we want to execute this code object. However, `code` objects cannot be called directly. They need to be tied to a function in order for them to be called. This is achieved by wrapping the preceding `lambda` function in an outer `lambda` function:

```
>>> (lambda f: (lambda x: [c for c in [].__class__.__bases__[0].__subclasses__() if c.__name__ == x])('code'))
<function <lambda> at 0x7f8b16a89668
```

Now our inner `lambda` function can be called in two steps:

```
>>> (lambda f=(lambda x: [c for c in [].__class__.__bases__[0].__subclasses__() if c.__name__ == x][0]): f('function')(f('code')))
<function <lambda> at 0x7fd35e0db7d0>
```

We finally invoke the `code` object via this outer `lambda` function by passing mostly default arguments. The code-string is passed as the string BOOM, which is, of course, a bogus code-string that causes the Python interpreter to segfault, producing a core-dump:

```
>>> (lambda f=(lambda x:
[c for c in [].__class__.__bases__[0].__subclasses__() if c.__name__
== x][0]):
f('function')(f('code')(0,0,0,0,'BOOM',(), (),(),'','',0,''),{})())()
Segmentation fault (core dumped)
```

This shows that `eval` in any context, even bereft of built-in module support, is unsafe, and can be exploited by a clever and malicious hacker to crash the Python interpreter, and thereby, possibly gain control over the system.

Note that the same exploit works in Python 3 as well, but we need some modification in the arguments to the `code` object, as in Python 3, `code` objects takes an extra argument. Also, the code-string and some arguments must be the `byte` type.

The following is the exploit running on Python 3. The end result is the same:

```
$ python3 test_eval.py
"(lambda f=(lambda x: [c for c in ().__class__.__bases__[0].__
  subclasses__()
  if c.__name__ == x][0]): f('function')(f('code')(0,0,0,0,0,b't\x00\
  x00j\x01\x00d\x01\x00\x83\x01\x00\x01d\x00\x00S',(),
  (),(),'','',0,b'')),{})())()"
Segmentation fault (core dumped)
```

Overflow errors

In Python 2, the `xrange()` function produces an overflow error if the range cannot fit into the integer range of Python:

```
>>> print xrange(2**63)
Traceback (most recent call last):
    File "<stdin>", line 1, in <module>
OverflowError: Python int too large to convert to C long
```

The `range()` function also overflows with a slightly different error:

```
>>> print range(2**63)
Traceback (most recent call last):
    File "<stdin>", line 1, in <module>
OverflowError: range() result has too many items
```

The problem is that `xrange()` and `range()` use plain integer objects (type `<int>`) instead of automatically getting converted to the `long` type, which is limited only by the system memory.

However, this problem is fixed in the Python 3.x versions, as types `int` and `long` are unified into one (`int` type), and the `range()` objects manage the memory internally. Also, there is no longer a separate `xrange()` object:

```
>>> range(2**63)
range(0, 9223372036854775808)
```

Here is another example of integer overflow errors in Python, this time for the `len` function.

In the following examples, we try the `len` function on instances of two classes A and B, whose magic method __len__ has been over-ridden to provide support for the `len` function. Note that A is a new-style class, inheriting from `object` and B is an old-style class:

```
# len_overflow.py

class A(object):
    def __len__(self):
        return 100 ** 100

class B:
    def __len__(self):
        return 100 ** 100


try:
    len(A())
    print("OK: 'class A(object)' with 'return 100 ** 100' - len
        calculated")
except Exception as e:
    print("Not OK: 'class A(object)' with 'return 100 ** 100' - len
        raise Error: " + repr(e))

try:
    len(B())
    print("OK: 'class B' with 'return 100 ** 100' - len calculated")
except Exception as e:
    print("Not OK: 'class B' with 'return 100 ** 100' - len raise
        Error: " + repr(e))
```

Here is the output of the code when executed with Python2:

```
$ python2 len_overflow.py
Not OK: 'class A(object)' with 'return 100 ** 100' - len raise Error:
OverflowError('long int too large to convert to int',)
Not OK: 'class B' with 'return 100 ** 100' - len raise Error:
TypeError('__len__() should return an int',)
```

The same code is executed in Python 3 as follows:

```
$ python3 len_overflow.py
Not OK: 'class A(object)' with 'return 100 ** 100' - len raise Error:
OverflowError("cannot fit 'int' into an index-sized integer",)
Not OK: 'class B' with 'return 100 ** 100' - len raise Error:
OverflowError("cannot fit 'int' into an index-sized integer",)
```

The problem in the preceding code is that `len` returns `integer` objects, and in this case, the actual value is too large to fit inside an `int`, so Python raises an overflow error. In Python 2, however, for the case when the class is not derived from `object`, the code executed is slightly different, which anticipates an `int` object, but gets `long` and throws a `TypeError` instead. In Python 3, both examples return overflow errors.

Is there a security issue with integer overflow errors such as this?

On the ground, it depends on the application code and the dependent module code used, and how they are able to deal with or mask the overflow errors.

However, since Python is written in C, any overflow errors which are not correctly handled in the underlying C code can lead to buffer overflow exceptions, where an attacker can write to the overflow buffer and hijack the underlying process, thereby gaining control over the application.

Typically, if a module or data structure is able to handle the overflow error and raise exceptions preventing further code execution, the chances of code exploitation are reduced.

Serializing objects

It is very common for Python developers to use the `pickle` module and its C implementation cousin `cPickle` for serializing objects in Python. However, both these modules allow unchecked execution of code, as they don't enforce any kind of type check or rules on the objects being serialized to verify whether it is a benign Python object or a potential command that can exploit the system.

 NOTE: In Python3, both the `cPickle` and `pickle` modules are merged into a single `pickle` module.

Here is an illustration via a shell exploit, which lists the contents of the root folder (/) in a Linux/POSIX system:

```
# test_serialize.py
import os
import pickle

class ShellExploit(object):
    """ A shell exploit class """
```

```
    def __reduce__(self):
        # this will list contents of root / folder.
        return (os.system, ('ls -al /',)

def serialize():
    shellcode = pickle.dumps(ShellExploit())
    return shellcode

def deserialize(exploit_code):
    pickle.loads(exploit_code)

if __name__ == '__main__':
    shellcode = serialize()
    deserialize(shellcode)
```

The previous code simply packages a `ShellExploit` class, which, upon pickling,
returns the command for listing the contents of the root filesystem / by way of the
`os.system()` method. The `Exploit` class thus masquerades malicious code into a
`pickle` object, which, upon unpickling, executes the code, and exposes the contents
of the root folder of the machine to the attacker. The output of the preceding code is
shown here:

Output of the shell exploit code for serializing using pickle, exposing contents of / folder.

As you can see, the output clearly lists the contents of the root folder.

What is the work-around to prevent such exploits?

First of all, don't use an unsafe module like `pickle` for serialization in your applications. Instead, rely on a safer alternative like `json` or `yaml`. If your application really is dependent on using the `pickle` module for some reason, then use sand-boxing software or code jails to create safe environments that prevent execution of malicious code on the system.

For example, here is a slight modification of the earlier code, now with a simple `chroot` jail, which prevents code execution on the actual root folder. It uses a local `safe_root/` subfolder as the new root via a context-manager hook. Note that this is a simple minded example. An actual jail would be much more elaborate than this:

```python
# test_serialize_safe.py
import os
import pickle
from contextlib import contextmanager

class ShellExploit(object):
    def __reduce__(self):
        # this will list contents of root / folder.
        return (os.system, ('ls -al /',))

@contextmanager
def system_jail():
    """ A simple chroot jail """

    os.chroot('safe_root/')
    yield
    os.chroot('/')

def serialize():
    with system_jail():
        shellcode = pickle.dumps(ShellExploit())
        return shellcode

def deserialize(exploit_code):
    with system_jail():
        pickle.loads(exploit_code)

if __name__ == '__main__':
    shellcode = serialize()
    deserialize(shellcode)
```

With this jail in place, the code executes as follows:

```
                                    Terminal                          – + ×
$ sudo python3 test_serialize_safe.py
$ ▮
```

Output of the shell exploit code for serializing using pickle, with a simple chroot jail.

No output is produced now, because this is a fake jail, and Python cannot find the ls command in the new root. Of course, in order to make this work in a production system, a proper jail should be set up, which allows programs to execute, but at the same time, prevents or limits malicious program execution.

How about other serialization formats like JSON ? Can such exploits work with them? Let's see using an example.

Here is the same serialization code written using the json module:

```python
# test_serialize_json.py
import os
import json
import datetime

class ExploitEncoder(json.JSONEncoder):
    def default(self, obj):
        if any(isinstance(obj, x) for x in (datetime.datetime,
                                            datetime.date)):
            return str(obj)

        # this will list contents of root / folder.
        return (os.system, ('ls -al /',))

def serialize():
    shellcode = json.dumps([range(10),
                            datetime.datetime.now()],
                           cls=ExploitEncoder)
    print(shellcode)
    return shellcode
```

```
def deserialize(exploit_code):
    print(json.loads(exploit_code))


if __name__ == '__main__':
    shellcode = serialize()
    deserialize(shellcode)
```

Note how the default JSON encoder has been overridden using a custom encoder named ExploitEncoder. However, as the JSON format doesn't support such serializations, it returns the correct serialization of the list passed as input:

```
$ python2 test_serialize_json.py
[[0, 1, 2, 3, 4, 5, 6, 7, 8, 9], "2017-04-15 12:27:09.549154"]
[[0, 1, 2, 3, 4, 5, 6, 7, 8, 9], u'2017-04-15 12:27:09.549154']
```

With Python3, the exploit fails as Python3 raises an exception.

```
$ python3 test_serialize_json.py
Traceback (most recent call last):
  File "test_serialize_json.py", line 27, in <module>
    shellcode = serialize()
  File "test_serialize_json.py", line 17, in serialize
    cls=ExploitEncoder)
  File "/usr/lib/python3.5/json/__init__.py", line 237, in dumps
    **kw).encode(obj)
  File "/usr/lib/python3.5/json/encoder.py", line 198, in encode
    chunks = self.iterencode(o, _one_shot=True)
  File "/usr/lib/python3.5/json/encoder.py", line 256, in iterencode
    return _iterencode(o, 0)
ValueError: Circular reference detected
$
```

Output of the shell exploit code for serializing using json, with Python3

Security issues with web applications

So far, we have seen four types of security issues with Python, namely, those with reading input, evaluating expressions, overflow errors, and serialization issues. All our examples so far have been with Python on the console.

However, almost all of us interact with web applications on a daily basis, many of which are written in Python web frameworks such as Django, Flask, Pyramid, and others. Hence, it is more likely that we are exposed to security issues in such applications. We will look at a few examples here.

Server Side Template Injection

Server Side Template Injection (SSTI) is an attack using the server-side templates of common web frameworks as an attack vector. The attack uses weaknesses in the way user input is embedded on the templates. SSTI attacks can be used to figure out internals of a web application, execute shell commands, and even fully compromise the servers.

We will see an example using a very popular web application framework in Python, namely, Flask.

The following is the sample code for a rather simple web application in Flask with an inline template:

```python
# ssti-example.py
from flask import Flask
from flask import request, render_template_string, render_template

app = Flask(__name__)

@app.route('/hello-ssti')
defhello_ssti():
    person = {'name':"world", 'secret':
'jo5gmvlligcZ5YZGenWnGcol8JnwhWZd2lJZYo=='}
    if request.args.get('name'):
        person['name'] = request.args.get('name')

    template = '<h2>Hello %s!</h2>' % person['name']
    return render_template_string(template, person=person)

if __name__ == "__main__":
    app.run(debug=True)
```

Running it on the console, and opening it in the browser allows us to play around with the `hello-ssti` route:

```
$ python3 ssti_example.py
 * Running on http://127.0.0.1:5000/ (Press CTRL+C to quit)
 * Restarting with stat
 * Debugger is active!
 * Debugger pin code: 163-936-023
```

First, let's try some benign inputs:

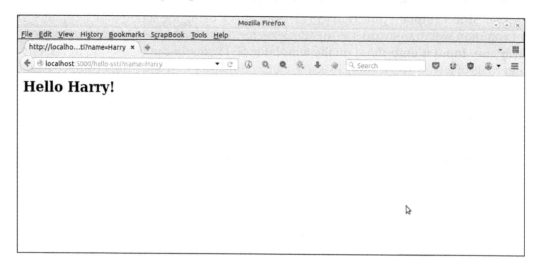

Here is another example.

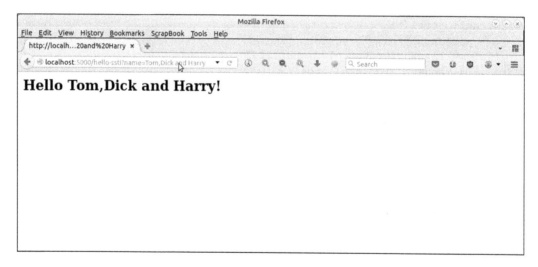

Next, let's try with some crafty inputs which an attacker may use.

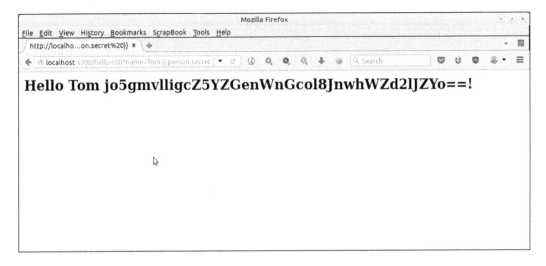

What is happening here?

Since the template uses unsafe `%s` string templates, it evaluates anything that is passed to it into Python expressions. We passed `{{ person.secret }}`, which, in the Flask templating language (Flask uses Jinja2 templating), got evaluated to the value of the key secret in the dictionary `person`, effectively exposing the secret key of the app!

We can perform even more ambitious attacks, as this hole in the code allows an attacker to try the full power of Jinja templates, including `for` loops. Here is an example:

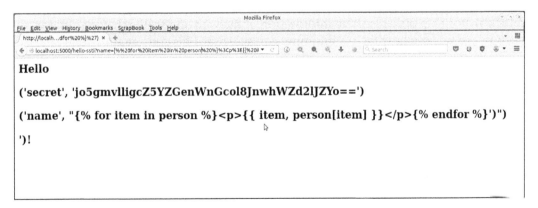

The URL used for the attack is as follows:

```
http://localhost:5000/hello-ssti?name={% for item in person %}<p>{{
item, person[item] }}</p>{% endfor %}
```

This goes through a for loop, and tries to print all contents of the `person` dictionary.

This also allows an attacker easy access to the sensitive server-side configuration parameters. For example, he can print out the Flask configuration by passing the name parameter as `{{ config }}`.

Here is the screenshot of the browser, printing the server configuration using this attack.

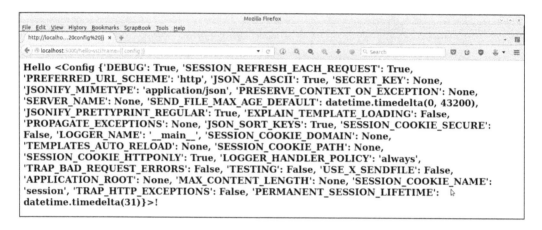

Server-Side Template Injection – Mitigation

We saw in the previous section some examples of using server side templates as an attack vector to expose sensitive information of the web application/server. In this section, we will see how the programmer can safeguard his code against such attacks.

In this specific case, the fix for this is to use the specific variable that we want in the template, rather than the dangerous, allow-all `%s` string. Here is the modified code with the fix:

```
# ssti-example-fixed.py
from flask import Flask
from flask import request, render_template_string, render_template

app = Flask(__name__)

@app.route('/hello-ssti')
defhello_ssti():
    person = {'name':"world", 'secret':
```

```
jo5gmvlligcZ5YZGenWnGcol8JnwhWZd2lJZYo=='}
    if request.args.get('name'):
        person['name'] = request.args.get('name')

    template = '<h2>Hello {{ person.name }} !</h2>'
    return render_template_string(template, person=person)

if __name__ == "__main__":
    app.run(debug=True)
```

Now the earlier attacks all fizzle off.

Here is the browser screenshot for the first attack:

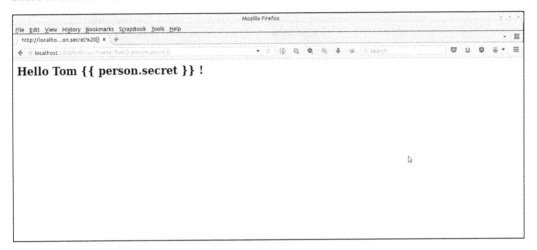

Here is the browser screenshot for the next attack.

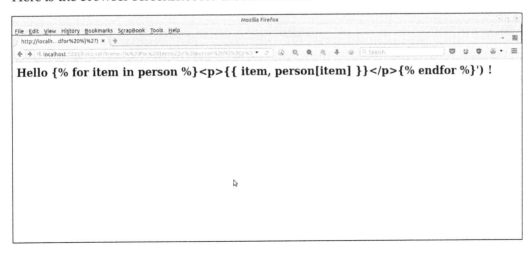

Denial of Service

Now let's look at another attack that is commonly used by malicious hackers, namely, **Denial of Service (DoS)**.

DoS attacks target vulnerable routes or URLs in a web application, and sends them crafty packets or URLs, which either force the server to perform infinite loops or CPU-intensive computations, or force it to load huge amounts of data from databases, which puts a lot of load on the server CPU, preventing the server from executing other requests.

> A DDoS or distributed DoS attack is when the DoS attack is performed in a choreographed way using multiple systems targeting a single domain. Usually thousands of IP addresses are used, which are managed via botnets.

We will see a minimal example of a DoS attack using a variation of our previous example:

```python
# ssti-example-dos.py
from flask import Flask
from flask import request, render_template_string, render_template

app = Flask(__name__)

TEMPLATE = '''
<html>
 <head><title> Hello {{ person.name }} </title></head>
 <body> Hello FOO </body>
</html>
'''

@app.route('/hello-ssti')
def hello_ssti():
    person = {'name':"world", 'secret':
'jo5gmvlligcZ5YZGenWnGcol8JnwhWZd2lJZYo=='}
    if request.args.get('name'):
        person['name'] = request.args.get('name')

    # Replace FOO with person's name
    template = TEMPLATE.replace("FOO", person['name'])
    return render_template_string(template, person=person)

if __name__ == "__main__":
    app.run(debug=True)
```

In the preceding code, we use a global template variable named TEMPLATE, and use the safer {{ person.name }} template variable as the one used with the SSTI fix. However, the additional code here is a replacement of the holding name FOO with the name value.

This version has all the vulnerabilities of the original code, even with the %s code removed. For example, take a look at the following screenshot of the browser exposing the {{ person.secret }} variable value in the body, but not in the title of the page.

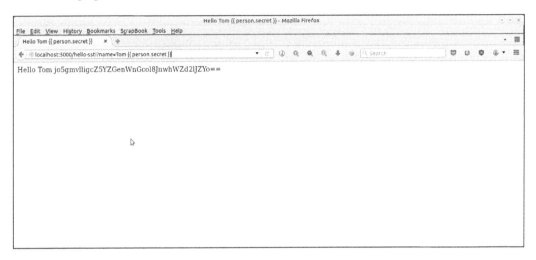

This is due to this following line of code that we added shown as follows:

```
# Replace FOO with person's name
template = TEMPLATE.replace("FOO", person['name'])
```

Any expression passed is evaluated, including the arithmetic ones. For example:

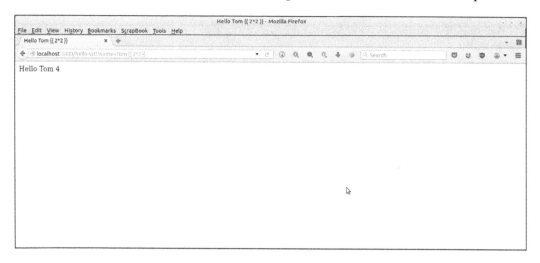

This opens up pathways to simple DoS attacks by passing in CPU-intensive computations that the server cannot handle. For example, in the following attack, we pass in a very large computation of a number, which occupies the CPU of the system, slows the system down and makes the application non-responsive:

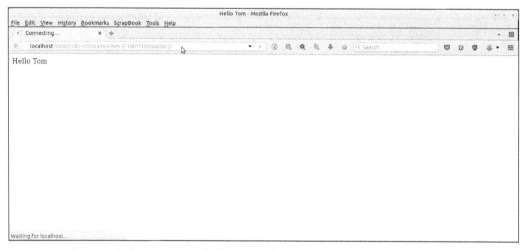

An example demonstrating a DoS style attack using computationally intensive code.

The URL used for this attack is `http://localhost:5000/hello-ssti?name=Tom {{ 100*100000000 }}`.

By passing in the arithmetical expression `{{ 100**100000000 }}`, which is computationally intensive, the server is overloaded and cannot handle other requests.

As you can see in the previous screenshot, the request never completes, and also prevents the server from responding to other requests; as you can see from how a normal request to the same application on a new tab opened on the right side is also held up causing the effect of a DoS style attack:

A new tab opened on the right side of the tab with attack vector shows
that the application has become unresponsive

Cross-Site Scripting (XSS)

The code that we used in the earlier section to demonstrate a minimalistic DOS attack is also vulnerable to script injection. Here is an illustration:

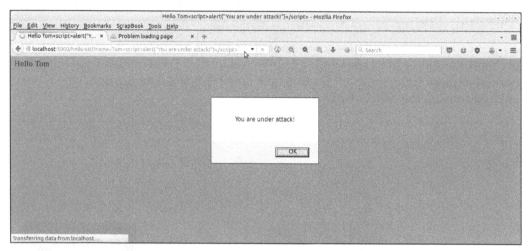

A simple demonstration of XSS scripting using server side templates and JavaScript injection

The URL used for this attack is as follows:

```
http://localhost:5000/hello-ssti?name=Tom<script>alert("You are under
attack!")</script>
```

These kinds of script injection vulnerabilities can lead to XSS, a common form of web exploit where attackers are able to inject malicious scripts into your server's code, which are loaded from other websites, and take control of it.

Mitigation – DoS and XSS

We saw a few examples of DoS attacks and simple XSS attacks in the previous section. Now let's look at how the programmer can take steps in his code to mitigate such attacks.

In the previous specific example that we have used for illustration, the fix is to remove the line that replaces the string FOO with the name value, and to replace it with the parameter template itself. For good measure, we also make sure that the output is properly escaped by using the escape filter, |e, of Jinja 2. Here is the rewritten code:

```
# ssti-example-dos-fix.py
from flask import Flask
from flask import request, render_template_string, render_template

app = Flask(__name__)

TEMPLATE = '''
<html>
 <head><title> Hello {{ person.name | e }} </title></head>
 <body> Hello {{ person.name | e }} </body>
</html>
'''

@app.route('/hello-ssti')
defhello_ssti():
    person = {'name':"world", 'secret':
'jo5gmvlligcZ5YZGenWnGcol8JnwhWZd2lJZYo=='}
    if request.args.get('name'):
        person['name'] = request.args.get('name')
    return render_template_string(TEMPLATE, person=person)

if __name__ == "__main__":
    app.run(debug=True)
```

Now that both of the vulnerabilities are mitigated, the attacks have no effect, and fail harmlessly.

Here is an screenshot demonstrating the DoS attack .

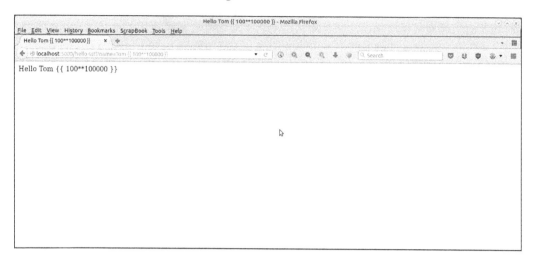

Here is the one, demonstrating the XSS attack.

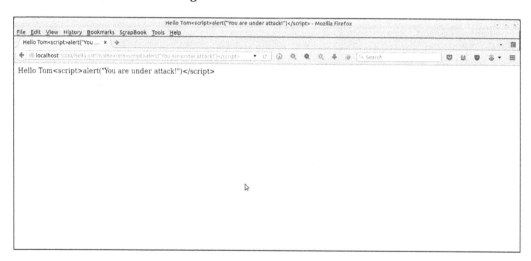

Similar vulnerabilities due to bad code in server side templates exist in other
Python web frameworks such as Django, Pyramid, Tornado, and others. However,
a step-by-step discussion on each of these is beyond the scope of this chapter. The
interested reader is directed to security resources on the web discussing such issues.

Strategies for security – Python

We have discussed quite a few vulnerabilities that exist in the core Python programming language, and also taken a look at some of the common security issues affecting Python web applications.

The time is ripe now to go through strategies—tips and techniques that a security architect can use so that their team can apply secure coding principles to mitigate security issues right from the stage of program design and development:

- **Reading input**: While reading console input, prefer raw input over `input`, as the former doesn't evaluate Python expressions, but returns input as plain strings. Any type conversions or validations should be done manually, and exceptions are thrown or errors returned if types don't match. For reading passwords, use libraries such as `getpass`, and also perform validations on the returned data. Any evaluation of the data can be safely done once the validations succeed.

- **Evaluating expressions**: As we've seen in our examples, `eval` always has loopholes whichever way it is used. Hence, the best strategy with Python is to avoid using eval and its cousin `exec`. If you have to use `eval`, make it a point to never use it with user input strings, or data read from third-party libraries, or APIs on which you have no control. Use `eval` only with input sources and return values from functions that you have control of and that you trust.

- **Serialization**: Don't use `pickle` or `cPickle` for serialization. Favor other modules such JSON or YAML. If you absolutely have to use `pickle`/`cPickle`, use mitigation strategies such as a chroot jail or sandbox to avoid the bad effects of malicious code execution, if any.

- **Overflow errors**: Guard against integer overflows by using exception handlers. Python doesn't suffer from pure buffer overflow errors, as it always checks its containers for read/write access beyond the bounds and throws exceptions. For overridden __len__ methods on classes, catch the overflow or `TypeError` exceptions as required.

- **String formatting**: Prefer the newer and safer format method of template strings over the older and unsafe `%s` interpolation.

For example:

```
def display_safe(employee):
    """ Display details of the employee instance """

    print("Employee: {name}, Age: {age},
            profession: {job}".format(**employee))

def display_unsafe(employee):
    """ Display details of employee instance """

    print ("Employee: %s, Age: %d,
            profession: %s" % (employee['name'],
                                        employee['age'],
                                        employee['job']))

>>> employee={'age': 25, 'job': 'software engineer', 'name':
'Jack'}
>>> display_safe(employee)
Employee: Jack, Age: 25, profession: software engineer
>>> display_unsafe(employee)
Employee: Jack, Age: 25, profession: software engineer
```

- **Files**: When working with files, it is a good idea to use the with context managers to make sure that the file descriptors are closed after the operation.

  For example, favor this approach:

  ```
  with open'somefile.txt','w') as fp:
  fp.write(buffer)
  ```

  And avoid the following:

  ```
  fp = open('somefile.txt','w')
  fp.write(buffer)
  ```

  This will also ensure that the file descriptor is closed if any exception occurs during file read or write instead of keeping open file handles in the system.

- **Handling passwords and sensitive information**: When validating sensitive information like passwords, it is a good idea to compare cryptographic hashes rather than comparing the original data in memory:

  ◦ This way, even if an attacker is able to pry out sensitive data from the program by exploits such as shell execution exploits or due to weaknesses in input data evaluation, the actual sensitive data is protected from immediate breach. Here is a simple approach for this:

```python
# compare_passwords.py - basic
import hashlib
import sqlite3
import getpass

def read_password(user):
    """ Read password from a password DB """
    # Using an sqlite db for demo purpose

    db = sqlite3.connect('passwd.db')
    cursor = db.cursor()
    try:
        passwd=cursor.execute("select password from passwds
where user='%(user)s'" % locals()).fetchone()[0]
        return hashlib.sha1(passwd.encode('utf-8')).
hexdigest()
    except TypeError:
        pass

def verify_password(user):
    """ Verify password for user """

    hash_pass = hashlib.sha1(getpass.getpass("Password:
").encode('utf-8')).hexdigest()
    print(hash_pass)
    if hash_pass==read_password(user):
        print('Password accepted')
    else:
        print('Wrong password, Try again')

if __name__ == "__main__":
    import sys
    verify_password(sys.argv[1])
```

A more cryptographically correct technique is to use strong password-hashing libraries with built-in `salt` and a fixed number of hashing rounds.

Here is an example using the `passlib` library in Python:

```python
# crypto_password_compare.py
import sqlite3
import getpass
from passlib.hash import bcrypt

def read_passwords():
    """ Read passwords for all users from a password DB """
    # Using an sqlite db for demo purpose

    db = sqlite3.connect('passwd.db')
    cursor = db.cursor()
    hashes = {}

    for user,passwd in cursor.execute("select user,password from passwds"):
        hashes[user] = bcrypt.encrypt(passwd, rounds=8)

    return hashes

def verify_password(user):
    """ Verify password for user """

    passwds = read_passwords()
    # get the cipher
    cipher = passwds.get(user)
    if bcrypt.verify(getpass.getpass("Password: "), cipher):
        print('Password accepted')
    else:
        print('Wrong password, Try again')

if __name__ == "__main__":
    import sys
    verify_password(sys.argv[1])
```

For the purpose of illustration, a `passwd.db` sqlite database has been created with two users and their passwords, as seen in the following screenshot:

```
Terminal                                             _  +  x
(env) $ sqlite3 passwd.db
SQLite version 3.11.0 2016-02-15 17:29:24
Enter ".help" for usage hints.
sqlite> select * from passwds;
jack|reacher123
frodo|ring123
sqlite>
```

Here is the code in action:

 Note that for purposes of clarity, the typed password is shown here—it won't be shown in the actual program, since it uses the `getpass` library.

Here is the code in action:

```
$ python3 crytpo_password_compare.py jack
Password: test
Wrong password, Try again

$ python3 crytpo_password_compare.py jack
Password: reacher123
Password accepted
```

- **Local data**: Wherever possible, avoid storing sensitive data local to functions. Any input validation or evaluation loophole in the functions can be exploited to gain access to the local stack, and hence, to the local data. Always store sensitive data encrypted or hashed separate modules.

The following is a simple illustration:

```
def func(input):
  secret='e4fe5775c1834cc8bd6abb712e79d058'
  verify_secret(input, secret)
  # Do other things
```

The above function is unsafe for the secret key 'secret', as any attacker gaining access to the function's stack can gain access to the secret as well.

Such secrets are better kept in a separate module. If you are using the secret for hashing and verification, the following code is much safer than the first, since it does not expose the original value of the 'secret':

```
# This is the 'secret' encrypted via bcrypt with eight rounds.
secret_hash='$2a$08$Q/1rMAMe14vETxJC1kmxp./JtvF4vI7/b/
VnddtUIbIzgCwA07Hty'
def func(input):
    verify_secret(input, secret_hash)
```

- **Race conditions**: Python provides an excellent set of threading primitives. If your program uses multiple threads and shared resources, follow these guidelines to synchronize access to resources to avoid race conditions and deadlocks:

    ○ Protect resources that can be writeable concurrently by a mutex (`threading.Lock`)

    ○ Protect resources that need to be serialized with respect to multiple, but limited, concurrent accesses by a semaphore (`threading.BoundedSemaphore`)

    ○ Use condition objects to wake up synchronize multiple threads waiting on a programmable condition or function (`threading.Condition`)

For programs using multiple processes, similar counterparts provided by the `multiprocessing` library should be used to manage concurrent access to resources.

- **Keep your system up to date**: Though this may sound clichéd, keeping up to date with respect to security updates of packages in your system and with security news in general, especially on packages that impact your application, is a simple way to keep your system and application secure. A number of websites provide constant updates on the state of security of a number of opensource projects including Python and its standard library modules.

These reports usually go by the name of **Common Vulnerabilities and Exposures (CVEs)** — and sites such as Mitre (`http://cve.mitre.org`) provide a constant stream of updates.

A search for Python on this sites shows 213 results:

Results for 'python' keyword search on Mitre CVE list

Architects, DevOps engineers, and webmasters can also tune in to their system package updates, and keep security updates always enabled by default. For remote severs, upgrading to the latest security patches every two to three months is highly recommended.

- Similarly, the Python **Open Web Application Security Project (OWASP)** project is a free, third-party project aimed at creating a hardened version of Python more resilient to security threats than the standard CPython. It is part of the larger OWASP initiative.

- The Python OWASP project makes available its Python bug-reports, tools, and other artifacts via the website and associated GitHub projects. The main website for this is, and most of the code is available from, the GitHub project page at: `https://github.com/ebranca/owasp-pysec/`.

Home page of the OWASP Python security project

It is a good idea for the stakeholders to keep track of this project, run their tests, and read their reports to keep up to date on Python security aspects.

Secure coding strategies

We are coming towards the end of our discussion on the security aspects of software architecture. It is a good time to summarize the strategies that one should try and impart to a software development team from a security architect's point of view. The following is a table summarizing the top 10 of these.

SL	Strategy	How it helps
1	Validate inputs	Validate inputs from all untrusted data sources. Proper input validation can eliminate a vast majority of software vulnerabilities.
2	Keep it simple	Keep program design as simple as possible. Complex designs increase the chances of security errors being made in their implementation, configuration, and deployment.
3	Principle of least privilege	Every process should execute with the least set of system privileges necessary to complete the work. For example, to read data from /tmp, one doesn't need root permission, but any unprivileged user is fine.
4	Sanitize data	Sanitize data read from and sent to all third-party systems such as databases, command shells, COTs components, third-party middlewares, and so on. This lessens the chances of SQL injection, shell exploit, or other similar attacks.
5	Authorize access	Separate parts of your application by roles that need specific authentication via login or other privileges. Don't mix different parts of applications together in the same code that requires different levels of access. Employ proper routing to make sure that no sensitive data is exposed via unprotected routes.
6	Perform effective QA	Good security testing techniques are effective in identifying and eliminating vulnerabilities. Fuzz testing, penetration testing, and source code audits should be performed as part of the program.
7	Practice defense in layers	Mitigate risks with multiple layers of security. For example, combining secure programming techniques with secure runtime configuration will reduce the chances of any remaining code vulnerabilities being exposed in the runtime environment.
8	Define security requirements	Identify and document the security constraints in the early lifecycle of the system, and keep updating them, making sure that any further features down the line keep up with these requirements.
9	Model threats	Use threat modeling to anticipate the threats to which the software will be subjected.
10	Architect and design for security policies	Create and maintain a software architecture that enforces a pattern of consistent security policies across your system and its subsystems.

Summary

In this chapter, we started by looking at the details of a system architecture that has information security built-in. We went on to define **secure coding**, and looked at the philosophies and principles behind the practice of secure coding.

We then studied the different types of security vulnerabilities encountered in software systems, such as buffer overflows, input validation issues, access control issues, cryptographic weaknesses, information leaks, insecure file operations, and so on.

We then went on to a detailed discussion on Python security issues with a lot of examples. We looked in detail at reading and evaluating input, overflow errors, and serialization issues. We then went on to look at the common vulnerabilities in Python web application frameworks by using Flask as the web application server for illustration. We saw how one can exploit the weaknesses on web application templates, and perform attacks such as SSTI, XSS, and DoS. We also saw few examples of how to mitigate these attacks.

We then went on to list specific techniques in Python for writing secure code. We looked in detail at managing cryptographic hashes of passwords and other sensitive data in code, and discussed a couple of examples of doing this the right way. The importance of keeping oneself updated with security news and projects, and keeping the system updated with security patches was also mentioned.

Finally, we summarized the top 10 secure coding strategies that a security architect can impart to their team in order to create secure code and systems.

In the next chapter, we take a look at one of the most interesting aspects of software engineering and design, namely that of Design Patterns.

7
Design Patterns in Python

Design patterns simplify building software by reusing successful designs and architectures. Patterns build on the collective experience of software engineers and architects. When faced with a problem that needs new code to be written, an experienced software architect tends to make use of the rich ecosystem of available design/architecture patterns.

Patterns evolve when a specific design proves successful in solving certain classes of problem repeatedly. When experts find that a specific design or architecture helps them to solve classes of related problems consistently, they tend to apply it more and more, codifying the structure of the solution into a pattern.

Python (given that it's a language which supports dynamic types and high-level object oriented structures such as classes and metaclasses, first-class functions, co-routines, callable objects, and so on) is a very rich playground for constructing reusable design and architecture patterns. In fact, as opposed to languages such as C++ or Java, you often find there are multiple ways of implementing a specific design pattern in Python. Also, more often than not, you find that the Pythonic way of implementing a pattern is more intuitive and illustrative than, say, copying a standard implementation from C++/Java into Python.

This chapter's focus is mostly on this latter aspect — illustrating how one can build design patterns which are more Pythonic than those in the usual books and literature on this topic. It doesn't aim to be a comprehensive guide to design patterns, though we would be covering most of the usual aspects as we head into the content.

The topics we plan to cover in this chapter are as follows:

- Design patterns elements
- Categories of design patterns
- Pluggable hashing algorithms
- Summing up pluggable hashing algorithms

- Patterns in Python – Creational
  - ° The Singleton pattern
  - ° The Borg pattern
  - ° The Factory pattern
  - ° The Prototype pattern
  - ° The Builder pattern

- Patterns in Python – Structural
  - ° The Adapter pattern
  - ° The Facade pattern
  - ° The Proxy pattern

- Patterns in Python – Behavioral
  - ° The Iterator pattern
  - ° The Observer pattern
  - ° The State pattern

Design patterns – elements

A design pattern attempts to record those aspects of a recurring design in object-oriented systems that solve a problem or a class of problems.

When we inspect design patterns, we find that almost all of them have the following elements:

- **Name**: A well-known handle or title, which is commonly used to describe the pattern. Having standard names for design patterns aids communication and increases our design vocabulary.

- **Context**: This is the situation in which the problem arises. A context can be generic such as *Develop a web application software,* or specific such as *Implementing resource-change notification in a shared memory implementation of the publisher-subscriber system.*

- **Problem**: Describes the actual problem that the pattern is applied to. A problem can be described in terms of its forces, which are as follows:

  ○ **Requirements**: The requirements that the solution should fulfill, for example, the *publisher-subscriber pattern implementation must support HTTP.*

  ○ **Constraints**: The constraints to the solution, if any, for example, the *Scalable peer-to-peer publisher pattern should not exchange more than three messages for publishing a notification.*

  ○ **Properties**: The properties of the solution which are desirable to have, for example, *The solution should work equally well on the Windows and Linux platforms.*

- **Solution**: Shows the actual solution to the problem. It describes the structure and responsibilities, the static relationships, and the runtime interactions (collaborations) of the elements making up the solution. A solution should also discuss which *forces* of the problem it solves and doesn't solve. A solution should also try to mention its consequences, that is, the results and trade-offs of applying a pattern.

 A design pattern solution almost never resolves all the forces of the problem leading to it, but leaves some of them open to related or alternate implementations.

Categories of design patterns

Design patterns can be categorized in different ways according to the criteria chosen. A commonly accepted way of categorizing patterns is based on their purpose. In other words, we ask the pattern what class of problem the pattern solves.

This kind of categorization gives us three neat varieties of pattern classes. These are as follows:

- **Creational**: These patterns solve the problems associated with object creation and initialization. These are problems that occur the earliest in the life cycle of problem solving with objects and classes. Take a look at the following examples:

  ○ **The Factory pattern**: The "How do I make sure I can create related class instances in a repeatable and predictable fashion?" question is solved by the Factory class of patterns.

○ **The Prototype pattern**: The "What is a smart approach to instantiate an object, and then create hundreds of similar objects by just copying across this one object ?" question is solved by Prototype patterns.

○ **Singleton and related patterns**: The "How do I make sure that any instance of a class I create is created and initialized just once" or "How do I make sure that any instances of a class share the same initial state ?" questions are solved by the Singleton and related patterns.

- **Structural**: These patterns concern themselves with the composition and assembling of objects into meaningful structures, which provides the architect and developer with reusable behaviors, where "the whole is more than the sum of its parts". Naturally, they occur in the next step of problem solving with objects, once they are created. Examples of such problems are as follows:

○ **The Proxy pattern**: "How do I control access to an object and its methods via a wrapper, behavior on top?"

○ **The Composite pattern**: "How can I represent an object which is made of many components at the same time using the same class for representing the part and the whole — for example, a Widget tree ?"

- **Behavioral**: These patterns solve the problems originating with runtime interactions of objects, and how they distribute responsibilities. Naturally, they occur at a later stage, once the classes are created, and then combined into larger structures. The following are a couple of examples:

○ **Using the Median pattern in the following case**: "Ensure that all the objects use loose coupling to refer to each other at runtime to promote run-time dynamism for interactions"

○ **Using the Observer pattern in the following case**: "An object wants to be notified when the state of a resource changes, but it does not want to keep polling the resource to find this out. There may be many such instances of objects in the system"

The order of Creational, Structural, and Behavioral patterns implicitly embeds the life cycle of objects in a system at runtime. Objects are first created (Creational), then combined into useful structures (Structural), and then they interact (Behavioral).

Let's now turn our attention to the subject of this chapter, namely, implementing patterns in Python in Python's own inimitable way. We will look at an illustrative example to get started.

Pluggable hashing algorithms

Let's look at the following problem.

You want to read data from an input stream—a file or network socket—and hash the contents in a chunked manner. You write some code as follows:

```
# hash_stream.py
from hashlib import md5

def hash_stream(stream, chunk_size=4096):
    """ Hash a stream of data using md5 """

    shash = md5()

    for chunk in iter(lambda: stream.read(chunk_size), ''):
        shash.update(chunk)

    return shash.hexdigest()
```

 All code is in Python3, unless explicitly mentioned otherwise.

```
>>> import hash_stream
>>> hash_stream.hash_stream(open('hash_stream.py'))
'e51e8ddf511d64aeb460ef12a43ce480'
```

So that works, as expected.

Now let's say you want a more reusable and versatile implementation, one that will work with multiple hashing algorithms. You first attempt to modify the previous code, but quickly realize that this means rewriting a lot of code, which is not a very smart way of doing it:

```
# hash_stream.py
from hashlib import sha1
from hashlib import md5

def hash_stream_sha1(stream, chunk_size=4096):
```

```
        """ Hash a stream of data using sha1 """

        shash = sha1()

        for chunk in iter(lambda: stream.read(chunk_size), ''):
            shash.update(chunk.encode('utf-8'))

        return shash.hexdigest()

    def hash_stream_md5(stream, chunk_size=4096):
        """ Hash a stream of data using md5 """

        shash = md5()

        for chunk in iter(lambda: stream.read(chunk_size), ''):
            shash.update(chunk.encode('utf-8'))

        return shash.hexdigest()
```

```
>>> import hash_stream
>>> hash_stream.hash_stream_md5(open('hash_stream.py'))
'e752a82db93e145fcb315277f3045f8d'
>>> hash_stream.hash_stream_sha1(open('hash_stream.py'))
'360e3bd56f788ee1a2d8c7eeb3e2a5a34cca1710'
```

You realize that you can reuse a lot of code by using a class. Being an experienced programmer, you may end up with something like the following after a few iterations:

```
# hasher.py
class StreamHasher(object):
    """ Stream hasher class with configurable algorithm """

    def __init__(self, algorithm, chunk_size=4096):
        self.chunk_size = chunk_size
        self.hash = algorithm()

    def get_hash(self, stream):

        for chunk in iter(lambda: stream.read(self.chunk_size), ''):
            self.hash.update(chunk.encode('utf-8'))

        return self.hash.hexdigest()
```

First let's try this with md5, as follows:

```
>>> import hasher
>>> from hashlib import md5
>>> md5h = hasher.StreamHasher(algorithm=md5)
>>> md5h.get_hash(open('hasher.py'))
'7d89cdc1f11ec62ec918e0c6e5ea550d'
```

Now let's use sha1:

```
>>> from hashlib import sha1
>>> shah_h = hasher.StreamHasher(algorithm=sha1)
>>> shah_h.get_hash(open('hasher.py'))
'1f0976e070b3320b60819c6aef5bd6b0486389dd'
```

As must be evident by now, you can build different hasher objects, each with a specific algorithm, which will return the corresponding hash digest of the stream (in this case, a file).

Now lets summarize what we just did here.

We first developed a function, hash_stream, which took in a stream object, and hashed it chunk-wise using the md5 algorithm. We then developed a class named StreamHasher, which allowed us to configure it using one algorithm at a time, thereby making the code more reusable. We obtained the hash digest by way of get_hash, which accepts the stream object as argument.

Now let's turn our attention to what else Python can do for us.

Our class is versatile with respect to different hashing algorithms, and is definitely more reusable, but is there a way to call it as if it were a function? That would be rather neat, wouldn't it?

The following is a slight reimplementation of our StreamHasher class, which does just that:

```
# hasher.py
class StreamHasher(object):
    """ Stream hasher class with configurable algorithm """

    def __init__(self, algorithm, chunk_size=4096):
        self.chunk_size = chunk_size
        self.hash = algorithm()

    def __call__(self, stream):
```

```
        for chunk in iter(lambda: stream.read(self.chunk_size), ''):
            self.hash.update(chunk.encode('utf-8'))

        return self.hash.hexdigest()
```

What did we do in the last code ? We simply renamed the `get_hash` function to `Get_Call`. Let's see what effect this has:

```
>>> from hashlib import md5, sha1
>>> md5_h = hasher.StreamHasher(md5)
>>> md5_h(open('hasher.py'))
'ad5d5673a3c9a4f421240c4dbc139b22'
>>> sha_h = hasher.StreamHasher(sha1)
>>> sha_h(open('hasher.py'))
'd174e2fae1d6e1605146ca9d7ca6ee927a74d6f2'
```

We are able to call the instance of the class as if it were a function by simply passing the file object to it.

So our class not only gives us reusable and versatile code, but also acts as if it were a function. This is done by making our class a callable type in Python by simply implementing the magic method `__call__`.

Callables in Python are any object that can be called. In other words, x is a callable if we can perform x() — with or without params, depending upon how the `__call__` method is overridden. Functions are the simplest and most familiar callables.

In Python, `foo(args)` is syntactic sugar for `foo.__call__(args)`.

Summing up pluggable hashing algorithm

So what does the previous example illustrate? It illustrates the power of Python in dealing with an existing problem, which would be solved traditionally in other programming languages, in a more exotic and powerful way due to the power of Python and the way it does things — in this case, by making any object callable by overriding a special method.

But what is the pattern we have achieved here? We said at the start of the chapter that something is a pattern only if it solves a class of problems. Is there a pattern hidden in this particular illustration?

Yes there is — this is an implementation of the Strategy behavioral pattern:

The Strategy pattern is used when we need different behaviors from a class and we should be able to configure a class with one of many available behaviors or algorithms.

In this particular case, we needed a class which supports different algorithms to perform the same thing — hashing data from a stream using chunks, and returning the digest. The class accepted the algorithm as a parameter, and since all algorithms support the same method for returning data (the `hexdigest` method), we were able to implement the class in a very simple way.

Let's continue our journey to discover some other interesting patterns we can write using Python, and its unique way of solving problems. We will follow the order of the Creational, Structural, and Behavioral patterns in this journey.

> Our approach to the discussion on patterns that follows is very pragmatic. It may not use the formal language used by the popular **Gang-of-Four (G4)** patterns — the most elemental approach to design patterns. Our focus is on demonstrating the power of Python in building patterns rather than getting the formalisms right.

Patterns in Python – creational

In this section, we will take a look at a few of the common creational patterns. We will start with Singleton, and then go on to Prototype, Builder, and Factory, in that order.

The Singleton pattern

The Singleton pattern is one of the most well-known and easily understood patterns in the entire pantheon of design patterns. It is usually defined as:

A Singleton is a class which has only one instance and a well-defined point of access to it.

The requirements of a Singleton can be summarized as follows:

- A class must have only one instance accessible via a well-known access point.
- The class must be extensible by inheritance without breaking the pattern.
- The simplest Singleton implementation in Python is shown next. It is done by overriding the `__new__` method of the base object type:

  ```
  # singleton.py
  class Singleton(object):
  ```

```
""" Singleton in Python """

_instance = None

def __new__(cls):
    if cls._instance == None:
        cls._instance = object.__new__(cls)
    return cls._instance
```

```
>>> from singleton import Singleton
>>> s1 = Singleton()
>>> s2 = Singleton()
>>> s1==s2
True
```

- Since we would be requiring this check for a while, let's define a function for the same:

```
def test_single(cls):
    """ Test if passed class is a singleton """
    return cls() == cls()
```

- Now let's see if our Singleton implementation satisfies the second requirement. We will define a simple subclass to test this:

```
class SingletonA(Singleton):
    pass

>>> test_single(SingletonA)
True
```

Cool! So our simple implementation passes the test. Are we done here now?

Well, the point with Python, as we discussed before, is that it provides a number of ways to implement patterns due to its dynamism and flexibility. So, let's stay with with Singleton for a while, and see if we can get some illustrative examples which would give us insights into the power of Python:

```
class MetaSingleton(type):
    """ A type for Singleton classes (overrides __call__) """

    def __init__(cls, *args):
        print(cls,"__init__ method called with args", args)
        type.__init__(cls, *args)
```

```
            cls.instance = None

    def __call__(cls, *args, **kwargs):
        if not cls.instance:
            print(cls,"creating instance", args, kwargs)
            cls.instance = type.__call__(cls, *args, **kwargs)
        return cls.instance

class SingletonM(metaclass=MetaSingleton):
    pass
```

The preceding implementation moves the logic of creating a Singleton to the type of the class, namely, its metaclass.

We first create a type for Singletons, named `MetaSingleton`, by extending the type and overriding the `__init__` and `__call__` methods on the metaclass. Then we declare that the `SingletonM` class, `SingletonM`, uses the metaclass.

```
>>> from singleton import *
<class 'singleton.SingletonM'> __init__ method called with args
('SingletonM', (), {'__module__': 'singleton', '__qualname__':
'SingletonM'})
>>> test_single(SingletonM)
<class 'singleton.SingletonM'> creating instance ()
True
```

The following is a peep into what is happening behind the scenes in the new implementation of the Singleton:

- **Initializing a class variable**: We can either do it at the class level (just after the class declaration) as we saw in the previous implementation, or we can put it in the metaclass `__init__` method. This is what we are doing here for the `_instance` class variable, which will hold the single instance of the class.

- **Overriding class creation**: One can either do it at the class level by overriding the `__new__` method of class as we saw in previous implementation, or, equivalently, we can do it in the metaclass by overriding its `__call__` method. This is what the new implementation does.

 When we override a class's `__call__` method, it affects its instance, and instances become callable. Similarly, when we override a metaclass's `_call_` method, it affects its classes, and modifies the way the classes are called – in other words, the way the class creates its instances.

Let's take a look at the pros and cons in the metaclass approach over the class approach:

- One benefit is that we can create any number of new top-level classes which get the Singleton behavior via the metaclass. Using the default implementation, every class has to inherit the top-level class Singleton or its subclasses to obtain the Singleton behavior. The metaclass approach provides more flexibility with respect to class hierarchies.

- However, the metaclass approach can be interpreted as creating slightly obscure and difficult-to-maintain code as opposed to the class approach. This is because fewer Python programmers understand metaclasses and metaprogramming when compared to those who understand classes. This may be a disadvantage with the metaclass solution.

Now let's think out of the box, and see if we can solve the Singleton problem in a slightly different way.

The Singleton – do we need a Singleton?

Let's paraphrase the first requirement of a Singleton in a slightly different way:

A class must provide a way for all its instances to share the same initial state.

To explain that, let's briefly look at what a Singleton pattern actually tries to achieve.

When a Singleton ensures it has only one instance, what it guarantees is that the class provides one single state when it is created and initialized. In other words, what a Singleton actually gives is a way for a class to ensure a single shared state across all its instances.

In other words, the first requirement of the Singleton pattern can be paraphrased in a slightly different form, which has the same end result as the first form.

A class must provide a way for all its instances to share the same initial state.

The technique of ensuring just a single actual instance at a specific memory location is just one way of achieving this.

Ah! So what has been happening so far is that we have been expressing the pattern in terms of the implementation details of less flexible and versatile programming languages. With a language such as Python, we need not stick pedantically to this original definition.

Let's look at the following class:

```
class Borg(object):
    """ I am not a Singleton """

    __shared_state = {}
    def __init__(self):
        self.__dict__ = self.__shared_state
```

This pattern ensures that when you create a class, you specifically initialize all of its instances with a shared state which belongs to the class (since it is declared at the class level).

What we really care about in a Singleton is actually this shared state, so `Borg` works without worrying about all instances being exactly the same.

Since this is Python, it does this by initializing a shared state dictionary on the class, and then instantiating the instance's dictionary to this value, thereby ensuring that all instances share the same state.

The following is a specific example of `Borg` in action:

```
class IBorg(Borg):
    """ I am a Borg """

    def __init__(self):
        Borg.__init__(self)
        self.state = 'init'

    def __str__(self):
        return self.state

>>> i1 = IBorg()
>>> i2 = IBorg()
>>> print(i1)
init
>>> print(i2)
init
>>> i1.state='running'
>>> print(i2)
running
>>> print(i1)
running
>>> i1==i2
False
```

By using `Borg`, we managed to create a class whose instances share the same state, even though the instances are actually not the same. And the state change was propagated across the instances; as the preceding example shows, when we change the value of state in `i1`, it also changes in `i2`.

What about dynamic values? We know they will work in a Singleton, since it's the same object always, but what about the Borg?

```
>>> i1.x='test'
>>> i2.x
'test'
```

So we attached a dynamic attribute `x` to instance `i1`, and it appeared in instance `i2` as well. Neat!

So let's see if `Borg` offers any benefits over Singleton:

- In a complex system where we may have multiple classes inheriting from a root Singleton class, it may be difficult to impose the requirement of a single instance due to import issues or race conditions — for example, if a system is using threads. The Borg pattern circumvents these problems neatly by doing away with the requirement for a single instance in memory.

- The Borg pattern also allows for simple sharing of state across the Borg class and all its subclasses. This is not the case for a Singleton, since each subclass creates its own state. We will see an example illustrating this next.

State sharing – Borg versus Singleton

A Borg pattern always shares the same state from the top class (Borg) down to all the subclasses. This is not the case with a Singleton. Let's see an illustration.

For this exercise, we will create two subclasses of our original Singleton class, namely, `SingletonA` and `SingletonB`:

```
>>> class SingletonA(Singleton): pass
...
>>> class SingletonB(Singleton): pass
...
```

Let's create a subclass of `SingletonA`, namely, `SingletonA1`:

```
>>> class SingletonA1(SingletonA): pass
...
```

Now let's create instances:

```
>>> a = SingletonA()
>>> a1 = SingletonA1()
>>> b = SingletonB()
```

Let's attach a dynamic property, x, with a value 100 to a:

```
>>> a.x = 100
>>> print(a.x)
100
```

Let's check if this is available on the a1 instance of the SingletonA1 subclass:

```
>>> a1.x
100
```

Good! Now let's check if it is available on the b instance:

```
>>> b.x
Traceback (most recent call last):
  File "<stdin>", line 1, in <module>
AttributeError: 'SingletonB' object has no attribute 'x'
```

Oops! So, it appears that SingletonA and SingletonB don't share the same state. This is why a dynamic attribute that is attached to an instance of SingletonA appears in the instance of its sub-classes, but doesn't appear on the instance of a sibling or peer subclass namely SingletonB – because it is a different branch of the class hierarchy from the top-level Singleton class.

Let's see if Borgs can do any better.

First, let's create the classes and their instances:

```
>>> class ABorg(Borg):pass
...
>>> class BBorg(Borg):pass
...
>>> class A1Borg(ABorg):pass
...
>>> a = ABorg()
>>> a1 = A1Borg()
>>> b = BBorg()
```

Now let's attach a dynamic attribute x to a with value 100:

```
>>> a.x = 100
>>> a.x
100
>>> a1.x
100
```

Let's check if the instance of the sibling class Borg also gets it:

```
>>> b.x
100
```

This proves that the Borg pattern is much better at state sharing across classes and sub classes than the Singleton pattern, and it does so without a lot of fuss or the overhead of ensuring a single instance.

Let's now move on to other creational patterns.

The Factory pattern

The Factory pattern solves the problem of creating instances of related classes to another class, which usually implements instance creation via a single method, usually defined on a parent Factory class and overridden by subclasses (as needed).

The Factory pattern provides a convenient way for the client (user) of a class to provide a single entry point to create instances of classes and subclasses, usually, by passing in parameters to a specific method of the `Factory` class: the factory method.

Let's look at a specific example:

```
from abc import ABCMeta, abstractmethod

class Employee(metaclass=ABCMeta):
    """ An Employee class """

    def __init__(self, name, age, gender):
        self.name = name
        self.age = age
        self.gender = gender

    @abstractmethod
```

```python
    def get_role(self):
        pass

    def __str__(self):
        return "{} - {}, {} years old {}".format(self.__class__.
            __name__,
                                                 self.name,
                                                 self.age,
                                                 self.gender)

class Engineer(Employee):
    """ An Engineer Employee """

    def get_role(self):
        return "engineering"

class Accountant(Employee):
    """ An Accountant Employee """

    def get_role(self):
        return "accountant"

class Admin(Employee):
    """ An Admin Employee """

    def get_role(self):
        return "administration"
```

We have created a general `Employee` class with some attributes and three subclasses, namely, `Engineer`, `Accountant`, and `Admin`.

Since all of them are related classes, a `Factory` class is useful to abstract away the creation of instances of these classes.

The following is our `EmployeeFactory` class:

```python
class EmployeeFactory(object):
    """ An Employee factory class """

    @classmethod
    def create(cls, name, *args):
```

```
""" Factory method for creating an Employee instance """

name = name.lower().strip()

if name == 'engineer':
    return Engineer(*args)
elif name == 'accountant':
    return Accountant(*args)
elif name == 'admin':
    return Admin(*args)
```

The class provides a single create factory method that accepts a name parameter, which is matched to the class's name and instance created accordingly. The rest of the arguments are parameters required for instantiating the class's instance, which is passed unchanged to its constructor.

Let's see our Factory class in action:

```
>>> factory = EmployeeFactory()
>>> print(factory.create('engineer','Sam',25,'M'))
Engineer - Sam, 25 years old M
>>> print(factory.create('engineer','Tracy',28,'F'))
Engineer - Tracy, 28 years old F

>>> accountant = factory.create('accountant','Hema',39,'F')
>>> print(accountant)

Accountant - Hema, 39 years old F
>>> accountant.get_role()

accounting
>>> admin = factory.create('Admin','Supritha',32,'F')
>>> admin.get_role()
'administration'
```

The following are a few interesting notes about our Factory class:

- A single factory class can create instances of any class in the Employee hierarchy.
- In the Factory pattern, it is conventional to use one Factory class associated to a class family (a class and its subclass hierarchy). For example, a Person class could use a PersonFactory, an automobile class could use AutomobileFactory, and so on.

- The factory method is usually decorated as a `classmethod` in Python. This way it can be called directly via the class namespace. For example:

```
>>> print(EmployeeFactory.create('engineer','Vishal',24,'M'))
Engineer - Vishal, 24 years old M
```

In other words, an instance of the `Factory` class is really not required for this pattern.

The Prototype pattern

The Prototype design pattern allows a programmer to create an instance of a class as a template instance, and then create new instances by copying or cloning this Prototype.

A Prototype is most useful in the following cases:

- When the classes instantiated in a system are dynamic, that is, they are specified as part of a configuration, or can otherwise change at runtime.
- When the instances only have a few combinations of initial state. Rather than keeping track of the state and instantiating an instance each time, it is more convenient to create prototypes matching each state and clone them.

A Prototype object usually supports copying itself via the `clone` method.

The following is a simple implementation of the Prototype in Python:

```
import copy

class Prototype(object):
    """ A prototype base class """

    def clone(self):
        """ Return a clone of self """
        return copy.deepcopy(self)
```

The `clone` method is implemented using the `copy` module, which performs a deepcopy on the object? and returns a clone.

Let's see how this works. For that, we need to create a meaningful subclass:

```python
class Register(Prototype):
    """ A student Register class """

    def __init__(self, names=[]):
        self.names = names


>>> r1=Register(names=['amy','stu','jack'])
>>> r2=r1.clone()
>>> print(r1)
<prototype.Register object at 0x7f42894e0128>
>>> print(r2)
<prototype.Register object at 0x7f428b7b89b0>


>>> r2.__class__
<class 'prototype.Register'>
```

Prototype – deep versus shallow copy

Now let's take a deeper look at the implementation details of our Prototype class.

You may notice that we use the deepcopy method of the copy module to implement our object cloning. This module also has a copy method, which implements shallow copying.

If you implement shallow copying, you will find that all objects are copied via a reference. This is fine for immutable objects such as strings or tuples, as they can't be changed.

However, for mutables such as lists or dictionaries, this is a problem since the state of the instance is shared instead of being wholly owned by the instance, and any modification of a mutable in one instance will modify the same object in the cloned instances as well!

Let's see an example. We will use a modified implementation of our Prototype class, which uses shallow copying, to demonstrate this:

```python
class SPrototype(object):
    """ A prototype base class using shallow copy """

    def clone(self):
        """ Return a clone of self """
        return copy.copy(self)
```

The SRegister class inherits from the new prototype class:

```
class SRegister(SPrototype):
    """ Sub-class of SPrototype """

    def __init__(self, names=[]):
        self.names = names



>>> r1=SRegister(names=['amy','stu','jack'])
>>> r2=r1.clone()
```

Let's add a name to the names register of instance r1:

```
>>> r1.names.append('bob')
```

Now let's check r2.names:

```
>>> r2.names
['amy', 'stu', 'jack', 'bob']
```

Oops! This is not what we wanted, but due to the shallow copy, both r1 and r2 end up sharing the same names list, as only the reference is copied over, not the entire object. This can be verified by a simple inspection:

```
>>> r1.names is r2.names
True
```

A deep copy, on the other hand, calls copy recursively for all objects contained in the cloned (copied) object, so nothing is shared, but each clone will end up having its own copy of all the referenced objects.

Prototype using metaclasses

We've seen how to build the Prototype pattern using classes. Since we've already seen a bit of meta-programming in Python in the Singleton pattern example, let's find out whether we can do the same in Prototype.

What we need to do is attach a clone method to all the Prototype classes. Dynamically attaching a method to a class like this can be done in its metaclass via the __init__ method of the metaclass.

This provides a simple implementation of Prototype using metaclasses:

```python
import copy

class MetaPrototype(type):

    """ A metaclass for Prototypes """

    def __init__(cls, *args):
        type.__init__(cls, *args)
        cls.clone = lambda self: copy.deepcopy(self)

class PrototypeM(metaclass=MetaPrototype):
    pass
```

The `PrototypeM` class now implements a Prototype pattern. Let's see an illustration by using a subclass:

```python
class ItemCollection(PrototypeM):
    """ An item collection class """

    def __init__(self, items=[]):
        self.items = items
```

First we create an `ItemCollection` object:

```python
>>> i1=ItemCollection(items=['apples','grapes','oranges'])
>>> i1
<prototype.ItemCollection object at 0x7fd4ba6d3da0>
```

Now we clone it as follows:

```python
>>> i2 = i1.clone()
```

The clone is clearly a different object:

```python
>>> i2
<prototype.ItemCollection object at 0x7fd4ba6aceb8>
```

And it has its own copy of the attributes:

```python
>>> i2.items is i1.items
False
```

Combining patterns using metaclasses

It is possible to create interesting and customized patterns by using the power of metaclasses. The following example illustrates a type which is both a Singleton as well as a Prototype:

```
class MetaSingletonPrototype(type):
    """ A metaclass for Singleton & Prototype patterns """

    def __init__(cls, *args):
        print(cls,"__init__ method called with args", args)
        type.__init__(cls, *args)
        cls.instance = None
        cls.clone = lambda self: copy.deepcopy(cls.instance)

    def __call__(cls, *args, **kwargs):
        if not cls.instance:
            print(cls,"creating prototypical instance", args, kwargs)
            cls.instance = type.__call__(cls,*args, **kwargs)
        return cls.instance
```

Any class using this metaclass as its type would show both Singleton and Prototype behavior.

It may look a bit strange to have a single class combine what look like conflicting behaviors into one, since a Singleton allows only one instance and a Prototype allows cloning to derive multiple instances, but if we think of patterns in terms of their APIs then it begins to feel a bit more natural:

- Calling the class using the constructor would always return the same instance – it behaves like the Singleton pattern.
- Calling `clone` on the class's instance would always return cloned instances. The instances are always cloned using the Singleton instance as the source – it behaves like the Prototype pattern.

Here, we have modified our `PrototypeM` class to now use the new metaclass:

```
class PrototypeM(metaclass=MetaSingletonPrototype):
    pass
```

Since `ItemCollection` continues to subclass `PrototypeM`, it automatically gets the new behavior.

Take a look at the following code:

```
>>> i1=ItemCollection(items=['apples','grapes','oranges'])
<class 'prototype.ItemCollection'> creating prototypical instance ()
{'items': ['apples'
, 'grapes', 'oranges']}
>>> i1
<prototype.ItemCollection object at 0x7fbfc033b048>
>>> i2=i1.clone()
```

The `clone` method works as expected, and produces a clone:

```
>>> i2
<prototype.ItemCollection object at 0x7fbfc033b080>
>>> i2.items is i1.items
False
```

However, building an instance via the constructor always returns the Singleton (Prototype) instance only as it invokes the Singleton API:

```
>>> i3=ItemCollection(items=['apples','grapes','mangoes'])
>>> i3 is i1
True
```

Metaclasses allow powerful customization of class creation. In this specific example, we created a combination of behaviors which included both Singleton and Prototype patterns into one class via a metaclass. The power of Python using metaclasses allows the programmer to go beyond traditional patterns and come up with creative techniques.

The Prototype factory

A prototype class can be enhanced with a helper **Prototype factory** or **registry class**, which can provide factory functions for creating prototypical instances of a configured family or group of products. Think of this as a variation on our previous Factory pattern.

The following is the code for this class. Notice that we inherit it from `Borg` to share state automatically from the top of the hierarchy:

```
class PrototypeFactory(Borg):
    """ A Prototype factory/registry class """

    def __init__(self):
```

```
                    """ Initializer """

                    self._registry = {}

            def register(self, instance):
                """ Register a given instance """

                self._registry[instance.__class__] = instance

            def clone(self, klass):
                """  Return cloned instance of given class """

                instance = self._registry.get(klass)
                if instance == None:
                    print('Error:',klass,'not registered')
                else:
                    return instance.clone()
```

Let's create a few subclasses of Prototype, whose instances we can register on
the factory:

```
class Name(SPrototype):
    """ A class representing a person's name """

    def __init__(self, first, second):
        self.first = first
        self.second = second

    def __str__(self):
        return ' '.join((self.first, self.second))


class Animal(SPrototype):
    """ A class representing an animal """

    def __init__(self, name, type='Wild'):
        self.name = name
        self.type = type

    def __str__(self):
        return ' '.join((str(self.type), self.name))
```

We have two classes: one, a Name class another, an animal class, both of which inherit from SPrototype.

First create a name and animal object:

```
>>> name = Name('Bill', 'Bryson')
>>> animal = Animal('Elephant')
>>> print(name)
Bill Bryson
>>> print(animal)
Wild Elephant
```

Now, let's create an instance of PrototypeFactory:

```
>>> factory = PrototypeFactory()
```

Now let's register the two instances on the factory:

```
>>> factory.register(animal)
>>> factory.register(name)
```

Now the factory is ready to clone any number of instances from the configured instances:

```
>>> factory.clone(Name)
<prototype.Name object at 0x7ffb552f9c50>

>> factory.clone(Animal)
<prototype.Animal object at 0x7ffb55321a58>
```

The factory, rightfully, complains if we try to clone a class whose instance is not registered:

```
>>> class C(object): pass
...
>>> factory.clone(C)
Error: <class '__main__.C'> not registered
```

 The factory class shown here could be enhanced with a check for the existence of the clone method on the registered class to make sure any class that is registered is obeying the API of the Prototype class. This is left as an exercise to the reader.

It is instructive to discuss a few aspects of the specific example we have chosen if the reader hasn't observed them already:

- The `PrototypeFactory` class is a Factory class, so it is usually a Singleton. In this case, we have made it a Borg, as we've seen that `Borg`s make a better fist of state sharing across class hierarchies.

- The `Name` class and `Animal` class inherit from `SPrototype`, since their attributes are integers and strings which are immutable; so, a shallow copy is fine here. This is unlike our first Prototype subclass.

- Prototypes preserve the class creation signature in the prototypical instance, namely the `clone` method. This makes it easy for the programmer, as he/she does not to have to worry about the class creation signature, the order and type of parameters to __new__, and hence, the __init__ methods, but only has to call `clone` on an existing instance.

The Builder pattern

A Builder pattern separates out the construction of an object from its representation (assembly) so that the same construction process can be used to build different representations.

In other words, using a Builder pattern one can conveniently create different types or representative instances of the same class, each using a slightly different building or assembling process.

Formally, the Builder pattern uses a `Director` class, which instructs the `Builder` object to build instances of the target class. Different types (classes) of builders help to build slightly different variations on the same class.

Let's look at an example:

```python
class Room(object):
    """ A class representing a Room in a house """

    def __init__(self, nwindows=2, doors=1, direction='S'):
        self.nwindows = nwindows
        self.doors = doors
        self.direction = direction

    def __str__(self):
        return "Room <facing:%s, windows=#%d>" % (self.direction,
                                                   self.nwindows)
class Porch(object):
```

```python
    """ A class representing a Porch in a house """

    def __init__(self, ndoors=2, direction='W'):
        self.ndoors = ndoors
        self.direction = direction

    def __str__(self):
        return "Porch <facing:%s, doors=#%d>" % (self.direction,
                                                 self.ndoors)

class LegoHouse(object):
    """ A lego house class """

    def __init__(self, nrooms=0, nwindows=0,nporches=0):
        # windows per room
        self.nwindows = nwindows
        self.nporches = nporches
        self.nrooms = nrooms
        self.rooms = []
        self.porches = []

    def __str__(self):
        msg="LegoHouse<rooms=#%d, porches=#%d>" % (self.nrooms,
                                                   self.nporches)

        for i in self.rooms:
            msg += str(i)

        for i in self.porches:
            msg += str(i)

        return msg

    def add_room(self,room):
        """ Add a room to the house """

        self.rooms.append(room)

    def add_porch(self,porch):
        """ Add a porch to the house """

        self.porches.append(porch)
```

Our example shows three classes, which are as follows:

- A `Room` and `Porch` class each representing a room and porch of a house — a room has windows and doors, and a porch has doors.

- A `LegoHouse` class representing a toy example for an actual house (We are imagining a kid building a house with lego blocks here, with rooms and porches.) The Lego house will consist of any number of rooms and porches.

Let's try and create a simple `LegoHouse` instance with one room and one porch, each with the default configuration:

```
>>> house = LegoHouse(nrooms=1,nporches=1)
>>> print(house)
LegoHouse<rooms=#1, porches=#1>
```

Are we done ? No! Notice that our `LegoHouse` is a class that doesn't fully construct itself in its constructor. The rooms and porches are not really built yet, only their counters are initialized.

So we need to build the rooms and porches separately, and add them to the house. Let's do that:

```
>>> room = Room(nwindows=1)
>>> house.add_room(room)
>>> porch = Porch()
>>> house.add_porch(porch)
>>> print(house)
LegoHouse<rooms=#1, porches=#1>
Room <facing:S, windows=#1>
Porch <facing:W, doors=#1>
```

Now you see that our house is fully built. Printing it displays not only the number of rooms and porches, but also details about them. All good!

Now, imagine that you need to build 100 such different house instances, each with different configurations of rooms and porches, and often the rooms themselves have varying numbers of windows and directions!

(Maybe you are building a mobile game which uses Lego Houses where cute little characters such as Trolls or Minions stay and do interesting things.)

It is pretty clear from the example that writing code like the last will not scale to solve the problem.

This is where the Builder pattern can help you. Let's start with a simple `LegoHouse` builder.

```python
class LegoHouseBuilder(object):
    """ Lego house builder class """

    def __init__(self, *args, **kwargs):
        self.house = LegoHouse(*args, **kwargs)

    def build(self):
        """ Build a lego house instance and return it """

        self.build_rooms()
        self.build_porches()
        return self.house

    def build_rooms(self):
        """ Method to build rooms """

        for i in range(self.house.nrooms):
            room = Room(self.house.nwindows)
            self.house.add_room(room)

    def build_porches(self):
        """ Method to build porches """

        for i in range(self.house.nporches):
            porch = Porch(1)
            self.house.add_porch(porch)
```

The following are the main aspects of this class:

- You configure the Builder class with the target class configuration — the number of rooms and porches in this case.
- It provides a `build` method, which constructs and assembles (builds) the components of the house — in this case, `Rooms` and `Porches`, according to the specified configuration.
- The `build` method returns the constructed and assembled house.

Now building different types of Lego Houses with different designs of rooms and porches is just two lines of code:

```
>>> builder=LegoHouseBuilder(nrooms=2,nporches=1,nwindows=1)
>>> print(builder.build())
LegoHouse<rooms=#2, porches=#1>
Room <facing:S, windows=#1>
Room <facing:S, windows=#1>
Porch <facing:W, doors=#1>
```

We will now build a similar house, but with rooms that have two windows each:

```
>>> builder=LegoHouseBuilder(nrooms=2,nporches=1,nwindows=2)
>>> print(builder.build())
LegoHouse<rooms=#2, porches=#1>
Room <facing:S, windows=#2>
Room <facing:S, windows=#2>
Porch <facing:W, doors=#1>
```

Let's say you find you are continuing to build a lot of Lego Houses with this configuration. You can encapsulate it in a subclass of the Builder so that the preceding code itself is not duplicated a lot:

```
class SmallLegoHouseBuilder(LegoHouseBuilder):
""" Builder sub-class building small lego house with 1 room and 1
    porch and rooms having 2 windows """

    def __init__(self):
        self.house = LegoHouse(nrooms=2, nporches=1, nwindows=2)
```

Now, the house configuration is *burned into* the new builder class, and building one is as simple as this:

```
>>> small_house=SmallLegoHouseBuilder().build()
>>> print(small_house)
LegoHouse<rooms=#2, porches=#1>
Room <facing:S, windows=#2>
Room <facing:S, windows=#2>
Porch <facing:W, doors=#1>
```

You can also build many of them (say 100, 50 for the Trolls and 50 for the Minions) as follows:

```
>>> houses=list(map(lambda x: SmallLegoHouseBuilder().build(),
range(100)))
>>> print(houses[0])
LegoHouse<rooms=#2, porches=#1>
```

```
Room <facing:S, windows=#2>
Room <facing:S, windows=#2>
Porch <facing:W, doors=#1>

>>> len(houses)
100
```

One can also create more exotic builder classes which do some very specific things. For example, the following is a builder class which creates houses with rooms and porches always facing north:

```python
class NorthFacingHouseBuilder(LegoHouseBuilder):
    """ Builder building all rooms and porches facing North """

    def build_rooms(self):

        for i in range(self.house.nrooms):
            room = Room(self.house.nwindows, direction='N')
            self.house.add_room(room)

    def build_porches(self):

        for i in range(self.house.nporches):
            porch = Porch(1, direction='N')
            self.house.add_porch(porch)
```

```
>>> print(NorthFacingHouseBuilder(nrooms=2, nporches=1, nwindows=1).
build())
LegoHouse<rooms=#2, porches=#1>
Room <facing:N, windows=#1>
Room <facing:N, windows=#1>
Porch <facing:N, doors=#1>
```

And, by using Python's multiple inheritance power, one can combine any such builders into new and interesting subclasses. The following, for example, is a builder that produces north-facing small houses:

```python
class NorthFacingSmallHouseBuilder(NorthFacingHouseBuilder,
SmallLegoHouseBuilder):
    pass
```

As expected, it always produces North-facing, small houses with 2 windowed rooms repeatedly. Not very interesting maybe, but very reliable indeed:

```
>>> print(NorthFacingSmallHouseBuilder().build())
LegoHouse<rooms=#2, porches=#1>
Room <facing:N, windows=#2>
Room <facing:N, windows=#2>
Porch <facing:N, doors=#1>
```

Before we conclude our discussion on Creational Patterns, let's summarize some interesting aspects of these creational patterns and their interplay, as follows:

- **Builder and Factory**: The Builder pattern separates out the assembling process of a class's instance from its creation. A Factory on the other hand is concerned with creating instances of different sub-classes belonging to the same hierarchy using a unified interface. A builder also returns the built instance as a final step, whereas a Factory returns the instance immediately, as there is no separate building step.

- **Builder and Prototype**: A Builder can, internally, use a prototype for creating its instances. Further instances from the same builder can then be cloned from this instance. For example, it is instructive to build a Builder class which uses one of our Prototype metaclasses to always clone a prototypical instance.

- **Prototype and Factory**: A Prototype factory can, internally, make use of a Factory pattern to build the initial instances of the classes in question.

- **Factory and Singleton**: A Factory class is usually a Singleton in traditional programming languages. The other option is to make its methods a class or static method so there is no need to create an instance of the Factory itself. In our examples, we made it a Borg instead.

We will now move on to the next class of patterns: Structural Patterns.

Patterns in Python – structural

Structural patterns concern themselves with the intricacies of combining classes or objects to form larger structures that are more than the sum of their parts.

Structural patterns implement this in these two distinct ways:

- By using class Inheritance to compose classes into one. This is the static approach.
- By using object composition at runtime to achieve combined functionality. This approach is more dynamic and flexible.

Python, by virtue of supporting multiple inheritance, can implement both of these very well. Being a language with dynamic attributes and using the power of magic methods, Python can also do object composition and the resultant method wrapping pretty well also. So, with Python, a programmer is indeed in a good place with respect to implementing structural patterns.

We will be discussing the following structural patterns in this section: Adapter, Facade, and Proxy.

The Adapter pattern

As the name implies, the Adapter pattern wraps or adapts an existing implementation of a specific interface into another interface which a client expects. The Adapter is also called a **Wrapper**.

You very often adapt objects into interfaces or types you want when you program, most often without realizing this.

Example:

Look at the following list containing two instances of a fruit and detailing how many:

```
>>> fruits=[('apples',2), ('grapes',40)]
```

Let's say you want to quickly find the number of fruits, given a fruit name. The list doesn't allow you to use the fruit as a key, which is a more suitable interface for the operation.

What do you do ? Well, you simply convert the list to a dictionary:

```
>>> fruits_d=dict(fruits)
>>> fruits_d['apples']
2
```

Voilà! You got the object in a form that is more convenient for you, adapted to your programming needs. This is a kind of data or object adaptation.

Programmers do such data or object adaptation almost continuously in their code without realizing it. Adaptation of code or data is more common than you think.

Let's consider a class Polygon, representing a regular or irregular Polygon of any shape:

```python
class Polygon(object):
    """ A polygon class """

    def __init__(self, *sides):
        """ Initializer - accepts length of sides """
        self.sides = sides

    def perimeter(self):
        """ Return perimeter """

        return sum(self.sides)

    def is_valid(self):
        """ Is this a valid polygon """

        # Do some complex stuff - not implemented in base class
        raise NotImplementedError

    def is_regular(self):
        """ Is a regular polygon ? """

        # True: if all sides are equal
        side = self.sides[0]
        return all([x==side for x in self.sides[1:]])

    def area(self):
        """ Calculate and return area """

        # Not implemented in base class
        raise NotImplementedError
```

This preceding class describes a generic, closed Polygon geometric figure in geometry.

We have implemented some basic methods such as perimeter and is_regular, the latter returning whether the Polygon is a regular one such as a hexagon or pentagon.

Let's say we want to implement specific classes for a few regular geometric shapes such as a triangle or rectangle. We can implement these from scratch, of course. However, since a Polygon class is available, we can try to reuse it, and adapt it to our needs.

Let's say the Triangle class requires the following methods:

- is_equilateral: Returns whether the triangle is an equilateral one
- is_isosceles: Returns whether the triangle is an isosceles triangle
- is_valid: Implements the is_valid method for a triangle
- area: Implements the area method for a triangle

Similarly the Rectangle class, needs the following methods:

- is_square: Returns whether the rectangle is a square
- is_valid: Implements the is_valid method for a rectangle
- area: Implements the area method for a rectangle

The following is the code for an adapter pattern, reusing the Polygon class for the Triangle and Rectangle classes.

The following is the code for the Triangle class:

```
import itertools

class InvalidPolygonError(Exception):
    pass

class Triangle(Polygon):
    """ Triangle class from Polygon using class adapter """

    def is_equilateral(self):
        """ Is this an equilateral triangle ? """

        if self.is_valid():
            return super(Triangle, self).is_regular()

    def is_isosceles(self):
        """ Is the triangle isosceles """
```

```
        if self.is_valid():
            # Check if any 2 sides are equal
            for a,b in itertools.combinations(self.sides, 2):
                if a == b:
                    return True
        return False

    def area(self):
        """ Calculate area """

        # Using Heron's formula
        p = self.perimeter()/2.0
        total = p
        for side in self.sides:
            total *= abs(p-side)

        return pow(total, 0.5)

    def is_valid(self):
        """ Is the triangle valid """

        # Sum of 2 sides should be > 3rd side
        perimeter = self.perimeter()
        for side in self.sides:
            sum_two = perimeter - side
            if sum_two <= side:
                raise InvalidPolygonError(str(self.__class__) + "is
invalid!")

        return True
```

Take a look at the following Rectangle class:

```
class Rectangle(Polygon):
    """ Rectangle class from Polygon using class adapter """

    def is_square(self):
        """ Return if I am a square """

        if self.is_valid():
            # Defaults to is_regular
            return self.is_regular()

    def is_valid(self):
```

```
    """ Is the rectangle valid """

    # Should have 4 sides
    if len(self.sides) != 4:
        return False

    # Opposite sides should be same
    for a,b in [(0,2),(1,3)]:
        if self.sides[a] != self.sides[b]:
            return False

    return True

def area(self):
    """ Return area of rectangle """

    # Length x breadth
    if self.is_valid():
        return self.sides[0]*self.sides[1]
```

Now let's see classes in action.

Let's create an equilateral triangle for the first test:

```
>>> t1 = Triangle(20,20,20)
>>> t1.is_valid()
True
```

An equilateral triangle is also isosceles:

```
>>> t1.is_equilateral()
True
>>> t1.is_isosceles()
True
```

Let's calculate the area:

```
>>> t1.area()
173.20508075688772
```

Let's try a triangle which is not valid:

```
>>> t2 = Triangle(10, 20, 30)
>>> t2.is_valid()
Traceback (most recent call last):
  File "<stdin>", line 1, in <module>
```

```
  File "/home/anand/Documents/ArchitectureBook/code/chap7/adapter.py",
line 75, in is_valid
    raise InvalidPolygonError(str(self.__class__) + "is invalid!")
adapter.InvalidPolygonError: <class 'adapter.Triangle'>is invalid!
```

 Its dimensions show it is a straight line, not a triangle. The `is_valid` method is not implemented in the base class, hence the subclasses need to override it to provide a proper implementation. In this case, we raise an exception if the triangle is invalid.

The following is an illustration of the `Rectangle` class in action:

```
>>> r1 = Rectangle(10,20,10,20)
>>> r1.is_valid()
True
>>> r1.area()
200
>>> r1.is_square()
False
>>> r1.perimeter()
60
```

Let's create a square:

```
>>> r2 = Rectangle(10,10,10,10)
>>> r2.is_square()
True
```

The `Rectangle`/`Triangle` classes shown here are examples of `class adapters`. This is because they inherit the class that they want to adapt, and provide the methods expected by the client, often delegating the computation to the base-class's methods. This is evident in the `is_equilateral` and `is_square` methods of the `Triangle` and `Rectangle` classes respectively.

Let's look at an alternative implementation of the same classes — this time, via object composition, in other words, `object adapters`:

```
import itertools

class Triangle (object) :
    """ Triangle class from Polygon using class adapter """

    def __init__(self, *sides):
        # Compose a polygon
        self.polygon = Polygon(*sides)
```

```
    def perimeter(self):
        return self.polygon.perimeter()

    def is_valid(f):
        """ Is the triangle valid """

        def inner(self, *args):
            # Sum of 2 sides should be > 3rd side
            perimeter = self.polygon.perimeter()
            sides = self.polygon.sides

            for side in sides:
                sum_two = perimeter - side
                if sum_two <= side:
                    raise InvalidPolygonError(str(self.__class__) +
                                                    "is invalid!")

            result = f(self, *args)
            return result

        return inner

    @is_valid
    def is_equilateral(self):
        """ Is this equilateral triangle ? """

        return self.polygon.is_regular()

    @is_valid
    def is_isosceles(self):
        """ Is the triangle isoscles """

        # Check if any 2 sides are equal
        for a,b in itertools.combinations(self.polygon.sides, 2):
            if a == b:
                return True
        return False

    def area(self):
        """ Calculate area """

        # Using Heron's formula
        p = self.polygon.perimeter()/2.0
        total = p
```

```
    for side in self.polygon.sides:
        total *= abs(p-side)

    return pow(total, 0.5)
```

This class works similarly to the other one, even though the internal details are implemented via object composition rather than class inheritance:

```
>>> t1=Triangle(2,2,2)
>>> t1.is_equilateral()
True
>>> t2 = Triangle(4,4,5)
>>> t2.is_equilateral()
False
>>> t2.is_isosceles()
True
```

The main differences between this implementation and the class adapter are as follows:

- The object adapter class doesn't inherit from the class we want to adapt from. Instead, it composes an instance of the class.

- Any wrapper methods are forwarded to the composed instance, for example, the `perimeter` method.

- All attribute access to the wrapped instance has to be specified explicitly in this implementation. Nothing comes for free since we are not inheriting the class. (For example, inspect the way we access the `sides` attribute of the enclosed `polygon` instance.)

 Observe how we converted the previous `is_valid` method to a decorator in this implementation. This is because many methods carry out a first check on `is_valid`, and then perform their actions, so it is an ideal candidate for a decorator. This also aids rewriting this implementation to a more convenient form, which is discussed next.

One problem with the object adapter implementation, as shown in the preceding implementation, is that any attribute reference to the enclosed adapted instance has to be made explicitly. For example, had we forgotten to implement the `perimeter` method for the `Triangle` class here, there would have been no method at all to call, as we aren't inheriting from the `Adapter` class.

The following is an alternate implementation, which makes use of the power of one of Python's magic methods, namely __getattr__, to simplify this. We are demonstrating this implementation on the Rectangle class:

```python
class Rectangle(object):
    """ Rectangle class from Polygon using object adapter """


    method_mapper = {'is_square': 'is_regular'}

    def __init__(self, *sides):
        # Compose a polygon
        self.polygon = Polygon(*sides)

    def is_valid(f):
        def inner(self, *args):
            """ Is the rectangle valid """

            sides = self.sides
            # Should have 4 sides
            if len(sides) != 4:
                return False

            # Opposite sides should be same
            for a,b in [(0,2),(1,3)]:
                if sides[a] != sides[b]:
                    return False

            result = f(self, *args)
            return result

        return inner

    def __getattr__(self, name):
        """ Overloaded __getattr__ to forward methods to wrapped
            instance """

        if name in self.method_mapper:
            # Wrapped name
            w_name = self.method_mapper[name]
            print('Forwarding to method',w_name)
            # Map the method to correct one on the instance
            return getattr(self.polygon, w_name)
        else:
```

```
                # Assume method is the same
                return getattr(self.polygon, name)

        @is_valid
        def area(self):
            """ Return area of rectangle """

            # Length x breadth
            sides = self.sides
            return sides[0]*sides[1]
```

Let's look at examples using this class:

```
>>> r1=Rectangle(10,20,10,20)
>>> r1.perimeter()
60
>>> r1.is_square()
Forwarding to method is_regular
False
```

You can see that we are able to call the method `is_perimeter` on the `Rectangle` instance even though no such method is actually defined on the class. Similarly, `is_square` seems to work magically. What is happening here?

The magic method `__getattr__` is invoked by Python on an object if it cannot find an attribute in the usual ways – by first looking up the object's dictionary, then its class's dictionary, and so on. It takes a name, and hence provides a hook on a class, to implement a way to provide method lookups by routing them to other objects.

In this case, the `__getattr__` method does the following:

- Checks for the attribute name in the `method_mapper` dictionary. This is a dictionary we have created on the class, which maps a method name that we want to call on the class (as a key) to the actual method name on the wrapped instance (as a value). If an entry is found, it is returned.

- If no entry is found on the `method_mapper` dictionary, the entry is passed as such to the wrapped instance to be looked up by the same name.

- We use `getattr` in both cases to look up and return the attribute from the wrapped instance.

- Attributes can be anything—data attributes or methods. For example, see how we refer to the `sides` attribute of the wrapped `polygon` instance as if it belonged to the `Rectangle` class in the method `area` and the `is_valid` decorator.

- If an attribute is not present on the wrapped instance, it raises an `AttributeError`:

```
>>> r1.convert_to_parallelogram(angle=30)
Traceback (most recent call last):
  File "<stdin>", line 1, in <module>
  File "adapter_o.py", line 133, in __getattr__
    return getattr(self.polygon, name)
AttributeError: 'Polygon' object has no attribute 'convert_to_
parallelogram'
```

Object adapters implemented using this technique are much more versatile, and lead to less code than regular object adapters where every method has to be explicitly written and forwarded to the wrapped instance.

The Facade pattern

A facade is a structural pattern that provides a unified interface to multiple interfaces in a subsystem. The Facade pattern is useful where a system consists of multiple subsystems, each with its own interfaces, but presents some high-level functionality, which needs to be captured, as a general top-level interface to the client.

A classic example of an object in everyday life which is a Facade is an automobile.

For example, a car consists of an engine, power train, axle and wheel assembly, electronics, steering systems, brake systems, and other such components.

However, usually, you don't have to bother whether the brake in your car is a disc-brake, or whether its suspension is coil-spring or McPherson struts, do you?

This is because the car manufacturer has provided a Facade for you to operate and maintain the car which reduces the complexity and provides you with simpler sub-systems which are easy to operate by themselves, such as the following:

- The ignition system to start the car
- The steering system to maneuver it
- The clutch-accelerator-brake system to control it
- The gear and transmission system to manage the power and speed

A lot of complex systems around us are Facades. Like the car example, a computer is a Facade, an Industrial Robot is another. All factory control systems are facades, supplying a few dashboards and controls for the engineer to tweak the complex systems behind it, and keep them running.

Facades in Python

The Python standard library contains a lot of modules which are good examples of Facades. The `compiler` module, which provides hooks to parse and compile Python source code, is a Facade to the lexer, parser, AST tree generator, and the like.

The following shows the help contents of this module:

```
anand@ubuntu-pro-book: ~/Documents/ArchitectureBook/code/chap7
File  Edit  View  Search  Terminal  Help
Help on package compiler:

NAME
    compiler - Package for parsing and compiling Python source code

FILE
    /usr/lib/python2.7/compiler/__init__.py

DESCRIPTION
    There are several functions defined at the top level that are imported
    from modules contained in the package.

    parse(buf, mode="exec") -> AST
        Converts a string containing Python source code to an abstract
        syntax tree (AST).  The AST is defined in compiler.ast.

    parseFile(path) -> AST
        The same as parse(open(path))

    walk(ast, visitor, verbose=None)
        Does a pre-order walk over the ast using the visitor instance.
        See compiler.visitor for details.

    compile(source, filename, mode, flags=None, dont_inherit=None)
        Returns a code object.  A replacement for the builtin compile() function.

    compileFile(filename)
        Generates a .pyc file by compiling filename.

PACKAGE CONTENTS
:
```

In the next page of the help contents, you can see how this module acts as a facade to other modules which are used to implement the functions defined in this package. (Look at PACKAGE CONTENTS at the bottom of the screenshot):

```
                          anand@ubuntu-pro-book: ~/Documents/ArchitectureBook/code/chap7
 File  Edit  View  Search  Terminal  Help

    parse(buf, mode="exec") -> AST
        Converts a string containing Python source code to an abstract
        syntax tree (AST).  The AST is defined in compiler.ast.

    parseFile(path) -> AST
        The same as parse(open(path))

    walk(ast, visitor, verbose=None)
        Does a pre-order walk over the ast using the visitor instance.
        See compiler.visitor for details.

    compile(source, filename, mode, flags=None, dont_inherit=None)
        Returns a code object.  A replacement for the builtin compile() function.

    compileFile(filename)
        Generates a .pyc file by compiling filename.

PACKAGE CONTENTS
    ast
    consts
    future
    misc
    pyassem
    pycodegen
    symbols
    syntax
    transformer
    visitor

(END)
```

Let's look at sample code for a Facade pattern. In this example, we will model a Car with a few of its multiple subsystems.

The following is the code for all the subsystems:

```python
class Engine(object):
    """ An Engine class """

    def __init__(self, name, bhp, rpm, volume, cylinders=4,
      type='petrol'):
        self.name = name
        self.bhp = bhp
        self.rpm = rpm
        self.volume = volume
        self.cylinders = cylinders
        self.type = type

    def start(self):
        """ Fire the engine """
```

```
        print('Engine started')

    def stop(self):
        """ Stop the engine """
        print('Engine stopped')

class Transmission(object):
    """ Transmission class """

    def __init__(self, gears, torque):
        self.gears = gears
        self.torque = torque
        # Start with neutral
        self.gear_pos = 0

    def shift_up(self):
        """ Shift up gears """

        if self.gear_pos == self.gears:
            print('Cannot shift up anymore')
        else:
            self.gear_pos += 1
            print('Shifted up to gear',self.gear_pos)

    def shift_down(self):
        """ Shift down gears """

        if self.gear_pos == -1:
            print("In reverse, can't shift down")
        else:
            self.gear_pos -= 1
            print('Shifted down to gear',self.gear_pos)

    def shift_reverse(self):
        """ Shift in reverse """

        print('Reverse shifting')
        self.gear_pos = -1

    def shift_to(self, gear):
        """ Shift to a gear position """

        self.gear_pos = gear
```

```python
        print('Shifted to gear',self.gear_pos)


class Brake(object):
    """ A brake class """

    def __init__(self, number, type='disc'):
        self.type = type
        self.number = number

    def engage(self):
        """ Engage the break """

        print('%s %d engaged' % (self.__class__.__name__,
                                  self.number))

    def release(self):
        """ Release the break """

        print('%s %d released' % (self.__class__.__name__,
                                   self.number))

class ParkingBrake(Brake):
    """ A parking brake class """

    def __init__(self, type='drum'):
        super(ParkingBrake, self).__init__(type=type, number=1)


class Suspension(object):
    """ A suspension class """

    def __init__(self, load, type='mcpherson'):
        self.type = type
        self.load = load

class Wheel(object):
    """ A wheel class """

    def __init__(self, material, diameter, pitch):
        self.material = material
        self.diameter = diameter
```

```
        self.pitch = pitch

class WheelAssembly(object):
    """ A wheel assembly class """

    def __init__(self, brake, suspension):
        self.brake = brake
        self.suspension = suspension
        self.wheels = Wheel('alloy', 'M12',1.25)

    def apply_brakes(self):
        """ Apply brakes """

        print('Applying brakes')
        self.brake.engage()

class Frame(object):
    """ A frame class for an automobile """

    def __init__(self, length, width):
        self.length = length
        self.width = width
```

As you can see, we have covered a good number of the subsystems in a car, or those which are essential, at least.

The following code for the `Car` class combines them as a Facade with two methods, to `start` and `stop` the car:

```
class Car(object):
    """ A car class - Facade pattern """

    def __init__(self, model, manufacturer):
        self.engine = Engine('K-series',85,5000, 1.3)
        self.frame = Frame(385, 170)
        self.wheel_assemblies = []
        for i in range(4):
            self.wheel_assemblies.append(WheelAssembly(Brake(i+1),
                                             Suspension(1000)))

        self.transmission = Transmission(5, 115)
        self.model = model
        self.manufacturer = manufacturer
        self.park_brake = ParkingBrake()
        # Ignition engaged
```

```
        self.ignition = False

    def start(self):
        """ Start the car """

        print('Starting the car')
        self.ignition = True
        self.park_brake.release()
        self.engine.start()
        self.transmission.shift_up()
        print('Car started.')

    def stop(self):
        """ Stop the car """

        print('Stopping the car')
        # Apply brakes to reduce speed
        for wheel_a in self.wheel_assemblies:
            wheel_a.apply_brakes()

        # Move to 2nd gear and then 1st
        self.transmission.shift_to(2)
        self.transmission.shift_to(1)
        self.engine.stop()
        # Shift to neutral
        self.transmission.shift_to(0)
        # Engage parking brake
        self.park_brake.engage()
        print('Car stopped.')
```

Let's build an instance of the `Car` first:

```
>>> car = Car('Swift','Suzuki')
>>> car
<facade.Car object at 0x7f0c9e29afd0>
```

Let's now take the car out of the garage and go for a spin:

```
>>> car.start()
Starting the car
ParkingBrake 1 released
Engine started
Shifted up to gear 1
```

From the preceding output you can see that our car has started.

Now that we have driven it for a while, we can stop the car. As you may have guessed, stopping is more involved than starting!

```
>>> car.stop()
Stopping the car
Shifted to gear 2
Shifted to gear 1
Applying brakes
Brake 1 engaged
Applying brakes
Brake 2 engaged
Applying brakes
Brake 3 engaged
Applying brakes
Brake 4 engaged
Engine stopped
Shifted to gear 0
ParkingBrake 1 engaged
Car stopped.
>>>
```

Facades are useful for taking the complexity out of systems so that working with them becomes easier. As the preceding example shows, it would've been awfully difficult if we hadn't built the `start` and `stop` methods the way we did in this example. These methods hide the complexity behind the actions involved with subsystems in starting and stopping a `Car`.

This is what a Facade does best.

The proxy pattern

A proxy pattern wraps another object to control access to it. Some usage scenarios are as follows:

- We need a virtual resource closer to the client, which acts in place of the real resource in another network, for example, a remote proxy.

- We need to control/monitor access to a resource, for example, a network proxy and an instance counting proxy.

- We need to protect a resource or object (protection proxy) because direct access to it would cause security issues or compromise it, for example, a reverse proxy server.

- We need to optimize access to results from a costly computation or network operation so that the computation is not performed every time, for example, a caching proxy

A proxy always implements the interface of the object it is proxying to, its target in other words. This can be either via inheritance or via composition. In Python, the latter can be done more powerfully by overriding the __getattr__ method, as we've seen in the Adapter example.

An instance-counting proxy

We will start with an example that demonstrates using the proxy pattern to keep track of instances of a class. We will reuse our Employee class and its subclasses from the Factory pattern here:

```python
class EmployeeProxy(object):
    """ Counting proxy class for Employees """

    # Count of employees
    count = 0

    def __new__(cls, *args):
        """ Overloaded __new__ """
        # To keep track of counts
        instance = object.__new__(cls)
        cls.incr_count()
        return instance

    def __init__(self, employee):
        self.employee = employee

    @classmethod
    def incr_count(cls):
        """ Increment employee count """
        cls.count += 1

    @classmethod
    def decr_count(cls):
        """ Decrement employee count """
        cls.count -= 1

    @classmethod
    def get_count(cls):
```

```
        """ Get employee count """
        return cls.count

    def __str__(self):
        return str(self.employee)

    def __getattr__(self, name):
        """ Redirect attributes to employee instance """

        return getattr(self.employee, name)

    def __del__(self):
        """ Overloaded __del__ method """
        # Decrement employee count
        self.decr_count()

class EmployeeProxyFactory(object):
    """ An Employee factory class returning proxy objects """

    @classmethod
    def create(cls, name, *args):
        """ Factory method for creating an Employee instance """

        name = name.lower().strip()

        if name == 'engineer':
            return EmployeeProxy(Engineer(*args))
        elif name == 'accountant':
            return EmployeeProxy(Accountant(*args))
        elif name == 'admin':
            return EmployeeProxy(Admin(*args))
```

 We haven't duplicated the code for the employee subclasses, as these are already available in the Factory pattern discussion.

We have two classes here: the EmployeeProxy and the original factory class modified to return instances of EmployeeProxy instead of employee. The modified factory class makes it easy for us to create proxy instances instead of having to do it ourselves.

The proxy, as implemented here, is a composition or object proxy, as it wraps around the target object (employee) and overloads __getattr__ to redirect attribute access to it. It keeps track of the count of instances by overriding the __new__ and __del__ methods for instance creation and instance deletion respectively.

Let's see an example of using the Proxy:

```
>>> factory = EmployeeProxyFactory()
>>> engineer = factory.create('engineer','Sam',25,'M')
>>> print(engineer)
Engineer - Sam, 25 years old M
```

 This prints details of the engineer via proxy, since we have overridden the __str__ method in the proxy class, which calls the same method of the employee instance.

```
>>> admin = factory.create('admin','Tracy',32,'F')
>>> print(admin)
Admin - Tracy, 32 years old F
```

Let's check the instance count now. This can be done either via the instances or via the class, since anyway it references a class variable:

```
>>> admin.get_count()
2
>>> EmployeeProxy.get_count()
2
```

Let's delete the instances, and see what happens!

```
>>> del engineer
>>> EmployeeProxy.get_count()
1
>>> del admin
>>> EmployeeProxy.get_count()
0
```

 The weak reference module in Python provides a proxy object which performs something very similar to what we have implemented, by proxying access to class instances.

The following is an example:

```
>>> import weakref
>>> import gc
>>> engineer=Engineer('Sam',25,'M')
```

Let's check the reference count of the new object:

```
>>> len(gc.get_referrers(engineer))
1
```

Now create a weak reference to it:

```
>>> engineer_proxy=weakref.proxy(engineer)
```

The `weakref` object acts in all respects like the object it's proxying for:

```
>>> print(engineer_proxy)
Engineer - Sam, 25 years old M
>>> engineer_proxy.get_role()
'engineering'
```

However, note that a `weakref` proxy doesn't increase the reference count of the proxied object:

```
>>> len(gc.get_referrers(engineer))
    1
```

Patterns in Python – behavioral

Behavioral patterns are the last stage in the complexity and functionality of patterns. They also come last chronologically in the object life cycle in a system since objects are first created then built into larger structures, before they interact with each other.

These patterns encapsulate models of communication and interaction between objects. These patterns allow us to describe complex workflows that may be difficult to follow at runtime.

Typically, Behavioral patterns favor object composition over inheritance as usually, the interacting objects in a system would be from separate class hierarchies.

In this brief discussion, we will look at the following patterns: **Iterator**, **Observer**, and **State**.

The Iterator pattern

An iterator provides a way to access elements of a container object sequentially without exposing the underlying object itself. In other words, an iterator is a proxy that provides a single method of iterating over a container object.

Iterators are everywhere in Python, so there is no special need to introduce them.

All container/sequence types in Python, that is, list, tuple, str, and set, implement their own iterators. Dictionaries also implement iterators over their keys.

In Python, an iterator is any object that implements the magic method __iter__, and also responds to the iter function returning the iterator instance.

Usually, the iterator object that is created is hidden behind the scenes in Python.

For example, we iterate through a list as follows:

```
>>> for i in range(5):
...             print(i)
...
0
1
2
3
4
```

Internally, something very similar to the following happens:

```
>>> I = iter(range(5))
>>> for i in I:
...             print(i)
...
0
1
2
3
4
```

Every sequence type implements its own iterator type as well in Python. Examples for this are given as follows:

- **Lists**:

  ```
  >>> fruits = ['apple','oranges','grapes']
  >>> iter(fruits)
  <list_iterator object at 0x7fd626bedba8>
  ```

- **Tuples**:

  ```
  >>> prices_per_kg = (('apple', 350), ('oranges', 80), ('grapes', 120))
  >>> iter(prices_per_kg)
  <tuple_iterator object at 0x7fd626b86fd0>
  ```

- **Sets**:

  ```
  >>> subjects = {'Maths','Chemistry','Biology','Physics'}
  >>> iter(subjects)
  <set_iterator object at 0x7fd626b91558>
  ```

Even dictionaries come with their own special key iterator type in Python3:

```
>>> iter(dict(prices_per_kg))
<dict_keyiterator object at 0x7fd626c35ae8>
```

We will explore a small example of implementing your own iterator class/type in Python now:

```
class Prime(object):
    """ An iterator for prime numbers """

    def __init__(self, initial, final=0):
        """ Initializer - accepts a number """
        # This may or may not be prime
        self.current = initial
        self.final = final

    def __iter__(self):
        return self

    def __next__(self):
        """ Return next item in iterator """
        return self._compute()

    def _compute(self):
```

```
""" Compute the next prime number """

num = self.current

while True:
    is_prime = True

    # Check this number
    for x in range(2, int(pow(self.current, 0.5)+1)):
        if self.current%x==0:
            is_prime = False
            break


    num = self.current
    self.current += 1

    if is_prime:
        return num

    # If there is an end range, look for it
    if self.final > 0 and self.current>self.final:
        raise StopIteration
```

This preceding class is a prime number iterator, which returns prime numbers between two limits:

```
>>> p=Prime(2,10)
>>> for num in p:
... print(num)
...
2
3
5
7
>>> list(Prime(2,50))
[2, 3, 5, 7, 11, 13, 17, 19, 23, 29, 31, 37, 41, 43, 47]
```

The prime number iterator without the end limit is an infinite iterator. For example, the following iterator will return all prime numbers starting from 2 and will never stop:

```
>>> p = Prime(2)
```

However by combining this with the itertools module, one can extract specific data that one wants from such infinite iterators.

For example here, we use it with the `islice` method of `itertools` to compute the first 100 prime numbers:

```
>>> import itertools
>>> list(itertools.islice(Prime(2), 100))
[2, 3, 5, 7, 11, 13, 17, 19, 23, 29, 31, 37, 41, 43, 47, 53, 59, 61,
67, 71, 73, 79, 83, 89, 97, 101, 103, 107, 109, 113, 127, 131, 137,
139, 149, 151, 157, 163, 167, 173, 179, 181, 191, 193, 197, 199, 211,
223, 227, 229, 233, 239, 241, 251, 257, 263, 269, 271, 277, 281, 283,
293, 307, 311, 313, 317, 331, 337, 347, 349, 353, 359, 367, 373, 379,
383, 389, 397, 401, 409, 419, 421, 431, 433, 439, 443, 449, 457, 461,
463, 467, 479, 487, 491, 499, 503, 509, 521, 523, 541]
```

Similarly, the following are the first 10 prime numbers ending with 1 in the unit's place using the `filterfalse` method:

```
>>> list(itertools.islice(itertools.filterfalse(lambda x: x % 10 != 1,
Prime(2)), 10))
[11, 31, 41, 61, 71, 101, 131, 151, 181, 191]
```

In a similar way, the following are the first 10 palindromic primes:

```
>>> list(itertools.islice(itertools.filterfalse(lambda x:
str(x)!=str(x)[-1::-1], Prime(2)), 10))
[2, 3, 5, 7, 11, 101, 131, 151, 181, 191]
```

Interested readers are referred to the documentation on the `itertools` module and its methods to find fun and interesting ways to use and manipulate data for such infinite generators.

The Observer pattern

The Observer pattern decouples objects, but at the same time allows one set of objects (Subscribers) to keep track of the changes in another object (the Publisher). This avoids one-to-many dependency and references while keeping their interaction alive.

This pattern is also called **Publish-Subscribe**.

The following is a rather simple example using an `Alarm` class, which runs in its own thread and generates periodic alarms every second (by default). It also works as a `Publisher` class, notifying its subscribers whenever the alarm happens.

```python
import threading
import time

from datetime import datetime

class Alarm(threading.Thread):
    """ A class which generates periodic alarms """

    def __init__(self, duration=1):
        self.duration = duration
        # Subscribers
        self.subscribers = []
        self.flag = True
        threading.Thread.__init__(self, None, None)

    def register(self, subscriber):
        """ Register a subscriber for alarm notifications """

        self.subscribers.append(subscriber)

    def notify(self):
        """ Notify all the subscribers """

        for subscriber in self.subscribers:
            subscriber.update(self.duration)

    def stop(self):
        """ Stop the thread """

        self.flag = False

    def run(self):
        """ Run the alarm generator """

        while self.flag:
            time.sleep(self.duration)
            # Notify
            self.notify()
```

Our subscriber is a simple `DumbClock` class, which subscribes to the `Alarm` object for its notifications and, using that, updates its time:

```
class DumbClock(object):
    """ A dumb clock class using an Alarm object """

    def __init__(self):
        # Start time
        self.current = time.time()

    def update(self, *args):
        """ Callback method from publisher """

        self.current += args[0]

    def __str__(self):
        """ Display local time """

        return datetime.fromtimestamp(self.current).
            strftime('%H:%M:%S')
```

Let's get these objects ticking:

1. First create the alarm with a notification period of 1 second. This allows:

    ```
    >>> alarm=Alarm(duration=1)
    ```

2. Next create the `DumbClock` object:

    ```
    >>> clock=DumbClock()
    ```

3. Finally, register the clock object on the alarm object as an observer so that it can receive notifications:

    ```
    >>> alarm.register(clock)
    ```

4. Now the clock will keep receiving updates from the alarm. Every time you print the clock, it will show the current time correct to the second:

    ```
    >>> print(clock)
    10:04:27
    ```

    After a while, it will show you the following:

    ```
    >>> print(clock)
    10:08:20
    ```

5. Then it will sleep for a while and print:

```
>>> print(clock);time.sleep(20);print(clock)
10:08:23
10:08:43
```

The following are some aspects to keep in mind when implementing observers:

- **References to subscribers**: Publishers can choose to keep a reference to subscribers or use a Mediator pattern to get a reference when required. A Mediator pattern decouples many objects in a system from strongly referencing each other. In Python, for example, this could be a collection of weak references or proxies or an object managing such a collection if both publisher and subscriber objects are in the same Python runtime. For remote references, one can use a remote proxy.

- **Implementing Callbacks**: In this example, the Alarm class directly updates the state of the subscriber by calling its update method. An alternate implementation is for the publisher to simply notify the subscribers, at which point they query the state of the Publisher using a get_state type of method to implement their own state change:

  This is the preferred option for a Publisher which may be interacting with subscribers of different types/classes. This also allows for decoupling code from the Publisher to the Subscriber as the publisher doesn't have to change its code if the update or notify method of the Subscriber changes.

- **Synchronous versus Asynchronous**: In this example, the notify is called in the same thread as the Publisher when the state is changed since the clock needs reliable and immediate notifications to be accurate. In an asynchronous implementation, this could be done asynchronously so that the main thread of the Publisher continues running; for example this may be the preferred approach in systems using asynchronous execution, which returns a future object upon notification, but the actual notification may occur sometime later.

Since we've already encountered asynchronous processing in *Chapter 5, Writing Applications That Scale*, we will conclude our discussion on the Observer pattern with one more example, showing an asynchronous example where the Publisher and Subscriber interact asynchronously. We will be using the asyncio module in Python for this.

For this example, we will be using the domain of news publishing. Our publisher gets news stories from various sources as news URLs which are tagged to certain specific news channels. Examples of such channels could be — "sports", "international", "technology", "India", and so on.

News subscribers register for news channels they're interested in, consuming news stories as URLs. Once they get a URL they fetch the data of the URL asynchronously. The publisher-to-subscriber notification also happens asynchronously.

The following is the source code for our publisher:

```python
import weakref
import asyncio

from collections import defaultdict, deque

class NewsPublisher(object):
    """ A news publisher class with asynchronous notifications """

    def __init__(self):
        # News channels
        self.channels = defaultdict(deque)
        self.subscribers = defaultdict(list)
        self.flag = True

    def add_news(self, channel, url):
        """ Add a news story """

        self.channels[channel].append(url)

    def register(self, subscriber, channel):
        """ Register a subscriber for a news channel """

        self.subscribers[channel].append(weakref.proxy(subscriber))

    def stop(self):
        """ Stop the publisher """

        self.flag = False

    async def notify(self):
        """ Notify subscribers """

        self.data_null_count = 0

        while self.flag:
            # Subscribers who were notified
            subs = []

            for channel in self.channels:
                try:
```

```
            data = self.channels[channel].popleft()
        except IndexError:
            self.data_null_count += 1
            continue

        subscribers = self.subscribers[channel]
        for sub in subscribers:
            print('Notifying',sub,'on channel',channel,'with
                    data=>',data)
            response = await sub.callback(channel, data)
            print('Response from',sub,'for
                    channel',channel,'=>',response)
            subs.append(sub)

    await asyncio.sleep(2.0)
```

The publisher's `notify` method is asynchronous. It goes through list of channels, finds the subscribers to each of them, and calls back to the subscriber using its `callback` method, supplying it with the most recent data from the channel.

The `callback` method itself being asynchronous, it returns a future and no final processed result. Further processing of this future occurs asynchronously inside the `fetch_urls` method of the subscriber.

The following is the source code for the subscriber:

```
import aiohttp

class NewsSubscriber(object):
    """ A news subscriber class with asynchronous callbacks """

    def __init__(self):
        self.stories = {}
        self.futures = []
        self.future_status = {}
        self.flag = True

    async def callback(self, channel, data):
        """ Callback method """

        # The data is a URL
        url = data
        # We return the response immediately
        print('Fetching URL',url,'...')
        future = aiohttp.request('GET', url)
```

```
        self.futures.append(future)

    return future

async def fetch_urls(self):

    while self.flag:

        for future in self.futures:
            # Skip processed futures
            if self.future_status.get(future):
                continue

            response = await future

            # Read data
            data = await response.read()

            print('\t',self,'Got data for URL',response.
                    url,'length:',len(data))
            self.stories[response.url] = data
            # Mark as such
            self.future_status[future] = 1

        await asyncio.sleep(2.0)
```

Notice how both the `callback` and `fetch_urls` methods are both declared as asynchronous. The `callback` method passes the URL from the publisher to the `aiohttp` module's GET method, which simply returns a future.

The future is appended as a local list of futures, which is processed again asynchronously by the `fetch_urls` method to get the URL data, which is then appended to the local stories dictionary with the URL as the key.

The following is the asynchronous loop part of the code.

Take a look at the following steps:

1. To get things started, we create a publisher and add some news stories via specific URLs to couple of channels on the publisher:

```
publisher = NewsPublisher()

# Append some stories to the 'sports' and 'india' channel

publisher.add_news('sports', 'http://www.cricbuzz.com/
cricket-news/94018/collective-dd-show-hands-massive-loss-to-
kings-xi-punjab')

publisher.add_news('sports', 'https://sports.ndtv.com/
indian-premier-league-2017/ipl-2017-this-is-how-virat-kohli-
recovered-from-the-loss-against-mumbai-indians-1681955')
```

```
publisher.add_news('india','http://www.business-standard.com/
article/current-affairs/mumbai-chennai-and-hyderabad-airports-put-
on-hijack-alert-report-117041600183_1.html')
    publisher.add_news('india','http://timesofindia.indiatimes.
com/india/pakistan-to-submit-new-dossier-on-jadhav-to-un-report/
articleshow/58204955.cms')
```

2. We then create two subscribers, one listening to the `sports` channel and the other to the `india` channel:

```
subscriber1 = NewsSubscriber()
subscriber2 = NewsSubscriber()
publisher.register(subscriber1, 'sports')
publisher.register(subscriber2, 'india')
```

3. Now we create the asynchronous event loop:

```
loop = asyncio.get_event_loop()
```

4. Next, we add the tasks as co-routines to the loop to get the asynchronous loop to start its processing. We need to add the following three tasks:

   ○ `publisher.notify()`:

   ○ `subscriber.fetch_urls()`: (one for each of the two subscribers)

5. Since both the publisher and subscriber processing loops never exit, we add a timeout to processing via its `wait` method:

```
tasks = map(lambda x: x.fetch_urls(), (subscriber1,
subscriber2))
    loop.run_until_complete(asyncio.wait([publisher.notify(), *tas
ks],                                     timeout=120))

    print('Ending loop')
    loop.close()
```

The following is our asynchronous Publisher and Subscriber(s) in action, on the console.

```
(env) $ python3 observer_async.py
Notifying <__main__.NewsSubscriber object at 0x7efbf5153f98> on channel india with data=> http://www.busin
ess-standard.com/article/current-affairs/mumbai-chennai-and-hyderabad-airports-put-on-hijack-alert-report-
117041600183_1.html
Fetching URL http://www.business-standard.com/article/current-affairs/mumbai-chennai-and-hyderabad-airport
s-put-on-hijack-alert-report-117041600183_1.html ...
Response from <__main__.NewsSubscriber object at 0x7efbf5153f98> for channel india => <aiohttp.client._Ses
sionRequestContextManager object at 0x7efbf53ded38>
Notifying <__main__.NewsSubscriber object at 0x7efbf691d2e8> on channel sports with data=> http://www.cric
buzz.com/cricket-news/94018/collective-dd-show-hands-massive-loss-to-kings-xi-punjab
Fetching URL http://www.cricbuzz.com/cricket-news/94018/collective-dd-show-hands-massive-loss-to-kings-xi-
punjab ...
Response from <__main__.NewsSubscriber object at 0x7efbf691d2e8> for channel sports => <aiohttp.client._Se
ssionRequestContextManager object at 0x7efbf4c68318>
Notifying <__main__.NewsSubscriber object at 0x7efbf5153f98> on channel india with data=> http://timesofin
dia.indiatimes.com/india/pakistan-to-submit-new-dossier-on-jadhav-to-un-report/articleshow/58204955.cms
Fetching URL http://timesofindia.indiatimes.com/india/pakistan-to-submit-new-dossier-on-jadhav-to-un-repor
t/articleshow/58204955.cms ...
Response from <__main__.NewsSubscriber object at 0x7efbf5153f98> for channel india => <aiohttp.client._Ses
sionRequestContextManager object at 0x7efbf39e0ca8>
Notifying <__main__.NewsSubscriber object at 0x7efbf691d2e8> on channel sports with data=> https://sports.
ndtv.com/indian-premier-league-2017/ipl-2017-this-is-how-virat-kohli-recovered-from-the-loss-against-mumba
i-indians-1681955
Fetching URL https://sports.ndtv.com/indian-premier-league-2017/ipl-2017-this-is-how-virat-kohli-recovered
-from-the-loss-against-mumbai-indians-1681955 ...
Response from <__main__.NewsSubscriber object at 0x7efbf691d2e8> for channel sports => <aiohttp.client._Se
ssionRequestContextManager object at 0x7efbf39e05e8>
      <__main__.NewsSubscriber object at 0x7efbf691d2e8> Got data for URL http://www.cricbuzz.com/crick
et-news/94018/collective-dd-show-hands-massive-loss-to-kings-xi-punjab length: 66230
      <__main__.NewsSubscriber object at 0x7efbf691d2e8> Got data for URL https://sports.ndtv.com/india
n-premier-league-2017/ipl-2017-this-is-how-virat-kohli-recovered-from-the-loss-against-mumbai-indians-1681
```

We now move on to the last pattern in our discussion of design patterns, namely the State pattern.

The State pattern

A State pattern encapsulates the internal state of an object in another class (**state object**). The object changes its state by switching the internally encapsulated state object to different values.

A State object and its related cousin, **Finite State Machine** (**FSM**) allow a programmer to implement state transitions seamlessly across different states for the object without requiring complex code.

In Python, the State pattern can be implemented easily, since Python has a magic attribute for an object's class: the __class__ attribute.

It may sound a bit strange, but in Python this attribute can be modified on the dictionary of the instance! This allows the instance to dynamically change its class, something which we can take advantage of to implement this pattern in Python.

The following is a simple example showing this:

```
>>> class C(object):
...       def f(self): return 'hi'
...
>>> class D(object): pass
...
>>> c = C()
>>> c
<__main__.C object at 0x7fa026ac94e0>
>>> c.f()
'hi'
>>> c.__class__=D
>>> c
<__main__.D object at 0x7fa026ac94e0>
>>> c.f()
Traceback (most recent call last):
   File "<stdin>", line 1, in <module>
AttributeError: 'D' object has no attribute 'f'
```

We were able to change the class of the object c at runtime. In this example, this proved dangerous, since C and D are unrelated classes, so this is never a smart thing to do in such cases. This is evident in the way c forgot its f method when it changed to an instance of class D (D has no f method).

However, for related classes, and more specifically, subclasses of a parent class implementing the same interface, this gives a lot of power, and can be used to implement patterns such as State.

In the following example, we have used this technique to implement the State pattern. It shows a computer which can switch from one state to another.

Notice how we are using an iterator to define this class since an iterator defines movement to the next position naturally according to its nature. We are taking advantage of this fact to implement our State pattern:

```python
import random

class ComputerState(object):
    """ Base class for state of a computer """

    # This is an iterator
    name = "state"
    next_states = []
    random_states = []

    def __init__(self):
        self.index = 0

    def __str__(self):
        return self.__class__.__name__

    def __iter__(self):
        return self

    def change(self):
        return self.__next__()

    def set(self, state):
        """ Set a state """

        if self.index < len(self.next_states):
            if state in self.next_states:
                # Set index
                self.index = self.next_states.index(state)
                self.__class__ = eval(state)
                return self.__class__
            else:
                # Raise an exception for invalid state change
                current = self.__class__
                new = eval(state)
                raise Exception('Illegal transition from %s to %s' %
(current, new))
        else:
            self.index = 0
            if state in self.random_states:
```

```
                self.__class__ = eval(state)
                return self.__class__

    def __next__(self):
        """ Switch to next state """

        if self.index < len(self.next_states):
            # Always move to next state first
            self.__class__ = eval(self.next_states[self.index])
            # Keep track of the iterator position
            self.index += 1
            return self.__class__
        else:
             # Can switch to a random state once it completes
            # list of mandatory next states.
            # Reset index
            self.index = 0
            if len(self.random_states):
                state = random.choice(self.random_states)
                self.__class__ = eval(state)
                return self.__class__
            else:
                raise StopIteration
```

Now let's define some concrete subclasses of the ComputerState class.

Each class can define a list of next_states which is a set of legal states the current state can switch to. It can also define a list of random states which are random legal states it can switch to once it has switched to the next state.

For example, the following is the first state: the off state of the computer. The next compulsory state is of course the on state. Once the computer is on, this state can move off to any of the other random states.

Hence the definition is as follows:

```
class ComputerOff(ComputerState):
    next_states = ['ComputerOn']
    random_states = ['ComputerSuspend', 'ComputerHibernate',
'ComputerOff']
```

Similarly, the following are the definitions of the other state classes:

```
class ComputerOn(ComputerState):
    # No compulsory next state
    random_states = ['ComputerSuspend', 'ComputerHibernate',
'ComputerOff']

class ComputerWakeUp(ComputerState):
    # No compulsory next state
    random_states = ['ComputerSuspend', 'ComputerHibernate',
'ComputerOff']

class ComputerSuspend(ComputerState):
    next_states = ['ComputerWakeUp']
    random_states = ['ComputerSuspend', 'ComputerHibernate',
'ComputerOff']

class ComputerHibernate(ComputerState):
    next_states = ['ComputerOn']
    random_states = ['ComputerSuspend', 'ComputerHibernate',
'ComputerOff']
```

Finally, the following is the class for the Computer which uses the state classes to set its internal state.

```
class Computer(object):
    """ A class representing a computer """

    def __init__(self, model):
        self.model = model
        # State of the computer - default is off.
        self.state = ComputerOff()

    def change(self, state=None):
        """ Change state """

        if state==None:
            return self.state.change()
        else:
            return self.state.set(state)

    def __str__(self):
        """ Return state """
        return str(self.state)
```

The following are some interesting aspects of this implementation:

- **State as an iterator**: We have implemented the ComputerState class as an iterator. This is because a state has, naturally, a list of immediate future states it can switch to and nothing else. For example, a computer in an Off state can move only to the On state next. Defining it as an iterator allows us to take advantage of the natural progression of an iterator from one state to next.

- **Random States**: We have implemented the concept of random states in this example. Once a computer moves from one state to its mandatory next state (On to Off, Suspend to WakeUp), it has a list of random states available to move on to. A computer that is On need not always be switched off. It can also go to Sleep (Suspend) or Hibernate.

- **Manual Change**: The computer can move to a specific state via the second optional argument of the change method. However, this is possible only if the state change is valid; otherwise an exception is raised.

We will now see our State pattern in action.

The computer is off to start with, of course:

```
>>> c = Computer('ASUS')
>>> print(c)
ComputerOff
```

Let's see some automatic state changes:

```
>>> c.change()
<class 'state.ComputerOn'>
```

And now, let the state machine decide its next states — note these are random states till the computer enters a state where it has to mandatorily move on to the next state:

```
>>> c.change()
<class 'state.ComputerHibernate'>
```

Now the state is Hibernate, which means the next state has to be On as it is a compulsory next state:

```
>>> c.change()
<class 'state.ComputerOn'>
>>> c.change()
<class 'state.ComputerOff'>
```

Now the state is Off, which means the next state has to be On:

```
>>> c.change()
<class 'state.ComputerOn'>
```

The following are all random state changes:

```
>>> c.change()
<class 'state.ComputerSuspend'>
>>> c.change()
<class 'state.ComputerWakeUp'>
>> c.change()
<class 'state.ComputerHibernate'>
```

Now, since the underlying state is an iterator, one can even iterate on the state using a module such as itertools.

The following is an example of this – iterating on the next five states of the computer:

```
>>> import itertools
>>> for s in itertools.islice(c.state, 5):
... print (s)
...
<class 'state.ComputerOn'>
<class 'state.ComputerOff'>
<class 'state.ComputerOn'>
<class 'state.ComputerOff'>
<class 'state.ComputerOn'>
```

Now let's try some manual state changes:

```
>>> c.change('ComputerOn')
<class 'state.ComputerOn'>
>>> c.change('ComputerSuspend')
<class 'state.ComputerSuspend'>

>>> c.change('ComputerHibernate')
Traceback (most recent call last):
  File "state.py", line 133, in <module>
      print(c.change('ComputerHibernate'))
  File "state.py", line 108, in change
      return self.state.set(state)
  File "state.py", line 45, in set
      raise Exception('Illegal transition from %s to %s' %
          (current, new))
Exception: Illegal transition from <class '__main__.ComputerSuspend'>
to <class '__main__.ComputerHibernate'>
```

We get an exception when we try an invalid state transition, as the computer cannot go directly from Suspend to Hibernate. It has to wake up first!

```
>>> c.change('ComputerWakeUp')
<class 'state.ComputerWakeUp'>
>>> c.change('ComputerHibernate')
<class 'state.ComputerHibernate'>
```

All good now.

We have completed our discussion of design patterns in Python, so it is time to summarize what we've learned so far.

Summary

In this chapter, we took a detailed tour of object-oriented design patterns, and found out new and different ways to implement them in Python. We started with an overview of design patterns and their classification into Creational, Structural, and Behavioral patterns.

We went on to see an example of a Strategy design pattern, and saw how to implement this in a Pythonic manner. We then began our formal discussion of patterns in Python.

In Creational patterns, we covered the Singleton, Borg, Prototype, Factory, and Builder patterns. We saw why Borg is usually a better approach than Singleton in Python due to its ability to keep state across class hierarchies. We saw the interplay between the Builder, Prototype, and Factory patterns, and saw a few examples. Everywhere possible, metaclass discussions were introduced, and pattern implementations were done using metaclasses.

In Structural patterns, our focus was on the Adapter, Facade, and Proxy patterns. We saw detailed examples using the Adapter pattern, and discussed approaches via inheritance and object composition. We saw the power of magic methods in Python when we implemented the Adapter and Proxy patterns via the __getattr__ technique.

In Facade, using a Car class, we saw a detailed example on how Facade helps programmers conquer complexity and provide generic interfaces over the subsystems. We also saw that many Python standard library modules are themselves facades.

In the Behavioral section, we discussed the Iterator, Observer, and State patterns. We saw how iterators are part and parcel of Python. We implemented an iterator as a generator for building Prime numbers.

We saw a simple example of the Observer pattern by using an `Alarm` class as a Publisher and a clock class as Subscriber. We also saw an example of an asynchronous observer pattern using the asyncio module in Python.

Finally, we ended our discussion of patterns with the State pattern. We discussed a detailed example, switching the states of a computer through allowable state changes, and how one can use Python's `__class__` as a dynamic attribute to change the class of an instance. In the implementation of State, we borrowed techniques from the Iterator pattern, and implemented the State example class as an Iterator.

In our next chapter, we move on from design to the next-higher paradigm of patterns in software architectures: architectural patterns.

Python – Architectural Patterns

Architectural patterns are the highest level of patterns in the pantheon of patterns in software. Architectural patterns allow the architects to specify the fundamental structure of an application. The architectural pattern chosen for a given software problem governs the rest of its activities, such as the design of systems involved, communication between different parts of the system, and so on.

There are a number of architectural patterns to choose from depending upon the problem at hand. Different patterns solve different classes or families of problems, creating their own style or class of architecture. For example, a certain class of patterns solves the architecture of client/server systems, another helps to build distributed systems, and a third helps to design highly decoupled peer-to-peer systems.

In this chapter, we will discuss and focus on a few architectural patterns that are encountered often in the Python world. Our pattern of discussion in the chapter will be to take a well-known architectural pattern, and explore one or two popular software applications or frameworks that implement it, or a variation of it.

We will not discuss a lot of code in this chapter—the usage of code will be limited to those patterns where an illustration using a program is absolutely essential. On the other hand, most of the discussion will be on the architectural details, participating subsystems, variations in the architecture implemented by the chosen application/framework, and the like.

There are any number of architecture patterns that we can look at. In this chapter, we will focus on MVC and its related patterns, event-driven programming architectures, microservices architectures, and pipes and filters.

We will be covering the following topics in this chapter:

- Introducing MVC:
  - ○ Model View Template — Django
  - ○ Flask microframework

- Event-driven programming:
  - ○ Chat server and client using select
  - ○ Event-driven versus concurrent programming
  - ○ Twisted

    Twisted chat server and client

  - ○ Eventlet

    Eventlet chat server

  - ○ Greenlets and gevent

    Gevent chat server

- Microservices architecture:
  - ○ Microservice frameworks in Python
  - ○ Microservice example
  - ○ Microservice advantages

- Pipe and filter architecture:
  - ○ Pipe and filter in Python — examples

Introducing MVC

Model View Controller (**MVC**) is a well-known and popular architectural pattern for building interactive applications. MVC splits the application into three components: the Model, the View, and the Controller.

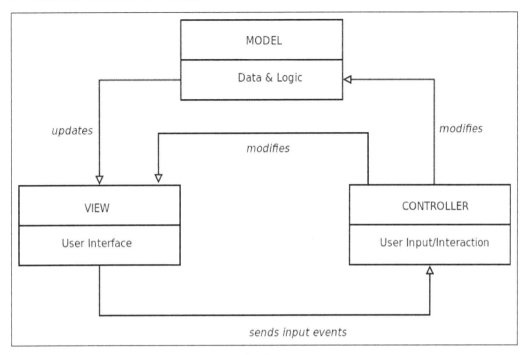

MVC architecture

The three components perform the following responsibilities:

- **Model**: The model contains the core data and logic of the application.
- **View**: The view(s) form the output of the application to the user. They display information to the user. Multiple views of the same data are possible.
- **Controller**: The controller receives and processes user inputs such as keyboard clicks or mouse clicks/movements, and converts them into change requests for the model or the view.

Separation of concerns using these three components avoids tight coupling between the data of the application and its representation. It allows for multiple representations (views) of the same data (model), which can be computed and presented according to user input received via the controller.

The MVC pattern allows the following interactions:

- A model can change its data depending upon inputs received from the controller.
- The changed data is reflected on the views, which are subscribed to changes in the model.

- Controllers can send commands to update the model's state, such as when making changes to a document. Controllers can also send commands to modify the presentation of a view without any change to the model, such as zooming in on a graph or chart.

- The MVC pattern implicitly includes a change propagation mechanism to notify each component of changes on the other dependent components.

- A number of web applications in the Python world implement MVC or a variation of it. We will look at a couple of them, namely Django and Flask, in the coming sections.

Model Template View (MTV) – Django

The Django project is one of the most popular web application frameworks in the Python world. Django implements something like an MVC pattern, but with some subtle differences.

The Django (core) component architecture is illustrated in the following diagram:

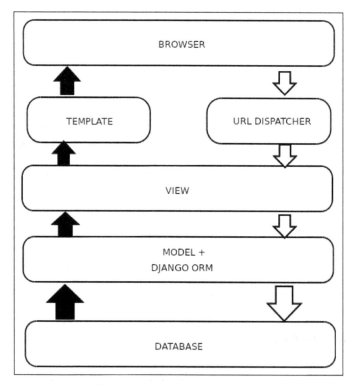

Django core component architecture

The core components of the Django framework are as follows:

- An **Object Relational Mapper** (**ORM**), which acts as a mediator between data models (Python) and the database (RDBMS) — this can be thought of as the **Model** layer.

- A set of callback functions in Python, which renders the data to the user interface for a specific URL — this can be thought of as the **VIEW** layer. The view focuses on building and transforming the content rather than on its actual presentation.

- A set of HTML templates to render content in different presentations. The view delegates to a specific template, which is responsible for how the data is presented.

- A regular expression-based **URL DISPATCHER**, which connects relative paths on the server to specific views and their variable arguments. This can be thought of as a rudimentary **Controller**.

- In Django, since the presentation is performed by the **TEMPLATE** layer and only the content mapping done by the **VIEW** layer, Django is often described as implementing the **MTV** framework.

- The Controller in Django is not very well defined — it can be thought of as the entire framework itself — or limited to the **URL DISPATCHER** layer.

Django admin – automated model-centric views

One of the most powerful components of the Django framework is its automatic admin system, which reads metadata from the Django models, and generates quick, model-centric admin views, where administrators of the system can view and edit data models via simple HTML forms.

For illustration, the following is an example of a Django model that describes a term that is added to a website as a `glossary` term (a glossary is a list or index of words that describes the meaning of words related to a specific subject, text, or dialect):

```python
from django.db import models

class GlossaryTerm(models.Model):
    """ Model for describing a glossary word (term) """

    term = models.CharField(max_length=1024)
    meaning = models.CharField(max_length=1024)
    meaning_html = models.CharField('Meaning with HTML markup',
                    max_length=4096, null=True, blank=True)
    example = models.CharField(max_length=4096, null=True, blank=True)

    # can be a ManyToManyField?
    domains = models.CharField(max_length=128, null=True, blank=True)

    notes = models.CharField(max_length=2048, null=True, blank=True)
    url = models.CharField('URL', max_length=2048, null=True,
blank=True)
    name = models.ForeignKey('GlossarySource', verbose_name='Source',
blank=True)

    def __unicode__(self):
        return self.term

    class Meta:
        unique_together = ('term', 'meaning', 'url')
```

This is combined with an admin system that registers a model for an automated admin view:

```python
from django.contrib import admin

admin.site.register(GlossaryTerm)
admin.site.register(GlossarySource)
```

The following is a screenshot of the automated admin view (HTML form) for adding a glossary term via the Django admin interface:

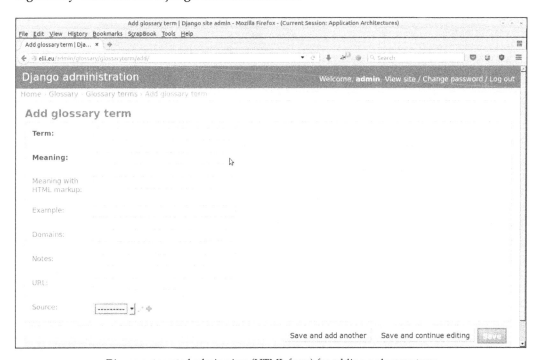

Django automated admin view (HTML form) for adding a glossary term

A quick observation tells you how the Django admin is able to generate the correct field type for the different data fields in the model, and generate a form for adding the data. This is a powerful pattern present in Django that allows one to generate automated admin views for adding/editing models with almost no coding effort.

Let's now look at another popular Python web application framework, namely Flask.

Flexible Microframework – Flask

Flask is a micro web framework that uses a minimalistic philosophy for building web applications. Flask relies on just two libraries: the Werkzeug (`http://werkzeug.pocoo.org/`) WSGI toolkit and the Jinja2 templating framework.

Flask comes with simple URL routing via decorators. The *micro* word in Flask indicates that the core of the framework is small. Support for databases, forms, and others is provided by multiple extensions that the Python community has built around Flask.

The core Flask can thus be thought of as an MTV framework minus the M (View Template), since the core does not implement support for models.

Here is an approximate schematic diagram of the Flask component architecture:

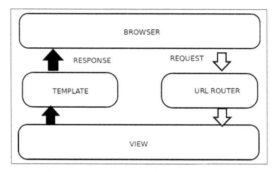

Schematic diagram of Flask components

A simple Flask application using templates looks something like this:

```
from flask import Flask
app = Flask(__name__)

@app.route('/')
def index():
    data = 'some data'
    return render_template('index.html', **locals())
```

We can find a few components of the MVC pattern right here:

- The `@app.route` decorator routes requests from the browser to the `index` function. The application router can be thought of as the controller.

- The `index` function returns the data, and renders it using a template. The `index` function can be thought of as generating the view or the view component.

- Flask uses templates like Django to keep the content separate from the presentation. This can be thought of as the template component.

- There is no specific model component in Flask core. However, this can be added on with the help of additional plugins.

- Flask uses a plugin architecture to support additional features. For example, models can be added on by using Flask-SQLAlchemy, RESTful API support using Flask-RESTful, serialization using Flask-marshmallow, and others.

Event-driven programming

Event-driven programming is a paradigm of system architecture where the logic flow within the program is driven by events such as user actions, messages from other programs, or hardware (sensor) inputs.

In event-driven architectures, there is usually a main event loop, which listens for events and then triggers callback functions with specific arguments when an event is detected.

In modern operating systems such as Linux, support for events on input file descriptors such as sockets or opened files is implemented by system calls such as `select`, `poll`, and `epoll`.

Python provides wrappers to these system calls via its `select` module. It is not very difficult to write a simple event-driven program using the `select` module in Python.

The following set of programs together implement a basic chat server and client in Python using the power of the select module.

Chat server and client using I/O multiplexing with the select module

Our chat server uses the `select` system call via the `select` module to create channels where clients can connect to and talk with each other. It handles the events (sockets) that are input ready–if the event is a client connecting to the server, it connects and performs a handshake; if the event is data to be read from standard input, the server reads the data, or else it passes the data received from one client to the others.

Here is our chat server:

```python
# chatserver.py

import socket
import select
import signal
import sys
from communication import send, receive

class ChatServer(object):
    """ Simple chat server using select """


    def serve(self):
        inputs = [self.server,sys.stdin]
        self.outputs = []


        while True:

            inputready,outputready,exceptready = select.select(inputs, self.outputs, [])




            for s in inputready:

                if s == self.server:
                    # handle the server socket
                    client, address = self.server.accept()

                    # Read the login name
                    cname = receive(client).split('NAME: ')[1]

                    # Compute client name and send back
                    self.clients += 1
                    send(client, 'CLIENT: ' + str(address[0]))
                    inputs.append(client)

                    self.clientmap[client] = (address, cname)
```

```
                        self.outputs.append(client)

                elif s == sys.stdin:
                    # handle standard input - the server exits
                    junk = sys.stdin.readline()
            break
                else:
                    # handle all other sockets
                    try:
                        data = receive(s)
                        if data:
                            # Send as new client's message...
                            msg = '\n#[' + self.get_name(s) + ']>> ' +
data

                            # Send data to all except ourselves
                            for o in self.outputs:
                                if o != s:
                                    send(o, msg)
                        else:
                            print('chatserver: %d hung up' %
s.fileno())

                            self.clients -= 1
                            s.close()
                            inputs.remove(s)
                            self.outputs.remove(s)

                    except socket.error as e:
                        # Remove
                        inputs.remove(s)
                        self.outputs.remove(s)

        self.server.close()

if __name__ == "__main__":
    ChatServer().serve()
```

Since the code of the chat server is big, we are only including the main function, namely the serve function here showing how the server uses select-based I/O multiplexing. A lot of code in the serve function has also been trimmed to keep the printed code small.

The complete source code can be downloaded from the code archive of this book from the book's website.

The chat server can be stopped by sending a single line of empty input.

The chat client also uses the `select` system call. It uses a socket to connect to the server, and then waits for events on the socket plus the standard input. If the event is from the standard input, it reads the data. Otherwise, it sends the data to the server via the socket:

```python
# chatclient.py
import socket
import select
import sys
from communication import send, receive

class ChatClient(object):
    """ A simple command line chat client using select """

    def __init__(self, name, host='127.0.0.1', port=3490):
        self.name = name
        # Quit flag
        self.flag = False
        self.port = int(port)
        self.host = host
        # Initial prompt
        self.prompt='[' + '@'.join((name, socket.gethostname().
split('.')[0])) + ']> '
        # Connect to server at port
        try:
            self.sock = socket.socket(socket.AF_INET, socket.SOCK_
STREAM)
            self.sock.connect((host, self.port))
            print('Connected to chat server@%d' % self.port)
            # Send my name...
            send(self.sock,'NAME: ' + self.name)
            data = receive(self.sock)
            # Contains client address, set it
            addr = data.split('CLIENT: ')[1]
            self.prompt = '[' + '@'.join((self.name, addr)) + ']> '
        except socket.error as e:
            print('Could not connect to chat server @%d' % self.port)
            sys.exit(1)

    def chat(self):
```

```
        """ Main chat method """

        while not self.flag:
            try:
                sys.stdout.write(self.prompt)
                sys.stdout.flush()

                # Wait for input from stdin & socket
                inputready, outputready,exceptrdy = select.select([0,
self.sock], [],[])

                for i in inputready:
                    if i == 0:
                        data = sys.stdin.readline().strip()
                        if data: send(self.sock, data)
                    elif i == self.sock:
                        data = receive(self.sock)
                        if not data:
                            print('Shutting down.')
                            self.flag = True
                            break
                        else:
                            sys.stdout.write(data + '\n')
                            sys.stdout.flush()

            except KeyboardInterrupt:
                print('Interrupted.')
                self.sock.close()
                break

if __name__ == "__main__":
    if len(sys.argv)<3:
        sys.exit('Usage: %s chatid host portno' % sys.argv[0])

    client = ChatClient(sys.argv[1],sys.argv[2], int(sys.argv[3]))
    client.chat()
```

[The chat client can be stopped by pressing *Ctrl* + *C* on the Terminal.]

In order to send data to and fro via sockets, both these scripts use a third module, named `communication`, which has a `send` and a `receive` function. This module uses pickle to serialize and deserialize data in the `send` and `receive` functions, respectively:

```python
# communication.py
import pickle
import socket
import struct

def send(channel, *args):
    """ Send a message to a channel """

    buf = pickle.dumps(args)
    value = socket.htonl(len(buf))
    size = struct.pack("L",value)
    channel.send(size)
    channel.send(buf)

def receive(channel):
    """ Receive a message from a channel """

    size = struct.calcsize("L")
    size = channel.recv(size)
    try:
        size = socket.ntohl(struct.unpack("L", size)[0])
    except struct.error as e:
        return ''

    buf = ""

    while len(buf) < size:
        buf = channel.recv(size - len(buf))

    return pickle.loads(buf)[0]
```

The following are some screenshots of the server running and two clients that are connected to each other via the chat server:

Here is the screenshot of client #1, named `andy`, connected to the chat server:

Chat session of chat client #1 (client name: andy)

Similarly, here is a client named `betty` who is connected to the chat server and is talking to `andy`:

Chat session of chat client #2 (client name: betty)

Some interesting points of the program are as follows:

- See how the clients are able to see each other's messages. This happens because the server sends the data sent by one client to all the other connected clients. Our chat server prefixes the messages with a hash (#) to indicate that this message is from another client.

- See how the server sends connection and disconnection information of a client to all other clients. This informs the clients when another client is connected to or disconnected from the session.

- The server echoes messages when a client disconnects saying that the client *hung up*.

> The preceding chat server and client example is a minor variation of the author's own Python recipe in the ASPN Cookbook at `https://code.activestate.com/recipes/531824`.

The simple select-based multiplexing is taken to the next level by libraries such as Twisted, Eventlet, and Gevent in order to build systems that provide high-level event-based programming routines to the programmer, typically based on a core event loop very similar to the loop of our chat server example.

We will discuss the architecture of these frameworks in the following sections.

Event-driven programming versus concurrent programming

The example we saw in the previous section uses the technique of asynchronous events as we saw in the chapter on concurrency. This is different from true concurrent or parallel programming.

Event programming libraries also work on the technique of asynchronous events. There is only a single thread of execution in which tasks are interleaved one after another based on the events received.

In the following diagram, consider a truly parallel execution of three tasks by three threads or processes:

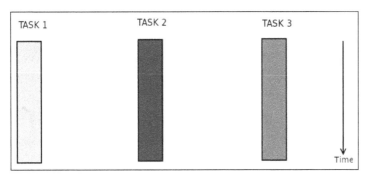

Parallel execution of three tasks using three threads

Contrast this with what happens when the tasks are executed via event-driven programming as depicted in the following diagram:

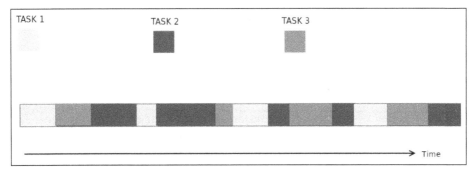

Asynchronous execution of three tasks in a single thread

In the asynchronous model, there is only one single thread of execution with tasks executing in an interleaved fashion. Each task gets its own slot of processing time in the event loop of the asynchronous processing server, but only one task executes at a given time. Tasks yield control back to the loop so that it can schedule a different task in the next time slice from the task that is being executed currently. As we have seen in *Chapter 5*, *Writing Applications that Scale*, this is a kind of cooperative multitasking.

Twisted

Twisted is an event-driven networking engine with support for multiple protocols, such as DNS, SMTP, POP3, IMAP, and so on. It also comes with support for writing SSH clients and servers, and to build messaging and IRC clients and servers.

Twisted also provides a set of patterns (styles) to write common servers and clients, such as web server/client (HTTP), publish/subscribe patterns, messaging clients and servers (SOAP/XML-RPC), and others.

It uses the Reactor design pattern, which multiplexes and dispatches events from multiple sources to their event handlers in a single thread.

It receives messages, requests, and connections coming from multiple concurrent clients, and processes these posts sequentially using event handlers without requiring concurrent threads or processes.

The reactor pseudo-code looks, approximately, as follows:

```
while True:
    timeout = time_until_next_timed_event()
    events = wait_for_events(timeout)
    events += timed_events_until(now())
    for event in events:
        event.process()
```

Twisted uses callbacks to call event handlers as and when an event happens. To handle a specific event, a callback is registered for that event. Callbacks can be used for regular processing, and also for managing exceptions (errbacks).

Like the `asyncio` module, Twisted uses an object such as futures in order to wrap the results of a task execution, whose actual results are still not available. In Twisted, these objects are called **Deferreds**.

Deferred objects have a pair of callback chains: one for processing results (callbacks) and one for managing errors (errbacks). When the result of an execution is obtained, a Deferred object is created, and its callbacks and/or errbacks are called in the order in which they were added.

Here is an architecture diagram of Twisted, showing the high-level components:

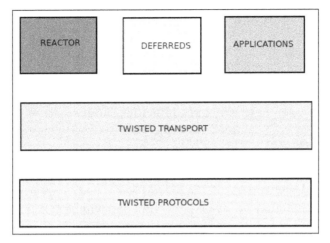

Twisted—Core Components

Twisted – a simple web client

The following is a simple example of a web HTTP client using Twisted, fetching a given URL and saving its contents to a specific filename:

```
# twisted_fetch_url.py
from twisted.internet import reactor
from twisted.web.client import getPage
import sys

def save_page(page, filename='content.html'):
    print type(page)
    open(filename,'w').write(page)
    print 'Length of data',len(page)
    print 'Data saved to',filename

def handle_error(error):
    print error

def finish_processing(value):
    print "Shutting down..."
    reactor.stop()

if __name__ == "__main__":
    url = sys.argv[1]
```

```
deferred = getPage(url)
deferred.addCallbacks(save_page, handle_error)
deferred.addBoth(finish_processing)

reactor.run()
```

As you can see in the preceding code, the getPage method returns a deferred, and not the data of the URL. To the deferred, we add two callbacks: one for processing the data (the save_page function) and another for handling errors (the handle_ error function). The addBoth method of the deferred adds a single function as both callback and errback.

The event processing is started by running the reactor. In the finish_processing callback, which is called at the end, the reactor is stopped. Since event handlers are called in the order that they are added, this function will be called only at the very end.

When the reactor is run, the following events happen:

- The page is fetched and the deferred is created.
- The callbacks are called in order on the deferred. First the save_page function is called, which saves contents of the page to the content.html file. Then a handle_error event handler is called, which prints any error string.
- Finally, finish_processing is called, which stops the reactor, and the event processing ends, exiting the program.

 At the time of writing, Twisted is not yet available for Python3, so the preceding code is written for Python2.

- When you run the code, you will see that the following output is produced:

```
$ python2 twisted_fetch_url.py http://www.google.com
Length of data 13280
Data saved to content.html
Shutting down...
```

Chat server using Twisted

Let's now see how we can write a simple chat server in Twisted on lines similar to our chat server using the select module.

In Twisted, servers are built by implementing protocols and protocol factories. A protocol class typically inherits from the Twisted Protocol class.

A factory is nothing but a class that serves as a factory pattern for protocol objects.

Using this, here is our chat server using Twisted:

```
from twisted.internet import protocol, reactor

class Chat(protocol.Protocol):
    """ Chat protocol """

    transports = {}
    peers = {}

    def connectionMade(self):
        self._peer = self.transport.getPeer()
        print 'Connected',self._peer

    def connectionLost(self, reason):
        self._peer = self.transport.getPeer()
        # Find out and inform other clients
        user = self.peers.get((self._peer.host, self._peer.port))
        if user != None:
            self.broadcast('(User %s disconnected)\n' % user, user)
            print 'User %s disconnected from %s' % (user, self._peer)

    def broadcast(self, msg, user):
        """ Broadcast chat message to all connected users except
        'user' """

        for key in self.transports.keys():
            if key != user:
                if msg != "<handshake>":
                    self.transports[key].write('#[' + user + "]>>> " +
msg)
                else:
                    # Inform other clients of connection
                    self.transports[key].write('(User %s connected
from %s)\n' % (user, self._peer))

    def dataReceived(self, data):
        """ Callback when data is ready to be read from the socket """

        user, msg = data.split(":")
        print "Got data=>",msg,"from",user
        self.transports[user] = self.transport
        # Make an entry in the peers dictionary
```

```
            self.peers[(self._peer.host, self._peer.port)] = user
            self.broadcast(msg, user)

    class ChatFactory(protocol.Factory):
        """ Chat protocol factory """

        def buildProtocol(self, addr):
            return Chat()

    if __name__ == "__main__":
        reactor.listenTCP(3490, ChatFactory())
        reactor.run()
```

Our chat server is a bit more sophisticated than the one before as it performs the following additional steps:

1. It has a separate handshake protocol using the special <handshake> message.
2. When a client connects, it is broadcast to other clients, informing them of the client's name and connection details.
3. When a client disconnects, other clients are informed about this.

The chat client also uses Twisted and uses two protocols — namely a ChatClientProtocol for communication with the server and a StdioClientProtocol for reading data from standard input and echoing data received from the server to the standard output.

The latter protocol also connects the former one to its input, so that any data that is received on the standard input is sent to the server as a chat message.

Take a look at the following code:

```
import sys
import socket
from twisted.internet import stdio, reactor, protocol


class ChatProtocol(protocol.Protocol):
    """ Base protocol for chat """

    def __init__(self, client):
        self.output = None
        # Client name: E.g: andy
        self.client = client
```

```
        self.prompt='[' + '@'.join((self.client, socket.gethostname().
split('.')[0])) + ']> '

    def input_prompt(self):
        """ The input prefix for client """
        sys.stdout.write(self.prompt)
        sys.stdout.flush()

    def dataReceived(self, data):
        self.processData(data)

class ChatClientProtocol(ChatProtocol):
    """ Chat client protocol """

    def connectionMade(self):
        print 'Connection made'
        self.output.write(self.client + ":<handshake>")

    def processData(self, data):
        """ Process data received """

        if not len(data.strip()):
            return

        self.input_prompt()

        if self.output:
            # Send data in this form to server
            self.output.write(self.client + ":" + data)


class StdioClientProtocol(ChatProtocol):
    """ Protocol which reads data from input and echoes
    data to standard output """

    def connectionMade(self):
        # Create chat client protocol
        chat = ChatClientProtocol(client=sys.argv[1])
        chat.output = self.transport

        # Create stdio wrapper
        stdio_wrapper = stdio.StandardIO(chat)
        # Connect to output
```

```python
        self.output = stdio_wrapper
        print "Connected to server"
        self.input_prompt()

    def input_prompt(self):
        # Since the output is directly connected
        # to stdout, use that to write.
        self.output.write(self.prompt)

    def processData(self, data):
        """ Process data received """

        if self.output:
            self.output.write('\n' + data)
            self.input_prompt()


class StdioClientFactory(protocol.ClientFactory):

    def buildProtocol(self, addr):
        return StdioClientProtocol(sys.argv[1])


def main():
    reactor.connectTCP("localhost", 3490, StdioClientFactory())
    reactor.run()


if __name__ == '__main__':
    main()
```

Here are some screenshots of the two clients andy and betty communicating using this chat server and client:

```
Terminal                                                          - + x
anand@mangu-probook:/home/user/programs/chap8$ python2 twisted_chat_client.py andy
Connection made
Connected to server
[andy@mangu-probook]>          ▶
(User betty connected from IPv4Address(TCP, '127.0.0.1', 39252))
[andy@mangu-probook]> hello betty
[andy@mangu-probook]>
#[betty]>>> hi andy
[andy@mangu-probook]> how are you ?
[andy@mangu-probook]>
#[betty]>>> I am good, and you ?
[andy@mangu-probook]> I am pretty fine
[andy@mangu-probook]>
#[betty]>>> Ok
[andy@mangu-probook]>
#[betty]>>> How about the dinner plan today ?
[andy@mangu-probook]> All good
[andy@mangu-probook]>
#[betty]>>> See you at 8 then
[andy@mangu-probook]> Sure, see you then
[andy@mangu-probook]>
#[betty]>>> bye andy
[andy@mangu-probook]> bye betty
anand@mangu-probook:/home/user/programs/chap8$
anand@mangu-probook:/home/user/programs/chap8$ █
```

Chat client using Twisted chat server — session for client #1 (andy)

Here is the second session, for the client betty:

```
Terminal                                                          - + x
anand@mangu-probook:/home/user/programs/chap8$ python twisted_chat_client.py betty
Connection made
Connected to server
[betty@mangu-probook]>
#[andy]>>> hello betty
[betty@mangu-probook]> hi andy
[betty@mangu-probook]>
#[andy]>>> how are you ?
[betty@mangu-probook]> I am good, and you ?
[betty@mangu-probook]>
#[andy]>>> I am pretty fine
[betty@mangu-probook]> Ok
[betty@mangu-probook]> How about the dinner plan today ?
[betty@mangu-probook]>
#[andy]>>> All good
[betty@mangu-probook]> See you at 8 then
[betty@mangu-probook]>
#[andy]>>> Sure, see you then
[betty@mangu-probook]> bye andy
[betty@mangu-probook]>
#[andy]>>> bye betty
[betty@mangu-probook]>
#[andy]>>> (User andy disconnected)
anand@mangu-probook:/home/user/programs/chap8$
anand@mangu-probook:/home/user/programs/chap8$ █
```

Chat client using Twisted chat server — session for client #2 (betty)

You can follow the flow of the conversation by alternately looking at the screenshots.

Note the connection and disconnection messages are sent by the server when user `betty` connects and user andy disconnects respectively.

Eventlet

Eventlet is another well-known networking library in the Python world that allows one to write event-driven programs using the same concept of asynchronous execution.

Eventlet uses co-routines for this purpose with the help of a set of so-called *green threads*, which are lightweight user-space threads that perform cooperative multitasking.

Eventlet uses an abstraction over a set of green threads, the `Greenpool` class, in order to perform its tasks.

The `Greenpool` class runs a predefined set of `Greenpool` threads (default is `1000`), and provides ways to map functions and callables to the threads in different ways.

Here is the multiuser chat server rewritten using Eventlet:

```python
# eventlet_chat.py

import eventlet
from eventlet.green import socket

participants = set()

def new_chat_channel(conn):
    """ New chat channel for a given connection """

    data = conn.recv(1024)
    user = ''

    while data:
        print("Chat:", data.strip())
        for p in participants:
            try:
                if p is not conn:
                    data = data.decode('utf-8')
```

```
                    user, msg = data.split(':')
                    if msg != '<handshake>':
                        data_s = '\n#[' + user + ']>>> says ' + msg
                    else:
                        data_s = '(User %s connected)\n' % user

                    p.send(bytearray(data_s, 'utf-8'))
            except socket.error as e:
                # ignore broken pipes, they just mean the participant
                # closed its connection already
                if e[0] != 32:
                    raise
        data = conn.recv(1024)

    participants.remove(conn)
    print("Participant %s left chat." % user)

if __name__ == "__main__":
    port = 3490
    try:
        print("ChatServer starting up on port", port)
        server = eventlet.listen(('0.0.0.0', port))

        while True:
            new_connection, address = server.accept()
            print("Participant joined chat.")
            participants.add(new_connection)
            print(eventlet.spawn(new_chat_channel,
                                 new_connection))

    except (KeyboardInterrupt, SystemExit):
        print("ChatServer exiting.")
```

 This server can be used with the Twisted chat client that we've seen in the previous example, and behaves in exactly the same way. Hence, we will not show running examples of this server.

The Eventlet library internally uses `greenlets`, a package that provides green threads on Python runtime. We will see greenlet and a related library, Gevent, in the following section.

Greenlets and Gevent

Greenlet is a package that provides a version of green or microthreads on top of the Python interpreter. It is inspired by Stackless, a version of CPython that supports microthreads called stacklets. However, greenlets are able to run on the standard CPython runtime.

Gevent is a Python networking library providing a high-level synchronous API on top of `libev`, the event library written in C.

Gevent is inspired by gevent, but it features a more consistent API and better performance.

Like Eventlet, gevent does a lot of monkey patching on system libraries to provide support for cooperative multitasking. For example, gevent comes with its own sockets, just like Eventlet does.

Unlike Eventlet, gevent also requires explicit monkey patching to be done by the programmer. It provides a method to do this on the module itself.

Without further ado, let's look at the multiuser chat server using gevent:

```python
# gevent_chat_server.py

import gevent
from gevent import monkey
from gevent import socket
from gevent.server import StreamServer

monkey.patch_all()

participants = set()

def new_chat_channel(conn, address):
    """ New chat channel for a given connection """

    participants.add(conn)
    data = conn.recv(1024)
    user = ''

    while data:
        print("Chat:", data.strip())
        for p in participants:
            try:
```

```
                    if p is not conn:
                        data = data.decode('utf-8')
                        user, msg = data.split(':')
                        if msg != '<handshake>':
                            data_s = '\n#[' + user + ']>>> says ' + msg
                        else:
                            data_s = '(User %s connected)\n' % user

                        p.send(bytearray(data_s, 'utf-8'))
                except socket.error as e:
                    # ignore broken pipes, they just mean the participant
                    # closed its connection already
                    if e[0] != 32:
                        raise
            data = conn.recv(1024)

        participants.remove(conn)
        print("Participant %s left chat." % user)

    if __name__ == "__main__":
        port = 3490
        try:
            print("ChatServer starting up on port", port)
            server = StreamServer(('0.0.0.0', port), new_chat_channel)
            server.serve_forever()
        except (KeyboardInterrupt, SystemExit):
            print("ChatServer exiting.")
```

The code for the gevent-based chat server is almost the same as the one using Eventlet. The reason for this is that they work in very similar ways, by handling control to a callback function when a new connection is made. In both cases the callback function is named `new_chat_channel`, which has the same functionality and hence very similar code.

The differences between the two are as follows:

- gevent provides its own TCP server class — `StreamingServer`-so we use that instead of listening on the module directly.

- In the gevent server, for every connection the `new_chat_channel` handler is invoked, hence the participant set is managed there.

- Since the gevent server has its own event loop, there is no need to create a while loop for listening for incoming connections as we had to do with Eventlet.

This example works exactly the same as the previous ones and works with the Twisted chat client.

Microservice architecture

Microservice architecture is an architectural style of developing a single application as a suite of small independent services, each running in its own process and communicating via lightweight mechanisms—typically, using HTTP protocol.

Microservices are independently deployable components, and usually have zero or minimalistic central management or configuration.

Microservices can be thought of as a specific implementation style for **Service Oriented Architectures (SOA)**, where, instead of building a monolith application top-down, the application is built as a dynamic group of mutually interacting, independent services.

Traditionally, enterprise applications were built in a monolithic pattern, typically consisting of these three layers:

1. A client-side **user interface (UI)** layer consisting of HTML and JavaScript.
2. A server-side application consisting of the business logic.
3. A database and data access layer, which holds the business data.

On the other hand, a microservices architecture will split this layer into multiple services. For example, the business logic, instead of being in a single application, will be split into multiple component services, whose interactions define the logic flow inside the application. The services might query a single database or independent local databases, with the latter configuration being more common.

Data in microservices architectures are usually processed and returned in the form of document objects—typically encoded in JSON.

The following schematic diagram illustrates the difference of a monolithic architecture from a microservices one:

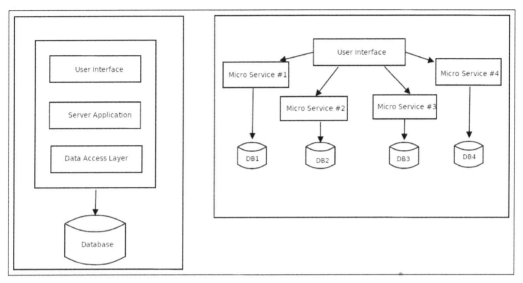

Monolithic (left) versus microservices (right) Architecture

Microservice frameworks in Python

With microservices being more of a philosophy or style of architecture, there are no distinct classes of software frameworks that one can say is the right fit for them. However, one can still make a few educated projections for the properties that a framework should have for it being a good choice for building a microservices architecture for your web application in Python. These properties include the following:

- The component architecture should be flexible. The framework should not be rigid in the component choices that it stipulates to make the different parts of the system work.

- The core of the framework should be lightweight. This makes sense, since if we start off with, say, a lot of dependencies for the microservices framework itself, the software starts feeling heavy right in the beginning. This may cause issues in deployment, testing, and so on.

- The framework should support zero or minimalistic configuration. Microservices architectures are usually configured automatically (zero configuration) or with a minimal set of configuration inputs that are available at one place. Usually the configuration is itself available as a microservice for other services to query and make the sharing of configuration easy, consistent, and scalable.

- It should make it very easy to take an existing piece of business logic, say, coded as a class or a function, and turn it into an HTTP or RCP service. This allows reuse and smart refactoring of code.

If you use these principles and look around in the Python software ecosystem, you will figure out that a few web application frameworks fit the bill, whereas a few don't.

For example, Flask and its single-file counterpart Bottle are good candidates for a microservices framework due to their minimal footprint, small core, and simple configuration.

A framework such as Pyramid can also be used for a microservices architecture since it promotes flexibility of choice of components and eschews tight integration.

A more sophisticated web framework such as Django makes a poor choice for a microservices framework due to exactly the opposite reasons–tight vertical integration of components, lack of flexibility in choosing components, complex configuration, and so on.

Another framework that is written specifically for implementing microservices in Python is Nameko. Nameko is geared toward testability of the application, and it provides support for different protocols for communication such as HTTP, RPC (over AMQP) – a Pub-Sub system, and a Timer service.

We will not be going into details of these frameworks. On the other hand, we will take a look at architecting and designing a real-life example of a web application using microservices.

Microservices example – restaurant reservation

Let's take a real-life example for a Python web application, and try to design it as a set of microservices.

Our application is a restaurant reservation app that helps users make a reservation for a certain number of people at a specific time in a restaurant close to their current location. Assume that reservations are only done for the same day.

The application needs to do the following:

1. Return a list of restaurants open for business at the time for which the user wants to make the reservation.

2. For a given restaurant, return enough meta information, such as cuisine choices, rating, pricing, and so on, and allow the user to filter the restaurants based on their criteria.

3. Once the user has made a choice, allow them to make a reservation at the selected restaurant for a certain number of people for a given time.

Each of these requirements is granular enough to have its own microservice.

Hence, our application will be designed with the following set of microservices:

- A service that uses the user's location, and returns a list of restaurants that are open for business and that support the online reservation API.

- A second service that retrieves metadata for a given hotel, given the restaurant ID. The application can use this metadata to compare against the user's criteria to see if it's a match.

- A third service, which, given a restaurant ID, the user's information, the number of seats required, and the time of reservation, uses the reservation API to make a reservation for seats, and returns the status.

The core parts of the application logic now fit these three microservices. Once they are implemented, the plumbing—in terms of calling these services and performing a reservation—will happen in the application logic directly.

We will not be showing any code for this application as that is a project on its own, but we will show the reader how the microservices look like in terms of their APIs and return data:

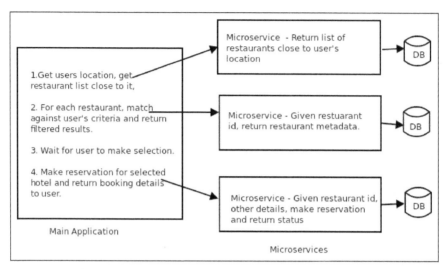

Architecture of restaurant reservation application using microservices

A microservice usually returns data in the form of JSON. For example, our first service, which returns a list of restaurants, would return a JSON similar to the one that follows:

```
GET /restaurants?geohash=tdr1y1g1zgzc

{
    "8f95e6ad-17a7-48a9-9f82-07972d2bc660": {
        "name": "Tandoor",
        "address": "Centenary building, #28, MG Road b-01"
        "hours": "12.00 - 23.30"
    },
   "4307a4b1-6f35-481b-915b-c57d2d625e93": {
        "name": "Karavalli",
        "address": "The Gateway Hotel, 66, Ground Floor"
        "hours": "12.30 - 01:00"
    },
    ...
}
```

The second service, which returns restaurant metadata, would mostly return a JSON like this one:

```
GET /restaurants/8f95e6ad-17a7-48a9-9f82-07972d2bc660

{

    "name": "Tandoor",
    "address": "Centenary building, #28, MG Road b-01"
    "hours": "12.00 - 23.30",
    "rating": 4.5,
    "cuisine": "north indian",
    "lunch buffet": "no",
    "dinner buffet": "no",
    "price": 800

}
```

Next is the interaction for the third one, which does a booking given the restaurant ID.

Since this service needs the user to provide information for the reservation, it needs a JSON payload with the details of booking. Hence, this is best done as an HTTP POST call:

```
POST  /restaurants/reserve
```

The service in this case will use the following given payload as the POST data:

```
{
    "name": "Anand B Pillai",
    "phone": 9880078014,
    "time": "2017-04-14 20:40:00",
    "seats": 3,
    "id": "8f95e6ad-17a7-48a9-9f82-07972d2bc660"
}
```

It will return a JSON like the following as a response:

```
{
    "status": "confirmed",
    "code": "WJ7D2B",
    "time": "2017-04-14 20:40:00",
    "seats": 3
}
```

With this design in place, it is not very difficult to implement the application in a framework of your choice, be it Flask, Bottle, Nameko, or anything else.

Microservices – advantages

So what are the advantages of using microservices over a monolithic application? Let's take a look at some of the important ones:

- Microservices enhance separation of concern by splitting the application logic into multiple services. This improves cohesion, and decreases coupling. There is no need for a top-down, upfront design of the system, since the business logic is not in a single place. Instead, the architect can focus on the interplay and communication between the microservices and the application, and let the design and architecture of the microservices itself emerge iteratively through refactoring.

- Microservices improve testability, since now each part of the logic is independently testable as a separate service, and hence is easy to isolate from other parts and test.

- Teams can be organized around the business capabilities rather than around tiers of the application or technology layers. Since each microservice includes logic, data, and deployment, companies using microservices encourage cross-functional roles. This helps to build a more agile organization.

- Microservices encourage decentralized data. Usually, each service will have its own local database or data store instead of the central database that is preferred by monolithic applications.

- Microservices facilitate continuous delivery and integration, and fast deployments. Since a change to business logic might often need only a small change in one or a few services, testing and redeployment can be often done in tight cycles, and in most cases, can be fully automated.

Pipe and Filter architectures

Pipe and Filter is a simple architectural style that connects a number of components that process a stream of data, each connected to the next component in the processing pipeline via a **Pipe**.

The Pipe and Filter architecture is inspired by the Unix technique of connecting the output of an application to the input of another via pipes on the shell.

The pipe and filter architecture consists of one or more data sources. The data source is connected to data filters via pipes. Filters process the data they receive, passing them to other filters in the pipeline. The final data is received at a **Data Sink**:

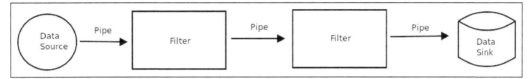

Pipe and Filter Architecture

Pipe and filter are used commonly for applications that perform a lot of data processing such as data analytics, data transformation, metadata extraction, and so on.

The filters can be running on the same machine, and they use actual Unix pipes or shared memory for communication. However, in large systems, these usually run on separate machines, and the pipes need not be actual pipes, but any kind of data channel such as sockets, shared memory, queues, and the like.

Multiple filter pipelines can be connected together to perform complex data processing and data staging.

A very good example of a Linux application that works using this architecture is gstreamer — the multimedia processing library that can perform a number of tasks on multimedia video and audio including play, record, edit, and stream.

Pipe and filter in Python

In Python, we encounter pipes in their most pure form in the multiprocessing module. The multiprocessing module provides pipes as a way to communicate from one process to another.

A pipe is created as a pair of parent and child connections. What is written on one side of the connection can be read on the other side and vice versa.

This allows us to build very simple pipelines of data processing.

For example, on Linux, the number of words in a file can be computed by this series of commands:

```
$ cat filename | wc -w
```

We will write a simple program that mimics this pipeline using the multiprocessing module:

```
# pipe_words.py
from multiprocessing import Process, Pipe
import sys

def read(filename, conn):
    """ Read data from a file and send it to a pipe """

    conn.send(open(filename).read())

def words(conn):
    """ Read data from a connection and print number of words """

    data = conn.recv()
    print('Words',len(data.split()))

if __name__ == "__main__":
    parent, child = Pipe()
    p1 = Process(target=read, args=(sys.argv[1], child))
    p1.start()
    p2 = Process(target=words, args=(parent,))
    p2.start()
    p1.join();p2.join()
```

Here is an analysis of the workflow:

1. A pipe is created, and two connections are obtained.
2. The read function is executed as a process, passing one end of the pipe (child) and the filename to be read.
3. This process reads the file, writing the data to the connection.
4. The words function is executed as a second process, passing the other end of the pipe to it.
5. When this function executes as a process, it reads the data from the connection, and prints the number of words.

The following screenshot shows the output of both the shell command and the preceding program on the same file:

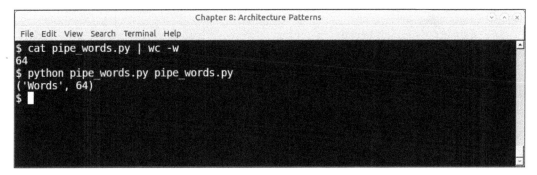

Output of a shell command using pipes and its equivalent Python program

You do not need to use an object that looks like an actual pipe in order to create pipelines. On the other hand, generators in Python provide an excellent way to create a set of callables, which call each other, and consume and process each other's data, producing a pipeline of data processing.

Here is the same example as the previous one, rewritten to use generators, and this time, to process all the files in the folder matching a particular pattern:

```python
# pipe_words_gen.py

# A simple data processing pipeline using generators
# to print count of words in files matching a pattern.
import os

def read(filenames):
    """ Generator that yields data from filenames as (filename, data)
tuple """

    for filename in filenames:
        yield filename, open(filename).read()

def words(input):
    """ Generator that calculates words in its input """

    for filename, data in input:
        yield filename, len(data.split())
```

```python
def filter(input, pattern):
    """ Filter input stream according to a pattern """

    for item in input:
        if item.endswith(pattern):
            yield item

if __name__ == "__main__":
    # Source
    stream1 = filter(os.listdir('.'), '.py')
    # Piped to next filter
    stream2 = read(stream1)
    # Piped to last filter (sink)
    stream3 = words(stream2)

    for item in stream3:
        print(item)
```

Here is a screenshot of the output:

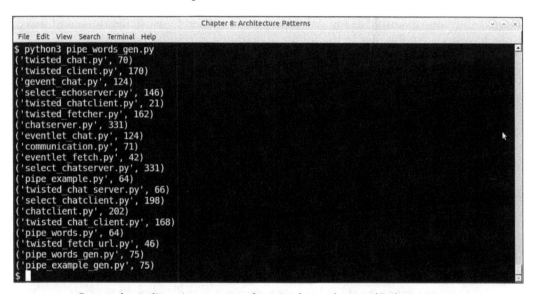

Output of a pipeline using generators that print the word count of Python programs

 One can verify the output of a program such as the preceding one using this command:

```
$ wc -w *.py
```

Here is another program that uses another couple of data filtering generators to build a program, which watches files matching a specific pattern and prints information about the most recent file — something similar to what is done by the watch program on Linux:

```
# pipe_recent_gen.py
# Using generators, print details of the most recently modified file
# matching a pattern.

import glob
import os
from time import sleep

def watch(pattern):
    """ Watch a folder for modified files matching a pattern """

    while True:
        files = glob.glob(pattern)
        # sort by modified time
        files = sorted(files, key=os.path.getmtime)
        recent = files[-1]
        yield recent
        # Sleep a bit
        sleep(1)

def get(input):
    """ For a given file input, print its meta data """
    for item in input:
        data = os.popen("ls -lh " + item).read()
        # Clear screen
        os.system("clear")
        yield data

if __name__ == "__main__":
    import sys

    # Source + Filter #1
    stream1 = watch('*.' + sys.argv[1])

    while True:
        # Filter #2 + sink
        stream2 = get(stream1)
        print(stream2.__next__())
        sleep(2)
```

The details of this last program should be self-explanatory to the reader.

Here is the output of our program on the console, watching over Python source files:

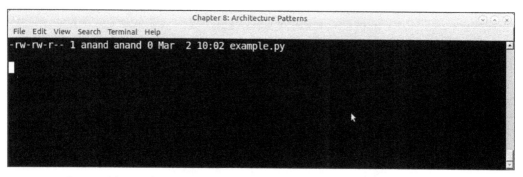

Output of the program that watches over recently modified Python source files

If we create an empty Python source file, say `example.py`, the output changes in two seconds:

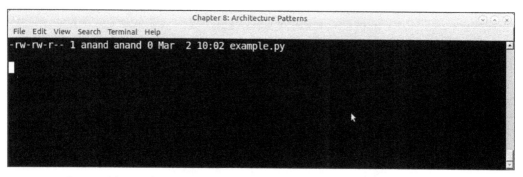

Output of the watch program changes, always showing the most recently modified file

The underlying technique of using generators (co-routines) to build such pipelines is to connect the output of one generator to the input of the next. By connecting many such generators in a series, one can build data processing pipelines that vary in complexity from simple to complex.

Of course, one can use a number of techniques for building pipelines apart from this. Some common choices are producer-consumer tasks connected using queues, which can use threads or processes. We have seen examples of this in the chapter on scalability.

Microservices can also build simple processing pipelines by connecting the input of one microservice to the output of another.

In the Python third-party software ecosystem, there are a number of modules and frameworks that allow you to build complex data pipelines. Celery, though a task queue, can be used to build simple batch processing workflows with limited pipeline support. Pipelining is not the main feature of Celery, but it has limited support for chaining tasks that can be used for this purpose.

Luigi is another robust framework that is written for complex, long-running batch processing jobs that require a pipe and filter architecture. Luigi comes with built-in support for Hadoop jobs, so it makes it a good choice for building data analytics pipelines.

Summary

In this chapter, we looked at some common architectural patterns of building software. We started with the Model View Controller architecture, and looked at examples in Django and Flask. You learned about the components of an MVC architecture, and learned that Django implements a variant of MVC using templates.

We looked at Flask as an example of a micro framework that implements the minimal footprint of a web application by using a plugin architecture with additional services that can be added on.

We went on to discuss the event-driven programming architecture, which is a kind of asynchronous programming using co-routines and events. We started with a multiuser chat example using the `select` module in Python. From there, we went on to discuss larger frameworks and libraries.

We discussed the architecture of Twisted and its components. We also discussed Eventlet and its close cousin gevent. For each of these frameworks, we saw an implementation of the multiuser chat server.

Next, we took up microservices as an architecture, which builds scalable services and deployments by splitting the core business logic across multiple services. We designed an example of a restaurant reservation application using microservices, and briefly looked at the landscape of Python web frameworks, which can be used to build microservices.

Toward the end of the chapter, we saw the architecture of using pipes and Filters for serial and scalable data processing. We built a simple example of actual pipes using the multiprocessing module in Python, which mimicked a Unix pipe command. We then looked at the technique of building pipelines using generators, and saw a couple of examples. We summarized techniques for building pipelines and frameworks available in the Python third-party software ecosystem.

This brings us to the end of the chapter on application architectures. In the next chapter, we will look at deployability, namely the aspect of deploying software to environments such as production systems.

9
Deploying Python Applications

Pushing code to production is often the last step in taking an application from development to the customer. Though this is an important activity, it often gets overlooked in the scheme of importance in a software architect's checklist.

It is a pretty common and fatal mistake to assume that, if a system works in the development environment, it will also work dutifully in production. For one thing, the configuration of a production system is often very different from that of a development environment. Many optimizations and debugging that are available and taken for granted in a developer's box, are often not available in the production setup.

Deployment to production is an art rather than an exact science. The complexity of deployment of a system depends on a number of factors, such as the language the system is developed in, its runtime portability and performance, the number of configuration parameters, whether the system is deployed in a homogeneous or heterogeneous environment, binary dependencies, geographic distribution of the deployments, deployment automation tooling, and a host of other factors.

In recent years, Python, as an open source language, has matured in the level of automation and support it provides for deploying packages to production systems. With its rich availability of built-in and third-party support tools, the pain and hassle for production deployments and maintaining deployment systems up to date has decreased.

In this chapter, we will discuss, briefly, deployable systems and the concept of deployability. We'll take some time to understand the deployment of Python applications, and the tools and processes that the architect can add to his repertoire in order to ease the deploying and maintenance of his production systems' running applications, written using Python. We will also look at techniques and best practices that an architect can adopt to keep his production systems chugging along healthily and securely, without frequent downtimes.

Here are the list of topics we will be talking about in this chapter.

- Deployability
    - ○ Factors affecting deployability
    - ○ Tiers of software deployment architecture
- Software Deployment in Python
    - ○ Packaging Python code

        PIP

        Virtualenv

        Virtualenv and PIP

        PyPI — the Python Package Index

        Packaging and submission of an application

        PyPA

    - ○ Remote deployments using Fabric
    - ○ Remote deployments using Ansible
    - ○ Managing remote daemons using Supervisor
- Deployment — patterns and best practices

Deployability

The deployability of a software system is the ease with which it can be taken from development to production. It can be measured in terms of the effort — in terms of man-hours, or complexity — in terms of the number of disparate steps required for deploying code from a development to production environment.

It is a common mistake to assume that a code that runs well in a development or staging system would behave in a similar way in a production system. It is not often the case due to the vastly dissimilar requirements that a production system has when compared to a development one.

Factors affecting deployability

Here is a brief look at some of the factors that differentiate a production system from a development one, which can often give rise to unexpected issues in deployment leading to *Production Gotchas*:

- **Optimizations and debugging**: It is very common for development systems to turn off optimizations in code.

    If your code is running in an interpreted runtime like Python, it is common to turn on debug configurations, which allows the programmer to generate generous tracebacks when an exception occurs. Also any Python interpreter optimizations are usually turned off.

    On the other hand, in production systems, the reverse is true – as optimizations are turned on and debugging is turned off. This usually requires additional configuration to be enabled for the code to work in a similar way. It is also possible (though rare) that the program gives a different behavior upon optimization under certain circumstances than it does when running unoptimized.

- **Dependencies and versions**: A development environment, usually, has a rich installation of development and support libraries for running multiple applications that a developer may be working on. Quite often, these may be dependencies which are themselves not stale, since developers often work on bleeding edge code.

    Production systems, on the other hand, need to be carefully prepared using a precompiled list of dependencies and their versions. It is quite common to specify only mature or stable versions for deployment on production systems. Hence, if a developer had relied on a feature or bug-fix which was available on an unstable (alpha, beta or release-candidate) version of a downstream dependency, one may find — too late — that the feature doesn't work in production as intended.

    Another common problem is undocumented dependencies or dependencies that need to be compiled from source code — this is often a problem with first-time deployments.

- **Resource configuration and access privileges**: Development systems and production systems often differ in level, privilege, and details of access of resources locally and in the network. A development system may have a local database, whereas, production systems tend to use separate hosting for application and database systems. A development system may use a standard configuration file, while, in production, the configuration may have to be generated specifically for a host or an environment using specific scripts. Similarly, in production, the application may be required to run with lesser privileges as a specific user/group, whereas, in development, it may be common to run the program as the root or superuser. Such disparities in user privileges and configuration may affect resource access and might cause software to fail in production, when it runs fine on the development environment.

- **Heterogeneous production environments**: Code is usually developed in development environments, which are usually homogeneous. But it may often be required to be deployed on heterogeneous systems in production. For example, software may be developed on Linux, but there may be a requirement for a customer deployment on Windows.

  The complexity of deployments increases proportionally to heterogeneity in environments. Well-managed staging and testing environments are required before such code is taken to production. Also, heterogeneous systems make dependency management more complex, as a separate list of dependencies needs to be maintained for each target system architecture.

- **Security**: In development and testing environments, it is somewhat common to give a wide berth to security aspects to save time and to reduce the configuration complexity for testing. For example, in a web application, routes which need logins may be disabled by using special development environment flags to facilitate quick programming and testing.

  Similarly, systems used in development environments may often use easy-to-guess passwords, such as database systems, web application logins, and others, to make routine recall and usage easy. Also, role-based authorization may be ignored to facilitate testing.

  However, security is critical in production, so these aspects require the opposite treatment. Routes which need logins should be enforced as such. Strong passwords should be used. Role-based authentication needs to be enforced. These can often cause subtle bugs in production where a feature which works in the development environment fails in production.

Since these and other similar problems are the bane of deploying code in production, standard practices have been defined to make the life of the DevOps practitioner a bit easier. Most companies follow the practice of using isolated environments to develop, test, and validate code and applications before pushing them to production. Let us take a look at this.

Tiers of software deployment architecture

To avoid complexities in taking the code from development to testing, and further to production, it is common to use a multitiered architecture for each stage of the life cycle of the application before deployment to production.

Let's take a look at some of the following common deployment tiers:

- **Development/Test/Stage/Production**: This is the traditional four-tiered architecture.
  - The developers push their code to a development environment, where unit tests and developer tests are run. This environment will always be on the latest trunk or bleeding edge of the code. Frequently, this environment is skipped and replaced with the local setup on developer's laptops.
  - The software is then tested by QA or testing engineers on a test environment using black-box techniques. They may also run performance tests on this environment. This environment is always behind the development environment in terms of code updates. Usually, internal releases, tags, or **code dumps** are used to sync the QA environment from the development environment.
  - The staging environment tries to mirror the production environment as closely as possible. It is the *pre-production* stage, where the software is tested on an environment as close as possible to the deployment one to identify issues that may occur in production in advance. This is the environment where usually stress or load tests are run. It also allows the DevOps engineer to test out his deployment automation scripts, cron jobs, and verify system configuration.

○ Production is, of course, the final tier where software that is tested from staging is pushed and deployed. A number of deployments often use identical staging/production tiers, and simply switch from one to the other.

- **Development and Test/Stage/Production**: This is a variation of the previous tier, where the development environment also performs the double duty of a testing environment. This system is used in companies with agile software development practices, where code is pushed at least once a week to production, and there is no space or time to keep and manage a separate testing environment. When there is no separate development environment – that is when developers use their laptops for programming – the testing environment is also a local one.

- **Development and Test/ Stage and Production**: In this setup, staging and production environments are exactly the same with multiple servers used. Once a system is tested and verified in staging, it is *pushed* to production by simply switching the hosts—the current production system switches to staging, and staging switches to production.

Apart from these, it is possible to have more elaborate architectures where a separate **Integration** environment is used for integration testing, a **Sandbox** environment for testing experimental features, and so on.

Using a staging system is important to ensure that software is well tested and orchestrated in a production-like environment, before pushing the code to production.

Software deployment in Python

As mentioned earlier, Python developers are richly blessed in the various tools offered by Python, and its third-party ecosystem in easing and automating the deployment of applications and code written using Python.

In this section, we will briefly take a look at some of these tools.

Packaging Python code

Python comes with built in support for packaging applications for a variety of distributions—source, binary, and specific OS-level packaging.

The primary way of packaging source code in Python is to write a `setup.py` file. The source can then be packaged with the help of the in-built `distutils` library, or the more sophisticated and rich `setuptools` framework.

Before we get introduced to the guts of Python packaging, let us get familiar with a couple of closely related tools, namely, `pip` and `virtualenv`.

PIP

PIP stands for the recursive acronym **PIP installs packages**. Pip is the standard and suggested tool to install packages in Python.

We've seen PIP in action throughout this book, but so far, we've never seen pip itself getting installed, have we?

Let's see this in the following screenshot:

```
                                  Chap 9  - Deployment                          ⌄ ⌃ ✕

 File  Edit  View  Search  Terminal  Help
$ wget https://bootstrap.pypa.io/get-pip.py
--2017-01-29 20:20:38--  https://bootstrap.pypa.io/get-pip.py
Resolving bootstrap.pypa.io (bootstrap.pypa.io)... 151.101.120.175
Connecting to bootstrap.pypa.io (bootstrap.pypa.io)|151.101.120.175|:443... connected.
HTTP request sent, awaiting response... 200 OK
Length: 1595408 (1.5M) [text/x-python]
Saving to: 'get-pip.py'

get-pip.py            100%[=======================>]   1.52M   642KB/s    in 2.4s

2017-01-29 20:20:41 (642 KB/s) - 'get-pip.py' saved [1595408/1595408]

$ sudo python3 get-pip.py
The directory '/home/anand/.cache/pip/http' or its parent directory is not owned by the
current user and the cache has been disabled. Please check the permissions and owner of
that directory. If executing pip with sudo, you may want sudo's -H flag.
The directory '/home/anand/.cache/pip' or its parent directory is not owned by the curre
nt user and caching wheels has been disabled. check the permissions and owner of that di
rectory. If executing pip with sudo, you may want sudo's -H flag.
Collecting pip
  Downloading pip-9.0.1-py2.py3-none-any.whl (1.3MB)
    100% |                                     | 1.3MB 646kB/s
Installing collected packages: pip
  Found existing installation: pip 8.1.1
    Uninstalling pip-8.1.1:
      Successfully uninstalled pip-8.1.1
Successfully installed pip-9.0.1
$ █
```

Downloading and installing pip for Python3

The `pip` installation script is available at `https://bootstrap.pypa.io/get-pip.py`.

The steps should be self-explanatory.

 In the preceding example, there was already a pip version, so the action upgraded the existing version instead of doing a fresh install. We can see the version details by trying the program with the `--version` option, as follows:

Take a look at the following screenshot:

Printing the current version of pip (pip3)

See how `pip` clearly prints its version number along with the directory location of the installation, plus the Python version for which it is installed.

 To distinguish between pip for the Python2 and Python3 versions, remember that the version installed for Python3 is always named `pip3`. The Python2 version is `pip2`, or just `pip`.

To install a package using PIP, simply provide the package name via the command `install`. For example, the following screenshot shows installing the `numpy` package using `pip`:

```
Chap 9 - Deployment
File  Edit  View  Search  Terminal  Help
$ sudo -H pip3 install numpy
Collecting numpy
  Downloading numpy-1.12.0-cp35-cp35m-manylinux1 x86 64.whl (16.8MB)
    100% |                                     | 16.8MB 38kB/s
Installing collected packages: numpy
Successfully installed numpy-1.12.0
$
```

We will not go into further details of using pip here. Instead, let's take a look at another tool that works closely with pip in installing the Python software.

Virtualenv

Virtualenv is a tool that allows developers to create sand-boxed Python environments for local development. Let's say that you want to maintain two different versions of a particular library or framework for two different applications you are developing side by side.

If you are going to install everything to the system Python, then you can keep only one version at a given time. The other option is to create different system Python installations in different root folders — say, /opt instead of /usr. However, this creates additional overhead and management headaches of paths. Also, it wouldn't be possible to get write permission to these folders if you want the version dependency to be maintained on a shared host where you don't have superuser permissions.

Virtualenv solves the problems of permissions and versions in one go. It creates a local installation directory with its own Python executable standard library and installer (defaults to pip).

Once the developer has activated the virtual environment thus created, any further installations goes to this environment instead of the system Python environment.

Virtualenv can be installed using pip.

The following screenshot shows creating a virtualenv named appvenv using the virtualenv command, and activating the environment along with installing a package to the environment.

The installation also installs PIP, setuptools, and other dependencies.

```
                        Chap 9 - Deployment
File  Edit  View  Search  Terminal  Help
$ virtualenv appenv
Running virtualenv with interpreter /usr/bin/python2
New python executable in /home/user/appenv/bin/python2
Also creating executable in /home/user/appenv/bin/python
Installing setuptools, pkg_resources, pip, wheel...done.
$ source appenv/bin/activate
(appenv) $ which python
/home/user/appenv/bin/python
(appenv) $ which pip
/home/user/appenv/bin/pip
(appenv) $ pip install numpy
Collecting numpy
  Downloading numpy-1.12.0-cp27-cp27mu-manylinux1_x86_64.whl (16.5MB)
    100% |                                 | 16.5MB 24kB/s
Installing collected packages: numpy
Successfully installed numpy-1.12.0
(appenv) $ pip --version
pip 9.0.1 from /home/user/appenv/local/lib/python2.7/site-packages (python 2.7)
(appenv) $ python --version
Python 2.7.12
(appenv) $ █
```

 See how the `python` and `pip` commands point to the ones inside the virtual environment. The `pip -version` command clearly shows the path of `pip` inside the virtual environment folder.

From Python 3.3 onwards, support for virtual environments is built into the Python installation via the new `venv` library.

The following screenshot shows installing a virtual environment in Python 3.5 using this library, and installing some packages into it. As usual, take a look at Python and pip executable paths:

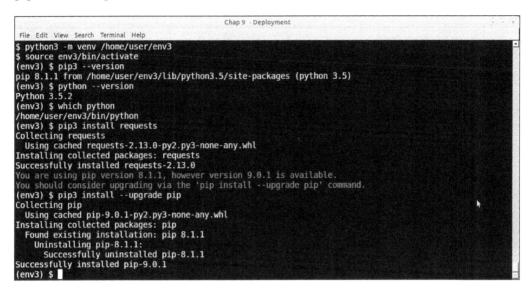

 The preceding screenshot also shows how to upgrade pip itself via the `pip` command.

Virtualenv and pip

Once you've set up a virtual environment for your application(s) and installed the required packages, it is a good idea to generate the dependencies and their versions. This can be easily done via the following command using pip:

```
$ pip freeze
```

This command asks pip to output a list of all the installed Python packages along with their versions. This can be saved to a requirements file, and the setup duplicated on the server for mirroring deployments:

```
                              Chap 9 - Deployment
  File  Edit  View  Search  Terminal  Help
(appenv) $ pip freeze | tee requirements.txt
appdirs==1.4.0
backports-abc==0.5
certifi==2017.1.23
numpy==1.12.0
packaging==16.8
pkg-resources==0.0.0
pyparsing==2.1.10
requests==2.13.0
singledispatch==3.4.0.3
six==1.10.0
tornado==4.4.2
(appenv) $
```

The following screenshot shows recreating the same setup in another virtual environment via the `-r` option of the `pip install` command, which accepts such a file as input:

```
                              Chap 9 - Deployment
  File  Edit  View  Search  Terminal  Help
(env3) $ pip3 install -r requirements.txt
Collecting appdirs==1.4.0 (from -r requirements.txt (line 1))
  Using cached appdirs-1.4.0-py2.py3-none-any.whl
Collecting backports-abc==0.5 (from -r requirements.txt (line 2))
  Using cached backports_abc-0.5-py2.py3-none-any.whl
Collecting certifi==2017.1.23 (from -r requirements.txt (line 3))
  Using cached certifi-2017.1.23-py2.py3-none-any.whl
Collecting numpy==1.12.0 (from -r requirements.txt (line 4))
  Downloading numpy-1.12.0-cp35-cp35m-manylinux1_x86_64.whl (16.8MB)
    100% |                                | 16.8MB 25kB/s
Collecting packaging==16.8 (from -r requirements.txt (line 5))
  Using cached packaging-16.8-py2.py3-none-any.whl
Requirement already satisfied: pkg-resources==0.0.0 in ./env3/lib/python3.5/site-packages (from -r requir
ements.txt (line 6))
Collecting pyparsing==2.1.10 (from -r requirements.txt (line 7))
  Using cached pyparsing-2.1.10-py2.py3-none-any.whl
Requirement already satisfied: requests==2.13.0 in ./env3/lib/python3.5/site-packages (from -r requiremen
ts.txt (line 8))
Collecting singledispatch==3.4.0.3 (from -r requirements.txt (line 9))
  Using cached singledispatch-3.4.0.3-py2.py3-none-any.whl
Collecting six==1.10.0 (from -r requirements.txt (line 10))
  Using cached six-1.10.0-py2.py3-none-any.whl
Collecting tornado==4.4.2 (from -r requirements.txt (line 11))
  Using cached tornado-4.4.2.tar.gz
Installing collected packages: appdirs, backports-abc, certifi, numpy, pyparsing, six, packaging, singled
ispatch, tornado
  Running setup.py install for tornado ... done
Successfully installed appdirs-1.4.0 backports-abc-0.5 certifi-2017.1.23 numpy-1.12.0 packaging-16.8 pypa
rsing-2.1.10 singledispatch-3.4.0.3 six-1.10.0 tornado-4.4.2
(env3) $
```

Our source virtual environment was in Python2, and the target was in Python3. However, pip was able to install the dependencies from the `requirements.txt` file without any issues whatsoever.

Relocatable virtual environments

The suggested way to copy package dependencies from one virtual environment to another is to perform a freeze, and install via `pip` as illustrated in the previous section. For example, this is the most common way to freeze Python package requirements from a development environment, and recreate it successfully on a production server.

One can also try and make a virtual environment relocatable so that it can be archived and moved to a compatible system:

```
                           Chap 9 - Deployment
 File  Edit  View  Search  Terminal  Help
$ virtualenv lenv
Running virtualenv with interpreter /usr/bin/python2
New python executable in /home/user/lenv/bin/python2
Also creating executable in /home/user/lenv/bin/python
Installing setuptools, pkg_resources, pip, wheel...done.
$ virtualenv --relocatable lenv
Running virtualenv with interpreter /usr/bin/python2
Making script /home/user/lenv/bin/python-config relative
Making script /home/user/lenv/bin/pip2.7 relative
Making script /home/user/lenv/bin/easy_install relative
Making script /home/user/lenv/bin/pip relative
Making script /home/user/lenv/bin/wheel relative
Making script /home/user/lenv/bin/pip2 relative
Making script /home/user/lenv/bin/easy_install-2.7 relative
$ cd lenv
$ ls
bin  include  lib  local  pip-selfcheck.json  share
$ source bin/activate
```

Creating a relocatable virtual environment

Here is how it works:

1. First, the virtual environment is created as usual.

2. It is then made relocatable by running `virtualenv -relocatable lenv` on it.

3. This changes some of the paths used by setuptools as relative paths, and sets up the system to be relocatable.

4. Such a virtual environment is relocatable to another folder in the same machine, or to a folder in a *remote and similar machine*.

A relocatable virtual environment doesn't guarantee that it will work if the remote environment differs from the machine environment. For example, if your remote machine is a different architecture, or even uses a different Linux distribution with another type of packaging, the relocation will fail to work. This is what is meant by the words *similar machine*.

PyPI

We learned that PIP is the standardized tool to do package installations in Python. It is able to pick up any package by name as long as it exists. It is also able to install packages by version, as we saw with the example of the requirements file.

But where does PIP fetch its packages from?

To answer this, we turn to the Python Package Index, more commonly known as PyPI.

Python Package Index (PyPI) is the official repository for hosting metadata for third-party Python packages on the Web. As the name implies, it is an index to the Python packages on the Web whose metadata is published and indexed on a server. PyPI is hosted at the URL `http://pypi.python.org`.

PyPI hosts close to a million packages at present. The packages are submitted to PyPI using Python's packaging and distribution tools, distutils, and setuptools, which have hooks for publishing package metadata to PyPI. A number of packages also host the actual package data in PyPI, although PyPI can be used to point to package data sitting in a URL on another server.

When you install a package using pip, it actually performs the search for the package on PyPI, and downloads the metadata. It uses the metadata to find out the package's download URL and other information, such as further downstream dependencies, which it uses to fetch and install the package for you.

Here is a screenshot of PyPI, which shows the actual count of the packages at the time of writing this:

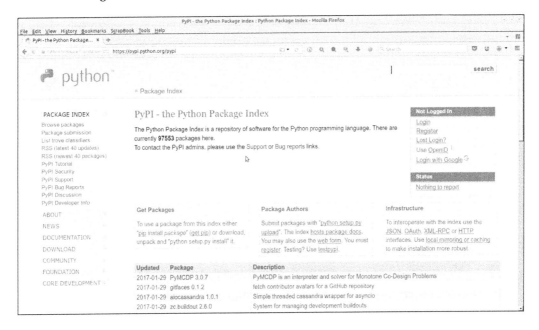

A developer can do quite a few things directly on the PyPI site:

1. Register using e-mail address and log in to the site.

2. After logging in, submit your package directly on the site.

3. Search for packages via keywords.

4. Browse for packages via a number of top-level *trove* classifiers, such as Topics, Platforms/Operating Systems, Development Status, Licenses, and so on.

Now that we are familiar with the suite of all Python packaging and installation tools and their relationships, let us try out a small example of packaging a trivial Python module and submitting it to PyPI.

Packaging and submission of an application

Remember that we had developed a mandelbrot program, which uses pymp to scale, in *Chapter 5, Writing Applications that Scale*. We will use it as an example of a program to develop a package, and a setup.py file, which we will use to submit the application to PyPI.

We will package the mandelbrot application in a main package consisting of two sub-packages as follows:

- mandelbrot.simple: The sub-package (sub-module) consisting of the basic implementation of mandelbrot

- mandelbrot.mp: The sub package (sub-module) having the PyMP implementation of mandelbrot

Here is our folder structure for the package:

```
                                    Chap 9: Deployment
 File  Edit  View  Search  Terminal  Help
$ pwd
/home/user/programs/chap9/mandelbrot
$ tree .
.
├── mandelbrot
│   ├── __init__.py
│   ├── mp
│   │   ├── __init__.py
│   │   └── mandelbrot.py
│   └── simple
│       ├── __init__.py
│       └── mandelbrot.py
├── README
└── setup.py

3 directories, 7 files
$
```

Folder layout of the mandelbrot package

Let us quickly analyze the folder structure of the application which we will be packaging:

- The top directory is named mandelbrot. It has an __init__.py, a README, and a setup.py file.

- This directory has two sub directories — mp and simple.

- Each of these subfolders consists of two files, namely, __init__.py and mandelbrot.py. These subfolders will form our sub-modules, each containing the respective implementation of the mandelbrot set.

 For the purpose of installing the mandelbrot modules as executable scripts, the code has been changed to add a main method to each of our mandelbrot.py modules.

The __init__.py files

The __init__.py files allow to convert a folder inside a Python application as a package. Our folder structure has three of them: the first one is for the top-level package mandelbrot, and the rest two for each of the sub-packages, namely, mandelbrot.simple and mandelbrot.mp.

The top-level __init__.py is empty. The other two have the following single line:

```
from . import mandelbrot
```

 The relative imports are to make sure that the sub-packages are importing the local mandelbrot.py module instead of the top-level mandelbrot package.

The setup.py file

The setup.py file is the central point of the entire package. Let us take a look at it:

```
from setuptools import setup, find_packages
setup(
    name = "mandelbrot",
    version = "0.1",
    author = "Anand B Pillai",
    author_email = "abpillai@gmail.com",
    description = ("A program for generating Mandelbrot fractal
images"),
    license = "BSD",
    keywords = "fractal mandelbrot example chaos",
    url = "http://packages.python.org/mandelbrot",
    packages = find_packages(),
    long_description=open('README').read(),
    classifiers=[
        "Development Status :: 4 - Beta",
        "Topic :: Scientific/Engineering :: Visualization",
```

```
                "License :: OSI Approved :: BSD License",
        ],
        install_requires = [
            'Pillow>=3.1.2',
            'pymp-pypi>=0.3.1'
            ],
        entry_points = {
            'console_scripts': [
                'mandelbrot = mandelbrot.simple.mandelbrot:main',
                'mandelbrot_mp = mandelbrot.mp.mandelbrot:main'
                ]
            }
    )
```

A full discussion of the setup.py file is outside the scope of this chapter, but do note these few key points:

- The setup.py file allows the author to create a lot of package metadata such as name, author name, e-mail, package keywords, and others. These are useful in creating the package meta information, which helps people to search for the package in PyPI once it's submitted.

- One of the main fields in this file is packages, which is the list of packages (and sub-packages) that is created by this setup.py file. We make use of the find_packages helper function provided by the setuptools module to do this.

- We provide the installment requirements in the install-requires key, which lists the dependencies one by one in a PIP-like format.

- The entry_points key is used to configure the console scripts (executable programs) that this package installs. Let us look at one of them:

  ```
  mandelbrot = mandelbrot.simple.mandelbrot:main
  ```

  This tells the package resource loader to load the module named mandelbrot.simple.mandelbrot, and execute its function main when the script mandelbrot is invoked.

Installing the package

The package can be now installed using this command:

```
$ python setup.py install
```

The following screenshot of the installation shows a few of the initial steps:

```
                              Chap 9: Deployment                            v ^ x
 File  Edit  View  Search  Terminal  Help
(env3) $ python setup.py install
running install
running bdist_egg
running egg_info
creating mandelbrot.egg-info
writing top-level names to mandelbrot.egg-info/top_level.txt
writing entry points to mandelbrot.egg-info/entry_points.txt
writing requirements to mandelbrot.egg-info/requires.txt
writing mandelbrot.egg-info/PKG-INFO
writing dependency links to mandelbrot.egg-info/dependency_links.txt
writing manifest file 'mandelbrot.egg-info/SOURCES.txt'
reading manifest file 'mandelbrot.egg-info/SOURCES.txt'
writing manifest file 'mandelbrot.egg-info/SOURCES.txt'
installing library code to build/bdist.linux-x86_64/egg
running install_lib
running build_py
creating build
creating build/lib
creating build/lib/mandelbrot
copying mandelbrot/__init__.py -> build/lib/mandelbrot
creating build/lib/mandelbrot/mp
copying mandelbrot/mp/mandelbrot.py -> build/lib/mandelbrot/mp
copying mandelbrot/mp/__init__.py -> build/lib/mandelbrot/mp
creating build/lib/mandelbrot/simple
copying mandelbrot/simple/mandelbrot.py -> build/lib/mandelbrot/simple
copying mandelbrot/simple/__init__.py -> build/lib/mandelbrot/simple
```

 We have installed this package to a virtual environment named env3.

Submitting the package to PyPI

The setup.py file plus setuptools/distutils ecosystem in Python is useful, not just to install and package code, but also to submit code to the Python package index.

It is very easy to register your package to PyPI. There are just the following two requirements:

- A package with a proper setup.py file
- An account on the PyPI website

We will now submit our new mandelbrot package to PyPI by performing the following steps:

1. First, one needs to create a `.pypirc` file in one's home directory containing some details – mainly the authentication details for the PyPI account.

   Here is the author's `.pypirc` file with the password obscured:

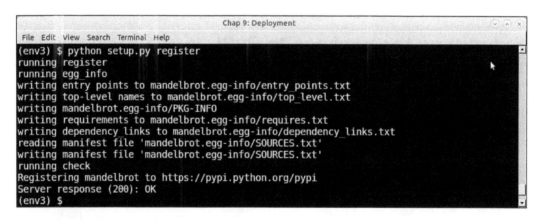

2. Once this is done, registration is as simple as running `setup.py` with the `register` command:

   ```
   $ python setup.py register
   ```

   The next screenshot shows the actual command in action on the console:

```
(env3) $ python setup.py register
running register
running egg_info
writing entry points to mandelbrot.egg-info/entry_points.txt
writing top-level names to mandelbrot.egg-info/top_level.txt
writing mandelbrot.egg-info/PKG-INFO
writing requirements to mandelbrot.egg-info/requires.txt
writing dependency_links to mandelbrot.egg-info/dependency_links.txt
reading manifest file 'mandelbrot.egg-info/SOURCES.txt'
writing manifest file 'mandelbrot.egg-info/SOURCES.txt'
running check
Registering mandelbrot to https://pypi.python.org/pypi
Server response (200): OK
(env3) $
```

However, this last step has only registered the package by submitting its metadata. No package data, as in the source code data, has been submitted as part of this step.

3. To submit the source code also to PyPI, the following command should
   be run:

```
$ python setup.py sdist upload
```

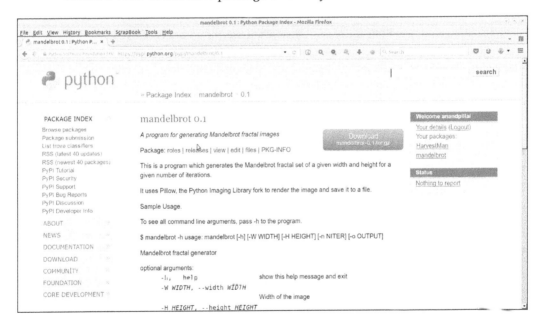

Here's a view of our new package on the PyPI server:

Now the package is installable via pip, completing the cycle of software
development: that is, first packaging, then deployment, and finally, installation.

PyPA

Python Packaging Authority (PyPA) is a working group of Python developers who maintain the standards and the relevant applications related to packaging in Python.

PyPA has their website at `https://www.pypa.io/`, and they maintain the application on GitHub at `https://github.com/pypa/`.

The following table lists the projects that are maintained by PyPA. You've already seen some of these, such as pip, virtualenv, and setuptools; others may be new:

Project	Description
`setuptools`	A collection of enhancements to Python distutils
`virtualenv`	A tool for creating sandbox Python environments
`pip`	A tool for installing Python packages
`packaging`	Core Python utilities for packaging used by pip and setuptools
`wheel`	An extension to setuptools for creating wheel distributions, which are an alternative to Python eggs (ZIP files) and specified in PEP 427
`twine`	A secure replacement for `setup.py` upload
`warehouse`	The new PyPI application, which can be seen at `https://pypi.org`
`distlib`	A low-level library implementing functions relating to packaging and distribution of Python code
`bandersnatch`	A PyPI mirroring client to mirror the contents of PyPI

Interested developers can go visit the PyPA site and sign up for one of the projects - and contribute to them in terms of testing, submitting patches and so on by visiting the github repository of PyPA.

Remote deployments using Fabric

Fabric is a command-line tool and library written in Python, which helps to automate remote deployments on servers via a set of well-defined wrappers over the SSH protocol. It uses the `ssh-wrapper` library, `paramiko`, behind the scenes.

Fabric works with Python 2.x versions only. However, there is a fork Fabric3 which works for both the Python 2.x and 3.x versions.

When using fabric, a DevOps user usually deploys his remote system administrator commands as Python functions in a `fabfile` named as `fabfile.py`.

Fabric works best when the remote systems are already configured with the ssh public keys of the user's machine from where he performs deployments, so there is no need to supply a username and password.

Here is an example of remote deployment on a server. In this case, we are installing our mandelbrot application on a remote server.

The fabfile looks as follows. See that it is written for Python3:

```python
from fabric.api import run

def remote_install(application):

    print ('Installing',application)
    run('sudo pip install ' + application)
```

Here is an example of running this, installing it on a remote server:

```
                              Chap 9: Deployment                          ⌄ ∧ ✕

 File  Edit  View  Search  Terminal  Help
(env3) $ fab remote_install:mandelbrot -H mylinode
[mylinode] Executing task 'remote_install'
Installing mandelbrot
[mylinode] run: sudo pip install mandelbrot
[mylinode] out: Downloading/unpacking mandelbrot
[mylinode] out:   Downloading mandelbrot-0.1.tar.gz
[mylinode] out:   Running setup.py (path:/tmp/pip-build-3RuBh1/mandelbrot/setup.py) egg_info for package m
[mylinode] out: Requirement already satisfied (use --upgrade to upgrade): Pillow>=3.1.2 in /usr/local/lib/
dist-packages (from mandelbrot)
[mylinode] out: Requirement already satisfied (use --upgrade to upgrade): pymp-pypi>=0.3.1 in /usr/local/l
.7/dist-packages (from mandelbrot)
[mylinode] out: Requirement already satisfied (use --upgrade to upgrade): olefile in /usr/local/lib/python
ackages (from Pillow>=3.1.2->mandelbrot)
[mylinode] out: Installing collected packages: mandelbrot
[mylinode] out:   Running setup.py install for mandelbrot
[mylinode] out:     Installing mandelbrot_mp script to /usr/local/bin
[mylinode] out:     Installing mandelbrot script to /usr/local/bin
[mylinode] out:   Could not find .egg-info directory in install record for mandelbrot
[mylinode] out: Successfully installed mandelbrot
[mylinode] out: Cleaning up...
[mylinode] out:


Done.
Disconnecting from mylinode... done.
(env3) $ ▮
```

DevOps engineers and system administrators can use a predefined set of fabfiles for automating different system and application deployment tasks across multiple servers.

 Though it is written in Python, Fabric can be used to automate deployment of any kind of remote server administration and configuration tasks.

Remote deployments using Ansible

Ansible is a configuration management and deployment tool written in Python. Ansible can be thought of as a wrapper over SSH with scripts with support for orchestration via tasks which can be assembled in easy-to-manage units called *playbooks* which map a group of hosts to a set of roles.

Ansible uses "facts" which are system and environment information it gathers before it runs tasks. It uses the facts to check if there is any need to change any state before running a task to get the desired outcome.

This makes it safe for Ansible tasks to be run on a server in a repeated fashion. Well-written Ansible tasks are *idempotent* in that they have zero to few side effects on the remote system.

Ansible is written in Python and can be installed using `pip`.

It uses its own hosts file, namely `/etc/ansible/hosts` to keep the host information against which it runs its tasks.

A typical ansible host file may look as follows:

```
[local]
127.0.0.1

[webkaffe]
139.162.58.8
```

The following is a snippet from an Ansible playbook named `dependencies.yaml` which installs a few Python packages via `pip` on a remote host named `webkaffeStyle`:

```
---
- hosts: webkaffe
  tasks:
    - name: Pip - Install Python Dependencies
      pip:
          name="{{ python_packages_to_install | join(' ') }}"

      vars:
          python_packages_to_install:
          - Flask
          - Bottle
          - bokeh
```

Here is an image of running this playbook on the command line using ansible-playbook:

```
(env) $ ansible-playbook --user=webkaffe -s dependencies.yaml

PLAY [webkaffe] ****************************************************************

TASK [Gathering Facts] ********************************************************
ok: [139.162.58.8]

TASK [Pip - Install Python Dependencies] **************************************
ok: [139.162.58.8]

PLAY RECAP ********************************************************************
139.162.58.8               : ok=2    changed=0    unreachable=0    failed=0

(env) $
```

Ansible is an easy and efficient way of managing remote dependencies and, due to its idempotent playbooks, is much better than Fabric at the task.

Managing remote daemons using Supervisor

Supervisor is a client/server system, which is useful to control processes on Unix and Unix-like systems. It consists mainly of a server daemon process named **supervisord** and a command-line client, which interacts with the server named **supervisorctl**.

Supervisor also comes with a basic webserver, which can be accessed via port 9001. It is possible to view the state of running processes, and also to start/stop them via this interface. Supervisor doesn't run on any version of Windows.

Supervisor is an application written using Python, and hence, is installable via pip. It runs only on Python 2.x versions.

Applications to be managed via supervisor should be configured via the supervisor daemons configuration file. By default, such files sit in the /etc/supervisor.d/conf folder.

However, it is possible to run Supervisor locally by installing it to a virtual environment, and keeping the configuration local to the virtual environment. In fact, this is a common way to run multiple supervisor daemons, each managing processes specific to the virtual environment.

We won't go into details or examples of using Supervisor, but here are some benefits of using Supervisor vs a traditional approach like system rc.d scripts:

- Decoupling process creation/management and process control can be achieved by using a client/server system. The supervisor.d file manages the processes via subprocesses. The user can get the process state information via supervisorctl, the client. Also, whereas most traditional rc.d processes require root or sudo access, supervisor processes can be controlled by normal users of the system via the client or through the web UI.

- Since supervisord starts processes via subprocesses, they can be configured to automatically restart upon crash. It is also easier to get a more accurate status of the subprocesses rather than relying on PID files.

- Supervisor supports process groups allowing users to define processes in a priority order. Processes can be started and stopped in a specific order as a group. This allows implementation of a fine-grained process control when there is a temporal dependency between creation of processes in an application. (Process B requires A to be running, C requires B to be running, and the like.)

We will complete the discussion in this chapter with an overview of the common deployment patterns, which an architect can choose from to solve common issues with deployability.

Deployment – patterns and best practices

There are different deployment approaches or patterns that can be used to address issues like down-times, reduce risks with deployment, and for a seamless development and deployment of software.

- **Continuous deployment**: Continuous deployment is a deployment model where software is ready to go live at any time. Continuous delivery is possible only if tiers, including development, testing, and staging, are integrated continuously. In a continuous deployment model, multiple production deployments can occur in a day, and automatically, via a deployment pipeline. Since one is constantly deploying incremental changes, the continuous deployment mode minimizes deployment risks. In agile software development houses, it also helps the customer to track progress directly by seeing live code in production almost as soon as it leaves development and testing. There is also the added advantage of getting user feedback faster allowing faster iterations to the code and features.

- **BlueGreen deployment**: We already discussed this in *Chapter 5, Writing Applications that Scale*. Blue green deployments keep two production environments, closely identical to each other. At a given instance, one environment is live (Blue). You prepare your new deployment changes to the other environment (Green), and, once tested and ready to go live, switch your systems—Green becomes active and Blue becomes the backup. BlueGreen deployments reduce deployment risks considerably, since, for anything that goes wrong with the new deployment, you just need to switch your router or load-balancer to the new environment. Usually, in typical BlueGreen systems, one system is the production (live) and other the staging, and you switch the roles between them.

- **Canary releases**: If you want to test the changes in your software on a subset of users before deploying it for the entire audience of your customers, you can use this approach. In canary release, the changes are rolled out to a small subset of users first. A simple approach is dogfooding, where the changes are rolled out internally to the employees first. Another approach is beta-testing, where a select group of audience is invited to test out your early features. Other involved approaches include selecting users based on their geographic location, demographics, and profiles. Canary releases, apart from insulating the company from sudden user reaction to badly managed features, also allow you to manage load and capacity scaling in an incremental way. For example, if a particular feature becomes popular, and starts driving, say, 100X users to your servers than before, a traditional deployment may cause server failures and availability issues as opposed to a gradual deployment using a Canary release. Geographical routing is a technique that can be used to select a subset of users if you don't want to do complex user profiling and analysis. This is where the load is sent more to nodes deployed in a particular geography or data center as opposed to other nodes. Canary release is also related to the concept of incremental rollout or phased rollout.

- **Bucket testing (A/B testing)**: This is the technique of deploying two dissimilar versions of an application or a webpage to production to test out which version is more popular and/or has more engagement. In production, a subset of your audience sees the A version of the app (or page)—the control or basic version—and the other subset sees the B version or the modified (variant) version. Usually, this is a 50-50 split, though, as with Canary releases, user profiles, geo locations, or other complex models can be used. User experience and engagement is collected using an analytics dashboard, and then it is determined whether the change had a positive, negative, or neutral response.

- **Induced chaos**: This is a technique of purposely introducing errors or disabling part of a production deployment system to test its resilience to failures and/or level of availability.

Production servers have the problem of drift—unless you use continuous deployment or similar approaches for sync, production servers, usually, tend to drift away from the standard configuration. One way to test your system is to intentionally disable part of the production system—this can be done, for example, by disabling a random 50% of the nodes in a load-balancer configuration, and see how the rest of the system performs.

A similar approach in finding out and weeding unused parts of code is to inject random secrets in parts of the configuration using, say, an API that you suspect is redundant and no longer required. You then observe how the application performs in production. Since a random secret will fail the API, if there is an active part of the application which still uses the dependent code, it will fail in production. Otherwise, it is an indication that the code can be safely removed.

Netflix has a tool called **Chaos Monkey**, which automatically injects failures in production systems, and then measures the impact.

Induced Chaos allows the DevOps engineer and architect to understand weak points in the system, learn about systems which are undergoing configuration drift, and find and weed out unnecessary or unused parts of an application.

Summary

This chapter was about deploying your Python code to production. We looked at the different factors that affect the deployability of a system. We went on to discuss the tiers in deployment architecture, such as the traditional four-tiered and the three- and two-tiered architectures, including combinations of development, testing, staging/QA, and production tiers.

We then went on to discuss the details of packaging Python code. We discussed the tools of PIP and virtualenv in detail. We looked at how pip and virtualenv can work together, and how to install a set of requirements using pip, and set up similar virtual environments using it. We also took a quick look at relocatable virtual environments.

We then went to discuss PyPI—the Python Package Index which hosts Python third-party packages on the web. We then went through a detailed example of setting up a Python package using setuptools and the `setup.py` file. We used the mandelbrot application as an example in this case.

We ended that discussion by showing how to register the package to PyPI using its metadata, and also how to upload the package data including its code. We also took a brief look at PyPA, the Python Packaging Authority and their projects.

After that, two tools, both developed in Python, were discussed—Fabric for remote automated deployments, and Supervisor for remote management of processes on Unix systems. We finished the chapter with an overview of the common deployment patterns that one can use to solve deployment problems.

In the final chapter of this book, we talk about a variety of techniques of Debugging your code to identify potential issues.

10
Techniques for Debugging

Debugging a program can often be as hard or, sometimes, even more difficult than writing it. Quite often, programmers seem to spend an awful amount of time hunting for that elusive bug, the reason for which may be staring them in the face, yet not revealing itself.

Many developers, even the good ones, find troubleshooting a difficult art. Most often, programmers resort to complicated debugging techniques when simple approaches such as properly placed print statements and strategically commented code would do the trick.

Python has its own set of problems when it comes to debugging code. Being a dynamically typed language, type-related exceptions, which happen due to the programmer assuming a type to be something (when it's something else), are pretty common in Python. Name errors and attribute errors fall in a similar category too.

In this chapter, we will exclusively focus on this lesser discussed aspect of software.

Here is a topic-wise listing of what we are going to encounter in this chapter:

- Maximum subarray problem:
    - The power of "print"
    - Analysis and rewrite
    - Timing and optimizing the code

- Simple debugging tricks and techniques:
    - Word searcher program
    - Word searcher program — debugging step 1
    - Word searcher program — debugging step 2
    - Word searcher program — final code

- Skipping blocks of code
- Stopping execution
- External dependencies — using wrappers
- Replacing functions with their return value/data (mocking)
- Saving to/loading data from files as cache
- Saving to/loading data from memory as cache
- Returning random/mock data
- Generating random patient data

- Logging as a debugging technique:
  - Simple application logging
  - Advanced logging — logger objects
  - Advanced logging — custom formatting and loggers
  - Advanced logging — writing to syslog

- Debugging tools — using debuggers:
  - A debugging session with pdb
  - Pdb — similar tools
  - iPdb
  - Pdb++

- Advanced debugging — tracing:
  - The `trace` module
  - The `iptrace` program
  - System call tracing using `strace`

Okay, so let's debug it!

Maximum subarray problem

For starters, let's look at an interesting problem. In this problem, the goal is to find the maximum contiguous subarray of an array (sequence) of integers having mixed negative and positive numbers.

For example, say we have the following array:

```
>>> a  = [-5, 20, -10, 30, 15]
```

It is pretty obvious with a quick scan that the maximum sum is for the subarray [20, -10, 30, 15], giving a sum of 55.

Let's say, as a first cut, you write this piece of code:

```
import itertools

# max_subarray: v1
def max_subarray(sequence):
    """ Find sub-sequence in sequence having maximum sum """

    sums = []

    for i in range(len(sequence)):
        # Create all sub-sequences in given size
        for sub_seq in itertools.combinations(sequence, i):
            # Append sum
            sums.append(sum(sub_seq))

    return max(sums)
```

Now let's try it out:

```
>>>  max_subarray([-5, 20, -10, 30, 15])
65
```

This output seems clearly wrong, as any manual addition of any subarray in the array doesn't seem to yield a number more than 55. We need to debug the code.

The power of "print"

In order to debug the preceding example, a simple, strategically placed `print` statement does the trick. Let's print out the subsequences in the inner `for` loop:

The function is modified as follows:

max_subarray: v1

```
    def max_subarray(sequence):
        """ Find sub-sequence in sequence having maximum sum """

        sums = []
        for i in range(len(sequence)):
            for sub_seq in itertools.combinations(sequence, i):
                sub_seq_sum = sum(sub_seq)
                print(sub_seq, '=>', sub_seq_sum)
                sums.append(sub_seq_sum)

        return max(sums)
```

Now the code executes and prints this output:

```
>>> max_subarray([-5, 20, -10, 30, 15])
((), '=>', 0)
((-5,), '=>', -5)
((20,), '=>', 20)
((-10,), '=>', -10)
((30,), '=>', 30)
((15,), '=>', 15)
((-5, 20), '=>', 15)
((-5, -10), '=>', -15)
((-5, 30), '=>', 25)
((-5, 15), '=>', 10)
((20, -10), '=>', 10)
((20, 30), '=>', 50)
((20, 15), '=>', 35)
((-10, 30), '=>', 20)
((-10, 15), '=>', 5)
((30, 15), '=>', 45)
((-5, 20, -10), '=>', 5)
((-5, 20, 30), '=>', 45)
((-5, 20, 15), '=>', 30)
((-5, -10, 30), '=>', 15)
((-5, -10, 15), '=>', 0)
((-5, 30, 15), '=>', 40)
((20, -10, 30), '=>', 40)
((20, -10, 15), '=>', 25)
((20, 30, 15), '=>', 65)
((-10, 30, 15), '=>', 35)
((-5, 20, -10, 30), '=>', 35)
((-5, 20, -10, 15), '=>', 20)
((-5, 20, 30, 15), '=>', 60)
((-5, -10, 30, 15), '=>', 30)
((20, -10, 30, 15), '=>', 55)
65
```

The problem is clear now by looking at the output of the print statements.

There is a subarray [20, 30, 15] (highlighted in bold in the preceding output), which produces the sum 65. However, this is *not a valid subarray*, as the elements are not contiguous in the original array.

Clearly, the program is wrong and needs a fix.

Analysis and rewrite

A quick analysis tells us that the use of itertools.combinations is the culprit here. We used it as a way to quickly generate all the subarrays of different lengths from the array, but using combinations *does not* respect the order of items, and generates *all* combinations producing subarrays that are not contiguous.

Clearly, we need to rewrite this. Here is a first attempt at the rewrite:

max_subarray: v2

```
def max_subarray(sequence):
    """ Find sub-sequence in sequence having maximum sum """

    sums = []

    for i in range(len(sequence)):
        for j in range(i+1, len(sequence)):
            sub_seq = sequence[i:j]
            sub_seq_sum = sum(sub_seq)
            print(sub_seq,'=>',sub_seq_sum)
            sums.append(sum(sub_seq))

    return max(sums)
```

Now the output is as follows:

```
>>> max_subarray([-5, 20, -10, 30, 15])
([-5], '=>', -5)
([-5, 20], '=>', 15)
([-5, 20, -10], '=>', 5)
([-5, 20, -10, 30], '=>', 35)
([20], '=>', 20)
([20, -10], '=>', 10)
([20, -10, 30], '=>', 40)
([-10], '=>', -10)
([-10, 30], '=>', 20)
([30], '=>', 30)
40
```

The answer is not correct again, as it gives the suboptimal answer 40, not the correct one, which is, 55. Again, the print statement comes to the rescue, as it tells us clearly that the main array itself is not being considered — we have an *off-by-one* bug.

An off-by-one or one-off error occurs in programming when an array index used to iterate over a sequence (array) is off either by *one less* or *one more* than the correct value. This is often found in languages where the index for sequences starts from zero, such as C/C++, Java, or Python.

In this case, the *off-by-one* error is in this line:

```
"sub_seq = sequence[i:j]"
```

The correct code should, instead, be as follows:

```
"sub_seq = sequence[i:j+1]"
```

With this fix, our code produces the output as expected:

```
# max_subarray: v2

def max_subarray(sequence):
    """ Find sub-sequence in sequence having maximum sum """

    sums = []

    for i in range(len(sequence)):
        for j in range(i+1, len(sequence)):
            sub_seq = sequence[i:j+1]
            sub_seq_sum = sum(sub_seq)
            print(sub_seq,'=>',sub_seq_sum)
            sums.append(sub_seq_sum)

    return max(sums)
```

Here is the output:

```
>>> max_subarray([-5, 20, -10, 30, 15])
([-5, 20], '=>', 15)
([-5, 20, -10], '=>', 5)
([-5, 20, -10, 30], '=>', 35)
([-5, 20, -10, 30, 15], '=>', 50)
([20, -10], '=>', 10)
([20, -10, 30], '=>', 40)
([20, -10, 30, 15], '=>', 55)
```

```
([-10, 30], '=>', 20)
([-10, 30, 15], '=>', 35)
([30, 15], '=>', 45)
55
```

Let us assume at this point that you consider the code to be complete.

You pass the code on to a reviewer, and they mention that your code, though called `max_subarray`, actually forgets to return the subarray itself, instead returning only the sum. There is also the feedback that you don't need to maintain an array of sums.

You combine this feedback and produce a version 3.0 of the code, which fixes both the issues:

max_subarray: v3

```
def max_subarray(sequence):
    """ Find sub-sequence in sequence having maximum sum """

    # Trackers for max sum and max sub-array
    max_sum, max_sub = 0, []

    for i in range(len(sequence)):
        for j in range(i+1, len(sequence)):
            sub_seq = sequence[i:j+1]
            sum_s = sum(sub_seq)
            if sum_s > max_sum:
                # If current sum > max sum so far, replace the values
                max_sum, max_sub = sum_s, sub_seq

    return max_sum, max_sub

>>> max_subarray([-5, 20, -10, 30, 15])
(55, [20, -10, 30, 15])
```

Note that we removed the print statement in this last version, as the logic was already correct, and so there was no need for debugging.

All good.

Timing and optimizing the code

If you analyze the code a bit, you'll find that the code performs two passes through the full sequence, one outer and one inner. So if the sequence contains *n* items, the code performs *n*n* passes.

We know from *Chapter 4, Good Performance is Rewarding!*, on performance that such a piece of code performs at the order of *O(n2)*. We can measure the real time spent on the code by using simple `context-manager` using the `with` operator.

Our context manager looks as follows:

```
import time
from contextlib import contextmanager

@contextmanager
def timer():
    """ Measure real-time execution of a block of code """

    try:
        start = time.time()
        yield
    finally:
        end = (time.time() - start)*1000
        print 'time taken=> %.2f ms' % end
```

Let's modify the code to create an array of random numbers of different sizes to measure the time taken. We will write a function for this:

```
import random

def num_array(size):
    """ Return a list of numbers in a fixed random range
    of given size """

    nums = []
    for i in range(size):
        nums.append(random.randrange(-25, 30))
    return nums
```

Let's time our logic for various sizes of arrays, beginning with 100:

```
>>> with timer():
... max_subarray(num_array(100))
... (121, [7, 10, -17, 3, 21, 26, -2, 5, 14, 2, -19, -18, 23, 12, 8,
     -12, -23, 28, -16, -19, -3, 14, 16, -25, 26, -16, 4, 12, -23, 26,
     22, 12, 23])
time taken=> 16.45 ms
```

For an array of 1,000, the code will be as follows:

```
>>> with timer():
... max_subarray(num_array(100))
... (121, [7, 10, -17, 3, 21, 26, -2, 5, 14, 2, -19, -18, 23, 12, 8,
     -12, -23, 28, -16, -19, -3, 14, 16, -25, 26, -16, 4, 12, -23, 26,
     22, 12, 23])
time taken=> 16.45 ms
```

So this takes about 3.3 seconds.

It can be shown that with an input size of 10,000, the code will take around 2 to 3 hours to run.

Is there a way to optimize the code? Yes, there is an $O(n)$ version of the same code, which looks like this:

```
def max_subarray(sequence):
    """ Maximum subarray - optimized version """

    max_ending_here = max_so_far = 0

    for x in sequence:
        max_ending_here = max(0, max_ending_here + x)
        max_so_far = max(max_so_far, max_ending_here)

    return max_so_far
```

With this version, the time taken is much better:

```
>>> with timer():
... max_subarray(num_array(100))
... 240
time taken=> 0.77 ms
```

For an array of 1,000, the time taken is as follows:

```
>>> with timer():
... max_subarray(num_array(1000))
... 2272
time taken=> 6.05 ms
```

For an array of 10,000, the time is around 44 milliseconds:

```
>>> with timer():
... max_subarray(num_array(10000))
... 19362
time taken=> 43.89 ms
```

Simple debugging tricks and techniques

We saw the power of the simple `print` statement in the previous example. In a similar way, other simple techniques can be used to debug programs without requiring to resort to a debugger.

Debugging can be thought of as a step-wise process of exclusion until the programmer arrives at the truth—the cause of the bug. It essentially involves the following steps:

- Analyze the code and come up with a set of probable assumptions (causes) that may be the source of the bug.

- Test out each of the assumptions one by one by using appropriate debugging techniques.

- At every step of the test, you either arrive at the source of the bug—as the test succeeds telling you the problem was with the specific cause you were testing for; or the test fails and you move on to test the next assumption.

- You repeat the last step until you either arrive at the cause or you discard the current set of probable assumptions. Then you restart the entire cycle until you (hopefully) find the cause.

Word searcher program

In this section, we will look at some simple debugging techniques one by one using examples. We will start with the example of a word searcher program that looks for lines containing a specific word in a list of files — and appends and returns the lines in a list.

Here is the listing of the code for the word searcher program:

```
import os
import glob

def grep_word(word, filenames):
    """ Open the given files and look for a specific word.
    Append lines containing word to a list and
    return it """

    lines, words = [], []

    for filename in filenames:
        print('Processing',filename)
        lines += open(filename).readlines()


    word = word.lower()
    for line in lines:
        if word in line.lower():
            lines.append(line.strip())

    # Now sort the list according to length of lines
    return sorted(words, key=len)
```

You may have noticed a subtle bug in the preceding code — it appends to the wrong list. It reads from the list "lines," and appends to the same list, which will cause the list to grow forever; the program will go into an infinite loop when it encounters even a single line containing the given word.

Let's run the program on the current directory:

```
>>> parse_filename('lines', glob.glob('*.py'))
(hangs)
```

On any day, you may find this bug easily. On a bad day, you may be stuck on this for a while, not noticing that the same list being read from is being appended to.

Here are a few things that you can do:

- As the code is hanging and there are two loops, find out the loop that causes the problem. To do this, either put a print statement between the two loops, or put a sys.exit function, which will cause the interpreter to exit at that point.

- A print statement can be missed by a developer, especially if the code has many other print statements, but sys.exit can never be missed of course.

Word searcher program – debugging step 1

The code is rewritten as follows to insert a specific sys.exit (...) call between the two loops:

```
import os
import glob

def grep_word(word, filenames):
    """ Open the given files and look for a specific word.
    Append lines containing word to a list and
    return it """

    lines, words = [], []

    for filename in filenames:
        print('Processing',filename)
        lines += open(filename).readlines()

    sys.exit('Exiting after first loop')

    word = word.lower()
    for line in lines:
        if word in line.lower():
            lines.append(line.strip())

    # Now sort the list according to length of lines
    return sorted(words, key=len)
```

When trying it out a second time, we get this output:

```
>>> grep_word('lines', glob.glob('*.py'))
Exiting after first loop
```

Now it's pretty clear that the problem is not in the first loop. You can now proceed to debug the second loop (we are assuming that you are totally blind to the wrong variable usage, so you are figuring out the issue the hard way, by debugging).

Word searcher program – debugging step 2

Whenever you suspect a block of code inside a loop to be causing a bug, there are a few tricks to debug this, and confirm your suspicion. These include the following:

- Put a strategic continue just preceding the block of code. If the problem disappears, then you've confirmed that the specific block or any next block is the issue. You can continue to move down your `continue` statement until you identify the specific block of code that is causing the issue.

- Make Python skip the code block by prefixing it with `if 0:`. This is more useful if the block is a line of code or a few lines of code.

- If there is a lot of code inside a loop, and the loop executes many times, print statements may not help you much, as a ton of data will be printed, and it would be difficult to sift and scan through it and find out where the problem is.

In this case, we will use the first trick to figure out the issue. Here is the modified code:

```
def grep_word(word, filenames):
    """ Open the given files and look for a specific word.
    Append lines containing word to a list and
    return it """

    lines, words = [], []

    for filename in filenames:
        print('Processing',filename)
        lines += open(filename).readlines()


    # Debugging steps
    # 1. sys.exit
    # sys.exit('Exiting after first loop')

    word = word.lower()
    for line in lines:
        if word in line.lower():
```

```
                words.append(line.strip())
                continue

        # Now sort the list according to length of lines
        return sorted(words, key=len)



>>> grep_word('lines', glob.glob('*.py'))
[]
```

Now the code executes, making it pretty clear that the problem is in the processing step. Hopefully, from there it is just one step to figure out the bug, as the programmer has finally got his eye on the line causing the issue by way of the process of debugging.

Word searcher program – final code

We have spent some time figuring out issues in the program by following a couple of debugging steps documented in the previous sections. With this, our hypothetical programmer was able to find the issue in the code and solve it.

Here is the final code with the bug fixed:

```
def grep_word(word, filenames):
    """ Open the given files and look for a specific word.
    Append lines containing word to a list and
    return it """

    lines, words = [], []

    for filename in filenames:
        print('Processing',filename)
        lines += open(filename).readlines()


    word = word.lower()
    for line in lines:
        if word in line.lower():
            words.append(line.strip())

    # Now sort the list according to length of lines
    return sorted(words, key=len)
```

The output is as follows:

```
>>> grep_word('lines', glob.glob('*.py'))
['for line in lines:', 'lines, words = [], []',
  '#lines.append(line.strip())',
  'lines += open(filename).readlines()',
  'Append lines containing word to a list and',
  'and return list of lines containing the word.',
  '# Now sort the list according to length of lines',
  "print('Lines => ', grep_word('lines', glob.glob('*.py')))"]
```

Let's summarize the simple debugging tricks that we've learned so far in this section, and also look at a few related tricks and techniques.

Skipping blocks of code

A programmer can skip code blocks that they suspect of causing a bug during debugging. If the block is inside a loop, this can be done by skipping execution with a `continue` statement. We've seen an example of this already.

If the block is outside of a loop, this can be done by using `if 0`, and moving the suspect code to the dependent block, as follows:

```
if 0:
    # Suspected code block
    perform_suspect_operation1(args1, args2, ...)
    perform_suspect_operation2(…)
```

If the bug disappears after this, then you're sure that the problem lies in the suspected block of code.

This trick has its own deficiency, in that it requires indenting large blocks of code to the right, which once the debugging is finished, should be indented back. Hence it is not advised for anything more than five or six lines of code.

Stopping execution

If you're in the middle of a hectic programming session, and you're trying to figure out an elusive bug, having already tried print statements, using the debugger, and other approaches, a rather drastic, but often fantastically useful, approach is to stop the execution just before or at the suspected code path using a function, `sys.exit` expression.

A `sys.exit(<strategic message>)` expression stops the program dead in its tracks, so this *can't be missed* by the programmer. This is often very useful in the following scenarios:

- A complex piece of code has an elusive bug depending upon specific values or ranges of input, which causes an exception that is caught and ignored, but later causes an issue in the program.

- In this case, checking for the specific value or range and then exiting the code using the right message in the exception handler via `sys.exit` will allow you to pinpoint the problem. The programmer can then decide to fix the issue by correcting the input or variable processing code.

  When writing concurrent programs, wrong usage of resource locking or other issues can make it difficult to track bugs like deadlocks, race conditions, and others. Since debugging multithreaded or multiple process programs via the debugger is very difficult, a simple technique is to put `sys.exit` in the suspect function after implementing the correct exception-handling code.

- When your code has a serious memory leak or an infinite loop, then it becomes difficult to debug after a while, and you're not able to pinpoint the problem otherwise. Moving a `sys.exit(<message>)` line from one line of code to the next until you identify the problem can be used as a last resort.

External dependencies – using wrappers

In cases where you suspect the problem is not inside your function, but in a function that you are calling from your code, this approach can be used.

Since the function is outside of your control, you can try and replace it with a wrapper function in a module where you have control.

For example, the following is generic code for processing serial JSON data. Let's assume that the programmer finds a bug with processing of certain data (maybe having a certain key-value pair), and suspects the external API to be the source of the bug. The bug may be that the API times out, returns a corrupt response, or in the worst case, causes a crash:

```
import external_api
def process_data(data):
    """ Process data using external API """

    # Clean up data—local function
    data = clean_up(data)
```

```
    # Drop duplicates from data—local function
    data = drop_duplicates(data)

    # Process line by line JSON
    for json_elem in data:
        # Bug ?
        external_api.process(json_elem)
```

One way to verify this is to *dummy* or *fake* the API for the specific ranges or values of the data. In this case, it can be done by creating a wrapper function as follows:

```
def process(json_data, skey='suspect_key',svalue='suspect_value'):
    """ Fake the external API except for the suspect key & value """

    # Assume each JSON element maps to a Python dictionary

    for json_elem in json_data:
        skip = False

        for key in json_elem:
            if key == skey:
                if json_elem[key] == svalue:
                    # Suspect key,value combination - dont process
                    # this JSON element
                    skip = True
                    break

        # Pass on to the API
        if not skip:
            external_api.process(json_elem)

def process_data(data):
    """ Process data using external API """

    # Clean up data—local function
    data = clean_up(data)
    # Drop duplicates from data—local function
    data = drop_duplicates(data)

    # Process line by line JSON using local wrapper
    process(data)
```

If your suspicion is indeed correct, this will cause the problem to disappear. You can then use this as a test code, and communicate with the stakeholders of the external API to get the problem fixed, or write code to make sure that the problem key-value pair is skipped in data sent to the API.

Replacing functions with their return value/ data (mocking)

In modern web application programming, you are never too far away from a blocking I/O call in your program. This can be a simple URL request, a slightly involved external API request, or maybe a costly database query and such calls can be the sources of bugs.

You may find either of the following situations:

- The return data from such a call could be the cause of an issue.
- The call itself is the cause of an issue, such as I/O or network errors, timeouts, or resource contentions.

When you encounter problems with costly I/O, replicating them can often be a problem. This is because of the following reasons:

- The I/O calls take time, so debugging this costs you a lot of wasted time, not allowing you to focus on the real issue.
- Subsequent calls may not be repeatable with respect to the issue, as external requests may return slightly different data every time.
- If you are using an external paid API, the calls may actually cost you money, so you cannot exhaust a lot of such calls on debugging and testing.

A common technique that is very useful in these cases is to save the return data of these APIs/functions, and then mock the functions by using their return data to replace the functions/APIs themselves. This is an approach similar to mock testing, but it is used in the context of debugging.

Let's look at an example of an API that returns *business listings* on websites, given a business address including details like its name, street address, city, and so on. The code looks like this:

```
import config

search_api = 'http://api.%(site)s/listings/search'

def get_api_key(site):
```

```
        """ Return API key for a site """

        # Assumes the configuration is available via a config module
        return config.get_key(site)

    def api_search(address, site='yellowpages.com'):
        """ API to search for a given business address
        on a site and return results """

        req_params = {}
        req_params.update({
            'key': get_api_key(site),
            'term': address['name'],
            'searchloc': '{0}, {1}, {1}'.format(address['street'],
                                                address['city'],
                                                address['state'])})
        return requests.post(search_api % locals(),
                             params=req_params)

    def parse_listings(addresses, sites):
        """ Given a list of addresses, fetch their listings
        for a given set of sites, process them """

        for site in sites:
            for address in addresses:
                listing = api_search(address, site)
                # Process the listing
                process_listing(listing, site)

    def process_listings(listing, site):
        """ Process a listing and analzye it """

        # Some heavy computational code
        # whose details we are not interested.
```

 The code makes a few assumptions, one of which is that every site has the same API URL and parameters. Note that this is only for illustration purposes. In reality, each site will have very different API formats including its URL and the parameters it accepts.

Note that in this last piece of code, the actual work is being done in the process_listings function, the code for which is not shown, as the example is illustrative.

Let's say you are trying to debug this function. However, due to a delay or error in the API calls, you find you are wasting a lot of valuable time in fetching the listings themselves. What are some of the techniques that you can use to avoid this dependency? Here are a few things that you can do:

- Instead of fetching listings via API, save them to files, to a database, or an in-memory store, and load them on demand.
- Cache the return value of the `api_search` function via a caching or memoize patterns so that further calls after the first call, return data from memory.
- Mock the data, and return random data that has the same characteristics as the original data.

We will look at each of these in turn.

Saving to / loading data from files as cache

In this technique, you construct a filename using unique keys from the input data. If a matching file exists on disk, it is opened and the data is returned; otherwise, the call is made and the data is written. This can be achieved by using a *file caching* decorator as the following code illustrates:

```python
import hashlib
import json
import os

def unique_key(address, site):
    """ Return a unique key for the given arguments """

    return hashlib.md5(''.join((address['name'],
                                address['street'],
                                address['city'],
                                site)).encode('utf-8')).hexdigest()

def filecache(func):
    """ A file caching decorator """

    def wrapper(*args, **kwargs):
        # Construct a unique cache filename
```

```
        filename = unique_key(args[0], args[1]) + '.data'

        if os.path.isfile(filename):
            print('=>from file<=')
            # Return cached data from file
            return json.load(open(filename))

        # Else compute and write into file
        result = func(*args, **kwargs)
        json.dump(result, open(filename,'w'))

        return result

    return wrapper

@filecache
def api_search(address, site='yellowpages.com'):
    """ API to search for a given business address
    on a site and return results """

    req_params = {}
    req_params.update({
        'key': get_api_key(site),
        'term': address['name'],
        'searchloc': '{0}, {1}, {1}'.format(address['street'],
                                             address['city'],
                                             address['state'])})
    return requests.post(search_api % locals(),
                         params=req_params)
```

Here's how this preceding code works:

1. The api_search function is decorated with filecache as a decorator.

2. Then filecache uses unique_key as the function to calculate the unique
    filename for storing the results of an API call. In this case, the unique_key
    function uses the hash of a combination of the business name, street, and city,
    plus the site queried for in order to build the unique value.

3. The first time the function is called, the data is fetched via API and stored in
    the file. During further invocations, the data is returned directly from the file.

This works pretty well in most cases. Most data is loaded just once, and on further
calls, returned from the file cache. However, this suffers from the problem of *stale
data*, as once the file is created, the data is always returned from it. Meanwhile, the
data on the server may have changed.

This can be solved by using an in-memory key-value store and saving the data there instead of in files on disk. One can use well-known key-value stores such as **Memcached**, **MongoDB**, or **Redis** for this purpose. In the following example, we'll show you how to replace the `filecache` decorator with a memory cached decorator using Redis.

Saving to / loading data from memory as cache

In this technique, a unique in-memory cache key is constructed using unique values from the input arguments. If the cache is found on the cache store by querying using the key, its value is returned from the store; or else the call is made and the cache is written. To ensure that data is not too stale, a fixed **time-to-live (TTL)** is used. We use Redis as the cache store engine:

```
from redis import StrictRedis

def memoize(func, ttl=86400):
    """ A memory caching decorator """

    # Local redis as in-memory cache
    cache = StrictRedis(host='localhost', port=6379)

    def wrapper(*args, **kwargs):
        # Construct a unique key

        key = unique_key(args[0], args[1])
        # Check if its in redis
        cached_data = cache.get(key)
        if cached_data != None:
            print('=>from cache<=')
            return json.loads(cached_data)
        # Else calculate and store while putting a TTL
        result = func(*args, **kwargs)
        cache.set(key, json.dumps(result), ttl)

        return result

    return wrapper
```

 Note that we are reusing the definition of `unique_key` from the previous code example.

The only thing that changes in the rest of the code is that we replace the `filecache` decorator with the `memoize` one:

```
@memoize
def api_search(address, site='yellowpages.com'):
    """ API to search for a given business address
    on a site and return results """

    req_params = {}
    req_params.update({
        'key': get_api_key(site),
        'term': address['name'],
        'searchloc': '{0}, {1}, {1}'.format(address['street'],
                                            address['city'],
                                            address['state'])})
    return requests.post(search_api % locals(),
                         params=req_params)
```

The advantages of this version over the previous one are as follows:

- The cache is stored in memory. No additional files are created.

- The cache is created with a TTL, beyond which it expires. So the problem of stale data is circumvented. The TTL is customizable, and defaults to a day (86,400 seconds) in this example.

There are a few other techniques for mocking external API calls and similar dependencies. Some of these are listed as follows:

- Using a `StringIO` object in Python to read/write data, instead of using a file. For example, the `filecache` or `memoize` decorators can be easily modified to use a `StringIO` object.

- Using a mutable default argument, such as a dictionary or a list, as a cache and writing results to it. Since a mutable argument in Python holds its state after repeated calls, it effectively works as an in-memory cache.

- Replacing an external API with a call to a replacement/dummy API call to a service on the local machine (`127.0.0.1` IP address) by editing the system's host file, adding an entry for the host in question, and putting its IP as `127.0.0.1`. The call to localhost can always return a standard (canned) response.

For example, on Linux and other POSIX systems, you can add a line like this in the /etc/hosts file:

```
# Only for testing—comment out after that!
127.0.0.1 api.website.com
```

 Note that this technique is a very useful and clever approach as long as you remember to comment out such lines after testing!

Returning random/mock data

Another technique, which is mostly useful for performance testing and debugging, is to feed functions with data that is *similar*, but *not the same* as the original data.

Let's say, for example, that you are working on an application that works with patient/doctor data for patients under a specific insurance scheme (say Medicare/Medicaid in the US, ESI in India) to analyze and find out patterns such as common ailments, top 10 health issues in terms of government expenses, and so on.

Let's say that your application is expected to load and analyze tens of thousands of rows of patient data from a database at one time, which is expected to scale to 1-2 million under peak load. You want to debug the application and find out performance characteristics under such a load, but you don't have any real data, as the data is in the collection stage.

In such scenarios, libraries or functions that generate and return mock data are very useful. In this section, we will use a third-party Python library to accomplish this.

Generating random patient data

Let's assume that for a patient we need the following basic fields:

- Name
- Age
- Gender
- Health issue
- Doctor's name
- Blood group
- Insured or not
- Date of last visit to doctor

The schematics library in Python provides a way to generate such data structures using simple types, which can then be validated, transformed, and also mocked.

The schematics library is installable via pip using the following command:

```
$ pip install schematics
```

To generate a model of a person with just their name and age is as simple as writing a class in schematics:

```
from schematics import Model
from schematics.types import StringType, DecimalType


class Person(Model):
    name = StringType()
    age = DecimalType()
```

To generate mock data, a mock object is returned, and a *primitive* is created using this:

```
>>> Person.get_mock_object().to_primitive()
{'age': u'12', 'name': u'Y7bnqRt'}
>>> Person.get_mock_object().to_primitive()
{'age': u'1', 'name': u'xyrh40EO3'}
```

One can create custom types using schematics. For the Patient model, for example, let's say that we are only interested in the age group 18-80, so we need to return age data in that range.

The following custom type does that for us:

```
from schematics.types import IntType


class AgeType(IntType):
    """ An age type for schematics """

    def __init__(self, **kwargs):
        kwargs['default'] = 18
        IntType.__init__(self, **kwargs)

    def to_primitive(self, value, context=None):
        return random.randrange(18, 80)
```

Also, since the names returned by the schematics library are just random strings, they have some room for improvement. The following NameType class improves upon it by returning names containing a clever mix of vowels and consonants:

```python
import string
import random

class NameType(StringType):
    """ A schematics custom name type """

    vowels='aeiou'
    consonants = ''.join(set(string.ascii_lowercase) - set(vowels))

    def __init__(self, **kwargs):
        kwargs['default'] = ''
        StringType.__init__(self, **kwargs)

    def get_name(self):
        """ A random name generator which generates
        names by clever placing of vowels and consontants """

        items = ['']*4

        items[0] = random.choice(self.consonants)
        items[2] = random.choice(self.consonants)

        for i in (1, 3):
            items[i] = random.choice(self.vowels)

        return ''.join(items).capitalize()

    def to_primitive(self, value, context=None):
        return self.get_name()
```

When combining both of these new types, our Person class looks much better when returning mock data:

```python
class Person(Model):
    name = NameType()
    age = AgeType()
```

```
>>> Person.get_mock_object().to_primitive()
{'age': 36, 'name': 'Qixi'}
>>> Person.get_mock_object().to_primitive()
{'age': 58, 'name': 'Ziru'}
>>> Person.get_mock_object().to_primitive()
{'age': 32, 'name': 'Zanu'}
```

In a similar way, it is rather easy to come up with a set of custom types and standard types to satisfy all the fields required for a Patient model:

```
class GenderType(BaseType):
    """A gender type for schematics """

    def __init__(self, **kwargs):
        kwargs['choices'] = ['male','female']
        kwargs['default'] = 'male'
        BaseType.__init__(self, **kwargs)


class ConditionType(StringType):
    """ A gender type for a health condition """

    def __init__(self, **kwargs):
        kwargs['default'] = 'cardiac'
        StringType.__init__(self, **kwargs)

    def to_primitive(self, value, context=None):
        return random.choice(('cardiac',
                              'respiratory',
                              'nasal',
                              'gynec',
                              'urinal',
                              'lungs',
                              'thyroid',
                              'tumour'))


import itertools

class BloodGroupType(StringType):
    """ A blood group type for schematics  """

    def __init__(self, **kwargs):
        kwargs['default'] = 'AB+'
```

```
        StringType.__init__(self, **kwargs)

    def to_primitive(self, value, context=None):
        return ''.join(random.choice(list(itertools.product(['AB','A',
'O','B'],['+','-'])))))
```

Now, combining all these with some standard types and default values into a `Patient` model, we get the following code:

```
class Patient(Model):
    """ A model class for patients """

    name = NameType()
    age = AgeType()
    gender = GenderType()
    condition = ConditionType()
    doctor = NameType()
    blood_group = BloodGroupType()
    insured = BooleanType(default=True)
    last_visit = DateTimeType(default='2000-01-01T13:30:30')
```

Now, creating random data of any size is as easy as invoking the `get_mock_object` method on the `Patient` class for any number *n*:

```
patients = map(lambda x: Patient.get_mock_object().to_primitive(),
range(n))
```

For example, to create 10,000 random sets of patient data, we use the following:

```
>>> patients = map(lambda x: Patient.get_mock_object().to_primitive(),
range(1000))
```

This data can be input to the processing functions as mock data until the real data is made available.

 Note: The Faker library in Python is also useful for generating a wide variety of fake data such as names, addresses, URIs, random text, and the like.

Let's now move on from these simple tricks and techniques to something more involved, mainly configuring logging in your applications.

Logging as a debugging technique

Python comes with standard library support for logging via the aptly named `logging` module. Though print statements can be used as a quick and rudimentary tool for debugging, real-life debugging mostly requires that the system or application generate some logs. Logging is useful because of the following reasons:

- Logs are usually saved to specific log files, typically, with timestamps, and remain at the server for a while until they are rotated out. This makes debugging easy even if the programmer is debugging the issue some time after it happened.

- Logging can be done at different levels—from the basic INFO to the verbose DEBUG levels—changing the amount of information output by the application. This allows the programmer to debug at different levels of logging to extract the information they want, and figure out the problem.

- Custom loggers can be written, which can perform logging to various outputs. At its most basic, logging is done to log files, but one can also write loggers that write to sockets, HTTP streams, databases, and the like.

Simple application logging

To configure simple logging in Python is rather easy and is shown as follows:

```
>>> import logging
>>> logging.warning('I will be back!')
WARNING:root:I will be back!


>>> logging.info('Hello World')
>>>
```

Nothing happens on executing the preceding code, because, by default, `logging` is configured at the **WARNING** level. However, it is pretty easy to configure logging to change its level.

The following code changes logging to log at the `info` level, and also adds a target file to save the log:

```
>>> logging.basicConfig(filename='application.log', level=logging.DEBUG)
>>> logging.info('Hello World')
```

If we inspect the `application.log` file, we will find that it contains the following lines:

```
INFO:root:Hello World
```

In order to add timestamps to the log lines, we need to configure the logging format. This can be done as follows:

```
>>> logging.basicConfig(format='%(asctime)s %(message)s')
```

Combining this, we get the final logging configuration as follows:

```
>>> logging.basicConfig(format='%(asctime)s %(message)s',
filename='application.log', level=logging.DEBUG)
>>> logging.info('Hello World!')
```

Now, the contents of `application.log` look something like the following:

```
INFO:root:Hello World
2016-12-26 19:10:37,236 Hello World!
```

Logging supports variable arguments, which are used to supply arguments to a template string supplied as the first argument.

Direct logging of arguments separated by commas doesn't work. For example:

```
>>> import logging
>>> logging.basicConfig(level=logging.DEBUG)
>>> x,y=10,20
>>> logging.info('Addition of',x,'and',y,'produces',x+y)
--- Logging error ---
Traceback (most recent call last):
  File "/usr/lib/python3.5/logging/__init__.py", line 980, in emit
    msg = self.format(record)
  File "/usr/lib/python3.5/logging/__init__.py", line 830, in format
    return fmt.format(record)
  File "/usr/lib/python3.5/logging/__init__.py", line 567, in format
    record.message = record.getMessage()
  File "/usr/lib/python3.5/logging/__init__.py", line 330, in getMessage
    msg = msg % self.args
TypeError: not all arguments converted during string formatting
Call stack:
  File "<stdin>", line 1, in <module>
Message: 'Addition of'
Arguments: (10, 'and', 20, 'produces', 30)
```

However, we can use the following:

```
>>> logging.info('Addition of %s and %s produces %s',x,y,x+y)
INFO:root:Addition of 10 and 20 produces 30
```

The earlier example works nicely.

Advanced logging – logger objects

Logging using the `logging` module directly works in most simple situations. However, in order to extract the maximum value out of the `logging` module, we should work with logger objects. It also allows us to perform a lot of customizations such as custom formatters, custom handlers, and so on.

Let's write a function that returns such a custom logger. It accepts the application name, the logging level, and two more options—the log filename, and whether to turn console logging on or not:

```
import logging
def create_logger(app_name, logfilename=None,
                                level=logging.INFO, console=False):

    """ Build and return a custom logger. Accepts the application
name,
    log filename, loglevel and console logging toggle """

    log=logging.getLogger(app_name)
    log.setLevel(logging.DEBUG)
    # Add file handler
    if logfilename != None:
        log.addHandler(logging.FileHandler(logfilename))

    if console:
        log.addHandler(logging.StreamHandler())

    # Add formatter
    for handle in log.handlers:
        formatter = logging.Formatter('%(asctime)s : %(levelname)-8s -
%(message)s', datefmt='%Y-%m-%d %H:%M:%S')

        handle.setFormatter(formatter)

    return log
```

Let's inspect the function:

1. Instead of using `logging` directly, it creates a `logger` object using the `logging.getLogger` factory function.

2. By default, the `logger` object is useless as it has not been configured with any handlers. Handlers are stream wrappers that take care of logging to a specific stream, such as the console, files, sockets, and so on.

3. The configuration is done on this logger object, such as setting the level (via the `setLevel` method) and adding handlers such as `FileHandler` for logging to a file and `StreamHandler` for logging to the console.

4. Formatting of the log message is done on the handlers, and not on the logger object per se. We use a standard format of `<timestamp>: <level>—<message>` using the date format for the timestamp of `YY-mm-dd HH:MM:SS`.

Let's see this in action:

```
>>> log=create_logger('myapp',logfilename='app.log', console=True)
>>> log
<logging.Logger object at 0x7fc09afa55c0>
>>> log.info('Started application')
2016-12-26 19:38:12 : INFO     - Started application
>>> log.info('Initializing objects...')
2016-12-26 19:38:25 : INFO     - Initializing objects...
```

Inspecting the app.log file in the same directory reveals the following contents:

```
2016-12-26 19:38:12 : INFO     —Started application
2016-12-26 19:38:25 : INFO     —Initializing objects...
```

Advanced logging – custom formatting and loggers

We looked at how we can create and configure logger objects according to our requirements. Sometimes, one needs to go over and above, and print extra data in the log lines, which helps debugging.

A common problem that arises in debugging applications, especially those that are performance critical, is to find out how much time each function or method takes. Now, though this can be found out by methods such as profiling the application using profilers and by using some techniques discussed previously like timer context managers, quite often, a custom logger can be written to do the trick.

Let's assume that your application is a business listing API server, which responds to listing API requests like the one we discussed in an earlier section. When it starts off, it needs to initialize a number of objects and load some data from the DB.

Assume that as part of performance optimization, you have tuned these routines, and would like to record how much time these take. We'll see if we can write a custom logger to do it for us:

```
import logging
import time
from functools import partial

class LoggerWrapper(object):
    """ A wrapper class for logger objects with
    calculation of time spent in each step """

    def __init__(self, app_name, filename=None,
                       level=logging.INFO, console=False):
        self.log = logging.getLogger(app_name)
        self.log.setLevel(level)

        # Add handlers
        if console:
            self.log.addHandler(logging.StreamHandler())

        if filename != None:
            self.log.addHandler(logging.FileHandler(filename))

        # Set formatting
        for handle in self.log.handlers:

            formatter = logging.Formatter('%(asctime)s [%(timespent)s]: %(levelname)-8s - %(message)s', datefmt='%Y-%m-%d %H:%M:%S')
            handle.setFormatter(formatter)


        for name in ('debug','info','warning','error','critical'):
            # Creating convenient wrappers by using functools
            func = partial(self._dolog, name)
            # Set on this class as methods
            setattr(self, name, func)

        # Mark timestamp
```

```
        self._markt = time.time()

    def _calc_time(self):
        """ Calculate time spent so far """

        tnow = time.time()
        tdiff = int(round(tnow - self._markt))

        hr, rem = divmod(tdiff, 3600)
        mins, sec = divmod(rem, 60)
        # Reset mark
        self._markt = tnow
        return '%.2d:%.2d:%.2d' % (hr, mins, sec)

    def _dolog(self, levelname, msg, *args, **kwargs):
        """ Generic method for logging at different levels """

        logfunc = getattr(self.log, levelname)
        return logfunc(msg, *args, extra={'timespent': self._calc_
time()})
```

We have built a custom class named LoggerWrapper. Let's analyze the code and see what it does:

1. The __init__ method of this class is very similar to our create_logger function written before. It takes the same argument, constructs handler objects, and configures logger. However, this time, the logger object is part of the outer LoggerWrapper instance.

2. The formatter takes an additional variable template named timespent.

3. No direct logging methods seem to be defined. However, using the partial functions technique, we wrap the _dolog method at the different levels of logging, and set them on the class as logging methods, dynamically, by using setattr.

4. The _dolog method calculates the time spent in each routine by using a marker timestamp—initialized the first time, and then reset in every call. The time spent is sent to the logging methods using a dictionary argument named extra.

Let's see how the application can use this logger wrapper to measure the time spent in critical routines. Here is an example that assumes a Flask web application:

```
# Application code
log=LoggerWrapper('myapp', filename='myapp.log',console=True)

app = Flask(__name__)
log.info("Starting application...")
log.info("Initializing objects.")
init()
log.info("Initialization complete.")
log.info("Loading configuration and data …")
load_objects()
log.info('Loading complete. Listening for connections …')
mainloop()
```

Note that the time spent is logged inside square brackets just after the timestamp.

Let's say that this last code produces an output like the following:

```
2016-12-26 20:08:28 [00:00:00]: INFO     —Starting application...

2016-12-26 20:08:28 [00:00:00]: INFO      - Initializing objects.

2016-12-26 20:08:42 [00:00:14]: INFO      - Initialization complete.

2016-12-26 20:08:42 [00:00:00]: INFO      - Loading configuration and data

...

2016-12-26 20:10:37 [00:01:55]: INFO      - Loading complete. Listening
for connections
```

From the log lines, it's evident that the initialization took 14 seconds, whereas the loading of configuration and data took 1 minute and 55 seconds.

By adding similar log lines, you can get a quick and reasonably accurate estimate of the time spent on critical pieces of the application. Being saved in log files, another added advantage is that you don't need to specially calculate and save it anywhere else.

 Using this custom logger, note that the time shown as time spent for a given log line is the time spent in the routine of the previous line.

Advanced logging – writing to syslog

POSIX systems such as Linux and Mac OS X have a system log file, which the application can write to. Typically, this file is present as /var/log/syslog. Let's see how Python logging can be configured to write to the system log file.

The main change that you need to make is to add a system log handler to the logger object like this:

```
log.addHandler(logging.handlers.SysLogHandler(address='/dev/log'))
```

Let's modify our create_logger function to enable it to write to syslog, and see the complete code in action:

```python
import logging
import logging.handlers

def create_logger(app_name, logfilename=None, level=logging.INFO,
                               console=False, syslog=False):
    """ Build and return a custom logger. Accepts the application
        name,
    log filename, loglevel and console logging toggle and syslog
toggle """

    log=logging.getLogger(app_name)
    log.setLevel(logging.DEBUG)
    # Add file handler
    if logfilename != None:
        log.addHandler(logging.FileHandler(logfilename))

    if syslog:
        log.addHandler(logging.handlers.SysLogHandler(address='/dev/
                    log'))

    if console:
        log.addHandler(logging.StreamHandler())

    # Add formatter
    for handle in log.handlers:
        formatter = logging.Formatter('%(asctime)s : %(levelname)-8s
                    - %(message)s',  datefmt='%Y-%m-%d %H:%M:%S')
        handle.setFormatter(formatter)



    return log
```

Now let's try to create a logger while logging to `syslog`:

```
>>> create_logger('myapp',console=True, syslog=True)
>>> log.info('Myapp - starting up…')
```

Let's inspect syslog to see if it actually got logged:

```
$ tail -3 /var/log/syslog
Dec 26 20:39:54 ubuntu-pro-book kernel: [36696.308437] psmouse serio1:
TouchPad at isa0060/serio1/input0 - driver resynced.
Dec 26 20:44:39 ubuntu-pro-book 2016-12-26 20:44:39 : INFO     - Myapp -
starting up...
Dec 26 20:45:01 ubuntu-pro-book CRON[11522]: (root) CMD (command -v
debian-sa1 > /dev/null && debian-sa1 1 1)
```

The output shows that it did.

Debugging tools – using debuggers

Most programmers tend to think of *debugging* as something that they ought to do with a debugger. In this chapter, we have so far seen that, more than an exact science, debugging is an art, which can be done using a lot of tricks and techniques rather than directly jumping to a debugger. However, sooner or later, we expected to encounter the debugger in this chapter—and here we are!

The Python Debugger, or pdb as it is known, is part of the Python runtime.

Pdb can be invoked when running a script from the beginning as follows:

```
$ python3 -m pdb script.py
```

However, the most common way in which programmers invoke pdb is to insert the following line at a place in the code where you want to enter the debugger:

```
import pdb; pdb.set_trace()
```

Let's use this, and try to debug an instance of the first example in this chapter, that is, the sum of the max subarray. We will debug the `O(n)` version of the code as an example:

```
def max_subarray(sequence):
    """ Maximum subarray - optimized version """

    max_ending_here = max_so_far = 0
    for x in sequence:
```

```
# Enter the debugger
import pdb; pdb.set_trace()
max_ending_here = max(0, max_ending_here + x)
max_so_far = max(max_so_far, max_ending_here)

return max_so_far
```

A debugging session with pdb

The debugger is entered in the very first loop immediately after the program is run:

```
>>> max_subarray([20, -5, -10, 30, 10])
> /home/user/programs/maxsubarray.py(8)max_subarray()
-> max_ending_here = max(0, max_ending_here + x)
-> for x in sequence:
(Pdb) max_so_far
20
```

You can stop the execution using s. Pdb will execute the current line, and stop:

```
> /home/user/programs/maxsubarray.py(7)max_subarray()
-> max_ending_here = max(0, max_ending_here + x)
```

You can inspect the variables by simply typing them and pressing *Enter*:

```
(Pdb) max_so_far
20
```

The current stack trace can be printed using w or where. An arrow ($\rightarrow$) indicates the current stack frame:

```
(Pdb) w
  <stdin>(1)<module>()
> /home/user/programs/maxsubarray.py(7)max_subarray()
-> max_ending_here = max(0, max_ending_here + x)
```

The execution can be continued until the next breakpoint by using c or continue:

```
    > /home/user/programs/maxsubarray.py(6)max_subarray()
-> for x in sequence:
(Pdb) max_so_far
20

(Pdb) c
```

```
> /home/user/programs/maxsubarray.py(6)max_subarray()
-> for x in sequence:
(Pdb) max_so_far
20
(Pdb) c
> /home/user/programs/maxsubarray.py(6)max_subarray()
-> for x in sequence:
(Pdb) max_so_far
35
(Pdb) max_ending_here
35
```

In the preceding code, we continued three iterations of the for loop until the max value changed from 20 to 35. Let's inspect where we are in the sequence:

```
(Pdb) x
30
```

We have one more item to go in the list, namely, the last one. Let's inspect the source code at this point using the l or the list command:

```
(Pdb) l
  1
  2      def max_subarray(sequence):
  3          """ Maximum subarray - optimized version """
  4
  5          max_ending_here = max_so_far = 0
  6  ->      for x in sequence:
  7              max_ending_here = max(0, max_ending_here + x)
  8              max_so_far = max(max_so_far, max_ending_here)
  9              import pdb; pdb.set_trace()
 10
 11          return max_so_far
```

One can traverse up and down the stack frames by using the u or up and d or *down* commands, respectively:

```
(Pdb) up
> <stdin>(1)<module>()
(Pdb) up
```

```
*** Oldest frame
(Pdb) list
[EOF]
(Pdb) d
> /home/user/programs/maxsubarray.py(6)max_subarray()
-> for x in sequence:
```

Let's now return from the function:

```
(Pdb) r
> /home/user/programs/maxsubarray.py(6)max_subarray()
-> for x in sequence:
(Pdb) r
--Return--
> /home/user/programs/maxsubarray.py(11)max_subarray()->45
-> return max_so_far
```

The return value of the function is 45.

Pdb has a lot of other commands than what we covered here. However, we don't intend for this session to be a fully fledged pdb tutorial. Interested programmers can refer to the documentation on the web to learn more.

Pdb – similar tools

The Python community has built a number of useful tools that build on top of Pdb, but add more useful functionality, developer's ease-of-use, or both.

iPdb

Basically, iPdb is iPython-enabled pdb. It exports functions to access the iPython debugger. It also has tab completion, syntax highlighting, and better traceback, and introspection methods.

iPdb can be installed with pip.

The following screenshot shows a session of debugging using iPdb, the same function as we did with pdb before. Observe the syntax highlighting that **iPdb** provides:

iPdb in action, showing syntax highlighting

Also note that iPdb provides a fuller stack trace as opposed to `Pdb`:

iPdb in action, showing a fuller stack trace than pdb

Note that iPdb uses iPython as the default runtime instead of Python.

Pdb++

Pdb++ is a drop-in replacement for pdb with features similar to iPdb, but it works on the default Python runtime instead of requiring iPython. Pdb++ is also installable via pip.

Once pdb++ is installed, it takes over at all places that import Pdb, so no code change is required at all.

Pdb++ does smart command parsing. For example, if there are variable names conflicting with the standard Pdb commands, Pdb will give preference to the command over displaying the variable contents. Pdb++ figures this out intelligently.

Here is a screenshot showing Pdb++ in action, including syntax highlighting, tab completion, and smart command parsing:

```
                            IPython: user/programs

File  Edit  View  Search  Terminal  Help
-> print(max_subarray([20, -5, -10, 30, 10]))
[1] > /home/user/programs/maxsubarray.py(6)max_subarray()
-> for x in sequence:
(Pdb++) max
              max                 max_ending_here  max_so_far      max_subarray
(Pdb++) max_so_far
20
(Pdb++) c
[1] > /home/user/programs/maxsubarray.py(6)max_subarray()
-> for x in sequence:
(Pdb++) c
[1] > /home/user/programs/maxsubarray.py(6)max_subarray()
-> for x in sequence:
(Pdb++) x
-10
(Pdb++) c
[1] > /home/user/programs/maxsubarray.py(6)max_subarray()
-> for x in sequence:
(Pdb++) max_s
            max_so_far    max_subarray
(Pdb++) max_so_far
35
(Pdb++) c
[1] > /home/user/programs/maxsubarray.py(6)max_subarray()
-> for x in sequence:
(Pdb++) c=x
(Pdb++) c
10
(Pdb++)
```

Pdb++ in action – Note the smart command parsing, where the c variable is interpreted correctly

Advanced debugging – tracing

Tracing of a program right from the beginning can often be used as an advanced debugging technique. Tracing allows a developer to trace program execution, find caller/callee relationships, and figure out all functions executed during the run of a program.

The trace module

Python comes with a default `trace` module as part of its standard library.

The trace module takes one of the `-trace`, `--count`, or `-listfuncs` options. The first option traces and prints all the source lines as they are executed. The second option produces an annotated list of files, which shows how many times a statement was executed. The latter simply displays all the functions executed by running of the program.

The following is a screenshot of the subarray problem being invoked by the `-trace` option of the `trace` module:

```
                              IPython: user/programs
 File  Edit  View  Search  Terminal  Help
$ python3 -m trace --trace maxsubarray.py
 --- modulename: maxsubarray, funcname: <module>
maxsubarray.py(2): def max_subarray(sequence):
maxsubarray.py(12): if    name    == "  main  ":
maxsubarray.py(13):     print(max_subarray([20, -5, -10, 30, 10]))
 --- modulename: maxsubarray, funcname: max_subarray
maxsubarray.py(5):       max_ending_here = max_so_far = 0
maxsubarray.py(6):       for x in sequence:
maxsubarray.py(7):           max_ending_here = max(0, max_ending_here + x)
maxsubarray.py(8):           max_so_far = max(max_so_far, max_ending_here)
maxsubarray.py(6):       for x in sequence:
maxsubarray.py(7):           max_ending_here = max(0, max_ending_here + x)
maxsubarray.py(8):           max_so_far = max(max_so_far, max_ending_here)
maxsubarray.py(6):       for x in sequence:
maxsubarray.py(7):           max_ending_here = max(0, max_ending_here + x)
maxsubarray.py(8):           max_so_far = max(max_so_far, max_ending_here)
maxsubarray.py(6):       for x in sequence:
maxsubarray.py(7):           max_ending_here = max(0, max_ending_here + x)
maxsubarray.py(8):           max_so_far = max(max_so_far, max_ending_here)
maxsubarray.py(6):       for x in sequence:
maxsubarray.py(7):           max_ending_here = max(0, max_ending_here + x)
maxsubarray.py(8):           max_so_far = max(max_so_far, max_ending_here)
maxsubarray.py(6):       for x in sequence:
maxsubarray.py(10):       return max_so_far
45
 --- modulename: trace, funcname:   unsettrace
trace.py(77):           sys.settrace(None)
$
```

Tracing program execution using the trace module by using its –trace option.

As you can see, the `trace` module traced the entire program execution, printing the lines of code one by one. Since most of this code is a `for` loop, you actually see the lines of code in the loop getting printed the number of times the loop was executed (five times).

The `-trackcalls` option traces and prints the relationships between the caller and callee functions.

There are many other options to the `trace` module such as tracking calls, generating annotated file listings, reports, and so on. We won't be having an exhaustive discussion regarding these, as the reader can refer to the documentation of this module on the web to read more about it.

The lptrace program

When debugging servers and trying to find out performance or other issues on production environments, what a programmer needs is not often the Python system or stack trace as given by the `trace` module, but to attach to a process in real time and see which functions are getting executed.

> `iptrace` can be installed using pip. Note that it doesn't work with **Python3**.

The `lptrace` package allows you to do this. Instead of giving a script to run, it attaches to an existing process running a Python program via its process ID, such as running servers, applications, and the like.

In the following screenshot, you can see `iptrace` debugging the Twisted chat server that we developed in *Chapter 8*, *Architectural Patterns – The Pythonic Approach*, live. The session shows the activity when the client andy has connected:

```
IPython: user/programs
File  Edit  View  Search  Terminal  Help
$ python3 -m trace --trackcalls maxsubarray.py
45

calling relationships:

*** /usr/lib/python3.5/trace.py ***
    trace.Trace.runctx -> trace._unsettrace
  --> maxsubarray.py
    trace.Trace.runctx -> maxsubarray.<module>

*** maxsubarray.py ***
    maxsubarray.<module> -> maxsubarray.max_subarray
$
```

The `iptrace` command debugging a chat server in Twisted

There are lots of log lines, but you can observe how some well-known methods of the Twisted protocol are being logged such as **connectionMade** when the client has connected. Socket calls such as *accept* can also be seen as part of accepting the connection from the client.

System call tracing using strace

`strace` is a Linux command, which allows a user to trace system calls and signals invoked by a running program. It is not exclusive to Python, but it can be used to debug any program. `strace` can be used in combination with `iptrace` to troubleshoot programs with respect to their system calls.

`strace` is similar to `iptrace` in that it can be made to attach to a running process. It can also be invoked to run a process from the command line, but it is more useful when running attached to a process such as a server.

For example, this screenshot shows the `strace` output when running attached to our chat server:

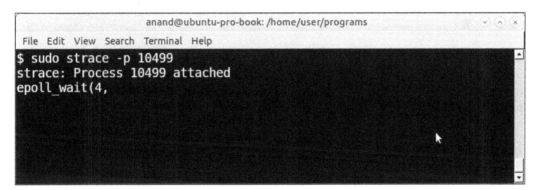

The `strace` command attached to the Twisted chat server

The `strace` command corroborates the conclusion of the `lptrace` command of the server waiting on an epoll handle for incoming connections.

This is what happens when a client connects:

```
anand@ubuntu-pro-book: /home/user/programs
File  Edit  View  Search  Terminal  Help

[{EPOLLIN, {u32=3, u64=14887175234342879235}}], 4, -1) = 1
accept(3, {sa_family=AF_INET, sin_port=htons(44874), sin_addr=inet_addr("127.0.0.1")}, [16
]) = 10
fcntl(10, F_GETFD)                    = 0
fcntl(10, F_SETFD, FD_CLOEXEC)        = 0
fcntl(10, F_GETFL)                    = 0x2 (flags O_RDWR)
fcntl(10, F_SETFL, O_RDWR|O_NONBLOCK) = 0
epoll_ctl(4, EPOLL_CTL_ADD, 10, {EPOLLIN, {u32=10, u64=14887175234342879242}}) = 0
accept(3, 0x7ffd17f2acd0, 0x7ffd17f2accc) = -1 EAGAIN (Resource temporarily unavailable)
epoll_wait(4, [{EPOLLIN, {u32=11, u64=14887175234342879243}}], 5, -1) = 1
recvfrom(11, "", 65536, 0, NULL, NULL) = 0
epoll_ctl(4, EPOLL_CTL_DEL, 11, 0x7ffd17f2aa60) = 0
shutdown(11, SHUT_RDWR)               = 0
close(11)                             = 0
epoll_wait(4,
```

The strace command showing system calls for a client connecting to the Twisted chat server

`strace` is a very powerful tool, which can be combined with tools specific for the runtime (such as lptrace for Python) in order to do advanced debugging in production environments.

Summary

In this chapter, we learned about different debugging techniques with Python. We started with the simple `print` statement and followed it with simple tricks to debug a Python program such as using the `continue` statement in a loop, strategically placing the `sys.exit` calls between code blocks, and so on.

We then looked at debugging techniques in some detail, especially on mocking and randomizing data. Techniques such as caching in files and in-memory databases such as Redis were discussed with examples.

An example using Python schematics library showed generating random data for a hypothetical application in the healthcare domain.

The next section was about logging and using it as a debugging technique. We discussed simple logging using the `logging` module, advanced logging using the `logger` object, and wrapped up the discussion by creating a logger wrapper with its custom formatting for logging the time taken inside functions. We also studied an example of writing to `syslog`.

The end of the chapter was devoted to a discussion on debugging tools. You learned the basic commands of pdb, the Python debugger, and took a quick look at similar tools that provide a better experience, namely, iPdb and Pdb++. We ended the chapter with a brief discussion on tracing tools such as lptrace and the ubiquitous `strace` program on Linux.

Index